DELINQUENCY AND JUSTICE

DELINQUENCY AND JUSTICE
A Psychosocial Approach

second edition

CURT R. BARTOL
Castleton State College

ANNE M. BARTOL
Castleton State College

PRENTICE HALL, UPPER SADDLE RIVER, NEW JERSEY 07458

Library of Congress Cataloging-in-Publication Data

Bartol, Curt R.
    Delinquency and justice : A psychosocial approach / Curt R.
    Bartol, Anne M. Bartol. — 2nd ed.
        p. cm.
    Includes bibliographical references and indexes.
    ISBN 0-13-841883-7
    1. Juvenile delinquency—United States—Prevention.   2. Juvenile
delinquents—United States—Psychology.   3. Juvenile delinquents—
United States—Attitudes.   4. Juvenile justice, Administration of—
United States.   I. Bartol, Anne M.   II. Title.
HV9104.B344   1998
364.36'0973—dc21   97-23352
                                                                CIP

Editorial Director: Charlyce Jones Owen
Editor in Chief: Nancy Roberts
Marketing Manager: Christopher DeJohn
Associate Editor: Sharon Chambliss
Editorial/Production supervision and interior design: Serena Hoffman
Manufacturing Buyer: Mary Ann Gloriande
Cover Design: Kiwi Design

This book was set in 10/12 Palatino by DM Cradle Associates
and was printed and bound by RR Donnelley & Sons Company.
The cover was printed by Phoenix Color Corp.

© 1998, 1989 by Prentice-Hall, Inc.
Simon & Schuster/A Viacom Company
Upper Saddle River, New Jersey 07458

Printed in the United States of America

10 9 8 7 6 5 4 3 2 1

ISBN 0-13-841883-7

Prentice-Hall International (UK) Limited, *London*
Prentice-Hall of Australia Pty. Limited, *Sydney*
Prentice-Hall Canada Inc., *Toronto*
Prentice-Hall Hispanoamericana, S.A., *Mexico*
Prentice-Hall of India Private Limited, *New Delhi*
Prentice-Hall of Japan, Inc., *Tokyo*
Simon & Schuster Asia Pte. Ltd., *Singapore*
Editora Prentice-Hall do Brasil, Ltda., *Rio de Janeiro*

Contents

5   Infrasystems: Developmental and Learning Factors   113

Preface

Delinquency and Justice is built on a social systems foundation. Social systems theory allows us to examine the vast amount of theory and research in juvenile delinquency within a unifying, thematic framework. It allows us to synthesize what we have learned from various academic disciplines and professional perspectives. This text argues that in order to understand, prevent, and treat delinquency, we must acknowledge the critical roles played by the family, peers, the school, neighborhood, community, and culture. Therefore, the text views the juvenile offender as being embedded and continually influenced by multiple systems within the social environment.

In contrast to the first edition, the second edition focuses more on: (1) prevention of juvenile offending and treatment strategies for dealing with juvenile offenders; (2) the victimization of juveniles, including the extent to which social problems like racism and sexism contribute to that victimization; and (3) current juvenile justice practices. For example, the text incorporates theories in criminology that question control-oriented policies applied to juveniles. The book takes a *psychosocial approach*, with considerable attention directed at psychological and social aspects of juvenile offending and victimization, and contemporary prevention and treatment programs that take a systems approach.

There are many ways of classifying juvenile offenders. One useful classification views the juvenile offender as belonging to one of two major groups: (1) the adolescent offending group, where offending is seen as a response to group and social pressures and is likely to wane as the youth grows older; and (2) the life-course-persistent offending group, where a lifelong pattern of antisocial behavior is apparent. Juveniles in the first group often need minimal intervention. Those who require more than the minimum often benefit from some of the current approaches to intervention. These current approaches have been less successful with juveniles in the second group, particularly if the intervention does not begin early in the life course. Effective intervention and treatment for either group require a multisystemic approach that focuses on the family as the central ingredient.

Chapter 1 defines delinquency and explains how it is usually measured. Chapter 2 discusses specific offense categories and provides statistics on the nature and extent of juvenile offending. Chapter 3 is devoted exclusively to alcohol and drug abuse by juveniles, including psychopharmacological effects; this chapter was added in response to requests from both students and instructors, who recommended that it be placed early in the book. Chapter 4 introduces the reader to social systems theory and its ramifications for delinquency. It describes individual or infrasystems, covering the available research on temperament, attention deficit/hyperactivity disorders, conduct disorders, and theories relating to these topics. Thereafter, the book moves from individual or infrasystems to broader and broader social systems.

Chapter 5 continues with individual systems from a child development perspective, focusing on learning and cognitive factors. Chapter 6 examines the microsystem of the family and its critical influence on the development of antisocial behavior and delinquency. The chapter addresses the topic of family violence and child abuse in considerable depth.

As we move up the systems ladder, the reciprocal influence of the many other systems becomes increasingly evident. Chapter 7 examines peer influence, with some focus directed at youth groups and gangs. The chapter also looks at the interactions among microsystems, such as peer and family, school and family, and family and work. Chapter 8 moves into higher-level systems involving the neighborhood, community, and culture. Throughout this odyssey, we try to be sensitive to the many young victims of adult and juvenile crime, especially minority victims living within the inner city.

Chapter 9 covers the contemporary prevention, intervention, and treatment programs that have been tried on at-risk children and delinquents. We discuss research that has evaluated the effectiveness of these programs. Chapter 10 describes the origins and functions of the juvenile justice system and identifies shifts in its focus over the years. Chapter 11 examines the early processing of juveniles and the various procedures in that process. In keeping with the prevention-intervention theme of the book, diversion programs and their effectiveness are critically examined. Chapter 12 provides details on delinquency hearings and criminal trials as they pertain to juvenile offenders. The chapter examines issues such as the death penalty for juveniles and the cultural shift toward punishment for juveniles. Chapter 13 expands on juvenile rehabilitation, focusing on community and institutional strategies.

Many individuals have helped significantly throughout the production of this book. Special thanks are due to Hope Liebhaber, who spent many hours searching the literature for relevant articles and manuscripts during the early phases of the project. Corey Belden provided invaluable assistance in *all* phases of the project; he obtained and suggested materials, conducted literature searches, gave helpful comments, and allowed us to take considerable advantage of his computer skills. Our daughter, Gina Bartol, carefully read the material and offered incisive comments and suggestions from her perspective as a professional social worker. Heather Howard provided many helpful comments from a student perspective. Sandy Duling, reference librarian at Castleton State College, was always there for us when it came to obtaining library materials.

The Prentice-Hall staff has offered encouragement, patience, and competent support throughout the project. We owe special thanks to Associate Editor Sharon Chambliss for her enthusiasm, support, and skill at managing the many whims of authors. We are grateful to Senior Project Manager Serena Hoffman who orchestrated the various phases of the project with great competence and professionalism.

Curt R. Bartol
Anne M. Bartol

DELINQUENCY AND JUSTICE

Defining and Measuring Delinquency

One major objective of this text is to cultivate in readers a patience to see the world from multiple perspectives and to provide the necessary concepts with which to refine these perspectives. Perspectives on behavior, including delinquent behavior, are strongly influenced by the political, economic, and social climate and by the dominant thinking of the times. Even in a pluralistic society, it is possible to identify social moods or trends that bear heavily on explanations of behavior.

A second major objective is to have the reader understand that juvenile delinquency has multiple causes, manifestations, and developmental pathways. These multiple causes reside in a very complicated way within the individual, the family, the school, peers, community, and the political and cultural context within which the child resides. It is critical to realize also that delinquency prevention and intervention, in order to be effective, must not only be tailored to the child's developmental level but also must address the significant influences of the social milieux. In a recent government document (Coordinating Council, 1996, p. 8), it was concluded that "To successfully reduce youth violence, prevention strategies must engage the entire spectrum of individuals and community systems impacting a young person's life, including families, schools, peers, and other adults in the community." The mission of this text, therefore, is to examine in some detail the individual and community systems, as well as the juvenile justice system and all its facets. For example, we review a wide variety of prevention efforts aimed at reducing serious juvenile offending.

We also examine the control exercised by agents of the juvenile justice system over juveniles whose offenses are less serious. As will be noted, first-time offenders or juveniles who run away from home or are truant continue to come before the juvenile courts in great numbers, and these courts are often reluctant to overlook their behavior. Finally, to some extent society's focus on a juvenile "crime wave" is a way of distracting attention from broader social problems, such as poverty and discrimination. Juvenile crime rates would be far lower if all juveniles in our society were given access to a good education and to a minimum standard of living. We will return to these themes throughout the book.

DEFINITIONS OF JUVENILE DELINQUENCY

"Delinquency" is both a legal and a social term. At first, one sentence, a simple legal definition, seems to suffice: *Delinquency is behavior against the criminal code committed by an individual who has not reached adulthood, as defined by state or federal law.* But the term "delinquency" has multiple definitions and meanings beyond this one-sentence definition. Additionally, in some states the legal definition also includes status offending, which is not behavior against the *criminal* code but is prohibited *only for juveniles*. Running away, violating curfew laws, and truancy are examples of status offending.

Stephen Toulman (1961), the distinguished philosopher of science, drew an analogy between definitions and belts. The shorter the belt, the more elastic it needs to be in order to accommodate all customers. Similarly, a short definition, when applied to a wide assortment of cases, must be expanded and contracted, qualified and reinterpreted, in order to fit every case. So it is here. We may start by defining juvenile delinquency briefly and concisely, but we will have to make adjustments as we go along. These adjustments lead us to a social definition of delinquency.

The social definition of delinquency comprises a plethora of youthful behavior deemed inappropriate (e.g., aggressive behavior, drug use, truancy, or petty theft). The behavior may or may not have come to the attention of police. Terms such as "antisocial behavior," "conduct disorder," and "aggressive or violent behavior," for example, are not synonymous with legal delinquency but do comport with social delinquency. They are also diagnostic labels placed on juveniles by mental health professionals.

Conduct disorder is a diagnostic term used to represent a cluster of behaviors characterized by habitual misbehavior, such as stealing, setting fires, running away from home, skipping school, destroying property, fighting, being cruel to animals and to other people, and frequently telling lies. The child may *or may not* have been arrested for these behaviors. In fact, some of these behaviors are not even against the criminal law. The term "conduct disorder" is more fully described in the American Psychiatric Association's *Diagnostic and Statistical Manual* (4th edition), commonly referred to as the *DSM-IV*. The *DSM-IV* divides conduct disorders into two categories, depending on the onset of the misbehaviors. If the misbehavior began in childhood (before age ten), it is called conduct disorder: childhood-onset type. If the misbehavior began in adolescence, it is called conduct disorder: adolescent-onset type.

The term **antisocial behavior** is usually reserved for more serious habitual misbehavior, especially a pattern of behavior that involves direct and harmful actions against others. It is to be distinguished, however, from **antisocial personality disorder**, a diagnostic label reserved for adults who displayed conduct disorders as children or adolescents. **Aggression** has many definitions, but for our purposes it will be used to mean physical attacks on another individual.

Legal definitions at first blush appear to offer the best avenue for defining clearly what delinquency is and is not. On closer examination, however, they are often imperfect. As noted earlier, they may or may not include status offending. Moreover, we soon confront other illustrations of the familiar cross-jurisdictional quagmire of inconsistent and contradictory provisions. State statutes vary widely, and federal statutes are different still. In addition, these statutes are periodically changed by legislatures or interpreted by courts. The legal definition of delinquency, then, is problematic; we must remind ourselves that the "belt" will need constant adjustment.

Even age is not a simple issue. Although no state considers anyone above 18 a delinquent, some have provisions for "youthful offenders," who are older, and some use 16 as the cutoff age. At this writing, four states give criminal courts, rather than juvenile courts, automatic jurisdiction over juveniles at age 16, and eight states do so at age 17. Several other states are considering changes. Furthermore, all states allow juveniles—some as young as age 7 (New York)—to be tried as adults in criminal courts under certain conditions and for certain offenses. Under federal law, juveniles may be prosecuted under the criminal law at age 15. Increasingly, however, more and more young offenders are moved to adult court in this manner. Under the legal definition of delinquency, the youths transferred to criminal courts are not delinquents. Their behavior, although not technically "delinquent," is clearly within the scope of this text.

A discernible shift toward moving troubled youth from juvenile jurisdiction to the adult domain has emerged since the mid-1980s. In 1994, for example, states introduced more than 700 bills to move more youthful offenders from specialized juvenile facilities to adult prisons (Krisberg, 1995). Moreover, the 1994 federal crime bill provided states with nearly $9 billion for prison construction and several billion more for adult boot camps, but juvenile corrections was hardly funded at all (Krisberg, 1995).

It will become obvious as we proceed through this chapter and others in the text that the measurement of delinquency and the determination of who is delinquent are extremely problematic. Delinquency is not a distinct entity easily located and studied. Whether defined legally or socially, delinquency is an artifact, ever changing and conceptually slippery. It is an imprecise, nebulous label for a wide variety of law- and norm-violating behaviors. Furthermore, the concept "delinquent" changes from society to society, culture to culture, and jurisdiction to jurisdiction. Youths who qualify as delinquents in one state may not in another state. In addition, society might resist calling a brutal killer a "delinquent." In general, however, legal definitions rest on social definitions of delinquents and delinquency. Laws are passed in response to societal values and demands. This legislative response may be a very gradual and conservative process, one that is almost invariably strongly influenced by society's perception. Traditionally, for example, society considered acting-out behavior on the part of girls as more unacceptable than the same behavior on the part of boys. These value judgments were reflected in statutes that allowed the longer incarceration of girls, compared with boys, for such offenses as running away from home. On the other hand, the legislative response may occur very quickly. Intensive media publicity given to a heinous crime committed by a juvenile has been known to precipitate changes in the law in response to public outrage.

Ultimately then, definitions of delinquency rest on two fundamental perspectives: the legal perspective and the social perspective. Delinquency is defined by law, which in turn is substantially influenced by the members of a particular society, state, or community. Consequently, delinquency is basically a sociolegal term.

Finally, we must be careful to distinguish between a delinquent and a delinquent *act*. The act—**delinquency**—is the behavior that violates the criminal code, whereas **delinquent** is the label we assign to a youngster who deviates from the prescribed norms. A youth who commits a legally defined delinquent act is not automatically a delinquent. A broken window or a stolen CD player does not automatically lead to labeling the youthful offender "delinquent." Usually, society reserves its judgment until there are a number of such acts over time. In general, we are inclined to consider a minor delinquent act here or there as a teenage prank or mischief, part of the rites of passage into adulthood.

Figures on crimes and status offenses committed by juveniles help us to separate the mild from the serious offenses, the violent from the nonviolent. In this way we can see trends in offending and identify types of offending in relation to time and place. Identifying the individual delinquent becomes much more difficult. Joseph Weis and John Sederstrom (1981) recommend that the most useful empirical distinction of the juvenile offender is between the serious and less serious (or petty) offender. Although the distinction between serious and less serious may seem reasonable, a better approach is to distinguish the child who begins showing antisocial behavior, aggressive conduct, and temperamental problems at an early age (usually by age three) from the youngster who begins to engage in delinquent behavior at the onset of puberty. Terrie Moffitt (1993a) refers to the first child as a **life-course-persistent delinquent** and the latter as the **adolescence-limited delinquent**. The life-course-persistent delinquent demonstrates an antisocial, criminal pattern very early in life and continues this pattern well into adulthood. The term "life-course-persistent" signifies that the antisocial behavior persists across the course of the person's life span and persists across a wide variety of situations. Adolescence-limited delinquents, on the other hand, engage in delinquent behavior during the teen years but show no previous history of antisocial behavior and normally terminate the delinquent behavior as they become young adults. We will adopt this very important distinction and will elaborate on it throughout the book.

QUANTITATIVE AND QUALITATIVE METHODS IN CRIMINOLOGY

In order for our knowledge about the juvenile offender to advance, various research strategies and methods are necessary. Howard Schwartz and Jerry Jacobs (1979) have outlined some of the differences between the various scientific methods used in the social sciences, including criminology and the study of deviant behavior. One of the most relevant distinctions is that between quantitative and qualitative methods. **Quantitative methods** assign numbers to observations, which allows researchers to analyze data systematically and to detect patterns and differences. Typically, quantitative methods collect measurements on variables and apply various statistical techniques to these measurements. Researchers using quantitative approaches might collect arrest and victimization data describing the distribution of delinquency in a particular city. Armed with these data, the researchers might do a statistical analysis to discover where delinquency is most heavily concentrated, what types of crimes are being committed, and who is most likely to be victimized. Quantitative methodology also allows us to gather data on the number of juveniles processed through juvenile courts, held in detention, or transferred to criminal courts. Through quantitative research we are also able to evaluate the effectiveness of various rehabilitative strategies, such as sex-offender treatment programs or juvenile boot camps.

Qualitative methods are quite different. Researchers using the qualitative approach minimize the use of numbers or statistics in their research observations. Rather, "Qualitative methodology refers to those research strategies, such as participant observation, in-depth interviewing, total participation in the activity being investigated, field work, etc., which allow the researcher to obtain first-hand knowledge about the empirical social world in question" (Filstead, 1970, p. 6). Researchers using qualitative methods most generally describe their observations in the "natural language" at hand. For example, some researchers try to gain the trust of a group of youths by interacting with their gang, hoping to acquire an "inside" view of how these youths perceive and construct their world. In this case, "natural language" would include the jargon, speech patterns, and symbols of the youths themselves, instead of the artificial categories and concepts imposed on them by the researcher. From this qualitative perspective, if we want to understand delinquents, it is important to know what they know, to see what they see, and to understand what they understand.

A good illustration of the qualitative approach can be found in the research conducted by Anne Campbell (1984) on the role of girls in New York street gangs. She writes, "I wanted to observe and interact with girl gang members and to represent their own views of their situations" (p. 1). After researching the nearly 400 known gangs in New York City, she selected three that seemed to represent the diversity of gang life: a street gang, a biker gang, and a religion-cultural gang. One was racially mixed, one was Puerto Rican, and one was black. She was introduced to the gangs by a police officer who knew them well or by agencies and youth-project members who worked with them. She spent several months with gang members, getting to know them and gaining their trust. She did not disguise her identity or purpose to the gang members, and data collection was accomplished through either field note taking or the use of a tape recorder. Much of her book, *The Girls in the Gang*, is written in the girls' "own words."

Campbell found some very interesting things about contemporary female gang members. She found them conservative in their attitudes, structure, and philosophy: pro–America, pro-capitalism, pro-education, pro-mainstream values. "The girls especially are subject to the dictates of fashion and consumer fetishism: substantial sums are spent on the 'right' jeans, hair perms—even cigarettes" (p. 241). They believe in American society and what it stands for. The girls accept the same roles within the gang as they probably would in the larger society. They were attached to male gangs, and the males were the central, pivotal figures; the females supported, nurtured, and sustained them.

Another illustration of qualitative research is an ethnographic study by Lisa Maher and Richard Curtis (1995). An **ethnographic study** is one in which researchers enter a cultural setting and, through observation and participation, provide a rich description of that setting. Ethnographers preserve the integrity and properties of the phenomena observed by utilizing the symbols and spoken language of their subjects.

Maher and Curtis took extensive fieldnotes based on in-depth interviews with residents of two drug-infested Brooklyn neighborhoods. Although the research was done primarily with adults, it nevertheless provides a good picture of what all residents, including juveniles, face in this environment. The researchers were interested in exploring whether women's roles in the street level drug economy had changed and whether they were becoming more violent. They learned that, far from being in positions of control, women and girls held low-level jobs in the drug economy, were in frequent physical danger, and were routinely victimized by drug buyers as well as by men who controlled the drug trade.

We will return to Campbell's study in Chapter 7 when we talk about peer groups, but at this point we wish to emphasize that both methods—qualitative and quantitative—are highly useful methods for the science and measurement of delinquency. According to Schwartz and Jacobs (1979, p. 5) " . . . quantitative methods are best for conducting a 'positive science'; that is, they allow for the clear, rigorous, and reliable collection of data and permit the testing of empirical hypotheses in a logically consistent manner." On the other hand, " . . . qualitative methods, which use natural language, are best at gaining access to the life-world of other individuals in a short time" (Schwartz & Jacobs, 1979, p. 5). Qualitative methods allow us to examine the motives, meanings, emotions, and other subjective aspects in the lives of youths. In short, they add life to our knowledge. It is important to realize, also, that one method does not necessarily have to be chosen over the other. David Silverman (1985, p. 17) asserts: ". . . it is not simply a choice between polar opposites that face us, but a decision about balance and intellectual breadth and rigour."

We will return repeatedly to qualitative research throughout the remainder of the book. In this chapter, however, we will focus on *quantitative* measures to obtain indices of juvenile offending.

THE MEASUREMENT OF DELINQUENCY

Quantitative methods may be divided into two major categories, official and unofficial. **Official statistics of crime** refer to recorded data published or supervised by governmental agencies. **Unofficial statistics of crime** refer to published data by private organizations or independent researchers. It is important to note that some types of measurement may fall into both categories. There are official as well as unofficial victimization studies, for example. In addition, it is important to note that relying on any *single* source of quantitative national data is likely to give rise to a limited perspective about delinquency. For that reason, criminologists often prefer to classify delinquency data according to their source: agencies of the juvenile or criminal justice system, victims, or offenders themselves. In that case, the categories are "official data," "victimization data," and "self-report data."

The most widely cited form of official statistics is the FBI's *Uniform Crime Reports* (UCR), which include law-enforcement data on reported crime and juvenile arrests. It is widely acknowledged that many crimes—adult or juvenile—are not reported to law enforcement, however. If reported, they are not necessarily followed by an arrest. Therefore, although statistics suggest that roughly 2.2 million juvenile arrests are made each year (FBI, 1996), we must keep in mind that the figure underestimates juvenile offending. Furthermore, the figures provide some estimate of the incidence, but not the prevalence, of delinquency, a distinction that will be explained shortly. Only about half of those arrested are referred to juvenile court; the others are not charged, or the charges against them are dropped. About 15 percent of the youths who reach juvenile court are referred by parents, school personnel, citizens, or social service agencies, usually for relatively minor offenses.

After referral to juvenile court, a decision is made as to whether to handle the case formally or informally. **Informal processing** is considered when the decision makers believe that accountability and rehabilitation can be achieved without the use of formal court intervention (Snyder & Sickmund, 1995). Of the total number of cases referred to juvenile court, about half are processed informally (Butts et al., 1995). **Formal processing** usually occurs when the juvenile is involved in more serious offenses, tends to be older, and often has longer court records. And, of the total cases certified for a formal hearing, about 3 in 5 result in a juvenile's being adjudicated—in some fashion—"delinquent."

Roughly, then, between 500,000 and 600,000 young people each year attain delinquency status. They may then be institutionalized, placed on probation, made to pay fines or make restitution, ordered to undergo counseling or to enroll in specified programs, or any combination of these (Snyder & Sickmund, 1995).

Many researchers argue that we lose valuable clues about delinquency if we define the delinquent population strictly according to legal rules, and they are, of course, correct. After all, only about 20 percent of those arrested ever reach delinquency status, and, as with adult crime, there is a **dark figure** representing young lawbreakers who never come to official attention at all. Dark figure is the term used in criminology to describe the amount of crime that is not measured by official statistics. Research by Elliott, Huizinga, and Ageton (1987) suggests that as many as 86 percent of American juvenile offenders escape detection, including the more serious and repeat offenders. The nonrandom sample designated "delinquent" severely misrepresents the population of true delinquents for other reasons as well. Widespread discretion exercised by police, court officials, and social service workers and differences in procedures mean that juveniles who have engaged in similar conduct will not necessarily be treated similarly. Furthermore, some juveniles may have been diverted from the court either by specific programs intended for that very purpose, or by the intervention of parents or guardians. In short, official figures based on legal definitions represent a special population of people under special circumstances and not the whole population of individuals about whom we are concerned. It is primarily for this reason that legal definitions or official figures alone should be used with caution.

OFFICIAL DATA

Surprisingly, comprehensive national data on youth crime and its control do not exist (Krisberg & Schwartz, 1983). Although a variety of different sources may be consulted, none gives us the total picture. The major source of official data on reported crime and arrests is the UCR (referred to previously). The primary source of data on juvenile corrections is a biennial census published as *Children in Custody*, whereas the primary source of information concerning activity in juvenile courts is the *Juvenile Court Statistics*, which includes data on juvenile probation.

The Uniform Crime Reports

The Federal Bureau of Investigation's *Uniform Crime Reports* (**UCR**), compiled since 1930, is the most-cited source of U.S. crime statistics. The UCR is an annual document (released to the public any time between late July and early September) containing information received on a voluntary basis from local and state law-enforcement agencies throughout the country. Interestingly, federal law enforcement agencies do not report through the traditional UCR program, although a revised reporting system is now being developed. This new system will be discussed shortly. The first UCR was published with data from fewer than 1,000 law-enforcement agencies; the 1994 UCR data collection was based on nearly 10,743 agencies, representing about 98 percent of the total U.S. population (FBI, 1996). The UCR represents the only major data source permitting a comparison of national aggregate data broken down by age, sex, race, and offense. The more recently developed FBI *Supplementary Homicide Report* contains data on victim and offender demographics, the offender-victim relationship, the weapon used, and the circumstances surrounding the homicide.

The UCR divides crime and arrest statistics a number of ways, including by age, sex, and race of the person arrested and city and region of the country where the crime was committed. Crimes are also categorized according to seriousness. Serious crimes are referred to as **index crimes** (or **Part I crimes**), nonserious as **non-index crimes** (or **Part II crimes**). Even this distinction is misleading, however. For example, larceny-theft, which includes shoplifting, is categorized as an index crime, whereas fraud and drug offenses are classified as non-index crimes. Table 1.1 contains definitions of some of the crimes reported in the UCR, specifically those that will be discussed in the text.

In order to be recorded in the UCR, a crime must (at a minimum):

1. Be perceived by the victim or by someone else
2. Be defined as a crime by the victim or the observer
3. In some way become known to a law-enforcement agency
4. Be defined by that law-enforcement agency as a crime
5. Be accurately recorded by the law-enforcement agency
6. Be reported to the FBI compilation center

It is important to stress the need to treat UCR data very gingerly. For a host of reasons, including possibly inaccurate reporting by local and state agencies and the fact that the data do not consider early discretionary decision making by law-enforcement officers, UCR data are misleading. Bernard Cohen (1981) has pleaded for a more accurate and precise indicator of the extent of national crime. "[This] is essential for the following reasons: (1) UCR crime rates are frequently used as an indicator of basic social problems; (2) they are the most influential of noneconomic indicators; (3) they are probably more than any other noneconomic indicator subject to public and official attention; (4) they are frequently cited by the press; (5) they are used extensively for scholarly research; and (6) they form the basis for far-reaching legislative proposals and decisions" (Cohen, 1981, p. 86).

The National Incident-Based Reporting System

During the late 1970s, the law-enforcement community called for the expanded use of the UCR and developed new guidelines for reporting crime statistics. These guidelines formed the basis of the **National Incident-Based Reporting System (NIBRS)**

TABLE 1.1   Definitions of Offenses in Uniform Crime Reporting

Index Crimes

Criminal homicide: Divided into two parts: (a) Murder and nonnegligent manslaughter refers to the willful (nonnegligent) killing of one human being by another; and (b) manslaughter by negligence refers to the killing of another person through gross negligence (traffic fatalities are excluded).

Forcible rape: The carnal knowledge of a female forcibly and against her will. Included are rapes by force and attempts or assaults to rape. Statutory offenses (no force used—victim under age of consent) are excluded.

Robbery: The taking or attempting to take anything of value from the care, custody, or control of a person or persons by force or threat of force or violence and/or by putting the victim in fear.

Aggravated assault: An unlawful attack by one person upon another for the purpose of inflicting severe or aggravated bodily injury. This type of assault usually is accompanied by the use of a weapon or by means likely to produce death or great bodily harm. Simple assaults are excluded.

Burglary; breaking or entering: The unlawful entry of a structure to commit a felony or a theft. Attempted forcible entry is included.

Larceny-Theft (except motor vehicle theft): The unlawful taking, carrying, leading, or riding away of property from the possession or constructive possession of another. Examples are thefts of bicycles or automobile accessories, shoplifting, pocket picking, or the stealing of any property or articles that are not taken by force and violence or by fraud. Attempted larcenies are included.

Motor vehicle theft: The theft or attempted theft of a motor vehicle. A motor vehicle is self-propelled and runs on the surface and not on rails. Specifically excluded from this category are motorboats, construction equipment, airplanes, and farming equipment.

Arson: Any willful or malicious burning or attempt to burn, with or without intent to defraud, a dwelling house, public building, motor vehicle or aircraft, personal property of another, and so on.

Common Non-Index Crimes of Juveniles

Other assaults: Assaults and attempted assaults wherein no weapon is used and that do not result in serious or aggravated injury to the victim.

Stolen property—buying, receiving, possessing: Buying, receiving, and possessing stolen property, including attempts to do so.

Vandalism: Willful or malicious destruction, injury, disfigurement, or defacement of any public or private property, real or personal, without the consent of the owner or persons having custody or control.

Weapons—carrying, possessing, and so on: All violations of regulations or statutes controlling the carrying, using, possessing, furnishing, and manufacturing of deadly weapons or silencers. Included are attempts.

Sex offenses (except forcible rape, prostitution, and commercialized vice): Statutory rape and offenses against chastity, common decency, morals, and the like. Attempts are included.

Driving under the influence (DUI): Driving or operating any vehicle or common carrier while drunk or under the influence of liquor or narcotics.

Liquor law violations: State or local liquor law violations, except drunkenness and driving under the influence. Federal violations are excluded.

Drunkenness: Offenses relating to drunkenness or intoxication. Excluded is driving under the influence.

Disorderly conduct: Breach of the peace.

Violations of curfew and loitering laws: Offenses relating to violations of local curfews or loitering ordinances where such laws exist.

Running away: Restricted to persons under age 18. Limited to less than into protective custody under provisions of local statutes.

SOURCE: Adapted from FBI *Uniform Crime Reports, 1995* (Washington, DC: U.S. Department of Justice, 1986), pp. 373–374.

under the Uniform Federal Crime Reporting Act passed by the U.S. Congress in 1988 (Public Law No. 100-690, 102 Stat. 4181). Congress required all federal law-enforcement agencies, including those law-enforcement agencies within the Department of Defense, to collect and report data to the FBI on two categories of offenses—Group A and Group B offenses. States were also invited to participate. For Group A offenses, reporting agencies must make Incident Reports for 22 offense categories, which are made up of 46 specific crimes (see Table 1.2). This new approach greatly expands the traditional 8 Part I categories found in the current UCR.

In the Group A Incident Report information, a crime is viewed along with all its aspects, including information about the victim, weapon, location of the crime, alcohol/drug influence, type of criminal activity, relationship of victim to the alleged offender, residence of victims and arrestees, and a description of property and its value. Presumably, this added information will become an indispensable tool for law-enforcement agencies and researchers, because it will provide them with detailed data about when and where crime takes place, what form it takes, and the characteristics of its victims and perpetrators.

For Group B offenses, reporting agencies must file arrest reports for eleven enumerated offenses: passing bad checks, driving under the influence of alcohol,

TABLE 1.2   The National Incident-Based Reporting System (NIBRS) Group A Offenses

Arson	Homicide offenses
Assault offenses	Murder/nonnegligent manslaughter
Aggravated assault	Negligent manslaughter
Simple assault	Justifiable homicide
Intimidation	Kidnapping/abduction
Bribery	Larceny-theft offenses
Burglary/breaking and entering	Pocket picking
Counterfeiting/forgery	Purse snatching
Destruction/damage/vandalism	Shoplifting
of property	Theft from building
Drug/narcotic violations	Theft from coin-operated machines
Drug/narcotic violations	Theft from motor vehicle
Drug equipment violations	Theft of motor vehicle parts/accessories
Embezzlement	Motor vehicle theft
Extortion/blackmail	Pornography/obscene material
Fraud offenses	Prostitution offenses
False pretenses/swindle	Prostitution
confidence game	Assisting or promoting prostitution
Credit card/ATM fraud	Robbery
Impersonation	Sex offenses, forcible
Welfare fraud	Forcible rape
Wire fraud	Forcible sodomy
Gambling offenses	Sexual assault with an object
Betting/wagering	Forcible fondling
Operating/promoting/assisting gambling	Sex offense, nonforcible
Gambling equipment violations	Stolen-property offenses
Sports tampering	Weapon law violations

SOURCE: *The National Center for the Analysis of Violent Crime, Annual Report, 1992* (Quantico, VA: FBI Academy, 1992), p. 22.

engaging in disorderly conduct, drunkenness, nonviolent family offenses, liquor law violations, Peeping Tom activity, runaway, trespass, and other offenses not specifically designated as Group A offenses. Group B arrest reports contain only information about the arrestee and the circumstances of the arrest.

State and federal agencies participating in the NIBRS use automated systems to report information on Group A and Group B offenses to the FBI on a monthly basis. Ultimately, this new approach is intended to be a paperless (electronic) reporting system. However, the new system is expected to take several more years to implement completely. As of May 1995, only nine states had been certified by the FBI for full NIBRS participation, and no federal law-enforcement agency had reported any data at all (MEGG Associates, 1996). Therefore, much of the crime and arrest data reported in this text will be based on the information provided in the most recent UCR.

Children in Custody

The principal source of data on incarcerated juveniles is the biennial census on children in both public and private juvenile correctional facilities, including detention and rehabilitation centers, throughout the 50 states and the District of Columbia. It is known as *Children in Custody* (CIC). In 1977 the Office of Juvenile Justice and Delinquency Prevention assumed sponsorship of the census, although the data are collected by the U.S. Bureau of the Census and are now analyzed by the Bureau of Justice Statistics. Mail questionnaires are sent to all institutions and agencies dealing with the incarceration of juveniles. Response rate usually ranges between 96 and 100 percent each year. The CIC questionnaire requests data from facility administrators on the number of youth admitted, their demographic characteristics, and pertinent budgeting information. A one-day count of residents also is sought.

The first two censuses in 1971 and 1973 were limited to gathering data only from public residential correctional facilities, but all subsequent censuses have included private facilities. The private and public facilities included in the tabulation are (1) "short-term" facilities like shelters, detention centers, and reception or diagnostic centers and (2) "long-term" facilities such as training schools, ranches, forestry camps, farms, and halfway houses. Generally, short-term facilities are for pre-adjudicated youth (before a court decision is reached), and long-term facilities are for those who have been adjudicated delinquent. It is not unusual, however, for nondelinquent youths to be housed with juvenile offenders, particularly in private institutions.

Excluded from the CIC census are juveniles in federal correctional institutions, foster homes, nonresidential facilities, and facilities designated exclusively for drug abusers, alcoholics, unwed mothers, the emotionally disturbed, and dependent or neglected children.

Juvenile Court Statistics

A variety of sources provide information on juvenile courts. These include the *Juvenile Court Statistics* series, first published in 1929 by the Children's Bureau of the U.S. Department of Labor, which depends on the voluntary support of courts with juvenile jurisdiction. The series describes the number and characteristics of delinquency and status offenses handled by courts with juvenile jurisdiction. Data reported in the document are not based on a nationally representative sample, and there is no way of determining the validity of the estimates (Snyder & Sickmund, 1995). In addition, the series does not provide any national estimates of the number of youth offenses committed in any given year or time period.

Juvenile courts in the United States handled an estimated 1.5 million delinquency cases in 1993, a 23 percent increase over the 1989 caseload (Butts, 1996). According to these data, the number of cases involving offenses against persons increased 52 percent between 1989 and 1993, while the number of property offense cases increased 15 percent. The number of homicide cases increased 45 percent during that same period of time. Slightly more than half the delinquency cases (53 percent) disposed by the U.S. courts with juvenile jurisdiction in 1993 were

FIGURE 1-1. Juvenile Court Processing of Delinquency Cases, 1993

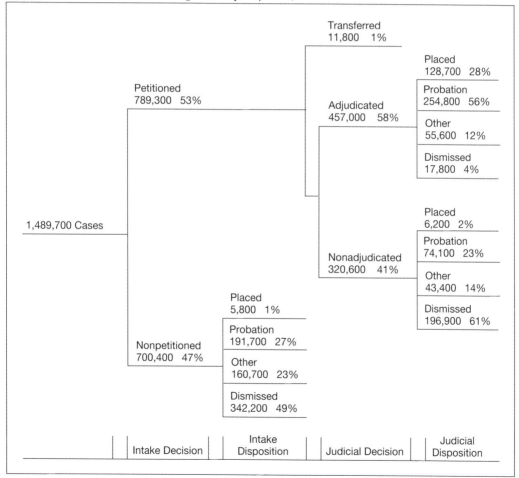

SOURCE: J.A. Butts, *Offenders in Juvenile Courts, 1993* (Washington, D.C.: U.S. Government Printing Office, 1996).

processed formally (Butts, 1996), meaning that a petition was filed formally charging the youth with delinquency; 58 percent of the petitions ended with an adjudication of delinquency.

Probation is the most common disposition given to juvenile offenders. Juvenile **probation** refers to the conditional freedom granted by the court in place of incarceration, as long as the juvenile meets certain conditions of behavior. **Parole** is a status granted an offender upon release from a correctional facility if his or her sentence has not expired. The term "parole" is rarely used in the juvenile justice system, however. Its equivalent is "aftercare," which refers to the ongoing community supervision of juveniles who have been in some type of juvenile facility. National data on probation and aftercare of juvenile offenders will be discussed more fully in Chapter 10.

VICTIMIZATION DATA

The main source of victimization data on delinquency is the *National Crime Victimization Survey* (NCVS). The Bureau of the Census interviews, on a staggered schedule, a large national sample of households (approximately 60,000) representing 136,000 persons over the age of 12. Crimes committed against children below age 12 are not counted for privacy reasons and because the designers of the survey believe that younger respondents are not as likely to provide accurate information as adults.

The households sampled are asked about personal crimes they experienced during the previous six months. The survey is currently designed to measure the extent to which persons and households are victims of rape, robbery, assault, burglary, motor vehicle theft, and larceny.

NCVS researchers use a **panel design**, a method that involves examining the same selected sample or group repeatedly over a certain length of time. In this case, each household is contacted twice a year for three years. The interviewers return to addresses (place of residence) rather than to individuals. That is, they contact (in person or by phone) the same housing unit every six months. If the family contacted during the last interview cycle has moved, the new occupants are interviewed. Housing units in the panel are visited a maximum of seven times, after which new units are selected.

The original impetus for the NCVS came from the President's Commission on Law Enforcement and Administration of Justice, which in 1966 commissioned the first national victimization survey. The commission wanted to supplement the annual UCR compiled by the FBI because of widespread dissatisfaction with this source. It was acknowledged that UCR data were to some extent unreliable and did not adequately measure the amount of crime. After considerable experimentation and a variety of pilot projects to test the method and its feasibility, the NCVS was fully implemented in 1973.

When respondents indicate that they have been victims of a crime, they are asked a series of detailed questions relating to the offense, including the offender's age if it is known. Specifically, the NCVS interviewer wants to know:

1.   Exactly what happened
2.   When and where the offense occurred
3.   Whether any injury or loss was suffered
4.   Whether the crime was reported to the police
5.   The victim's perceptions of the offender's sex, race, and—most important for us—age

NCVS data show that in 1991, victims age 12 and older reported that the offender was a juvenile (under age 18) in nearly one-third of personal crimes (Snyder & Sickmund, 1995). These victims also reported that a large majority (about 90 percent) of the offenders were male. Furthermore, the NCVS data revealed that persons who reported being victimized by a juvenile in a violent crime said that more than half of the incidents involved a group of offenders.

These data, as very rough estimates of juvenile crime, are dependent on (1) the victim's actually seeing the offender and (2) the victim's correct perceptions of the age of the offender. Unfortunately, these important potential shortcomings undermine the accuracy of the NCVS data to some extent. More important, the omission of children under age 12 not only reflects a lack of sophistication about children's cognitive development but also allows a large number of crimes committed by and against juveniles to go unreported. Crimes committed by juveniles often have younger juveniles as victims. In addition, the omission of children under 12 as victims limits our information on the sensitive issue of intrafamily violence and child abuse.

SELF-REPORT DATA

It is doubtful that any researcher believes that official or victimization statistics provide an accurate picture of crime and juvenile delinquency. As we noted earlier, a vast majority of adult and juvenile offending, for a variety of reasons, goes undetected or hidden from the official figures reported in the UCR. Victimization studies offer additional information, but they are limited in a number of ways, including the willingness of victims to reveal what happened to them and the fact that they may not know the age of the person who victimized them. Some researchers maintain that a third procedure for estimating the "true" delinquency rate is even better: It involves having juveniles in the general population simply reveal the extent of their own misconduct. This procedure, called the **self-report method** (hereafter abbreviated **SR**), is extremely important in the measurement (and definition) of delinquency. Currently, the SR method continues to be the dominant method of measurement in studies focusing on the extent and cause of delinquency.

The usual procedure is to prepare a list of questions asking about specific forbidden behavior. The list is then presented to youths, most often in a written questionnaire form, but occasionally in an interview setting. Very often, the youths are "captive" subjects in public schools or juvenile detention or treatment facilities. The SR method is also used to evaluate the effectiveness of an intervention or treatment program. For example, youths who have gone through a program designed to provide them with alternatives to violence may be contacted six months or a year later to see if they have remained free of violent behavior.

In SR measures, subjects usually are asked to indicate whether they have engaged in any of the specified activities and, if so, how frequently. Some studies ask whether the activities resulted in police contacts. In most cases, anonymity is guaranteed. Interestingly, Michael Hindelang and his colleagues (1981) found in their research that anonymity did not increase significantly the accuracy of the responses.

Gwynn Nettler (1984) noted that the numerous international studies employing the SR procedure (with adults as well as juveniles) have consistently drawn the following three conclusions: (1) almost everyone, by his or her own admission, has violated some criminal law; (2) the amount of "hidden crime" (the dark figure) is huge; and, most important, (3) most of the infractions are minor. Current research continually emphasizes that the statistics collected through SR methods indicate that official measures, such as arrest records, reflect merely the tip of a massive iceberg of offending. Undetected rates of adolescent offending are enormous. They are so high that they appear to be a normal part of being a teenager.

SR studies also continually show that the proportions of respondents involved in serious (defined primarily as violent) crimes are relatively small but that those juveniles who do commit serious, violent crimes are quite busy (Weis & Sederstrom, 1981). Carl F. Jesness (1987) suggests that some offenders must be working overtime to accumulate the large numbers of offenses they report. In short, he finds some self-reports very hard to believe and recommends that criminologists be cautious about accepting the validity of SR questionnaires. In any event, it is clear that a majority of serious or violent juvenile crime is committed by a small portion of the juvenile population. Furthermore, contrary to common belief, the SR investigations indicate that there is no "offense specialization" among delinquents. That is, active juvenile offenders do not concentrate on a specific criminal activity, such as robbery; they show considerable versatility in criminal involvement, committing a wide variety of offenses, violent as well as nonviolent.

Much of this serious, violent offending is probably committed by the life-course-persistent (LCP) individuals referred to earlier in the chapter. LCP youths show a childhood-onset of serious antisocial behaviors that encompass a wide variety of behaviors across a wide variety of situations (Moffitt, 1993b; Moffitt et al., 1996). These youths demonstrate a persistence in offending that baffles the experts looking for explanations, and their longstanding propensity to offend continues throughout their lifetimes. Based on available data, the number of LCPs in the male juvenile offender population is between 5 and 10 percent (Moffitt et al., 1996).

SR data also underscore the observation that serious juvenile delinquency is not evenly distributed across the country, nor across cities or communities (Weis & Sederstrom, 1981). Youthful offenders are more prevalent in some communities and neighborhoods than in others. Certain communities, sectors of cities, and neighborhoods tend to have criminal careers of their own, even with turnovers of population. By inference, then, if we are to accept the information gleaned from SR studies, some neighborhoods and communities may play a key role in the development of crime and delinquency.

Although advocates of the SR method believe that SR measures are more accurate indices of delinquency than other methods, we would be cautious about accepting this claim without further examination. Psychologists and sociologists have for many years wrestled with the troubling problems of SR questionnaires. For at least a hundred years, for instance, psychologists attempting to measure personality via SR methods have continually encountered myriad problems. For one thing, individuals attach a wide range of interpretations to the wording of questions. For another, they enter a test situation displaying widely different attitudes about answering questions. These pretest attitudes are called "response sets." An offender, then, may (1) misinterpret a question and (2) approach the questionnaire or the interview with suspicion, determined not to be honest. Sociologists, too, have recognized these problems. They have examined the many pitfalls in survey research in general, realizing that the quality of this research depends on many things, including the content of the questions and the manner in which they are asked. Thus, images of delinquent conduct drawn from SR studies vary according to who is drawing them, with which methods, and to which population they apply (Nettler, 1984).

IDENTIFYING THE SERIOUS DELINQUENT

There appear to be two very broad categories of juvenile offenders—those who offend frequently and persistently (**life-course-persistent delinquents**) and those who offend during their teen years and then stop (**adolescence-limited delinquents**). Finer distinctions are desirable but are very difficult to make at this point in research knowledge. At this juncture, it will be beneficial to describe two important cohort studies that provide a beginning thumbnail sketch of those who offend frequently and persistently and those who offend during their teens. One study, a classic in the field of criminology, was conducted some years ago by Marvin E. Wolfgang and his associates; the other, a more recent project, was conducted by Donna Martin Hamparian and her associates.

Cohort Studies

Wolfgang and his colleagues (Wolfgang, Figlio, & Sellin, 1972; Wolfgang, 1983) actually carried out two massive cohort studies. The term "cohort" refers to a group of subjects having one or more characteristics in common. In the two Wolfgang projects, the subjects had been born in the same year. The first birth cohort consisted of 9,945 males born in 1945 who resided in Philadelphia from their tenth to their eighteenth birthdays.

The second birth cohort consisted of 13,160 males and 14,000 females born in 1958 who also lived in Philadelphia from their tenth to their eighteenth birthdays. Essentially, the 1958 project was a "replication" of the 1945 one. In the social sciences, a replication occurs when researchers "copy" the procedure and methodology of a previous study as closely as possible to see if they will obtain similar results. The researchers also conducted an important third study in which they followed up 10 percent of the 1945 cohort until age 30.

Wolfgang followed the members of these cohorts through their adolescent years to discover who became delinquent and who did not. He collected data about their personal backgrounds and delinquency history from three sources: schools, police, and juvenile courts. Background data pertaining to race, sex, date of birth, and residential history were obtained from school records. Delinquency involvement was checked through the records of the Juvenile Aid Division of the Philadelphia Police Department. These data consisted of all recorded police contacts in which the youth was taken into custody, whether or not the contact resulted in an actual arrest. In Philadelphia, as in most jurisdictions, when a police officer has contact with a juvenile, he or she has the option of handling the offender informally or making an arrest. Delinquency, in the Wolfgang studies, was defined exclusively by the number of police contacts. The records of the Juvenile Court Division of the Court of Common Pleas for Philadelphia were also examined to determine how a case was handled.

Of the 13,160 males in the 1958 cohort, 4,315 or 33 percent had at least one police contact before reaching their 18th birthdays, a ratio very close to that of the 1945 cohort of 34 percent. Females were not included in the 1945 cohort analysis, but the 1958 data revealed that male adolescents were two and one-half times more likely to have a police contact than female adolescents. Of the 14,000 females, 1,972 or about 14 percent had at least one police contact.

In both studies, Wolfgang differentiated among three groups of offenders based on the frequency of police contacts: one-time offenders, nonchronic recidivists (two to four police contacts), and chronic recidivists (five or more police contacts). Because a recidivist is technically a person who commits more crime after having been convicted and punished, Wolfgang took some liberty with the term. Subsequent researchers must be careful to recognize this small but important deviation in terminology. Wolfgang's recidivists had not necessarily been adjudicated delinquent. In any event, he concluded that 6 percent were chronic recidivists.

In the 1958 cohort, the distribution of delinquents was 42 percent one-time offenders, 35 percent nonchronic recidivists, and 23 percent chronic recidivists. In the 1945 cohort, 46 percent were one-time offenders, 35 percent nonchronic recidivists, and 18 percent chronic recidivists. Thus, in both studies, the distributions were similar. Female delinquents in the 1958 cohort were 60 percent one-time offenders, 33 percent nonchronic recidivists, and 7 percent chronic recidivists.

One of the most important findings of both cohort studies pertains to the chronic recidivists, a group whose members qualify as serious delinquents. In the 1945 cohort analysis, male chronic recidivists constituted only 18 percent of the delinquent sample (and 6% of all boys in the cohort), yet they were responsible for more than 52 percent of all juvenile offenses. Even more striking, these chronic offenders accounted for 71 percent of the homicides, 73 percent of the rapes, 82 percent of the robberies, and 69 percent of the aggravated assaults. Similar statistics were found for the 1958 cohort. Although 1958 male chronics constituted only 23 percent of the delinquent group, they were responsible for 61 percent of all juvenile offenses. They were also involved in 61 percent of the juvenile homicides, 75 percent of the rapes, 65 percent of the aggravated assaults, and 73 percent of the robberies. In sum, a relatively small number of males seemed to be responsible for the bulk of the serious, violent delinquency. This finding, you will recall, has also been consistently reported in SR studies.

In a separate study, Wolfgang and his associates (Wolfgang, Thornberry, & Figlio, 1987) focused on 10 percent of the 1945 cohort and followed their records to the age of 30. The youths described as "chronic offenders"' in the original study comprised 70 percent of a group called "persistent offenders" in the follow-up study. The "chronics" in the early group had an 80 percent chance of becoming adult offenders. Furthermore, these offenders were arrested for the most serious crimes, such as murder, rape, and robbery. This follow-up research provided strong evidence that many juveniles who are involved in repeated offending carry this forward into adulthood.

Donna M. Hamparian and her colleagues (1978, 1982) conducted a longitudinal cohort analysis of 1,222 males and females born between the years 1956 and 1960 and arrested, as juveniles, for at least one violent offense. They found that violent offenders accounted for just over 30 percent of all the juvenile arrests. However, nearly one-third of the cohort qualified as chronic offenders (five or more arrests). And these chronic offenders accounted for two-thirds of all reported juvenile arrests in the birth cohort.

As in the SR data discussed earlier, the Hamparian project also found that the subjects did not specialize in the types of crimes they committed. The violent offenders did not repeat only violent acts, for example. Rather, they engaged in a variety of illegal acts, ranging from violence to petty larceny.

Like Wolfgang and his colleagues, the researchers tracked the offenders into their adult years to determine whether they had continued their criminal activity. They learned that approximately 60 percent of the males and less than one-third of the females were arrested for felonies as adults. Those who went on to be arrested as adults tended to have more arrests as juveniles, to have begun their delinquent careers at an earlier age, and to have been involved in the more serious types of violent offenses as juveniles. Significantly, three-fourths of those juveniles who had qualified as chronic offenders continued their criminal activity into adulthood. Thus, there appears to be a clear continuity between juvenile and adult criminal careers for some individuals.

Following the Juvenile Over Time: Longitudinal Studies

The Wolfgang and Hamparian projects both were longitudinal studies, meaning that they involved repeated measures or continual follow-up of the same individuals or groups over a specific length of time. Typically, investigators conducting longitudinal studies follow a group of youths over a number of developmental milestones in an effort to identify features that explain eventual delinquency. Because we will encounter the longitudinal method frequently in the pages ahead, it is important that we review some of its major characteristics.

There are two major types of longitudinal methods, retrospective and prospective. In **retrospective investigations**, individuals are identified after the events of interest have already taken place. The researchers look back to an earlier time period and follow up to a specified stopping point. In most retrospective studies, researchers rely on records that often are incomplete. When the retrospective procedure involves some self-report, as it often does, individuals are asked to remember events (e.g., delinquent offenses) that occurred earlier in their lifetimes, often covering a span of many years. Accuracy of recall, of course, becomes a critical factor in this method. Although human memory has an incredibly extensive storage capacity, it is also replete with distortions, misrepresentations, and biases. This is particularly true of memory about one's childhood. In **prospective studies**, on the other hand, subjects are identified before the event of interest occurs, and data are collected as relevant incidents are happening. For example, researchers might select 500 first-graders in a community and follow them through high school graduation to see who becomes involved in delinquency. The prospective approach is often preferred over the retrospective because of its reliance on recent memory and events in contrast to "old" memory or records, but it is also far more expensive and time-consuming.

Both approaches have advantages and disadvantages. David Magnusson and Vernon Allen (1983, p. 379) assert: "Both approaches are valuable and should be used; the one cannot replace the other." They go on to say that it all depends on the issue being examined, the nature of the data, and the resources available. The simultaneous application of both prospective and retrospective longitudinal studies may be necessary in some cases.

Some writers (e.g., Gottfredson & Hirschi, 1987) subsume retrospective studies into the same category as cross-sectional studies, which gather information about subjects at one point in time. A researcher using a cross-sectional procedure might select groups of 10-, 14-, and 18-year-old delinquents and compare them with groups of same-age nondelinquents to see if there are any discernible differences in their background. In effect, this method cuts a "cross-section" through time. For organizational purposes we will treat retrospective studies as variants of the longitudinal method, because they generally look back at more than one point in time. The Gottfredson–Hirschi position will be discussed again later in the book.

Desirable Features of Longitudinal Studies

David P. Farrington, Lloyd E. Ohlin, and James Q. Wilson (1986) recommend four features that should be part of any longitudinal design. First, they argue that ideally the study should be prospective. Suppose we wished to design a longitudinal study to explore the effects of parental abuse on frequent, persistent delinquency.

Obviously, we would want to design a study that allows us to sample subjects randomly, without exercising too much bias in the selection process. We would hope, then, to select our subjects before there was evidence of child abuse or before they demonstrated delinquent or nondelinquent patterns. We would want to keep close tabs on the subjects as they grow up. In short, we would want a prospective design.

Second, Farrington, Ohlin, and Wilson recommend that the longitudinal investigation collect data from a number of different sources, such as self-report questionnaires, court or police records, and interviews with teachers, peers, and parents. Material from different sources provides checks on the accuracy of the information and helps fill gaps in information. A high agreement among various sources offers consensual validation of the data.

A third desirable feature is that the sample size (the number of subjects in the study) be large—at least 100. In our proposed study, if we were to select only 50 youths, we might find ourselves with very few frequent, persistent delinquents—perhaps none. Similarly, we might also find little evidence of child abuse. Our research, then, would run the risk of having limited applicability to the study of delinquency. When a study can be generalized to other similar populations (e.g., serious delinquents), researchers say that it has high **external validity**. Low external validity indicates that the data are not representative. Consequently, a longitudinal design should include as large a percentage of the relevant youth population as time and money will allow.

A fourth desirable feature is that the longitudinal project cover a significant amount of time in the life course of the subjects—the longer the better. Farrington, Ohlin, and Wilson recommend that the project cover at least five years of development. Presumably, short longitudinal studies do not allow researchers to discover satisfactorily what is contributing to delinquency. Magnusson and Allen (1983) believe that for any longitudinal study to be effective, (1) it must cover the total critical periods of development for the behaviors of concern (in this case, delinquency), and (2) observations must be made frequently enough so as not to miss any of these critical periods of development. In essence, this means that longitudinal studies continue over rather long periods of time. It is not very meaningful, for example, to begin examining the effects of child abuse during early adolescence without knowing how much earlier in the child's development the abuse began, and how it affected that development.

Examples of Longitudinal Studies

Farrington, Ohlin, and Wilson were able to identify only 11 American studies on crime and delinquency that met the four desirable features outlined previously. The Wolfgang and Hamparian projects were not among them, because they relied primarily on written records. Several of the 11 studies are classics in the study of delinquency and will be discussed in detail in Chapter 8. Three were conducted by Sheldon and Eleanor Glueck (1930, 1934, 1937, 1943, 1950, 1968). Although Farrington, Ohlin, and Wilson classify the Glueck studies as prospective, they are, strictly speaking, both prospective and retrospective, because the

Gluecks selected their subjects after they were labeled "delinquent" and then carried out extensive follow-ups. The longest-lasting American longitudinal study, also a classic, was the Cambridge–Somerville Youth Study, designed by Robert C. Cabot and carried on by Edwin Powers and Helen Witmer (1951). It is called " . . . one of the most famous criminological experiments of all time" (Farrington, Ohlin, and Wilson, 1986, p. 65). Joan and William McCord (1959) achieved fame in the field of criminology by reviewing and analyzing its results. The Cambridge–Somerville boys and their offspring were followed for 25 years thereafter (McCord, 1986) and are still followed today.

Two other longitudinal studies were conducted by the psychologist Starke Hathaway and the sociologist Elio Monachesi (1957, 1963), who assessed the personalities of predelinquent boys. Personalities were measured by an extensive inventory, the Minnesota Multiphasic Personality Inventory (MMPI), which Hathaway helped develop. The researchers administered the MMPI to nearly 2,000 ninth-grade boys in Minneapolis public schools and then followed them and their official delinquency records throughout high school. In a second study, the research team tested another 5,700 ninth-grade boys, using the same basic procedure. They discovered ultimately, however, that their personality measures were not reliable predictors of delinquency. Another longitudinal project was conducted by Emmy Werner and her colleagues (1971, 1977, 1982, 1987) on nearly 700 Hawaiian children. This research will be reviewed in Chapter 6. Other longitudinal designs include the work of Langner, Gersten, and Eisenberg (1977), Lefkowitz et al. (1977), and Kellam et al. (1981).

The preeminent contemporary longitudinal study is the well-executed and informative **National Youth Survey** (NYS) (Ageton, 1983; Elliott & Huizinga, 1983, 1984), which also is one of the best SR surveys undertaken to date. The NYS is based on SR and official data collected on 1,725 youths who were between the ages of 11 and 17 when the project began in 1977. The survey involves a panel design in which the same youth are sampled repeatedly over a 5-year period. The NYS self-report questions were constructed to address many of the major criticisms usually directed at SR measures of delinquency. For example, critics often complain that self-report questionnaires ask about status or trivial offenses such as running away, violations of sexual mores, acting out in school, occasional drinking of alcohol, or disobeying parents. Others complain that questions are ambiguous or that the choices are unclear or inappropriate.

An even more ambitious longitudinal study sponsored by the National Institute of Juvenile Justice and Delinquency Prevention began in 1988. Substantial grants were awarded to the State University of New York at Albany, the University of Pittsburgh, and the University of Colorado to track seventh and eighth graders (ages 11–13) in three American cities over a period of four years. The project, called the **Rochester Youth Development Study**, is a longitudinal study designed to examine the development of delinquent behavior and drug use in a high-risk urban sample (Smith & Krohn, 1995). Researchers interview the children and the primary caretaker at six-month intervals. Additional data are gathered from a variety of psychological, social, and community resources. The objective is to identify the causes of delinquency and nondelinquency in city children and recommend effective strategies for intervention and prevention.

Another very important study is the **Chicago Youth Development Study**, a longitudinal study of the development of serious delinquent behavior among inner-city male adolescents, especially those youths representing diverse ethnic and socioeconomic backgrounds. This longitudinal study applies a multilevel, multiwave assessment to evaluate the interactions between individual, family, peer, community, and social variables affecting boys' involvement in antisocial behavior (Gorman-Smith et al., 1996). Most longitudinal studies have not included minority youths or include only a small segment of minority population in the sample. The Chicago Youth Development Study is one very prominent exception. We will be reviewing many of the findings of this project throughout the course of the book.

Although we have discussed only American studies up to this point, the reader should be aware that longitudinal research is a hallmark of criminology in Great Britain and the Scandinavian countries. Among the best-known British studies are those directed by Donald West and David Farrington (1973, 1977) and the National Survey of Health and Development (Douglas, Ross, & Simpson, 1968) carried on by M. E. J. Wadsworth (1975, 1979). We will encounter material from these investigations periodically in the course of the book.

Perhaps one of the most informative international research investigations is the **Dunedin Multidisciplinary Health and Development Study** (Silva, 1990). This project is a longitudinal study of the health, development, and behavior of children born between April 1, 1972, and March 31, 1973, in Dunedin, New Zealand, a city of approximately 120,000. The Dunedin sample, consisting of 1,037 males and females, has been continually evaluated through a diverse battery of psychological, medical, and sociological measures about every two or three years since the births. The findings of this very important, well-designed project will also be referred to frequently throughout the text.

A cautionary note is necessary before we proceed. Although most criminologists endorse the prospective longitudinal method, some are very critical. Michael Gottfredson and Travis Hirschi (1987), for example, argue that longitudinal research is not a necessary or even a valuable procedure to use in the study of crime and delinquency. They are convinced that cross-sectional procedures are more efficient and equally effective in gathering data about crime and delinquency. Other criminologists accept the value of longitudinal research but do not agree with the Farrington, Ohlin, and Wilson requirements for data collection and quantification. Instead, they believe that verbal descriptions and other **qualitative data** offer as many insights about delinquency as numerical data. In other words, they contend that research designs which allow researchers to talk informally and perhaps even live among their subjects over a period of time without collecting extensive numerical data also supply valuable material.

Summing up the Findings of Longitudinal Studies

At this point, we should assess what existing longitudinal studies tell us about delinquency. According to Farrington and his colleagues, longitudinal research indicates that juveniles involved in a high rate of offending represent a small proportion of the entire juvenile population. Furthermore, frequent offenders do not seem to specialize in any one particular kind of offending, such as theft or larceny. Instead, they tend to be involved in a wide assortment of offenses, ranging from minor property crimes to violent actions. Each of these points was stressed earlier in the chapter. Longitudinal research suggests also that these offenders are unusually troublesome in school, earn poor grades, have inadequate or inappropriate social skills, come from adverse family backgrounds, and receive poor parenting and supervision. Moreover, these troublesome behaviors began at an early age (usually they emerge by age three), and the more persistent and violent the offender, the earlier the childhood patterns appeared. There is strong evidence, for instance, that aggressive and violent behavior is well developed at approximately eight years of age (Eron, Huesmann, & Zelli, 1991). This should *not* be interpreted to mean that effective intervention after that age cannot be achieved, however. Nor should it be assumed that a particular aggressive child will be a violent delinquent. We must be very wary of labeling young children, especially in classrooms and other group environments.

In some children, the patterns of going "against the environment" extend into adolescence, frequently resulting in the youth's dropping out of school and being unable to maintain steady employment. These offenders very often use drugs and alcohol regularly. In sum, longitudinal research has consistently shown that a very small number of males engage in high rates of delinquent behavior across time and place. The research also confirms that another very large group of males engage in delinquency, sometimes engaging in frequent or even violent delinquent actions, but only during their teenage years. Before their teen years, and after, they are not involved in the criminal behaviors that are measured by official, victimization, or self-report data.

THE SERIOUS DELINQUENT

Up to this point, we have used the term "serious" rather loosely, with no attempt to define it carefully. Who, precisely, is the serious offender? Is he the 13-year-old who tries to hold up the local grocer with a toy gun? Is he the high school junior who has built an impressive rock-music collection from shoplifted CDs? Is she the gang member who has been arrested four times for simple assault? Law-enforcement officers, the public, victims, and researchers might all differ in their responses. Yet criminologists invariably express concern about the serious delinquent and draw conclusions about his or her background. For example, some believe that serious delinquents tend to come from families characterized by marital conflict, divorce, or poor parental supervision, or that gangs are prominent in their lives. Others observe that serious delinquents come from high-crime communities with ineffective informal social control and support systems. It will be important, when we assess these contributions to the criminological literature, to recognize how seriousness is being defined.

The Wolfgang and Hamparian studies discussed earlier emphasized frequency of offending as an adequate feature of the serious delinquent. The frequency of the offending, however, may not be the critical issue in identifying the serious, career offender. The developmental perspective (as represented by Terrie Moffitt, David Farrington, Rolf Loeber, Gerald Patterson, and others) contends that crime and delinquency follow at least two primary developmental courses, one with an early childhood onset and the other with later adolescent onset. Serious offenders usually begin their antisocial behavior early in their childhoods and continue this early antisocial behavior through adolescence and beyond. The early antisocial behavioral patterns may include a difficult, uncontrolled temperament, a lack of self-control, and cruelty to animals and peers. Children who demonstrate antisocial behaviors very early in their lives (around age three) are good candidates for a criminal career, especially if this behavior persists through adolescence. According to Moffitt et al. (1996, p. 399), "almost all violent and predatory adult antisocial careers originate in juvenile conduct problems." It should be emphasized, however, that more than 50 percent of the children who demonstrate antisocial behaviors in their early childhoods do *not* continue to demonstrate antisocial behaviors into adulthood. However, those who do become serious, violent offenders generally have exhibited early antisocial behaviors.

Those offenders who start an antisocial pattern early and persist at a high level through adolescence are termed life-course-persistent (LCP) offenders, as briefly described earlier. This small subgroup consists of offenders who mostly are male. The LCP's antisocial style often accumulates into rejection by peers, school failure, and continual problems with parents, teachers, and authorities. This escalating pattern continues throughout the LCP's life, thereby qualifying the individual for the label "career criminal."

Research finds that males who abstain from delinquency are rare and out of the norms for male adolescence (Moffitt et al., 1996). A very large majority (90 to 95 percent) of juveniles commit their offenses during the growing adjustments and social pressures characteristic of puberty. They do not exhibit antisocial behaviors during childhood, and, once through adolescence, these boys generally stop their delinquent conduct. As mentioned earlier in the chapter, these offenders are called adolescence-limited (AL) offenders. Throughout their adolescence they remain in school, do well or reasonably well academically, continue to develop friends, and are generally close to their families. Although they often are found in the delinquency statistics, they do not follow the life course of the chronic offender.

We will follow the developmental perspective throughout the book in distinguishing between the serious offender and the offender who statistically shows up during adolescence but stops persistent offending thereafter. It is important, therefore, that the reader keep the LCP and AL distinction in mind as we go through the text material. It is also important to realize, as we turn to the nature and extent of juvenile offending, that both LCP and AL offenders will be indistinguishable in much of the quantitative and qualitative research and data collection. Researchers and government agencies very rarely separate the two groups.

KEY CONCEPTS

adolescence-limited delinquent
aggression
antisocial personality disorder
antisocial behavior
Chicago Youth Development Study
conduct disorder
dark figure
delinquency
delinquent
Dunedin Multidisciplinary Health and
    Development Study
ethnographic study
external validity
formal processing
index crimes
informal processing
life-course-persistent delinquent
National Crime Victimization Survey
    (NCVS)

National Incident-based Reporting
    System (NIBRS)
National Youth Survey
non-index crimes
official statistics of crime
panel design
Part I crimes
prospective studies
qualitative data
qualitative methods
quantitative methods
retrospective investigations
Rochester Youth Development Study
self-report data
SR
Uniform Crime Reports (UCR)
victimization data
Wolfgang birth cohort studies

The Nature and Extent
of
Juvenile Offending

<h1>2</h1>

On August 9, 1996, a front-page story in the *New York Times* by Fox Butterfield proclaimed: "The nationwide rate of juvenile violent crime fell slightly last year for the first time in almost a decade, and the rate of homicide by juveniles decreased for the second year in a row, down by 15.2 percent, Attorney General Janet Reno said yesterday." No one, however, really could explain the drop, although some political posturing was evident. Law-enforcement agencies, for example, claimed the news was evidence that efforts in community policing were beginning to pay off. President Bill Clinton, during a campaign stop, attributed the drop to his administration's war on crime. School administrators credited various school programs for reducing the violent-crime rate. In the final analysis, no convincing explanation for the decline was found. Although some intervention and prevention programs may have had an effect on the juvenile violent-crime rate, the apparent decrease could also have been due to random fluctuation in crime reporting, data gathering, and overall statistics.

The decline was not large when we consider total juvenile offending, and, despite the reported drop, the juvenile violent-crime rate continues to remain uncomfortably high in the United States. In response to the reduction in juvenile offending reported in the *New York Times*, the University of Nebraska criminologist Chris Eskridge asserted: "You ain't seen nothing yet. It's going to be big-time. We're in the lull. There is a predatory group that is coming down the pipeline" (Rodriquez, 1996, p. B4). Eskridge believes that the reported drop is essentially a statistical fluke that had nothing to do with changes in public policy, community policing, or attempts at prevention. In similar fashion, John DiIulio, Jr. (1995), a public policy analyst, has drawn considerable media attention by predicting increases in a population of juvenile "super predators" the criminal justice system is unprepared to handle. Are these fears justified?

In this chapter, we will review what is known about the nationwide juvenile crime rates and trends, and what these data may tell us as we move into the twenty-first century. In addition, we will examine the major demographic variables that play significant roles in putting youth at risk, such as poverty, minority status, age, and gender. We will not describe in any detail specific offense categories, such as rape, aggravated assault, or robbery. Rather, we will divide offense categories into four very broad categories: violent, property, status, and drug offenses. **Violent offenses** are those that involve physical harm or the threat of physical harm. **Property offenses** are crimes directed at physical property and do not involve the physical harm, even though the victim may be present. A bicycle theft, for example, is a property offense. A robbery, on the other hand, is a *violent* offense because it involves force or the threat of force. **Status offenses** are violations of the law specifically restricted to juveniles, such as breaking of curfew, engaging in truancy, and running away. The trend in recent years has been to remove status offenses from juvenile court jurisdictions, but the jurisdiction remains in some states. Therefore, even though status offenses are a category that is slowly being phased out, it is important that we be familiar with the term because of its long, controversial history in juvenile justice. Furthermore, there is evidence that many juvenile court judges are resistive of this "letting go" of status offenders. This issue will be discussed in later chapters. **Drug offenses** pertain to the use and abuse of illegal drugs and alcohol.

We will cover violent and property offenses broadly because serious juvenile offenders rarely restrict their behavior to one type of offense category. Persistent juvenile offenders (LCPs), like persistent adult offenders, engage in a wide variety of offenses, specializing in none. Consequently, it will be more meaningful if we focus on *general patterns* of offending to get a better picture of offending characteristics, rather than focus on statistical detail and characteristics concerning a particular offense. We will let the tables, figures, and charts do that. There will be two exceptions to this restriction: arson and larceny-theft. Arson is covered in some detail in this chapter because it has the highest percentage of juvenile involvement of any other index crime, is often neglected in the literature on delinquency, and highlights very well some of the points on child development we plan to emphasize throughout the book. Larceny-theft, which includes such varied offenses as theft of bicycles, shoplifting, and grand larceny, will be highlighted because it represents by far the most commonly committed offense by juveniles.

The major characteristics of violent and property offenses will be described in this chapter. The status offenses will also be briefly described. Drug offenses, because they are so very important to understanding juvenile offending, will be discussed in considerable detail in the next chapter. We will begin with juvenile crime rates and trends pertaining to violent crimes.

JUVENILE ARREST RATES AND TRENDS: VIOLENT CRIMES

In 1995, the UCR crime index total was 13.9 million reported offenses, which was 1 percent lower than the 1994 total and 7 percent lower than the 1991 total. Violent crimes (murder and nonnegligent manslaughter, forcible rape, robbery, and aggravated assault) decreased 3 percent from 1994 to 1995. Aggravated assaults accounted for 61 percent and robberies for 32 percent of all violent crimes reported. Forcible rapes accounted for 5 percent and murder less than 2 percent.

In 1995, more than 3 million juveniles (under age 18) were arrested, with more than 800,000 of the arrests occurring for index crimes (FBI, 1996). (See Table 2.1.) In 1995, 69 million persons in the United States were below age 18, the group commonly referred to as juveniles. By the year 2010, the juvenile population is expected to reach 74 million (Bureau of the Census, 1995). According to the FBI, juvenile arrest rates have continually increased during the past ten years (with the unexplained exception of 1995). This increase is expected to continue for the next 10 to 20 years unless something quite substantial is done to reduce offending rates.

Most discouraging is the amount of violence allegedly perpetrated by the young. The rate of criminal homicide attributed to individuals under age 18 has more than doubled during the 7-year period from 1985 to 1992 (Blumstein, 1995), and it is expected to have doubled again within the 5-year period from 1993 to 1998.

We must be very careful not to assume that a person arrested and charged with a crime is guilty of that crime. An arrest merely indicates that a law enforcement officer had probable cause to believe a crime had been committed and that the person arrested committed it. Nevertheless, the increasing appearance of juveniles in arrest records is disturbing.

When we combine the projected growth rate in the juvenile population with the increasing arrest rates, the overall number of serious juvenile crime arrests is expected to more than double by the year 2010 (Snyder, Sickmund, & Poe-Yamagata, 1996). More specifically, the juvenile arrests for murder are expected to increase by 145 percent, forcible rapes by 66 percent, robbery arrests by 58 percent, and aggravated assault by 129 percent (Snyder, Sickmund, & Poe-Yamagata, 1996). If juvenile violent crime follows its current trajectory, the turn of the century will be very bleak for the safety of American youth, particularly those living in urban, poverty conditions.

TABLE 2.1   Total arrest trends and arrest trends for persons under 18 years of age, 1986–1995

| | Number of persons arrested | | | | | |
| | Total all ages | | | Under 18 years of age | | |
Offense charged	1986	1995	Percent change	1986	1995	Percent change
Total	88,870,709	10,362,736	+16.8	1,446,133	1,881,586	+30.1
Murder and nonnegligent manslaughter	14,297	15,384	+7.6	1,255	2,383	+89.9
Forcible rape	26,284	24,106	-8.3	3,994	3,853	-3.5
Robbery	113,671	128,089	+13.3	25,607	41,841	+63.4
Aggravated assault	260,451	399,414	+53.4	32,598	58,113	+78.3
Burglary	324,002	266,363	-17.8	113,921	93,484	-17.9
Larceny-theft	988,925	1,056,145	+6.8	309,746	353,667	+14.2
Motor vehicle theft	115,898	137,233	+18.4	44,675	57,209	+28.1
Arson	12,689	13,569	+6.9	5,095	7,137	+40.1
Violent crime[a]	414,703	567,713	+36.9	63,454	106,190	+67.3
Property crime[b]	1,441,523	1,473,310	+2.2	473,437	511,497	+8.0
Crime index total[c]	1,856,226	2,041,023	+10.0	536,891	617,687	+15.0
Other assaults	488,005	883,870	+81.1	69,554	146,543	+110.7
Forgery and counterfeiting	64,005	84,068	+31.3	5,968	6,103	+2.3
Fraud	245,779	295,584	+20.3	17,010	17,918	+5.3
Embezzlement	8,857	10,832	+22.3	608	896	+47.4
Stolen property: buying, receiving, possessing	97,711	114,982	+17.7	24,372	29,358	+20.5
Vandalism	175,589	208,705	+18.9	75,252	94,213	+25.2
Weapons: carrying, possessing, etc.	124,888	170,335	+19.5	22,437	39,309	+75.2
Prostitution	91,764	74,644	-18.7	1,945	976	-49.8
Sex offenses (except rape and prostitution)	72,517	66,018	-9.0	11,616	11,180	–3.8
Drug-abuse violations	636,821	1,048,319	+64.6	61,960	113,323	+115.2
Gambling	24,321	14,653	-39.8	552	1,093	+98.0
Offenses against family and children	39,055	84,637	+116.7	2,287	4,077	+78.3
Driving under the influence (DUI)	1,215,983	917,167	-24.6	18,695	9,565	–48.8
Violation of liquor laws	372,532	394,621	+5.9	94,791	77,969	–17.7
Drunkeness	661,943	489,385	-26.1	23,474	14,252	–39.3
Disorderly conduct	t470,361	487,073	+3.6	65,517	109,305	+66.8
Vagrancy	31,264	19,582	-37.4	2,266	2,612	+15.3
All other offenses (except traffic)	2,001,618	2,677,432	+33.8	237,068	285,401	+20.4
Suspicion	10,596	7,901	-25.4	1,866	1,383	– 25.9
Violation of curfew and loitering	58,930	103,436	+75.5	58,930	103,436	+75.5
Runaways	114,940	176,370	+53.4	114,940	176,370	+53.4

SOURCE: *FBI Uniform Crime Reports—1995* (Washington, DC: U.S. Department of Justice, 1996), p. 212.

[a]Violent crimes are offenses of murder, forcible rape, aggravated assault, and robbery.
[b]Property crimes are offenses of burglary, larceny-theft, motor vehicle theft, and arson.
[c]Includes arson.

Figure 2.1 lists the offenses for which juveniles are most often arrested, in descending order. As you can readily see, larceny-theft tops the list by a wide margin, whereas violent offenses are comparatively low. Figure 2.1 also represents arrest rates per 1,000 juveniles ages 10 to 17 in parentheses for all juveniles in 1995.

In 1991, the *National Crime Victimization Survey* (NCVS) revealed that victims of personal crimes (e.g., rape, robbery, aggravated assault, and theft from a person) reported that approximately 28 percent of the offenders were juveniles (under age 18) (Snyder & Sickmund, 1995).

When juveniles commit murder, a majority of their victims are friends (53 percent) (Snyder & Sickmund, 1995). Thirty-two percent of juvenile murder victims are strangers, and 15 percent are family members. When juveniles commit murder within the family, they typically kill fathers or stepfathers (30 percent) or brothers (17 percent) (Snyder & Sickmund, 1995).

Weapons and Violence

In 1990, the Centers for Disease Control (CDC) asked a representative sample of high school students if they had carried weapons during the previous 30 days (Centers for Disease Control, 1991). The CDC survey found that one in five high schoolers reported carrying a weapon (gun, knife, razor, club) at least once during the previous month. Males, compared with females, were four times more

FIGURE 2.1   1995 total arrests for juveniles

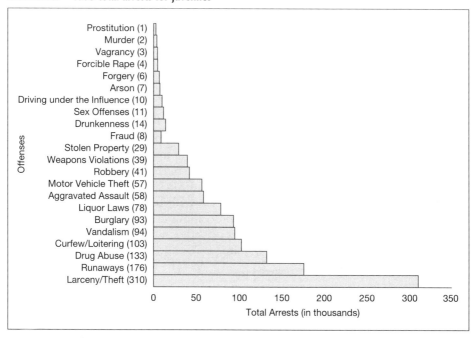

SOURCE: FBI *Uniform Crime Reports—1995* (Washington, DC: U.S. Department of Justice, 1996), p. 212.

likely to report carrying a weapon (Snyder & Sickmund, 1995). The weapons most often carried were knives or razors (55 percent), followed by clubs (24 percent), and firearms (21 percent). Firearms are the most dangerous and most closely associated with violence.

Research (e.g., Lester, 1991; Berkowitz, 1994) consistently reveals that the availability of firearms in a particular nation is strongly related to that country's homicide rate. For example, total firearms in the United States is estimated to be 222,000,000, compared with Britain's 409,000 (McGuire, 1996). The rate of firearms per 100,000 people in the United States is 5.25, compared with the British rate of 0.116. The total murders in the United States due to firearms averages around 14,000 per year, compared with Britain, where there are fewer than 100 annually. By any measure, the United States has the highest homicide rate of any Western industrialized country in the world. The firearm homicide rate in the United States is twice as high as that in France, more than 5 times higher than Canada's, and more than 10 times higher than Switzerland's (Berkowitz, 1994).

Despite these revealing statistics, we cannot assume that the availability of guns automatically results in an increase in violence. Violence and the fear of violence prompt at least some citizens to obtain guns to protect or defend themselves or to improve their status. In any event, the data do not allow a determination of causality, but the *correlation* between guns and crime is evident.

Firearms are used in about 60 to 65 percent of the murders committed by juveniles, and a vast majority of these offenders use handguns. More discouragingly, not only is the use of firearms by juveniles increasing each year, but the use of high-caliber automatic or semiautomatic weapons is also growing. Firearms appear to be especially troublesome for minorities. Research has consistently shown that African Americans are greatly overrepresented in homicide cases, both as victims and offenders, and that three-quarters of these deaths are a result of firearms (Berkowitz, 1994).

The rise in firearm homicide rates among the young is frequently attributed to increases in drug traffic and drug use, but some researchers believe that drug trafficking is rarely the primary cause of the growing juvenile deaths due to firearms (Block & Block, 1993; Berkowitz, 1994). For example, gang wars over territorial conflicts are often the principal reason for many firearms homicides, independent of disputes over the sale and use of drugs.

Fortunately, research evidence indicates that only a small fraction of the juvenile population commits violence with a weapon. We will find as we go through the text that juveniles who commit crimes with weapons tend to be the more serious life-course-persistent offenders who engage in a lifelong assortment of antisocial and violent behaviors.

JUVENILE ARREST RATES AND TRENDS: PROPERTY CRIMES

Most of the index crimes committed in the United States are not violent crimes but crimes against property. Property crimes, totaling 12 million, accounted for nearly 90 percent of the index crimes reported in 1995. Approximately $15.6 billion worth of property was stolen, an average of $1,251 per offense reported. The most frequently reported property crime is larceny-theft, which makes up 66 percent of the total property crime. Burglary accounted for 22 percent of property crime totals and motor vehicle theft for 12 percent. About 2 out of every 3 burglaries are residential in nature, and more than half (52 percent) occurred during the daylight hours. Juvenile burglaries most commonly occur between 3:00 P.M. and 6:00 P.M., obviously after-school hours. There were approximately 1.5 million thefts of motor vehicles reported in 1995, with more than two-thirds of them being auto-mobiles.

Larceny-Theft

Larceny-theft is defined as the "unlawful taking, carrying, leading, or riding away of property from the possession or constructive possession of another" (UCR, 1993, p. 43). Larceny-theft differs from **burglary**, which is defined as the *unlawful entry* of a structure, with or without force, with intent to commit a felony or theft.

Larceny-theft includes picking pockets, purse snatching, shoplifting, and stealing from vending machines or from motor vehicles. Theft of property left outdoors, such as bicycles, pedigreed dogs, and lawnmowers is also included. The unauthorized taking of property from a person's home is in this category if the thief is in the home legitimately. A youth who steals his friend's father's pocketwatch while visiting the friend is committing larceny. Larceny-theft constitutes approximately two-thirds of all property crimes reported and accounts for more than 58 percent of the entire FBI Crime Index arrests. It is the offense resulting in the most arrests of persons under the age of 18 (Figure 2.1). Thirty-three percent of those arrested for larceny-theft in 1995 were under age 18, and 15 percent percent were under age 15. Figure 2.2 depicts the offenses for which juveniles under 15 are arrested.

FIGURE 2.2   Total arrests of persons under age 15 during 1995

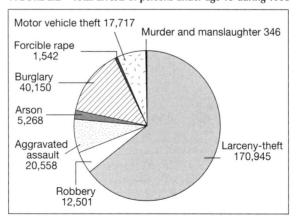

SOURCE: *FBI Uniform Crime Reports—1995* (Washington, DC: U.S. Department of Justice, 1996), p. 224.

Shoplifting

Although the majority of shoplifting incidents involve a small dollar amount, the total dollar loss across North America is enormous. It is estimated to be in the billions. The Retail Council of Canada estimates that in Canada, merchandise totaling $3 million in value is shoplifted each day (Lo, 1994). Cox et al. (1993) speculate that consumers shoplift about $12 billion worth of merchandise from U.S. retailers every year. In response, retailers implement a number of security measures to reduce the incidence of theft; among these are the use of security guards, electronic tags, video cameras, and undercover floor walkers. Retailers also employ a variety of legal threats, such as "Shoplifters Will be Prosecuted" signs.

As described by Lo (1994), the shopping mall has become a way of life in North America and has also become a major hangout area for teenagers. Furthermore, shoplifting represents the largest crime committed at malls, with the greatest amount of the shoplifting occurring in major anchor stores and large chain stores. There is a widespread belief that a vast majority of shoplifters are teenagers, and that they are more likely to commit the crime in groups.

Lo (1994) reports that teenagers shoplift primarily for fun and thrills and that peer pressures also substantially influence this behavior. Cox et al. (1993) disagree with this assessment, arguing that teenagers shoplift because they wish to emulate peers who shoplift and/or they have inadequate attachment to caretakers in their lives.

The causes of juvenile shoplifting are probably multiple. One thing is clear, however. Shoplifting activity decreases for a vast majority of individuals with age. This observation holds whether we are talking about arrest data or self-report data. Arrests for shoplifting are most frequent in the age 11–15 group, and then show a steady decline throughout the life cycle, especially after age 20 (Klemke, 1992). Although some may argue that these data reflect the heightened watchfulness of store personnel to younger shoppers, self-report data show a similar age-related trend. In fact, self-report data suggest that shoplifting may peak before age 10 for a majority of youth, and then show a decline through the life cycle (Klemke, 1992). Interestingly, data from college bookstores indicate that first-year students are more likely to be apprehended for shoplifting than other college students (Klemke, 1992).

ARSON

Arson is defined "as any willful or malicious burning or attempt to burn, with or without intent to defraud, a dwelling house, public building, motor vehicle or aircraft, or personal property of another" (UCR, 1993, p. 53). Arson joined the list of UCR index crimes in 1978, signifying both its seriousness and frequency. One-fifth of all property loss in the United States is due to arson, exceeding $2 billion annually. Residential property is most commonly involved, with the majority of juvenile arsons directed at single-family dwellings (see Table 2.2). In 1995, the monetary value of property damaged due to reported arson averaged around $11,000 per offense. Tragically, arson also claims at least 700 to 800 lives a year.

TABLE 2.2   **Arson offenses cleared by arrests of persons under 18 years of age, 1995**

Property classification	Total clearances	Percent under 18
Total	14,808	47.2
Total Structure	9,666	45.3
Single-occcupancy resident	4,178	36.6
Other residential	1,793	34.5
Storage	705	64.1
Industrial/manufact.	105	45.7
Other commercial	718	37.7
Community/public	1,554	73.6
Other structure	613	51.5
Total Mobile	1,709	28.1
Motor vehicles	1,502	26.5
Other mobiles	207	39 6
Other	3,433	62.0

SOURCE: *FBI Uniform Crime Reports—1995* (Washington, DC: U.S Department of Justice, l996), p. 54.

A total of 95,000 arson offenses were reported in 1995, and approximately 50 percent of those cleared were attributed to juveniles under the age of 18; 38 percent were attributed to juveniles under the age of 15. However, it is generally acknowledged that only a small proportion of fires set by young people are ever reported, probably fewer than 10 percent (Adler et al., 1994).

Fascination and experimentation with fire appear to be a common feature of normal child development. Kafrey (1980) discovered that fascination with fire appears to be nearly universal in children between five and seven years old. Furthermore, this fascination with fire begins early, with one in five children setting fires before the age of three. Firesetting behavior usually declines after age seven, probably in part because of frequent admonishments of its dangers by parents and other adults. The children who continue to set fires tend to demonstrate poor social skills, poor judgment, and impulsiveness compared with their peers (Kolko, 1985; Kolko & Kazdin, 1986). In general, persistent fire setters are more likely to demonstrate attention deficit hyperactivity disorders (AD/HD)(Forehand et al., 1991), and many are considered to have "conduct problems" by their teachers. Nearly all children who set fires beyond the normal fascination stage tend to have poor relationships with their parents and also appear to be victims of physical abuse (Jackson, Glass, & Hope, 1987). Kolko (1985) in his comprehensive review suggests that fire setting may be closely associated with parental ineffectiveness and faulty or nonexistent supervision. In a retrospective study by Saunders and Awad (1991), the records of 13 adolescent girls referred to the Toronto Family Court Clinic for setting fires were examined. The authors discouragingly concluded:

> Reading through the 13 charts was a depressing experience even for those of us who have worked for years with families who have many problems and serious difficulties meeting their children's basic needs. These parents had a history of marital problems, separation, violence against the spouse and the children, criminal behaviour, drug and/or alcohol abuse, and inability to take care of the children (Saunders & Awad, 1991, p. 403).

Interestingly, a very large majority of fire setters known to the juvenile justice system have committed many other serious juvenile acts besides arson (Ritvo, Shanok, & Lewis, 1983). Some researchers report that persistent fire setting is a sign of an advanced antisocial trajectory (Forehand et al., 1991). That is, persistent fire setting indicates that the individual is well into his or her delinquent or criminal career. As might be expected, a large portion of the continual fire setters are boys, probably at least 80 percent (Kolko, 1985).

Adult arsonists who began seting fires as children tend to be unassertive, have limited interpersonal skills, be underemployed or unemployed, and be prone toward depression and feelings of helplessness (Murphy & Clare, 1996). In general, research findings continually find that as a group, arsonists are inadequate socially and interpersonally, although the exact nature of the inadequacy varies between individuals (Jackson, Glass, & Hope, 1987).

Research suggests that fire setters (adolescent or adult) have little or no effective means for influencing their environment and find themselves in highly undesirable situations (Jackson, Glass, & Hope, 1987). Consequently, the arsonist experiences feelings of worthlessness and social ineffectiveness. Some researchers suggest that setting fires may provide conditions whereby the person feels that he or she can experience control or at least some influence over the environment.

The continual fire setter follows the behavioral pattern of the life-course-persistent (LCP) offender, discussed previously. Thus, there appear to be two very broad classes of fire setters: those who engage in setting fires for curiosity during an early developmental period of their lives and then stop, and those who continue to use fire in an attempt to gain something, such as revenge or intimidation.

STATUS OFFENSES

Status offenses, mentioned earlier, are acts that only juveniles are prohibited from committing. The same act if committed by an adult results in no sanctions. Typical status offenses range from specific misbehaviors, such as violating town- or city-established curfews, running away from home, using tobacco or alcohol, and engaging in truancy, to loosely defined offenses such as unruliness and unmanageability that are responded to with wide discretion.

Historically, much of the discretion has been based on gender differences. Law-enforcement officials as well as representatives of the judicial system have treated male and female status offenders differently, for example. Adolescent girls have often been detained for incorrigibility or running away from home, when the same behavior in adolescent boys has been ignored or tolerated. Traditionally, many more girls have been detained for status offenses than boys (U.S. Department of Justice, 1983). Self-report data tell a different story, however. Self-report information from eleventh- and twelfth-grade students indicates that so-called status offending is equally distributed between males and females (Kratcoski & Kratcoski, 1996).

In recent years, as a result of suits brought on behalf of juvenile girls, many courts have put authorities on notice that this discriminatory approach is unwarranted, and overtly the practice appears to be diminishing. Under federal law, juveniles are no longer subject to official sanction for status violations. Nevertheless, some research suggests that officials circumvent the rules by reaching for ways to bring adolescents, particularly girls, under the aegis of juvenile courts (Chesney-Lind, 1986; Schwartz, 1989). Furthermore, though some states (7 at this writing) have removed status offenses from the jurisdiction of the courts, many (30 including the District of Columbia) have also replaced statutes concerning these offenses with statutes allowing the detention and/or supervision of youngsters who are presumably in need of protection either from their own behavior or the behavior of others. These statutes are usually referred to as PINS, CHINS, MINS, or YINS laws (the acronymns mean, respectively, person, child, minor, or youth in need of supervision). Under these laws, runaways or "incorrigible" youngsters are subject to juvenile court jurisdiction, often at the instigation of their parents, and even though they may not have violated a criminal code.

Should we be concerned about the status offender or the "incorrigible" adolescent? For our purposes, we should be only if these youths are also involved in criminal conduct. This is not to say that society should not be concerned, for status offenders and children in need of supervision often have been and continue to be abused, emotionally and physically. Humane intervention may be required, but it should not be accomplished through use of criminal sanctions or without regard to the rights of the juveniles or their families. Ironically, officially labeled juvenile delinquents have been given a greater measure of constitutional protections than have children determined to be "in need of supervision."

JUVENILES AT RISK: SOME DEMOGRAPHICS

In this section, we will examine the demographics (the statistical study of human populations) of the American juvenile offender. Although each demographic variable will be presented separately, it is important to keep in mind that none of them operates in isolation. They interact and influence one another in complex ways. For example, race and ethnicity cannot be separated from poverty in many instances, nor can they be separated from the social discrimination and occupational biases that may operate in any given society.

Poverty, Social Class, and Delinquency

Social class has been a central focus in research studies of crime and delinquency for many years. Most pre-1960 sociological theories of delinquency included it as a crucial ingredient in explanations for crime and delinquency. Specifically, these theories predicted an inverse or negative relationship between social class and criminal involvement: the lower the social class, the greater the likelihood of involvement in criminal or delinquent behavior. During the mid-1950s and early

1960s, researchers began to wonder if the social class–delinquency connection was as strong as originally supposed. Much of this doubt stemmed from the development of self-report studies, which indicated that juvenile offending was as prevalent among middle-class youth as it was among lower-class youth.

As the self-report data rolled in, the controversy soon shifted to the definition of social class. What precisely, researchers asked, is meant by social class, and how can it be measured? The new term **"socioeconomic status"** (**SES**), defined by the educational, occupational, or income level of the father, mother, or both, gradually began to replace "social class" in the literature. However, because the term "SES" had so many different meanings, it actually presented as many problems as "social class." Researchers continued to debate the best way to measure the terms, and few could agree on the best methods to use.

Other criminologists moved away from the class-crime connection altogether, arguing cogently that the poor were being placed under the research microscope while the crimes of the economically advantaged were being ignored. A conflict or critical school of criminology that challenged many assumptions of mainstream theorists developed rapidly. Representatives of this conflict approach preferred to examine how a society decides what is prohibited as well as how groups and individuals with power maintain that power at the expense of the disadvantaged. The contributions and insights of conflict criminologists will be highlighted in a later chapter and should be considered in the context of the material to follow.

There is little doubt, though, that poverty has a strong connection to persistent, violent delinquency as measured by official, victimization, and self-report data. Today, accumulating research evidence strongly indicates that poverty is one of the most robust predictors of adolescent violence for both males and females (Sampson & Wilson, 1993; Hammond & Yung, 1994; Hill et al., 1994). The poverty–violence relationship holds whether we are discussing victims or offenders. Youth living under conditions of poverty are more likely to be victimized, and youth living under conditions of poverty are more likely to be offenders. Preschool children living in a low-income family characterized by poor housing and unemployment are especially at high risk to become delinquent and/or to become victimized (Dodge, 1993a; Farrington, 1991).

It is extremely important to keep in mind, however, that crime—including violent crime—perpetrated by middle and upper strata in society is much less likely to be reflected in the statistics. There are many reasons for this. With reference to arrest data, for example, it is well recognized that law enforcement polices poor neighborhoods in the inner city very differently from middle and upper income neighborhoods. "Street crimes" are treated differently from "suite crimes." Moreover, actions of the rich and powerful that victimize society are far less likely to be made crimes; if criminalized, they are less likely to be prosecuted. With respect to juvenile offending, the children of the middle class are almost invariably given favorable treatment by the juvenile justice system. We have grave concerns, therefore, about perpetuating the misconceptions that the poor or minority groups in society are to be blamed for crime, and we cannot emphasize enough the need to be cautious.

Poverty—broadly defined—refers to a situation where the basic resources to maintain an average standard of living are lacking. This may include the absence of sufficient income to meet basic necessities of life. Currently, there are two slightly different versions of the U.S. measure of poverty: the poverty thresholds and the poverty guidelines. The **poverty thresholds** are updated each year by the Bureau of the Census and are used primarily for statistical reports. The thresholds are essentially monetary cutoffs that define what a family needs in order to meet basic needs in various regions of the United States.

The **poverty guidelines** are issued each year in the Federal Register by the Department of Health and Human Services. The guidelines are fundamentally a simplification of the poverty thresholds and are used largely for administrative purposes, such as determining eligibility for certain federal programs, including Head Start, the Food Stamp Program, and the National School Lunch Program. The 1995 poverty threshold for a family of four within the 48 contiguous states and the District of Columbia was $15,150. In 1995, juveniles made up 26 percent of the U.S. population but made up 40 percent of all persons living below the poverty threshold.

The exact nature of the relationship between poverty and serious, violent juvenile offending is not well understood. It certainly is far more complicated than it seems. For example, poverty is often accompanied not only by inequities in resources, but also by discrimination, racism, family disruption, unsafe living conditions, joblessness, social isolation, and limited social-support systems (Hill et al., 1994; Sampson & Lauritsen, 1994). Youth living under conditions of poverty are more likely to drop out of school, to be unemployed, to carry a firearm, and to be involved in violence. In addition, poverty affects people differently. The values of different ethnic and cultural groups, for instance, provide a contextual backdrop wherein poverty is viewed differently (Guerra et al., 1995). As noted by Hawkins (1993), it appears that economic inequality and lack of opportunity, rather than the absolute level of material deprivation, are more strongly related to group differences in violence. If subgroups or minority groups perceive everyone as being in the "same boat," the amount of material deprivation is more acceptable. In fact, violence rates are highest for countries and regions in which the difference in the levels of material wealth between the rich and the poor is greatest (Hawkins, 1993; Eron & Slaby, 1994). This observation may be a bad omen for the United States, where the gap between the wealthy and the poor is widening and where harmful actions of the wealthy are perceived (very often accurately) as going unpunished.

Poverty influences the family in numerous ways. Perhaps most critically, it influences children through its impact on parents' behavior toward children. For example, the stress caused by poverty in urban settings is believed to diminish parents' capacity for supportive and consistent parenting (Hammond & Yung, 1994). This situation may lead to coercive and aggressive methods of child control. Coercive methods of child control are more direct and immediate, and require less energy and time to administer, than methods that require sensitivity and interpersonal skills and understanding. To put it more simply, it is easier to slap than it is to explain and employ more thoughtful parenting techniques. Furthermore, the aggressive, forceful methods often provide aggressive models and a violent context that promote the cycle of violence in future generations. Also, living in disadvantaged urban settings can lead to the belief that economic survival through conventional channels is not possible. Disadvantaged youth may come to believe that aggressive, violent behavior may be the most feasible choice for gaining status or material rewards or for simply coping with the fear of victimization (Guerra et al., 1995).

We now turn our attention to the complex relationship among minorities, poverty, and crime. Before we proceed, however, it is important to emphasize at the outset that ethnic minority groups are extremely heterogeneous and reflect very wide cultural differences in beliefs, perceptions, attitudes, and behavior.

Minorities, Poverty, and Delinquency

African American Youth   Minority juveniles are more likely to live in poverty than nonminority juveniles. In 1995, 47 percent of African American juveniles lived in poverty, compared with 17 percent of white juveniles. Furthermore, official crime statistics continually reveal that African American youths are disproportionately involved in delinquency for youths under the age of 18. Although they make up only 12 percent of the U.S. population, they constitute about 30 percent of all arrests for index crimes and about 50 percent of all arrests for violent crimes in 1995. Several explanations have been offered to explain the disparity in delinquency between African Americans and whites. A common argument focuses on what is perceived to be widespread discrimination and bias on the part of the criminal justice system itself. Other explanations focus on the conditions in inner cities that block opportunities for minority youth and effectively consign them to a marginal status in society. Jonathan Kozol (1992, 1995) has documented with brutal reality the plight of poor children and their families in American society.

U.S. Latino Youth   Latinos represent approximately 22.4 million people, or about 9 percent of the total U.S. population, and are presently one of the largest and fastest-growing minorities in the United States (Garcia, 1991; Soriano, 1994). The U.S. Latino population is expected to surpass the U.S. African American population by the year 2010. Yet Latinos are sometimes called the "invisible minority" because so little is known at the national level about them (Soriano, 1994). In terms of country of origin, the Mexican subgroup is the largest Latino subgroup in the United States today, making up 63 percent of the U.S. Latino population (Soriano, 1994). Persons of Puerto Rican ancestry, who represent 11 percent of the U.S. Latino population, constitute the second-largest Latino subgroup, followed by the Cuban subgroup, which constitutes 5 percent of the U.S. Latino population. In recent years, there has been a steady influx of Latinos into the United States from Central and South America.

Available data suggest that at least 40 percent of U.S. Latino youth live in poverty (Soriano, 1994; Snyder & Sickmund, 1995). There is also some evidence to suggest that Latinos ages 15 to 19 may have the highest homicide victimization rates of any minority group (Block, 1988; Soriano, 1994). Because violence-related national data were not systematically collected on ethnic groups other than African Americans until recently, little is known about the extent of risk and the experience of violence against Latinos and the other minority groups. *Uniform Crime Reports—1996*, the most recent edition, does differentiate arrest data for some minorities besides African Americans: namely Native Americans, Asians, and Pacific Islanders (Table 2.3).

TABLE 2.3   Total arrests, distribution by race, 1995

	Total arrests				
Offense charged	*Total*	*White*	*Black*	*American Indian or Alaskan Native*	*Asian or Pacific Islander*
Total	11,386,627	7,607,522	3,523,409	129,843	125,853
Murder and nonnegligent manslaughter	16,691	7,245	9,047	134	238
Forcible rape	26,519	14,739	11,234	260	286
Robbery	137,761	53,370	81,957	692	1,742
Aggravated assault	437,686	260,778	167,857	4,152	4,899
Burglary	291,901	195,486	90,421	2,765	3,229
Larceny-theft	1,162,647	753,868	377,143	12,811	18,852
Motor vehicle theft	148,899	87,159	57,060	1,743	2,937
Arson	14,931	11,083	3,543	150	155
Violent crime	618,657	336,132	270,122	5,238	7,165
Property crime	1,618,405	1,047,596	528,167	17,469	25,173
Crime index total	2,237,062	1,383,728	798,289	22,707	32,338
Other assaults	973,672	613,098	338,038	11,983	10,553
Forgery and counterfeiting	91,782	59,630	30,336	509	1,307
Fraud	319,404	207,473	110,920	1,559	2,452
Embezzlement	11,599	7,529	3,840	71	159
Stolen property: buying, receiving, possessing	127,624	74,837	50,285	933	1,569
Vandalism	232,387	170,647	55,611	3,139	2,990
Weapons: carrying, possessing, etc.	187,046	111,123	72,494	1,235	2,194
Prostitution and commercialized vice	81,050	49,334	29,866	439	1,411
Sex offenses (except forcible rape and prostitution)	72,171	54,141	16,342	783	905
Drug-abuse violations	1,143,148	709,704	421,346	5,286	6,812
Gambling	15,673	8,360	6,468	72	773
Offenses against family and children	104,122	67,857	33,506	1,010	1,749
Driving under the influence (DUI)	1,019,226	880,635	110,839	15,626	12,160
Liquor laws	433,585	345,127	75,137	10,212	3,109
Drunkenness	526,742	425,514	86,608	12,749	1,871
Disorderly conduct	560,809	352,965	196,919	7,539	3,386
Vagrancy	20,517	10,749	9,225	463	80
All other offenses (except traffic)	2,915,568	1,840,568	1,012,616	30,274	23,110
Suspicion	9,055	4,697	4,032	35	21
Curfew and loitering law violations	114,702	86,902	24,445	1,519	1,836
Runaways	189,649	145,904	35,977	1,700	6,068

SOURCE: *FBI Uniform Crime Reports—1995* (Washington, D.C.: U.S. Deopartment of Justice, 1996), p. 227.

Native American Youth   Statistics are even more difficult to obtain concerning Native Americans, the smallest and among the most diverse of all American minorities. There are an estimated 124 major federally recognized tribes and bands in the United States, and at least another 450 smaller subgroups (Yung & Hammond, 1994). The available but sketchy data on economics of this minority group suggest that they may be the poorest minority group of all (Yung & Hammond, 1994).

Just as with Latinos, obtaining comprehensive national crime data on Native Americans is difficult. Although the UCR is beginning to report arrest statistics for "American Indians," most of the existing data have been gathered from regional or tribal studies. A few studies (e.g., Sloan et al., 1988; Becker et al., 1990) have suggested that violent crime among Native Americans may be the highest of all minority groups. However, research specifically focusing on the effects of violence or abuse on Native American youths and adolescents continues to be sparse (Yung & Hammond, 1994), and many more data are required before conclusions about Native American violence can be advanced.

Asian and Pacific Island American Youth   Very little is known about the effects of violence and crime on Asian and Pacific Island American youth (Chen & True, 1994). The Asian and Pacific Island (A/PI) population certainly represents a very heterogeneous group in terms of its members' history, language, culture, socioeconomic status, needs, and problems (Takaki, 1989; Chen & True, 1994). Asian Americans account for 95 percent of the A/PI population, representing 28 ethnic groups, consisting of persons of Chinese, Japanese, Korean, Filipino, Asian Indian, and Vietnamese ancestry (Chen, 1992; Chen & True, 1994).

In spite of the lack of national violence-related data on the A/PI group, Chen and True (1994) contend that A/PIs are at considerable risk of experiencing interracial violence. For example, although Chinese American and Japanese American families have relatively high incomes overall, there is considerable poverty among some A/PI subgroups. Specifically, new refugees and immigrants from southeast Asia continue to be among the highest poverty groups in America. Furthermore, many A/PI refugee or immigrant youths have been exposed to violent atrocities in their countries of origin, such as tortures, brutal assaults, rape, and the murder of their parents and loved ones (Chen & True, 1994). In the United States, a significant number of A/PI children are also subject to hate (bias) crimes, resulting in physical, social, and psychological attacks. As Chen and True (1994, p. 153) note, when refugees become victimized, "the new traumas reawaken and compound their past psychic traumas, which are often manifested as severe anxiety reactions, depressive symptoms, psychosomatic symptoms, and behavior problems."

Available data do suggest that the overall incidence of child abuse and sexual abuse among the A/PI family groups appears to be substantially lower than reported in the general U.S. population (Chen & True, 1994). Involvement of A/PI youth in gangs and gang-related violence also appears low, despite media publicity about reported increases in A/PI gang activity. And there is reason to believe that A/PI adolescents use alcohol and drugs at levels significantly below those of the U.S. youth population in general.

AGE AND CRIMINAL CAREER PATHS

The age factor has been instrumental in the increased use of the longitudinal study as the preferred method of criminological research. **Cross-sectional investigations**, wherein researchers examine several age groups only once rather than follow them over a period of years, are insensitive to age effects. Thus, many criminologists today view cross-sectional approaches as flawed, because these approaches are unable to detect developmental or social trends.

As is apparent from Figure 2.3, which is based on 1995 UCR data, arrest rates for index property crimes peak at around age 16 and then show a sharp drop after age 20. With increasing age, the property crime arrest rate shows a continual, gradual decline. The violent-crime arrest rate increases gradually to age 18 and shows a more gradual decline with age. Notice also that the violent-crime arrest rates are substantially lower than property crime arrest rates during the adolescent years. The relationship between age and crime has been observed as far back as any crime statistics have been kept.

FIGURE 2.3   Index crime arrests by age group

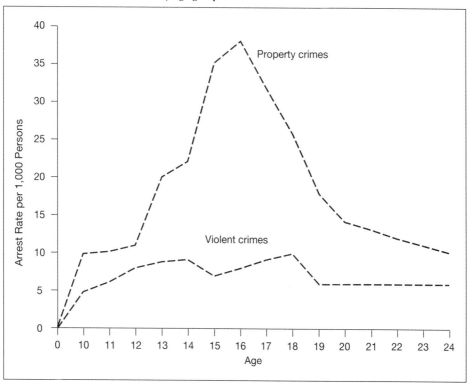

SOURCE: Based on data from *FBI Uniform Crime Reports*, three-year average, 1993–1995.

Note that Figure 2.3 illustrates arrest rates—in this case the number of arrests made for every 1,000 persons between 10 and 24. Arrest rates adjust for changes in population across age groups. The 14- to 16-year-old population may be much larger in one five-year period than in another. If there were no adjustment for these differences, an increase in the number of arrests would be misleading—it would reflect simply the fact that there is a larger population rather than any increase in the prevalence of offending. In the early 1960s, for example, the post–World War II baby boom generation reached adolescence. In 1960, the total population of adolescents (ages 14 to 17) in the United States was about 11 million. In 1970, it jumped to 16 million, and in 1975 the total population of adolescents peaked at about 17 million. Since that time, the adolescent population has steadily decreased every year. Failure to take these fluctuations into consideration might lead us to conclude that juvenile crime has similarly decreased since 1975.

Explanations for the consistently reported relationship between age and crime may be placed roughly into two theoretical camps. One camp is collectively known as the **general theory of crime** perspective, espoused by Travis Hirschi and Michael Gottfredson (1983; Gottfredson & Hirschi, 1990). The other represents a much larger group, consisting of Terrie Moffitt, Daniel Nagin, David Farrington, Alfred Blumstein, Rolf Loeber, and many others. This group is sometimes referred to as the **developmental theory of antisocial behavior** group or the **criminal career path** group. An understanding of the two positions is important because they imply very different strategies for research and intervention policy. We will begin by describing the general theory perspective.

General Crime Theory: The Invariant Hypothesis

In 1983 Travis Hirschi and Michael Gottfredson began an article asserting that virtually no criminologist, regardless of theoretical persuasion, disagrees that crime, as generally defined, is disproportionately committed by the young. They added that criminologists also generally agree, as noted previously, that the age distribution across the life cycle has a distinct shape: There is a sharp increase in crime during adolescence, it peaks during mid- to late adolescence, shows a sharp decline in early twenties, then follows a slow but steady decline thereafter (see Figure 2.3). This is consistently supported in aggregate data across gender, geographical areas, and socioeconomic status.

Hirschi and Gottfredson (1983; Gottfredson & Hirschi, 1990) argued that this age distribution is *invariant* (to be explained shortly), a position that—to their critics—has unsettling implications for the future direction of research, policy, and intervention on juvenile delinquency.

Hirschi and Gottfredson also comment that, in light of consistent support for the age distribution, age could well replace social class as the "master variable" of sociological theories of crime. According to Hirschi and Gottfredson, age seems to be emerging as the principal criterion on which the adequacy of theories of crime and delinquency are judged. In other words, a "good theory" must be able to account for the consistently reported observation that involvement in crime decreases after late adolescence. Hirschi and Gottfredson noted that failure to account for this downward swing in offending has rendered some theories weak in explaining crime and delinquency.

To Hirschi and Gottfredson longitudinal research is unnecessary. According to them, those who use maturation or age changes as a criterion of theoretical and research adequacy are misguided, because the age effect is *invariant* across all social and cultural conditions, regardless of the offense. That is, the relationship between age and offending is the same, regardless of the country or culture being discussed or the period in history being reviewed. The form of the age distribution (a rapid rise to a peak, then a steady decline) occurs again and again, wherever, however, or whenever it is measured. "If the form of the age distribution differs from time to time and from place to place, we have been unable to find evidence of this fact," commented Hirschi and Gottfredson (1983, p. 555). Hirschi and Gottfredson further maintained that the invariance of the age–crime relationship applies across gender and race. Again, it is important to emphasize that we are talking about the *shape* of the age distribution, not about frequencies or rates of offending. In other words, the *amount* of delinquency may be higher in the United States than it is, say, in Denmark, but the *shape* of the curve will peak at 16 to 18, regardless of the country or culture.

Let us be careful about what is being said here. The "invariance hypothesis" specifically reads that "the age distribution of the tendency to commit criminal acts is invariant across social and cultural conditions" (1983, p. 561, note 9). A critical phrase is "tendency to commit criminal acts." This point is underscored because, although crime commission is strongly related to age, there may be circumstances that prevent the commission of the criminal act itself, even though the *tendency* within adolescents remains the same. It is, therefore, more accurate to state that the *tendency* to engage in antisocial behavior is a function of age. Teenagers, according to the hypothesis, have a higher innate tendency to commit antisocial acts than any other age group.

In considering this hypothesis we must again point to the lack of attention given to the adult criminal activity that too often escapes the attention of crime statisticians. Official, victimization, and self-report data rarely report on perjury, obstruction of justice, bribe-taking, price-fixing, tax evasion, fraudulent business practices, or the vast array of violations of regulatory law.

Hirschi acknowledges that even his own control theory (to be covered in Chapter 6) cannot satisfactorily explain the age factor. Neither, of course, can any other theory of crime and delinquency that assumes that correlations between age and offending can be explained by processes inherent in the culture, society, or social experience. Hirschi and Gottfredson propose that age effects will occur across a large sample of subjects, independent of shifts in economic, political, or social events, or independent of individual developmental factors. The invariant hypothesis also implies that the traditional etiological division between juvenile and adult crime—that is, that different factors cause each—is unlikely to be useful, because the causes of crime are likely to be the same at any age. Therefore, although correlated with crime, age is not useful in predicting involvement in crime over the life cycle of offenders. According to the invariant hypothesis, to know that a child of 10 has committed delinquent acts is no more useful for predicting subsequent involvement than to know that a child of 15 has done so.

According to Hirschi and Gottfredson, developmental theories as explanations of delinquency are of questionable value. Criminologists traditionally have placed great importance on the point at which an individual first engages in criminal activity. For example, the **age-of-onset hypothesis** predicts that the earlier the child begins to offend, the more serious and persistent the criminal career will be. David Farrington (1979), for example, writes that boys first convicted at the earliest ages tended to become the most persistent offenders as adults. Hirschi and Gottfredson charge that there is very little value in developing theories based on the age-of-onset hypothesis. They insist that no special explanations for age of onset are needed because all groups share a common age/crime distribution. In other words, according to Hirschi and Gottfredson's invariance hypothesis, if a youth begins criminal activity at age 13, he or she will peak between ages 16 and 18; if the youth begins at age 8, he or she will still peak between ages 16 and 18.

David Greenberg (1985, 1991, 1992) finds the invariance hypothesis particularly troubling in its postulation that the age-crime relationship holds regardless of the economic and social context. Greenberg (1977) argues that the increasing level of juvenile crime in the United States and other Western countries could be explained by the "structural position" of juveniles in an advanced capitalist economy. More specifically, Greenberg objects strongly to the idea that age variations in criminality are a result of biological or psychological reactions to the physiological changes of adolescence. To Greenberg, the age–crime relationship is primarily the result of social forces within a given culture. He suggested that the detachment of adolescents from their families, along with the extensive advertising directed at them, increased their need to finance their social activities. Theft and related activities helped both male and female adolescents to meet their social needs for entertainment and material goods. Greenberg saw violence, primarily a male enterprise, as a product of "masculine status anxiety." He posited that certain economic conditions evoke anxiety in males, especially males of low socioeconomic status. They fear unemployment and being without occupational status, and thus being unable to fulfill what they see as their traditional gender-role expectations. One result of this masculine status anxiety, Greenberg posits, is increased violence.

Greenberg theorized that as adolescents get older, they are deterred from criminal activity by the prospects of apprehension. Interpersonal relationships, jobs, and other social benefits are too much to lose; thus, their criminal behavior decreases. According to Greenberg, this is what accounts for the age–crime relationship. In his view, the relationship between age and crime will change from culture to culture, society to society, depending upon the economic and political conditions. It will also change across time, as differential values are emphasized.

Developmental Theory: Age-at-Onset Hypothesis

Developmental theory argues that age is essential to the understanding of antisocial behavior and delinquency. The theory posits that the life course of antisocial behavior differs from individual to individual, and that simply assuming that the tendency for antisocial behavior is the same for everyone at roughly the same age does not lead to a satisfactory understanding of crime and delinquency. According to this perspective, antisocial behavior that begins at mid-adolescence is not qualitatively the same as antisocial behavior that begins during the preschool years. More important, each will require different strategies for prevention, intervention, and treatment. Consequently, and in contrast to the general theory argument, longitudinal research methods are necessary to characterize the qualitatively different developmental paths of antisocial participation from childhood to adulthood (Jeglum Bartusch, et al., in press).

In order to illustrate the developmental perspective more comprehensively, let us take two examples. As noted in Chapter 1, Terrie Moffitt (1993) has identified two developmental paths of antisocial behavior: the **adolescence-limited** (AL) path and **life-course-persistent** offender (LCP) path. The AL offender is one who begins antisocial behavior at the time of puberty (around age 12 to 15), continues antisocial behavior during adolescence, and then usually terminates offending as he or she moves into young adulthood. In essence, the AL offender follows the offending curve as outlined by the general theory of crime and the official group delinquency data compiled by the federal government (Figure 2.3).

On the other hand, LCP offenders do not demonstrate the offending pattern of AL offenders. Those in the much smaller population group of LCP offenders display problem behaviors early in life (as early as age three) and continue on through adolescence and well into adulthood. Treatment and intervention strategies that are used for AL offenders are applied too late to be effective for LCP offenders. In addition, the events that precipitate LCP patterns are very different from those found in the AL patterns. There is some evidence to suggest that the LCP pattern may be largely due to some combination of family adversity and neuropsychological deficits, whereas the AL pattern may be largely due to mimicking the delinquent behavior of deviant peer models (Moffitt, 1993a). If the developmental theory is correct, prevention and intervention of antisocial conduct will require decidedly different strategies for dealing with the two groups.

Another example of the importance of the developmental perspective in understanding delinquency is found in a study conducted by Daniel Nagin and Kenneth Land (1993). Through some very sophisticated statistics, these researchers were able to identify four developmental paths in British boys: the **never-convicted** (NCs), the **adolescence-limiteds** (ALs), the **high-level chronics** (HLCs), and the **low-level chronics** (LLCs). The offending paths of the AL followed the conventional contour: Offending began late, reached a peak at age 16, and then showed a precipitous decline to zero by age 22 (Nagin, Farrington, & Moffitt, 1995). The LLC curve showed a rise through early adolescence, reached a plateau, and remained at the same level well past age 18. The HLC group (essentially the same as Moffitt's LCP) showed an early and frequent antisocial and offending pattern that began early in life, continued through adolescence at a high rate, and remained high well into adulthood. Each of these developmental trajectories reflects an offending pattern that would be missed if we relied solely on the information provided by the cross-sectional data illustrated by the offending curve (Figure 2.3). The developmental theory data argue that different youths offend for different reasons and do not have an innate propensity toward antisocial actions that reaches a peak during their teens.

Summing Up

In conclusion, the controversy among researchers is not whether the age–crime relationship exists, but rather whether it is invariant. If it is invariant, as Hirschi and Gottfredson claim, the value of longitudinal studies is lessened. Moreover, invariance would have important implications for policy setting, as the two have illustrated in an article on the merit of programs aimed at incapacitating "career criminals" (Gottfredson & Hirschi, 1986). It makes little sense, they say, to target individuals who are making a lifetime career of crime, because they are in the minority; most criminals reduce their involvement as they age. The developmentalists agree that most youth offenders do follow the traditional contour, peaking at age 16 and dropping thereafter. However, they also contend that there are a small number of offenders who not only show a decidedly different age curve but probably commit a majority of the violent crimes throughout their lifetimes. Preventive and intervention strategies that work for AL offenders are not likely to work for LCP offenders, not only because of the age difference in the two groups' offending histories but also because of the differences in causes.

The position taken in this book is that longitudinal studies are extremely valuable in the discovery of developmental patterns involved in the formation of crime and delinquency. We will learn, for example, that serious, violent offenders take a decidedly different developmental path from that of individuals who engage in nonviolent offending or minor offending.

GENDER AND JUVENILE OFFENDING

As early as 1842, Lambert Adolphe Jacques Quetelet, a Belgian social statistician, noted that arrest data decidedly "favored" males by a 4-to-1 margin; that is, four men were arrested for every one woman. Since that time, data have continually indicated that males commit far more crime than females, regardless of culture or period in history. In fact, males have been so overrepresented in violent crimes (approximately a 9-to-1 ratio) for so long that some theorists have suggested that hormonal factors are the most logical explanation for these gender differences (Wilson & Herrnstein, 1985). Juvenile crime statistics show a similar trend, although the male-to-female ratio diminishes when status offenses are included in the data. Girls, in fact, appear in the official runaway statistics more than boys, but there is no indication that they are as assaultive. With reference to the gender differential consistently reported, John Hagan writes, "The correlation of gender with criminal and delinquent behavior was one of the few findings from the beginnings of criminological research that although questioned, never was doubted

THE NATURE AND EXTENT OF JUVENILE OFFENDING

seriously" (Hagan, 1987, p. 3). Victimization data (Hindelang, 1979), self-report data (Smith & Visher, 1980), and official data (Steffensmeier, 1978, 1980) all support this gender gap in criminal offending.

Until the late 1960s, most explanations for these differences were based on biological or psychological assumptions about the nature of women or girls, and this "nature" invariably had a negative taint (Klein, 1973). Cesare Lombroso (with W. Ferrero) (1895) wrote that women were closer than men to their atavistic origins and were not shrewd enough to commit crime. Women who did, however, were even more evil than men, because they were acting against their "nature." W. I. Thomas (1923) believed that girls were more apt than boys to be maladjusted and thus less likely to be accused of roguelike delinquent behavior. The "inherent nature" explanation for the gender gap was perpetuated by Otto Pollak, whose book *The Criminality of Women* was published in 1950. Pollak believed that the gap was an illusion, however. He suspected that women commit as much crime as men, but are able to escape detection because of what he saw as their "devious, concealing nature." He believed as well that when they were detected, the male-dominated criminal justice system was reluctant to arrest, prosecute, or punish them.

In the mid-1970s, some researchers suggested that the gender gap would disappear primarily because of the effect of the women's liberation movement (Adler, 1975; Simon, 1975). Others strongly disagreed with these assertions. Today, we can say with confidence that the female–male ratios in offending have not changed dramatically. There continue to be gaps between the male and female arrest rates, although they are smaller for some offenses. Darrell Steffensmeier and Renee Hoffman Steffensmeier (1980) combined national arrest statistics with juvenile court, self-report, and field observational data to evaluate the general trends in female delinquency between 1965 and 1975. They reported that, based on these varied sources of data, there had been no increase in female violence or in the traditionally male-dominated gang-related delinquency. "Generally, females are *not* catching up with males in the commission of violent, masculine, or serious crimes" (Steffensmeier & Steffensmeier, 1980, p. 80). When status offenses are excluded, female delinquency rates have remained generally unchanged in most offense categories. Smith and Visher (1980), however, noted that the gender difference is not as strong for children as for adults, and they suggest that this may reflect shifting gender roles due to differences in socialization and expectations during development.

Coramae Mann (1984, p. 7) observes: "In the past twenty years the arrests of females, according to official data, have not varied by more than five percentage points as a proportion of total arrests." This observation holds for both juveniles and adults and is especially the case for violent crimes, where males clearly predominate. Mann adds that any slight increases that have occurred for women and girls are almost entirely in the area of larceny-theft (see Table 2.4). Likewise, in an analysis of arrest and incarceration data from 1960–1990, Darrell Steffensmeier (1995) reports that female crime continues to be less violent than male crime.

It seems clear on the basis of our present knowledge that the persistent gender differential continues, particularly for serious offenses. And this relationship

TABLE 2.4 Total juvenile arrests by gender in 1995 (in 1,000s)

Male	Offense	Female
214	Larceny	102
74	Burglary	8
53	Liquor law violations	22
81	Vandalism	10
84	Disorderly conduct	28
108	Drug abuse	16
57	Runaways	77
74	Curfew/loitering	31
45	Motor vehicle theft	8
41	Aggravated assault	10
35	Robbery	4
12	Drunkenness	2
7	DUI	1
13	Fraud	4
10	Sex offenses	1
6	Arson	1
4	Forgery	2
3	Forcible rape	0.07
2	Vagancy	0.30
3	Murder	0.10
0.43	Prostitution	0.43

SOURCE: Adapted from *FBI Uniform Crime Reports—1995* (Washington, DC: U.S. Department of Justice, 1996), p. 215.

holds for both adults and juveniles, provided that status offenses are controlled for in the latter group. After a comprehensive review of the literature on gender and crime, Nagel and Hagan (1983) concluded, "Female crime rates remain, in absolute terms, far below those for men" (p. 94). The next step is to explain why this gender differential might exist.

As we have seen, some early explanations of the gap between male and female offending rates focused on unsupported assumptions about the nature of women or on their differential treatment by the criminal justice system. Most theories, however, did not try to explain the gender gap. In fact, most theories ignored female delinquency and crime altogether. They were formulated almost entirely on the basis of data about the behavior of boys, particularly lower-class boys. One explanation for this is that, because girls simply do not violate the law very much, why develop a theory for such a small group? Another explanation: It was assumed that the causal factors identified for boys would apply to girls as well. Eileen Leonard (1982), however, systematically reviewed each of the major theories in criminology—unexplainably with the exception of Hirschi's social control theory—and concluded that none satisfactorily explains female crime or delinquency. Leonard then proposed a feminist theory to explain female crime, one that focuses on the marginal economic status of women offenders. Feminist theories, as they apply to juvenile girls, will be discussed in later chapters, particularly Chapters 7 and 10.

Research by developmental psychologists, which will be discussed in more detail in Chapter 4, sheds considerable light on the gender differential in juvenile offending. There is growing recognition, however, that biology is not the primary factor—or even a significant factor—in explaining the differences in gender violence (Adams, 1992; Pepler & Slaby, 1994). Research by Eleanor Maccoby (1986), for example, suggests that girls and boys learn different types of prosocial behavior, with girls accommodating others more than boys do. The current work of cognitive psychologists suggests that there may be socialized differences in the way girls and boys construct their worlds. Social learning theorists have long held that girls are "socialized" differently from boys, or taught not to be aggressive. Anne Campbell (1993, p. 19) contends that "boys are not simply more aggressive than girls; they are aggressive in a different way." According to Campbell, boys and girls are born with the potential to be equally aggressive, but girls are socialized not to be aggressive, whereas boys are encouraged to be aggressive.

In any event, the evidence strongly indicates that cultural and psychosocial factors play a very major role in determining differences in gender aggression and violence. Biological and genetic factors appear to play a less significant role than previously believed.

SUMMARY AND CONCLUSIONS

Scientists can now point with confidence to a large list of risk factors associated with juvenile delinquency, but no one single variable on the list is the overwhelming favorite as the cause of the problem (Zigler, Taussig, & Black, 1992). Clearly, it is the interaction of a number of risk factors that leads to crime and delinquency.

In this chapter, we described juvenile arrest rates and trends for violent crimes and property crimes. We focused on two offense categories often overrepresented by juveniles: arson and shoplifting. Status offenses were briefly outlined here, but will be discussed in more detail in Chapters 10 and 11 because they are greatly dependent on characteristics of the juvenile justice system and state and federal statutes. Drug offending will be discussed in the next chapter.

Also in this chapter we began to examine some of the demographic factors involved in the development of delinquency. Among those factors are poverty and social class. It is difficult to disentangle poverty and social class, however, from race or ethnicity as independent predictors of crime and delinquency. As we learned, economic inequality between the rich and poor, rather than absolute levels of material wealth, appears to be one of the strongest demographic predictors of violence. More specifically, economic discrimination and occupational biases against the poor and other minority groups are stronger predictors of violence than single measures of poverty. Single measures of poverty (e.g., family incomes) do not tell the whole story. Discrimination, racism, family disruption, unsafe living conditions, joblessness, social isolation, and limited social networks all play roles in the formation and development of delinquency.

Attention was also directed at ethnic or group minorities as demographic variables that are related to crime and delinquency. Little or no research has identified unique psychological, biological, or behavioral characteristics among ethnic or minority groups that might explain differential occurrences of crime and violence (Eron & Slaby, 1994). Populations of children who are especially susceptible to becoming perpetrators or victims of violence experience sociocultural conditions that restrict opportunity and prevent them from achieving developmental milestones.

We must stress once again, however, that data on juvenile crime underestimate the participation of middle- and upper-class juveniles. Police, intake workers, juvenile judges, probation officers, and lawyers exhibit differential responses to juveniles in different social and economic situations and often to juveniles on the basis of gender. This theme will be reiterated throughout the text.

The general theory of crime advocated by Hirschi and Gottfredson was discussed, particularly the invariant hypothesis as an explanation for the effects of age on crime. The general theory maintains that the factor underlying the propensity toward crime is the same for all ages. The developmental perspective argues that there is no universal innate propensity for crime. According to this perspective, antisocial behavior that begins at mid-adolescence is not qualitatively the same as antisocial behavior that begins during the preschool years. More important, both will require different strategies for prevention, intervention, and treatment.

Finally, we looked at gender differences in juvenile offending. Clearly, boys outnumber girls in almost all offense categories, some by a substantial margin. There is very little evidence that these differential offending rates are due primarily to biological factors. Rather, the differences can be best explained by sociocultural factors, especially culturally mandated gender roles and the accompanying social reinforcements for demonstrating these behaviors and attitudes.

KEY CONCEPTS

adolescence-limiteds (ALs)
adolescent-limited offender (AL)
age-of-onset hypothesis
arson
burglary
career criminals
cross-sectional investigations
criminal career path group
developmental theory of antisocial
    behavior
drug offenses
general theory of crime
high-level chronic offender (HLC)

larceny-theft
life-course-persistent offender (LCP)
low-level chronic offender (LLC)
never-convicted group (NCs)
poverty
poverty thresholds
poverty guidelines
property offenses
socioeconomic status (SES)
shoplifting
status offenses
violent offenses

3

Drugs and Delinquency

On August 21, 1996, a front-page story in *USA Today* (Friend, 1996) reported that illicit drug use among 12- to 17-year-olds had more than doubled since 1992 and that drugs have become so widespread among teens that in a classroom of 25, three were drug users. The most heavily used drug in these reports was marijuana.

The "drug problem" remains a very serious one in the United States. By all accounts, the levels of substance abuse in the United States are estimated to be the highest found in any developed country in the world (Inaba & Cohen, 1995). This substance abuse appears to be especially acute among the youth. Urban juvenile detention facilities are filled with juveniles who are involved with drugs. For example, about 85 percent of the juveniles in the San Francisco Youth Guidance Center are there because of drugs—either using, under the influence, dealing, or committing another offense while under their influence (Inaba & Cohen, 1995).

Drug abuse is an issue for both genders. In 1994, the overall percentage of 15- to 20-year-old female arrestees testing positive for at least one drug ranged from 23 to 68 percent with a median of 33 percent, depending on what part of the country the arrests took place in (National Institute of Justice, 1995). The overall percentage for 15- to 20-year-old males that same year ranged from 50 to 73 percent, with a median of 60 percent.

While the "drug problem" exists, getting accurate figures is very difficult. Surveys often contradict one another, and anyone examining the numbers must read carefully, especially the "fine print." For example, when percentages are reported in the survey, are the percentages referring to once-in-a-lifetime experimentation or to current, regular use?

Some surveys do suggest that the use of illicit drugs has decreased in recent years. Illicit drugs are psychoactive substances that are considered illegal within a given jurisdiction or region. This definition is intended to include the nonmedical use of psychoactive substances, such as amphetamines, antidepressants, or barbiturates, by persons without legal prescriptions.

According to the *National Household Survey on Drug Abuse* (NHSDA; Substance Abuse and Mental Health Services Administration, 1995), the peak year for illicit-drug use was 1979, when there were an estimated 25 million current users, representing nearly 14 percent of the U.S. population. Since that time there has been a steady decline to the point where only about 6 percent of the U.S. population are current illicit-drug users. A similar pattern of illicit-drug use is also noted for youths 12 to 17 years old, reaching a peak of 18.5 percent of all youth using drugs in 1979 but continually dropping to around 10 percent in 1994. In 1994, the survey reported that the rate of illicit-drug use by Americans was highest among persons 16 to 21 years old. The survey also discovered that although the use of marijuana among adolescents declined between 1979 and 1992, the rate of marijuana use among youths 12 to 17 years old nearly doubled between 1992 and 1994.

In 1993, 43 percent of all high school seniors in the United States reported that they had used illicit drugs at least once in their lifetimes (Snyder & Sickmund, 1995). These data are based on an annual school survey of eighth, tenth, and twelfth graders conducted by the University of Michigan Institute for Social Research. The survey, known as *Monitoring the Future* (MTF), samples 50,000 students in 420 public and private schools. A recent MTF (1995) found that marijuana was the most commonly used illicit drug, followed by inhalants. Heroin was the least commonly used illicit drug. In the same survey, approximately 90 percent of the high school seniors said they had tried alcohol at least once. In addition, 28 percent of the seniors admitted to engaging in heavy drinking (defined as five or more drinks in a row) during the preceding two weeks. Interestingly, 14 percent of eighth graders also reported heavy drinking sometime during the previous two weeks. Table 3.1 provides additional information about self-reported illegal drug use among high school seniors.

The MTF data are supported by the *National Household Survey on Drug Abuse*. Other national surveys, such as the *National Health Interview Survey* and the *Youth Risk Behavior Survey* (YRBS), report similar findings. The *National Health Interview Survey* provides data on the relationship between drug use and health status. The *Youth Risk Behavior Survey* collects data from a nationally representative sample of youths and young adults, aged 12 to 21 years, and focuses on the prevalence of a variety of unhealthy behaviors, including alcohol, tobacco, marijuana, and cocaine use. The survey collects data by administering questionnaires to a representative sample of the population at their place of residence. The YRBS still has its problems, such as its failure to sample satisfactorily certain populations who use certain drugs, including heroin and phencyclidines (PCPs), which will be discussed shortly. Still, the YRBS is one of the most comprehensive sources of statistical information on the use of illegal drugs by Americans.

It is estimated that about one in five Canadians has used an illegal substance at least once over his or her lifetime (McKenzie & Williams, 1995). As in the United States, the most widely used illicit drug is cannabis (marijuana or hashish), which is used by 20 percent of the Canadian population over their lifetimes (Adlaf, 1993). Approximately 10 percent of Canadian youth between the ages of 15 to 19 used cannabis in 1993, with notable differences among the individual provinces. In Ontario, nearly 13 percent of the students in grades 7, 9, 11, and 13 reported using cannabis once in their lifetimes (Adlaf, Smart, & Walsh, 1993), whereas in British Columbia, 23 percent of the adolescents reported experimenting with cannabis (British Columbia Ministry of Health and Ministry Responsible for Seniors, 1992).

Although tobacco use is less prevalent than alcohol use among the youth, still in 1993 62 percent of high school seniors and 30 percent of eighth graders in the United States had tried cigarettes. Moreover, 15 percent of the seniors, 11 percent of the tenth graders, and 6 percent of the eighth graders reported that they were regular smokers (Snyder & Sickmund, 1995).

The NHSDA does demonstrate one very important aspect: Drug use is correlated with cognitions (attitudes and beliefs) about drugs. For example, rates of drug use are much higher in populations that did not perceive great risk of harm than in populations that did perceive great risk of harm. Thus, explanations for the significant increase in marijuana use in recent years often center on the belief that there is very little harm in the use of the drug.

Before adolescents become dependent on alcohol, tobacco, or any illicit substance, they pass through a stage of **experimental substance use** (ESU; Petraitis,

TABLE 3.1   **Reported illegal drug use by American high school seniors, 1993**

	Used within the past	
Drug	12 months	30 days
Marijuana	26.0%	15.5%
Cocaine	2.9	1.2
Crack	1.5	0.7
Hallucinogens	7.4	2.7
Heroin	0.5	0.2
Other opiates	3.6	1.3
Inhalants	7.0	2.5
Stimulants	8.4	3.7
Sedatives	3.4	1.3
Tranquilizers	3.5	1.2
Steroids	1.2	0.7

SOURCES: *National Institute on Drug Abuse; BJS Sourcebook of Criminal Justice Statistics, 1995.*

Flay, & Miller, 1995). Events and variables that determine who experiments with substances during adolescence are multiple and include the availability of drugs, family history, peer pressures, social attitudes concerning drug use, the social and economic context, and individual differences in biopsychological/psychological makeup. Because of the enormous complexity involved in ESU, many theories have been proposed to explain the phenomenon. However, very few of them have ever been empirically tested or have provided cogent explanations for why some youth experiment with drugs and others do not.

The association between drugs and crime is a complex one in another sense as well. Thus far we have discussed drug *use*. Nadelman (1991) identifies four possible connections between drugs and crime. First, the possession, production, selling, buying, and consumption of illegal drugs is itself a crime. Second, users may commit other crimes to finance their illegal drug purchases. A person addicted to heroin and having to finance a $150-a-day habit, for example, may resort to robbery, burglary, or prostitution to pay for the drug. In the case of prostitution, the person also may commit the crime in exchange for drugs. Third, persons under the influence of drugs may commit crimes, including violent crime. Fourth, the drug trafficking world itself is intimidating and violent, leading to assaults, robberies, and homicides among those involved in the business.

The above distinctions are important, and research on delinquency is just beginning to explore them. Experimental drug abuse among juveniles, though a major concern, requires a different response from serious involvement in both use and trafficking, both of which are likely to lead to additional crime.

In discussing the complex relationships among juveniles, drugs, and crime, it is critical that we consider not only the illegal behavior of the juveniles, but also the extent to which they are victimized by adult suppliers and traffickers. Youths in inner city ghettoes have been particularly hurt in this way. It is well recognized, for example, that during the heroin epidemic that hit some inner cities in the 1950s, organized crime imported large quantities of heroin and marketed it extensively to low-income minority youth (Rouse & Johnson, 1991). Many of today's street youths who are immersed in the drug culture are runaways who have histories of physical and sexual abuse and have turned to prostitution in exchange for drugs. This is particularly a problem with girls. Finally, because of increasingly tough penalties, adult traffickers use more and more juveniles, both boys and girls, to run drugs (Nadelman, 1991). Any discussion of the connection between drugs and delinquency, therefore, must take these complex issues into consideration.

A study by Altshuler and Brounstein (1991), illustrates some of this complexity. The researchers studied 387 minority youths, all males, from Washington, D.C. They conducted in-person interviews with the youths and examined their school, police, and court records. The boys were divided into users and nonusers as well as traffickers and nontraffickers. Although more than one-half the youths reported involvement in crime over the past year, only one-fifth used or sold drugs.

Heavy users were significantly more likely to commit property crimes than nonusers, but involvement in crimes against persons was not significantly different between the two groups. Youths involved in drug trafficking, however, were significantly more likely than those not involved in selling to report crimes against persons. Of all the boys in the sample, those who both used and sold were the most involved in committing crimes against persons and property, and at high rates.

Altshuler and Brounstein also learned that, among the drug users, crimes committed while the youth was on drugs were the exceptions rather than the rules, usually hovering around the 15 percent mark. Additionally, only a small proportion of the juveniles said they committed crimes to finance the purchase of drugs.

CLASSIFICATIONS OF PSYCHOACTIVE DRUGS

Four major categories of psychoactive drugs will be covered. However, to keep the chapter within manageable limits, we will focus on only one or two representative drugs within each group, usually the one most often associated with delinquency.

The **hallucinogens** or **psychedelics**, which include LSD (lysergic acid diethylamine), mescaline, psilocybin, phencyclidine, ketamine, marijuana, and hashish, will be our first category. The hallucinogens are chemicals that lead to a change in consciousness involving an alteration of reality, sometimes generating hallucinations. In some respects, they replace the present world with an alternative one, although persons using them can generally attend simultaneously to their altered state and to reality. Marijuana is classified as a hallucinogen. Because of its widespread use and the public's tendency mistakenly to associate it with crime and bizarre behavior, marijuana will be the main drug covered under the hallucinogens category. We will also include phencyclidine (PCP), a powerful drug that was linked to crime during the 1980s.

Next, we will discuss the **stimulants**, so called because they appear to stimulate central nervous system functions. They include amphetamines, clinical antidepressants, cocaine, caffeine, and nicotine. Again, because of an alleged relationship with crime, the amphetamines and cocaine will be highlighted.

The third group includes the **opiate narcotics**, which generally have sedative (sleep-inducing) and analgesic (pain-relieving) effects. Heroin will be featured in this section. The heroin addict appears frequently in crime statistics, as it is believed that he or she often turns to crime—particularly to property crime—to finance this expensive habit.

Finally, alcohol will represent the **sedative-hypnotic** chemicals that depress central nervous system functions. In most instances, the sedative-hypnotics are all capable of sedating the nervous system and reducing anxiety and tension.

The relationship between drugs and crime is complicated by a threefold interaction: (1) the pharmacological effects of the drug, which refer to the chemical impact of the drug on the body; (2) the psychological characteristics of the individual using the drug; and (3) the psychosocial conditions under which the drug is taken. Pharmacological effects include features of the nervous system, such as the amount of neurotransmitter substances within neurons, and body weight, blood composition, and other neurophysiological features that significantly influence the chemical effects of the drug. Psychological variables include the mood of the person at the time the drug is consumed, previous experience with the drug, and the person's expectations of the drug's effects. Psychosocial variables include the social atmosphere under which the drug is taken. The people who are present and their expectations, moods, and behavior all may influence an individual's reactions to a drug.

In order to understand the effects of any drug, therefore, one must take into account the pharmacological, psychological, and psychosocial variables. Considering the fact that antisocial behavior and delinquency are complex to begin with, deciphering the delinquency–drug connection becomes very difficult, and the conclusions are elusive and tentative.

The relationship between drugs and delinquency is likely to be further complicated by the cultural and subcultural aspects of drug consumption. Very little research has focused on the contributions of gender or ethnicity to the experimental use of alcohol or marijuana by youths (Petraitis, Flay, & Miller, 1995). Differences in the use of hard drugs are beginning to emerge. We should keep in mind, though, that substance preferences shift and change depending on drug availability, law enforcement priorities, and changes in cultural attitudes.

Among adults, certain professional criminal groups often prefer one drug over another. Professional pickpockets, shoplifters, and burglars, for example— when they use drugs—have a distinct preference for those that steady their nerves and provide relief from the pressures of their occupation (Inciardi, 1981). Professional pickpockets often consider opiates instrumental in furthering their careers. To some extent, this has a cyclical effect, since their material gain from their crimes is used to obtain the drugs.

In light of research such as that of Altschuler and Brounstein (1991), however, it may be too simplistic to assume that juveniles either finance their drug habits through crime or commit crime under the influence of drugs to the same degree and in the same way as adults. Although it is clear that juveniles who are seriously involved in the drug trade are also likely to be seriously involved in other crime, the type of criminal behavior is often very different. We will return to this issue in our discussion of juveniles and crack cocaine.

Drug Tolerance and Dependence

Before proceeding, we must distinguish netweem two terms that are consistently used in the drug literature: **tolerance** and **dependence**. Drug tolerance is the "state of progressively decreased responsiveness to a drug" (Julien, 1975, p. 29). Tolerance is indicated if the individual requires a larger dose of the drug to reach the same effects he or she has previously experienced. In other words, the person has become psychologically and physiologically used to, or habituated to, the drug.

Dependence may be physical, psychological, or both. In simple terms, **physical dependence** refers to the physiological distress and physical pain a person suffers if he or she goes without the drug for any length of time. **Psychological dependence** is difficult to distinguish from physical dependence, but it is characterized by an overwhelming desire to use the drug for a favorable effect. The person is convinced that he or she needs the drug in order to maintain an optimal sense of well-being. The degree of psychological dependence varies widely from person to person and from drug to drug. In its extreme form, the person's life is permeated with thoughts of procuring and using the drug, and he or she may resort to crime in order to obtain it. In common parlance, the person who is extremely psychologically and/or physically dependent is an addict.

Secondary psychological dependence may also develop. While primary dependence is associated with the reward of the drug experience (positive reinforcement), secondary dependence refers to expectancies about aversive withdrawal or the painful effects that will accompany absence of the drug. Thus, to avoid the anticipated pain and discomfort associated with withdrawal, the individual continues to take the drug (negative reinforcement).

THE HALLUCINOGENS: CANNABIS

Marijuana, which apparently originated in Asia, is among the oldest and most frequently used intoxicants. It is the most popular illegal drug used in the United States, and, as of this writing, it is the most popular illegal drug used by eighth graders. The earliest reference to marijuana was found in a book on pharmacy written by the Chinese Emperor Shen Nung in 2737 B.C. (Ray, 1972). It was called the "Liberator of Sin" and recommended for such ailments as "female weakness," constipation, and absent-mindedness. The word "marijuana" is commonly believed to have derived from "mary jane," Mexican slang for cheap tobacco, or from the Portuguese word *mariguano*, meaning intoxicant.

The drug is prepared from the plant **cannabis**, an annual that is cultivated or grows freely as a weed in both tropical and temperate climates. There are at least three species of cannabis—sativa, indica, and ruderalis—each differing in psychoactive potency. The psychoactive (intoxicating) properties of the plant reside principally in the chemical **Delta-9 tetrahydrocannabinol (THC)**, found mainly in its resin. Thus, the concentration and quality of THC within parts of the plant determine the potency or psychoactive power of the drug.

THC content varies from one preparation to another, partly because of the quality of the plant itself but also because of its environment. The strain of the plant (there are more than 200), the climate, and the soil conditions all affect THC content. For example, the resin is believed to retard the dehydration of the flowering elements and thus is produced in greater quantities in hot, tropical climates (Hofmann, 1975). Consequently, cannabis grown in the tropics (Mexico, Colombia, Jamaica, and North Africa) presumably has greater psychoactive potential than American-grown hemp. However, THC potency appears to be more a feature of the species of the cannabis plant than of geographic area or climatic conditions (Ray, 1983).

The cannabis extracts used most commonly in the United States are marijuana and hashish. Marijuana is usually prepared by cutting the stem beneath the lowest branches, air drying, and stripping seeds, bracts, flowers, leaves, and small stems from the plant. This procedure results in a green, brown, or gray mixture of dried material. The female cannabis plant produces more resin than the larger male plant but slows down resin production once it is fertilized. Therefore, knowledgeable marijuana growers usually separate the male and female plants before pollination occurs, thereby allowing the female plant to continue producing higher levels of THC (although it remains seedless). The higher THC content in the female plant is not found in the leaves or stems but in the buds. Sinsemilla, which is Spanish for "without seeds," is a potent form of marijuana produced by harvesting the resinous buds from the female plant; it is becoming extremely popular among youth.

Hashish, the Arabic word for "dry grass," is produced by scraping or in some other way extracting the resin secreted by the flowers. Therefore, hashish, which is usually sold in the United States in small cubes, cakes, or even cookie-like shapes, has more THC content than marijuana, with a range as high as 28 percent.

Enterprising horticulturists in the 1990s have been able to develop cannabis strains that easily contain 15 percent or more THC. Not only have marijuana growers been successful in raising THC levels, but they have also been able to breed cannabis strains that have a set of particular psychological and physiological effects, much the same way that winemakers breed grapes that produce a particular flavor or bouquet in wine (Weisheit, 1992).

Hashish oil (red oil) is produced by repeated extractions of cannabis plant materials, a process that results in a dark, viscous liquid with an average THC content of 16 percent and with a range as high as 43 percent. A drop or two on a regular cigarette usually produces the effect of one marijuana cigarette.

When exposed to air over a period of time, marijuana appears to lose its psychoactive potency, because THC is converted to cannabinol and other inactive compounds (Mechoulam, 1970). One study found that marijuana exposed to light and air over the course of year lost more than half of its THC (Weisheit, 1992). Moreover, marijuana with higher levels of THC appears to deteriorate more rapidly than marijuana with lower THC.

In the United States, marijuana and hashish are usually smoked, most often in hand-rolled cigarettes (commonly called a joint or a nail), in a pipe, or in a "bong." A common practice in some countries is to consume cannabis as tea or mixed with other beverages or food. In recent years, some youth have developed the method of slicing open a cigar and replacing the tobacco with marijuana, making what they call a "blunt." In a national survey conducted in 1994, approximately 16 percent of American youth between the ages of 12 and 17 years acknowledged being current users of marijuana (Substance Abuse and Mental Health Services Administration, 1995). A current user means that the individual has used the drug within the past month. Among twelfth graders, nearly 40 percent acknowledged having tried marijuana at least once, and 19 percent were current users. The average age of first use is about 13.5 years of age. A similar statistic for first use is reported for Canadian youth (McKenzie & Williams, 1995).

There are a wide variety of slang names for marijuana (at last count, more than 200), with some of them changing almost monthly. Some terms from almost a generation ago are still used, such as pot, herb, grass, Mary Jane, weed, and reefer; some new names include boom, gangster, kif, ganja, skunk, and Aunt Mary. There is an assortment of street names for the different strains, such as Texas tea, Maui wowie, and chronic.

The psychological effects of cannabis are so subjective and dependent on such a wide range of variables that any generalizations must be accompanied by the warning that there are numerous exceptions. Reactions to cannabis, like reactions to all psychoactive drugs, depend on the complex interactions of both pharmacological and extrapharmacological factors. As we noted, these include the mood of the user, the user's expectations of the drug, the social context in which it is used, and the user's experiences with the drug. The strong influence of these extrapharmacological factors, together with the widespread variation in THC content in any sample of cannabis, makes it exceedingly difficult to obtain comparable research data. Essentially, the effects of cannabis are unique to each individual. Except for increases in heart rate, increases in peripheral blood flow, and reddening of the membranes around the eyes, there are few consistent physiological changes reported for all persons.

The person who uses marijuana must learn to use the drug in order to reach a euphoric "stoned" or "high" state. Ray (1983) reports that a three-stage learning process is involved. First, users must inhale the smoke deeply and hold it in their lungs for 20 to 40 seconds. Then, they must learn to identify and control the effects. Finally, they must learn to label the effects as pleasant. Some users (even experienced ones) may suffer acute anxiety and paranoid thoughts with high levels of THC; these reactions wear off within a few hours.

Although the psychoactive effects last only four to six hours, traces of THC (metabolites) may remain in the body for up to six months after one has smoked a single joint. These long-term traces are absorbed by the fatty tissues of the body. Consequently, the traces rarely can be detected by standard urine testing, because they are usually eliminated by the digestive system.

Cannabis and Delinquency

Public concern about the connection between cannabis and crime was stimulated by a number of articles printed in a New Orleans newspaper as long ago as 1926 (Ray, 1972). The Harrison Narcotics Act had been passed in 1914 and was followed by similar legislation in most states. In 1931, a popular article concluded that one out of every four persons arrested in New Orleans was addicted to cannabis. With public interest activated, a drive to get the "dangerous" drug outlawed was soon under way. It was spearheaded by the Commissioner of Narcotics at that time (Harry Anslinger), who convinced Congress and many states that marijuana often led to serious crime and was a threat to the "moral fabric" of American society.

During this time (the 1930s), marijuana use was often linked with both violent and "perverted" crime.

In 1937, Congress passed the Marijuana Tax Act, which was a bill intended to add muscle to antimarijuana laws that by then existed in 46 states and had the effect of criminalizing marijuana possession. The Tax Act did not actually outlaw cannabis, but it taxed the grower, distributor, seller, and buyer prohibitively. It also established so many requirements that it was nearly impossible to have anything to do with any form of cannabis (Ray, 1972). Interestingly, none of the attitudes or regulations were supported by comprehensive scientific investigations or by evidence that marijuana was harmful. The information communicated was anecdotal; the "documentation" consisted of testimony of the "I know a case where" variety.

In 1939, Bromberg published results of a study conducted in New York between 1932 and 1937. Out of a total of 16,854 prisoners, only 67 said they were cannabis users and only 6 of those had been convicted of a violent crime. Bromberg concluded that the relationship between marijuana use and crime could not be substantiated. However, staunch advocates of the marijuana–crime connection were not swayed.

Numerous research projects directed at the effects of cannabis were launched during the 1950s, 1960s, and early 1970s. Many of these studies had methodological shortcomings and did not control for parity of dosage levels, means of administering the drug, and THC content in the drug itself. Psychological factors associated with the subjects were not considered carefully enough, and experimental settings and instructions were haphazard. At first, some of the research did suggest a relationship between cannabis use and criminal behavior. However, with more sophisticated statistical analyses that controlled for demographic and criminal background variables, the earlier results were found to be spurious (National Commission, 1972). Both independent research and investigations conducted by government-sponsored commissions strongly indicate that marijuana does not directly contribute to criminal behavior. After an extensive review of available literature, the National Commission on Marihuana and Drug Abuse (1972, p. 470) came to this conclusion: "There is no systematic empirical evidence, at least that is drawn from the American experience, to support the thesis that the use of marijuana either inevitably or generally causes, leads to or precipitates criminal, violent, aggressive or delinquent behavior of sexual or nonsexual nature." The Commission Report (p. 470) adds: "If anything, the effects observed suggest that marijuana may be more likely to neutralize criminal behavior and to militate against the commission of aggressive acts."

One of the predominant effects of THC is relaxation, resulting in a marked decrease in physical activity. THC induces muscular weakness and an inability to sustain physical effort, so that the user wishes nothing more strenuous than to stay relatively motionless. As Tinklenberg and Stillman (1970, p. 341) note, "'being stoned' summarizes these sensations of demobilizing lethargy." It is difficult to imagine "stoned" users engaging in assaultive or other violent activity. If anything, THC should reduce the likelihood of criminal activity, particularly aggressive conduct.

Although the empirical evidence so far indicates that cannabis does not, as a rule, stimulate aggressive behavior or other criminal actions, whenever we deal with human behavior there will be exceptions. Individuals have reported occasional negative experiences produced by THC. Although the phenomenon is rare, some people do describe feelings of panic, hypersensitivity, feelings of being out of contact with their surroundings, and bizarre behavior. Some individuals have experienced rapid, disorganized intrusions of irrelevant thoughts, which prompted them to feel as if they were losing control of their minds. Under these conditions, it is plausible that one would interpret the actions of others as threatening. It is also possible that these panicked individuals might attack those around them.

However, those who investigate cannabis effects usually agree that people who act violently under the influence of the drug were probably predisposed to act that way, with or without the drug. The evidence indicates that violent marijuana users were violent prior to using cannabis. In other words, they learned the behavioral pattern independently of cannabis.

Marijuana does have adverse effects on many of the skills for driving a car and may lead to reckless driving, resulting in serious and fatal car accidents. These accidents can lead to criminal charges. It is widely acknowledged, however, that violations of motor vehicle laws attributed to marijuana use are low compared to those attributed to alcohol (Jonas, 1991).

In summary, there is no solid evidence to indicate that cannabis contributes to or encourages violent or property crime, in spite of continuing beliefs that such a relationship exists. In fact, there is evidence to suggest that cannabis users are *less* criminally or violently prone under the influence of the drug than users of other drugs, such as alcohol and amphetamines. There are also no supportive data that cannabis is habit-forming to the point where the user must get a "fix" and will burglarize or rob to obtain funds to purchase the drug.

Jonas (1991, p. 170) notes that marijuana is a special case among the currently illegal drugs. "Its use causes many people to become lawbreakers solely to obtain the drug or raise their own." Because it is relatively inexpensive it is unlikely that people break the law in order to obtain money to buy the drug, as is the case with other illegal drugs.

Delinquent or antisocial youth do appear to be more inclined to use marijuana and its derivatives, compared with other youth. However, the primary reason is that marijuana provides a quick, relatively cheap, easy, and certain short-term pleasure for those adolescents looking for immediate gratification. The use of the substance can also represent a form of rebellion from adult society.

Phencyclidine (PCP)

Phencyclidine or PCP may be classified as a central nervous system depressant, anesthetic, tranquilizer, or hallucinogen. It has many effects, but most pronounced are its barbiturate-like downer effect, perceptual distortions and hallucinations, and its amphetamine-like upper effects (such as excitation and hyperactivity). An overdosed person, for example, may show signs of moving from upper to downer effects while having hallucinations.

PCP was first synthesized in 1957 but, because of its psychotic and hallucinogenic reactions, it was taken off the market for human consumption in 1965 and limited to veterinary medicine as an animal-immobilizing agent. Between 1973 and 1979 its popularity increased but then declined briefly between 1979 and 1981. PCP then showed a resurgence in popularity between 1982 and 1990 but has shown a strong decrease in recent years (Substance Abuse and Mental Health Services Administration, 1995).

The behavior of some individuals under the influence of PCP is highly unpredictable and may lead to life-threatening situations. Under the influence of a PCP psychosis, it is not uncommon for an individual to experience delusions of superhuman strength, persecution, and grandiosity. On occasion, individuals may use weapons to defend themselves and commit acts of violence. However, the incidence of violence caused by PCP influence is unknown.

There is wide variation in degree of purity and dosage forms of PCP manufactured in clandestine laboratories. It comes in capsules, tablets, liquids, or powders. It may be administered orally, by inhalation, and at times by intravenous injection. Users usually combine PCP with other drugs, particularly marijuana and alcohol. PCP can cause death, although the majority of fatal doses have occurred when it was combined with alcohol (Brunet et al., 1985–86). Because of its adverse and negative effects, the reasons for its popularity remain obscure.

The available evidence clearly indicates that PCP users tend to be multiple illicit-drug users (polydrug users). In addition, PCP continues to be one of the more common drugs found in arrestee populations. Wish (1986) reports that in a urinalysis study of nearly 5,000 male arrestees in Manhattan (New York City) in 1984, 12 percent showed evidence of having used PCP. Furthermore, 49 percent of those using PCP were also using other drugs at the time of the arrest, usually cocaine. In a similar project conducted in Washington, D.C., 30 percent of the male arrestees were found to be using PCP. In both studies, the vast majority of the subjects were arrested for goal-oriented, income-generating crimes rather than for violent offenses. The extent to which PCP propels a person toward a life of crime is largely unknown, but it does not seem likely that the PCP user regularly engages in crime to support his or her habit. PCP is cheap and readily available. PCP users are generally polydrug users who have demonstrated a variety of antisocial conduct prior to PCP usage.

AMPHETAMINES AND COCAINE

Amphetamines and cocaine are classified as central nervous system stimulants and have effects that are highly similar. Amphetamines are part of a group of synthetic drugs known collectively as **amines**. Cocaine (coke, snow, candy) is a chemical extracted from the coca plant (*Erythroxylon coca*), an extremely hardy plant native to Peru. The amines in particular produce effects in the sympathetic nervous system, a subdivision of the autonomic nervous system. These effects arouse the person to action that might include fighting or fleeing from a frightening situation. Amphetamines are traditionally classified into three major categories: (1) amphetamine (Benzedrine); (2) dextroamphetamine (Dexedrine); and (3) methamphetamine (Methedrine or Desoxyn). Of the three, Benzedrine is the least potent. All may be taken orally, inhaled, or injected, and all act directly on the central nervous system, particular the reticular activating system (Bloomquist, 1970). Once the drug is taken, it is rapidly assimilated into the bloodstream, but it is metabolized and eliminated from the body relatively slowly. Both psychological and physiological reactions to these drugs vary dramatically with the dose. In addition, the effects of massive quantities intravenously injected differ substantially from those of low doses administered orally. Reactions to the drugs also vary widely among individuals. For our purposes, we will refer to amphetamines in the broad sense, including all three categories.

The common slang terms for amphetamines include bennies, dexies, copilots, meth, speed, white cross, uppers, "A," pep pills, diet pills, jolly beans, black bombers, truck drivers, eye openers, wakeups, hearts, footballs, bombitas, crossroads, cartwheels, coasts-to-coasts, splash, and purple hearts. The slang names are derived from the various effects, procedures used, the shape and color of the drug, or the trade names applied by the manufacturers.

The American pharmaceutical industry produces an estimated 8 to 10 billion doses of amphetamines annually (Julien, 1995). This figure is believed to be considerably higher than the estimated number of amphetamine prescriptions dispensed during the same period of time. Prescriptions reached an all-time high in 1965 (24.5 million), but this figure has declined steadily since then because of widespread concern about misuse of the drug and its effect. A sizeable portion of all amphetamines produced end up on the black market for distribution. Because the drug is a synthetic compound, unlike cannabis or cocaine, it can easily be produced by individuals for large-scale illegal distribution. Therefore, it is exceedingly difficult to estimate the quantity of amphetamines consumed each year in the United States.

Cocaine has traditionally been much more expensive than amphetamines, partly because it is a natural organic substance and cannot be produced synthetically. The coca plant from which it is extracted thrives at elevations of 2,000 to 8,000 feet with heavy rainfall (100 inches per year). It is an evergreen shrub, growing to about 3 feet tall, and generally found in the eastern slopes of the Andes. It has long been used by Peruvians living in or near the Andes. Indigenous populations in the region have traditionally chewed coca leaves almost continually and commonly kept them tucked in their cheeks. Coca leaves are also used for tea. There are at least 200 strains of coca plants, but the vast majority contain little if any cocaine. However, because of the high demand for cocaine, South American growers and entrepreneurs have developed not only vast new areas for the cultivation of coca but also new, more vigorous strains of the plant (Inciardi, 1986).

In the United States and Canada, cocaine is usually administered nasally (sniffing), by inhalation (smoking), or intravenously. Cocaine taken orally is poorly absorbed because it is hydrolyzed (neutralized) by gastrointestinal secretions. Smoking cocaine was first tried in America around 1914, but the high temperature (198 degrees C) required to burn the chemical resulted in the destruction of most of its psychoactive properties (Inaba & Cohen, 1993). As a consequence, cocaine smoking (in the form of "crack") did not become popular in the United States until the mid-1970s. Crack is produced in such way that the cocaine ingredient can be smoked without the potency's being destroyed.

Light users normally sniff the drug to obtain their "high," and chronic sniffing can result in nasal irritation and inflammation. The common unit in the black market is the "spoon," which approximates one gram of the diluted drug. In most cases, cocaine is diluted 20 to 30 times its weight. It is estimated that in the United States 20 to 30 million people have used cocaine (Julien, 1995), 6 million (3 percent of the population) are regular cocaine users (White & Azel, 1989), and 2 million are "hard core" cocaine users (Julien, 1995).

Around the turn of the last century, cocaine was used in soft drinks (such as Kos-Kola, Wiseola, and Care-Cola) and in cigarettes, cigars, various tonics, foods, sprays, and ointments (Smart, 1986). In fact, Coca-Cola contained cocaine as an active ingredient until 1903, when caffeine was substituted (Kleber, 1988). The famous drink "Vin Mariani" so popular among the wealthy at the time was a combination of French wine and cocaine. However, cocaine began to fall into disfavor when people became concerned about its dangerous and undesirable effects. By 1910, cocaine had fast become the most hated and feared drug in North America (Kleber, 1988). The Harrison Narcotics Act of 1914 in the United States and the Propriety and Patents Medicines Act of 1908 in Canada sharply curtailed or terminated its usage, and the popularity of cocaine correspondingly declined until the 1960s.

In national surveys conducted in the early 1980s in Canada, about 4 percent of the college students and 3 percent of the adults said they had used cocaine at least once during the year (Smart, 1986). More recent research suggests that the high level of cocaine use in Canada during the 1980s seems to have declined during the early 1990s (Smart & Adlaf, 1992). In the United States, the incidence is high, with about 16 to 20 percent of the college students using cocaine at least once during the year (Substance Abuse and Mental Health Services Administration, 1995). Recall from Table 3.1 that 2.9 percent of high school seniors in 1993 reported using cocaine within the past year, and 1.5 percent reported using crack.

Psychological Effects

Both amphetamines and cocaine increase wakefulness, alertness, and vigilance, improve concentration, and produce a feeling of clear thinking. There is generally an elevation of mood, mild euphoria, increased sociability, and a belief that one can do just about anything. In large doses, the effects may be irritability, hypersensitivity, delirium, panic aggression, hallucinations, and psychosis. Injected at chronically high doses, these drugs may precipitate "toxic psychosis," a syndrome with many of the psychotic features of paranoid schizophrenia. With the metabolization and elimination of the drug, the psychotic episode usually dissipates.

Heavy users of amphetamines typically prefer to inject the drug directly into the bloodstream, cranking up with several hundred milligrams at one time. During these speed "runs" the user may engage in aggressive or violent behavior (Tinklenberg & Stillman, 1970; National Commission on Marihuana and Drug Abuse, 1973; Hofmann, 1975). Ellinwood (1971) studied the case histories of 13 persons who committed homicides under amphetamine intoxication and found that, in most instances, the homicidal act was directly related to the effects of the amphetamine itself.

Crack

The most common form of cocaine smoking in the United States is produced through a process called freebasing. There are two popular methods used to produce freebase cocaine. In one method, the freebase is prepared by dissolving cocaine hydrochloride in water and then adding a strong base such as ammonia or baking soda to the solution (Weiss & Mirin, 1987). The solution is then heated. This method, sometimes referred to as "cheap basing" or "dirty basing," does not remove many of the impurities or residues such as the baking soda. The second method involves dissolving cocaine hydrochloride in highly flammable chemicals, such as ether, to extract the cocaine. The ether is then removed by drying the solution, leaving crystals of freebase cocaine. This method creates a purer form of the drug because any additives are filtered out by the process. The result is a product ranging from 37 to 96 percent purity (Weiss & Mirin, 1987).

Crack has two chemical properties sought by users. First, crystallized cocaine has a lower melting point than the powdered form, so it can be heated easily in a glass pipe and vaporized to form smoke at a lower temperature (Inaba & Cohen, 1993). The second chemical property provided by freebase cocaine is that it is more fat-soluble than powdered cocaine. Therefore, it is more readily absorbed by the fatty brain tissue, causing a more immediate and intense reaction (Inaba & Cohen, 1993).

Crack is, according to Howard Abadinsky (1993), the drug abuser's answer to fast food. The drug is called "crack" because it produces a crackling sound when smoked (Gold, 1984; Abadinsky, 1993). Several times more pure than ordinary street cocaine, crack smoking generates a very rapid intense state of euphoria that peaks in about 5 minutes. The psychological and physical effects of crack are as powerful as those of any intravenously injected cocaine. However, the euphoria is short-lived, ending in about 10 to 20 minutes after inhalation, and is followed by depression, irritability, and often an intense craving for more. Although most users limit themselves to one or two "hits" at a given time, some users seek multiple hits. Crack smokers, in order to stay high, often find a place where crack can be safely smoked, such as a "crack house," because the smoke and smell are difficult to hide. An overdose of freebase cocaine usually results in very rapid heartbeat and hyperventilation. Often these physiological reactions are accompanied by an overwhelming feeling of impending death. Experts agree that crack is extremely dangerous to the user and may result in a number of life-threatening neurophysiological reactions, such as rapid, irregular heartbeat, respiratory failure, seizures, or a cerebral hemorrhage.

It is estimated that there are about 500,000 regular crack users in the United States, with most of the users being between 18 and 25 years old (Substance Abuse and Mental Health Services Administration, 1995). One of the major reasons why youth are more drawn to crack than cocaine involves economics. Although crack is no less expensive than cocaine when sold by weight alone, it is sold in smaller units, such as small fractions of a gram, making the price more manageable for teenagers.

Some experts regard crack as the most addictive drug currently available on the street (Weiss & Mirin, 1987). Moreover, the craving for the drug may become so severe for some individuals that the user will lie, steal, or commit acts of violence in order to obtain more of it (Rosecan, Spitz, & Gross, 1987). Its popularity probably resides in the instantaneous psychological effects it provides, its inexpensiveness, and its wide availability throughout most major U.S. cities. The drug also provides tremendous profit for the sellers. For example, twenty dollars' worth of cocaine powder may easily return a profit of sixty dollars (Ratner, 1993). In recent years, about one-third of all arrests made by the New York City Narcotics Division involved cocaine, and more than half of them involved crack (Cohn, 1986). Because it is so inexpensive and available, it has become a very popular drug for the young—including preteenagers.

Some researchers exploring the connection between delinquency and crack have focused upon the consequences of sex-for-crack exchanges that characterize adolescent drug use in inner cities. Studies by John Inciardi and his colleagues (1991) help shed light on the connection between crack and delinquency and raise serious concerns about HIV transmission among serious delinquents. The researchers studied 611 Miami youths, both males and females, who were heavily involved in the drug business, including dealing, manufacturing, and smuggling. All were current drug users (defined as any use during the 90 days prior to the interview) and almost all (98 percent) were using at least three different types of drugs. The four most commonly used drugs were marijuana (100 percent of the sample), crack (84 percent), cocaine powder (75 percent), and alcohol (70 percent). Ninety-one percent of the youths were using some form of cocaine on a regular basis, defined as three or more times a week. All were seriously involved in profit-making crimes, with a mean total of 702 offenses per subject.

The researchers looked closely at two behaviors that put juveniles at high risk of contracting HIV: sexual activity with multiple partners and intravenous (IV) drug use. Gender differences were apparent in both behaviors; 87 percent of the girls reported regular involvement in prostitution, compared with 5 percent of the boys. The female mean was 431 sexual acts, while the male mean was 26 acts. Intravenous drug use was prevalent, particularly among females and black males. Almost all black females and one-third of the white females acknowledged intravenous use; about one-third of the black males acknowledged it. Only 6 percent of the white males, however, reported intravenous drug use. Altogether, 69 percent of the IV users were African-American, 20 percent were white, and 12 percent were Latino.

Inciardi and his colleages (1991, p. 231) expressed grave concerns about rising rates of HIV infection among inner-city juveniles and the failure of community agencies and the criminal justice system to respond effectively to this crisis. They call for "strenuous outreach prevention/intervention programs," including drug treatment directed toward street populations of youth.

The relationship between crack and delinquency has many facets. One thing that emerges clearly from the research literature is that crack users are often **polydrug users**. Furthermore, persistent offenders tend to be polydrug users. Although it is difficult at this point in our knowledge to determine which comes first, drug use or involvement in delinquency or crime, the evidence strongly suggests that persistent offenders have engaged in a variety of illegal activities and troublesome conduct throughout their lifetimes, probably beginning before the onset of drug abuse.

NARCOTIC DRUGS

The word **"narcotics"** usually provokes intense negative reactions and very often is quickly associated with crime. Like the word "dope," it is widely misused to denote all illegal drugs. In this chapter, "narcotic drugs" refers only to the derivatives of (or products pharmacologically similar to products of) the opium or poppy plant, *Papaver sominferum*.

Narcotic drugs can be divided into three major categories on the basis of the kind of preparation they require: (1) natural narcotics, which include the grown opium; (2) semisynthetic narcotics, which include the chemically prepared heroin; and (3) synthetic narcotics, which are wholly prepared chemically and include methadone, meperidine, and phenazocine. All are narcotics because they produce similar effects: relief of pain, relaxation, peacefulness, and sleep (*narco*, of Greek origin, means "to sleep"). In fact, the opium poppy was named after Somnis, the Roman god of sleep.

The narcotics are highly addictive for some individuals, to the point where they develop a relentless and strong craving for the drug. Many heavy narcotic users, however, lead productive lives, without significant interference in their daily routine. There does not appear to be a single type of opium user, as a wide variety of people use the drug for various purposes.

Heroin

The most heavily and consistently used illegal narcotic in the United States is heroin. A heroin epidemic hit inner cities in the 1950s, particularly among youth. Drug abuse, including heroin abuse, spread to the suburbs in the 1960s. (Inciardi, 1991). Since 1979, estimates of lifetime heroin prevalence have fluctuated between

1.7 million and 2.7 million users, with no clear pattern over time (Substance Abuse and Mental Health Services Administration, 1995). Similarly, estimates of current users fluctuate between 245,000 to 550,000 Americans. The recent *Monitoring the Future* survey indicates that heroin was the least commonly used illicit drug among grade schoolers and high schoolers. Research by Joseph (1995), however, finds that heroin may still be used heavily by Latino and African American teens living within the inner cities.

Heroin, a white, crystalline material, is characterized by the bitter taste of alkaloid. Its appearance is largely dictated by its diluents, which in most cases make up 95 to 98 percent of its total weight. Heroin is rarely taken orally, not only because of its very bitter taste but also because the absorption rate is slow and incomplete. It may be administered intramuscularly, subcutaneously ("skin popping"), or intravenously ("mainlining"), or it may be inhaled ("snorted").

The effects of heroin depend on the quantity taken, the method of administration, the interval between administrations, the tolerance and dependence of the user, the setting, and the user's expectations. The experienced heroin user strongly prefers mainlining because of the sensational thrill, splash, rush, or kick it provides. Moreover, the effects of mainlining are immediate (15 to 30 seconds), compared with those of skin popping, which take about 5 to 8 minutes to occur. Effects usually wear off in from 5 to 8 hours, depending on the user's tolerance.

Like all the narcotics, heroin is a central nervous system depressant. For many users, it promotes mental clouding, dreamlike states, light sleep punctuated by vivid dreams, and a general feeling of "sublime contentment." The body may become permeated with a feeling of warmth, and the extremities may feel heavy. There is little inclination toward physical activity; the user prefers to sit motionless and in a fog.

Heroin and Crime

No other drug group is as closely associated with crime as the narcotics, particularly heroin. The image of the desperate junkie looking for a fix is familiar to everyone. Furthermore, because of the adverse effects of the drug, it is assumed that the heroin user is bizarre, unpredictable, and therefore dangerous. However, high doses of narcotics produce sleep rather than the psychotic or paranoid panic states sometimes produced by high doses of amphetamines. Therefore, narcotics users rarely become violent or dangerous. Early research strongly indicates that addicts do not, as a general rule, participate in violent crimes such as assault, rape, or homicide (Tinklenberg & Stillman, 1970; Canadian Government's Commission of Inquiry, 1971; National Commission on Marihuana and Drug Abuse, 1973; National Institute on Drug Abuse, 1978). Research evidence does indicate, however, a relationship between heroin addiction and money-producing crime, including prostitution, drug dealing, and larceny. A study in Miami of 573 narcotics users found that they were responsible for almost 6,000 robberies, 6,700 burglaries, 900 stolen vehicles, 25,000 instances of shoplifting, and 46,000 other events of larceny and fraud (Inciardi, 1986).

Self-report surveys also find that heroin users report financing their habits largely through "acquisitive crime" (Jarvis & Parker, 1989; Mott, 1986). Parker and Newcombe (1987) studied crime patterns and heroin use in the English community of Wirral, located in northwestern England. They found that many heroin users were from the poor sections of the community and were young. The researchers were also able to divide their sample into three groups: (1) the largest group, which consisted of young offenders who were not known to be using heroin but were highly criminally active; (2) heroin users who engaged in considerable acquisitive crime but were involved in this type of crime prior to their heroin addiction; and (3) heroin users who started engaging in acquisitive crime after beginning drug use in order to support their habit. The Parker–Newcombe investigation suggests that some heroin addicts do support their habit through crime.

Ball, Shaffer, and Nurco (1983) found that heroin addicts committed more money-producing crime when they were addicted than when they were not. Still, it may be misleading to examine the heroin–crime relationship in isolation without considering the possible interactions between polydrug use and crime, or to conclude that heroin addiction causes crime. All we can say with some confidence at this point is that those who use heroin also seem to be deeply involved in money-producing crime. Heroin users, however, are not necessarily driven to crime by the needs of their addiction. Heroin users, particularly polydrug users, *may* run counter to society's rules and expectations in multiple ways, drug use and larceny among them. It could be that *most* heroin-addicted offenders were involved in crime and antisocial behavior before they became addicted. Research by Faupel (1991) supports this hypothesis. However, studies also suggest that, although many heroin users have criminal records prior to their addiction, their criminal activity increases substantially during periods of heavy drug consumption (Faupel, 1991). Furthermore, polydrug users tend to switch from drug to drug, depending on what is available and inexpensive at the time, and do not seem physiologically desperate for any one particular drug. They simply substitute one drug for the other. Overall, the relationship between heroin use and criminal behavior is a complex one and varies throughout the addict's career.

THE DEPRESSANTS: ALCOHOL

Despite the public concern over heroin, opium, marijuana, cocaine (especially crack) and amphetamines, the number one drug of abuse by both adults and juveniles has been and continues to be alcohol (ethanol, ethyl alcohol, grain alcohol). According to the 1994 National Household Survey on Drug Abuse, 13 million Americans (6.2 percent of the population) had 5 or more drinks per occasion on 5 or more days in a given month (Substance Abuse and Mental Health Services Administration, 1995). Other surveys indicate that one-third of American families have problems with alcohol (Peele, 1984). Alcohol is responsible for more deaths and violence (it is the third major cause of death) than all other drugs combined. However, in recent years the number of alcohol-related traffic deaths have shown a dramatic decrease. According to the Centers for Disease Control and Prevention, during the peak year of 1982 approximately 25,000 individuals were killed in traffic accidents involving alcohol. Overall, 57 percent of all traffic fatalities were linked to alcohol use during that year. However, by 1993, the number of deaths had fallen to approximately 17,400 and alcohol was a factor in only 44 percent of traffic fatalities. The change in the minimum legal drinking age has been credited for this drop, but it is certainly not the only contributing factor. During the early 1980s, the minimum legal drinking age in many states was 18. Today, all 50 states have a legal drinking age of 21. Increases in penalties for alcohol-related traffic violations have also helped to curb the fatalities. However, seatbelt laws and even more sturdily built cars have also helped to lower the death rate.

The usual way to determine if an individual is intoxicated is by measuring his or her blood-alcohol concentration (BAC). A blood-alcohol concentration of .10 percent means there are 100 milligrams of alcohol per 100 milliliters of blood. For example, a 165-pound man would reach a BAC of .10 percent if he had about five drinks within 1 hour on an empty stomach. (A drink is defined as $1^1/_2$ ounces of liquor, a 12-ounce beer, or a 5-ounce glass of wine). In most states, a driver is considered intoxicated if his or her BAC is .10 percent, and in some states the cutoff is .08 percent.

Psychological Effects

The social, psychological, and psychobiological effects of excessive alcohol use can be just as destructive to the individual, his or her family, and society in general as those associated with heroin abuse. Similar to heroin users, the alcoholic can develop a strong psychological and physical dependence on the drug. Society's attitudes toward alcohol are dramatically different from its attitudes toward other drugs of abuse, however. In virtually every part of the United States, it is legal and socially acceptable to consume the drug. In public, drinking behavior is generally unregulated unless it involves heavy intoxication and correspondingly unacceptable conduct (e.g., disturbing the peace or operating a motor vehicle). In private, one can get as drunk as one wishes, a privilege presumably not granted with respect to other drugs.

In reality, the private use of illegal drugs is tolerated much less in some contexts than in others. Police raids of inner-city crack houses are a frequent occurrence compared to raids of hotel suites, condominiums, and private residences where cocaine, heroin, and other illegal drugs are consumed.

The effects of alcohol are extremely complex. Miczek and his colleagues (1994) write that the effects of alcohol depend on ". . . a host of interacting pharmacologic, endocrinologic, neurobiologic, genetic, situational, environmental, social, and cultural determinants" (p. 382). Consequently, we can provide only a cursory review of this complicated topic here.

At low doses (two or four ounces of whiskey, for example), alcohol seems to act as a stimulant on the central nervous system. Initially, it appears to affect the inhibitory chemical process of nervous system transmission, producing feelings of euphoria, good cheer, and social and physical warmth. In moderate and high quantities, however, alcohol begins to depress the excitatory processes of the central nervous system, as well as its inhibitory processes. Consequently, the individual's neuromuscular coordination and visual acuity are reduced, and he or she perceives pain and fatigue. The ability to concentrate is also impaired. Very often, self-confidence increases and the person becomes more daring, sometimes foolishly so. It is believed that alcohol at moderate levels begins to "numb" the higher brain centers that process cognitive information, especially judgment and abstract thought. It should be emphasized at this point that the levels of intoxication are not necessarily dependent on the amount of alcohol ingested; as for other psychoactive drugs, the effects depend on many interacting variables.

Alcohol and Crime

The belief that alcohol is a major cause of crime appears to be deeply embedded in American society. Surveys suggest that more than 50 percent of the population is convinced that alcohol is a major factor in crimes of violence (Critchlow, 1986). This pervasive belief appears to be based on the premise that alcohol either instigates aggressive conduct in some individuals or somehow diminishes the checks and balances of nonaggressive, nonviolent behavior.

Coleman (1976) calls alcohol a "catalyst for violence," noting that about one out of every three arrests in the United States results from alcohol abuse. A survey of state prisons in 1974 found that 43 percent of all inmates had been drinking when they committed the crime for which they were serving time (Law Enforcement Assistance Administration, 1976). In a Missouri study, 55 percent of all males charged with capital or first degree murder over a three-year period were taking alcohol, drugs, or a combination of both at the time of the homicide (Holcomb & Anderson, 1983). Cole, Fisher, and Cole (1968) reported that 51 percent of a sample of California women arrested for homicide had been drinking at the time of their offense. Fifty-five percent of those convicted for murder in Britain (Gillies, 1965) and 51 percent of those convicted in France (Derville et al., 1961) were drinking at the time of the violence. Nichol et al. (1973) found that the more severe the drinking problem, the more serious the violent offense. Mayfield (1976) reports that 57 percent of a sample of convicted American murderers were drinking when they killed. Rada (1975) cites evidence that 50 percent of a sample of rapists were drinking at the time of their offense. Tinklenberg (1973) found that 53 percent of a sample of California youth under age 19 convicted of murder, manslaughter, or assault were under the influence of alcohol at the time of their offense. A national survey of 12,000 inmates indicated that 38 percent were daily or almost daily drinkers in the year prior to their incarceration. Approximately 50 percent had been drinking just prior to the offense that resulted in their incarceration (Kalish, 1983). Glaser (1978, p. 275) estimates that "about half of the people arrested on any charge in the United States either are under the influence of alcohol when taken into custody, or are held for acts committed when drunk, or both."

One of the most consistent findings in the research across the world is that alcohol appears to play a significant role in family abuse and violence (Miczek et al., 1994). Interestingly, the available evidence suggests that this phenomenon occurs only in humans. Intoxicated lab animals may act violently toward members outside their families, but very rarely do they attack members within their family.

Overall, the evidence clearly shows that approximately half of all offenders who commit violent crime were drinking at the time of offense, and many were highly intoxicated. After an extensive literature review, Reiss and Roth (1993, p. 185) concluded: "In studies of prison inmates, those classified as 'heavy' or 'problem' drinkers had accumulated more previous arrests for violent crime, and reported higher average frequencies of assaults, than did other inmates." And the National Institute on Alcohol Abuse and Alcoholism (1990, p. 92) asserts: "In both animal and human studies, alcohol, more than any other drug, has been linked with a high incidence of violence and aggression."

While the relationship between alcohol and violence has long been suspected, the landmark study by Wolfgang (1958) on 588 Philadelphia homicides brought the alcohol–violence relationship into clear focus and stamped it with some scientific confirmation. The Wolfgang survey reported that in 9 percent of the homicides the victims had been drinking alcohol at the time of the offense, while 11 percent of the offenders had been drinking. More important, however, alcohol was present in *both* the offender and the victim in an additional 44 percent of the cases surveyed. The Wolfgang findings suggest that people become volatile under the influence of alcohol and that the danger increases greatly when both parties have been drinking. Research continues to support this finding.

High blood-alcohol concentration (BAC) has often been consistently reported in about 50 percent of homicide victims (Fisher, 1951; Cleveland, 1955; Bowden, Wilson, & Turner, 1958; Bensing & Schroeder, 1960). In a recent study (Welte & Abel, 1989), 46 percent of the homicide victims had significant amounts of alcohol, and many had substantial amounts. Specifically, 70 percent of the 46 percent had BAC amounts higher than 0.10. This was especially the case for victims involved in fight-related homicides. We should not assume that the BAC–victim connection supports the conclusion that most victims precipitate their own demise. Although this may be the case in some violent events, the relationship should also be viewed as underscoring the importance of the social context within which violence occurs. Violence frequently occurs in social situations in which drinking is heavy, physiological arousal (such as anger) is high, interpersonal conflict is evident, and cognitive processes—especially judgment and abstract reasoning—are impaired.

Research in the psychology laboratory also finds strong evidence that drinking alcohol *facilitates* (not causes) physical aggression. In the typical laboratory experiment, subjects are placed in a variety of conditions and can administer simulated electric shocks to another person. To create another common design, researchers may place subjects into aroused (usually anger) and nonaroused conditions.

Research using these paradigms has consistently found that drinking alcohol facilitates aggression (Taylor & Leonard, 1983; Taylor & Sears, 1988).

Furthermore, as the quantity of alcohol consumed increases, so does the tendency to be aggressive, at least up to the point when the subject "passes out."

It should be mentioned that the alcohol–violence connection appears to be strongest in the United States, even though the amount of alcohol consumption in this country is by no means the highest in the world. Many countries, including France, Italy, Spain, Germany, Portugal, and Russia, consume substantially more alcohol per capita than the United States. In addition to obvious cultural differences between the countries, however, drinking patterns are also different. In some countries, alcohol consumption is spread out across the day, including at mealtimes, whereas in the United States drinking is generally reserved for the end of the day, particularly during weekends and holidays. Think of the drinking patterns of some college students, who traditionally let loose on weekends with heavy consumption of alcohol and partying. It appears to be this episodic heavy drinking pattern that is most strongly related to aggression, violence, and antisocial behavior.

The relationship between episodic heavy drinking of alcohol and aggression or violence is well supported, but how is it explained? Many models and theories have been proposed during the past twenty years, but a majority can be subsumed into two major categories: **disinhibitory models** and **social-cognitive models**. Disinhibitory models contend that alcohol, directly or indirectly, influences neurological or psychological mechanisms that normally control aggressive and antisocial behavior. One disinhibitory perspective hypothesizes that alcohol chemically influences the portion of the brain that controls the expression of aggression: The more intoxicated the people are, the less control they have of their behavior. Another disinhibitory perspective, and by far the most popular in American society, supposes that certain people have a particular sensitivity or susceptibility to alcohol. This perspective views problem drinking as a biological abnormality or disease. This approach, known as the "American disease model" (Miller & Hester, 1989), is deeply entrenched in American society and forms the fundamental assumption of Alcoholics Anonymous (AA). Polls show, for example, that 79 percent of Americans believe that alcoholism is a disease, requiring medical treatment (Peele, 1984). The basic AA version is that chronic problem drinking is a disease reflected in an individual's inability to control alcoholic drinking, an affliction that exists within the individual even before the first drink is taken because it has a genetic basis. Furthermore, "The condition is irreversible and progressive and requires complete and utter abstinence" (Peele, 1984, p. 1339).

All disinhibitory models assume that alcohol has the power to disinhibit impulses that are normally held in check, and consequently this disinhibition may result in drink-induced criminal behavior (Critchlow, 1986). Alcohol may provide a powerful excuse for undesirable behaviors that are often accompanied by such pleas as "I couldn't help myself" or "Alcohol always does this to me."

While disinhibitory viewpoints focus on internal influences or predispositions, social cognitive models emphasize the interactions between subjective belief systems and the social environment. Social cognitive models reject the disease or loss-of-control assumptions basic to the disinhibitory models. Social-cognitive models argue that problem drinking and much of the psychoactive influences of alcohol are learned and situationally determined. According to this view, the contention that one cannot help oneself or that alcohol directly instigates a loss of control is a subjective, cognitive expectancy that feeds on itself, as opposed to being a disease. A person's expectations or cognitions influence how he or she responds to alcohol. Alcohol serves as a cue for acting intoxicated and doing things one normally would not do. In other words, you act the way you *believe* alcohol makes you act.

There is considerable empirical support for social-cognitive models of drinking behavior and actually very little empirical support for disinhibitory models. For example, disinhibitory models advocate total abstinence if alcoholic-prone people are to control themselves; otherwise, "one drink leads to one drunk." However, a large body of research shows that the most effective treatment for heavy drinkers is to train them to be responsible light to moderate drinkers rather than to have them abstain completely over their lifespans (see Peele, 1984). Research continually shows that total abstinence has a poor track record over the long haul, especially for younger single men, because the abstinence requirement does not fit into their lifestyles and the opportunities and pressures they face to drink (Peele, 1984).

Among the proponents of social-cognitive theory are Marlatt and Rohsenow (1980) and Lang and his colleagues (1975), who found that the amount of alcohol consumed may not be as important as what the person expects from the drug. Independent of the pharmacological effects, some people expect to become giddy or boisterous after one or more drinks. Some anticipate acting more aggressively under the influence because alcohol is "supposed" to have that effect. According to Lang, if a person expects alcohol to influence behavior in a preconceived way, it probably will. Moreover, as mentioned earlier, the person avoids blame for some of his or her actions, because society tends to accept the "I was drunk" explanation unless a serious crime is committed. In fact, Sobell and Sobell (1973) suggested that one of the rewarding aspects of heavy drinking is that it provides a socially acceptable excuse for engaging in inappropriate behavior.

In the Lang et al. (1975) experiment, half of the subjects were told they would be drinking alcohol, which actually was either vodka or tonic water. The other half were told they would be drinking tonic water, not alcohol. However, half the members of this second group were actually given vodka, whereas the other half received the tonic water they expected. Results indicated that "the only significant determinant of aggression was the expectation factor; subjects who believed they had consumed alcohol were more aggressive than subjects who believed they had consumed a non-alcoholic beverage, regardless of the actual alcohol content of the drinks administered" (p. 508).

Therefore, according to social-cognitive theory, the consumer's expectancy becomes the crucial factor. As long as consumers believe they are drinking alcohol, they expect to feel intoxicated. Because they are "intoxicated," they tend to feel less responsible for their behavior, including violent or criminal behavior. Interestingly, convicted murderers who were intoxicated during the crime often claim that they cannot remember the incident at all (Schacter, 1986). Whether these claims of amnesia are genuine or not remains very much in question.

Critchlow (1986) asserts that the pharmacological action of alcohol cannot account for the many transformations in social behavior that occur when people drink, as those transformations vary widely from culture to culture and in the same culture across time periods. She argues that the effects of alcohol on social behavior are found largely at the cultural level. Expectations about what alcohol can do behaviorally can be learned by anyone through a particular culture, even before taking the first drink. Critchlow writes:

> On a cultural level, it seems to be the negative consequences of alcohol that hold the most powerful sway over our thinking. . . . Thus, by believing that alcohol makes people act badly, we give it a great deal of power. Drinking becomes a tool that legitimates irrationality and excuses violence without permanently destroying an individual's moral standing or society's systems of rules and ethics (pp. 761–62).

While cognitive expectancies play an extremely important role, we should not downplay the pharmacological effects of alcohol. Alcohol does affect the neurochemistry of the central nervous system by depressing many functions. Anyone who has tried to act sober with marginal success, no matter how he or she has tried, can attest to this effect. Research confirms that alcohol has a strong pharmacological effect on behavior, somewhat independent of subjective expectancies. For example, Shuntich and Taylor (1972) found that actually intoxicated subjects were more aggressive than both subjects who consumed a placebo beverage (thinking they had consumed alcohol) and subjects who did not consume any beverage. Zeichner and Pihl (1979, 1980) also found that subjects in a nonalcohol condition were as aggressive as placebo subjects who thought they had consumed alcohol.

Social cognitive theory also predicts that the amount of alcohol consumed should make little difference on overall behavior. If subjects believe they are consuming large amounts, they will, correspondingly, act more intoxicated (and hence more aggressively). If, on the other hand, they do not believe they have consumed much alcohol, even though they actually have, they will be less aggressive and less likely to act intoxicated. In other words, the misled subjects will behave at the level of aggressiveness that corresponds with their expectations, regardless of the amount of alcohol they consume.

In evaluating this implication, a series of studies by Stuart Taylor and his associates (Taylor & Gammon, 1975; Taylor, Gammon, & Capasso, 1976) is instructive. The Taylor projects found that small doses of alcohol (e.g., 0.5 ounces of vodka or bourbon per 40 pounds of body weight) tend to inhibit aggression, whereas larger doses (1.5 ounces per 40 pounds) tend to facilitate aggression. Therefore, depending on the amount, alcohol may either inhibit or facilitate expressions of aggression and violence.

The Taylor experiments are in agreement with the known pharmacological effects of alcohol. At small amounts, alcohol appears to stimulate the central nervous system, generating mild euphoria and a sense of well-being. This good cheer becomes readily apparent at a party when, after the first round of drinks, people tend to take on a happy frame of mind. As alcoholic intake increases, however, the integrating functions of the cortex are depressed, causing some disorganization and impairment of complex cognitive functions. At extreme levels of intoxication, even simple cognitive processes like attention and sustained concentration break down, eventually ending in stupor and sleep. Therefore, violent behavior, if it is to occur, will most likely occur at moderate levels of intoxication.

In the Taylor investigation, when subjects were informed that they would be consuming alcohol, aggression was positively related only to the amount of alcohol actually consumed, not to the amount they thought they had consumed (Taylor & Gammon, 1975). In a later study (Taylor, Gammon, & Capasso, 1976) subjects were informed that they would be consuming one of three drugs: alcohol, marijuana, or a tranquilizer. Therefore, all subjects within each group had the same drug expectancy. They then received either a high or low dose of THC or alcohol. The results demonstrated that the high dose of alcohol facilitated aggression, whereas the high dose of THC suppressed it.

Overall, Taylor's data strongly suggest that the aggression demonstrated by intoxicated subjects is a joint function of the pharmacological state produced by alcohol and cognitive and situational factors. The researchers maintain that alcohol consumption by itself does not produce aggressive behavior (Taylor & Leonard, 1983). Physiological effects of alcohol do influence behavior, but they also interact with expectancies and with what is happening in the person's environment at any given time.

Emotions may be important also. Jaffe, Babor, and Fishbein (1988) observe that alcoholics exhibit more aggressive, violent behavior than do nonalcoholics, especially when drinking. Beyond this, however, the researchers also noted that alcoholics frequently report highly negative emotions when drinking, such as anger and depression. They concluded, "Thus it is possible that when these states are experienced by alcoholics with a prior history of aggressive behavior, the likelihood of alcohol-related aggression increases and such behavior can be predicted with some degree of reliability" (p. 217). Similarly, unhappy or depressive thoughts presumably activate other negative memories and feelings and therefore are likely to promote aggressive, violent inclinations (Berkowitz & Heimer, 1989).

Situational factors are crucial. None of Taylor's studies supported an automatic aggression–alcohol relationship, even alcohol in large amounts. Subjects were provoked, threatened, or in the presence of aggressive cues before they displayed aggressive behavior. Therefore, in order for aggression to occur, there must be provocative, incitive, or instigative cues along with intoxication. Something or someone must anger, threaten, or in some other way arouse the intoxicated subject. Internal cues, such as thoughts, beliefs, or even imagined slights or provocations, can also serve as instigating cues for aggressive or violent behavior.

SUMMARY AND CONCLUSIONS

This chapter reviewed the relationship between delinquency and substance use. Four major drug categories were identified: (1) the hallucinogens; (2) the stimulants; (3) the opiate narcotics; and (4) the sedative-hypnotics. Rather than discuss most of the drugs in each category, we considered only those believed to be connected with delinquent conduct. We did not examine in depth the crimes of drug possession and distribution, crimes associated with the drug trafficking trade, or crimes committed to support a habit. We were mainly concerned with whether the substance itself facilitates or instigates illegal action, especially violence. The sale of drugs may lead to violence and other antisocial conduct, especially if the participants are members of gangs or cohesive groups. The National Institute on Drug Abuse, for instance, estimates that about 10 percent of homicides occur during drug sales (Eron & Slaby, 1994). However, we will discuss the relationship between violence and gangs—including the relationship between drug trafficking and violence—in Chapter 7.

In this chapter we tried to answer such questions as: Are persons under the influence of marijuana more violent than they are normally? Or, to what extent does alcohol directly contribute to loss of control or reduce self-regulatory mechanisms? Cannabis, which includes marijuana and hashish, is a relatively mild hallucinogen with few psychological or physiological side effects. No significant relationship between cannabis use and delinquency has been consistently reported in the research literature. If anything, marijuana seems to reduce the likelihood of violence, because its psychoactive ingredient, THC, induces relaxation and peacefulness and promotes feelings of lethargy.

Amphetamines and cocaine (especially crack) represent the stimulant group. Most illegal users do not participate in crime other than the possession or sale of these drugs. Similar to marijuana, amphetamines are plentiful and inexpensive. However, there are some documented cases in which heavy users of amphetamines entered psychological states that presumably predisposed them to paranoia and violence. In addition, several studies have found correlations between violent offenders and a history of amphetamine abuse. Cocaine, a natural drug that grows only in certain parts of the world, has traditionally been quite expensive. In recent years, cocaine has become widely available and its cost less prohibitive because of crack. There is no hard evidence, however, that cocaine generally renders people more violent, more out of control, or more likely to engage in property crimes than they would be without taking the drug. Research evidence consistently shows that youths who are highly aggressive or violent under the influence of any drug were highly aggressive and violent before taking the substance.

We discussed heroin as the representative of the opiate narcotics. Like most other narcotics, heroin appears to be highly addictive, particularly in the sense that it creates a strong psychological dependency. Narcotics in general are so addictive and so expensive that substantial funds are needed to support a user's habit. Thus, some researchers have found a moderate correlation between narcotics and various income-generating crimes. Others have noted that most addicts turned to drugs only after they had developed criminal patterns.

Of all the drugs reviewed, alcohol—representing the sedative-hypnotic group—shows the strongest relationship with violent offending. At intermediate and high levels, alcohol appears to impair or disrupt the brain operations responsible for self-control. However, it is likely that violent behavior associated with alcohol use is a joint function of pharmacological effects, cognitive expectancies, experiences, and situational influences. If the individual expects that alcohol will make him or her act aggressively, and if the social environment provides appropriate cues, aggression or violent behavior will be facilitated. Again, however, the evidence indicates that youths who exhibit high levels of aggression and violence under the influence of alcohol also display aggressive and violent behavior when not under the influence.

The relationships between crime and all the drugs discussed in this chapter are complex, involving interactions between numerous pharmacological, social, and psychological variables. Research is beginning to ease some data out of the complexity, but additional studies employing well-designed methodology are greatly needed to understand the many possible influences of psychoactive drugs on human behavior, particularly delinquent and criminal behavior. Numerous theories concentrate on explaining adolescent substance use and abuse, but very little effort has been made to fit them together (Petraitis, Flay, & Miller, 1995). Consequently, the causes of substance use and abuse among youth remain a puzzle with numerous pieces missing. The contributions of gender and ethnicity factors to drug use is especially unknown and await further research. Males, for example, are more likely to abuse drugs than females (although gender differences are shrinking), but we do not know why.

One thing we do know from the research literature: Childhood aggression is highly predictive of later substance abuse (O'Donnell, Hawkins, & Abbott, 1995). Specifically, aggressiveness in boys at ages five to seven is predictive of frequent drug use in adolescence and drug problems in adulthood. Children who are highly aggressive and demonstrate many antisocial behaviors often grow up to be poly-drug abusers well into adulthood. It appears, therefore, that drugs do not cause aggression, violent, or serious delinquency. Rather, individuals prone to be antisocial often abuse drugs. Drugs provide immediate, easy, and certain short-term pleasures that antisocial individuals often seek (Gottfredson & Hirschi, 1990).

KEY CONCEPTS

amines	phencyclidine (PCP)
cannabis	physical dependence
crack	polydrug users
delta-9 tetrahydrocannabinol (THC)	psychedelics
dependence	psychoactive drugs
disinhibitory models of alcohol effects	psychological dependence
experimental substance use (ESU)	secondary psychological dependence
heroin	sedative-hypnotics
hallucinogens	sex-for-crack exchanges
Monitoring the Future (MTF)	social cognitive models of alcohol effects
narcotics	stimulants
National Household Survey on Drug Abuse	tolerance
opiate narcotics	Wolfgang study

4

Systems Theory
and Delinquency

Reviews of the literature summarizing interventions and treatment of juvenile delinquency have continually come to one overriding conclusion: Most current interventions and treatment strategies simply do not work in the sense of reducing recidivism, particularly among serious delinquents. Many that do show some promise are effective in the short term. However, once the treatment or intervention stops, positive effects are often lost within a year or two.

Although it may appear that we are beginning this chapter on a pessimistic note, there is—to quote the title of a recent book—"reason to hope" (Eron, Gentry, & Schlegel, 1994). Promising treatment programs that tackle serious delinquency at various levels are rapidly emerging. These will be reviewed in Chapter 9. Additionally, it is important to remember that the great majority of delinquents are adolescence-limited offenders who grow out of crime once they have survived the turmoil of the adolescent years (Bernard, 1992; Moffitt, 1993a). Many of these juveniles require a minimum of intervention. We will return to this theme in Chapters 10 and 11.

There is rapidly accumulating evidence that the causes of delinquency, its prevention, and effective treatment depend on viewing the problem from a perspective that emphasizes the many influences on the developmental path of the child and recognizes the multiple levels of these influences. By multiple levels we mean the family, the peer system, the school system, the neighborhood, the community, and the society as a whole. It is clear that there is no one single cause of delinquency, and it is even debatable whether any one factor emerges as the most powerful influence on the offending history of a child or an adult.

We must also recognize that the contexts of development vary from child to child. Individual differences in developmental sequences are important, but so are the rich cultural and ethnic differences found within various social groups. For example, prevention programs designed for the inner-city minority child are likely to be very different from those designed for the child living in a small town.

Moreover, all childhood peer groups create their own culture. Children obviously pick up substantial local language, customs, and habits from their peers. This peer-group culture or "gang" is apt to have significant influences on its members, especially during the early teen years. These peer groups should be considered in any intervention or treatment program designed to prevent delinquency.

SOCIAL SYSTEMS THEORY

Systems theory has adherents in a variety of disciplines, spanning the natural and social sciences. The biologist Ludwig von Bertalanffy (1968) is credited with developing the most comprehensive systems approach. Currently, social systems theory is particularly well articulated by the developmental psychologist Urie Bronfenbrenner. Bronfenbrenner's approach, slightly modified to include an individual perspective, will be used throughout the remainder of the text. We chose the Bronfenbrenner model because it is based on human development, and juvenile delinquency is, ultimately, a developmental problem which is strongly influenced by social factors. The model is also highly compatible with **interactionism**, a perspective that describes the mutual and ongoing influence of the psychosocial environment on the individual, and the individual's influence on the environment. We will refer to interactionism frequently throughout the remainder of the book.

It is important to recognize that there are many formulations and variants of systems theory. Sociologists are displaying one variant when they refer to micro- and macroanalyses. **Microanalysis** focuses on explanations of behavior at the individual or psychological level. Motivation, socialization, attachment, and learning are all concepts that involve microanalysis. **Macroanalysis** concentrates on collective behavior, such as the patterns of large groups or social institutions. "Social structure" is a key concept in this approach. Studies examining social class, socioeconomic status, value conflict, social disorganization, and social ecology are examples of macroanalysis. Although microanalysis might focus on the individual attributes of delinquents, macroanalysis is more concerned with the big picture—the time, space, and social context of delinquent behavior.

In order to understand crime and delinquency, is it more helpful to develop theory at the microlevel or the macrolevel? Criminologists differ. Traditionally, there has been a major debate over whether theory developed at the two levels (the microlevel and macrolevel) can be combined. Some argue that it should be (e.g., Elliott, Ageton, & Canter, 1979; Elliott, 1985; Pearson & Weiner, 1985), whereas others insist that cross-level integration is not possible (e.g., Hirschi, 1979, 1987; Short, 1979). Currently, it is difficult to integrate information obtained from research at different levels of analysis into *one* grand theory of delinquency, although with increasing knowledge this goal will be attainable.

Bronfenbrenner (1979, 1986b) has outlined a social systems theory that has considerable relevance to the study of delinquency. Bronfenbrenner specifically applied his ideas to research in child development. Psychological explanations that view delinquency within a developmental context, then, seem most obviously in tune with Bronfenbrenner. However, Bronfenbrenner's theory is relevant to all human behavior within any social environment as well as to the social environments themselves. Systems theory can comfortably accommodate a wide range of perspectives, from those that see delinquency as a result of unique, individual factors to those that indict the structure of society as a whole.

Microsystems

Bronfenbrenner's view of the social environment is more complex than the view of those who discuss the relative merits of micro- and macroanalysis. He conceives of society as a set of nested structures, which are called "systems" because they involve interrelationships and mutual, ongoing influences. The nested systems exist at different levels of abstraction, from the concrete and specific to the abstract and general. Each requires a different level of analysis. Families, schools, neighborhoods, cities, nations, and the world all exist at increasingly larger or more abstract levels of description.

The immediate setting, which contains the person, is called a **microsystem**. It is, to Bronfenbrenner, the smallest unit for social analysis. Microsystems are patterns of activities, roles, and interpersonal relations that take place within settings directly experienced by an individual. Each person is an active participant in his or her microsystems; these might be as varied as family, anthropology class, juvenile gang, or poker group. The microsystem consists of how the person acts with and reacts to others within these groups. The microsystems also contain "subsystems," such as how Lucia reacts to her twin brother or how Larson reacts to his teacher. Therefore, although the immediate family as a whole represents a microsystem, this social system also has partner, parent–child, and sibling components or subsystems to it. Of these three family subsystems, the relationship between parents or parent figures is regarded by many as the core of family solidarity and the key element in determining the quality of family life (Erel & Burman, 1995).

An important phrase contained in the definition of microsystem is "experienced by an individual." Bronfenbrenner (1979, p. 22) states:

> The term [experienced] is used to indicate that the scientifically relevant features of any environment include not only its objective properties but also the way in which these properties are perceived by the persons in that environment. . . . Very few of the external influences significantly affecting human behavior and development can be described solely in terms of objective physical conditions and events; the aspects of environment that are most powerful in shaping the course of psychological growth are overwhelmingly those that have meaning to the person in a given situation.

By implication, if we are to understand delinquent behavior, or any human behavior, we must appreciate how different people perceive, interpret, and reconstruct their environments. Although social pressures and influences are critically important, so too are the personal interpretations of those pressures and influences.

Mesosystems

Also important in Bronfenbrenner's theory are interrelationships among microsystems. The child does not remain within the family microsystem; he or she goes to school, to the homes of relatives and friends, to grocery stores, to amusement parks. Each of these settings influences the child, and they in turn are influenced by him or her.

Bronfenbrenner calls these interrelationships between microsystems **mesosystems**. Thus, a wider social environment must always be kept in mind when considering the child and his or her family, because what goes on beyond its immediate boundaries invariably affects and is affected by what transpires within it. Consider how the safety of a neighborhood playground can influence the freedom parents grant their children in playing there, away from their careful supervision. Child-rearing practices, in turn, affect how the child approaches other children in the neighborhood playground.

Mesosystem models take into account the joint effects of processes occurring within and between two or more settings, in each of which the developing person is an active participant (Bronfenbrenner, 1986b). In essence, a mesosystem is a system of microsystems, or a network of relationships among our microsystems. Bronfenbrenner argues that researchers interested in child development have concentrated on microsystems without commenting on the relationships among them.

Exosystems

Bronfenbrenner notes that systems beyond the micro- and mesosystems also affect one's development, feelings, thoughts, and actions, even though one may not directly participate in them. These **exosystems** include at least one setting that does not directly involve the person as an active participant. For example, what happens at the parent's place of work has considerable impact on the child at home, even if the child never visits that workplace or has direct contact with it. Recent research indicates that there is often a robust **spillover effect** from one situation to another. That is, there is a direct transfer of mood, affect, or behavior from one setting to another. Examples of this include a troubled marital relationship's spilling over and negatively affecting the parent–child relationship (Erel & Burman, 1995), or a parent's bringing home all the negative moods accumulated during a conflict-filled day at work. Research by Melvin L. Kohn (1977) illustrates this point very well. It indicates that the type of work engaged in by a parent may strongly influence the development of everyone within the home (e.g., Kohn, 1977). For instance, Kohn found that occupations allowing considerable freedom and personal autonomy seem to have a significantly different impact on parenting styles from that of occupations requiring conformity and personal constraints. We cannot assume this without more empirical evidence, however. Kohn found that working-class men whose jobs involved compliance with authority tended to demand unquestioning obedience from their children. On the other hand, middle-class fathers who held jobs encouraging self-direction and independence expected similar behaviors from their children. This is a good illustration of the influence of an exosystem on lower-level systems, particularly the family. Of course, the fathers may have done some self-selection of their own by choosing the nature of the work, independent of any major influences of the job on the father's personality or family style. More likely, though, the situation is likely to be bi-directional. The father does some selection and influencing, and the work system influences the father and his role at home. Although Kohn's research was limited to fathers, similar principles *might* apply in the case of mothers. We cannot make this assumption without empirical research to support it, however.

The family's outside social supports (such as friends, relatives, adequate health care, social guidance) strongly influence the home microsystem. A child may never meet the members of his parent's Alcoholics Anonymous group, but what happens to the parent at the group meeting ultimately affects the parent–child relationship. James Garbarino (1976) suggests an association between maternal child abuse and the degree to which mothers receive adequate social support in parenting—the less adequate the social support, the higher the probability of abuse. When both male and female parents are in the home, abuse—if it happens—is far more likely to be perpetrated by the male than by the female parent or parent-figure (Weis, 1989). Social support systems may be just as important for the male, but the research in this area is sparse. Abuse by men has been linked more to factors such as unemployment, problems in the workplace, or their need to exert dominance over the family unit.

Neighborhoods may also qualify as exosystems (as well as microsystems) according to Bronfenbrenner's scheme. The neighborhood as a whole, with its many clusters of groups, represents the larger exosystem. However, peer groups or gangs within a neighborhood—say, the Neighborhood Watch Group or the group that gathers to play basketball every weekend—represent microsystems to their participants. Ever since the pioneering work of Burgess, Shaw, and McKay (to be discussed in Chapter 8), scientists have recognized the importance of the neighborhood in the development of crime and delinquency. To this day, the ecological perspective points to robust relationships among such factors as deteriorated residential areas, the percentage of people living below the poverty line, the extent of unemployment, fear of crime, and rates of delinquency. Therefore, we must also consider the neighborhood when explaining delinquency.

Macrosystems

At an even higher level of analysis, Bronfenbrenner suggests clusters of interrelated exosystems that form **macrosystems**. In Bronfenbrenner's scheme, macrosystems are the belief systems, expectations, customs, attitudes, and associated ideologies that pervade a subculture or culture. Latino, African American, Native American, Pacific Islander, and Asian cultures all represent macrosystems, as do their numerous and heterogenous subcultures. For example, cultures differ in their expectations of boys and girls. For some cultures, little boys are expected to start acting "masculine" (as defined by their culture) within the first two years of life. Little girls are expected to act "feminine." Hence, gender stereotypes of accepted behavior, as an aggregate variable across American culture, represent a component of the macrosystem.

Over the past 20 years, a significant body of theory and research from feminist criminologists has given us important insights into gender differences in both the commission of crime and victimization (e.g., Chesney-Lind, 1995; Daly & Chesney-Lind, 198S; Simpson, 1996). These contributions are almost invariably from a macrosystem perspective. Recall the study by Inciardi et al. (1991) discussed in Chapter 3, which examined sex-for-crack exchanges in a sample of Miami youth. Inciardi and his colleagues found that 87 percent of the girls, compared with 5 percent of the boys, reported involvement in prostitution. A feminist analysis of these findings would focus on the exploitation of the girls and the high risk of HIV infection that they face.

Classical Examples of the Macrosystem Approach to Delinquency   One classical example of macrosystem study is **strain theory**. The theory, which originated in the classical writing of sociologist Émile Durkheim and was developed by Robert Merton, is based on the observation that humans, as a whole, accept the values promoted by any given society. For instance, in American society the advocated goal is to acquire wealth, status, and power. However, the legitimate means for reaching these goals are not universally available to everyone. Strain results from the fact that one wants the goals but does not have access to the acceptable means. Some persons choose illegitimate means, and deviance becomes the reasonable recourse. Thus, strain theory views the offender as being forced into crime by culturally induced (macrosystem) desires that cannot be otherwise satisfied. With reference to delinquency, strain theory assumes that both delinquents and nondelinquents are bonded to the social order, but deviance occurs because the road to success and material acquisition is blocked.

Strain theory is essentially a social-class or minorities-based theory, because many minority groups and individuals of low SES are often more likely to have limited access to opportunity. In recent years, however, modernized versions of strain theory have rendered it applicable across all social classes (Agnew, 1996; Messner & Rosenfeld, 1994).

Chronosystems

In 1986 Bronfenbrenner (1986a) revised his model to add the **chronosystem**. The chronosystem accounts for changes across time. He found this concept necessary in order to account for the obvious changes that occur in time across all four systems outlined previously. Historically, developmental psychologists have treated the passage of time as synonymous with chronological age. The developmental sequence of a child, of course, is extremely critical in understanding delinquency. Fire setting by a curious 4-year-old is likely to represent very different behavior from that exemplified by fire setting by a 16-year-old. In current research designs, time appears not merely as an attribute of the developing person but also as a property of the surrounding environment (Bronfenbrenner, 1986b). Neighborhoods change, communities change, cities change, and cultures change. The school environment is different in September from the way it is in June. First-borns experience a different home environment when later children are born. A child's adjustment to school may be affected by several factors. These factors include apprehension about the first day (microsystem), the death of a mother (mesosystem, representing the relationship between home and school), the fact that a father suddenly becomes unemployed (exosystem), or the society that becomes torn by racial tension (macrosystem). Each person's life course involves numerous transitions that accumulate and interact to affect his or her emotions, cognitions, behaviors, and overall perceptions of the social world at any given point in time. We will discuss a very important chronosystem later in this chapter (and throughout the book) exemplified by the **developmental theory** of delinquency. Bronfenbrenner distinguishes between two types of chronosystems: those that most people experience (normative) and those that are rare or unexpected (non-normative). Normative chronosystems include school entry, puberty, entering the labor force, marriage, and retirement; non-normative chronosystems include a death, a severe illness in the family, divorce, sexual assault, and winning the sweepstakes. Non-normative events may have decidedly different effects from normative events on one's life.

It is important to keep in mind that some of the controversy in theory and empirical research we shall review may stem from the confusion surrounding what system is being defined or explained. Delinquency patterns gleaned from large collections of aggregate data across the nations—macrosystems—are apt to provide a different picture from that gleaned from delinquency patterns gathered at the neighborhood or exosystem level. Macrosystem analysis offers different clues about delinquency from those of microsystem analysis. For example, part of the controversy about the strengths and weaknesses of the self-report (SR) method of obtaining information about delinquency and official statistics is that SR data are gathered at the individual levels by asking individuals their *perceptions* about their involvement in crime. Official statistics are collected from agencies and large organizations over a wide cross-section of society. These methods approach the issue from two different levels, requiring different perspectives. In this sense, whether self-report data support official data or not may not be all that important. They are most helpful in what they reveal about the respondents.

Individual Systems

Bronfenbrenner's basic framework does not conceptualize the individual as a system within him- or herself. This is a significant omission. We have adjusted his theory, therefore, adding an **infrasystem**, wherein personal constructs, beliefs, or schema interact with temperament and genes to form a "personality." "Whatever else personality may be, it has the properties of a system" (Allport, 1961, p. 109). The personal system changes and continually interacts with higher-level systems, particularly the microsystems and mesosystems. It is sometimes tempting to conclude that social environments dictate who we are or what we do. Yet it is not wise to overlook the fact that each person has a personal version of the world, conceptualized and organized in a unique way. The environment provides us with information and experience, but how these are integrated and stored is itself a system. It is premature then, to attribute most behavior to either social or individual factors. Figure 4.1 illustrates Bronfenbrenner's systems with the addition of the infrasystem.

FIGURE 4.1   Illustration of systems theory

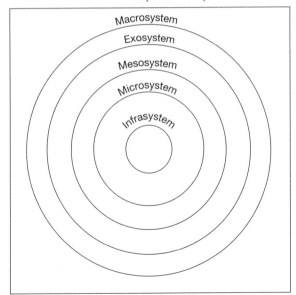

In order to understand and effectively prevent delinquency, we must approach its study in a way that recognizes the multiple social systems impinging on each human life. The sociologist Albert J. Reiss Jr. writes: "If our understanding of crime and criminal behavior and its control is to advance, governmental data collection and scholarly research must be designed to collect individual, organizational, and community-level information" (1986, p. 27). Elsewhere, Charles Wellford (1987, p. 7) asserts: "[W]e must develop theories of criminal behavior that take seriously the notion that there are biophysical effects on criminal behavior, psychological effects, social effects, cultural effects or any other organized effects that we wish to identify through our specification of the appropriate categories or levels of analysis."

One of the best ways to launch us into the individual or infrasystem is to examine Terrie Moffitt's **developmental theory of delinquency** (1993a, 1993b). The Moffitt theory encourages us to view delinquency as proceeding along at least two developmental paths (or chronosystems). On one path we see a child developing a lifelong trajectory of delinquency and crime at a very early age, probably around 3 or younger. Moffitt (1993a, p. 679) writes: "Across the life course, these individuals exhibit changing manifestations of antisocial behavior: biting and hitting at age 4, shoplifting and truancy at age 10, selling drugs and stealing cars at age 16, robbery and rape at age 22, and fraud and child abuse at age 30." These individuals, whom Moffitt labels **life-course-persistent** (**LCP**) delinquents or criminals (mentioned in Chapter 1), continue their antisocial ways across all kinds of conditions and situations. Many of these LCP persons exhibit minor neuropsychological problems during their childhoods, such as difficult temperaments as infants, attention deficit disorders or hyperactivity as children, and learning problems in school. Judgment and problem-solving deficiencies are often evident when the children reach adulthood. Clinicians and mental-health professionals may diagnose these individuals with conduct disorders in childhood, and with antisocial personality disorders in adulthood. LCP delinquents commit a wide assortment of aggressive and violent crimes across their life spans. LCP children miss opportunities to acquire and practice prosocial and interpersonal skills at each stage of development, partly because they are rejected and avoided by their childhood peers, and partly because their parents and other adults become frustrated and give up on them (Coie, Belding, & Underwood, 1988; Coie, Dodge, & Kupersmith, 1990; Moffitt, 1993a). And, as noted by Moffitt (1993a, p. 684), ". . . if social and academic skills are not mastered in childhood, it is very difficult to later recover from lost opportunities." Furthermore, disadvantaged homes, schools, and neighborhoods are factors that are likely to exacerbate the ongoing and developing antisocial behavioral pattern.

The great majority of "delinquents" are those individuals who begin offending during their adolescent years and who appear to stop offending around their eighteenth birthdays. Moffitt calls these individuals **adolescence-limited** (**AL**) delinquents. Their developmental histories do not demonstrate the early and persistent antisocial problems that members of the LCP group manifest. However, the frequency—and in some cases, the violence—of the offending during the teen years may be as high as that of the LCP youth. In fact, the teenage offending pattern of the AL and that of the LCP may be indistinguishable (Moffitt et al., 1996).

"The two types cannot be discriminated on most indicators of antisocial and problem behavior in adolescence; boys on the LCP and AL paths are similar on parent-, self-, and official records of offending, peer delinquency, substance abuse, unsafe sex, and dangerous driving" (Moffitt et al., 1996, p. 400). That is, one could not identify the group (AL or LCP) by looking at juvenile arrest records, self-reports, or information provided by parents, unless there was early involvement of delinquent or antisocial activities. Early involvement carries a high probability that the individual will engage in crime well into adulthood. If the offending began sometime during adolescence, then the probability is high that the individual will cease offending as he or she approaches young adulthood. There is some evidence to suggest, however, that some ALs may continue to commit some offenses that have a low risk of detection by police and that do not jeopardize their jobs and marriages (Nagin, Farrington, & Moffitt, 1995).

According to Moffitt, AL antisocial behavior is motivated by the gap between biological maturity and social maturity. It is learned from antisocial peer models and sustained through peer-based rewards and reinforcements. The biological–social maturity gap refers to the emerging realization by teens that, although they have the biological maturity to reproduce and be of equal physical stature and strength as adults, the desirable adult privileges are forbidden.

According to Moffitt et al. (1996), the AL delinquent is most likely, during the teen years, to be involved in crimes that symbolize adult privilege and demonstrate autonomy from parental control. Examples are vandalism, drug and alcohol offenses, theft, and "status" offenses such as running away or truancy. Furthermore, AL delinquents are likely to be involved in antisocial actions in situations where such behaviors seem profitable or rewarding to them, but they also have the ability to abandon these antisocial actions when prosocial styles become more rewarding. For example, the onset of young adulthood brings on opportunities not attainable during the teen years, such as leaving high school for college, obtaining full-time jobs, and entering a relationship with a prosocial person. AL delinquents are quick to learn that they have something to lose if they continue offending. During childhood, AL delinquents have also learned to get along with others. They normally have a satisfactory repertoire of social skills that enable them to "get ahead." Therefore, the developmental histories and personal traits of the AL youth allow them the option of exploring new life pathways, an opportunity not usually afforded the LCP adolescent.

Because the LCP offender shows a distinctive developmental history, we will begin by focusing on some of the early childhood influences often associated with these criminal careers. We begin by examining one of the earliest factors: temperament.

TEMPERAMENT

A child's temperament—defined very loosely for the moment as a "natural" mood disposition—may offer important clues about delinquency. How we approach and interact with our social environment influences how that environment will interact with us. This is true even of very young children. Parents, teachers, physicians, and caretakers know very well that infants and young children differ in activity, emotionality, and general sensitivity to stimuli. A smiling, relaxed, interactive child is apt to initiate and maintain a different social response from that of a fussy, tense, and withdrawn one. A consistently ill-tempered child may become so frustrating to his or her parents that they feel overwhelmed and helpless in dealing with the child. Their own resulting irritability may feed into the behavior of the child in a reciprocal fashion, producing a serious disruption in the parent–child relationship. Frustration may progress into physical or emotional abuse or neglect.

Research has suggested with some regularity that poor parent–child relationships and a home with considerable tension and conflict are common, although not inevitable, ingredients in delinquency. It is suggested here that temperament may increase or decrease the probability of delinquency, not that it determines whether an individual will or will not be delinquent. Nor should it be assumed that poor temperament is a necessary condition of delinquency. As Robert Hogan and Warren Jones (1983, pp. 6–7) write: "It is easy to imagine that a child who is very emotional, active, unsociable, and impulsive might be constantly in trouble with his or her adult caretakers and perhaps predisposed to delinquency." The temperament model ". . . is interactional in the best sense of the word; it does not maintain that certain temperaments cause delinquency, but rather that the concurrence of these temperaments and certain kinds of family environments may lead to delinquent outcomes."

As it is currently used in the research, "temperament" is assumed to: (1) have a constitutional or biological basis; (2) appear in infancy and continue throughout life; and (3) be influenced by the environment (Bates, 1980). Most experts today believe that temperament has biological underpinnings that are best discerned at birth (Goldsmith et al., 1987). Most of the contemporary research on temperament, therefore, focuses on the infant, because the connection between temperament and behavior seems uncomplicated at this stage and becomes more complex as the child matures.

Among researchers, there is no universally accepted definition of temperament. It is generally operationally defined (clearly enough so anyone can observe the behavior) by identifying the behaviors commonly associated with it. There is little disagreement that **activity** and **emotionality** are two of those behaviors. Activity, the most widely studied, refers to gross motor movement across a variety of settings and times, such as the movement of arms and legs, squirming, crawling, or walking. Children who exhibit an inordinate amount of movement compared with their peers may be labeled "hyperactive" or as having an **attention deficit disorder** (commonly referred to as **attention deficit hyperactivity disorder** or **ADHD**). ADHD will be discussed in more detail shortly. "Emotionality" refers to such features as irritability, sensitivity, soothability, and general intensity of emotional reactions. Researchers disagree as to what other behaviors should be included in descriptions of temperament. Some argue that temperament should not be defined according to demonstrated behaviors in the first place. This disagreement has splintered current psychological research into four somewhat overlapping perspectives.

The Thomas and Chess Perspective

One of the most influential perspectives has been advanced by Alexander Thomas and Stella Chess (1977), who define temperament as a behavioral tendency rather than a concept measured by a cluster of behavioral acts. To Thomas and Chess, temperament is an innate readiness to respond across a variety of situations. It is continually evolving along with other psychological attributes (cognitive and emotional). During its maturation, temperament is strongly influenced by the intra- and extrafamilial environment.

Thomas and Chess asked parents to report on nine characteristics of their infant children: (1) rhythmicity of biological functions, such as the regularity of bowel movements, sleep cycles, and feeding times; (2) activity level; (3) approach to or withdrawal from new stimuli; (4) adaptability; (5) sensory threshold; (6) predominant quality of mood; (7) intensity of mood expression; (8) distractibility; and (9) attention span or persistence. It is important to note that the researchers assumed that these were temperamental predispositions. They then classified infant temperament into three personality styles: (1) the easy child, (2) the difficult child, and (3) the slow-to-warm-up child.

Table 4.1 summarizes the characteristics of each style. The easy child is characterized by high rhythmicity, positive moods, high approachability, high adaptability, and low intensity. The difficult child shows the opposite patterns: irregular biological functioning, initial aversion and slow adaptability to environmental changes, high intensity in emotional expression, and more generally a negative mood (Bates, 1980). The slow-to-warm-up child displays high activity, withdrawal, low adaptability, negative mood, and low intensity.

"Difficult children," according to the Thomas–Chess viewpoint, represent a specific cluster of inborn temperamental attributes that make child rearing more difficult for most, though not all, of their parents. Such children are at higher risk for developing behavior problems, particularly the LCP delinquent.

The research support for the Thomas and Chess typology is mixed (Campos et al., 1983). The existence of the "difficult child syndrome" is a matter of consid-

TABLE 4.1.   Thomas-Chess categories of child temperaments

	Easy child	Difficult child	Slow-to-warm-up child
Rhythmicity	Regular	Irregular	Regular
Moods	Positive	Negative	Negative
Approach to others	High	Low	Low
Adaptability	Rapid	Slow	Slow
Intensity	Low	High	Low

SOURCE: Adapted from Thomas, A., & Chess, S., *Temperament and Development* (New York: Brunner/Mazel, 1977).

erable debate. Bates (1980) reports that factor analysis does reveal that soothability, fussiness, and intensity of protest do emerge with some consistency and are statistically significant. Furthermore, he notes that no matter which parent considers a child as being difficult, frequent fussing and crying continually crop up as the repetitive theme. However, Bates emphasizes that the parent–child relationship is an interactive one, strongly influenced by the parent's perception of why the child is fussy. Some parents see fussiness as a normal developmental stage or a result of environmental changes, and therefore something that will pass or can be moderated. Others ascribe it to innate, enduring tendencies that last a lifetime. According to Bates, the parent's explanations relate to how he or she reacts. Thus, the parent's own temperament, parenting styles, and beliefs are also significant. The existence of the **difficult child syndrome**, therefore, may hinge more on the subjective interpretations of each parent than on objective, measurable features in the child. This possibility may account for why the research on the difficult child syndrome is highly inconclusive and controversial, particularly because it generally gathers data from parental reports.

The Buss and Plomin Perspective

A second perspective is represented by Arnold Buss and Robert Plomin (1975, 1984), who identify three basic dimensions of temperament: emotionality, activity, and sociability. Each is conceptualized as existing on a continuum. **Emotionality** ranges from a stoic, almost total lack of reaction to intense emotional reactions that are out of control. At the higher levels of emotionality, a child demonstrates frequent crying and tantrums, may have breath-holding spells, and cannot be easily soothed. The child at the lower end of the spectrum is very quiet and easy to soothe and rarely shows anger. The **activity** continuum ranges from lethargy to extremely energetic behavior. The best measures of activity are the amplitude of speech and the rate of motion, displacement of body movements, and the duration of energetic behavior. **Sociability** refers to the extent an individual likes to be with others. Individuals at the high extreme of the continuum seek to share activities with others, to receive attention, and to be involved in the back-and-forth responsivity that characterizes social interaction. Typical measures of sociability are the frequency of attempts to initiate social contacts, number of affiliations, the amount of time spent with others, and reactions to isolation.

According to Buss and Plomin, the three dimensions that characterize temperament types are inheritable personality traits. They may be observed in animals, older children, adults, and infants. The traits may change somewhat over the course of childhood, however. For example, as the individual grows in size, strength, and endurance, activity is apt to increase. As a child grows older, he or she also tends to have more opportunities to seek out others, and thus sociability increases. In other words, the child's microsystems increase in variety and number. Finally, as the nervous system matures and socialization practices have an effect, emotionality becomes less intense. Despite these changes in development and experience, however, Buss and Plomin maintain that the basic personality core remains stable. The most outgoing child in kindergarten is expected to have a wide circle of friends in high school. Sociability, however, is of little relevance to Buss and Plomin's conception of the "difficult child." For them, that child is one who is highly emotional and active. Emotional children are problematic because they often have frequent temper tantrums and are, therefore, difficult to handle and socialize with. Children high in activity are problematic because they continually press against limits, become easily bored, and may wear out parents with their energy. A reasonable prediction is that an active child will be a risk taker, one who likes excitement—such as taking chances and pulling pranks. Perhaps it is this child who is prone to engage in minor, mischievous kinds of delinquency. On the other hand, it is reasonable to suppose that the nasty, emotional, impulsive child will be more *inclined* toward violent or serious delinquency.

Buss and Plomin go far beyond outlining behavioral descriptions that accompany various temperaments. They see a major role for temperament, arguing that it interacts with the social environment in a dynamic and bi-directional way. Temperament continually influences the social environment and the social environment continually influences temperament in a reciprocal fashion. As discussed earlier, a child elicits certain types of parental behaviors and the parent elicits certain behaviors from the child. The impact of such parental behaviors varies as a function of the child's temperament. How well things work out over the long haul is a function of a good match in the temperament and behavioral styles between parents and the child. For example, a parent with low tolerance for a hyperactive child would be a poor match compared with a more tolerant and patient one.

In many ways the Buss and Plomin position is similar to that advocated by Sandra Scarr and Kathleen McCartney (1983), who view temperament as an inherited trait. They claim that genes play a substantial role in directing development and experiences. Individuals with certain temperaments will receive certain kinds of parenting, evoke certain responses from others, and select certain aspects from the available environments. The environment and its experiences strongly influence human development, but the genetic makeup of the individual in part determines which environment that individual will be exposed to. According to Scarr and McCartney, genes organize and direct one's development and experiences. Babies and children with high needs for stimulation, for example, seek out and create environments that best meet those needs. Others may prefer to play by themselves, be aloof toward parents, and seek out quiet, sedentary activities.

The Rothbart Perspective

A third major perspective on temperament is represented by the psychologist Mary Klevjord Rothbart (Rothbart & Derryberry, 1982; Rothbart, 1986). She defines temperament as a relatively stable, constitutionally based construct representing individual differences in (1) reactivity of the nervous system and (2) self-regulation of that reactivity. The term "constitutional" emphasizes the enduring biological makeup of the individual, influenced over time by heredity, maturation, and experience. **Reactivity** of the nervous system refers to the innate excitability of the nervous system to stimuli. **Self-regulation** refers to processes, such as attention, approach, avoidance, and inhibition, that enhance or inhibit reactivity.

Like Thomas and Chess, Rothbart developed her theory primarily on the basis of parental reports. According to Rothbart, temperament can be observed in all age groups as individual differences in patterns of emotionality, activity, and attention. The behavioral expression and personal experience of temperament will be influenced by the degree of stimulation and regulation provided by that environment. For example, a young child who is highly reactive with few self-regulative controls must rely heavily on the parent as an outside source of regulation, until self-control is established. If those external controls are not introduced or do not succeed in modifying the child's high reactivity, the result may be a lifelong pattern of inadequate control of impulses or temperament. This might be illustrated by "impulsive" violent delinquent behavior.

Rothbart also introduces the concept of **niche picking**. Temperament will influence the circumstances under which individuals feel comfortable and happy, and thus will influence the situation—or niches—they choose to enter or avoid. Temperaments are strongly influential in one's choice of friends. Niche picking will also be relevant in the discussion of the microsystem of peer groups and its influence on delinquency.

The Goldsmith and Campos Perspective

In a fourth perspective of temperament, Hill Goldsmith and Joseph Campos (1982) consider temperament to be emotionality—nothing more. "Temperament" refers to individual differences in the expression of primary emotions—anger, sadness, fear, joy, pleasure, disgust, interest, and surprise—and in the experience of emotional arousability. Emotionality lays the foundation for personality characteristics. For example, temperamental proneness to anger influences the development of aggression; temperamental persistence affects the motivation to achieve; fear may affect one's willingness to take risks, make career moves, or even move to another part of the country.

Research by Olweus (1980) lends support to Goldsmith and Campos's perspective. In his investigation of the determinants of aggressive behavior in adolescent boys, Olweus had parents rate (retrospectively) the childhood temperaments of their offspring as "hot-headed" or "calm." The hot-headed ratings predicted later aggression. Moreover, early activity and emotionality indirectly predicted aggression through its tendency to encourage parents to permit aggressive behavior. Parents and caretakers often become discouraged and resigned to the continual temperamental onslaught of aggression. Thus, individual differences in children produce differences in parental behavior, and these, in turn, affected later development. A major difficulty with the Olweus research design, as with many studies of temperament, was its reliance on parental reports of their children's behavior. Retrospective reports based on parental recall are notoriously inaccurate when compared with other documentation, such as when a child began walking, talking, and so forth.

Neither Goldsmith and Campos nor Rothbart saw any need to consider the "difficult child" pattern as a meaningful concept. Rothbart believed there were serious problems in defining it. Goldsmith and Campos argued that there was little value in discussing such a pattern independent of the context in which it occurs.

McCall (cited in a symposium reported by Goldsmith et al., 1987) summarizes the concept of temperament very well. He states that at the least, temperament consists of relatively consistent basic dispositions inherent in the person and that these dispositions underlie and modulate the expressions of activity, reactivity, emotionality, and sociability. The biological elements of temperament are strongest early in life, but as development proceeds the expressions of temperament are influenced increasingly by experience and context.

Temperament and Delinquency

Despite the disagreements in definition, temperament has captured the attention of many researchers in recent years. Robert McCall (Goldsmith et al., 1987) makes the valid point that definitions should not be simply valid or invalid, confirmable or refutable. Instead, they are more or less useful. For our purposes the concept of temperament is of use in that it encourages us to consider the possibility that individual differences *may* be critical in the early formation of delinquency and crime. In other words, temperament is a viable causal agent in the delinquency complex. "Difficult children"—even if this label comes strictly from subjective parental perceptions—may be at higher risk to engage in delinquency than "easy" children. Temperamentally emotional and hyperactive adolescents *may* present handling problems for caretakers and the social environment, whereas adolescents at the lower end of these dimensions may not. Interactions between the person and his or her environment merit consideration in any comprehensive attempt to explain delinquency.

Recent research does suggest that a difficult temperament in early childhood predisposes a child to become aggressive and delinquent in later childhood (Pepler & Slaby, 1994). It is likely, therefore, that certain temperamental dispositions of activity, reactivity, emotionality, and sociability observed at an early age carry high probabilities that the individual will engage in behaviors that run counter to society's expectations and regulations. Highly active children move into (and often against) their environments at a higher pace and perhaps more impulsively than less active children. Because of their high activity levels, the probability is greater that they will collide with the wishes of parents and society. Furthermore, children with highly irritable, nasty temperaments and children with relaxed, pleasant ones are apt to create environments and to influence parenting in significantly different ways. Olweus (1980), for example, discovered that mothers of boys with difficult temperaments became increasingly more permissive with their children's aggressive behaviors, and this permissiveness, in turn, increased the opportunity for the boys to become even more aggressive and delinquent.

Failure to acknowledge these dispositional variables at the individual systems level may leave us with an incomplete picture of the etiology of delinquency, especially in the case of the person who demonstrates a persistent pattern of violent or serious offending. Bill Henry et al. (in press), using data from the Dunedin (New Zealand) Multidisciplinary Health and Development Study, found that children considered temperamentally explosive and lacking in self-control were more likely to become violent adolescents, compared with their more temperamentally stable peers.

Likewise, the temperament of parents must also be considered as a possible component in the development of the delinquent child. Moffitt (1993b) suggests that parents and their offspring often resemble each other in temperament and personality. An irritable, temperamental child may have a high probability of being born to highly irritable, temperamental parents. Thus, parents of difficult children often lack the necessary psychological and physical resources to cope effectively with a difficult child.

HYPERACTIVITY AND ATTENTION DEFICITS

One area that remains an intriguing temperamental mystery is that of the hyperactive child. The terms "hyperactivity" and "attention deficit hyperactivity disorder" (ADHD) are used interchangeably to refer to children who demonstrate a heterogeneity of problem behaviors. The central three behaviors have traditionally been (1) inattention (does not seem to listen or is easily distracted); (2) impulsivity (acts before thinking, shifts quickly from one activity to another); and (3) excessive motor activity (cannot sit still, fidgets, runs about, is talkative and noisy). Educators note that ADHD children have difficulty staying on task, remaining cognitively organized, sustaining academic achievement in the school setting, and maintaining control over their behavior.

ADHD is a puzzling problem that some scientists argue is closely related to temperament. Some scientists contend that ADHD children are born with the tendency; others maintain that some children are exposed to environmental events that damage the nervous system. Rolf Loeber (1990) illustrates how exposure to toxic substances during the preschool years often retards or negatively influences children's neurological development, potentially engendering symptoms of ADHD. For instance, children exposed to low levels of lead toxicity (from certain paints) were more distractible, hyperactive, impulsive, and easily frustrated. They also had difficulty following simple instructions.

Some researchers argue that the schema or cognitive constructs of ADHD children have been hampered in their development. ADHD youth, it seems, do not possess effective strategies and cognitive organization with which to deal with the daily demands of both school and work. They often have particular difficulty in abstract thinking. ADHD children also do not seem to possess cognitively organized ways for dealing with new knowledge. Unfortunately, these often-reported conclusions about ADHD children may lead to expectations that they will fail in the academic environment rather than strategies to help them succeed.

Other, more psychoneurologically inclined researchers assert that ADHD is largely a problem of neurological dimensions. Although many behaviors have been identified as accompanying ADHD, the overriding theme is that ADHD children are perceived as annoying and aversive by those around them. Although children with ADHD are socially busy, continually seeking and prolonging interpersonal contacts, they also manage to irritate and frustrate the people with whom they interact (Henker & Whalen, 1989). More often than not, ADHD children, especially if they are aggressive, are rejected by peers (Henker & Whalen, 1989). This peer rejection appears to be stable and ongoing throughout the developmental years (Reid, 1993).

In recent years it has become clear, therefore, that ADHD is not so much a disorder of activity as it is a disorder of interpersonal relationships. Even those individuals who are not aggressive and who manage to control some of their "hyperactivity" still have problems in their social interactions. As noted by Henker and Whalen (1989), they seem to lack friendship and intimacy. The most common problem associated with ADHD is not emotional or psychological disorder, such as serious depression or schizophrenia, but delinquency and substance abuse. Terrie Moffitt (Moffitt & Silva, 1988; Moffitt, 1993b) reports that a very large proportion of ADHD children report delinquent behaviors in early adolescence. She has also found that children between the ages of five and seven who demonstrate the characteristics of both ADHD and antisocial behavior not only have special difficulty with social relationships but also have a high probability of consistent serious delinquency into adolescence and beyond (Moffitt, 1990). The data suggest that youth with a combined ADHD–antisocial symptomology are at very high risk for developing the most lengthy and serious criminal careers (Moffitt, 1990; Satterfield et al., 1994). David Farrington (1991) found that violent offenders often have a history of hyperactivity, impulsivity, and attention problems. Interestingly, for some unknown reason Canadian ADHD youth seem to be less prone toward delinquency than their American counterparts (Henker & Whalen, 1989). This suggests that the *reaction* to ADHD, rather than the disorder itself, is the key to understanding the relationship.

The common method of treatment for ADHD is stimulant medication (methylphenidate or Ritalin). However, this approach is marked by limited success and myriad side effects, some of them severe. Counseling and psychotherapy are also used frequently, but they too have had very limited success with this puzzling phenomenon, especially over the long term. ADHD children can demonstrate multiple social problems which require a treatment strategy that encompasses all the systems within the child's social world. A multicomponent, multisystemic approach offers the best hope for helping ADHD youngsters in their social development and education. Promising interventions of this nature will be discussed in more detail in Chapter 9.

CONDUCT DISORDERS

Hyperactivity or ADHD co-occurs with conduct disorders at a high rate (Offord, Boyle, & Racine, 1991; Reid, 1993). The term "conduct disorder" is not synonymous with the legal term "delinquency," but the behaviors that characterize it are frequently associated with delinquent behavior. As defined in Chapter 1, **conduct disorder** is a diagnostic term often used by mental-health professionals to represent a cluster of behaviors characterized by persistent misbehavior. Examples of such behavior include stealing, fire setting, running away from home, skipping school, destroying property, fighting, being cruel to animals and to other people, and frequently telling lies. According to the *Diagnostic and Statistical Manual–IV* (*DSM–IV*), published by the American Psychiatric Association (1994), the essential feature of conduct disorder is the *repetitive* and *persistent* pattern of behavior that violates the basic rights of others.

The *DSM-IV* identifies four major behavioral groupings to help in the diagnosis of a conduct disorder. The first group refers to "aggressive conduct that causes or threatens physical harm to other people or animals" (APA, 1994, p. 85). The second group refers to "nonaggressive conduct that causes property loss or damage" (APA, 1994, p. 85). Behavioral patterns characterized by deceitfulness or theft make up the third group. And the fourth group refers to behavior that demonstrates serious violations of rules, such as the rules set by the school or parents. An example of the fourth group would be truancy or running away from home for a night or two. Remember, the key words in these behavioral patterns are "repetitive" and "persistent." The behaviors must be committed repeatedly and across many different situations, such as at home, in the school, and in the community. The *DSM-IV* posits that at least three of these behaviors must be present during the past 12 months to qualify for conduct disorder.

Behavioral signs of conduct disorder (CD) can be observed in the context of interaction with parents well before school entry (Reid, 1993). For example, children who are aggressive, difficult to manage, and generally noncompliant in the home at age three continue to have similar problems when entering school (Reid, 1993). These behaviors show remarkable continuity right into adolescence and beyond. CD children often have significant problems with academic performance. As reported for ADHD children, aggressive CD youth are at high risk for quick and decisive rejection by their peers (Reid, 1993). This rejection often lasts throughout the school years and is difficult to change (Reid, 1993). Children who are consistently rejected obviously miss opportunities to develop normal interpersonal and social skills.

We should caution that a conduct disorder diagnosis does not overlook events in the child's social environment, which may provide the best explanations for the child's behavior. The three-year-old who demonstrates antisocial behavior may be abused, may witness violence in the home or the neighborhood on a regular basis, or may be victimized by older youths or adults outside the immediate family circle. It is not the intent here to suggest that young children are themselves responsible for their unacceptable behavior.

The *DSM-IV* is consistent with LCP (life-course-persistent) and AL (adolescence-limited) antisocial behavioral patterns observed by Moffitt, Reid, and others. That is, the *DSM-IV* outlines two subtypes of conduct disorders based on the onset of the repetition and persistence of the misbehavior, the **childhood-onset type** and **adolescent-onset type**. Childhood-onset CD occurs when at least one of the behavioral patterns begins prior to age ten. The adolescent-onset type, on the other hand, is characterized by the *absence* of any patterns before age ten.

According to the *DSM-IV*, poor frustration tolerance, irritability, temper outbursts, and recklessness are frequent accompanying features. Early onset of sexual activity, drinking, smoking, and use of illegal substances are also very common. The disorder, especially the childhood-onset type, is more common among boys. Interestingly, the *DSM-IV* notes that the disorder is more frequent among urban than rural youth, suggesting the significance of social conditions to which urban youth are exposed. Finally, if the onset of the conduct disorder is during early childhood, the prognosis is not good, compared with the prognosis for a later onset.

An estimated 6 to 16 percent of the male population is believed to have many features of CD. The prevalence in girls ranges from 4 to 9.2 percent, depending on the study (Cohen, Cohen, & Brook, 1993; Zoccolillo, 1993). A recent study by Anna Bardone and her colleagues (in press) indicates that CD in girls is a strong predictor of a lifetime of problems, including poor interpersonal relations with partners/spouses and peers, criminal activity, early pregnancy without supportive partners, and frequent job loss and firings. Similar to CD boys, CD girls appear destined for a life of conflict with others and with society in general.

In summary, the diagnosis "conduct disorder" shows some characteristics very similar to those of the juvenile offender distinctions of LCP and AL outlined earlier. A worthwhile venture at this point is an examination of some longitudinal studies that have looked at the relationships between temperament and delinquency.

GENERAL THEORY OF CRIME

Michael Gottfredson and Travis Hirschi (1990) have proposed a theory of crime that follows very closely many of the behavioral features described for developmental theory, ADHD, and conduct disorder. The theory is called the **general theory of crime**, often abbreviated GTC.

According to Gottfredson and Hirschi, the central core of antisocial behavior is low self-control. Individuals who lack self-control will tend to be impulsive, insensitive, short-sighted risk-takers. They do not possess or value cognitive, verbal, or academic skills. They engage in delinquent or criminal acts that are exciting, risky, or thrilling and that quickly provide gratification of desires. Individuals with low self-control "tend to smoke, drink, use drugs, gamble, have children out of wedlock, and engage in illicit sex" (Gottfredson & Hirschi, 1990, p. 90). They tend to have minimal tolerance for frustration and prefer to use quick, simple, physical strategies for dealing with conflict.

These descriptions sound very similar to those found in the previous discussion on life-course-persistent offenders, ADHD, and conduct disorder. They also sound highly similar to the behavioral descriptions of adult criminal psychopaths outlined by Robert Hare (1983; Hare, McPherson, & Forth, 1988; Hare, Forth, & Stachan, 1992), suggesting that the general theory of crime falls in line with the observations made by many other scientists.

From another perspective, however, a major weakness of the "self-control" approach is its failure to recognize the crucial connection between delinquency and the victimization of juveniles. The out-of-wedlock births that concern Gottfredson and Hirschi are not simply a symptom of low self-control. Instead, they are far more likely to result from sexual victimization or a naive desire to "be cool" or to possess something of one's own in a confusing world. It can also be argued that some out-of-wedlock births reflect the fact that segments of society and the law are restricting juvenile girls' access to abortion, which may be viewed as a form of victimization. The assumption that juveniles merely lack self-control overlooks the complex social factors that impinge upon their lives.

LONGITUDINAL STUDIES CONNECTING TEMPERAMENT WITH DELINQUENCY

In the Kauai longitudinal study, Emmy Werner and her collaborators (Werner, Bierman, & French, 1971; Werner & Smith, 1977, 1982; Werner, 1987) followed a cohort of 698 children living on the Hawaiian island of Kauai from birth to adulthood. This prospective longitudinal study spanned the years 1954–86 and included data from pediatricians, psychologists, public health personnel, and social workers. The project identified a number of personality, constitutional, and environmental variables that presumably distinguished children who became delinquent from those who did not. Problems arise, however, when we look at the Werner measure of delinquency. Of the 698 children, 102 were labeled "delinquent" based solely on official records or police and family court files. A vast majority of these 102 "juvenile offenders" (both males and females) committed relatively minor offenses, such as traffic violations or running away. This word of caution should be kept in mind as we review the findings of the study.

Werner (1987) states that a combination of about a dozen variables provides the best predictor of eventual delinquency. For example, children with a history of a difficult temperament, hyperactivity, substandard living conditions, low IQ, or unstable, conflictful home life were more likely to be delinquent than children without these background variables. However, a significant number of these children (a total of 72) with 4 or more of these features in their background did *not* become delinquent, indicating that making predictions of delinquency on the basis of background variables is risky business.

Werner divides those children with four or more high-risk variables into a "resilient" group (those who did not become delinquent) and a "vulnerable" group (those who became delinquent). One difference between the two groups was the mother's perception concerning the child's temperament. Mothers of the resilient children perceived them as affectionate, cuddly, good-natured, and easy to handle. Furthermore, these children seemed to have a positive social orientation toward others. The families of the resilient children also had fairly extensive social support systems. That is, they had many supportive adults and caretakers available to them when problems arose. On the other hand, mothers of vulnerable children perceived them as being difficult to handle. These mothers reported that their children exhibited more temper tantrums and eating and sleeping problems. The children's orientation toward others was negative and aggressive. Overall, the families of vulnerable children seemed to have meager support systems.

We should note that the perceptions of the *fathers* were not discussed. As a result, the possibility that they, too, perceived the children in the same way as the mothers did remains unexplored. It is important to make this point because of the subtle negative connotation given to the perceptions of the mothers of the vulnerable group. Mothers seem to be blamed for the subsequent delinquency of the children. Mothers are not lauded for the *non*delinquency of the resilient group, however. In this case, family support systems and the community share the credit.

Another prospective longitudinal study, by George Spivack and Norma Cianci (1987), used a cohort of 660 kindergarten children and analyzed the extent to which behavioral patterns observed in kindergarten were predictive of later delinquency. Delinquency was defined as a "police contact" with the Philadelphia Police Department before age 17. Each offense was coded for seriousness using a research-based scoring method (the Sellin–Wolfgang method).

Spivack and Cianci found that excessive aggressive and antisocial behavior at an early age is a modest predictor of the same behavior at a later age. The finding most relevant to our present topic, however, was that delinquency-prone children were more likely to exhibit a "difficult temperament," as reflected in their impatience, impulsiveness, annoying interpersonal behavior, poor adaptability, and moodiness. From another perspective, however, we could say that these children might have had very good reasons for being any or all of the above.

In conclusion, Spivack and Cianci recommend that future research focus on ". . . the issue of 'match' between parental child rearing styles and child temperament, hypothesizing that the high-risk pattern will emerge with greatest frequency when children with a 'difficult' temperament have parents who perceive such behavior in a negative light . . . and thus respond to the child impatiently, punitively, and without understanding of the child's needs and feelings" (1987, p. 69). In addition, both the Kauai and the Spivack–Cianci studies emphasize the bi-directionality (**reciprocity**) of the child's influencing the parents and the parents' influencing the child.

The Caspi Study: Developmental Paths of Ill-tempered People

Avshalom Caspi, Glen Elder, and Daryl Bem (1987) distinguish between two kinds of person–environment interactions. One type is reciprocal and dynamic: The person acts, the environment reacts, and the person reacts back, and so forth, in a causal loop. For example, a child's temper tantrums may coerce others into offering short-term payoffs as temporary appeasement. However, this immediate appeasement precludes the learning of more controlled behaviors that would, in the long run, be more effective. Caspi, Elder, and Bem suggest that temper tantrums reflect an interactional style that evokes reciprocal, reinforcing responses from others. The explosive, undercontrolled style that appears as temper tantrums in early childhood may later manifest itself in undercontrolled rages when the individual again confronts frustration or controlling authority in adulthood, such as in the work setting or the marital or partner relationship.

The second type of interaction between the person and the environment relates to the stability of temperament. Here, the individual's innate dispositions systematically select environments that reinforce and sustain them. Persons with ill-tempered or antisocial dispositions may deliberately select environments that condone and immediately reinforce antisocial approaches to the world. The ill-tempered boy drops out of school and associates with boys who do not challenge or care about this ill temper. The group of boys may, in fact, display the same feature, thereby reinforcing a sense of belonging. In this sense, ill-tempered children represent high-risk candidates for delinquency: Their behavior increasingly channels them into environments that facilitate antisocial conduct.

Caspi, Elder, and Bem followed the life course of 87 boys and 95 girls in a project initiated in 1928 by the Institute of Human Development of the University of California at Berkeley. Most subjects were white, Protestant, middle-class children when the project began. A major finding of this longitudinal study was that ill-tempered children became ill-tempered adults. Whatever had been involved in childhood patterns of temper tantrums or uncontrolled behavior had carried over into adulthood. The uncontrolled behavior was evoked in adult roles and settings, especially those requiring a high degree of subordination (e.g., military and employment settings) and those requiring negotiation of interpersonal conflicts (e.g., marital and parenthood settings).

The researchers found gender differences in their results. Ill-tempered compared with even-tempered boys were substantially less likely to complete a formal education, to maintain a job for any length of time, or to remain married. Their lives reflected erratic work habits and little persistence on tasks. In the study by Caspi and his colleagues, ill-tempered men were twice as likely to have been divorced by age 40 and were more likely to be judged inadequate parents by their spouses. They were inclined to "resolve" interpersonal conflicts with demonstrations of anger and aggression. The Caspi group also discovered a progressive deterioration in SES for ill-tempered boys. As a group, they showed downward class mobility; most came from middle-class families, but by age 40 they had fallen to working-class status. Part of this downward mobility could be attributed to their lack of formal education and their inability to maintain steady employment. Ill-tempered men were significantly more likely to be unemployed, to hold a variety of short-term jobs, and to express less satisfaction with their careers and their supervisors than even-tempered men. On the other hand, recent evidence (Snarey & Vaillant, 1985) suggests that working-class even-tempered boys tend to move upward in SES over the years.

The pattern for women was similar to that for men, but there were some differences. Movement on the SES scale was confounded by the cultural and social forces that dictated different proper roles for women during the years covered in the study. For women, movement along the SES spectrum hinged primarily on the jobs and SES of their husbands. Women were expected to move up by marrying higher-SES men, not through their own efforts, and they were expected to maintain the ideal home. Caspi and his colleagues did discover that 40 percent of women with frequent childhood tantrums married down (as measured by occupational status of husbands), compared with only 24 percent of their even-tempered peers. Other trends emerged from the data. Ill-tempered girls grew up to be ill-tempered women. The relationship between childhood temper tantrums and achievement in later life, however, was not nearly as strong as that found for men. Similar to ill-tempered men, ill-tempered women experienced deterioration in marital and personal relationships. Twenty-six percent of ill-tempered women were divorced by age 40, compared with only 12 percent of even-tempered women. Furthermore, they reported more marital conflicts, were generally more dissatisfied with their marriages, and were more likely to be ill-tempered parents, according to their own reports.

Although the Caspi–Elder–Bem investigation did not directly examine the amount of delinquency and criminal conduct in the sample, some inferences could be drawn based on their findings. The evidence certainly indicates that ill-tempered people are in store for a life of inordinate strife and general dissatisfaction. Ill-tempered, irritable youngsters characterized by temper tantrums and "poor impulse control" appear to be prime candidates for serious delinquency. We can anticipate that ill-tempered people, because of their tendency to react to things with explosive tirades and temper tantrums, will be more involved in violent "solutions" to frustrations. Sheldon and Eleanor Glueck (1950) found that serious delinquents were nearly six times more likely to exhibit "temper tantrums" than nondelinquent peers. D. Zillman (1979, 1983) hypothesizes that individuals prone to temper tantrums temporarily suspend their rational thinking processes and do things they would normally not do.

Compounding the problem is the finding by the Caspi group that ill-tempered people fail at educational and occupational endeavors, a background feature often associated with the adult criminals who are the most likely to appear in official statistics. Delinquents also have a higher rate of school failure, as reflected by poor grades, truancy, conduct problems, and dropping out completely. The issue of temperament, temper tantrums, and poor impulse control leads us to the biosocial theory of Hans J. Eysenck.

EYSENCK'S THEORY OF CRIMINALITY

In 1977, the British psychologist Hans J. Eysenck proposed a theory of crime and delinquency that clearly fits into the individual system category of social systems theory. It is a temperament perspective built upon a genetic-biological platform: Innate temperamental traits influence in part all personality and behavior pat-

SYSTEMS THEORY AND DELINQUENCY **105**

terns. According to Eysenck, antisocial behavior is the result of an interaction between certain environmental conditions and inherited personality traits. Eysenck (1996, p. 150) writes: "The theory suggests an **interaction** between social and psychophysiological factors; not a 100% biological chain of causation."

Eysenck believes that any comprehensive theory of crime and delinquency must advocate a careful examination of both the biological makeup and the socialization history of each individual. Because clearly we inherit morphological, physiological, and biochemical properties through genes, there is no reason not to believe that we also inherit personality traits or temperamental predispositions to antisocial behavior (Eysenck, 1983). He asserts: "No serious student can doubt the relevance of both the *biological* and the *social* aspects of an individual's behaviour" (Eysenck, 1984, p. 90).

People obviously differ in the degree to which they indulge in antisocial conduct, from those who never do to the habitual criminal who continually and frequently displays such conduct. Most people, according to Eysenck, lie somewhere between these extremes. The majority occasionally indulge in antisocial conduct, but only to a minor degree and when chances of detection are minuscule.

Basically, Eysenck believes that most people do not participate regularly in antisocial behavior because they have developed a conscience. Furthermore, Eysenck argues that conscience forms as a result of classical conditioning. An explanation of the conditioning process and the formation of the conscience would take us too far from our focus here. The interested reader, however, is encouraged to read Eysenck's theory on this topic in the original version (see Eysenck & Gudjonsson, 1989).

Eysenck contends that people are born with nervous system characteristics that (1) are significantly different from those of the general population and (2) affect their ability to conform to social expectations and rules. With an effective learning schedule (conditioning), just about any person, regardless of his or her nervous system characteristics, can be made to conform to societal needs. It will take longer and require more concentrated learning for some—but it can be done.

Eysenck's theory is similar in many ways to the theoretical concepts of temperament discussed previously. Eysenck believes that nervous systems differ in their reactivity, sensitivity, and excitability. It is these features that predispose—but not cause—a person to act antisocially. But antisocial action is not dictated by the temperamental characteristics of the nervous system working in isolation. Innate features of the nervous system, influenced by experience and the social environment, render certain persons more at risk for delinquent and criminal action than others.

Eysenck's theory sensitizes us to the possible role of biological and genetic factors in the etiology of delinquency. The concept of temperament does the same. But let us be clear about what is being said here. Certain persons may be "wired up" in such a way as to increase the *probability* that they will engage in frequent misconduct, depending on their experiences with the social environment. In other words, some criminologists believe it is unlikely that human beings are neutral, passive pawns waiting for social forces to shape them. Rather, human beings come into the world with predispositions to resist or accept some of the shaping. Some are full of energy and activity and mood shifts. Some are pleasant, whereas others are irritable. These factors affect those caregivers and others around them, setting up a dynamic, interactive chain of events. To those contemporary criminologists who hold this perspective, the etiology of delinquency begins in biological predispositions, but the social environment plays the major role in its overall development.

GENETICS

Social scientists, especially criminologists, support a longstanding tradition of animosity toward biological-genetic explanations of human behavior (Rowe & Osgood, 1984; Raine, 1993). Moreover, "Most sociological texts on crime and delinquency discuss genetic explanations only as bad examples, the reprehensible products of a less-enlightened era" (Rowe & Osgood, 1984, p. 526). What is not often recognized or emphasized is that the earlier assumptions and contentions of a bygone era (e.g., those of Lombroso, Goddard, and Sheldon) are also not acceptable to most biologists, psychobiologists, or psychologists today. Contemporary scientists find the assumptions made by these early writers untenable and their research methods crude. Genes influence human behavior, but the influence is modified by, even buried under, multiple psychosocial influences. And the likelihood of any single, all-encompassing influence or determinant is extremely remote.

Attempts to Disentangle the Genetic-Environmental Thicket: Twin Studies

If genetics play a substantial role in behavior, that role should be identifiable in the conduct of identical and fraternal twins. That assumption underlies the work of researchers who have conducted empirical research on crime and delinquency among twins. Fraternal twins (dizygotic twins) develop from two different fertilized eggs and genetically are no more alike than ordinary siblings. Identical twins (or monozygotic twins) develop from a single egg; they are always the same sex and share the same genes. Presumably, then, if genes are determinative, identical twins should display highly similar behavior. Twin researchers report their results in concordance terms. **Concordance**, in genetics, is the degree to which pairs of related subjects share a particular behavior or condition. It is usually expressed in percentages. For example, assume that we wish to determine the concordance of intelligence between 20 pair of fraternal twins and 20 pair of identical twins. If 10 pairs of the identical twins obtained approximately the same IQ score, but only 5 pair of the fraternal twins obtained the same score, the concordance for identical twins would be 50 percent and for fraternal twins 25 percent. The concordance for identical twins would be twice that for fraternal twins, suggesting that hereditary factors play a role in the formation of intelligence. If, however, the concordance for identical twins was about the same as that for fraternals, genetic factors could be presumed unimportant, at least as represented by that sample and measured by our methodology.

One of the earliest twin–criminality studies was conducted by the German psychiatrist Johannes Lange in 1929 on inmates in Bavarian prisons. He discovered a 77 percent concordance for criminality for identical twins and a 12 percent concordance for fraternal twins. Many subsequent twin studies (there have been at least 13) have confirmed Lange's findings. On the average, investigations reported a concordance rate of 50 percent for identical twins and about 20 percent for fraternal twins (Raine, 1993).

In spite of these findings, many researchers are hesitant to accept the genetic implications of twin research. Most twin studies have lacked rigid sampling or testing procedures, leaving their results questionable. Gordon Trasler (1987) observes that the more carefully designed a twin study is, the less pronounced are the concordance differences in offending between monozygotic and dizygotic twins. For example, early investigations—such as the one by Lange—were handicapped by unreliable methods of determining whether twin pairs were monozygotic or dizygotic. Now, with increased sophistication in blood and serum testing, the large differences reported in the earlier studies have dropped substantially. For instance, Dalgard and Kringlen (1976), in contrast to Lange, report an offending concordance rate of only 26 percent for monozygotic twin pairs, compared with 15 percent for dizygotic twin pairs. The twin method assumes that the environment exerts a similar influence on each member of the set, whether the twins are identical or fraternal. Differences, then, must be due to genetic factors. Many critics have noted, however, that identical twins are so alike physically that it is very likely they elicit more similar social responses than fraternal twins. Similar behavior could just as easily be due to environmental influences. In fact, when Dalgard and Kringlen adjusted their data to take into account the effects of the social environment (whether the twins were treated alike, dress alike, and so forth), the concordance differences in offending disappeared. Their conclusion: "These findings support the view that *hereditary factors are of no significant importance in the etiology of common crime*" (1976, p. 231). Overall, because of these questions about the twin method and the failure of the studies to separate decisively genetic from environmental effects, many if not most criminologists are suspicious about the genetic implications of twin research.

Further Attempts to Disentangle: Adoption Studies

Another method used to identify relevant variables in the interaction between heredity and environment is the adoption study, which assumes that, if siblings are raised apart, similarities in their behavior may be due to genetic influences. Theoretically, adoption studies should be especially useful for determining what kinds of environments are most conducive to criminality. More than 15 fairly well-executed adoption studies have been carried out in recent years, most of them in Denmark, Sweden, and the United States. Other studies are being conducted in Germany, Japan, England, Holland, Finland, and Norway.

Almost all of the studies completed so far suggest that there may be some degree of genetic predisposition to crime (Raine, 1993). However, it is clear that genetic factors alone are not capable of providing an adequate explanation of delinquency. In the three studies with a large enough sample size to separate violent from nonviolent crime, it was found that genetics appear to play a larger role in petty property crimes than violent crimes. Adrian Raine (1993, p. 66) writes: "This seems counterintuitive since one would imagine that violent, more serious offending, being more extreme, would be more "hard-wired" and have a higher heritability than property offending, which one could imagine is more driven by social and economic factors." Raine's very tentative explanation is that property offenses appear to be associated with genetic factors in some mysterious way, whereas violent offending appears to be more related to environmental stressors, such as brain damage, unstable home environments, and child abuse. This intriguing finding awaits more research.

BODY BUILD AND DELINQUENCY

The belief that personality or temperament is somehow closely related to bodily appearance has been expressed in a variety of forums for at least 2,000 years (Montemayor, 1978). In criminology, the view is associated primarily with W. H. Sheldon, a physician who theorized that body structure and delinquency were closely related. Sheldon developed a classification system based on the shape of the body and related these "body types" directly to a genetic propensity to engage in delinquency. After extensively and painstakingly collecting physical measurements and documenting them with photographs, Sheldon delineated three basic body builds in both males and females: **ectomorphic** (thin and fragile), **mesomorphic** (muscular and hard), and **endomorphic** (fat and soft). The reader with some background in embryology will recognize that the terms refer to layers of the embryo. The ectodermal layer evolves into the nervous system. The ectomorph, therefore, has a well-developed brain and central nervous system compared with the rest of his or her tall and thin body. The mesodermal layer of the embryo develops into muscle, and, therefore, the muscular body that is tough and well equipped for strenuous activity is labeled the mesomorph. The endodermal embryonic layer develops primarily into the digestive tract, and thus individuals who are flabby and fat (endomorphs) are associated with the digestive system.

Somatotypes: Indexing Body Shapes

Sheldon did not make sharp, abrupt distinctions between the body types (which he called "somatotypes"). Rarely did a person's body structure fall exclusively into one of the three "pure" somatotypes described in the preceding paragraph. Rather, most individuals had features of all three to varying degrees. Sheldon ranked his subjects on a 7-point scale, with 7 representing maximum features of the body type and 1 representing the minimum. A "pure" mesomorph would have a somatotype of 1–7–1. A 3–2–5 person would be primarily endomorphic (5) but would have some features of ectomorphy (3) and of mesomorphy (2). Notice that the first score reflects ectomorphy, the second, mesomorphy, and the third, endomorphy. Sheldon assigned a 4–4–4 to the average body. This indicated constitutional "balance."

Furthermore, while we used whole numbers in the examples, the actual indexes usually contained decimals, such as 3.6–4.8–5.5. Sheldon claimed that he discovered a strong correlation between personality (or what he termed "temperament") and somatotype, and he proceeded to describe personality types that were linked with body types: cerebrotonia to the ectomorphic, somatotonia to the mesomorphic, and viscerotonia to the endomorphic. In Sheldon's theory, the cerebrotonic person is inhibited, reserved, self-conscious, and afraid of people. A somatotonic person ordinarily needs muscular and vigorous physical activity, risk, and adventure. A person with this temperament is likely to be aggressive, ruthless, and callous in relationships with others and to be relatively indifferent to pain. Mesomorphs are associated with these features. The third personality, the viscerotonic, loves comfort, food, affection, and people. This type of person, according to Sheldon, is usually even-tempered and easy to get along with, traits that describe the endomorph.

Testing the Theory

Sheldon began to test his theory of delinquency in 1939 by exploring the relationship between delinquency and body type. He published the results ten years later, in his book *Varieties of Delinquent Youth* (Sheldon, Hartl, & McDermott, 1949). He had classified the body structures of 200 "more-or-less delinquent boys" from the Hayden Goodwill Inn, a Boston rehabilitation home for the "incorrigible" and the "disappointing." Each boy was assigned an index. Results were compared with indexes of 4,000 male college students. As predicted, Sheldon found a preponderance of mesomorphs and very few ectomorphs in his delinquent sample compared with his normal college sample. The average somatotype of the 200 "delinquents" was 3.5–4.6–2.7, compared to an average somatotype of 3.2–3.7–3.5 for college males. Sheldon identified a special group of boys as definite "criminals"; their average somatotype was 3.4–5.4–1.8.

"Whatever else may be true of the delinquency I saw in Boston, it is mainly in the germ plasm," Sheldon concluded (1949, p. 872). He was convinced that genetics, as reflected in body structure, were the primary causal factor of delinquency and a life of crime. He discussed the desirability of "thoroughbredness in the human stock" and recommended that serious consideration be given to selective breeding. Consequently, Sheldon's work was widely and severely criticized.

Sutherland (1956a) asserted that Sheldon's conclusions were simply unwarranted on the basis of the data. He called *Varieties of Delinquent Youth* "useless," adding, "This book fails completely to add anything to scientific knowledge except the evidence from which the conclusion can be drawn that in this particular group of 200 youth, variations in civil delinquency are not related to variations in the basic indices of Sheldon's constitutional psychology" (Sutherland, 1956a, p. 289). Other critics pointed to the numerous flaws in the project, such as the subjective and unreliable criteria for determining delinquency. Sheldon did not merely select youths who "violated the law"; he preferred his own subjective method and vague criteria for selecting the "delinquent" sample. At one point, Sheldon had arbitrarily eliminated 200 other Hayden residents because their records were "less than complete" but did not elaborate.

Also contaminating his results was the fact that his subjects, being early to mid-adolescent males, were most likely experiencing dramatic growth spurts and undergoing physical changes. This could be said of any research on the body appearance of juveniles. Finally, the college males in Sheldon's control group were older than the delinquent boys, making comparisons difficult at best (Montemayor, 1978). In sum, Sheldon's method of somatotyping was so confusing and subjective that his measures of body type lacked both validity and reliability. Even researchers sympathetic to Sheldon's approach resorted to other measures or variations of his procedure.

Shortly after Sheldon's work was published, Sheldon and Eleanor Glueck (1950, 1956) reported on their own scheme for somtatotyping applied in their classic and extensive study of delinquent boys, which we cover in some detail in Chapter 5. The Gluecks classified 60 percent of their delinquent sample as mesomorphs, compared with 30 percent of the control group. Other researchers followed suit. Gibbens (1963) studied English borstal boys and discovered an unexpectedly large percentage of mesomorphs, but he was unable to somatotype his control sample for comparison purposes. Cortes and Gatti (1972) reported that delinquents (100 boys adjudicated by juvenile court) were preponderantly more mesomorphic than nondelinquents (100 male high school seniors). They classified 57 percent of the delinquent group as mesomorphic compared with 19 percent of the nondelinquents. Epps and Parnell (1952) compared the physiques of 177 female delinquents with those of 123 Oxford undergraduates and found the delinquents to be shorter, heavier, and more muscular or fat, suggesting mesomorphy and endomorphy.

Another body of more sophisticated research reached very different results. McCandless, Persons, and Roberts (1972) found physique unrelated to either self-reported delinquency or to the seriousness of criminal offenses. Wadsworth (1979), using data from the British National Survey, reported that delinquents, especially those who committed serious offenses, were generally smaller in stature and appeared to reach puberty later than their nondelinquent peers. While no somatotyping was done, the results suggest that the delinquents were not mesomorphs, because mesomorphs reportedly reach puberty before the other body types (Rutter & Giller, 1984). Finally, in their longitudinal study of working-class boys in London, West and Farrington (1973) reported little association between delinquency and either height–weight ratios or physical strength.

Some contemporary writers (e.g., Wilson & Herrnstein, 1985; Eysenck & Gudjonsson, 1989) suggest that body build and delinquency data provide good evidence that constitutional factors correlate with crime and delinquent behavior and, therefore, represent a constitutional basis to crime. "Similarly," Raine (1993, p. 203) writes, "most commentaries on the body build–crime literature have almost universally linked body build to genetic and constitutional interpretations of crime." However, such interpretations are gross simplifications of a very complicated problem and fail to recognize the enormous influence of psychosocial factors.

For example, body build may be linked to delinquency because having a larger, more muscular body build allows bullying to be an effective strategy in winning social conflicts in the playground setting. Early reinforcement of this behavior may encourage the use of force and violence later in life (Raine, 1993, p. 203).

In summary, the body build–delinquency connection is weak, contradictory, and divisive in disciplinary terms; does not lead to a deeper understanding of delinquency; and is not helpful in developing prevention programs.

SUMMARY AND CONCLUSIONS

In this chapter, the systems approach was introduced. A system is an arrangement of things that are related to one another. The concept of "system" is a human creation that is used to describe regularities or consistencies found in the world. A system is a conceptual tool used, for convenience, to put order into an otherwise chaotic mass of events and situations. Social systems theory, the theoretical framework for this text, will allow us to examine the vast amount of theoretical and empirical work in juvenile delinquency with some thematic orientation; it offers a tentative structure for the many topics to be covered.

A social systems approach facilitates a synthesis of what we know about delinquency across the disciplines and viewpoints, whether we are talking about social class, neighborhood, community, culture, family, school, peers, or the individual. The social systems framework will accommodate all. Furthermore, this approach urges us to realize that research concentrating at the community, societal, or macrolevel is not superior to research at the family or individual level. Rather, each research project or theoretical endeavor is at a *different* level of study and explanation, and each has merit. Superiority based on level of study is not tenable in this scheme.

Nonetheless, criminology is increasingly becoming recognized as a policy science, and research in the field is continually used in making public policy decisions. Furthermore, researchers at all systems levels compete for private and public grants to continue their work. When choices have to be made, the suggestion that no research approach is superior to others is not helpful. It makes sense, therefore, to consider the *implications* of various research endeavors. There is considerable debate today, for example, over the wisdom of giving money to researchers who are investigating biological and/or neurological factors that may predispose a person to violence. Some opponents fear that violent individuals will not be held accountable for their offenses. Others fear that such biological approaches will take attention away from needed changes at higher systems levels, such as changes in society's cultural fascination with violence. Although the debate is far more extensive than we have portrayed here, it is used to illustrate the need to consider the *implications* of theory and research at any systems level.

In this chapter we have begun to review the individual or infrasystem based on the biological and genetic factors. There is some evidence that biological and genetic components play a role in the equation, but the overwhelming evidence indicates that psychosocial factors play substantially greater roles. A "difficult" temperament, when combined with other risk factors—such as poor parenting, an inadequate educational system, a delinquent peer group—may predispose a child to a developmental trajectory of delinquency and violence. Research on temperament not only recognizes the bi-directional, reciprocal influences between child and parent, but it is beginning to explore other influences as well, such as the self-selection of social environments by the participants themselves. Similarly, ADHD features may alienate some children from prosocial peers and teachers, a behavioral pattern that puts these children at a disadvantage for developing academic and social skills.

Some other biological factors were reviewed in this chapter, but it must be emphasized that human behavioral patterns are partially influenced by millions of genes sharing a very small effect (Trasler, 1987). Thus, we are not talking about one single gene or a small number of genes having significant effects on human conduct. We are talking about an incalculable number of genes and their combinations possibly having some small effect on behavior against a backdrop of enormous environmental influences. Attempts to group people on the basis of genetic differences are, at best, risky and full of error. "The potential for genetic differences between individuals is staggering, even within a family. The numbers of genetically different types of sperm and egg which any one individual could in principle produce is many millionfold more than the number of humans who have ever lived. This extraordinary genetic uniqueness of the individual must apply to all his attributes. . . ." (W. Bodmer, cited by Trasler, 1987, p. 106). Trasler (1987, p. 106) concludes: "We might venture the comment that social scientists often think in excessively simple terms about the respective influences of genetic and environmental factors in controlling the delinquent."

It is important to be ever mindful that when it comes to human behavior, cognitive or mental factors take precedence over genetic-biological or neurological ones. In recent years, there has been a discernible shift toward the cognitive underpinnings of antisocial and delinquent behavior (Tolan, Guerra, & Kendall, 1995). The next chapter will focus on these factors.

KEY CONCEPTS

activity	infrasystem
adolescence-limited (AL)	interactionism
adolescent-onset type	life-course-persistent (LCP)
attention deficit disorder	macroanalysis
attention deficit hyperactivity disorder (ADHD)	macrosystems
	mesomorphic
childhood-onset type	mesosystems
chronosystem	microanalysis
concordance	microsystem
conduct disorder	niche picking
developmental theory of delinquency	reactivity
difficult child syndrome	reciprocity
ectomorphic	self-regulation
emotionality	sociability
endomorphic	spillover effect
exosystems	strain theory
general theory of crime	

5

Infrasystems: Developmental and Learning Factors

More than 30 years ago, George A. Kelly (1963) theorized that humans look at their worlds through mental images similar to transparent patterns or templates. We create these templates and try to fit them over the reality of the world. Often the fit is not very good. Yet, without our templates, the world would appear chaotic, unpredictable, and fragmented. Thus, even a "poor fit" is more helpful than none at all. Kelly called these cognitive templates **constructs**. Constructs enable us ". . . to chart a course of behavior, explicitly formulated or implicitly acted out, verbally expressed or utterly inarticulate, consistent with other courses of behavior or inconsistent with them, intellectually reasoned or vegetatively sensed" (Kelly, 1963, p. 9).

Constructs, then, are mental representations of the environment. They are our mental shorthand or summaries of what we know about the world. Constructs make us liberal or conservative, optimistic or pessimistic, jaded or naïve, for whatever those labels are worth. Because constructs are dynamic and interrelated, they are cognitive *systems*.

Juvenile offenders, especially life-course-persistent offenders, are apt to have cognitions, beliefs, and attitudes about others and their worlds that contribute to their offending patterns. For example, highly aggressive children often have a **hostile attributional bias**. That is, children prone to unusually aggressive actions are more likely to interpret ambiguous actions as hostile and threatening than are their less aggressive counterparts (Dodge, 1993b). Research consistently indicates that highly aggressive and violent adolescents "typically define social problems in hostile ways, adopt hostile goals, seek few additional facts, generate few alternative solutions, anticipate few consequences for aggression, and give higher priority to their aggressive solutions" (Eron & Slaby, 1994, p. 10). These hostile cognitive styles, combined with deficient interpersonal skills, are more likely to result in aggression and violence in certain social situations.

We begin this chapter with brief attention to basic principles of learning and to the specific area of social learning, illustrated by theories in psychology and sociology. Following that we move to moral development, and the labeling perspective. What these seemingly diverse views have in common is they all emphasize the cognitive systems and styles of thinking about the world.

SOCIAL LEARNING AND DELINQUENCY: PSYCHOLOGICAL PERSPECTIVES

The many variants of social learning theory can generally be divided into two categories: (1) those based on social reinforcement, derived from principles articulated by Burrhus Frederick (B. F.) Skinner and (2) those based on social imitation. Both positions have their roots in classical behaviorism as articulated by John B. Watson and later Skinner.

Social learning theory can be traced as far back as the late nineteenth century to the writings of the child psychologist James Mark Baldwin and the social psychologist Gabriel Tarde. The fundamental principle of social learning is that people learn their behavior from the social environment: from parents, peers, teachers, and significant others. Theories based on *social* reinforcement and *social* imitation were stated most explicitly by psychologists during the early 1960s (Cairns, 1983), but they were also implicit in the work of the sociologist Edwin Sutherland, which will be discusssed later in this chapter. Today, no single discipline can claim exclusive guardianship of the basic ideas of social learning. Theorists from both psychological and sociological perspectives have tried to reformulate or expand various aspects of earlier approaches. Because there are some subtle differences in their views, though, we will separate them in this chapter.

Gerwitz (1961) and Bijou and Baer (1961) adapted B. F. Skinner's classical behaviorism to emphasize the influence of **social reinforcement** in child development, especially concerning prosocial and deviant behavior. The **social imitation** school of thought was led by Albert Bandura and Richard Walters (1963), who emphasized—as Baldwin had earlier—the important element of **modeling** the behavior of significant others in the social environments. Because there is so much confusion and misunderstanding among students of crime and delinquency about Skinner, operant conditioning, and behaviorism in general, it will be worthwhile to begin this section by briefly addressing these topics.

CLASSICAL BEHAVIORISM: THE ROOTS OF SOCIAL LEARNING

Behaviorism "officially" began in 1913 with the publication of a landmark paper by John B. Watson, "Psychology as the Behaviorist Views It." The paper, which appeared in *Psychology Review*, is considered the first definitive statement on behaviorism. Thus, Watson is acknowledged as the "father" of this very influential perspective.

In this paper, and in subsequent writings and public appearances, Watson continually declared that psychology is the *science* of behavior. He argued that psychologists should eliminate the "mind" and all of its related "vague" concepts from scientific consideration, because they could not be observed directly or measured. Watson was convinced that the fundamental goal of any behavioral science was to understand, predict, and control human behavior; and only a rigorous scientific approach could reach this goal. He also asserted that any behavioral science must mimic closely the physical sciences if it was to accomplish the extensive explanation and control achieved by those sciences.

Greatly influenced by Ivan Pavlov's research on classical conditioning, Watson thought the behavioral sciences should focus exclusively on the relationship between stimulus and response. A stimulus is any object or event that elicits behavior. A response is the elicited behavior. Watson was convinced that all behavior—both animal and human—was controlled by the external environment in a way similar to that described by Pavlov in his initial study—a stimulus produces a response (sometimes called S-R psychology). For Watson, classical (or Pavlovian) conditioning was the key to understanding, predicting, and controlling behavior, and its practical applicability was unlimited.

The chief spokesperson for behaviorism for well over half a century was B. F. Skinner, who is one of the best known American psychologists of the twentieth century. For many years, the Skinnerian perspective dominated the application of "behavior modification" in both adult and juvenile correctional facilities and in residential facilities for the mentally handicapped or severely emotionally disturbed. Eventually, practices associated with behavior modification were strongly challenged and very often curtailed, because they often involved a restriction of rights. For example, a juvenile in a detention facility might have blankets removed as punishment for unacceptable behavior. Some comprehensive theories on the causes of delinquency (e.g., Akers, 1977, 1985) have tried to integrate Skinnerian behaviorism with sociological perspectives.

Skinner was a strong situationist. He believed that all behavior is at the mercy of stimuli in the environment and that individuals have no control or self-determination. Independent thought and free will are myths that humans use to delude themselves into thinking that they are under their own control. Both animals and humans react, like complicated robots, to their environments. For Skinner, crime and delinquency are exclusively the result of certain forces within the environment and are not due to any personal predisposition or personality trait.

According to Skinner, people do things simply to get rewards and avoid punishment. Of course Skinner was by no means the first to draw attention to the simple principle that people do things to get rewards and avoid things when punishment is involved. In the late eighteenth century, the philosopher Jeremy Bentham observed that human conduct seemed to be controlled by the seeking of pleasure and the avoidance of pain: People do things solely to receive rewards and to avoid punishment. The rewards may be physical (e.g., material goods, money), psychological (e.g., feelings of competence), or social (e.g., improved status, acceptance by peers).

The ideas of Bentham and Cesare Beccaria were embodied in the classical school of criminology, which saw crime as an expression of the exercise of free will. According to this approach, people chose to commit crime after weighing the costs and benefits. The role of society, then, was to make the choice of committing crime unappealing. One way to do this, according to Beccaria and Bentham, was to make punishment swift, certain, and severe. They cautioned that punishment must not be too severe or disproportionate to the crime, however, a point that is often overlooked by modern-day supporters of the classical school.

Skinner refers to rewards as **reinforcements**, defined as anything that increases the probability of future responding. Reinforcement could be either positive or negative. In **positive reinforcement** one gains something desired as a consequence of certain behavior. Nicole disciplines herself to train faithfully for the track team and is rewarded with a varsity position. In **negative reinforcement**, one avoids an unpleasant event or stimulus as a consequence of certain behavior. Fred successfully avoids what he anticipates will be an unpleasant day at school by feigning illness. The behaviors of both Nicole and Fred were reinforced and are thus likely to be used again—in the one case to gain rewards, in the other to avoid events that are anticipated to be unpleasant or painful. Both positive and negative reinforcement can increase the likelihood of a particular behavior.

Negative reinforcement must be distinguished from "punishment" and "extinction." In punishment, a person receives noxious or painful stimuli as a consequence of something he or she does. In extinction, a person receives nothing, neither reinforcement nor pain. Skinner argues that punishment is an ineffective way to eliminate or change behavior, because it merely suppresses it temporarily. At a later time, under the right context, the response is likely to occur again. Extinction, he believes, is a far better procedure for the elimination or alteration of behavior. Once the person learns that a particular behavior brings no reinforcement, that behavior will eventually drop out of the repertoire of possible responses for that set of circumstances. For example, once six-year-old Georgie realizes that temper tantrums at the checkout counter of the local supermarket will not gain the anticipated chewing gum, the behavior should drop out of his response pattern.

The premise that operant conditioning is the basis for the origins of delinquent behavior is deceptively simple: Delinquent behavior is learned behavior. It is behavior that is learned through the principles of operant conditioning. It is behavior that brings rewards for the respondent. According to Skinner, human beings are born neutral—neither bad nor good. Culture, society, peers, parents, and the whole social environment reward and shape behavior. Delinquent behavior is a result of rewards received from the social environment.

According to Skinner, delinquent behavior is a social problem, not an individual one. He is convinced that searches for individual dispositions or personalities that lead to misbehavior will be fruitless because people are completely determined by the environment in which they live. He did not entirely discount the role of genetics in the formation of human behavior but saw it as very minor. According to Skinner and his followers, if we wish to eliminate delinquency and crime, we must change society through behavioral engineering based on a "scientific conception of humankind." Skinner believed we must design a society in which members learn very early that reinforcement will not occur if they violate prescribed rules and regulations but will occur if they abide by them.

Contemporary psychology has grown cool toward the Skinnerian perspective as an explanation of human behavior. The theory is, in the eyes of many theorists and practitioners, too narrow and restrictive in explanation to account adequately for the constellation of factors that are characteristic of human behavior. Skinner's brand of behaviorism tends to see humans as robots. It should be noted that when Skinnerian theory was introduced, Ludwig von Bertalanffy, the founder of general systems theory, argued vehemently against it. "The organism is not a passive but an intrinsically active system," he wrote (1968, p. 208). "The robot model . . . only partly covers animal behavior and does not cover an essential portion of human behavior at all" (1968, p. 209).

SOCIAL LEARNING VERSUS BEHAVIORISM

In contrast to Skinnerian behaviorism, social learning theorists see humans as active problem solvers who perceive, encode, interpret, and make decisions on the basis of what their environment has to offer. To understand delinquency, social learning theorists tell us that we must examine perceptions, thoughts, expectancies, competencies, and values. Viewing humans as "reinforcement maximizers" who consider only the ratio of rewards to punishments before making decisions is overly simplistic and not in line with present research on cognitive processes.

To explain human behavior, social learning theorists emphasize cognitive variables, such as the internal processes we commonly call thinking and remembering. They note that classical behaviorism ignores what transpires between the time the person perceives a stimulus and the time he or she responds or reacts to it.

The term "social learning" reflects the theory's strong assumption that we learn primarily by observing and listening to people around us—the social environment. In fact, social learning theorists believe that the social environment is the most important factor in the *acquisition* of most human behavior. They do accept the necessity of reinforcement for the *maintenance* of behavior. Delinquent behavior, for example, may be initially acquired through association and through observation. However, whether or not it is maintained will depend primarily upon reinforcement. We will elaborate on this process when we discuss the imitational aspects of social learning.

EXPECTANCY THEORY

Julian Rotter is best known for drawing attention to the importance of expectations (cognitions) about the consequences (outcome) of behavior, including the reinforcement that will be gained from the behavior. In other words, before doing anything, we ask, "What has happened to me before in this situation, and what will I gain this time?" According to Rotter, whether a specific pattern of behavior occurs will depend upon our expectancies and how much we value the outcomes. Rotter puts considerable emphasis on social reinforcement, as opposed to social imitation. To predict whether someone will behave a certain way, we must estimate that person's expectancies and the importance he or she places on the rewards gained by behavior. Often, the person will develop "generalized expectancies" that are stable and consistent across relatively similar situations. For example, Luke has learned to expect that passivity and silence bring the best outcomes while in the presence of his dominating father or aggressive older boys. On the other hand, Luke expects confrontation to bring negative outcomes, such as physical abuse by his father or fights with neighborhood boys.

The foregoing hypothesis may be important in the study of delinquency. Juveniles, according to Rotter's perspective, engage in misconduct because they expect to gain something in the form of status, power, affection, material goods, or living conditions. The social reinforcement perspective sees delinquent behavior as a situation in which the individual has learned to value goals or reinforcements that, although bringing the disapproval of the larger society, lead to approval and acceptance of those in the delinquent's reference group (Phares, 1972). "Thus, quite simply, he engages in such activity because of the expectancy that it will lead to the rewards of approval and recognition from those people who are particularly reinforcing for him. In short, the principles by which he becomes a criminal are the same as those that turn someone else into a social conformist. He is not deviant in terms of his own subculture" (Phares, 1972, p. 648). The Rotterian version of social learning, therefore, reflects a **cultural deviance orientation**, a position also embraced by some sociologists.

IMITATIONAL ASPECTS OF SOCIAL LEARNING

According to Albert Bandura (1973), an individual may acquire behavior simply by watching others in action, as opposed to actually receiving direct reinforcement. Bandura calls this process **observational learning** or **modeling**. Thus, Bandura belongs to the social imitation brand of social learning. Bandura contends that much of our behavior is *initially* acquired by watching others, who are labeled *models*. For example, a child may learn how to shoot a gun by imitating TV characters. He or she then rehearses and fine tunes this behavioral pattern by practicing with toy guns. The child then watches the models again for confirmation about his or her behavior. The behavior is likely to be maintained if peers also play with guns and reinforce one another for doing so.

According to Bandura, the more respected the models, the greater their impact on one's behavior. Relevant models include parents, teachers, siblings, friends, and peers, as well as symbolic models like literary characters or, more likely, media heroes. Rock stars, entertainment celebrities, and famous athletes are modeled by many young people, which is one reason why our society is exposed to so many public figures touting everything from cosmetics to a drug-free life.

Reinforcement has its place in Bandura's version of social learning. The observed behavior of the model is more likely to be imitated if the observer thinks that the model is rewarded for the behavior. Conversely, a model is less likely to be imitated if that model is punished. Bandura believes—much like Rotter—that once a person has made the decision to use a newly acquired behavior, whether he or she actually performs it and maintains it will depend on the situation and the expectancies for potential gain (reinforcement). This "potential gain" may come from outside in the form of praise from others or financial profit or from within in the form of self-satisfaction.

Television, the Mass Media, and Violence

An ever-present source of aggressive models is television. Recent surveys show that approximately 98 percent of American households have television and that many of these homes have multiple sets (Huston et al., 1992; Donnerstein, Slaby, & Eron, 1994). These same surveys discovered that within these homes television watching averages about 28 hours per week for children (ages 2 to 11 years) and 23 hours for teens. Television viewing occupies more of children's time than any other nonschool activity. More important, many of the poorest and potentially most vulnerable children are the heaviest viewers of television because of lack of alternative activities (Kuby & Csikszentmihalyi, 1990; Donnerstein, Slaby, & Eron, 1994). Current research finds that by the end of elementary school, the average child has watched more than 8,000 TV murders and 100,000 other violent acts (Huston et al., 1992). It is estimated that by the time a youth nears the end of his or her teens, he or she has viewed more than 200,000 violent acts.

Do all this television watching and mass media influence the development of aggressive and violent behavior in children and adolescents? To answer, lets's begin with a classic study conducted by Albert Bandura (1965) many years ago. In this famous study, 66 nursery school children were divided into three groups and shown one of three five-minute films. All three films depicted an adult verbally and physically assaulting a "BoBo," a large inflatable doll with a sand base. One group saw the adult model being rewarded with candy and a soft drink after displaying aggressive behavior. A second group observed the model being spanked and reprimanded verbally. A third group witnessed a situation in which the model received neither punishment nor reward.

After the children saw the film, they were permitted to engage in free play for ten minutes in a playroom of toys, including a BoBo doll. The group that had witnessed the adult model being rewarded for aggressive behavior exhibited more aggression than the other two groups. In addition, boys were more aggressive than girls. The group that saw the adult model being punished exhibited the least amount of aggression in the playroom. Bandura interpreted the gender differences as due to prior socialization and observational learning from significant social models.

Bandura's subsequent research, which included variations on the aforementioned basic design, consistently demonstrated this modeling effect. Furthermore, numerous follow-up studies not only replicated his findings but also suggested that media violence may have a strong influence on real-life violence in many situations (Baron, 1977). There has also been some evidence that even new reports of violence may have a **contagion effect**, a tendency for some people to model or copy an activity portrayed by the entertainment media. Contagion effect is said to occur when action depicted in the media is evaluated by certain individuals as a good idea and they then try to mimic the action. For example, an ingenious bank robbery, dramatized on television, might be imitated.

As aggressive or antisocial children become less popular at school with peers and teachers and begin to fail academically, they begin to drop out of the school scene and become more regular television viewers. Researchers have found that aggressive children do watch television more regularly, watch more media violence, identify more with violent characters, and believe more that the violence they observe reflects real life than nonaggressive children (Huesmann & Eron, 1986; Huesmann, 1988).

In general, experimental studies clearly reveal that television violence has a significant impact on the frequency and type of aggressive and antisocial behavior expressed by some adults and some children. Repeatedly, numerous well-designed research projects over the past 25 years have found that the mass media, including MTV and some RAP lyrics, are significant contributors to the aggressive and antisocial attitudes of many children, adolescents, and adults (Surgeon General, 1972; National Institute of Mental Health, 1982; Huston et al., 1992; Donnerstein, Slaby, & Eron, 1994).

Repeated exposure to violence on television may also habituate heavy viewers to violence. It may also distort one's perception of the world. Heavy television viewers respond to violence with less physiological arousal than do light viewers, suggesting that repeated exposure has desensitized them to violent effects. Furthermore, television programs tend to be heavily populated with villainous and unscrupulous people, portrayals that may give frequent viewers a jaded view of the world. There is some evidence that heavy viewers, compared with light viewers, are less trustful of others and overestimate their chances of being criminally victimized (Gerbner & Gross, 1976).

Although television and the mass media do not directly cause aggression and violence, they contribute to these behaviors by reinforcing certain values and beliefs. Television and the media show people being aggressive and violent and being rewarded. They also show that aggressive behavior is a quick and easy way to solve problems.

SOCIAL LEARNING AND DELINQUENCY: SOCIOLOGICAL PERSPECTIVES

Edwin H. Sutherland is regarded by many scholars and students as one of the great masters of theory in American criminology. In some circles, he is considered the "father of criminology." Sutherland's major contributions include both the earliest published research on white-collar crime and a comprehensive statement on the formation of crime known as **differential association theory**. The theory itself was a way of bringing attention to white collar crime, because Sutherland maintained that it explained *all* criminal behavior, not only violent crime or the crimes of the poor.

Sutherland stated his theory in a series of propositions that were designed to have universal application across culture and time. His theory-building approach differed from those of early psychologists in that he tried to explain criminal behavior, not behavior in general. Nevertheless, he was not constrained by the adjective "criminal." In fact, he argued strongly that many behaviors that society does not label crimes really *should be* crimes. He was directing this argument particularly at corporations and individuals who violated the laws of regulatory agencies, such as the Food and Drug Administration or the Federal Trade Commission. Although these were administrative or civil violations and not technically crimes, Sutherland saw them as illustrations of criminal behavior that often had a more harmful effect on society than common street crimes. It should be noted, also, that Sutherland did not believe it was useful to distinguish between juvenile and adult criminal conduct. Sutherland believed that adult and juvenile offenders followed the same principles of development. Both juvenile and adult criminal behavior, he believed, were learned by exposure to events and persons conducive to the development of antisocial action.

Sutherland strongly endorsed the idea that criminal behavior is learned, not inherited, and that it is not due to psychopathology. Criminal behavior is learned in interactions with other persons. The social influences of associations with others dictate what one believes and does, according to Sutherland. The decision-making ability, thoughts, and unique cognitive features of an individual were irrelevant to Sutherland, as they had been to the classical behaviorist. "If a person is self-determinative, science is impossible and criminal behavior cannot be explained" (Sutherland, 1973, p. 43).

Sutherland's **differential association theory** is set forth in nine propositions, beginning with the proposition that "Criminal behavior is learned." The core of the theory can be found in proposition six: "A person becomes delinquent because of an excess of definitions favorable to violations of law over definitions unfavorable to violation of law. This is the principle of differential association" (Sutherland & Cressey, 1974). The term "association" signifies the critical importance that intimate contacts with others have in determining one's behavior. The term "differential" was introduced to emphasize the importance of a *ratio*, specifically of favorable to unfavorable definitions or contacts. The theory explains that adolescents become delinquents or adults become criminals because associations with criminal behavior patterns outnumber associations with anticriminal patterns. Sutherland did *not* postulate that persons engage in criminal conduct because they are simply exposed to criminal behavior patterns. Rather, individuals become criminals because of an *overabundance* of such associations, in comparison with noncriminal behavior patterns. The critical aspect of Sutherland's theory is that a higher *ratio* of associations with criminal behavior patterns promotes criminal activity in people. If the association ratio is in reverse (the ratio is in favor of noncriminal patterns over criminal patterns), the person will not be criminal. Furthermore, Sutherland did not say that persons become delinquent simply because of excessive associations with delinquents. The critical aspect lies in the associations one has with *patterns of behavior*, regardless of the character of the person presenting them. Adolescents can learn antisocial conduct from persons who are not criminals or delinquents (even from well-meaning parents) and can likewise learn anticriminal patterns from criminals and hard-core delinquents. A father may verbalize that it is wrong to break the law but may display a reckless disregard for the property of others. On the other hand, an individual labeled "delinquent" may demonstrate honesty and integrity in most situations and generally be a "good" model except for his or her rare transgressions.

Sutherland, continually refining his theory, found it necessary to qualify the term "association," because it was excessively broad and vague. A simple, differential ratio of criminal associations over anticriminal associations are not enough to explain criminal conduct. Therefore, Sutherland proposed that associations also vary in their frequency, duration, priority, and intensity. Frequency and duration are self-explanatory, though still not easy to measure. "Intensity" refers to the prestige and significance of the models with whom one associates. The behavior patterns of respected models have more influence (and thus are more "intense" in impact) than those of less respected models. "Priority" refers to Sutherland's belief that behavior learned in early childhood has more impact on a person's overall conduct than behavior learned later in life.

Let us stop at this point to illustrate the complexity of Sutherland's theory. Consider the case of six-year-old Preston, who had an excess of associations with firesetting behavior. Presumably, he would learn from these associations more than from associations with firefighters the following year. On the other hand, we could easily complicate this scenario by supposing that his uncle, to whom he has recently been introduced and whom he idolizes, happens to be a firefighter. Can this new intense association with noncriminal behavior patterns outweigh the earlier frequent associations? What appeared to be intuitively sensible has now become a Gordian knot.

Critics have identified many vague areas in Sutherland's theory. The theory's lack of clarity and precision makes empirical investigations nearly impossible to carry out, although researchers have attempted to test it. Even the later spokesperson for the theory, Donald R. Cressey, admitted (1960, p. 3): "The current statement of the theory of differential association is neither precise nor clear." Although the proposition that criminal behavior is learned has appeal, researchers have been at a loss to measure frequency, duration, intensity, and priority of associations.

In answer to some of the criticism, Sutherland asserted that criminal or delinquent behavior is not always a result of excessive associations with law-breaking behaviors. The tendency to engage in delinquency and crime may also be influenced by "opportunity." There are unexpected times when a person may be pushed toward criminal action, even without a high ratio of criminal-to-anti-criminal associations. Jock, a "good" 14-year-old with nary a police contact, visits his cousin Jay for a week. One evening, along with a group of Jay's cohorts, the cousins notice that a store is unattended. Jock steals a $622 camera and ends up in juvenile court. On the other hand, a delinquent with a strong propensity toward criminal action as a result of numerous associations with criminal patterns may not have the opportunity to engage in criminal conduct. Thus, in some cases, differential association is not a "sufficient" explanation for criminal behavior.

DIFFERENTIAL ASSOCIATION-REINFORCEMENT THEORY

When psychologists discuss social learning theory, they invariably cite Bandura and Rotter. When sociologists discuss social learning theory, they invariably cite Sutherland and Ronald Akers (1977, 1985; Burgess & Akers, 1966). Akers proposed a social learning theory of deviance that tries to integrate core ingredients of Skinnerian behaviorism, the social learning theory as outlined by Bandura, and the differential association theory of Edwin Sutherland. Akers calls his theory **differential association-reinforcement (DAR)**. He postulates that people learn to commit deviant acts through experiences with significant others.

As you will recall, Sutherland believed that criminal or deviant behavior is learned in the same way that all behavior is learned. The crucial factors are: (1) with whom a person associates; (2) for how long; (3) how frequently; (4) how personally meaningful the associations are; and (5) how early these social experiences occur in an individual's development. According to Sutherland, people observe, imitate, and manifest the needs and values of the subgroups with which they associate, a process, you will recall, he called differential association. If the attitudes and values learned are socially undesirable and if the behaviors are unlawful, and if these values and behaviors outweigh desirable and lawful attitudes and behaviors, the individual is likely to engage in unlawful activities. Note that deviant or delinquent behavior does not invariably develop out of association or contacts with "bad companions" or a criminal element. The ratio factor is crucial. Contact with unlawful or deviant patterns must *outweigh* contacts with lawful patterns of behavior.

Sutherland's theory, although intuitively appealing, was widely criticized by criminologists, who found it vague and impossible to submit to empirical falsification. Burgess and Akers (1966) and ultimately Akers alone (1977, 1985) tried to correct some of these problems by reformulating differential association theory. Akers proposed that most deviant behavior is learned according to the stimulus-response principles outlined in classical behaviorism. Furthermore, the strength of the deviant behavior is a direct function of the amount, frequency, and probability of reinforcement the individual has experienced by performing the behavior in the past. The reinforcement may be positive or negative, in the Skinnerian meanings of the terms.

Critical to the Akers position is the role played by *social* reinforcement, in contrast to other forms of reinforcement. "[M]ost of the learning relevant to deviant behavior is the result of social interactions or exchanges in which the words, responses, presence, and behavior of other persons make reinforcers available, and provide the setting for reinforcement . . ." (Akers, 1977, p. 47). It is also important to note that most of these social reinforcements are symbolic. Very often these reinforcements are verbal rewards for participating in or for agreeing with group norms and expectations. For example, Dalton longs for acceptance by his "deviant" peers. He burglarizes his neighbor's home, a behavior in accordance with their norms, and is rewarded by their admiration and by entry into their social circle.

Deviant behavior, then, is most likely to develop as a result of social reinforcements given by significant others, usually within one's peer group. The group first adopts **normative definitions** about what conduct is good or bad, right or wrong, justified or unjustified. These normative definitions become internal, cognitive guides to what is appropriate and will most likely be reinforced by the group. In this sense, normative definitions operate as **discriminative stimuli**—social signals transmitted by subcultural or peer groups to indicate whether certain kinds of behavior will be rewarded or punished within a particular social context.

According to Akers, two classes of discriminative stimuli operate in promoting deviant behavior. First, "positive" discriminative stimuli are the signals (verbal and nonverbal) that communicate appropriate behaviors as determined by the subgroup. Not surprisingly, positive discriminative stimuli follow the principle of positive reinforcement: The individual engaging in them gains social rewards from the group. Akers's second type, "neutralizing" or "justifying" discriminative stimuli, neutralize society's warnings that certain behaviors are inappropriate or unlawful. According to Akers, they "make the behavior, which others condemn and which the person himself may initially define as bad, seem all right, justified, excusable, necessary, the lesser of two evils, or not 'really' deviant after all" (Akers, 1977, p. 521). Statements like "Society gave us a bum rap," "Cops are on the take; we just want our fair share," or "She deserved it" reflect the influence of neutralizing certain stimuli.

The more that people define their behavior as positive or justified, the more likely they are to engage in it. If the deviant activity (as defined by society at large) has been reinforced more than the conforming behavior (also defined by society) and if it has been justified, it is likely that deviant behavior will be maintained. In essence, behavior is guided by the norms the individual has internalized and for which he or she expects to be socially reinforced by significant others. Akers agrees with Bandura that modeling is a crucial factor in the initial acquisition of deviant behavior. Its continuation, however, will depend greatly upon the frequency and personal significance of social reinforcement, which comes from association with others.

Akers' theory has received its share of criticism. Some sociologists consider it tautological: Behavior occurs because it is reinforced, but it is reinforced because it occurs. Kornhauser (1978) declared that the theory was not empirically supported. Akers himself stressed the need for longitudinal research to test the theory and began to do such research himself in a series of studies of drug use among adolescents.

COGNITIVE AND MORAL DEVELOPMENT

In 1983 Albert Bandura added a significant clarification to social learning theory. He emphasized that individuals are able to exercise cognitive control over their behavior. In other words, the fact that behavior has been learned by imitation and maintained by reinforcement does not guarantee that it will be performed. This is not a new position taken by Bandura; it was in his earlier versions of the theory. However, it was an aspect that was frequently misunderstood.

From the social learning perspective, cognitive processes enable the individual to transcend the present and think about both the future and the past, even in the absence of immediate environmental stimuli. This conceptual ability allows the individual to guide his or her behavior by thinking about its possible outcomes. Nevertheless, circumstances do sometimes weaken cognitive control and facilitate "impulsive" actions. This self-regulatory process presumes the development and refinement of cognitive structures, to which we now turn.

Moral Development

How people acquire, internalize, and develop personal values are key concerns to some who study the delinquent. Some philosophers and social scientists argue that we develop our concepts of right and wrong through a series of cognitive stages, with the highest levels being reached through lifelong periods of logic and self-discovery. They contend that through the principles of logic and continual learning, humans can discover and cognitively construct ethical and moral principles of fairness, responsibility, and empathy toward others.

The most widely cited early research on moral character was conducted in 1924 by Hugh Hartshorne, a professor of religious education at the University of Southern California, and Mark A. May, a professor of psychology at Columbia University. They examined the qualities of honesty, generosity, and self-control in children. To their surprise, they discovered that these desirable traits, which they associated with moral behavior, were *not* consistent across situations. Instead, they found that a child may conduct him- or herself in a moral fashion in one situation but not in a different situation. Hartshorne and May concluded that no child is universally honest or dishonest, generous or selfish, self-controlled or impulsive. Instead, conduct is largely controlled by the situation.

For many years, the Hartshorne–May data were used to support assumptions that behavior is situational. Later statistical analyses of the Hartshorne–May data revealed that the researchers' original conclusion of situation specificity may have been unjustified, however (Burton, 1963, 1976; Eysenck, 1977). The current research suggests that although the situation often plays an extremely powerful role in determining what individuals do, personality components, including the influence of learning, also play a crucial role. The question becomes, does one outweigh the other?

Subsequent investigations of moral development focused on moral judgment and reasoning. The Swiss psychologist Jean Piaget (1948) was a pioneer in studying how we symbolize and organize social rules and make judgments based on that organization. He hypothesized that morality develops in a series of steps or stages, each one depending on the completion of previous steps and upon the intellectual equipment and social experiences of the individual. Much of Piaget's thinking was strongly influenced by the forgotten James Mark Baldwin, whom he freely acknowledged throughout his works. The developmental psychologist Lawrence Kohlberg (1976) revised Piaget's theory and revived research in moral development. Like Piaget, Kohlberg postulated that moral development evolves in sequential stages. The sequence is *invariant*, with each stage following another in an orderly fashion. "Invariant" in this context means that a person cannot reach a higher stage without going through earlier stages in an orderly, progressive sequence. The individual must develop the features and skills of a lower moral stage before attaining a higher one. Before we can appreciate *why* society needs rules and regulations, we have to learn what behaviors are approved or disapproved.

Kohlberg identified three primary stages: **preconventional**, **conventional**, and **postconventional**. Each primary stage comprises two substages, which we will refer to here as "early" and "late." During the **early preconventional** stage, the child acts only to obtain rewards and avoid punishment. In essence, the child has not developed any moral reasoning and is basically amoral. According to Kohlberg, this amoral orientation characterizes children below age seven, but it may be seen at any age in some individuals. During the **late preconventional** stage, the right action is that which satisfies one's own needs. This stage reflects a selfish orientation that considers the needs of others only to the extent that favors will be returned. In other words, the individual will be helpful or ostensibly "moral" to others only when it clearly serves his or her personal interests. According to Kohlberg (1976, 1977), human relationships at this stage are viewed not with loyalty, gratitude, or justice but with the goal of using others to obtain something.

The **early conventional** stage is referred to as the "good boy" or "good girl" orientation. The individual's behavior is directed toward gaining social approval and acceptance, especially from peers, and he or she conforms to a stereotyped image of what the majority of the cultural group regards as acceptable behavior. To obtain social rewards and avoid punishment, a person at this stage believes that she or he must conform precisely to what is expected. The conscience, or the ability to feel guilty, begins to emerge. At the **late conventional** stage the person acts out of duty and respect for the authority of others. Certain rules and regulations are acknowledged as necessary to ensure the smooth functioning of society; if one is derelict in performing his or her duty, dishonor and blame will result. This late conventional state is often labeled "law and order" morality, because of its strong emphasis on unquestioning respect for authority, conventionalism, and rigid rules of conduct.

The final and highest primary stage of moral developmen—the postconventional—is, in Kohlberg's estimation, reached by few people. To reach these stages one must have the cognitive ability to abstract and to perceive issues in "gray shades" rather than in a strict "black and white" dichotomy. During the **early postconventional** stage, correct action is determined by principles that reflect an appreciation for the general rights of individuals as well as the standards that have been critically examined and agreed on by society. Note that there is a strong assumption running throughout Kohlberg's theory that there is consensus in society about what is right and wrong.

Kohlberg believed that individuals at the early postconventional stage had achieved a mature balancing of individual and societal rights. In addition to considering what is democratically agreed upon, the early postconventional person relies on personal values to consider the rightness and wrongness of behavior. These personal values may not be in agreement with those of society. Kohlberg asserted that individuals act in accordance with the laws but also believe that unjust laws can be changed.

The **late postconventional** person demonstrates an orientation "toward the decisions of conscience and toward self-chosen ethical principles appealing to logical comprehensiveness, universality, and consistency" (Kohlberg, 1977, p. 63). The moral principles are highly abstract and ethical, and they reflect universal principles of justice as well as the reciprocity and equality of human rights. Persons at the late postconventional stage rely on their own personally developed ethical principles and show respect for the dignity of human beings as individuals.

According to Kohlberg, people go through the stages at different rates and thus reach them at different ages of their lives. Some never go beyond the preconventional stage, and most never reach the postconventional. The development of moral judgment depends on intellectual capacity and life experiences. Thus, someone may possess the cognitive ability to develop high stages of moral development but lack sufficient social experiences. On the other hand, despite adequate moral upbringing, the individual may lack the cognitive ability to abstract and generalize the moral principles involved at the higher stages. It is unclear, however, what constitutes "adequate" moral upbringing or "adequate" life experiences. Kohlberg contends that a large majority of juvenile delinquents are at the preconventional stage (Kohlberg & Freundlich, 1973).

It is important to realize that Kohlberg's theory is specifically related to moral *judgment* and the person's rationale for his or her behavior. Although an outside observer may view an act as unethical or immoral, the individual may perceive his or her action as morally sound. Therefore, Kohlberg argues that we must try to understand *intentions* before we draw conclusions about another's *actions*.

Kohlberg measured moral development by presenting his subjects with dilemmas and asking them to choose a solution and explain why they chose it. One item on the test reads:

> In Europe, a woman was near death from a special kind of cancer. There was one drug that the doctors thought might save her. It was a form of radium that a druggist in the same town had recently discovered. The drug was expensive to make, but the druggist was charging 10 times what the drug cost him to make. He paid $200 for the radium and charged $2,000 for a small dose of the drug. The sick woman's husband, Heinz, went to everyone he knew to borrow the money, but he could only get together about $1,000, which is half of what it cost. He told the druggist that his wife was dying and asked him to sell it cheaper or let him pay him later. But the druggist said, "No, I discovered the drug and I'm going to make money from it." So Heinz gets desperate and considers breaking into the man's store to steal the drug for his wife (Colby et al., 1983, p. 75).

The subject is then asked such questions as "Should Heinz steal the drug?" and "Why or why not?"

For his doctoral dissertation, Kohlberg administered his moral development test to boys in custody awaiting juvenile hearings. He found that they were at lower levels of moral development than their nondelinquent peers. A high percentage of the boys in detention, who were charged with repetitive car theft, burglary, and assault and robbery, were functioning at the preconventional stage. Later, Kohlberg (1978) concluded that the conventional stage insulates the adolescent against social pressures toward delinquency. In other words, at the conventional stage the adolescent's cognitive development has matured to a point where internal reasoning overrides outside influence. Adolescents with more principled normative reasoning are better able to think through their own options for each situation, relatively independent of social pressures.

Research support for Kohlberg's theory has depended on the sample of adolescents used. Studies of institutionalized or officially labeled delinquents support his theory, whereas studies using self-report data do not. Hudgins and Prentice (1973) discovered that boys with official delinquency records (such as repetitive auto theft or burglary) exhibited lower moral development than boys with no official records. Interestingly, although mothers of both groups scored higher than their sons on a moral development scale, the mothers of delinquent sons scored lower than the mothers of nondelinquent sons. (How the *fathers* scored is left unsaid.) Campagna and Harter (1975) compared the moral development of institutionalized delinquent boys who had the temperamental and behavioral characteristics of a conduct disorder (impulsivity, hyperactivity, pathological lying) with that of nondelinquent boys. They found that the delinquent boys were significantly lower in moral reasoning than their matched peers. Moreover, the delinquent boys, compared with their matched peers, scored significantly lower in all verbal sections of an IQ test (Wechsler Intelligence Scale for Children), suggesting that they had less adequate language skills and vocabulary. (Recall that one of Kohlberg's requirements for higher levels of moral development is good abstract ability.) Jurkovic and Prentice (1977), using 120 institution-alized delinquent boys, found that psychopathic delinquents lagged consider-ably behind both nonpsychopathic delinquent boys and nondelinquent peers in moral reasoning.

All the studies mentioned here used subjects who had been adjudicated juvenile delinquents for serious offenses. Merry Morash (1981) went a step fur-ther. She studied 201 youths charged with committing misdemeanors or minor juvenile offenses. All were white males, 14 to 16 years of age. Morash adminis-tered Kohlberg's moral development scale as well as a self-report survey devel-oped by Elliott and Voss (1974) to measure the extent of the youths' prior delin-quent behavior. When the results of the self-report questionnaire were taken into account, Morash found that most of the boys (78 percent) were functioning at the conventional stage of moral development rather than at the preconventional stage, in contrast to what Kohlberg would have predicted.

Delorto and Cullen (1985) tested moral development theory on a sample of 109 high school students from a rural Illinois community. They measured delin-quency with the self-report scale developed by Elliott and Ageton (1980) and moral reasoning with Rest's Defining Issues Test (DIT) (Rest, 1979). The DIT con-sists of 6 hypothetical scenarios of moral dilemmas (similar to the druggist exam-ple described earlier). Respondents read stories and then completed 12 questions that followed. On the self-report survey, students were asked if they had commit-ted any of 45 listed offenses within the last year, running from very minor offens-es to serious ones. The delinquency score was compiled in relation to the number of different offenses in which they had participated. In line with Elliott and Ageton, the researchers grouped the overall delinquency measures into 6 sub-scales. One subcategory related to predatory crimes against persons, and another involved hard drug use. Both subcategories represent serious offenses. The other 4 subcategories consisted almost exclusively of minor offenses. Most of the Elliott–Ageton scale (both versions) taps minor delinquency, a point we should very much keep in mind. Unfortunately, Delorto and Cullen did not ask the sub-jects how often they engaged in the listed offenses.

The Delorto–Cullen data did not reveal any association between self-report delinquency and moral reasoning, a finding that held for both minor offenses and serious offenses. This is not surprising because, as noted in Chapter 1, self-report measures of delinquency suggest that a very large proportion of the adolescent population commits acts that may be defined as "minor delinquent." A delin-quency–moral development connection is more likely to surface in self-report studies that measure chronic or repetitive serious offense. Delorto and Cullen did not measure this aspect of juvenile offending. However, the research that has con-centrated on repetitive serious offenders has found signs that moral reasoning is linked to delinquency (see Jennings et al., 1983). In a statistical review of the liter-ature on morality and delinquency, Nelson, Smith, and Dodd (1990) report that the moral reasoning of juvenile delinquents appears lower relative to that of non-delinquents. One factor that is not clear from the review, however, is to what extent repetitive violent offenders (life-course-persistent offenders) differ from other offenders (adolescence-limited offenders) in their moral development. The LCP and AL difference is a critical factor and needs to be examined in future research dealing with moral development.

Criticisms of Kohlberg's Theory

Albert Bandura (1977) and other social learning theorists question Kohlberg's contention that moral development follows a universal and invariant stage sequence of cognitive construction. Bandura argues that moral judgment can be acquired and modified through imitative and observational learning processes, including the powerful influence of peer models. Although he admits that personal experiences and changing social demands produce cognitive development with age, he considers "universal" stage development of morality far-fetched. Moral reasoning is highly dependent on culture and the social milieu, and it is surely unique for each individual. The stages of morality constructed by Kohlberg, if anything, reflected *his* personal construct systems and beliefs. They represent what he as a theorist conceived of as the correct way of dealing with certain issues. Social learning theorists contend that it is unlikely that the Kohlberg stages represent universal, transcultural, and transtemporal principles that reside in nature as a given form of "natural justice."

Others have proposed theories of moral reasoning and judgment not dependent on universal stages. For example, the researchers Carol Gilligan (1982), Norma Haan (1977, 1978), and Merry Morash (1983) have all theorized that an additional, "other-oriented" dimension is needed to explain moral conduct. Gilligan calls this dimension "contextual relativism," Haan calls it "interpersonal morality," and Morash prefers "other-oriented reasoning." Regardless of the label used, each dimension focuses upon the extent to which a person has developed responsibility, concern, and care for others. The other-oriented dimension appears to have considerable validity in helping us understand the behavior of delinquents. For example, highly aggressive children and those with conduct disorders often show a deficit in affective perspective taking (that is, understanding the emotions of others) and social perspective taking (that is, understanding the reasoning of another) (Dodge, 1993b).

Gilligan believes there are gender differences in these areas. She argues that men tend to focus on abstract, rational principles such as justice and respect for the rights of others. Women, on the other hand, tend to see morality more as a matter of caring and compassion and are more concerned about general human welfare.

Other researchers studying the other-oriented dimension have also reported intriguing findings with respect to gender differences. They contend, for example, that boys develop an ethic of care for others at a later time than girls, usually sometime after adolescence (Morash, 1983). Research by Hoffman (1977) indicates that empathy is better developed in females than males at all ages, although Eisenberg and Lennon (1983) point out that this finding may be attributed to Hoffman's method of measurement. More specifically, self-report questionnaires consistently revealed that females were more empathetic than males, but behavioral observations showed few gender differences. Males may be more reluctant to admit that they care. Gender differences could shed light on the consistent finding that males commit proportionately more violent crime than females.

Morash (1983) notes that the family is especially important in developing concern, empathy, and an other-oriented perspective in children. Interestingly, Kohlberg (1969) emphasized the substantial importance of inductive reasoning as a stimulus for moral development while insisting that family life in general had minimal or no importance (Morash, 1983). We will discuss family influences on delinquency in considerable detail in the next chapter.

CONSTRUCT SYSTEMS

Several decades ago, the psychologist George A. Kelly (1955) began to write about personal constructs, which he conceived of as basic mental building blocks that represent individualized versions of the world. He suggested that all of one's present interpretations of the universe and social world are forever subject to revision or replacement. Objective reality and absolute truth are figments of the imagination. Each of us acquires new experiences that lead us to restructure and reinterpret our environment. This process of experiencing, interpreting, and structuring is referred to as "construing." Those constructs that seem to make sense of the world we keep; those that do not, we discard.

Nelson Goodman (1978) explained human thought in similar fashion when he referred to "worldmaking." Each person constructs a personal world on the basis of his or her own experience and unique mental structure. There are many world versions, and it is foolhardy to presume that these versions can be reduced to a single, common perspective.

The anthropologist Edward Sapir (1921) hypothesized that a person's thinking processes are structured, if not controlled, by the properties of the language he or she speaks. The language habits of our community, culture, or subculture predispose us to what we see, hear, or otherwise experience. Sapir's student Benjamin Lee Whorf (1956) developed his mentor's ideas further by hypothesizing that no individual is free to describe nature with absolute impartiality. Rather, we are all constrained to certain modes of interpretation by the properties of our language and our habitual ways of thinking. Sapir and Whorf believe that the language used by a group is a principal determinant of the belief structures and the ways of thinking of that population. One's language is the guide to social reality.

Children's construct systems vary with age. As experiences with the environment accumulate, the number, quality, and organization of these constructs likewise change. Over the course of development, interpersonal construct systems should become: (1) increasingly differentiated (contain a greater number of constructs); (2) increasingly abstract (contain constructs pertaining to the more psychological, subtle aspects of other persons and their motives); (3) increasingly organized (contain constructs that are more interconnected with one another); and (4) increasingly perspectivistic (contain constructs less directed at self-involvement and self-reference) (Werner, 1957; Applegate et al., 1985). Research in cognitive psychology has provided consistent support for these theoretical propositions (Applegate et al., 1985).

Contemporary research has found that aggressive antisocial children process social information differently from the way other children do (Reid, 1993). This tendency appears to begin during the preschool years in most children. Highly aggressive children, for instance, repeatedly fail to respond adaptively to minor provocations of others. They seem to have a "hostile attribution bias" in ambiguous situations and are inclined to perceive even slight transgressions of others as threatening. Unclear intentions from peers are often met with aggressive overreactions. Highly aggressive children appear to be less equipped cognitively for dealing with ambiguous or conflict situations. Research strongly indicates that highly aggressive and antisocial children possess biases and cognitive deficits for dealing with others and in their social problem solving (Pepler, Byrd, & King, 1991). Research also shows that delinquent offenders are deficient in being able cognitively to put themselves in the place of others (Pepler, Byrd, & King, 1991). They are deficient in role-taking skills and lack the ability to empathize. As a result, these youths are less concerned about the negative consequences of violence, such as the suffering of the victim or their possible rejection by peers.

Some people seem to possess more structure about the world than others; this is another way of saying that some people are more cognitively complex. People with many sophisticated structures evaluate behavior and world events in more complex ways than people with a few, crude structures. Nevertheless, one's language, cultural background, cognitive sophistication, and, more generally, one's versions of the world are all likely to have an extremely important connection to delinquency. For example, Charles King (1975) conducted a qualitative study of 10 adolescent murderers whose average age was 14 years. The 9 boys and 1 girl had committed unusually brutal murders (e.g., a dismembering with a machete, a gasoline burning) that appear senseless to an outsider. To the consternation of authorities, none of the teenagers had expressed any guilt or remorse. Their families, although intact, were characterized by turmoil, conflict, and excessive drinking by caretakers. Parents and caretakers exhibited unpredictable mood swings and physical violence, especially when drinking.

On the basis of interview data, King determined that these youngsters were "confused" about their environment, viewing it as chronically hostile and largely unpredictable. Most surprising, however, were the psychological evaluations. Although these adolescents had average IQ scores, ". . . every youth was most severely retarded in reading, and drastically stunted in language skills" (p. 136). This finding led King to conclude that lack of language skills and cognitive constructs may have interfered with the youths' ability to interpret and interface adequately with the world. Such cognitive deficits, he believed, contributed to poor judgment and little realization of the consequences for their actions. Furthermore, these youngsters seemed to be unable to conceptualize their victims as persons. To the offenders, the victims were merely nonperson objects or targets. King maintains that the poverty of language may have directly contributed to the adolescents' actions. Their versions of the world seemed to be simplistic, black-and-white conceptions in which hostility reigned and compassion was for "suckers."

This study illustrates the potential value of studying language development and the construct systems of serious delinquents. Far-reaching generalizations from a single study are, of course, unwarranted. Furthermore, we are not implying that "intelligent people" do not commit crimes. Rather, individuals with limited cognitive constructs and language skills may be less able to mediate and get along in their social worlds, compared with others with a richer cognitive structure and process.

LABELING THEORY

Cognitive constructs are the basic foundation of the labeling perspective. It was Frank Tannenbaum's 1938 book *Crime and the Community* that contained the seeds of the **labeling perspective**. In it, Tannebaum argued that the proper study of crime and delinquency was not the behavior itself but society's reaction to it. Tannenbaum maintained that once individuals are "tagged" or labeled deviants or delinquents, others begin to see them as such and treat them accordingly. The reactions of others become the primary source of the individual's conduct. "The process of making the criminal, therefore, is a process of tagging, defining, identifying, segregating, describing, emphasizing, making conscious and self conscious; it becomes a way of stimulating, suggesting, emphasizing, and evoking the very traits that are complained of . . . the person becomes the thing he is described as being" (Tannenbaum, 1938, pp. 19–20).

Tannenbaum believed that, initially, children are usually involved merely in mischief, but some are labeled "bad" as a result. These children then come to see themselves as bad and to take on the role behaviors associated with "badness." This process, which he called "the dramatization of evil," was a slow and gradual one and represented the transformation of an offender's self-identity as a doer of mischief to a doer of evil. As the community's definition of a youth changed from one who occasionally misbehaves to one who is a delinquent, so the youth's own self-definition changes. Eventually the youth comes to believe that he or she is basically evil, quite possibly beyond salvation.

Edwin M. Lemert was one of the earliest to outline in detail the labeling perspective, which he preferred to call the "societal reaction perspective," in his book *Social Pathology* (1951). *Social Pathology* was not taken seriously by criminologists and sociologists in general until ten years after its publication. During the 1960s, the labeling perspective gained favor under the influence of Howard S. Becker, Erving Goffman, John Kitsuse, Kai T. Erikson, and Edwin Schur.

In *Social Pathology*, Lemert distinguished between two kinds of deviant behavior, primary and secondary deviation. **Primary deviation** is neither identified nor punished by anyone in authority. In a sense, it is "hidden" or "secret." Although the behavior violates a norm, it remains undetected and thus escapes the reactions of others. In Lemert's view, deviant behavior in society is ubiquitous and secret, because most forbidden behavior goes unobserved and unsanctioned. Not even the offender may consider the behavior representative of inner personality or self-concept. Consider Kingston, who regularly and skillfully lifts CDs from the unattended music counter in a nationwide chain store and has never been apprehended. According to Lemert, Kingston may not see himself as a thief; he sees his "violations" as really not violations at all but as occasional lapses of forgetfulness, reactions to boredom, or an adventure peripheral to his cognitive constructs, his perceptions of himself. They are, in essence, behaviors largely foreign to Kingston's "true self." Sykes and Matza (1957), in contrast, would say that Kingston "neutralized" temporarily his own standards of conduct and that he would likely experience some guilt.

Rule-breaking behavior profoundly changes the individual when it receives negative recognition from the outside world. Detection of Kingston's conduct by the store detective begins to change his self-image. The unpleasant identity of "thief" or "delinquent," even if not officially imposed by a juvenile court, prompts Kingston to defend his actions as nothing serious or not in character: "I am not a thief!" However, with continued societal reactions to the transgressions—notification of police and/or parents, contact with a juvenile court judge—Kingston gradually comes to believe that he is, in fact, a thief. Gradually, Kingston incorporates these "societal reactions" into his existing cognitive structure. It is at this point, according to Lemert, that he may begin to do the things and play the role that others associate with him. Kingston then enters into a pattern of additional violations of the norms, or what Lemert calls **secondary deviance**. "When a person begins to employ his deviant behavior or a role based upon it as a means of defense, attack, or adjustment to the . . . problems created by the consequent societal reaction, his deviation is secondary" (Lemert, 1951, p. 76).

There is, then, a significant difference between the experience of one who shoplifts and is not caught and one who is certified a thief. Secondary deviance affects the self-concept or inner belief system as well as the performance of social roles. Lemert stressed, however, that secondary deviance does not follow from a single reaction to an individual but rather after a long and sustained process. Kingston is a good candidate for secondary deviance after his parents do not let him forget what happened. Lemert believed that we tend to see ourselves as others see us and tend to act on this self-definition. The person labeled deviant comes to see him- or herself as deviant and to behave accordingly. Labeling leads to "symbolic reorganization" (or construct rearrangement). Primary deviance, which is not detected, usually does not affect one's self-concept or social roles, nor does it initiate symbolic reorganization.

Being publicly or officially labeled a deviant is socially stigmatizing, adversely affecting social relationships and opportunities. The young vandal may find her circle of nondelinquent friends dwindling if parents warn their children not to associate with her. Employers rarely hire known deviants or delinquents. Thus, according to Lemert, the initial societal reactions precipitate a chain of events, perceptions, identities, and actions that call forth new interactions that reinforce the delinquent label. "Interactions" is a critical word here, because it underscores the complicated interplay of the deviance process. It transforms "deviance" from a simple cause-and-effect relationship—you steal, therefore you are a thief—to a complex process that continually feeds on the individual's own constructs along with those of others.

Lemert believed that the "societal reaction process" is affected by many factors, including age, gender, SES, race, manner of dress, and neighborhood. Each may influence the responses of legal authorities to the young offender. For example, the police officer who realizes that a youth is the son in one of the model (and powerful) families in the community may be more likely to ignore his behavior. Youth from less powerful families, perceived as "continually breeding trouble," will not have that advantage.

In 1979, Lemert credited Howard Becker as the real initiator of the labeling perspective. "Becker's ideas of labeling took precedence over mine so far as popular acceptance and recognition were concerned. At the same time his writings seem to have been the target for more criticism than mine" (Lemert, 1983, p. 125). Lemert also admitted that he became uninterested in the societal reaction approach because ". . . it was becoming too psychological" (Lemert, 1983, p. 126). It was never developed to its full potential to show the reciprocal effects of the labeling process, Lemert said. Instead, it focused too much on the self-concept issue and not enough on the interplay with the labelers. "Without looking at this—the way the labeled persons respond, and problems created for the agents of social control by their responses—it is difficult to study changes in patterns of deviance, policy, and social control" (Lemert, 1983, p. 126).

Lemert would likely say that we are illustrating his point by placing the labeling perspective in a chapter that focuses on the individual rather than on the macrolevel. Recall that we began this section with the statement that cognitive constructs are the basic foundation of the labeling perspective. This statement reflects the premise that the individual's reactions to being tagged as a deviant are at the root of the deviant behavior, even though there is a continual process of labeling and relabeling. Lemert, like Tannenbaum before him and Becker after him, wanted to put *those who do the labeling* at the root of the behavior.

Lemert's observation concerning the popularity and influence of Becker's writings is probably an accurate one. Becker's book *Outsiders* (1963) was one of the two most frequently cited criminology books of the period between 1945 and 1972 (Downes & Rock, 1982). The term "outsiders" refers to those people who are judged deviant by others and therefore stand outside the circle of "normal" members of a group. Becker, more than Lemert, succeeded in moving deviance far "outside" of the individual, treating it not as a quality of the person or his or her acts but as a social problem. The police, the courts, correctional personnel, and welfare agencies are the principal culprits; their labeling and dehumanizing produced deviance in those they considered outside mainstream society. These stigmatizing social labels placed on the rule violator by institutional powers push the offender into additional deviant behavior, a deviant way of life, and, basically, a deviant identity.

Although Lemert delineated two categories of deviants, primary and secondary, Becker (1963) outlined four: (1) those who have violated a rule and have been sanctioned, or the "pure" deviants; (2) those who have violated a rule but have escaped sanction for the violation, the so-called secret deviants—they have committed improper acts not noticed or reacted to by others; (3) those who have not violated a rule but who have been negatively sanctioned anyway—this category includes the falsely accused, such as a girl labeled a delinquent because her two best friends have a record of police contacts; and (4) those who have neither violated a rule nor been negatively sanctioned. The last category represents conforming behavior. Becker was recognizing that conforming behavior, under certain conditions, may be deviant behavior, as when someone obeys orders beyond the commander's intentions. An example would be an instance in which a subordinate takes it upon himself to do things he thinks his commander wants done, although the commander did not have that intention.

The most controversial type is Becker's "hidden deviant," who differed from the primary deviant described by Lemert. According to Becker, secret deviants have so labeled themselves, even though others are unaware of their behavior. For example, Becker describes the sadomasochistic fetish market that not only publishes expensive, high-quality catalogues, but has a large clientele as well. A person who is detected using these fetishes for sexual pleasure may be labeled a "sexual deviant," but the thousands of individuals who browse through and purchase items from the catalogue but who remain undetected are examples of secret deviants.

Becker also makes the distinction between a "master status" and a "subordinate status" to emphasize that some statuses in a society override all others and have a certain priority. Race, he said, is an example. According to Becker, membership in the black race normally takes priority over other status considerations. Regardless of whether a person is a physician, a plumber, a lawyer, a husband, or a wife, being black remains the master status for many African Americans in American society. This same "master status" identity may develop for deviants. If one received the status of "deviant" as a result of breaking rules, this self-identification may come to be more important in one's daily life than other "subordinate" statuses combined.

Becker was trying to shift the focus from the individual being labeled deviant to the society that imposes the label. "[S]ocial groups create deviance by making the rules whose infraction constitutes deviance, and by applying those rules to particular people and labeling them as outsiders" (1963, p. 9). The rules themselves are enforced differentially, therefore, depending upon who is breaking them.

George Vold (1979) notes that the labeling perspective has been criticized on several fronts. First, it overemphasizes the importance of the official labeling process. Second, it assumes that deviants resent the deviant label. Actually, perhaps particularly in the case of juveniles, deviance may allow the person to gain status or approval from peers or even from significant adults. Third, reducing the labeling process may create more crime than it eliminates, because it waters down the effect of general deterrence. This criticism assumes that most people do not commit crime because they fear the stigma that would result, a questionable assumption in light of the research on general deterrence.

COGNITIVE CONSTRAINTS AND NEUTRALIZATIONS

Under normal circumstances, we perceive, interpret, compare, and act on the basis of cognitive structures, which we will refer to here as personal standards. If we do not like what we are doing, we can change our behavior, justify it, or try to stop thinking about it. We can also reward and punish ourselves for our conduct. Self-punishment is expressed as guilt or remorse following actions we consider alien to our standards. In most instances, however, we prefer self-reinforcement to self-punishment; therefore, we behave in ways that correspond to our cognitive structures. We anticipate the feelings of guilt we will experience for "bad" actions and thus restrain ourselves. Therefore, each of us develops personal standards or codes of conduct that are maintained by self-reinforcement or self-punishment, as well as by external reinforcement and punishment. Walter C. Reckless's "containment theory" addresses the balance between internal (cognitive) and external controls of behavior, and Sykes and Matza talk about psychological neutralizations of internal controls. We now turn our attention to these two theories.

Containment Theory

Walter C. Reckless (1961, 1973) describes delinquent and nondelinquent behavior as "functions" of personality and social/family influences, both of which serve to "contain" the individual. This "containment theory" is based on two sources of constraints. One source originates from within the person, a kind of self-regulatory mechanism that prevents us from acting out our impulses or desires. This source is called "inner" containment. A second source originates from outside the person and is found within the social institutions of the family, friends, church, school, and generally the community. This source, which represents informal social control, is termed "outer" containment.

Reckless assumes that strength in one source of containment compensates for weaknesses in the other. For example, a youngster with strong inner containment—which Reckless describes variously as self-concept, goal orientation, frustration tolerance, sense of responsibility, and resistance to distractions—will be prevented from engaging in delinquent behavior, even under circumstances of weak external containment. Outer containment, in order to be strong, must offer effective supervision and discipline and a reasonable set of social expectations and activities, as well as good social role models. Similarly, if inner containment is weak, a strong outer containment will compensate and hold the adolescent in check.

Reckless acknowledges that in our mobile society, with external circumstances changing frequently, the individual is forced to rely upon internal standards more than ever. Hence, Reckless affirms, the most important prevention of delinquency in contemporary society is the development of strong inner constraints. Of greatest importance in inner containment, Reckless tells us, is a solid self-concept, a product of favorable socialization by parents or parent figures.

Reckless and Dinitz (1967) tested the role of self-concept in delinquency using a group of predominantly white boys living in high-delinquency areas of Columbus, Ohio. Reckless and Dinitz found that, over a four-year period, boys with a "good" self-concept, as measured by an inventory of self-concept developed by the investigators, had significantly fewer contacts with the juvenile court system compared with boys with a poor self-concept. Reckless and Dinitz concluded that a good self-concept is ". . . indicative of a residual favorable socialization and a strong inner self, which in turn steers the individual away from bad companions and street corner society, toward middle class values, and to awareness of the possibility of upward movement in the opportunity structure" (p. 196).

Containment theory does offer a plausible explanation for some delinquent behavior. For example, it is reasonable to assume that some juveniles resist serious and even minor delinquent behavior, even given ample opportunity in a high-crime area, because of strong inner containment. But why do some juveniles with strong outer containments or informal social controls, such as found in middle-class and upper-class cohesive, stable families and neighborhoods, engage in delinquent behavior? According to containment theory, the strong outer constraints provided by such environments should override any factors of a weaker inner containment, and delinquency should not occur. Likewise, why do some juveniles in high-delinquency areas (weak outer containment) who give every indication of also having weak inner containment (poor self-concept, lack of goals, etc.) remain uninvolved in self-reported delinquency or officially-recorded delinquent acts?

Containment theory is also weak in clearly defining inner and outer containment. Reckless throws in an armory of vague terms to describe each, but direct measurement of them is nearly impossible. This may be one reason why the theory, although often cited, has drawn exceedingly little research.

Techniques of Neutralization

The criminologists Gresham Sykes and David Matza (1957) enumerated five major strategies people use to avoid self-blame and blame from others. These are common methods used, alone or in combination, to separate or disjoin our construct systems from our action. Sykes and Matza called these personal strategies **techniques of neutralization** and applied them specifically to delinquents. They are: denial of injury, denial of the victim, denial of responsibility, condemnation of the condemners, and appeal to higher loyalties. Sykes and Matza believed that delinquents are at least partially committed to the dominant social order and therefore susceptible to experiencing guilt or shame when they engage in deviant acts. However, they protect themselves from these unpleasant feelings by rationalizing that their violations are acceptable.

According to Sykes and Matza, each delinquent has a preferred strategy that he or she applies across situations. A youth may excuse his act of vandalism, for example, by convincing himself (and others) that "I didn't really hurt anybody." The youth is convinced that what he did was just "a prank" or that it constituted only "mischief." On the other hand, he might conclude that the person whose property has been damaged or destroyed can well afford it. Both reactions describe **denial of injury**. The **denial of the victim** technique usually is expressed in the form of rightful retaliation or punishment. The victim is transformed into one deserving of injury: "He had it coming to him."

Denial of responsibility involves such perceptions as "I couldn't help myself" or "I didn't mean it." Delinquents who use this strategy see themselves as billiard balls—or better yet, soccer balls—helplessly propelled or kicked from event to event. They are not actors as much as they are acted upon. **Condemnation of the condemners** includes the belief that "The cops are out to get me" or "Society gave me a bum rap." These delinquents shift attention away from their own deviant acts to the motives and behavior of those who disapprove of the violation. In this view, the condemners are often hypocrites and violators of the law themselves. Finally, the delinquent using **appeal to higher loyalties** will convince him- or herself, "I didn't do it for myself," or "I did it because my buddies and I are all in this together," or "My mother needed the money."

Sykes and Matza's theory is an offshoot of strain theory (to be discussed in Chapter 9), because it assumes that society has dominant values and that these have been internalized. In fact, these values may be internalized to such an extent that the techniques of neutralization are not effective enough to shield juveniles completely from their force and from the reactions of those around them who conform to the dominant values. Therefore, many—if not most—will suffer some shame and guilt about violating the rules of the dominant social order.

In Sykes and Matza's view, the learning of the techniques is a crucial step; such learning allows the juvenile to become delinquent in the first place. He or she has accepted the validity of the dominant value system and internalized it to a large extent. He or she then rationalizes to suspend the adopted values temporarily. This viewpoint is in direct opposition to the subcultural position, which argues that the delinquent rejects the values of the dominant culture and adopts and internalizes those of a particular subculture. The theory regards learning as important, but does not explain how the techniques are learned.

The Sykes and Matza position has some appeal, but it may not apply to very many situations. Moreover, it has not been tested to any great extent. Therefore, its validity as an explanation of delinquency remains unclaimed. In order for techniques of neutralization to have explanatory power, one would have to demonstrate that the delinquents employed these techniques *before* they committed their delinquent acts. Instead, they are used as justifications after the fact. While research examining techniques of neutralization as "causes" of delinquency is sparse, treatment programs directed at trying to change these constructs are widely used. For example, juvenile sex-offender treatment programs commonly try to get the juvenile to empathize with the victim and take responsibility for the behavior. We discuss these programs in Chapter 9.

IQ AND DELINQUENCY

In 1977, the criminologists Travis Hirschi and Michael Hindelang took the sociological perspective on delinquency to task for ignoring a persistent and statistically significant negative correlation between IQ scores and delinquency. After reviewing major official and self-report studies (e.g., Reiss & Rhodes, 1961; Hirschi, 1969; Wolfgang, Figlio, & Sellin, 1972; West & Farrington, 1973), Hirschi and Hindelang concluded that IQ was as strong a predictor of delinquency as social class and race. Throughout their literature search, they continually uncovered a negative correlation: The lower the IQ, the higher the incidence of delinquency, whether official or self-reported. In their article, Hirschi and Hindelang hypothesized that an *indirect* causal relationship exists between IQ and delinquency. By "indirect," the writers meant that a low IQ leads to poor performance and attitudes toward school, and these in turn lead to delinquency. A high IQ leads to good performance and attitudes toward school, and these in turn lead to conformity (or at least to nondelinquency). Thus, Hirschi and Hindelang saw school performance and attitudes as "intervening variables" that mediate between IQ and delinquency. Furthermore, they asserted that in spite of vehement denials of an IQ–delinquency relationship, most mainstream criminological theories implicitly assume that it exists.

Hirschi and Hindelang's 1977 paper is one of the most challenging and misunderstood in the modern literature on the relationship between IQ and delinquency. Ronald Simons (1978) accused the authors of reviving the long-forgotten connection between "genetic IQ" and delinquency, and he chastised Hirschi and Hindelang for concluding that IQ is a stable ability that is largely independent of cultural and social influences. A careful reading of the article reveals that Hirschi and Hindelang did *not* conclude that IQ is inherited or independent of cultural or social influences, however. If anything, their paper "pointedly ignores" heritability (Hirschi & Hindelang, 1978). The principal point that Hirschi and Hindelang made was that the inverse relationship between IQ score and delinquency continues to be substantiated in the research, *for whatever reason*. They urged criminologists to address the relationship and try to explain it rather than deny it exists. Interestingly, current research continues to support Hirschi and Hindelang's observation (see Neisser et al., 1996). The important question is, how should this persistent relationship be interpreted?

We must focus first on the meaning of "IQ." Traditionally, the term is an abbreviation of the **intelligence quotient** derived from a numerical score on an "intelligence test." The term originated out of what is now called, in psychology, the **psychometric approach**, which searches for psychological differences in people through the use of intelligence tests, scholastic aptitude tests, school achievement tests, personality inventories, and specific abilities tests. The tests are used for many purposes, such as selection, diagnosis, and evaluation. The psychometric approach is widely used by practicing psychologists and mental-health professionals (Neisser et al., 1996). Increasingly, the term "**psychometric intelli-**

gence," abbreviated **PI**, is preferred to the traditional term "IQ," primarily because the latter possesses a variety of surplus meanings.

The relationship between PI test scores and school performance is strong and consistent. "Wherever it has been studied, children with high scores on tests of intelligence tend to learn more of what is taught in school than their lower-scoring peers" (Neisser et al., 1996, p. 82). Teaching practices and what is taught are critical variables in the learning process. Children in Japan and China, for instance, know a great deal more math than American children even though their average intelligence test scores are similar (Stevenson & Stigler, 1992). Schools also help develop certain intellectual skills and attitudes. Quality schools generally have positive effects on intelligence scores, for example. Preschool programs (e.g., Headstart) show significant positive effects—and the most recent research in this area is promising in that the gains do not fade when the program is over as long as there is periodic intervention during the child's school years.

There is also a relationship between psychometric intelligence and years of education, and, to a lesser extent, between social status and income. Perhaps the most striking observation made by researchers in recent years is there has been a steady worldwide rise in PI scores. In what is known as the "Flynn effect" (after James Flynn who first noticed the increase), youth in technologically advanced countries have shown a gain of about three PI points per decade. In the United States, however, while psychometric intelligence continues to increase, scores on scholastic aptitude tests (such as the SAT) have decreased or, at best, remained the same.

Average PI scores also vary between ethnic groups. For example, many studies using different tests and samples typically show African Americans scoring significantly lower than whites (Neisser et al., 1996). Recent studies show that this psychometric-intelligence gap has been consistently decreasing since 1980 (Vincent, 1991). Asian Americans and whites, on average, score about the same on intelligence tests; Native Americans score slightly lower than the other groups on verbal skills, but this slight difference is likely a result of chronic middle-ear infections common among Native American children (McShane & Plas, 1984a, 1984b). Latinos, who make up the second-largest and fastest-growing minority group in the United States, typically score somewhere between African Americans and whites. It is unclear what these differences mean, but there is no evidence to support the view that ethnic differences in psychometric intelligence are due to genetics or biological factors. Although genetics *may* play a role in individual differences in psychometric intelligence, there is no evidence for ethnic *group* differences.

Group differences in psychometric intelligence are most likely due to a combination of factors, dominated by cultural and social influences. For example, according to Boykin (1986, 1994), the African American culture is often in conflict with the constriction and competition expected in American schools. To varying degrees, the black culture "includes an emphasis on such aspects of experience as spirituality, harmony, movement, verve, affect, expressive individualism, communalism, orality, and a socially defined time perspective" (Neisser et al., 1996, p. 95). According to Boykin, black children often find their cultural background in conflict with the culture of the school system, and consequently they become alienated from both the process and products of that educational system.

Poverty factors—such as poor nutrition, inadequate prenatal care, lack of adequate child-care facilities, and inaccessibity to educational, occupational, and training opportunities—also play critical but unknown roles. In the final analysis, we really don't know much about psychometric intelligence, although its relationship to socioeconomic status, educational level, and academic achievement does clearly exist.

The Concept of Intelligence

Although research has shown that juvenile delinquents as a group do not do well on standardized PI tests, people who work with them often find them "intelligent" in other areas, especially those activities that interest them. Brazilian street children, for example, are capable of doing the math required for survival in their street business even though they have failed mathematics in school (Carraher, Carraher, & Schliemann, 1985; Neisser, et al., 1996).

It is widely accepted that standardized intelligence tests do not sample all forms of intelligence, such as creativity, wisdom, practical sense, social sensitivity, and musical ability. Most psychologists today would agree that PI scores are strongly influenced by social, educational, and general culture background (Neisser et al., 1996). PI tests, then, are "culture biased," in spite of recurring efforts to develop culture-free instruments. Furthermore, PI scores typically are crude indices of mainstream language skills that are strongly influenced by academic and language development experiences. In general, rich and varied experiences increase PI scores, and limited experiences decrease them (Garbarino & Asp, 1981; Neisser, et al., 1996). School experiences, if positive, may increase language skills; if negative, they may stagnate, or even decrease, language skills. Rosenbaum (1975) assessed the effects of educational tracking or ability grouping on intellectual development and PI scores. The sample consisted of white, working-class high school youths, a choice that eliminated the potentially confounding variables of race and social class. The youths had been placed in one of five possible educational groupings (or tracks) based on past school performance. Rosenbaum discovered that the PIs of students who were in the lower three tracks declined, whereas those of students in the upper two educational tracks increased. In addition, the variance (or individual differences) of the upper two tracks increased, but it decreased in the lower three. Good environments and enhanced opportunity to refine mental constructs raised the PI averages and increased the differences, whereas less enriching environments and limited cognitive opportunity decreased the mean and variance (Garbarino & Asp, 1981). Thus, PI tests are largely measuring educational experiences, acquired skills, and attitudes. "Children who are unsuccessful in—and hence alienated from—school may be more likely to engage in delinquent behaviors for that very reason, compared to other children who enjoy school and are doing well" (Neisser et al., 1996, p. 83).

Multiple Forms of Intelligence

It is apparent that "Individuals differ from one another in their ability to understand complex ideas, to adapt effectively to the environment, to learn from experience, to engage in various forms of reasoning, to overcome obstacles by taking thought" (Neisser et al., 1996, p. 77). Furthermore, although these differences can be substantial, they are rarely consistent. A person's intellectual performance will vary on different occasions, in different domains, as judged by different criteria. The concept of "intelligence" is nothing more than an attempt to clarify and organize this complex set of phenomena (Neisser et al., 1996). So far, attempts at clearly and convincingly defining intelligence have not been successful. Ask two dozen prominent scientists studying the phenomenon of intelligence what "intelligence" is, and you will get two dozen different answers. However, there has been a concentrated effort in recent years to develop the idea of broader, multiple intelligences, rather than just one single intelligence, and for an appreciation of abilities that previously either were ignored or considered not very important in understanding human behavior.

Today, it is becoming increasingly apparent that intelligence exists in multiple forms and relates to a wide assortment of abilities. Howard Gardner in his book *Frames of Mind* (1983), for example, describes seven independent intelligences or talents. They are linguistic, logical-mathematical, spatial (used in getting from one place to another or in packing a suitcase), musical, bodily kinesthetic (such as what athletes and dancers have), insight into oneself, and understanding of others. Standard intelligence tests measure only the first three. Gardner added that there are probably many others. For example, how do we account for wisdom, synthesizing ability, intuition, metaphoric capacities, humor, and good judgment (Gardner, 1986, 1993)?

Gardner considered the last two of the seven—insight into oneself and understanding of others—features of **emotional intelligence**, and a deficiency in this form of intelligence may play a prominent role in human violence. Individuals who continually engage in violence may lack significant insight into their own behavior and possess little sensitivity toward others. They tend to misread emotional cues from others and become confused and angry in social situations.

Robert Sternberg's (1985) **triarchic theory** proposes three fundamental aspects of intelligence: analytic, creative, and practical. Whereas Gardner considered the seven intelligences to be largely independent of one another, Sternberg emphasizes the extent these three aspects work together. Moreover, the triarchic theory considers how experience interacts with them. Only the first—analytic or academic intelligence—has been tested to any great extent by mainstream intelligence testing. The second aspect of intelligence is the capacity to use problem-solving skills that require creative thinking, the ability to deal with new situations, and the ability to learn from experience. The third aspect is the capacity to use practical thinking skills that help a person adjust to and cope with his or her social and cultural environment.

Sternberg (1995) proposes that the three components of intelligence serve three functions in real-world contexts: adapting ourselves to our existing environments, shaping our existing environments to create new environments, and selecting new environments. "Intelligent" people know their strengths and weaknesses and find ways to capitalize on their strengths and either compensate for or remediate their weaknesses. For example, some youth may use their interpersonal skills to deal with and to create new environments, whereas others may use their athletic skills and physical prowess to do the same.

Summing Up

Howard Gardner (1983, pp. 17–18) summarizes incisively IQ and aptitude testing in general: ". . . the IQ movement is blindly empirical. It is based simply on tests with some predictive power about success in school and, only marginally, on a theory of how the mind works." Intelligence testing has been primarily, if not exclusively, concerned with establishing a predictive relationship between a score and grades in school. If a score on the exam predicts with *some* accuracy how well people do in school, then it is considered by many to be a "valid" and useful instrument. Most often, there is no further attempt to decipher how the mind works in obtaining that score. Intelligence tests, for example, rarely assess skill in assimilating new information or in solving new problems (Gardner, 1983).

It is extremely important that the distinction between psychometric intelligence and the many forms of other intelligence be carefully recognized. The so-called "IQ–delinquency connection" refers to a correlation between a test score and official and self-reported delinquency. The IQ–delinquency connection is not between the broader meaning of "intelligence" and delinquency, although some mistakenly make that inference. There is often very little match between intelligence tests and "intelligence" broadly defined. Moreover, the PI score will vary depending upon the type of test used, its content, the many attributes and conditions of the testing situation, the examinee's interpretation of the reasons for the testing, and so forth. Similarly, the definitions of juvenile delinquency used by the researchers will vary. Still, even with these variations, the mysterious inverse relationship occurs: As IQ goes down, the probability of misconduct goes up, and vice versa. But what this relationship means exactly remains unclear.

Hirschi and Hindelang (1977) postulated that IQ contributes to school failure, and this, in turn, contributes to delinquency. In another examination of this position, Menard and Morse (1984) discovered that "institutional practices" (such as tracking, promoting, and grading) contributed more to delinquency than did individual characteristics of school failure. Menard and Morse contend that PI scores and academic performance are linked to delinquent behavior only because of the responses of school officials to the different PI scores and the levels of academic performance. School officials may negatively label children with a low PI score. This initial labeling follows a child through his or her school career. The institutional practice of attaching a negative label and selectively denying access to desirable social roles may lead to delinquent behavior. Menard and Morse speculate that if these social reactions to low PI scores could be eliminated, the relationship between PI scores and delinquency might also be eliminated.

SUMMARY AND CONCLUSIONS

In this chapter we have reviewed the mental or cognitive side of the individual system and related it to several theories of delinquency. Understanding the individual's construct system is highly important in explaining why certain "delinquents" engage in antisocial conduct. For example, violence may be but is not necessarily triggered by individual characteristics of temperament, biological predispositions, or personality factors. It is more likely to be a function of the way in which an individual "perceives these events, makes meaning of them, anticipates others' reactions, and chooses to act on these events" (Eron & Slaby, 1994, p. 10). From the preschool years, highly aggressive or violent individuals have been found to show habits of thought that reflect lower levels of social problem-solving skills and higher endorsement of beliefs that support the use of violence. Leonard Eron and Ronald Slaby (1994, p. 10) write: "Highly aggressive children and violent adolescent offenders typically define social problems in hostile ways, adopt hostile goals, seek few additional facts, generate few alternative solutions, anticipate few consequences for aggression, and give higher priority to their aggressive solutions."

Theories built on an individual system perspective are invaluable for explaining (or speculating) why particular juveniles lack empathy, have a hostile attributional bias, and engage in a series of brutal, violent attacks that are sometimes difficult to understand. Aggressive, antisocial children place value on aggressive acts and upon their acceptability (Cairns & Cairns, 1991). Furthermore, these values tend to be shared by the other persons with whom they associate, whether in the family or peer groups. If they are reinforced by the culture of society, such as media images, the individual is all the more at risk of acting violently.

If the importance of the cognitive processes is recognized, we can develop intervention and treatment strategies that will help reduce the violent behavior. Cognitive-behavior therapies that are designed to deal with these processes have been quite successful in changing antisocial and violent behavior in children and adolescents, as we will discuss in Chapter 9.

It should be emphasized that the statements and theories discussed in this chapter provide only a *partial* explanation of delinquency. Their predictive and explanatory power should not be overestimated. The overestimation of the value of one social system over another has sometimes created unnecessary tension between the individual or psychological perspective and the societal or sociological perspective. The grand mistake of the individual perspective is assuming that individual systems can explain patterns of delinquency. They cannot. The mistake of the societal perspective is in dismissing the potential contribution of its counterpart. Individual systems represent but one level in the interacting levels of stratification within any social phenomenon. Moral development, social learning theories, interpersonal-maturity theory, PI measures, labeling theory, containment theory, and neutralization techniques are all basically anchored at the same level of explanation: the individual. Fundamentally, the labeling perspective framed by Lemert and Becker is a macrolevel approach, however.

Criminology can best be construed as a family of related sciences focusing at different levels, accepting different tasks, and employing different methodologies. The individual level adds immeasurably to the picture, but the overall picture is an interactive and stratified one. Preschool children are at high risk if they have experienced combinations of adverse factors, such as financial deprivation in the form of low family income, poor housing, high-crime neighborhoods, inadequate school systems, poor health care, poor nutrition, and lack of protection from toxic elements. The risk increases further if they are subjected to child abuse, maltreatment, domestic violence, and poor monitoring and supervision.

Typically, textbooks include in the discussion of delinquency theories their weaknesses and their supposedly "fatal flaws." Although the present text does this to some extent, it is more intent on emphasizing that theories are often directed at different levels. Researchers who cherish aggregate data criticize individual-based theorists and researchers for being too narrow, too reductionistic, and too psychological in their efforts to understand delinquency. Those who persist with individual explanations claim that the aggregate or macrolevel approach is misguided; it will never understand delinquency and especially the delinquent without recognizing individual differences. Still another view holds that the individuals and groups that hold the most power in a given society define crime and delinquency and control the behavior of the powerless. Until we acknowledge and address these power differentials, they say, we will make little progress toward social change.

We must recognize that stratification of explanation is necessary in order to make substantial inroads into the prevention and treatment of delinquency and antisocial behavior. The point is that we can criticize endlessly without agreement or solution. It is more worthwhile to construct systems developed for a specific levels of explanation. In the next chapter, we plan to move up one more rung in the ladder of explanation.

KEY CONCEPTS

appeal to higher loyalties
condemnation of the condemners
constructs
contagion effect
conventional
cultural deviance orientation
denial of the victim
denial of injury
denial of responsibility
differential association theory
differential association-reinforcement (DAR)
discriminative stimuli
early preconventional stage
early postconventional stage
early conventional stage
emotional intelligence
hostile attributional bias
intelligence quotient (IQ)
labeling perspective

late postconventional stage
late preconventional stage
late conventional stage
modeling
negative reinforcement
normative definitions
observational learning
positive reinforcement
postconventional
preconventional
primary deviance
psychometric intelligence (PI)
psychometric approach
reinforcement
secondary deviation
social reinforcement
social imitation
techniques of neutralization
triarchic theory

6

Microsystems:
The Family

The family represents the second step (the infrasystem being the first) in our upward climb along the social systems ladder toward broader contexts. The microsystem of the family may be the single most important system in the development of delinquency. The family is, after all, the principal context in which human development takes place. Throughout most of the twentieth century, popular literature (e.g., *Better Homes and Gardens*, *Ladies' Home Journal*, the *Saturday Evening Post*) has concluded that parental neglect and faulty training at home have been the principal causes of delinquency (Gordon, 1971). Surprisingly, however, the family has not been regarded as very important from the perspective of many midcentury criminologists, at least as evidenced by the amount of research. Traditionally, peer groups and neighborhoods have dominated the work of the sociologically oriented theorists, and individual systems have dominated that of psychologically oriented theorists. Between these two orientations there exists a void of knowledge about delinquent development, although in recent years there has been some renewed interest in the structure and process of the family and delinquency. In this chapter we will try to fill some of this void with some emphasis directed at the few 'classics' in family–delinquency investigations. We then move on to family structure and delinquency, concluding with an examination of family process.

James Garbarino (1982) contends that children who are exposed to social impoverishment and lack the basic psychological necessities of life are at **socio-cultural risk** of becoming developmentally impaired. Garbarino is particularly concerned about deprivation in any of the following areas: (1) important relationships (as may happen when one parent is absent); (2) experiences that lead to self-esteem (a deprivation that happens when children are rejected or neglected by significant people in their lives or are alienated from significant social settings, such as the school); and (3) values and experiences that contribute to socialization and the development of competence (as happens when children do not learn the value of reading or of work). Garbarino believes that children who are thus impaired are susceptible to academic, occupational, and personal failure as well as to alienation from mainstream society.

Garbarino warns that it is no easy task to understand the complicated chain of events that results when a child's basic needs are not met. "It requires a multidisciplinary understanding of how the many parts of a child's life—home, neighborhood, school, government, and the world of work—all fit together" (Garbarino, 1982, p. 632). In poverty-stricken neighborhoods, for example, pressures from the street and the ubiquity of despair may far overshadow positive influences in the home (Johnstone, 1980). On the other hand, in more affluent communities, unstable family relationships may be seriously detrimental to the normal development of a child's life.

The remainder of this text looks for clues about how these influences interact with the individual system described in Chapter 4 to provide a comprehensive, multidisciplinary picture of the juvenile delinquent. This will require familiarity with contemporary research and theory in such diverse fields as developmental psychology, sociology, and ecological criminology. Once again this approach will be structured within a social systems framework.

THE FAMILY, DELINQUENCY, AND RECIPROCAL INFLUENCE

After a careful review of the research literature, Walter Gove and Robert Crutchfield (1982, p. 302) concluded, "The evidence that the family plays a critical role in juvenile delinquency is one of the strongest and most frequently replicated findings among studies of deviance." Although we cannot isolate the family as the principal causal agent of juvenile delinquency, we can be quite sure that its role is significant. The family is the context in which children often spend most time and establish their most long-lasting and influential interpersonal relationships. Whatever the variations in the structure and process of the family at different times and in different places, it is after all the basic socialization group in all human societies (Yorburg, 1973). Families provide children with their initial experiences with other human beings and with their earliest definitions of themselves and the world in which they are destined to live.

Within the family context, we especially have to be mindful of the chronosystem, which produces change over time. According to Bronfenbrenner, you will recall, each life course experiences normative and non-normative (traumatic) transitions. Entering school is a normative transition that shifts some influence away from the family to the school environment. Teachers, school officials, and peers become increasingly important to each child as his or her microsystems expand. During adolescence, peers become highly influential on one another's behavior, often more so than parents or school. These microsystems—school and peers—will be discussed in Chapter 7, along with the relationships among them: the mesosystems.

A family's physical, social, and economic situation has considerable impact on the way parents carry out their parenting functions and on the nature of parent-child interactions. In addition, the family in which children are abused or neglected or which is otherwise inadequate in meeting its children's needs is desperately in need of community support systems. Some of the early sociologists of the Chicago School believed that some families could not properly socialize their children to society because they lacked the necessary resources and social support systems.

FAMILY STRUCTURE VERSUS FAMILY PROCESS

The contemporary sociological and psychological literature on the relationship between the family and delinquency is voluminous and confusing. The empirical work can be roughly dichotomized into studies that examine **family structure** and those that examine **family process**, and there is some disagreement about which is more important. Studies of structure examine such variables as family size, birth order, spacing of siblings, number of natural parents living with the children, place of residence, and socioeconomic status. Process studies explore parent-child interactions, support provided by family members, communication among family members, parenting styles, discipline, the quality of marital relationships, and the general emotional tone within the family. The dynamics of family violence certainly qualify as important process variables, and they will also be discussed later in the chapter. While we do know quite a bit about the relationship between family structure and delinquency, we know little about family process—how the family *works*—or about the significance of this process to delinquent behavior.

Gorman-Smith et al. (1996) propose that it might be useful to fine tune the current family research by distinguishing parental styles and practices from the more general family process. Specifically, they suggest that **parental styles and practices** focus on the parental behaviors used to manage and socialize the child. For instance, such parental practices as poor supervision, extensive use of coercive discipline, and inconsistent discipline have been found to be significantly more prominent in families of antisocial youth compared with the families of youth not displaying these behaviors (Patterson, 1982, 1986b). **Family processes**, on the other hand, should refer to the beliefs and values held by the family, emotional warmth between family members, psychological support provided by family members, and communication among family members. Low cohesion, high conflict, and low levels of family warmth and affection within the family have been linked to higher rates of antisocial youth (Tolan & Lorion, 1988). Gorman-Smith et al. (1996) argue that by separating the family process variables from parenting practices and family relationship characteristics, researchers will be better able to examine the ethnic and socioeconomic differences in families and the roles these differences play—if any—in the development of delinquency. We will return to this topic later in the chapter.

Lawrence Rosen (1985) writes that the debate over the relative merits of structure or process in explaining delinquency represents an erroneous preoccupation with finding one major cause of delinquency. Both—structure and process—are important. David Farrington (1989) found that both family structure (economic status, parental criminality) *and* family process factors (harsh discipline, authoritarian child rearing, parental disagreements on discipline) were associated with violent offending. An exclusive focus on structure offers a static construction that does not consider the continuous interactions through which the behavior of participants in the family system is instigated, sustained, and developed. On the other hand, exclusive focus on process ignores the possibility that much of the development of antisocial behavior might be explained by structure. A family's area of residence may have a strong influence on the modes of discipline used by the parents. In a high-crime area, for example, some parents will place strict controls—such as early curfews—on their children's activities. Conversely, the parents' philosophy of discipline may influence their choice of neighborhood in the first place. Which is more important, structure or process? It is apparent that both warrant further examination.

To appreciate why delinquency occurs, we must view the family as a complicated, dynamic social system nestled within other social systems. It is a complex unit varying widely in composition and cohesion from family to family as well as from culture to culture. Moreover, the family contains constantly changing, dynamic social subsystems. A brother and sister close in age may harangue and harass each other incessantly when they are in the fifth and sixth grades; in high school, they may be each other's main source of emotional support. Examinations of both structure and process will yield the maximum information about this complex system. Our task, therefore, is to decide what family structures *and* what processes are significantly linked to delinquency.

Before probing the complexities of the family-delinquency relationship, it is worthwhile to repeat that family influences do not flow in one direction; they are apt to be multidirectional, a feature referred to as **reciprocal influence**. For example, whereas the parents affect the development of the child, the child also affects the development and growth of the parents, including their marital relationship, relationships with friends, and even level of job satisfaction. As James Snyder and Gerald Patterson (1987, p. 219) observe, "The antisocial child is a product and an architect of his environment." As we have seen, certain characteristics of family members (e.g., temperament, ADHD, CD) influence the whole family system. Reciprocal influence implies that the social environment influences an individual and that the individual, in turn, has an impact on the social environment. This reciprocal influence extends across several levels of the general social system, although one's personal effect diminishes as he or she encounters higher levels of the system. A child's impact on the state, for example, is obviously weaker than his or her impact on the neighborhood.

In a systems approach, the factors that influence the individual are conceptualized and measured at a number of different levels. Choosing the relevant factors and most meaningful level of analysis remains one of the most challenging problems of systems analysis. With respect to the family at the microsystem level, research has focused very heavily on the single-parent family, a structural variable that, it is maintained here, is certainly not the most relevant in the development of delinquency. Before reviewing this research, it will be instructive to review critically four of the classic studies on family variables and delinquency: the works by the Gluecks, the McCords, F. Ivan Nye, and Travis Hirschi.

EARLY STUDIES OF FAMILY AND DELINQUENCY

The Gluecks of Harvard

Sheldon Glueck, born in Warsaw, Poland, in 1896, was a Harvard Law professor throughout most of his professional career, until his retirement in 1963. Dr. Eleanor Touroff Glueck was a research associate in criminology until her 1964 retirement. This husband–wife team worked together for more than 36 years and became widely known in American criminology as "the Gluecks of Harvard." They published more than 14 books, but their work on family factors and delinquency is the most relevant to our present purpose.

In 1939, the Gluecks began to collect data on a sample of 500 boys incarcerated in training or correctional schools for serious delinquents. For comparison purposes, data were also gathered on a control group of 500 nondelinquent boys attending public schools in the area. The two all-white groups were matched in age, ethnic origin, area of residence, and IQ (as measured by the Wechsler–Bellevue Intelligence Test). Four kinds of data were collected: (1) sociocultural (which included family variables); (2) physical (body type and size); (3) intellectual; and (4) emotional-temperamental. A wide variety of measures was used, including IQ tests, Rorschachs (inkblots), and personal interviews. The Gluecks observed and analyzed the home environment, looking for discipline techniques, marital relationships, conduct standards, family pride, cultural refinements, recreational outlets, and cohesiveness; they even took notes as to which was the dominant parent. The results of this massive project were published in the classic monograph *Unraveling Juvenile Delinquency*, published in 1950.

No specified theory of delinquency appeared to guide the collection of data, although the Gluecks clearly were biased in favor of individual (infrasystem) or dispositional variables. The Gluecks analyzed reams of data and concluded that family factors were among the most critical in the formation of delinquency. More precisely, they found that the following were significantly related to delinquency: the discipline of the boy by the father (whether it was overstrict or erratic, lax, or firm but kindly); supervision of the boy by the mother (unsuitable, fair, suitable); affection of the father for the boy (indifferent or hostile; warm, including overprotective); affection of the mother for the boy; and family cohesion (unintegrated, some elements of cohesion, cohesive). Delinquent boys had parents whose disciplinary tactics varied between extremes of laxity and harshness. Parental discipline, in general, was more closely related to delinquent behavior than any other family variable.

Parents of delinquents were also seen as careless, sometimes negligent, in their supervision of their children. A high proportion of the delinquent families was disorganized as opposed to cohesive. This family disorganization was typified by a lack of warmth and respect for the integrity of each member. "Since the family is the first and foremost vehicle for the transmission of values of a culture to the young child, non-cohesiveness of the family may leave him without ethical moorings or convey to him a confused and inconsistent cultural pattern" (Glueck & Glueck, 1950, p. 280).

The Glueck data also suggested that delinquent boys tend to come from families in which fathers, mothers, and siblings had been indifferent or hostile toward them. Most of the boys were not attached to their parents and felt that they were not concerned about their welfare. Compared with nondelinquent boys, twice as many of the delinquent boys did not look upon their fathers as acceptable symbols for emulation.

In sum, the "obvious inferiority of the families of delinquents" contributed greatly—though not exclusively—to delinquency. Although the Gluecks did find a small relationship among delinquency and father's presence, family size, and the boy's ordinal position (which are all structural features), the most significant associations existed between delinquency and process variables—parental discipline, maternal supervision, affection of both the father and the mother for the boy, and family cohesion.

The Gluecks declared, however, that these features of the home environment do not act on the child in isolation. Rather, the environment interacts with the child's constitutional and personality traits to produce delinquency. Specifically, the Gluecks believed that the traits of mesomorphy, restlessness, and impulsiveness predispose youth toward delinquency. Interestingly, these last two behaviors are highly similar to those found in ADHD children.

Soon after the publication of *Unraveling Juvenile Delinquency*, stinging criticisms of the entire project and its conclusions appeared throughout the professional literature (e.g., Rubin, 1951; Reiss, 1951a; Peterson & Becker, 1965; Hirschi & Selvin, 1967). Could the results on these 500 white boys from specific social areas and ethnic backgrounds be valid predictors for all boys from all social areas, across all ethnic groups, and across all time? Obviously, criminologists did not think so. Moreover, the Glueck study did not address the delinquency of girls, a fact which was not noted by these critics. Among the more influential critiques was that by Sol Rubin (1951), who attacked the Gluecks' methodology. The study, Rubin said, did little more than compare boys who had been institutionalized an average of 7 months with boys who had not been institutionalized. Rubin argued that the Gluecks had failed to recognize the psychological and social effects of an institution on a 13-year-old boy. For example, the observed personality differences between delinquents and nondelinquents could have easily been due to the effects of institutionalization or of being labeled delinquent rather than to any inherent personality traits. A far better procedure, Rubin said, would have been to compare institutionalized delinquents with both non-institutionalized delinquents and nondelinquents so that the effects of being in a training school could be more properly evaluated. Non-institutionalized delinquents then might have been more similar to the nondelinquents than to delinquents in institutions.

Critics also chastised the Gluecks for making "unwarranted" conclusions about cause-and-effect relationships, and they excoriated them for attempting to formulate a "scientific law" on the basis of correlational analyses. According to the "Glueck Law," boys who (1) are physically mesomorphic (solid and muscular) in constitution; (2) are temperamentally restless, impulsive, extroverted, and aggressive; and (3) come from homes displaying little understanding, affection, stability, and moral fiber were destined to become delinquents. The Gluecks advanced this "law" tentatively and with the admonishment that it needed much more testing, but nevertheless they provoked the ire of criminologists well versed in scientific methods (e.g., Reiss, 1951a; Hirschi & Selvin, 1967).

The criticisms directed at the Glueck project were effective. Today many criminology textbooks hardly mention the study except to note its flawed assumptions, design, and conclusions. Still, the Glueck study has value and deserves to be recognized in the criminology literature. It directed attention to a possible relationship between family variables (both structural and process) and delinquency. Despite their flawed methodology, the Gluecks were cited heavily by researchers interested in studying the importance of family systems (e.g., Peterson & Becker, 1965; Nye, 1958; Hirschi, 1969). Although the limitations of the Glueck study were well-recognized, other researchers took their cue from the two and began to examine, with more methodological rigor, the role of the family in the development of delinquency. As Lawrence Rosen (1985, p. 554) notes, ". . . there is little question that [the Gluecks'] study served to reestablish the credibility of the central role of family dynamics in delinquency etiology."

The Cambridge-Somerville Youth Study

Another classic in the family-delinquency literature is William and Joan McCord's *Origins of Crime* published in 1959. The book represents a further examination of the **Cambridge-Somerville Youth Study**, a project begun in the 1930s that "attempted to prevent delinquency and develop character by means of friendly guidance" (McCord, McCord, & Zola, 1959, p. vi). The project, which was launched in 1936, was conceived, initiated, and financed by Robert Clark Cabot, professor of social ethics and clinical medicine at Harvard University. Cabot hypothesized that delinquency could be prevented if a close and caring friendship were developed between a youngster and an adult counselor. He reasoned that if intensive family and individual counseling were provided, buttressed by proper medical care, recreational facilities, and other social services, delinquency could be prevented.

The study focused on the 2,000 *boys*, ages 6 to 12, attending schools in the factory-dominated cities of Cambridge and Somerville, Massachusetts. Six hundred and fifty boys were eventually selected for the experiment. They were divided randomly into two groups by the flip of a coin. One group, the "experimental group," received treatment and social services, beginning in 1939. The other group, the "control group," did not receive counseling and services. Between 1939 and 1945, counselors visited the homes of both groups twice a month, filing comprehensive and detailed reports of everything observed, including the physical conditions of the neighborhood. Unfortunately, World War II interfered with the project. For example, many of the counselors, social workers, and older boys in the experiment were drafted into or enlisted in the armed services. When the project was terminated in 1945, only 75 boys remained. A follow-up study was launched in 1951 by Edwin Powers and Helen L. Witmer (1951), and later by William and Joan McCord (McCord, McCord, & Zola, 1959).

It is difficult to evaluate the success of the treatment because of the many problems the experiment faced. The McCords concluded that the experiment failed, despite its being one of the most extensive and costly experiments tried anywhere on the prevention of delinquency. According to the McCords, the experiment ". . . failed primarily because it did not affect the basic psychological and familial causes of crime" (p. vi). Interestingly, 30 years after termination of the program, many of the boys remembered their counselors, often with considerable fondness (McCord, 1978). "Were the Youth Study program to be assessed by the subject judgment of its value as perceived by those who received its services, it would rate high marks" (McCord, 1978, p. 288). However, none of the objective measures revealed that treatment had a significant effect on improving the lives of the boys. In fact, some of the data are quite disturbing. For instance, men who had been in the treatment program were more likely to commit further crime than men who had not received treatment. The reasons for this unexpected finding remain a mystery.

In addition, the McCords felt that their study was on more solid theoretical footing than previous investigations, because they used information gathered through multiple "observations" by psychologists, psychiatrists, and social workers. Observations consisted of sifting through the many records and written documents available on the boys. Therefore, the McCords claimed, bias was kept to a minimum. However, it is likely that these clinicians had a strong bias in favor of individual factors, and this bias probably influenced their search to a great extent.

Overall, the McCords found the following:

- Intelligence was not strongly related to crime
- Social factors (e.g., neighborhood conditions, SES) were not strongly related to crime

- Broken homes (the term for single-parent families which was then in use) were not strongly linked to crime
- A child's "home atmosphere" (cohesiveness, affection, conflict) was not strongly related to crime
- Erratic, punitive discipline was related to crime
- The father's personality had an important effect on crime (warm fathers and passive fathers produced very few criminals)
- The mother's personality had the greatest effect on the genesis of criminality (maternal love led to low crime; maternal passivity, cruelty, absence, or neglect led to high crime)

The McCords, like the Gluecks, were critical of sociological viewpoints of crime and delinquency, and they apparently relished disposing of the sociological theories that prevailed at the time. These theories focused on explanatory factors like social disorganization, conflicting cultural values, gangs, and blocked opportunities for success. All were subtly attacked. This is probably one reason why the McCord research—like the Glueck research—has also failed to receive much recognition in the criminological literature, which has been predominantly sociological in orientation.

F. Ivan Nye and the Sociology of the Family

F. Ivan Nye (1958), a sociologist at Washington State University specializing in family relations, conducted an SR (self-report) study in 1955 in an effort to evaluate family characteristics associated with delinquency. The study is often cited in the criminological literature, especially in reference to the connection between parental marital happiness and delinquency. Nye and his colleagues administered several questionnaires to high schoolers (grades 9 through 12) living in three small cities (population 10,000 to 30,000) in the state of Washington. He was able to gather information from 780 predominately white students representing a cross-section of the SES characteristics.

Nye correlated items on mothers' employment, broken homes, family structure (birth order, family size), SES, discipline, parental appearance, parental character, and values with the 23-item SR questionnaire designed to measure delinquency. He found that girls committed only a fraction of the delinquent behavior committed by boys, and he attributed the difference to differential parental practices relating to boys and girls. Parents exerted more social control on girls than boys. He also found a "U-shaped" relationship between discipline and delinquency. Too much or too little discipline was related to delinquency, with a balance between harsh and lax discipline showing the lowest delinquency. Furthermore, a child's strong identification with parents is associated with low delinquency.

Nye's analysis revealed a large discrepancy between the proportion of children from broken homes incarcerated in state training schools (48 percent) and the proportion who fall into the most delinquent high school group (23.6 percent). The discrepancy, Nye concluded, was probably the result of differential treatment of children from broken homes received from the police, courts, parents, and neighbors. In addition, delinquent children (still in high school) were *slightly* more likely to come from broken homes than were nondelinquent high school students. However, Nye asserted that the broken home per se did not necessarily contribute to delinquency. Rather, the happiness of the marriage makes the difference. Unhappy homes in which parents quarrelled and argued were more likely to produce delinquent children than the more happy, less conflictful homes. This finding has become one of the most widely cited of the Nye study.

However, before we rush to tell parents that they must not quarrel or fight lest they produce delinquent kids, several qualifications need to be made about the Nye project. First, examination of the 23-item delinquency scale reveals that it measured very minor juvenile "offenses," some of which just about every American high school student has committed at some point during adolescence. For example, there were questions about whether the student has ever defied his or her parents' authority (to their face), or if he or she has ever disobeyed parents, ever told a lie, ever skipped school without a legitimate excuse, ever taken little things (worth less than $2), or bought or drank beer, wine, or liquor. Other items inquired as to whether the respondent ever had sexual relations with persons of the opposite sex or of the same sex, or went hunting or fishing without a license, or driven a car without a driver's license or permit. More "serious" questions asked about running away from home, fistfights, gang fights, taking a car for a ride without the owner's knowledge (including parents'), using narcotic drugs, theft (more than $50), and vandalism.

Most of these items do not qualify as serious juvenile offending, even if committed frequently. Nye's conclusions, then, are generally based on "common," nonserious juvenile actions, mingled with some status offenses.

Second, Nye's "marital happiness" finding is predicated on a single-item estimate by the adolescent of the marital happiness of each parent. Furthermore, he found no relationship between another nine-item questionnaire measuring parental quarreling and delinquency for boys, and only a weak relationship for girls. It is difficult to know precisely what "quarreling" and "arguing" mean. Mildly acting-out adolescents may raise havoc with any stable, "happy" home, and quarrels may be a common parental response to this behavior. In conclusion, Nye's finding concerning family "happiness" and delinquency seems to be on shaky ground and should not be employed as supportive documentation for a marital discord–delinquency connection without considerable caution.

Social Control Theory

In 1969, Travis Hirschi published his well-known book *Causes of Delinquency*. Control or bond theories contend that delinquency occurs when the child's ties to the conventional order are weakened or broken. The control or bonding begins within the family system and then branches out to include others within the neighborhood and community. When delinquency occurs, it is primarily because the appropriate socialization process has not occurred. More specifically, it is because the necessary socialization process within the family has not taken place. Delinquency—and deviance in general—occurs when people have not been adequately indoctrinated with the rules and expectations of a given society, and when the external social constraints are lacking.

Hirschi set out to identify and empirically test the concepts of his control theory, using adolescent *boys* as his subjects. As will be noted later in the chapter, the theory was later tested with girls. He proposed four basic elements of the bonding process: (1) **attachment** to parents, teachers, and peers; (2) **commitment** to conventional lines of activity, such as educational and occupational aspirations; (3) **involvement** in that conventional activity; and (4) **belief** about the legitimacy and morality of the social rules and laws. Hirschi speculated that these elements had an additive effect: the more attachment, commitment, involvement, and belief the more likely the individual is to be bonded to society. Consequently, the less likely he or she is to engage in delinquent activity. Hirschi posited that the more a youth was tied or bonded to conventional society by one element, the more likely he or she was to be bonded by the others.

"**Attachment**" refers to the degree of sensitivity a youth has to the opinions of others. According to Hirschi, the most important persons within a child's social environment are parents, peers, and school officials, with parents being the most critical. ". . . [T]he fact that delinquents are less likely than non-delinquents to be closely tied to their parents is one of the best documented findings of delinquency research" (Hirschi, 1969, p. 85). Insensitivity on the part of the youth to what these groups think and feel is a sign of weakened or nonexistent bonds to the conventional social order.

Commitment involves the physical and emotional investment a person puts into the normative, conventional way of life. It includes such activities as studying, building up a business, saving money, acquiring a reputation for virtue and honesty, and generally doing those things encouraged and expected by conventional others. The more a person commits him or herself to these activities, the less likely the person is to engage in acts that ultimately jeopardize his or her position in the social order. "The person becomes committed to a conventional line of action, and he is therefore committed to conformity" (Hirschi, 1969, p. 21).

"**Involvement**" refers to the amount of time and energy expended in the pursuit of conventional activities. According to Hirschi, a person heavily involved in conventional endeavors has neither the time nor the energy to engage in deviant behavior. "The person involved in conventional activities is tied to appointments, deadlines, working hours, plans, and the like, so the opportunity to commit deviant acts rarely arises. To the extent that he is engrossed in conventional activities, he cannot even think about deviant acts, let alone act out his inclinations" (Hirschi, 1969, p. 22). Thus, the juvenile involved in recreational, social, religious, and school endeavors has little time to engage in delinquent acts. In some ways, Hirschi sees male delinquents as members of a leisure class, plagued with free time and characterized by ". . . a search for kicks, disdain for work, a desire for the big score, and the acceptance of aggressive toughness as proof of masculinity" (Hirschi, 1969, pp. 22–23).

Belief is the degree to which a person internalizes and accepts the common value system of the society or group. The value system includes sharing, sensitivity to the rights of others, respect for and acceptance of laws and rules, and concern for the plight of others.

Hirschi proposed that there were many variations in the extent to which people believe they should obey the rules of society. Beliefs in the rules are not all-or-nothing things. Beliefs exist on continua, ranging in degrees of conviction. According to Hirschi, the less a person is committed to the rules (the weaker the bonds), the more likely he or she is to violate them.

Hirschi tested his control theory in 1964 in a study of 1,300 junior high and high school boys living in an urban California county. He used data from both official and self-report sources. The boys were administered questionnaires in which they were asked about their involvement in delinquency. In addition, Hirschi included a number of questions that were designed to measure the four elements of his bond to society. For example, attachment was measured by such questions as: "Would you like to be the kind of person your father is?" Commitment was measured primarily by the importance the boys placed on grades, involvement by the amount of time they devoted to school activities, and belief by their degree of respect for police and the law.

The most striking finding of Hirschi's study was the importance of identification with the male parent. Boys who reported that they discussed their plans and shared their thoughts and feelings with their fathers were much less likely to engage in delinquent acts than boys who reported less intimate communication. The *amount* of communication was less significant than the *closeness* or the intimacy as perceived by the boys.

The Hirschi data suggested that relationship with the father was possibly the most important factor in the development of male delinquency. A close and intimate relationship between father and son was correlated with nondelinquency, regardless of the relationship with the mother. A similar finding has been reported by Alayne Yates et al. (1983). These researchers discovered that a vast majority of the 339 young male offenders (ages 18 to 20) reviewed described their early relationships with their fathers as more important than their early relationships with their mothers. Interestingly, in Hirschi's study, boys whose parents themselves engaged in criminal behavior were no more likely to be delinquent than those boys whose parents were noncriminal. Hirschi explained this by speculating that all parents—criminal and noncriminal—communicate allegiance to the societal norms, even though they may not conform to them personally.

The Hirschi survey also uncovered a complex relationship among parents, the child, the school, and peers. Boys who did poorly in school tended to lack intimate communication with parents. Hirschi disagreed with theorists who concluded that dislike for school was a source of motivation to delinquency, or that delinquency was a means of relieving frustration generated by unpleasant school experiences. Success in school, Hirschi said, depended upon how competent the boy believed himself to be. These perceptions of competence stemmed partly from the parent's perceptions of his competence as they were communicated to him. If parents communicated that the boy was competent and should do his best, then school became tolerable and even pleasant. Although teachers and peers played significant roles, parental influences were paramount. In this sense, Hirschi emphasized the important role of mesosystems—or interactions between microsystems—in the development of delinquency.

In sum, attachment to parents became a central tenet in Hirschi's control theory: Strong attachment essentially precluded delinquency. Furthermore, attachment to parents was associated with other relationships, both within and away from home. Attachment to parents was often associated with attachment to peers, for example. And Hirschi found that the closer the boy was to his peers, the less delinquent he tended to be. This would not be predicted by cultural deviance theory, which suggested an inverse relationship between attachment to parents and to peers: Children unattached to parents were more likely to be influenced by those outside the family. Hirschi also found a negative relationship between ambition and delinquency: The more ambitious a boy was, the less likely he was to become delinquent.

Michael J. Hindelang (1973) conducted a quasi-replicative study of Hirschi's survey, using both male and female adolescents in a rural New York state community. We call Hindelang's project "quasi-replicative" because some of the questions were worded slightly differently from the original study, and the resources available to Hindelang were not nearly as extensive as Hirschi's. Even so, and despite the fact that the surveys were conducted nearly ten years apart and in different parts of the country, Hindelang's results were remarkably similar to those of Hirschi. Attachment to parents, teachers, and school officials; commitment to "adult" activities and conventional activities; involvement in school-related activities; and conventional beliefs produced results very similar to Hirschi's. One contrast between the Hirschi and Hindelang studies was Hindelang's finding that the greater the peer attachment among his rural subjects, the higher the reported delinquency.

We now turn our attention to three prominent family structure variables that have played significant roles in the causes-of-delinquency debate. We begin with the highly debated single-parent family issue and then move to family size and birth order effects.

THE SINGLE-PARENT FAMILY

Criminologists interested in the study of delinquency have given a great deal of attention to the family that has experienced divorce, separation, desertion, or the death of one parent. Many researchers are now using "single- (or one-) parent family" as a substitute for the term "broken family," and this is the term we use here.

Karen Wilkinson (1974) noted that the relationship between delinquency and single-parent homes has historically been characterized by periods of acceptance followed by periods of rejection. During the first 30 years of this century, it was widely accepted that these homes led directly to delinquency. Shaw and McKay (1932), writing an influential review of the research between 1900 and 1932, summarized the thinking during that period with this comment: "It is significant only to note that the belief that the broken home is one of the most important causes of delinquency is widely accepted" (p. 514). Research by Breckinridge and Abbott (1912) reported that 44 percent of all delinquent boys brought before the Juvenile Court of Cook County (Illinois) lived in homes that were "broken" by death of one or both parents, desertion, divorce, or separation. Healy (1915; Healy & Bronner, 1926) claimed that his delinquent samples contained anywhere between 36 and 49 percent of children from such families. Shideler (1918) found that more than 50 percent of the delinquents he studied were from single-parent homes. Monahan (1957) reviewed 14 studies published between 1903 and 1933 and reported that, indeed, all of them affirmed a strong association between the absence of one parent and delinquency.

Articles by Shaw and McKay (1931, 1932), Joanna Colcord (1932), and Katharine Lenroot (1932) marked the beginning of serious questioning of the dogma that single-parent homes led directly to a delinquent and criminal way of life. In their 1931 monograph, Shaw and McKay asserted that the these homes were not necessarily conducive to delinquency unless there were additional complicating factors, such as low morale, poverty, or a physically deteriorating neighborhood. The combination of these factors, not the structure of the family alone, was more likely to draw children into delinquency. According to Shaw and McKay, a vast majority of the early research neglected to use control groups of comparable nondelinquent youths. Moreover, the early investigations did not distinguish between homes "broken" because of parental conflict and those "broken" because of death.

The British criminologist Herrmann Mannheim, after an exhaustive review of the literature, wrote (with apparent discouragement):

> No other term [broken home] in the history of criminological thought has been so overworked, misused, and discredited as this. For many years universally proclaimed as the most obvious explanation of both juvenile delinquency and adult crime, it is now often regarded as the "black sheep" in the otherwise respectable family of criminological theories, and most writers shamefacedly turn their backs to it (Mannheim, 1965, p. 618).

Wilkinson (1974) noted (as do Wilson and Herrnstein, 1985) that the major theories on crime and delinquency developed during this period did not for the most part include family factors as important variables. Differential social class, economic opportunities, the operations of the criminal justice systems, and peergroup patterns were all considered much more relevant to the search for the causes of delinquency. To Wilkinson, the neglect of family factors was inconsistent with the traditional interest of sociologists in the family. She speculated that the lack of interest in familial variables might be explained by the strong aversion of sociologically oriented criminologists to psychologically oriented explanations of behavior. Familial relationships, such as those between the parent and the child, were too psychological for their research tastes.

Wilson and Herrnstein (1985) attribute the lack of attention to family factors to the political climate of the 1950s and 1960s. In the 1950s, Americans were worried about violence connected with organized crime. During the 1960s, the country's attention turned to civil rights and economic opportunity. "Gangs, race prejudice, social class, and criminal justice were concepts that seemed close to the problem and amenable to change. By contrast, the family as a concept suffered from two defects: It was not on the public agenda and it was not clear how its practices might be altered" (p. 216).

The work of F. Ivan Nye (1958) and Travis Hirschi (1969) prompted a resumed interest in sociological investigations of the relationship between delinquency and the family. Since the 1970s, sociological researchers have had a particular interest in reexamining what some see as an intuitively appealing relationship between the single-parent family and delinquency.

The research on the relationship has continued to yield equivocal and conflictful findings, however. Grinnell and Chambers (1979), using official statistics to measure delinquency, found little or no relationship between single-parent homes and white middle-class delinquency. Gibson (1969) found no higher incidence of delinquency among London schoolboys from low-income single-parent homes than among boys from low-income two-parent homes. Rankin (1983) found a positive relationship between single-parent homes and delinquency, but only for certain offenses (e.g., running away, truancy, auto theft) and for certain types of homes (specifically, those in which neither biological parent was present). Hennessy et al. (1978) conducted a self-report study with middle-class high school students of both sexes and found no significant relationship between single-parent homes and delinquent behavior.

Some research (e.g., Toby, 1957; Wadsworth, 1979) on official delinquency has suggested that the earlier the parental break occurs in the developmental history of the child, the greater its impact on the development of delinquency (Wells & Rankin, 1985). This is compatible with studies in child development which suggest that age at time of parental discord and separation is a relevant factor in determining its effect on the child. Older children, because they have formulated friendships with peers and have achieved some degree of personal autonomy from parents, appear to find separation less traumatic than younger children (Kellam et al., 1982). Younger children experiencing divorce not only have fewer experiences outside the home but also lack the cognitive and social competencies to understand and deal with the dissolution of their parents' marital relationship (Belsky, Lerner, & Spanier, 1984). Child development research suggests that the coping styles of children of different ages vary as a function of their cognitive and social competencies. Young children, for example, may blame themselves for causing the separation and otherwise be unable to evaluate the divorce situation accurately (Belsky, Lerner, & Spanier, 1984). The few self-report studies conducted on the topic are at odds with the official studies; the self-report research does not support this age–divorce hypothesis (e.g., Nye, 1958; Rankin, 1983).

A child's temperament may also be a factor in how he or she reacts to a divorce situation. In a study by Hetherington, Cox, and Cox (1978), children who exhibited the highest level of behavioral problems as a result of divorce or marital discord were those who (1) were described by their mothers as having had, during their infancies, a prevalence of fussiness and crying; (2) adapted slowly to new situations and showed distress under those conditions; and (3) displayed biological irregularities in sleeping, feeding, and eliminating. Possibly, some combination of marital disharmony and individual temperament produced a high-risk environment for the development of delinquency.

One frequent observation is that delinquent girls come from single-parent families more often than delinquent boys (Rodman & Grams, 1967), suggesting that parental discord and separation may have a greater negative impact on girls. Jackson Toby (1957) argued that this difference is due to the greater control parents maintain over girls—when separation occurs, the contrast effects (from control to much less control) have a stronger impact on girls. Most of the studies finding gender effects were based on official delinquency records, however (Wells & Rankin, 1985). Some investigators (e.g., Datesman & Scarpitti, 1975; Rankin, 1983), therefore, have suggested that the gender difference may be due to the family-related bias in the official processing of female delinquents. Girls are more likely than boys to be referred to juvenile authorities and to receive official sanctions for such "ungovernable" behaviors as sexual misconduct, running away, and truancy, all of which are likely to be affected by the family situation (Wells & Rankin, 1985). Datesman and Scarpitti (1975) did find some gender differences in the effect of paternal absence, but the relationship is weak. Austin (1978) replicated the study with a larger sample and found support only for the hypothesis that paternal absence would have a stronger negative effect on white girls than on white boys.

There is some evidence that boys are more strongly affected by divorce than girls (Emery, 1982) and that family conflict is as important in male as in female delinquency (Norland et al., 1979). Self-report studies in general, however, are less convincing about these reported gender differences. Wells and Rankin (1985, p. 256) summarize the empirical research with this comment: ". . . the simple proposition that family break up has a greater negative effect on girls than on boys is too simple to be meaningful." They add that the relationship between delinquency and the absence of one parent may itself be nothing but an artifact of official processing procedures.

The reasons for frequent and frustrating inconsistencies in the research are multiple. A complete review of the reasons would take us too far afield from the main topic, but it is instructive to review briefly some of them because they underscore the complex relationship between structural and process variables associated with the family.

Conceptual Problems

The terms "broken home" or "single-parent family" are so broad that they may be virtually meaningless for research purposes. Research clearly suggests, for example, that more serious childhood problems are present in homes "broken" by divorce, separation, or desertion than in homes "broken" by death (Emery, 1982). But even if one concedes that homes in which one parent has died probably constitute a nonsignificant minority in any given sample, it still is not justifiable to treat separation, desertion, or divorce as part of a unitary concept. Ideally, research focused on structure should clearly delineate *how* the homes in its sample are "broken."

Even this, however, assumes that all divorces, all desertions, and all separations affect families in the same way. Furthermore, the term broken home does not cover the family which never had a father (or mother) in the home. It is for these reasons that some researchers prefer to examine process variables rather than structural variables in family research.

This is not easily done. Research on the effects of divorce in general often fails to acknowledge that the legal formality of divorce usually follows long after alienation (psychological and physical) between the spouses (Lamb, 1977). There are, however, exceptions, and the research does not tell whether these exceptions are significant. Furthermore, although the stresses and strains of divorce generally occur gradually, including the psychological separation between the children and the conflictful parents, this is not invariably the case. The absent parent may continue to maintain a significant relationship with both the separated spouse and the child or children, with or without a shared-custody arrangement. It is also not unusual for parental conflict to continue unabated after the home has been formally "broken." Some research indicates that children of divorced parents who remain in conflict after the divorce decree are more likely to be delinquent than children from low-conflict divorces (Hetherington, Cox, & Cox, 1979). Structural research—that which focuses simply on whether the family is broken or intact—does not address these fine points.

Emery (1982) and Gove and Crutchfield (1982) concluded after extensive literature reviews that it is parental conflict rather than separation per se that results in delinquency. Children from single-parent, conflict-free homes are less likely to be delinquent than children from conflict-ridden "intact" homes.

To continue with definitional problems, investigators far too often have treated "intact" families as though they were a homogeneous collection. Some children live with both of their biological parents; others live in restructured nuclear families, in which a step-parent has entered the family, or in "blended families," in which two adults each bring offspring into the new nuclear group. Recent studies (Dornbusch, et al., 1985; Johnson, 1986) suggest a strong link between the presence of a stepfather and delinquency. Stepfathers, for reasons unknown, appear to engender delinquent behavior in their stepchildren. If one wishes to pursue this line of research, it may be more meaningful to classify families on the basis of whether they are "original" intact families or "restructured nuclear" families.

In addition, single-parent homes are invariably defined from the reference point of children vis-à-vis their relationship with parents, whereas siblings and extended-family members who might be living in the household (e.g., grandparents, aunts, and uncles) are ignored (Wells & Rankin, 1986). Some research is beginning to pay attention to some of these factors. Neilsen and Gerber (1979) found that brothers and sisters of chronic truants tended to be truant as well. G. R. Patterson (1986b), after reviewing the literature, concluded that the evidence so far suggests that siblings are similar across a considerable range of behavior, including involvement in delinquency.

Even the word "parent" is not sufficiently defined in much of the existing literature. Some researchers study only homes of biological parents, whereas others discount the primacy of biological ties, counting as parents any adults who effectively carry out parental tasks and perform the necessary care-giving functions (Wells & Rankin, 1986). The most frequent version of the single-parent home defines parents in biological terms (West, 1982; Wilgosh & Paitich, 1982; Wells & Rankin, 1986), but noteworthy studies have expanded the definition to include anyone considered to be parents by the children in the home (e.g., Blechman, 1982; Gove & Crutchfield, 1982; Matsueda, 1982).

Parental absence is a condition that encompasses a wide variety of situations. The absence may be due to occupational demands, military service, hospitalization, or incarceration. It may be total or partial (e.g., shared custody, visitation privileges, correspondence), temporary or long-term, voluntary or involuntary (Wells & Rankin, 1986). Also, research rarely considers distinctions between father-absent and mother-absent homes, although the implicit assumption is that single-parent homes are generally father-absent households. Such variations in "absence" may have differential effects on the child's development and possible misconduct.

FAMILY SIZE, BIRTH ORDER, AND DELINQUENCY

A sizeable amount of evidence suggests that both family size and birth order are linked to delinquency (Ernst & Angst, 1983). "Family size" refers to the number of siblings within one family. "Birth order" refers to the ordinal position in the birth sequence among siblings (e.g., first-born, second-born, last-born, only-born, etc.).

The Gluecks (1950) found that their delinquent group was more likely to come from a large family than was their nondelinquent group. Hirschi (1969, pp. 239–40) concluded from his SR study of delinquency that ". . . children from large families are more likely than children from small families to have committed delinquent acts." West and Farrington (1973) reported similar findings. In their very extensive review of the research literature, Rolf Loeber and Magda Stouthamer-Loeber (1986) concluded that delinquents often come from large families. At the same time, they could not locate a single study that tried to investigate *why* this relationship exists. They were unaware of any study that has concentrated on the familial processes that contribute to the family size–delinquency connection.

Research further shows that if one sibling is delinquent, there is a high probability that the other siblings will be as well. Therefore, "delinquent families" contribute disproportionately to the delinquency rate. For example, Harriet Wilson

(1975) found in her study of disadvantaged inner-city British families that 16 percent of the families produced 62 percent of the delinquent children. Similarly, David Farrington and his colleagues (1975) reported that about 4 percent of the families from a working-class neighborhood in London produced 47 percent of the convicted delinquents. Loeber and Stouthamer-Loeber found that siblings engage in pretty much the same delinquent activities, such as substance abuse, burglary, and shoplifting.

The evidence for birth order effects is also quite robust. Middle-born boys are overrepresented in delinquency (Glueck & Glueck, 1950; Lees & Newson, 1954; West & Farrington, 1973; Ernst & Angst, 1983). William and Joan McCord (with I. K. Zola) (1959) also found that middle-born boys were more likely to be delinquent. The McCords speculated that the middle-born children are forgotten during times of heavy family burden. Others have speculated about the many possible reasons for the birth order effect, but research has yet to examine the processes through which middle-born children are potentially more prone toward delinquent behavior. We also do not know from the available research whether birth order is related to serious delinquency, nonserious delinquency, or both.

Again, we have a reported significant relationship between family structure and delinquency, but little empirical evidence as to *why* it exists. Until further research focuses more on the family process involved, we can only speculate on what these connections mean. The causal chain, however, is unlikely to be as simple as: Family size (or birth order) causes delinquency. M. Wadsworth (1979), for example, found that family size appears to be most strongly associated with delinquency in disadvantaged families (measured by income and father's occupation), and only weakly with middle-class families. There are likely to be many other contributing, co-determining variables in the equation.

PROCESS STUDIES ON FAMILY AND DELINQUENCY

Gerald Patterson (1982, 1986a) concluded years ago that the families of aggressive children support the use of antisocial behavior in their children by inadvertently reinforcing such behaviors and by failing to reinforce prosocial ones. Within such families, reciprocally aversive exchanges were noted between parents and the aggressive children, suggesting that these children may be both the architects and the victims of aggressive interactions (Pepler & Slaby, 1994).

Other researchers have discovered that the lack of parental supervision appears to be a strong predictor of serious, violent delinquency (Loeber & Stouthamer-Loeber, 1986; Pepler & Slaby, 1994). A lack of parent–child involvement and parental rejection have also been found to be strong predictors of serious delinquency (Farrington, 1991). Furthermore, factors such as inconsistent parental disciplinary practices (McCord, 1979) and harsh, physical punishment by parents are strongly correlated with delinquency (Straus, 1991; Pepler & Slaby, 1994). Murray Straus (1991) concluded that although harsh physical punishment produces some conformity in children in the short term, over time it tends to increase the probability of violent delinquency and crime. Straus further found that parents who believe in physical punishment not only hit the child more often but are more likely to go beyond ordinary physical punishment and assault. For example, they may resort to punching and kicking, which, of course, carry a greater risk of injury to the child. Research by Leonard D. Eron and his colleagues (Eron, Huesmann, & Zelli, 1991) reveals that this cycle of violence and aggression remains in aggression-prone families for at least three generations. In one of the few studies examining the process variables of minority families living within the inner city, Gorman-Smith et al. (1996) found that some aspects of family relationship characteristics and parenting practices are consistently linked to violent delinquency, regardless of ethnic or socioeconomic characteristics. Three of the most prominent factors are poor parental monitoring, poor discipline, and lack of family cohesion. "Regardless of ethnic or socioeconomic group, it is important for parents to be involved, to monitor their child's whereabouts, and to use effective and consistent discipline" (Gorman-Smith et al. 1996, p. 125).

It must be stressed that the relationships discussed here do not occur in isolation. After all, Straus (1991) also reports the results of several surveys which indicate that more than 90 percent of the parents of three- and four-year-olds in the United States use physical punishment as a disciplinary tactic. If there were a simple, direct relationship between the parental method of physical punishment and violent delinquency, the crime conditions in the United States would be far worse than they are now.

However, much of the family process research supports the theory that serious delinquency and violent behavior are at least partly learned through the behavior of the parents. In short, "[P]arents teach children aggression by the models of behavior they present, the reinforcements they provide for aggressive behavior, and the conditions they furnish in the home that frustrate and victimize the child" (Eron, Huesmann, & Zelli, 1991, p. 170).

The Johnstone Studies: Relationships Between Microsystems

John Johnstone (1978, 1980) examined the simultaneous effects of environmental and family factors on different forms of delinquent behavior. Johnstone viewed delinquent behavior as the end product of three sets of forces: peer-group influences, family influences, and community-norm pressures. Community-norm pressure was measured by the prevalence of poverty-level families, the unemployment rate, and the number of single-parent, female-headed households within the area in which the youngsters lived. Measures of family integration, attachment to a delinquency-prone peer group, and participation in law violations were all measured by questionnaire responses from the adolescents themselves.

Johnstone's contextual analysis demonstrated that the influence of the family varied both with the type of delinquent behavior and with the community setting in which the adolescent lived. In reference to the type of delinquent behavior, there was an inverse relationship between the seriousness of the delinquency and the importance of the family to the child. When it came to serious offenses (burglary, larceny, robbery, and assault), the environment had the strongest effect. In other words, serious offenses were predicted better by characteristics of the community than by characteristics of the family. Adolescent participation in serious offenses seems to be rooted in the wider social environment. On the other hand, less serious offenses (status offenses), minor drug infractions, and property violations were more likely to be determined by characteristics of the family.

Johnstone concludes that in communities that are crowded and deteriorated and where poverty is constant and ubiquitous, the family's influence over the adolescent appears to be minimal. In communities characterized by stability, security, safety, and moderate affluence, disrupted or conflictful family conditions can and do generate delinquency, usually of the minor variety. Thus, "Deteriorated families seem to have a stronger impact on youngsters in benign than in hostile ecological settings" (Johnstone, 1980, p. 92).

The Dornbusch Studies: Can Mother Do It Alone?

Sanford Dornbusch and his colleagues (1985) have conducted a series of important studies on the relationship between single-parent (primarily mother-present) homes and adolescent deviance or delinquency. In one study, Dornbusch explored the interrelationships among family structure, patterns of family decision making (process), and deviant behavior. He used data from a nationwide sample of 7,514 subjects drawn from a population of 23 million non-institutionalized youth between the ages of 12 and 17. The sample was representative of the U.S. population for sex, race, region, population density, and population growth.

Dornbusch hypothesized that mother-only households would differ from two-parent households in their ability to control adolescents. Researchers administered questionnaires to both adolescents and to their parents. They sought to ascertain the extent to which parents exerted direct control over adolescent decision making. A lack of control by parents was assumed to lead to adolescent deviance and delinquency. Measures of delinquency included number of contacts with the law, number of arrests, frequency of running away from home, truancy, and frequency of disciplinary actions by school officials.

The proportion of delinquency among mother-only households was greater than the proportion of deviants in households with two biological parents, even when social class and income level were taken into account. This held for both males and females. More important, the presence of a second adult in the mother-only households substantially *reduced* adolescent deviance. The data further suggested that the second adult could be anyone—grandmother, friend, aunt—*other than a stepfather*. Furthermore, there were sex differences in the stepfather arrangement. Boys with stepfathers living in the home engaged in as much deviance and delinquency as those in mother-alone families and more than those in two-parent families. On the other hand, girls in step-parent families exhibited more deviance than their male counterparts in two-parent families but less than girls living in mother-alone families. Dornbusch concludes that the internal processes of families with stepfathers have a stronger negative impact on male than on female adolescents.

In addition to the foregoing family structure variables, Dornbusch examined family decision-making processes as an index of parental control. In an earlier study (1983), he had found that family decision-making style was *partly* related to socioeconomic status (SES). Higher-income families were more likely to demonstrate joint decision-making patterns. However, Dornbusch noted that in the 1983 study, mother-only families constituted a high percentage of the lower-SES families, confounding any conclusions about income and decision-making processes. In the 1985 study, the data continued to reveal that mother-only households showed less control over the adolescent, regardless of SES. The adolescent was making decisions independent of the mother's input. It appears that mothers, faced with the problem of controlling adolescents without another adult, are more likely to allow their children to make their own decisions. Adolescents making their own decisions, according to Dornbusch, are more likely to be deviant.

Findings such as these should not be used to blame mothers raising their children alone for their children's delinquency. Mothers are far more likely than fathers to be responsible for the care of the children, which is one reason why researchers find so many mother-only homes in the first place. Additionally, the need for income to support the family can lead to long hours away from home. Society needs to recognize that placing limitations on entitlements and forcing mothers into workfare programs—while they may have beneficial effects—can also harm the children involved. If we are to do this successfully, it is critical that support services like child care and school and community after-school programs be available.

The Steinberg Study: Is the Family Enough?

Laurence Steinberg (1987) concurs with some of the conclusions drawn from the Dornbusch study. In a self-report survey of 865 adolescents in Madison, Wisconsin, Steinberg discovered that those living in step-parent families were as much at risk of becoming deviant as their peers living in single-parent households. Results supported the assumption that two-biological-parent households are more effective in controlling (or producing less) deviant behavior than other forms of family structure. This was especially the case for girls of all age groups. Steinberg's data did not strongly support the "additional adult" hypothesis (that other adults living in single-mother households diminish deviance). The hypothesis did hold for sixth-grade girls, but not for boys and girls in the other age groups. According to Steinberg, there is a possible link between family structure and adolescent deviance: "Family structure may affect adolescents' susceptibility to antisocial peer pressure, which in turn may affect their involvement in deviant or delinquent activity" (Steinberg, 1987, p. 274).

The recent evidence suggests that children living in homes with both biological parents are significantly less likely to become involved in delinquent or deviant behavior. It does not suggest that delinquency or deviance are products of any unitary concept such as the the single-parent home, however. Researchers are just beginning to uncover the complicated interplay among the myriad variables that influence the family system. Variations in patterns of child rearing, social support systems, reciprocal interchanges between child and parent, and the influences of siblings on one another are uncharted areas of research. Furthermore, even if a single-parent–delinquency association were clear, it would be dangerous and unfair to blame the caregiver. Individual single parents may be excellent caregivers, but as a microsystem, their household may be insufficient unless it is augmented to produce a fuller, richer range of roles, activities, and relationships for the child. Sufficient income is also a critical factor. Single-parent homes with adequate finances and adequate social support systems are likely to be as effective in promoting prosocial behavior as the two-biological-parent household.

FAMILY VIOLENCE AND CHILD ABUSE

When it comes to violent crime, children are far more likely to be victimized than adults (Finkelhor & Dziuba-Leatherman, 1994). The rates of violent crime (assault, rape, and robbery) against those age 12 to 19 are 2 to 3 times higher than for the adult population as a whole. In fact, children and teenagers suffer more victimizations than do adults in virtually every category of violent crime, including physical abuse, sibling assaults, bullying, sexual abuse, and rape (Eron & Slaby, 1994). Homicide is the exception; teenagers (as a whole) are slightly less vulnerable to this violence than adults.

It is clear that victimization can disrupt the course of child development in very fundamental ways (Boney-McCoy & Finkelhor, 1995). In addition to physical injury and neurological damage, severely abused children often suffer emotional and psychological trauma that follows them throughout their lifetimes. For example, chronic anxiety, sadness, school problems, aggressive peer relations, and lower self-esteem have been closely linked to childhood abuse (Briere, 1992; Boney-McCoy & Finkelhor, 1995). Furthermore, individuals with a childhood history of parental abuse are three times more likely to engage in substance abuse than their peers (Scott, 1992; Finkelhor & Dziuba-Leatherman, 1995). Likewise, Widom (1992) reports that a childhood history of abuse may increase the odds of future delinquency and adult criminality by 40 percent. More recent research (Weiler & Widom, 1996) suggests that children who have been abused and/or neglected are prone to be highly aggressive and violent throughout their lifetimes. In another study (Coordinating Council, 1996), adolescents from families reporting multiple forms of violence were more than twice as likely as their peers from nonviolent homes to report committing violent acts.

Even witnessing family violence appears to have a profound effect on the socioemotional development of the child (Feindler & Becker, 1994). Available research indicates that exposure to family violence is related to a greater tendency to engage in aggressiveness, destructiveness, and rebelliousness. It is also reasonable to assume that children who have been abused are more likely to grow up to be abusive parents themselves. More research is necessary before we can determine the nature and extent of these relationships. Research evidence also indicates that neglected children are as likely to grow up violent as children who have been physically abused (Coordinating Council, 1996). Eight out of ten maltreated youths arrested for violent offenses were neglected during their childhoods.

Incidence of Childhood Abuse

Estimates on the prevalence and incidence of family violence differ widely, generally because different terms, concepts, and methodologies are used to gather the data. In addition, abuse and neglect directed at teenagers are often underreported or unrecognized because the teens may try to deal with the unpleasant circumstances by running away, engaging in drug abuse, attempting suicide, or shoplifting.

In 1986, a National Incidence Study (NIS), sponsored by the National Center on Child Abuse and Neglect, reported that more than 1.5 million American children had been neglected or abused the previous year. More recent data are even more disturbing. In 1994, it was estimated that as many as 3 million children were abused or neglected that year (Coordinating Council, 1996). In reference to the total abuse figures reported by the NIS in 1986, 675,000 were found to be abused children, including 358,000 physically abused children, 155,900 sexually abused children, and 211,100 emotionally abused children. Physical abuse includes broken bones, head injuries, lacerations, intestinal perforations, and burns. Emotional abuse consists of three kinds of maltreatment: (1) close confinement; (2) verbal or emotional assault; or (3) other. "Close confinement" refers to incidents in which the child was tied or bound, or confined in a closet or very small enclosure for long periods of time. "Verbal or emotional assault" refers to cases in which the child was habitually belittled, denigrated, made to be a scapegoat, or threatened with sexual or physical abuse. "Other" refers to cases in which the basic necessities of food, water, shelter, or sleep were withheld for extended periods or in which an attempted physical or sexual assault took place. Most of the research up to now has focused on sexual abuse, almost to the exclusion of other kinds of childhood victimization and despite the fact that it accounts for only about one-sixth of all child-abuse reports (Boney-McCoy & Finkelhor, 1995).

TABLE 6.1 Incidence of child abuse and neglect, by age group

	Ages 0–11 Victimizations	Ages 12–17 Victimizations
Child abuse and neglect	387,000	482,000
Fatal	1,180	75
Sexual abuse	97,000	88,000
Physical abuse	194,000	161,000
Emotional abuse	105,000	233,000

SOURCE: T. R. Miller, M. A. Cohen, & B. Wiersema (1996). *Victim costs and consequences: A new look.* Washington, DC: National Institute of Justice, U.S. Government Printing Office.

The NIS reported that approximately 1,100 cases of physical injury resulted in the death of the child, and more recent data suggest that as many as 5,000 children die (most under age 4) annually as a result of maltreatment (Reiss & Roth, 1993). The NIS classified another 160,000 cases as serious because the injuries were evaluated as life-threatening. These injuries included loss of consciousness, breathing cessation, dangerous broken bones, third-degree burns, or extensive second-degree burns over the child's body. Another 952,000 children (15.1 for every 1,000 children) received moderate injury from physical abuse. "Moderate injury" refers to tissue damage, bruises, burns, or pain that persists for at least 48 hours. Additional data (Finkelhor & Dziuba-Leatherman, 1994) indicate that about 58 out of every 1,000 children are subjected to serious violence from their parents, including being kicked, bitten, hit with a fist or object, or threatened with a knife or gun. Female children were subjected to more abuse of all three kinds (physical, sexual, and emotional) than male children. In addition, female preschool children are more frequently homicide victims of their mothers than are male preschoolers (Mann, 1993).

Sibling and Child-to-Parent Abuse

Violence between siblings is believed to be the most common form of intrafamilial violence, but surprisingly little is known about it (Gelles, 1982; Ohlin & Tonry, 1989). Although professionals may recognize parent-to-child or spouse-to-spouse intrafamilial violence, they often find it difficult to recognize sibling violence and abuse.

Child-to-parent abuse is increasingly becoming an important topic. Three teenagers (ages 15 to 17) in 100 (3.5 percent) were reported as kicking, biting, punching, hitting with an object, beating up, threatening, or using a gun or knife against a parent (Gelles, 1982). The killing of parents (parricide) is usually committed by sons (Pagelow, 1989) and is the rarest form of intrafamily homicide. Mothers are killed (matricide) far more often than fathers (patricide) by both adolescents and adult sons and daughters.

Multiassaultive Families

According to recent statistics, at least 7 percent of all intact families are multiassaultive (Hotaling & Straus, 1989). That is, some families are characterized by continual cycles of intrafamilial physical aggression and violence. Siblings hit one another, parents hit the children, and the older children hit the parents. Research findings support the hypothesis that assault is a generalized pattern in interpersonal relations that crosses settings. Family members assault not only one another but the family unit as well (Hotaling & Straus, 1989). Males who have witnessed, participated in, or been victimized by violence in their own families are five times more likely to have also assaulted a nonfamily person than are men in nonassaultive families. A similar pattern holds for women from multiassaultive families, although the relationship is not as strong. Sibling violence is particularly higher in families in which child assault and spousal assault are present, with boys displaying significantly more assaultive behavior (Hotaling & Straus, 1989). Furthermore, children from multiassaultive families engage in an inordinately high rate of assault against nonfamily members. These children are also more likely to be involved in property crime, to have adjustment problems in school, and to be more involved with the police (Hotaling & Straus, 1989).

Intervention

Adolescent physical abuse is commonly linked to rigidity in family relations and parents' poor understanding of teenage development, including unrealistic expectations of their children and poor problem-solving skills (Feindler & Becker, 1994). Successful treatment of child-abusive parents must make use of cognitive restructuring approaches in addition to skills training in child management (Feindler & Becker, 1994). Effective intervention and prevention requires that abusive parents be trained, or be retrained, to parent.

This focus on changing the behavior of the parents is unlikely to have long-term beneficial effects if it is unaccompanied by social support systems, however. Parents without adequate income or community resources to turn to may remain at risk of abusing their children, despite the parenting training they may have received. These community and societal support systems will be discusssed in the following two chapters.

Although there have been some attempts to develop and study strategies for dealing with parents, there has been serious neglect in doing the same for abused children and adolescents. As noted by Feindler and Becker (1994, p. 410), there are "precious few studies of psychological treatment interventions for abused children." Feindler and Becker believe that this omission is partly due to the tendency of practitioners to remove abused children from the home and place them in foster care, primarily for the safety of the children. Approximately one out of five maltreated children are removed from their homes in the United States and placed in foster care for protection. Rarely are the children provided psychotherapy. We should not assume that they need it, however. The absence of research or knowledge on the treatment of abused children is also partly due to the emphasis on working with the entire family, rather than concentrating on only one member of the family.

SUMMARY AND CONCLUSIONS

In this chapter we examined the principal context in which human development takes place: the family. It is apparent from the available research that the family is a major force in the development of delinquency. In the chapter, we summarized four classic studies that have analyzed the family–delinquency connection. The Glueck and McCord projects, although massive and extensive in their detail and data collection, have remained largely ignored in the delinquency literature, primarily because of their attention to individual-level variables.

The two classics that have made inroads into the delinquency literature and prompted greater attention to family factors were the works by F. Ivan Nye and Travis Hirschi. Hirschi especially has had an enormous impact in stimulating thinking and research that centers on the many aspects of family and social control in recent years.

We then looked at family structure and its relationship to delinquency. The family structure variable receiving the bulk of attention has been the single-parent family. Despite this attention, however, the empirical results are not entirely clear on how this variable contributes directly to delinquency.

Family structure variables are important. They highlight what needs to be studied, but they do not, by themselves, encourage theoretical development and cogent explanations of delinquent behavior. Investigations into family processes offer the greater promise for a deeper and more systematic understanding of delinquency. Family processes provided a forum for determining bi-directional, interactional influences, and direct and indirect causal influences.

Current research on prevention and intervention programs strongly indicates that strategies which focus on family processes show the greatest promise in the reduction of delinquency. But let us not be too myopic and overemphasize family influences to the exclusion of other systems. Work by Jeffrey Fagan and Sandra Wexler (1987), for example, indicates that the role of families in the development of many violent delinquents may have been overstated in recent years. Their data imply that much of the learning for violence may occur outside the family within peer groups, neighborhoods, and schools. Fagan and Wexler suggest that families by themselves may be powerless to mitigate well-entrenched neighborhood social processes in the development of serious delinquency, and they recommend that policymakers look beyond the family to the social domain of school, peer, and community in establishing ways to prevent delinquent behavior.

The causes and effective prevention of delinquency continue to be elusive, however. The problem probably stems in part from the tendency to look for cause at only one level of the world's stratification. Causes of human behavior are the result of an enormous range of interacting structures and multilevel systems. We often isolate partial causes, such as faulty practices in parental discipline, or deviant construct systems, or modeling, but this approach is not comprehensive enough. Most past and current explanations of delinquent behavior are not rich enough to account for the myriad causal factors, be they physical, biological, psychological, or sociological. To repeat a statement made by the criminologist Charles F. Wellford (1987, p. 7), ". . . we must develop theories of criminal behavior that take seriously the notion that there are biophysical effects on criminal behavior, psychological effects, social effects, cultural effects or any other organized effects that we wish to identify through our specialization of the appropriate categories or levels of analysis." And as the psychologists Peter T. Manicas and Paul F. Secord (1983, p. 405) write: "Identification of structures and their dynamics can only be accomplished by the *multilevel* application of imaginative theory that simultaneously guides observation, analysis, and experiment" (emphasis added).

KEY CONCEPTS

attachment (control theory)
belief (control theory)
bond theory
Cambridge-Somerville Youth Study
commitment (control theory)
control theory
Dornbusch studies
family process
family structure
Glueck studies

involvement (control theory)
Johnstone studies
National Incidence Study
Nye survey
parental styles
parental practices
reciprocal influence
sociocultural risk
Steinberg study

7

Microsystems and Mesosystems

PEER GROUPS AND YOUTH GANGS

As noted by Irving Spergel (1995), the definition of youth gangs proposed by Malcolm Klein nearly 30 years ago is still in common use today. Klein (1971, p. 111) defined a youth gang as "any denotable adolescent group of youngsters who (a) are generally perceived as a distinct aggregation of others in the neighborhood, (b) recognize themselves as a denotable group (almost invariably with a group name), and (c) have been involved in a sufficient number of delinquent incidents to call forth a consistent negative response from neighborhood residents and/or law enforcement agencies."

Contemporary Gang Demographics

No national-level data are collected on the number of gangs or gang members, nor is there national information on the characteristics of gangs. Although an increasing number of local and state agencies are collecting juvenile-gang statistics, this collection has very little consistency in criteria or uniformity of procedures. Therefore, estimates of gang crime are very rough and subject to considerable error.

The number of gangs in the United States is estimated to be at least 5,000 with a membership of well over 250,000 and growing (Snyder & Sickmund, 1995). The U.S. Department of Justice estimates that there may be as many as 175,000 to 200,000 gang members in California alone. Juvenile gangs are found in every state and are an urban, suburban, and rural phenomenon (Goldstein & Soriano, 1994). These national numbers seem exceedingly small, especially in view of the fact that Frederick Thrasher, a well-known theorist on gang behavior, talked about 1,313 gangs in Chicago alone at the turn of the century. Furthermore, Thrasher was convinced that about one-tenth of Chicago's 350,000 boys between the ages of 10 and 20 were influenced by gangs. One of the major problems in estimating gang numbers is that gang membership is in continual flux, depending on the social, economic, and political climate of a particular geographic region at any given time.

A very large number of the gangs and their membership consist of ethnic minorities. According to Spergel et al. (1989), more than half of gang members are African American, and another third are U.S. Latinos. In recent years, the Latino gang membership in Los Angeles has expanded at a rate 2.5 times faster than the African American membership. This pattern appears to be characteristic of other major urban areas in the United States (Spergel, 1995). Asian gangs, especially Vietnamese, Cambodian, and Laotian gangs, also seem to be expanding rapidly, particularly in California.

Until the mid-1970s, juvenile gangs consisted primarily of members ranging in age from 12 to 21 years. Currently, the age range of membership has expanded at both ends, with members now as young as 9 and older than 30 (Goldstein, 1991). Young members are often used as runners, weapons carriers, and lookouts and in similar capacities because if they are caught, the criminal justice system is likely to respond with considerable leniency. In some gangs, prospective members are required to commit a drive-by shooting or some other form of violence. Older members frequently remain in the gang because employment opportunities for disadvantaged populations remain low in the legitimate economy.

Gang size is the result of several interacting factors, including the size of the youth population within a given area, the presence or absence of police and community pressure, and the nature and visibility of the group. For decades, male gang members have outnumbered females by a ratio of nearly 20 to 1 (Goldstein, 1991). Spergel (1995) argues that the ratio of female gang members to male gang members has remained basically the same over the decades, even though the news media contend that there have been substantial increases in female gang involvement in recent years.

In the past, female gang members functioned in a manner largely auxiliary to their associated male counterparts. They were used as weapons carriers, lookouts, and social and sexual targets. Today, there are increasing numbers of independent or unaffiliated female gangs. Females join gangs later than do males, and they leave earlier (Goldstein, 1991).

Research on peer influences on delinquent behavior has almost invariably focused on sizeable juvenile groups or gangs. Virtually no one has studied very small groups, such as delinquent or nondelinquent dyads or triads. Even research on adult crime partnerships is scarce. Therefore, although we should recognize that some delinquent behavior is displayed by two or three juveniles working in collusion, the concentration in this chapter will be on larger groups.

YOUTH GANGS AND CRIME

Although there have been peaks and valleys in gang violence over the years, the amount of violence perpetrated by gang members in recent years appears to be on the increase (Spergel, 1995). Part of the current increase is due to the availability of guns, especially semiautomatic ones, such as A.K. 47s, Tech-9s, Uzis, and other high-powered weapons. Gangs today are also more mobile, riding around in cars and looking for opposing gang members to confront.

The relationships among gang membership, drug use, drug selling, and violence are unclear (Spergel, 1995). The news media and law enforcement agencies have for years claimed a close connection between violence and gang involvement in drugs. The research evidence, however, does not support these claims (Klein, Maxson, & Cunningham, 1988; Institute for Law and Justice, 1994; Spergel, 1995). The relationships are much more complicated than is commonly assumed. Many gang members engage in drug use and/or trafficking, but many do not.

Why do adolescents join gangs? Goldstein and Soriano (1994, p. 318) conclude: "Largely to obtain what all adolescents appropriately seek: peer friendships, pride, identity development, self-esteem enhancement, the acquisition of resources, and family and community tradition." Perspectives and theories differ in the importance and influence that gangs attribute to these motivations. In the following pages, we will examine some of the varying viewpoints that explain the development of juvenile gangs and why individuals join them. Exceedingly little gang-focused literature exists that is of a psychological nature (Goldstein & Soriano, 1994). Research and theory on youth gangs springs largely from a sociological perspective, most of it before the 1980s.

THE CLASSICS ON YOUTH GANGS

All intellectual paths on group delinquency originated with the pioneering efforts in Chicago of Frederick M. Thrasher, who published his observations in the well-received classic *The Gang* (Geis, 1965). At a time when psychologically oriented criminologists treated gang behavior as a throwback to primitive man roaming in herds, Thrasher dramatically shifted the discussion. Gang behavior, he said, was one way for youths to react to economic and social conditions. Although his colleagues at the Chicago School were drawing similar conclusions about delinquency in general, Thrasher studied only gangs. He observed that gangs emerged and thrived in the interstitial areas of cities, particularly those areas lying between adjacent commercial and residential neighborhoods. Thrasher essentially equated gangs with group delinquency, because virtually all of the gangs he studied engaged in criminal activities.

Thrasher wrote that gangs represented the spontaneous effort of young people to create a society for themselves that offered excitement and adventure in the company of peers. Gangs provided the medium for stimulation, thrills, and togetherness that were not readily available in impoverished neighborhoods. Because a majority of the Chicago gangs engaged in unconventional and delinquent behavior, Thrasher's gangs were an appropriate unit for the study of delinquency as group behavior. Of the 1,313 gangs he studied, 530 could be classified as delinquent and another 609 as "often delinquent." Unfortunately, he did not explain the criteria for these classifications.

Thrasher concluded that faulty social controls were at the root of gang delinquency. Specifically, the youths who violated norms had been ineffectively or weakly socialized by their families, churches, and schools. The social void thus created prompted the youths to seek one another's company and form groups. Believing themselves free of traditional social controls, youth gangs did what they wanted, subject only to the social constraints of their own subculture. Thrasher also observed that female gangs were exceedingly rare (he could locate only six that were independent of male gangs). He attributed the rarity of female gangs to the closer supervision that families—including single-parent families—gave to girls.

Following Thrasher's pioneering work, interest in gang delinquency ebbed, peaked, and ebbed once again. Interest was high in the 1950s and the 1960s, and several provocative theories were proposed. Since the mid-1960s, precious few new theories of gang delinquency have been advanced, nor has there been much research on the topic. Thus, our knowledge in this area is limited. Mark Stafford (1984) cites two primary reasons for the lost interest. First, the study of gang delinquency has been hampered by its parochialism. Researchers and theorists have focused almost exclusively on low-SES urban boys, and this focus has limited the scope of any potential theory of group delinquency. A notable exception is the work of Anne Campbell (1984), who studied group delinquency among girls. Second, there is considerable disagreement over the use of the word "gang." For example, what are the social boundaries of a gang? Where does it begin and where does it end? Members are not always easy to identify, and membership often fluctuates. Furthermore, it is not clear how a gang differs from a formal group or even, in some cases, a youth organization.

A rather exasperated Walter B. Miller (1980), whose work on gang delinquency will be discussed shortly, noted also that there is no systematic procedure for identifying and characterizing different kinds of law-violating youth groups. Unfortunately, there has been little attempt to develop such a procedure. Although criminologists often conclude that most delinquency is committed in groups (Miller, 1980; Hansell & Wiatrowski, 1981), we are able to obtain only very rough estimates of the amount of group delinquency in the United States or elsewhere. The sparse available information has been gathered from self-report research or field observation, not from official tabulations. Although there is a sense that groups of juveniles operate together, and virtually every law enforcement official is personally familiar with the phenomenon of group delinquency, quantifiable data are hard to find. Some of the best work on gangs in recent years has take a *qualitative* tack, such as Campbell's (1984) work, which is discussed later in the chapter.

SOCIAL ABILITY VERSUS SOCIAL DISABILITY MODELS

Stephen Hansell and Michael Wiatrowski (1981) called attention to a major theoretical disagreement about the nature of delinquent group relationships. Some criminologists believe that most gang members have average social and interpersonal skills and generally belong to strong, cohesive groups. Group solidarity, close friendships, and loyalties are assumed to be features of the delinquent gang. In this sense, delinquent groups are not unlike nondelinquent groups. Other criminologists perceive delinquents as loners and social isolates with below-average interpersonal skills. Members are perceived as social outcasts who gravitate to other deviant and socially inept peers, eventually forming gangs. Because the members constituting them are socially inadequate, the gangs remain unstable, chaotic, disorganized bands of youths who cannot establish close, intimate relationships with one another.

Theories that view delinquent gang members as socially normal and their groups as cohesive and close-knit are **social ability models** in Hansell and Wiatrowski's terminology. Those theories that consider delinquent gang members outcasts and socially inept adolescents who make little attempt to develop cohesive groups are called **social disability models**. Examples of social ability models are the classic theories of Albert K. Cohen, Walter B. Miller, Richard Cloward and Lloyd Ohlin, and Herbert Bloch and Arthur Niederhoffer. Social disability models are best represented in the work of James Short Jr. and Fred Strodbeck, and more recently by Gerald Patterson.

SOCIAL ABILITY MODELS

Cohen: Delinquent Boys and the Strains of the Working Class

The concepts of subculture, social class, and status deprivation are central themes in Albert K. Cohen's book on male delinquency, *Delinquent Boys: The Culture of the Gang* (1955). The book is an extensive revision of the author's doctoral dissertation, which was completed at Harvard University in 1951. Although Cohen's primary intent was to outline a general theory of subcultures, the book is most commonly regarded as a classic statement on the causation of delinquency, falling under the **strain** perspective. We should keep in mind that Cohen's statement refers specifically to lower-SES *male* delinquency.

Cohen stipulated that the basic cause of lower-SES male delinquency rested with the very limited opportunities for lower-SES youths to gain access to mainstream, middle-class society. This limited opportunity resulted in the male's feeling alienated from mainstream society. Thus, like Merton's theory, Cohen's was fundamentally a strain theory. Whereas Merton concentrated upon the goal of material wealth, Cohen emphasized the importance of additional or higher status. According to Cohen, lower-SES youth were ascribed a low status by their families of origin. Upon entering society, these youth realized that they were unable to achieve status because they had not been socialized in the manner of the dominant class and were not privy to the proper behavior needed to get ahead. Middle-class parents had taught their children self-control, postponement of gratification, and effective planning for the future. Parents had communicated to their children that if they worked hard, were patient, and did what was expected, "good things" would come to them in the long run. Lower-class children had no such advantage. Lower-class boys were impulsive, hedonistic, and concerned with immediate gratification. They had been socialized to the tenet "Get what you can when you can get it. Tomorrow will be too late." Cohen's stereotypical assumptions about lower-class socialization have been widely criticized.

Cohen believed that lower-SES children were at a serious disadvantage in the schools, where all children were constantly evaluated against the "middle-class measuring rod" (Cohen, 1955, p. 84). This concept referred to the set of social expectations regarding the characteristics of "good children." One could meet this abstract standard only if one displayed responsibility, ambition, courtesy, and the proper control of aggression. According to Cohen, lower-SES children were unable to do this.

The low ascribed status and the inability to achieve status among both law-abiding peers and adults created strain in the lower-class boy. He realized that his upbringing had not emphasized order, punctuality, and time consciousness. He had learned to be easygoing and spontaneous, to be unconcerned about achieving the long-term material goals desired by most of society. He had also learned to solve his problems with physical aggression and threats. Thus, the lower-class boy began to feel alienated from middle-class children, school officials, and other middle-class adults. Eventually, he found other lower-class boys who felt the same way. They formed the groups that, according to Cohen, were the essence of the delinquent subculture.

Cohen described the delinquent subculture as nonutilitarian, malicious, negativistic, and versatile. It was further characterized by **short-run hedonism** and **group autonomy**. These features differed significantly from Merton's conception of anomie. Merton, for example, assumed that lower-class members of society stole for material gain and therefore to be in tune with mainstream America. Cohen suggested that delinquent boys, more often than not, stole "for the hell of it." In fact, they often discarded, destroyed, or gave away stolen property. Delinquent boys valued the status they obtained from their fellow gang members, not material gain. This was the nonutilitarian feature of the delinquent subculture. Its members usually acted with no discernible purpose.

Delinquent subcultures, according to Cohen, were also generally malicious. They seemed to delight in the discomfort of others—nongang peers and adults—

and enjoyed defying societal taboos. "[T]here is keen delight in terrorizing 'good' children, in driving them from playgrounds and gyms for which the gang itself may have little use, and in general in making themselves obnoxious to the virtuous" (Cohen, 1955, p. 28). Teachers often received the brunt of the malice. "There is an element of active spite and malice, contempt and ridicule, challenge and defiance, exquisitely symbolized, in an incident described to the writer by Mr. Henry D. McKay, of defecating on the teacher's desk" (Cohen, 1955, p. 28).

Cohen's term "negativisitic" was closely related to maliciousness. Delinquent subcultures flouted the values and norms of mainstream society. Delinquents did things in spite of expectations and against mainstream norms. "The delinquent's conduct is right, by the standards of his subculture, precisely *because* it is wrong by the norms of the larger culture" (Cohen, 1955, p. 28).

"Versatility," which Cohen referred to as the "spirit" of the delinquent subculture, signified the **diversity** of the antisocial behavior exhibited by the delinquent gang. Delinquents did not "specialize" in one activity. They were involved in many different irritating or illegal activities, often using ingenious strategies and devious plots.

"Short-run hedonism" underscored the lack of long-term planning, patience, or socialized ability to control the impulse of the moment, which Cohen believed characterized the delinquent subculture as well as the lower social class in general. Members of the delinquent gang typically congregated—with no specific purpose in mind—at some street corner or hangout spot. They responded impulsively to suggestions or spontaneous events. Typically, they did not like organized or supervised recreation or being told what to do by the adult world. They enjoyed the "fun" of the moment, without regard for the consequences. Cohen recognized that this characteristic was common for adolescents across all social classes but said, ". . . it reaches its finest flower" in the delinquent gang (Cohen, 1955, pp. 30–31).

Another feature not entirely specific to the delinquent gang was its "group autonomy," which referred to intolerance of restraint from persons or institutions outside the immediate circle of gang members. According to Cohen, gang relationships were intense, showing solidarity and commitment, features that place Cohen's theory into Hansell and Wiatrowski's social ability category. Relationships with other groups tended to be indifferent, hostile, or rebellious. Cohen warned that he was not referring to an individual's autonomy from parents or other social agents but specifically to the autonomy of the gang as a social unit. "For many of our subcultural delinquents the claims of the home are very real and very compelling. The point is that the gang is a separate, distinct and often irresistible focus of attraction, loyalty and solidarity" (Cohen, 1955, p. 31).

In Cohen's view, the frustrations inherent in status deprivation and the limited opportunity to change it within mainstream society *may* lead to the formation of the delinquent subculture. Notice that the word "may" is emphasized here. This is because status frustration does not lead automatically to delinquency. Cohen maintains that juveniles plagued by status frustration are more likely to join delinquent subcultures than others.

Cohen was also a student of Edwin Sutherland. Reflecting Sutherland's differential association theory, Cohen believed that boys learned delinquent behavior from one another; they looked for "signs" or gestures of support (definitions) from their fellow group members. As those signs gradually appeared, the group became progressively committed to a set of new behaviors—a process Cohen called "mutual conversion." Cohen believed that Merton treated the deviant act as a sudden, discontinuous change of state, a leap from a state of strain and anomie to a state of deviance (Cohen, 1965). From Cohen's perspective, deviance and delinquency developed gradually. "Human action, deviant or otherwise, is something that typically develops and grows in a tentative, groping, advancing, backtracking, sounding out process. People taste and feel their way along" (Cohen, 1980, p. 162).

In summary, Cohen explained that a large segment of delinquency was a reaction against middle-class values and occurred as a function of participation in a delinquent subculture. Boys of similar circumstance formed a subculture, complete with a system of beliefs and values engendered by a process of "communicative interaction." The similar circumstance—more often than not—was membership in the lower social class, where access to mainstream opportunity was severely limited. Frustrated in their attempts to gain status, lower-SES boys allied themselves with gangs that engaged in a wide assortment of delinquent activity. In essence, the delinquent subculture was a way of dealing with the "problems of adjustment"; it provided a criterion of status that the boys could meet and with which they were reasonably comfortable. Within the gang, they could flout middle-class values and standards with peer support. Together, members could reject school, religious institutions, and anything representative of the middle-class system.

Cohen added a surprising twist to his theory, suggesting that the rejection of middle-class norms was a kind of "reaction formation." "Reaction formation," a concept used in the psychological and psychiatric literature, refers to one of the defense mechanisms that humans are said to use in order to ward off threatening levels of anxiety. Sigmund Freud identified it as a hypothetical process that results in the person's overtly stressing behaviors that are antithetical to his or her unconscious desires. The person who employs reaction formation presumably does not have to acknowledge his or her unconscious wishes. If these wishes were to come into awareness, they would cause considerable anxiety or guilt. "[W]e would expect the delinquent boy who, after all, has been socialized in a society dominated by a middle-class morality and who can never quite escape the blandishments of middle-class society, to seek to maintain his safeguards against seduction" (Cohen, 1955, p. 133). Thus, reaction formation takes the form of an "irrational" and "malicious" behavior against all symbols and agents of middle-class society. Cohen believed, therefore, that gang delinquents never actually repudiated conventional norms and standards. Subconsciously, they had the same goals and the same material interests as the rest of society.

Critics often point out that one major weakness in Cohen's theory is its inability to account for middle-class or female delinquency. Contemporary criminologists see these as major flaws in early theories of crime and delinquency. Focusing on the lower class ignored the fact that youth in all classes commit crime; focusing on boys ignored the possibility that girls may commit delinquency for different reasons than boys. In his book *Delinquent Boys*, Cohen did acknowledge that practically all children, regardless of social class, commit delinquent acts. However, he also argued that delinquency is certainly more heavily concentrated in the working class. Viable theories of delinquency, he said, should begin there.

Although Cohen acknowledged the existence of female delinquents, he argued that their delinquency was overwhelmingly sexual in nature and not to be explained by his theory. "Stealing, 'other property offenses,' 'orneriness' and 'hell raising' in general are primarily practices of the male" (p. 45). Cohen, not unlike others during that era, believed that a woman's adjustment in society was dependent upon her ability to form a satisfying relationship with a male. "[A] female's station in society, the admiration, respect and property that she commands, depends to a much greater degree on the kinds of relationships she establishes with members of the opposite sex" (p. 14). "Boys collect stamps, girls collect boys" (p. 142). Female delinquency represented a failure on the part of the girl to fulfill her proper role. Cohen believed that the "true" delinquent was the "rogue male" (p. 140). As we will see in Chapter 10, these interpretations of the "proper role" of women and girls have been widely shared throughout much of the twentieth century and have led to a punitive response to girls by the juvenile justice system.

Walter B. Miller and Lower-SES Gangs

The Harvard cultural anthropologist Walter B. Miller disagreed with Cohen's contention that delinquency was a reaction against middle-class standards and values. To Miller, who also restricted his study to boys, delinquency was an adaptive effort to achieve success within the constraints of lower-SES membership. Based on the data he collected on delinquent gangs in the slums of Boston, Miller concluded that delinquency was little more than lower-class adolescents' modeling the behavior and adopting the beliefs of lower-class adults. In an article published in 1958, Miller argued that the prime motivation of delinquent activity was the desire to realize the values of the lower-class community itself, not a defiant response directed at the middle class. These values, however, were considered deviant.

Miller analyzed the lower-class value system as an anthropologist would study a culture in East San Loa. The American lower class, according to Miller, is a long-established, distinctively patterned tradition with an integrity of its own. He suggested that it may comprise as many as four to six subcultures. About 15 percent of Americans represented a real "hard core" lower-class group from which most male gang delinquency evolved.

Miller's gang theory revolved around two important structural variables that he saw as central ingredients of lower-class culture: (1) female-dominated households and (2) single-sex peer groups. A majority of the households he studied were clearly dominated by a woman (mother, grandmother, or sibling). The male authority figure either was entirely absent from the home or appeared only sporadically. When present, he took little or no part in the care and support of the children. Furthermore, the dominant woman in the household would generally have a stream of sexual partners, in or out of wedlock. According to Miller, boys brought up in this female-based world lacked an adequate male identity and sex role. To discover their places in the masculine world, they "hung out" and eventually became members of street-corner gangs, all composed of male adolescents seeking their proper roles. Within this gang structure, the boys would not rail against the middle class, as Cohen suggested. Instead, they emulated and modeled what males they could find in the lower-class culture, including older boys in their gang. There was very little concern about middle-class attainment.

Miller believed that gang delinquency was a natural product of lower-class culture, which had six **focal concerns**, none of which appeared in the middle class. The lower SES gave widespread attention to these concerns, which were (1) trouble, (2) toughness, (3) smartness, (4) excitement, (5) fate, and (6) autonomy. All of these concerns were embraced by the gang and could be observed easily by field researchers.

"Trouble" referred to how much difficulty one had with the law. Miller asserted that members of the lower SES assigned one another a "trouble index," indicating where someone fell along some hypothetical "trouble dimension." This index was so important that it dictated how others related to the person. If a woman's daughter was spending time with a boy, it was normal for the mother to be concerned about how much "trouble" the boy had faced in the past and was likely to face in the future. The trouble index also influenced a boy's status within the gang; some gangs responded positively to a high index but others did not.

A second focal concern of the lower SES was **toughness**, or physical prowess, strength, endurance, and athletic skill. Miller believed that the lower SES, especially lower-SES males, demonstrated excessive concerns about masculinity, a feature that may be attributed to the predominance of female-based households. An excessive concern with masculinity could reflect a "compulsive reaction formation," a term that Miller, like Cohen, borrowed from the currently fashionable psychology of the day.

Smartness designated a capacity to outsmart, outfox, outwit, dupe, or generally "con" others. Whereas the middle class emphasized intellectual ability, the lower-SES was concerned about the ability to outsmart others and, more generally, society. Miller contended that this trait had a long tradition in lower-SES culture and was demonstrated in such practices as card playing and other forms of gambling.

A fourth focal concern was the constant search for **excitement** and thrills. This search was exhibited by excessive use of alcohol, gambling of all kinds, interest in music, and sexual adventuring. Fighting was also a feature of the need to take risks and seek danger. Gangs looking for trouble were an obvious product of this focal concern.

The last two focal concerns—fate and autonomy—referred to control over one's life. Miller posited that lower-class people as a group strongly felt that their lives were subject to a set of forces over which they had little control. Whatever happened was solely a matter of fate, and hence, any directed effort at a long-term goal was ultimately futile. Persons of lower SES lived for the moment and took whatever came their way. On the other hand, they insisted on autonomy and resented the idea of external controls or restrictions on behavior. Lower-SES people say they do not like to be "pushed around," yet they expected it as part of their fate.

Male adolescents had two additional concerns: **belonging** and **status**. Miller described these two as "higher order concerns" because before one could "belong" or have "status" within a gang, one had to demonstrate toughness, smartness, and similar attributes. "Belonging" means a boy is "part of the club" or has in-group membership in the gang—"he hangs with us" was the terminology used by Miller. Violation of the group's code of conduct and beliefs results in exclusion. "Status" refers to the boy's ranking within the group, which is tested constantly by means of a set of status-ranking activities. One gains status within the group by demonstrating superiority in one of the six basic concerns described previously.

In sum, Miller saw the lower-SES boy as belonging to a gang in order to prepare for lower-SES adulthood. Such membership was a normal part of growing up in poverty. In response to the high incidence of gang-related violence, Miller (1975, 1982) came to believe that juvenile gangs had become significant threats to a normal society.

Like Cohen, Miller can be faulted for perpetuating the stereotypical notion that the values of the lower class are different and deviant. It is not unusual for male students today to read Miller's work and recognize themselves in the descriptions of the focal concerns, regardless of their socioecoonic status.

Bloch and Niederhoffer: Psychodynamic Aspects of Gangs

In 1958, the same year that Miller published his theory in the *Journal of Social Issues*, Herbert A. Bloch, a sociologist, and Arthur Niederhoffer, a police lieutenant, published *The Gang: A Study in Adolescent Behavior*. Their approach was distinct from others in two respects: It took a decidedly psychological perspective, and it was not limited to lower-SES delinquent behavior. According to Bloch and Niederhoffer, adolescence is a psychological stage of development that all youths throughout the world experience. It is characterized by a role "strain" toward obtaining adult status. Bloch and Niederhoffer maintained that adolescents were constantly testing their upcoming adult roles. If adults hampered or interfered with this testing, adolescents were forced to seek alternate forms of behavior, including delinquency. Parents might hamper the adolescent's development of adult roles by not allowing them to try things that they (the adolescents) perceive as adultlike behavior, including smoking, drinking, driving cars, swearing, engaging in sexual behavior, and so forth.

According to Bloch and Niederhoffer, adolescents who lacked adult support turned to gangs, and these associations eased their transition to adult society.

Gangs fulfilled the same psychological function as formalized rituals, such as puberty rites. For example, the investigators noticed that many gang members displayed tattoos or other identifying marks, signifying a rite of passage or an initiation. Bloch and Niederhoffer observed that gangs were close-knit and cohesive, with an organized hierarchy of leadership and status. Thus, the gang satisfied deep-seated needs of adolescents in all cultures. In fact, like Thrasher, Block and Niederhoffer virtually equated delinquency with gangs: Gangs almost automatically led to delinquency, and delinquent acts were usually committed by gangs.

Bloch and Niederhoffer disagreed with Cohen's descriptions of lower-class gangs. They did not believe, for example, that delinquent behavior was nonutilitarian. From their observations and experiences with gangs, they concluded that most delinquent behavior either had material value or great "psychological utility" in satisfying personal needs and tensions. They also found little evidence of Cohen's short-run hedonism; many gangs not only had long-range plans but also would forego immediate pleasures to attain them. Finally, many of the descriptive features of Cohen's lower-SES delinquency (malice, hatred, versatility, non-utility, and short-run hedonism) could be just as readily applied to middle- and upper-class gangs.

The authors tried to incorporate popular psychological developmental theories into their explanations of gangs and delinquency. They particularly favored psychoanalytic theory. For example, they asserted that gangs allowed members to release forces and urges that were suppressed and repressed in nongang boys. Bloch and Niederhoffer did not convince many criminologists that their perspective had merit, however. Those amenable to gang theory were attending to the work of Cohen, Miller, and soon after to the work of Cloward and Ohlin.

Cloward and Ohlin: Opportunity Theory

A book that had considerable impact on gang theory was *Delinquency and Opportunity: A Theory of Delinquent Gangs*, written by Richard Cloward and Lloyd Ohlin (1960). The book—and the differential opportunity theory contained therein—was developed from field studies. The authors conducted the studies in two juvenile institutions in New York, one private (Children's Village) and the other public (Warwick). Cloward and Ohlin set out to explore the various types of delinquent subculture that they believed existed; other subcultural theorists had acknowledged only one type. Cloward and Ohlin hypothesized that different institutional environments produced different kinds of inmate subcultures. They predicted that the social climate and structure of the public institution would elicit a significantly different subculture from the social climate and structure of the private one. Hence, the Cloward and Ohlin theory was formulated on institutionalized youngsters and generalized to community gangs. "Thus it was a transfer of basic theoretical notions we were developing in the institutions, that we developed further and applied by analogy to the community" (Ohlin, 1983a, p. 211).

Cloward and Ohlin, both former students of Sutherland, were impressed with theories of Durkheim and Merton as well as the ecological work of the

Chicago School. The Cloward–Ohlin theory of differential opportunity incorporates concepts from each of these. It was, in fact, one of the earliest attempts to integrate different perspectives into a unified theory.

Cloward and Ohlin believed that "pressures toward the formation of delinquent subcultures originate in the marked discrepancies between culturally induced aspirations among lower-class youth and the possibilities of achieving them by legitimate means" (Cloward & Ohlin, 1960, p. 78). Thus, they accepted Merton's position that the fundamental sociological cause of strain is blocked opportunity to achieve socially valued goals. In this sense, the Cloward–Ohlin theory is often subsumed under the strain theory perspective. They also acknowledged Merton's very helpful distinction between cultural goals and institutionalized means and the interchange between them. The means are the approved ways of reaching the desired goals. The social structure of a society establishes the patterned relationships in which individuals are involved, such as the divisions of social class on the basis of wealth, power, or prestige. Cloward and Ohlin theorized that individuals had differential opportunities for reaching the cultural goals, depending upon their position in the social structure as well as their abilities. Consequently, individuals experienced differential pressure toward deviance. Under some conditions, lower-class youth were under great strain toward deviance, but this was not as universal as earlier theorists had maintained. "It is our view that many discontented lower-class youth do not wish to adopt a middle-class way of life or to disrupt their present associations and negotiate passage into middle-class groups. The solution they seek entails the acquisition of higher position in terms of lower-class rather than middle-class criteria" (Cloward & Ohlin, 1960, p. 92).

Cloward and Ohlin emphasized that the formation of delinquency did not follow a simple or universal pattern. Like their mentor Sutherland, Cloward and Ohlin believed that delinquency was learned in the everyday interaction with others and that the nature of that interaction varied substantially among groups. They saw a strong relationship among the social environment, the economic structure, and the behavioral choices that were available. To put it another way, subcultures had differential accessibility to both legitimate *and* illegitimate means of achieving higher status or positions. Not only were the legal and socially approved opportunities blocked for some, but so too were illegal opportunities. Even the illegitimate means to success were unevenly distributed. For example, some lower-class neighborhoods provided greater opportunity for illegal gain than did others.

Cloward and Ohlin proposed that three general delinquent subcultures existed. They labeled these the **criminal**, **conflict**, and **retreatist** subcultures. Each not only had its specific features but also advocated different forms of criminal behavior. Members of the criminal subculture were interested in instrumental gains, such as money that would allow them to obtain the material wealth advocated by society. Cloward and Ohlin believed that the criminal subculture depended heavily upon illegitimate success models—persons who were highly visible to lower-class youth and willing to establish a relationship with them.

These success models were usually older lower-class youth who had obtained material goods through one of the few avenues available to them: theft, robbery, prostitution, or other instrumental crimes. Thus, whereas middle-class youth had such middle-class success models as lawyers, bankers, physicians, and other educated persons, lower-class adolescents generally had only illegitimate models to imitate. One way to avoid a life of deprivation and frustration was to acquire the values and skills of successful deviants.

Cloward and Ohlin noted that learning the values and skills of the criminal subculture would not necessarily ensure successful acquisition of the desired material goods, however. Individuals also needed the support of other members of the criminal subculture. For example, they often had to have middlemen, fences, and partners, and they needed access to lawyers and bondsmen. To qualify for membership in the criminal subculture, a person had to be able to conform to the standards of the group and control undisciplined, unpredictable, or erratic behavior. Impulsive acts had no place in the pursuit of a successful criminal career. Individuals also had to prove themselves by engaging in criminal activities that would meet with the group's approval. In this social context, theft was a way of "expressing solidarity with the carriers of criminal values . . . and a way of acquiring the various concrete skills necessary before the potential criminal can gain full acceptance in the group to which he aspires" (Cloward & Ohlin, 1960, p. 309). This contrasted sharply with Cohen's belief that delinquent activity was nonutilitarian.

According to Cloward and Ohlin, not all boys could become successful criminals. Some, because of personality features, beliefs, or physical skills, were locked out of the illegitimate avenue toward desired goals. Furthermore, reflecting the influence of the Chicago School, Cloward and Ohlin maintained that some neighborhoods were more likely to support the criminal subculture than others. Illegitimate avenues were most available in lower-class neighborhoods that were integrated and organized. Youth living in lower-class neighborhoods that lacked unity and cohesion—socially disorganized neighborhoods—were frustrated in their quest for both conventional and criminal opportunities.

Heightened frustration, according to Cloward and Ohlin, became the chief motivator of participation in the conflict subculture. Youths deprived of both conventional and criminal opportunities were outcasts of both the criminal minority and the cultural majority, and their behavior reflected this frustration. The illegal activity of the conflict subculture tended to be unorganized, petty, and unprotected. Members of this subculture often endangered their own lives and the lives of others for minimal gain. They caused extensive property damage and were especially prone to impulsive violence. Violence, in fact, was the hallmark of the conflict subculture. It was often displayed in gang warfare.

The third subculture, the retreatist, typically comprised drug users and social isolates. Their criminal activities were often individualistic. Social contacts were made only to secure sufficient drugs or money to maintain a retreatist lifestyle. Members of the retreatist subculture suffered from "double failure"—not only were they unable to participate in conventional or illegal activities, but they were also likely to alienate all others in their social world.

The general source of social strain was the same for all three subcultures: anomie produced by blocked legitimate opportunities (Pfohl, 1985). What differed was the specific channel each subculture used to adapt to its plight.

When Hansell and Wiatrowski (1981) discussed the social ability and social disability models of gang delinquency, they placed the Cloward–Ohlin theory in the former group. The criminal subculture clearly deserves this characterization, because it suggests that group solidarity and mutual assistance are needed for success. It is less clear that the conflict and retreatist subcultures have these features. Retreatists in particular would fall more convincingly into the social disability model.

SOCIAL DISABILITY MODELS

Short and Strodtbeck: The Sociology of Gangs

One of the most extensive studies ever undertaken on gang delinquency was conducted in Chicago by James F. Short Jr. and Fred L. Strodtbeck during a three-year period (1959–62). This classic study, published in the book *Group Process and Gang Delinquency* (1965), grew out of the detached-worker program sponsored by the YMCA of metropolitan Chicago. Social workers and volunteers working in the community were asked to conduct systematic, detailed observations of youth gangs and monitor "the flow of events." The Short–Strodtbeck project collected data on 16 gangs, ranging in size from 16 to 68 members and totaling 598 boys. Eleven of the gangs were black gangs, totaling 464 boys. Additional data were collected on another 12 black and 10 white gangs. Gang members were almost entirely of lower SES; Short and Strodtbeck could not locate a single middle-class gang. "Gangs of middle class youngsters apparently are rare, however, despite mounting public concern over middle class delinquency" (p. 15).

Although the YMCA detached-worker program of Chicago was modeled after the Cloward–Ohlin theory, Short and Strodtbeck were unable to locate the neat categories suggested by the theory. They were also unable to identify any of the group solidarity discussed by other theorists. The image of the gang as a carefree, close-knit, all-for-one-and-one-for-all group was not supported. Instead, Short and Strodtbeck found that gang members were socially disabled individuals alienated from mainstream society. They were, according to these researchers, social misfits. "Our gang boys failed often in schools, on the job, in conventional youth-serving agencies, and in the eyes of law enforcement officials. . . . They fail more often in each of these respects than do the non-gang boys we have studied, both middle and lower class" (Short & Strodtbeck, 1965, p. 230). Short and Strodtbeck also claimed that gang boys, compared with nongang boys, were less self-assertive, slightly more neurotic and anxious, less gregarious, and generally had few of the qualities that engender confidence and nurturing relationships with others. Overall, they lacked fundamental social or interpersonal skills. The boys also exhibited limited verbal skills and appeared to be significantly below average in cognitive development.

According to Short and Strodtbeck, the emotional atmosphere of the gangs was similar to that reported for the lower-SES culture, accentuated by a strong distrust of both "insiders" and "outsiders." The gangs also seemed to be socially isolated from social networks beyond immediate gang members and had limited meaningful contacts with adults.

Patterson's Two-Stage Process

Patterson and his colleagues (Patterson, 1982; Patterson, Dishion, & Bank, 1984; Snyder & Patterson, 1987) consider delinquency to be largely a result of faulty socialization. This faulty socialization occurs in two stages. The first stage takes place during childhood and primarily within the home setting. This stage is a consequence of inept parenting, such as the enmeshed and lax parental styles and the inadequate monitoring discussed earlier. Inept parenting fosters poor interpersonal, academic, and work skills in children. Because the child lacks the necessary skills to adapt under normal daily living conditions, he or she is likely to move into the second stage of antisocial training. The child's hostility and inadequate interpersonal approach toward others "turns people off," encouraging and accelerating rejection by others. This social and emotional rejection restricts opportunity to acquire the necessary skills to adjust or achieve in society, resulting in a kind of catch-22. Rejected by mainstream society and closed off from adjusting within it, these youth are drawn toward other unskilled, socially disabled children. This association increases opportunity ". . . to acquire, perform, and hone antisocial behavior" (Snyder & Patterson, 1987, p. 219). Consequently, antisocial and delinquent behaviors, under the watchful eyes and encouragement of other deviant peers, become more frequent, varied, and serious. Thus, the relationship between skills deficits and delinquent behavior becomes reciprocal within the context of a deviant, socially disabled peer group.

Synder and Patterson admonish that their two-stage model is very incomplete. It is based almost exclusively on their assessment of the development of male delinquent behavior. The factors and processes outlined may be substantially different for females. Furthermore, they acknowledge that we simply do not know enough about the reciprocal processes of family, parenting, and peer interactions to be confident that the model represents the complicated dynamics of delinquency development. One attempt to understand these dynamics is found in peer network analysis.

DEVELOPMENTAL THEORY

Developmental theory also discusses gang delinquency. Recall the life-course-persistent (LCP) youth, who during the preteen years was rejected by peers. During the teen years, however, the LCP adolescent is seen by many teens as independent from adult supervision and authority, a situation other teens seek but don't have. The LCP teen has very little parental or adult supervision, constantly flouts authority, and seems able to do pretty much what he or she wants. In essence, the LCP teen becomes a "magnet" for other teens to cluster around. Moffitt (1993a, p. 688) writes: "A magnet role would imply that children who were rejected and ignored by others should experience newfound 'popularity' as teens, relative to their former rejected status." These formerly rejected teens become role models for a network of novice delinquents, a network that eventually develops into delinquent gangs. The foregoing scenario suggests that many delinquent gangs do not come together primarily for supportive friendships or surrogate parenting but primarily to model the wayward magnet in demonstrating independence and resistance to adult authority and values. In most instances, however, the adolescence-limited (AL) teen will do his or her anti-authority demonstration (such as larceny, school vandalism, curfew violations, shoplifting, motor vehicle theft, or substance abuse) and then shift into a relatively crime-free young adulthood. The danger, of course, is that some rebellious AL youth become so caught up in the juvenile justice or criminal justice system that they seriously damage their social and occupational futures. They may find it extremely difficult to extricate themselves from the entanglement of societal labels, restrictions, and expectations that often accompany delinquent or crime adjudication. In these cases, intervention, rehabilitation, and treatment programs would be extremely helpful in changing the career path.

PEER GROUPS: ACCEPTANCE AND REJECTION

In a comprehensive review of peer relations, Willard W. Hartup (1983) reported available research which suggests that antisocial children are unpopular and often excluded from peer groups. "A repertoire of friendly, prosocial, and competent social behaviors is clearly predictive of social acceptance, while devious, aversive reactions to other children enhance one's chances of social rejection" (Hartup, 1983, p. 135). Olweus (1978) found that bullies are not popular and are socially isolated. Patterson (1982) also found "hyperaggressive" children to be social isolates. M. Roff and Sells (1968), in a longitudinal study of 40,000 schoolchildren in Minnesota and Texas, reported that boys who eventually became delinquent (defined as having had official contact with juvenile court) were not liked or accepted by their peers. In another study, M. Roff (1975) discovered that the same relationship holds for girls: Later delinquency seems to increase as their peer status at school decreases. Some additional research has suggested this relationship holds for both boys and girls regardless of SES (J. D. Roff & Wirt, 1984). Conversely, children liked by peers very rarely became delinquent. Conger and Miller (1966) found that delinquents-to-be had more difficulty getting along with peers, both in individual one-to-one contacts and in group situations. In addition, youth who later became delinquent were considerably less interested in organized parties, school functions, or organizations. West and Farrington (1973) observed that boys judged most dishonest by their peers were more likely to become delinquent. In a literature review, Eleanor Maccoby (1986, p. 275) concluded: "[I]t is not participation in the boys' culture, but failure to participate in it, that is associated with certain kinds of predelinquent activity." In another extensive literature review, Jeffrey Parker and Steven Asher (1987, p. 371) conclude: "[T]he evidence for a link between early peer-relationships disturbance and later criminality is generally very good. The . . . studies reviewed show that the backgrounds of criminals of all types show a history of aggressiveness and poor peer regard that in some cases extends as far back as the point of the child's entry into formal schooling."

In hindsight, relevant data in human development suggest that delinquents were less integrated into their social networks and had less developed mesosystems than their peers. This literature alone also suggests that delinquents tend to be socially disabled in comparison with counterparts. It is unclear, however, to what types of delinquency researchers were referring, how often the delinquency was committed, or how it was measured. Most psychological research focuses on aggression and antisocial behavior. Both terms imply acts against others, usually in a violent or harmful manner. It is the ostracized antisocial youth who usually commit violent acts against persons. Consequently, the social disability model may be most relevant to serious or LCP delinquency. The social ability model may pertain more to the AL delinquency.

All of this assumes that groups or gangs are homogeneous and that pre-adolescents and adolescents are attracted to and remain in youth groups whose members are very similar to them. Hartup (1983) suggests that this assumption is warranted. There is, he says, a great deal of similarity both in activities and values among members of youth groups. Group members often have attitudes, personality traits, abilities, physical characteristics, and behaviors (such as drug use) in common. The three attributes that appear to be the most consistently shared by these youth groups are age, gender, and race. Behavioral and attitudinal similarities, although important, do not occur with the same consistency and strength as these three.

Denise Kandel (1986), however, admonishes that assessments designed to determine which attributes draw youngsters together must carefully consider what stage of the friendship is being evaluated. Personality attributes seem to be most important in the beginning of a friendship, shared values emerge as crucial later in the relationship, and shared construct systems become the most important later on (Duck & Craig, 1978).

Why do birds of a feather flock together? Hartup suggests three reasons. First, youths *select* their groups, and they likely select groups with which they feel most compatible and comfortable. This tendency is particularly prominent during late pre-adolescence. Second, early relationships based on similarity appear to continue over time, at least until late adolescence. Third, noted similarities may perpetuate themselves. That is, group members may generate and reinforce attitudinal and behavioral concordances in a reciprocal fashion. In short, they may socialize one another. Further, peer groups generate their own norms, applying them only to themselves, beginning around middle childhood.

In her comprehensive series of studies of adolescent friendships, Denise Kandel (1986) found that adolescents who share certain characteristics are more likely to become friends, and those who regularly associate with one another become even more alike over time. Thus, selection and socialization *both* appear important in the process of adolescent friendships.

GENDER DIFFERENCES IN GANG OR GROUP BEHAVIOR

The gang theories of Thrasher, Cohen, Miller, Cloward and Ohlin, and Short and Strodtbeck were all formulated with boys as subjects of study. There is a general assumption in the literature that girls engage in delinquent behavior less frequently and that girl gangs are rare. Criminologists have spent little energy discussing this phenomenon, a noteworthy exception being Anne Campbell (1984).

Anne Campbell: Girls in the Gang

Campbell's "girl gang" study was described briefly in Chapter 1 as an example of qualitative research. Her work represents one of the very few studies on youth gangs in recent years. During the 1980s, Campbell spent six months observing and talking with members of three gangs in New York City, particularly the girls. She reported her results, often in the girls' own words, in her book *The Girls in the Gang*. Although Campbell focused on girls, she also made interesting observations about contemporary gang characteristics in general. Furthermore, she noted that youth gangs are primarily an American phenomenon. Although other cultures have youth groups, they lack the structure, demarcated roles, rules, and territoriality of American gangs. Nor do they have the initiation rites, the gang names, the "colors," the long-term commitment, or the specific philosophies found in American youth gangs.

The gangs she observed had a traditional pyramidal power structure with males as the head and female members as subordinates. Gang members—both male and female—spent many hours a day in front of television sets, watching game shows, soap operas, and other depictions of American "life." The girls almost worshipped clothes and makeup and took particular care of the clothes they had. Despite their failure to fit into mainstream society, the gang members were conservative and displayed an "American capitalistic society is all right" attitude. Certain illegal acts, such as selling soft drugs, were not considered wrong, but burglary, robbery, rape, and assault generally were. When the gang was warring with another gang, however, any criminal activities against the opposing group were acceptable. Gang members claimed to keep the streets safe and the neighborhood clean. At the same time, they did not seem to mind being portrayed to the public as rebellious, tough, and persecuted.

Although gang members most generally came from backgrounds of poverty, minority status, unemployment, and unfinished educations, this pattern was especially evident for female members. Campbell's girls came from homes characterized by geographic and emotional instability, a pattern more typical of girls than boys. During their childhoods, their families had moved frequently and they had attended a series of schools. Family life had been consistently stormy and unhappy, and physical violence was common. Physical aggression between parents was particularly frequent, and the girls often grew up fearing abuse themselves. Alone and alienated, the girls had gravitated to the gang in the hope of fining "sisters" who were like them and who were willing to treat them with respect.

Campbell did not find the girls in the gang to be violent, overly aggressive, or independent. Their main reason for belonging to the gang was to have companionship and security. Members had dreams but believed that these dreams would probably never be fulfilled in light of their current skills, education, and living arrangements. Finally, the girls accepted the traditional double-standard approach with respect to the sexes. They believed that men were naturally aggressive and dominant, and they tolerated this behavior without question from the males in their lives. The roving, unfaithful "nature" of men was expected and tolerated. It is interesting to note, however, how the macrosystem (the society at large) influenced the values and philosophies of the microsystem of the gangs, although largely in one direction. The macrosystem, primarily through television, greatly affected how the gang members should dress, think, and live.

Maccoby: Why Boys Join Gangs More Often Than Girls

Eleanor Maccoby (1986) outlined several cultural reasons that may explain why boys become more involved in gang delinquency than girls. First, boys tend to congregate in public places. They are generally outdoors, whereas girls are often indoors. Boys meeting in public places—parks, playgrounds, or street corners—are more likely to escape adult supervision. Maccoby suggests that when girls are outdoors, they are more likely to be kept around their homes under the watchful eyes other adults. Meda Chesney-Lind (1986) suggests that this parental control factor may account for the consistent research finding that girls are less delinquent than boys. The premise is supported by Mawby (1980), who studied self-reported delinquency in England and noted that families exerted greater control over the behavior of their daughters than over their sons.

Second, Maccoby notes that research in developmental psychology consistently reveals that boys tend to play in large groups, whereas girls tend to play in groups of two or three. There also appears to be a qualitative difference between males and females in the nature and significance of friendships. The friendships of girls are sometimes called "intensive," whereas those of boys are "extensive." Specifically, girls are more likely to have one or two close "best" friends who play important roles in their lives. They seem to place greater emphasis on emotional sharing and intimacy in their friendships. On the other hand, the friendships of boys tend to be multiple and to be closely associated with group activities and group games (Bell, 1981). They develop their identities through an alliance with a gang or group. Friendships among boys appear to be more oriented toward a shared struggle for independence from adult authority (Stokes & Levin, 1986).

The third reason why more boys become involved with gangs is the tendency of boys' groups to fight more than girl gangs (Maccoby & Jacklin, 1980). This appears to be more a feature of the interactive behavior of boys within social groups than any kind of individual predisposition on the part of boys to be aggressive. Social encounters among boys often center on issues of dominance and the formation of an order of status. The play of girls, on the other hand, tends to be oriented toward a strong convention of taking turns and compromising.

Fourth, Maccoby suggests that even the social speech of boys and girls is different and serves different functions. Summarizing the research on speech among girls, she notes that they learn to do three important things with words: "(1) to create and maintain relationships of closeness and equality; (2) to criticize others in acceptable ways, and (3) to interpret accurately the speech of other girls. Symptomatic of these functions are the facts that girls frequently express agreement with others' ideas, let others have a turn to talk, and acknowledge what others have said when they speak; in other words, girls use speech as a means of cooperation" (Maccoby, 1986, pp. 272–73). Boys, on the other hand, tend to use speech to (1) assert status or dominance, (2) attract and maintain an audience, and (3) assert themselves when others have the floor.

Research does suggest that boys do indeed seek the company of delinquent peers more than girls do. Does this reflect an inability on the part of parents to control their sons? Is group joining by boys encouraged by the culture? Is it "more natural" for boys to seek out others when they are rejected by families or by society? Although we might speculate as to the answers to these questions, there is very little evidence to apply. To repeat, classic criminology theories focusing on gang behavior were formulated with boys in mind, and group or gang delinquency among girls has received very little study. Although developmentalists have shed some light on intergender group behavior, it is premature to draw conclusions about gang delinquency among girls without additional research.

THE FAMILY–PEER MESOSYSTEM

Theorists often assume that delinquents are "lost" to their parents because of the parents' neglect, ill treatment, lack of sophistication, or incompetence. To fill this void, the children find peers who are in similar circumstances. Bixenstine et al. (1976, p. 235) reflected this position when they stated:

> The clear implication is that it is not an advancing regard for and loyalty to peers that accounts for a child's growing readiness to affirm peer-sponsored antisocial behavior, but an intense disillusionment with adult veracity, strength, wisdom, importance, good will, and fairmindedness. The child is not won away from parents to children, rather he is, at least for a time, lost to parents.

Some research suggests, however, that this is a questionable assumption. Thomas Berndt (1979) concluded that the adolescent lives in two separate worlds, one for family and one for peers. Hans Sebald (1986) claimed that middle-class white adolescents seek parental advice in matters of finances, education, and career plans, but in making decisions about their social lives—dress, drinking, dating, drugs—adolescents overwhelmingly want to be attuned to the opinions and standards of their peers. Sebald discovered that adolescents are under considerable pressure from peers to conform to peer standards about social life, but not about other matters.

In her large-scale longitudinal survey of adolescents in New York state, Denise Kandel (1986) examined the extent to which adolescent development is influenced by parents and by peers. Students from 18 public high schools were given self-administered questionnaires in their classrooms twice during the school year. Parents of each student also received questionnaires through the mail, and approximately two-thirds returned them for analysis. Students were asked about their relationships with parents and friends. The purpose was to reconstruct social dyads and triads between and among the adolescent subjects (called the "focal adolescents"), their parents, and their peers. The dyads and triads were then examined to obtain specific information about shared values, attitudes, and characteristics. Kandel was able to establish 4,033 adolescent–parent dyads, 1,879 best-friend dyads, and 1,112 triads among the focal adolescent, best friend, and parent. In a sense, she was conducting a form of network analysis.

The most frequent attributes shared by friends were not values and attitudes but sociodemographic characteristics such as age and gender. These same sociodemographic attributes seem to be the most important among adults as well (Fischer, 1982). Behavior was the next important attribute shared by adolescent friends. In other words, the adolescents were drawn to others who liked to do the same things, such as go to movies, play basketball, drive around, or drink. Use of illicit drugs was the most important shared behavior. Kandel found that the least-shared attributes were psychological factors, such as feelings of self-esteem and confidence and attitudes, such as political orientation.

What are the areas of influence for friends and what are the areas of influence for parents? Peers are more influential in some things, parents in others. Like Sebald, Kandel found that peers are most influential in settling issues of immediate relevance to the adolescent's life, such as whether to become involved in drugs. For issues relevant to basic values, including future plans, occupational choice, religion, and education, parents play the crucial role.

The attraction of adolescents to peers who like to do similar things is important, because it involves the use of illicit drugs and provides some clues on the relative importance of peers vis-à-vis that of parents. Two explanations of an adolescent's involvement in illicit drugs have been suggested in the literature. One argues that adolescent drug use results predominantly, if not exclusively, from peer influences. Sutherland would predict, for example, that participation in a drug subculture and the heavy association with peer drug users will almost certainly result in heavy drug use by each member of the subculture. A second argument suggests that parental influence, not the peer group, is the most important component in drug behavior. Adolescents act primarily in accordance with family values and standards. Therefore, if parents use drugs (e.g., alcohol, marijuana, cocaine, or heavy prescription drugs), the children will likewise be inclined to use drugs.

In the previously mentioned study, Kandel (1984) tried to determine from the questionnaires the relative influences of peers and parents on drug use. She found that only 15 percent of her focal adolescents reported having used marijuana if their best friends reported never having used it. However, when best friends had used marijuana 60 times or more, 79 percent of the focal adolescents also used marijuana. This result indicates that a peer group is the strongest determinant of substance abuse. The highest rate of adolescent marijuana use (70 percent) occurred when both parents and peers admitted to considerable drug use. In contrast, the lowest rate (12 percent) occurred when neither peers nor parents admitted drug use. Kandel also found that girls were slightly more influenced by their peer relationships than boys. This comports with research findings that girls do not report stronger bonds to their parents than boys (Cantner, 1981). Kandel concluded that, despite peer substance abuse, parents still have a moderate influence on the adolescent. Teenagers of non–drug-using parents were somewhat less likely to use drugs than their peers, whereas teenagers of drug-using parents were somewhat more likely to do so. The same patterns occurred for adolescent alcohol use.

Ronald Akers (1985), in a test of his theory of differential association-reinforcement, discussed in Chapter 5, found that the extent to which individuals approved or disapproved of alcohol and marijuana use was most strongly related to the norms of their significant peers. The norms of parents and others also played a smaller role. When actual self-reported drinking and marijuana use were studied, however, the results were mixed. Parental influence was only slightly below that of peers in drinking behavior, and, with respect to marijuana use, the influence of peers was far above that of parents.

Richard Johnson and his associates (Johnson, Marcos, & Bahr, 1987) also found that peers have considerable influence on the frequency and type of drug use. They conclude, "It is not so much that adolescents use drugs because the drug use of their friends makes drug use seem right or safe; rather, they apparently use drugs *simply because their friends do*" (p. 336).

In summary, peers do seem to have the overriding influence on drug use in adolescents, particularly in the case of nonalcoholic drugs. Although it is unclear which comes first—the use of drugs and the seeking out of compatible peers or the association with peers who influence drug use—the data indicate a strong association between drug use and drug-using peers.

Kandel found opposite patterns of influence for educational aspirations, where parents were far more influential than the adolescent's best friends. In follow-up studies, however, Kandel reports indications that, over time, parents may have the greater effect on both drug use and educational aspirations. R. Jessor (1986) conducted a longitudinal study of seventh-, eighth-, and ninth-grade boys and girls drawn from three junior high schools in a small Rocky Mountain city, beginning in 1969. He found that about 50 percent of the men who had been problem drinkers as adolescents were no longer problem drinkers as young adults. For women, the shift was even more dramatic: About 75 percent of adolescent problem drinkers were no longer so as young adults. Problem drinkers were defined as those who reported being drunk six or more times in the past year, or who had experienced significant negative consequences—such as coming to the attention of law-enforcement officials—at least twice in the past year. According to Jessor, the long-term influence of parents and increased responsibilities appear to be the major determinants of changes in behavior.

The Kandel project demonstrated that interaction with parents and interaction with peers could coexist. In other words, as Berndt (1979) had observed, adolescents did seem to live in two worlds.

Furthermore, in an earlier study, Kandel (1978) discovered that adolescent groups differed drastically in both behavioral preferences and values and that future considerations of gang behavior must be highly sensitive to these striking differences. Gangs were not simply groups of adolescents seeking to fill the social void in their lives; they varied widely in orientation and social network systems. However, Kandel did find that groups characterized by heavy marijuana use performed significantly less well in school (they also held more liberal political views) compared with non–marijuana-using groups.

Kandel's research highlights the interplay between the family and peers, a critical mesosystem in the development and maintenance of behavior. More research of this type and magnitude will promote better understanding of the important family–peer mesosystem in delinquent behavior. As Kandel emphasizes, we are only at a modest beginning in this endeavor.

THE SCHOOL AND DELINQUENCY

The school, like the family and peer group, is an important microsystem in the child's social network. Criminologists have consistently reported a strong correlation between delinquency and school failure (Schafer & Polk, 1967; Kelly, 1980; Wilson & Herrnstein, 1985). Delinquents, compared with nondelinquents, have far more trouble performing adequately within the school setting. This is not surprising. What is surprising, however, is that little research has been directed at explaining this oft-cited correlation. One explanation, advanced without much empirical documentation, is that the delinquent child is intellectually handicapped or at least ill prepared for the rigors of school. We shall refer to this as the "student deficit hypothesis." Another explanation is the "school deficit hypothesis," which places the blame on the shoulders of the educational system.

The **student deficit hypothesis** suggests that poor and minority children are especially prone to intellectual deficits. Their deficiency is presumed to arise from any number of causal factors, including faulty parenting, inadequate genes, limited intellectual capacity, cultural deprivation, poor attitudes and motivation, or some combination of these. Whatever the reasons, the disadvantaged child enters school ill equipped to succeed, begins to experience failure, becomes frustrated and angry, and often drops out as soon as possible. Somewhere along the line, usually before dropping out, the child begins to engage in delinquent conduct.

In 1992, 11 percent of all 16 to 24-year-olds had dropped out of school before receiving a high school degree. Four in 10 dropouts said they left high school because they did not like school or because they were failing (Snyder & Sickmund, 1995). The rate is much higher for Latinos (29 percent) than for African Americans (14 percent) or whites (8 percent). Native Americans may have the highest dropout rate of all, with some estimates as high as 70 percent for some Native American nations or communities. In some instances, however, many Native American children have been required to attend boarding schools that have often been situated at great distances from their families (Yung & Hammon, 1994), which contributes to their dropping out.

As Laurence Sternberg and his co-workers (1984) assert, dropout rates for many minorities are primarily due to the child's difficulty with the English language and to cultural orientation, not to intellectual deficiency of some kind. The dropout rates are substantially higher among 16- to 24-year-old Latinos who speak Spanish at home than among Latinos who speak English at home. The dropout rate is about 62 percent for those Latinos who speak English poorly and 83 percent for those who do not speak English at all (Snyder & Sickmund, 1995). Another viable explanation for the high dropout rates among minorities is anchored in the conflicts that have existed between mainstream American culture and the cultures of certain minority groups for many years. School systems rarely address subcultures, especially if the subcultures are represented by a very small segment of the community.

Still, the tendency to drop out is related to delinquency. Potential dropouts are more likely to be involved in delinquency than their peers who eventually graduate (Elliott & Voss 1974; Carnegie Council, 1979; Camp 1980). Note that we are referring to potential dropouts here. Delbert Elliott and Harwin Voss (1974) found that youths appeared to engage in less delinquency after they left school than before. Furthermore, Elliott and Voss concluded that the school is the critical social context for the development of delinquent behavior. Academic failure and difficulty at school seem to be participating factors in delinquency—at least in boys. The pattern for girls was not as clear. To Elliott and Voss, male delinquency is primarily a response to school failure. Specifically, delinquency is a way of coping with the social stigma and loss of self-esteem associated with this failure. In addition, Elliott and Voss did not find that delinquents dropped out of school because they felt socially alienated and isolated. Instead, "Respondents with the highest rates of delinquency were youth who had strong commitment to peers and weak commitment to parents" (p. 205). In fact, they seemed "overcommitted" to peers. If anything, school peer networks seemed to be launching pads for entering delinquent groups. Academic and behavioral problems may prompt individuals to seek the company of those in similar circumstances. Once the individual dropped out of school, however, contacts with peers remaining in school (and his or her involvement in delinquency) were significantly reduced. Despite these observations, the relationship between delinquency and the school remains unclear. Delinquent behavior is related to many things; how much the school contributes to the equation remains ambiguous.

The **school deficit hypothesis** places the blame for school failure upon the school and many of its supporting groups. It predicts that the school system sets the stage early for the disadvantaged child's failure as well as for actions and reactions that often lead to delinquency. Specifically, the school is said to cultivate the failure process for some children by using negative labels such as "slow learner," "disadvantaged," "special learner," or "academically handicapped" and reacting to the child accordingly. The child assumes the label and also begins to act accordingly, as do others, including parents and peers. Once this process has begun, ". . . students who fail tend to be progressively shunned and excluded by other achieving students, by individual teachers, and by the 'systems as a whole'" (Schafer & Polk, 1967, p. 230). Because of this negative labeling process, the targeted children find themselves caught up in a deteriorating downward spiral. School becomes aversive and frustrating, and the child begins to violate its rules and regulations, as well as those of society.

Advocates of the school deficit hypothesis accept that some children begin school at a disadvantage, usually because of lack of preparation, but it is the school system that exacerbates the condition. The school deficit position, best represented in the work of Walter Schafer and Kenneth Polk (1967), also assumes that much of the curriculum is irrelevant to the child's life.

Other researchers point to the use of heavy and inflexible school rules in the classroom as a contributing factor (Pepler & Slaby, 1994). Additionally, the relationships between teachers, the amount of teacher hostility, and the rapport among staff members all affect the school social environment. Hostility and poor staff–teacher relationships encourage school aggression and dropout.

Which better explains dropout rates, the student deficit hypothesis or the school deficit hypothesis? Before answering, we need to sidetrack a bit. In Chapter 5 we reviewed construct systems and their ramifications for perceiving the world and for acting. It was suggested that intellectual capacity can be defined in many ways and probably cannot be measured. Accordingly, dropping out of school may reflect not lack of capacity or ability but rather of orientation (Bernstein, 1974). As alluded to earlier, youngsters from different subcultures and different neighborhoods who have been subjected to different family styles and have spoken different languages are apt to have different orientations and constructs about the world and acceptable ways of acting. The anthropologist John U. Ogbu (1974) studied middle- and lower-SES sections of Stockton, California. The lower-class section, Burgherside, comprised mostly African Americans and Mexican-Americans. Ogbu learned that the children of Burgherside almost universally did not feel it was important to do the best they could on exams or achievement tests in school. They did not try to get better-than-average grades. The vast majority of Burgherside children, from the elementary to the high school levels, received grades of C or D in classroom work. Very few received a single A. The Burgherside youth wanted to get by and get school over with, and there was little attempt to maximize their scores and grades. Ogbu rejected any notion of intellectual deficit or handicap. He believed the youths' way of seeing the world simply did not dovetail with that of middle-class whites, who felt it important to get the best grades possible.

Middle-class Stocktonians were generally convinced that Burgherside parents had low expectations for their children and that it was this attitude which resulted in poor school performance. Interviews with the Burgherside parents, however, revealed they did indeed have high occupational and educational hopes for their children and did urge the children to do the best they could in school. Why, then, the poor performance? According to Ogbu, the Burgherside parents seemed to be giving their children double messages. While urging them to do well in school, they also communicated that they (the children) would continually be victims of discrimination. An implicit message proclaimed, "No matter how hard you work, you probably won't get ahead." Widespread and pervasive discriminatory practices would not abate. Although this second message was not stated explicitly, it was often embedded in comments or stories about discriminatory practices encountered by the parents themselves or by acquaintances. Thus, part of the problem may be ascribed to parental deficits rather than to a school or student deficit.

From another perspective, the deficit is not a parental one, however. The double messages identified by Ogbu may represent the parents' attempts to be realistic with their children, in the sense of recognizing the pervasive effects of discrimination in society. Should the parents *not* recount stories about discriminatory practices? Shouldn't the children be prepared for what they might encounter and be helped to deal with what they already are encountering? It could be argued that the parents were urging their children to achieve in the hope that, once successful, they could challenge discriminatory practices. Furthermore, it is significant that the middle-class Stocktonian parents were convinced that the Burgherside parents had low expectations for their children. One might wonder whether middle-class teachers of the Burgherside children shared these assumptions as well, and whether that might have contributed to the findings of the study.

Good school systems today recognize the value of cultural diversity in the classroom. Rather than assuming that cultural groups place different values on education, they see that parents across all levels of social stratification and across all ethnic, racial, and religious groups want the same for their children: a safe learning environment and educational preparation for the future. To accomplish this, schools need to start where the children are and guide them—preferably in partnership with parents or parent figures—through their developing years. When that mission is shared by all within the school system, dropout rates should plummet.

Some investigators have found that as many as 75 percent of school dropouts demonstrate intellectual or cognitive skills sufficient to do passing or even superior schoolwork (Elliot, Voss, & Wendling, 1966; Garbarino & Asp, 1981). Furthermore, although some studies have reported that delinquents are plagued by learning disabilities, one literature review (Murray, 1976, p. 61) concluded that the "disparity of estimates fairly reflects the disparity of definitions, procedures, and analyses in the studies." Researchers were unable to derive reasonable estimates of learning disabilities. To date no study has demonstrated that the average delinquent even was more likely to suffer from a learning disability than his or her nondelinquent counterpart. The evidence for a causal link between learning disability and delinquency is feeble. So, too, is the evidence for the student deficit hypothesis in general.

Wholesale indictments of the educational system are not new. There is no question that some schools do manage to welcome and accommodate children from various backgrounds and subcultures. Nevertheless, some youngsters do not catch the current. They get washed ashore, often quite early in the flow of things. Intellectual capacity has little to do with this. At this point, the school deficit hypothesis gets more support than the student deficit hypothesis.

THE SCHOOL-FAMILY MESOSYSTEM

Bronfenbrenner (1979, 1986a) has emphasized the importance of the mesosystem of the family and the school in the development of the child and his or her performance in school. The greater the frequency of contacts between family and the school, the stronger the mesosystem and the more integrated the child will be into the system. "The available research evidence suggests that a powerful factor affecting the capacity of a child to learn in the classroom is the relationship existing between the family and the school" (Bronfenbrenner, 1986, p. 735). Elsewhere, Garbarino and Asp conclude in much the same vein:

> The school–home mesosystem is of great developmental significance for the child. In general, we would expect enhanced development in cases where this mesosystem was characterized by a lot of interaction between parents and school personnel, where more was known to members of both settings, and where home and school communicate frequently (Garbarino & Asp, 1981, p. 27).

In an investigation of the school system in Stockton, Ogbu (1974) found that the relationships between the Burgherside families and the school was ". . . characterized by social distance, mutual stereotyping, and lack of effective communication" (p. 159). Communications with the school were one way and authoritarian: The school did the communication, and parents were expected to listen. Although the school sent Burgherside families messages by way of phone calls, notes, and personal visits, parents felt that they were not given opportunities to state their concerns or positions. Teachers decided when, where, why, and how they interacted with parents. Many mothers expressed a wish to establish a bidirectional link with the school, but they found school officials cold, unsympathetic, and unresponsive. Parents complained that they were made to feel "dumb" by school officials. This observation corroborates the one made by Schafer and Polk (1967), who report that lower-income parents frequently perceived the school as hostile, cold, and alien. Moreover, the black and Mexican American fathers in the Burgherside community generally thought that involvement with the school was part of the woman's role and consequently made little or no attempt to contact the school.

Bronfenbrenner (1979) cited Ogbu's work as important in our understanding of the interconnections among the school, family, and neighborhood, as well as the influence of economic conditions and community attitudes on school effectiveness. "Moreover, he [Ogbu] looks at the nature of the processes involved in these connections rather than merely at the statistical correlations between low income, minority status, and poor school performance" (Bronfenbrenner, 1979, p. 254). The research on the relationship between the family–school mesosystem and delinquency is virtually nonexistent. More attention to this kind of research would bring us much closer toward understanding the social system of delinquency.

FAMILY, WORK, AND DELINQUENCY

The mesosystem between family and work and its effect on delinquency has received scant attention. Research that has examined it has often failed to appreciate the complexities of and interplay between the relationships. Early research on the links between work and its effects on family life assumed a simplistic relationship: Maternal employment was bad for the developing child. If the mother is at work, so goes this theory, she cannot be home rearing her children, and therefore her children will be more prone toward delinquent behavior. Conversely, paternal unemployment was considered bad for the child (Bronfenbrenner & Crouter, 1982). A despondent, irritable, unemployed father could add only an unhealthy element to the home environment.

Research focused on maternal employment or paternal unemployment and delinquency and that considers the labyrinth of relationships is exceedingly rare. As mentioned previously, a vast majority of the research has proceeded on a narrow path, looking only at maternal employment or what is considered maternal unemployment ("housewives") to see what effects they have on the delinquency rate. Studies examining the connection between paternal unemployment (or employment) and delinquency are virtually nonexistent.

Glueck and Glueck (1957) reported a higher incidence of delinquency among boys of employed mothers. This pattern was especially evident if the mothers worked "occasionally" or "sporadically." Interestingly, the Gluecks suggested that the effect of the working mothers was most damaging when the boy was physically ectomorphic and temperamentally sensitive and prone to worry. However, the Gluecks (1950, 1957) implied that an arrangement for proper supervision (such as that provided by a relative or neighbor) could neutralize any negative effects of maternal employment. Nye (1958) also found that youngsters of working mothers tend to engage in more delinquency, but the behavior was minor and the relationship was weak. He suggested that maternal employment seemed to have a more adverse effect on girls than it did on boys. Even after Nye controlled for many of the background variables, such as SES, mother's education, and family size, a small relationship persisted. Nye speculated that the maternal employment–delinquency relationship was due to a loss of direct control and supervision associated with the absence of the mother. Hirschi (1969) also cites a significant link between maternal employment and SR delinquency, although it was not particularly strong. He suggested that "physical proximity" of the mother may be a factor. More specifically, a youngster may feel less controlled if his mother works 70 blocks as opposed to her working only 5 blocks away. More recently, Hirschi (1983) suggests that the maternal employment–delinquency relationship might also be due to a "destruction of the nest" effect, whereby the unoccupied house may become less attractive to adolescents, prompting them to spend more time away from home. Some research (e.g., Bandura & Walters, 1959; West & Farrington, 1973; Wadsworth, 1979) reported no signficant relationship between delinquency and the working status of the mother. A few writers (e.g., Rutter & Giller, 1984) have concluded that the relationship is unsupported and need not be investigated further, especially if it focuses on employment of the *mother*.

It is indeed debatable whether this is a research area worth pursuing. It is common in today's society for parents to work outside the home, often out of economic necessity. One rarely sees a study evaluating the effects of *paternal* employment on delinquency; the research cited previously invariably looked at maternal employment, presumably because it was considered against the norm. Rather than pursue this employment–delinquency connection, it would be far more prudent to establish community support systems for working parents, including after-school programs and high quality day care centers. Some research on "latchkey kids" suggests that this would be a wise policy approach. (This term has been used to describe children who arrive from school and find no adult on the premises because parents are at work.) Laurence Steinberg (1986) learned that latchkey kids without adult supervision are more prone toward minor delinquent actions than latchkey kids who have some type of adult supervision, primarily because of the former group's apparent increased susceptibility to peer pressures. Even if working parents just call home after school, this strategy appears to have an effect on lowering delinquency rates. We do not know, however, what effect different levels of adult supervision will have on serious delinquency.

INTERACTIONISM: A SUMMING UP

The most productive strategy in our quest for explaining, preventing, and treating delinquency may lie in **interactionism**. It is important to realize that interactionism is not a new approach. Its many variants were used in the first half of the twentieth century by James Mark Baldwin, George Herbert Mead, C. H. Cooley, Herbert Blumer, William James, Kurt Lewin, and John Dewey—to mention only a few. More recently, the principles of interactionism have been expressed most clearly by David Magnusson and his colleagues (1981, 1983).

"Interactionism" refers to the continually ongoing, bi-directional influence that goes on between systems. The most obvious illustration is the interactionism between the individual system (the person) and the microsystem (the immediate environment). Magnusson and Allen (1983, p. 370) state, ". . . the person–environment interaction process is an open system that consists of a dynamic process in which mutual influence and change are taking place continuously." The person influences the microsystem and the microsystem influences the person in a continual stream of influences across time. The individual and the environment are inseparable. They form an indivisible whole or totality. Therefore, to illustrate interactionism correctly, we need more than a linear, static, two-way interaction.

We need a series of "causal loops" connected across time (see Figure 7.1). In this sense, the development of delinquency can be conceptualized as a spiral or helix.

"The process of person–environment interaction is a system, as we have noted; but it must be remembered that this system is embedded within a hierarchy of other systems, some of which are at a higher, and others at a lower, level than the person–environment system itself" (Magnusson & Allen, 1983, p. 370). Thus, the development of delinquency is best conceptualized as spirals within spirals (like funnel clouds of tornados within increasingly larger funnel clouds), each influencing the others. The larger, more powerful funnel clouds (e.g., macrosystems) influence the inner funnels more than the inner funnels influence the outer. In order to understand delinquency development adequately, ". . . we need to know as much as possible about the degree and frequency of penetration from other systems at different levels into the systems being studied" (Magnusson & Allen, 1983, pp. 370–71).

As we have described in this chapter, the family, school, and peer systems interact with one another and with the larger systems (the community) and smaller systems (the person), forming a rich tapestry of mesosystems. The delinquent is not an isolated entity of deviance but rather is embedded among swirls of other systems. The delinquent is a totality who views the world from a certain perspective, functions as an ongoing system, and interacts with other systems.

Terence Thornberry (1987) ties interactionism to theory and research on delinquency. Thornberry asserts that most theories of delinquency, classical and contemporary, are plagued by three fundamental limitations. First, they tend to be unidirectional in their explanations rather than reciprocal. They describe adolescents as being propelled along a single one-way path. Early factors affect later ones in a single direction. Falling into the company of bad peers or limited opportunity, for instance, pushes the child toward a life of delinquency and crime. Second, most theories of delinquency fail to recognize the important developmental changes that occur over the life course. They fail to consider that ". . . as the developmental process unfolds, life circumstances change, developmental milestones are met (or, for some, missed), new social roles are created, and new networks of attachments and commitments emerge" (Thornberry, 1987, p. 881). Third, most theories assume uniform causal effects throughout the social structure (such as race, class, and community of residence). In other words, most theories ignore the person's position in

FIGURE 7.1 Illustration of person–environment interactionism

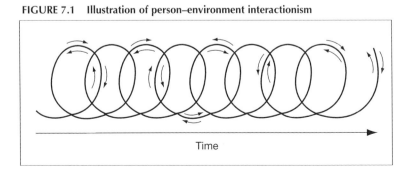

Time

a given society and "fail to provide an understanding of the sources of initial variation in both delinquency and its presumed causes" (p. 864). Many youngsters are at a decidedly greater disadvantage in relation to commitment to family, school, and conventional beliefs others. This may be—but is not necessarily—related to position in the socioeconomic structure. An emotionally-neglected child of wealthy parents, who finds no caring adult in his world, may be at very high risk of serious delinquency. Thornberry argues that many theories are not sensitive to the initial systems network within which one begins life.

According to Thornberry, a viable theory of delinquency must take into consideration reciprocity, developmental changes across time, and the initial setting for a person's developmental sequence. Two concepts are emphasized in the model: the concept of reciprocity and the initial starting place to begin describing this reciprocity or interactionism. In other words, at what point should we begin describing the interactive course toward delinquency? He begins with the weakening of social controls.

Thornberry's interactional theory ". . . asserts that the fundamental cause of delinquency lies in the weakening of social constraints over the conduct of the individual. . . . The weakening of controls simply allows for a much wider array of behavior, including the continued conventional action, failure as indicated by school dropout and sporadic employment histories, alcoholism, mental illness, delinquent and criminal careers, or some combination of these outcomes" (p. 865). Thus, weakened social controls reduce the behavioral restrictions, encouraging the individual to experiment with any variety of nondeviant and deviant behaviors. For delinquency to occur, the individual must find him- or herself in an ". . . interactive setting in which delinquency is learned, performed, and reinforced" (p. 865). In this sense, Thornberry is including both control and Akers's social learning in his model. He is careful to emphasize that he is not integrating the two theories but simply engaging in "theoretical elaboration." That is, Thornberry is "extending" the theories to fit with empirical findings.

Thornberry focuses upon the interrelationships among six concepts: (1) attachment to parents, (2) commitment to school, (3) belief in conventional values, (4) associations with delinquent peers, (5) adoption of delinquent values, and (6) engaging in delinquent behavior. The first three are from Hirschi's social control theory. The next two are from Akers' social learning theory. When attachment to parents, commitment to school, and belief in conventional values are strong, the person's behavior is channeled toward conventional society. When one or more of these bonds are weakened, behavioral freedom increases, and the probability of delinquent involvement correspondingly increases. Involvement in delinquency, in turn, reduces the bonds to parents, school, and conventional society. Thus, whereas weakening of bonds initially causes engagement in delinquency, delinquency eventually becomes its own indirect cause because it influences (weakens more) the individual's bonds to family, school, and conventional beliefs. Unless this causal loop is interrupted, higher and higher rates of delinquent involvement are likely.

Thornberry also suggests that concerning child development, parental influences have their greatest impact during the early formative years and become less as the child grows older. "The family declines in relative importance as the adolescent's own world of school and peers takes on increasing significance" (p. 879). In other words, the social systems of the child change and the networks and microsystems grow larger, more complicated, and more influential with age. This observation has the substantial support of many developmental psychologists (e.g., Bronfenbrenner, 1979; Garbarino, 1982; Hartup, 1983).

Finally, theories must consider where each person begins his or her developmental journey. "[Y]ouths from middle-class families, given their greater stability and economic security, are likely to start with a stronger family structure, greater stakes in conformity, and higher chances of success, and all of these factors are likely to reduce the likelihood of initial delinquent involvement. In brief, the initial values of the interactional variables are systematically related to the social class of origin" (p. 885). Children deprived of family stability, a decent physical and comfortable environment, a caring social network, adequate nutrition and medical care, and a neighborhood in which crime is held in check begin the interactional course at a decidedly different place from that of children with these advantages.

SUMMARY AND CONCLUSIONS

Principal concepts in this chapter were microsystems, mesosystems, and networks. Our goal was to demonstrate how juvenile delinquency is associated with each. A microsystem is limited to processes taking place within the individual's single, immediate setting—the family, the classroom, the peer group, the work environment. A mesosystem takes into account the joint effect of processes occurring within and between two or more settings, such as family and school, family and peers, family and work, and family and the neighborhood. We discussed delinquency in relation to each. "Social networks" refers to the social relationships within or between groups.

The growing research confirms the frequent observation that the causes and prevention or treatment of juvenile delinquency requires an ecological perspective that recognizes multiple influences on child development and multiple levels of those influences. We also know that unidirectional causes between and among social variables are often an oversimplification, and that social environments are always changing. And we know that substantial sensitivity to cultural and ethnic differences is required for any comprehensive understanding of delinquency.

In this chapter we focused on the extant literature that has studied primarily male youth gangs and peer groups. As a group, classical sociological theories have suggested that youths form or join gangs in response to being denied opportunities in middle-class society. Most theories also conclude that the affiliation with peers and the imitation of peer models continue all through childhood and adolescence. Youth strive to dress, speak, and behave like their same-sex peers. Highly aggressive and antisocial children, however, are shunned by less aggressive peers. We learned that antisocial (especially LCP) children are unpopular among peers during the early and middle school years but may become popular during the teen years. In some instances, LCP teens may be the core members in certain gangs or deviant groups. However, the LCP popularity drops off dramatically during the late teens and early adulthood, and most teens (including the adolescence-limited offender) leave for a more traditional life course. It should be emphasized that many (about 50 percent) of the highly aggressive children "mellow" during their late teens and do not continue at elevated aggression levels or escalate to serious antisocial behavior (Tolan & Thomas, 1995).

We discussed gender differences in peer associations and learned that these differences are primarily due to socialization factors. The precise mechanisms and processes implicated in the development of delinquency vary not only by gender but also by demographic variables. Delinquency develops through the interaction of demographic variables and developmental factors. Growing up in disadvantaged urban settings, for example, may encourage individual beliefs that promote aggression and violence. A code of violence often prevails among youth in impoverished urban areas whereby violence is seen as a legitimate and appropriate behavior in social interactions (Anderson, 1990). It would be a mistake to assume that this code is accepted by all who live in these areas, however.

Some recent research on the prevention of delinquency reports that intervention methods which use the peer system as a change agent are not successful. More specifically, despite the importance of peer relationships in development, using peer pressure to change antisocial behavior has not been effective so far. It is very likely, however, that part of the problem is the lack of systematic knowledge on the peer process itself. Consequently, much more research is needed before scientists will be able to use the untapped resource of peer influences in the future.

KEY CONCEPTS

autonomy (secondary focal concern)
belonging (focal concern)
Campbell study
conflict subculture
criminal subculture
diversity
excitement (focal concern)
fate (secondary focal concern)
focal concern
group autonomy
interactionism
Kandel studies
Maccoby study
malicious (gang characteristic)
negativistic (gang characteristic)

nonutilitarian (gang characteristic)
reaction formation
retreatist subculture
school deficit hypothesis
short-run hedonism
smartness (focal concern)
social disability models of gang
    delinquency
social ability models
status (focal concern)
strain perspective
student deficit hypothesis
toughness (focal concern)
trouble (focal concern)
versatile (gang characteristic)

8

Higher-Order Systems

THE ECOLOGICAL APPROACH TO DELINQUENCY: THE CHICAGO SCHOOL

Late one rainy and bleak afternoon in 1890, Albion W. Small, president of Colby College in Waterville, Maine, met with the newly appointed president of the University of Chicago, William Rainey Harper. Harper was a man of leadership, inventiveness, and daring. He was also the close personal friend of John D. Rockefeller. The latter, already in possession of his Standard Oil fortune, wanted to build and endow a small college to provide moral training in the Baptist tradition (Faris, 1967). Harper, a Yale professor of Greek and Hebrew, had agreed to administer the project, but he had a vision much greater than that of Rockefeller. Harper immediately began to scour the country for bright, energetic faculty, with the goal of building a great university.

The main topic of discussion between Small and Harper that afternoon was a faculty position for Small when the new university opened its doors, the projected date being the fall of 1892. Small was interested only on one condition, to which Harper readily agreed: The university must include a department of sociology. The first department of sociology in the United States was thus established at the University of Chicago, with Small as head professor. Several other universities quickly followed suit, but the Chicago department was to dominate the intellectual and professional development of sociology for almost half a century. It became known as the "Chicago School of Sociology."

An Early Psychosocial View of Delinquency: W. I. Thomas

The four best-known sociologists during the Chicago School's very early years were Small, George Vincent, Charles Henderson, and William I. Thomas. Of these, the work of Thomas is most relevant to the study of crime and delinquency. All four had theology backgrounds, but they soon directed their energies toward the more secular goal of building a new science of social behavior (Faris, 1967). They, their students, and the prolific and energetic faculty who would join them created and promoted a scientific discipline based on direct observation. As head professor, Small stressed the importance of theory and research to both faculty and students, and he strongly encouraged them to venture outside the confines of the department. The city of Chicago, he said, should be their laboratory.

Thomas was the youngest member of the department. He received his Ph.D. from the school in 1896 and immediately joined the faculty, where he remained until his forced resignation amidst scandal in 1918 after being discovered in one of Chicago's brothels during a police raid. Finestone (1976a) notes that this unfortunate event cost Thomas even a publication, because a book he wrote, *Old World Traits Transplanted*, appeared under the name of his Chicago colleagues Robert E. Park and Herbert A. Miller (1921). Because of the scandal, Thomas could not be credited.

Thomas was initially interested in folk sociology and ethnology. During the early stages of his professional development, and in line with the dominant scholarly thought of the time, he preferred biological explanations of individual behavior. He considered humans creatures of instinct whose most natural behaviors were roving, fighting, and hunting. The needs for food and sex were humans' chief motivating forces, as they were for all animals. Emphasis on these biological needs would be untenable for contemporary sociologists, but we should keep in mind that in their infancy, sociology, psychology, and psychiatry all were responsive to the dominant Darwinian perspective. Consequently, representatives of these three disciplines were sometimes indistinguishable from one another. The Darwinian perspective argued that most human behavior, including human social behavior, is the result of innate biological urges emerging from our animal ancestry. In short, the perspective contends that humans differ from the animals (subhumans) only slightly. It was not until the early 1930s that sociology began to break away from an individual perspective and emphasize the importance of the social environment.

Eventually, Thomas abandoned his food and sex theory of motivation and replaced it with his "four wishes" theory. The new wishes, or innate needs, according to Thomas, were for recognition, response, new experience, and security (Thomas, 1931). **Recognition** was the general need for people to struggle for positions of status within their social group. This struggle added significantly to the development of personality. "**Response"** referred primarily to the innate desire for sex and love, a combination of physiological and emotional needs. **New experience** was a need to obtain exciting and adventurous events from one's environment. **Security** was the need for a stable, predictable environment in which one could develop regular habits and a systematic work routine. Thomas thought that all human action, including delinquency, could be accounted for by these four wishes. The wishes had a biological basis, but they could be modified by the social environment.

One controversial aspect of Thomas's work was his emphasis on gender differences in human needs. He has been criticized extensively for drawing a sharp distinction between male and female "needs" and applying this distinction to juvenile delinquency, which he believed was predominately a male endeavor (Klein, 1973; Leonard, 1982; Chesney-Lind, 1986). Boys, Thomas said, naturally crave excitement and adventure, and under the right conditions, they might disregard the prevailing social standards to get these needs met. In contrast, Thomas noted in his *Unadjusted Girl* that the beginning of delinquency in girls was usually the result of an impulse to obtain amusement, pretty clothes, favorable notice, distinction, and freedom in the larger world that presents so many allurements. Sexual passion, according to Thomas, did not play a role in the delinquent behavior of girls—only in that of boys.

THE CONCEPT OF SOCIAL DISORGANIZATION

In his later writings, Thomas began to give credit to the role played by the environment, leaning toward a more solid sociological perspective. In his classic book *The Polish Peasant in Europe and America* (Thomas & Znaniecki, 1927), Thomas described the concept of **social disorganization**, which became central to much of the work of the Chicago School despite the fact that Thomas had by then moved elsewhere. Social disorganization was a nebulous concept that was not clearly defined by the Chicago group, however (Carey, 1975). Despite this ambiguity, it has been used extensively in the formulation of many theories of juvenile delinquency and is often cited as an implicit or explicit cause of delinquency.

To Thomas, social disorganization was a breakdown in the influence of existing rules of conduct on individual members of a group. It was caused by erosion of standards and values as a particular subculture encountered an alien environment to which it was ill-adapted. With reference to the Polish culture that Thomas studied, social disorganization reflected the disrupting influence of an urban industrial environment. Children were deprived of any effective guide to behavior, and the amount of control the nuclear family had over its members was greatly reduced. Delinquency was the result of ineffective socialization by the family. It was random and "wild" behavior without parental or social control. It was also behavior instigated by temperamental tendencies and swayed by momentary moods (Finestone, 1976a). Thus, Thomas had not lost his psychological perspective, nor had he apparently modified his belief in the influence of the four wishes.

Thomas observed in the Polish peasant family—as well as in other families he studied—that social disorganization in the broader subculture led to decreased control of the family unit over the children's behavior. However, disorganization was not inevitable when old-world values clashed with those of the new world; it occurred only if the old-world subculture lost its force with exposure to the American urban environment. Delinquency was one by-product of this decrease in social control.

ECOLOGICAL FOUNDATIONS OF DELINQUENCY: BURGESS AND PARK

Two individuals who were especially crucial in laying the groundwork for the sociological study of crime and delinquency were Ernest W. Burgess and Robert E. Park. Park joined the faculty in 1914, under the strong recommendation of W. I. Thomas. This was a year after Burgess had received his degree from the school. Burgess taught at other colleges for three years, then returned to his alma mater as a professor in the department of sociology. The two men were office mates, with little in common other than their love of sociology and their work-intensive habits, which led them to collaborate on one of the most influential sociological textbooks ever written. *Introduction to the Science of Sociology* (1921) is a hefty, green-covered volume that sociology students for decades afterward called "the green bible."

Burgess, 22 years younger than Park, was a slight man who rarely left the office. He was so caught up in his work, to the exclusion of everything else, that he always looked pale, worn, and harried. A lifelong bachelor, he lived with his father and sister. Finestone (1976a) notes that Burgess once joked that his unmarried status lent objectivity to his studies of the family, because he would not be generalizing from personal experience.

Park, a former newspaper reporter, led a sedentary life, chronically thinking about and planning research (Faris, 1967). He was the prototypical absent-minded professor. His unruly white hair was long and wild-looking. At times he appeared before his classes with traces of shaving soap on his face, often wearing wrinkled and disheveled clothes. Faris (1967) repeats an anecdote in which Park continued to lecture without breaking stride while a student walked to the front of the room and tied and adjusted the professor's necktie, which had been dangling loose from his collar. The students were both amused and impressed.

During his 12 years as a newspaper reporter, Park became intrigued by the city of Chicago, particularly its structure. He sincerely wanted to improve the city but believed that his newspaper work was not the way to do it. Publicity, he concluded, aroused interest and stirred the emotions of the public, but it rarely led directly to constructive action. Park enrolled at Harvard University, studying psychology and philosophy, then went to Germany (Berlin and Heidelberg), where he studied sociology and completed a doctoral dissertation on "The Crowd and the Public."

Park was fascinated with theories of plant ecology and their possible application to humans. Park hoped to apply this study to urban life. He believed, for example, that the process of invasion, dominance, and succession demonstrated by plant species in taking over regions of the world might have relevance to the growth of populations in urban regions. Eventually he framed a theory of "human ecology," speculating that the city was a super-organism, with its physical structure, people, and institutions constituting separate, interlocking parts.

Ecological studies of Chicago began with Park's article "The City: Suggestions for the Investigation of Human Behavior in the Urban Environment." It was published in the *American Journal of Sociology* in 1916, the year Burgess was welcomed back to the University of Chicago as a member of its faculty. Burgess was intrigued with Park's theory. In an effort to test it, the two set out to gather as much information as they could about the city, using the student power at their disposal to do so. They demanded high-quality term papers, encouraging students to focus on information about Chicago. "Students made spot maps, rate maps, conducted interviews, attended meetings, and in various ways observed and systematically recorded phenomena of the city" (Faris, 1967, p. 54). Within a short period of time, many of these students were enrolled in the graduate program at the university, and the department was accumulating large sets of data, both quantified and descriptive. The Chicago School became well known internationally for its "urban ecological" focus, although the interests of its members were broad and diversified. It was the ecological orientation, however, that led to sociology's dominance in the field of crime and delinquency.

Researchers at the Chicago School began to discover that extremes in poverty, illness, and crime were found disproportionately in particular parts of the city. According to the maps, both male and female juvenile delinquents lived and operated in certain locations and were less conspicuous in others. At first, juvenile court officials and youth workers in other cities were skeptical about these findings (Burgess & Bogue, 1967). They maintained that although these strange patterns might be characteristic of Chicago, delinquency in *their* cities was distributed evenly. Studies of these other cities, however, revealed the same disproportionate patterning (Morris, 1957). In urban areas, delinquency seemed to be concentrated where buildings deteriorated, poverty was widespread, and the population was in transition. It was almost nonexistent in the "better" residential neighborhoods.

Moreover, delinquency seemed to fit neatly into a pattern of circular zones around the centermost part of the city, called in Chicago the Loop.

Burgess, then, began to fine tune the ecological theory and propose his **concentric circles theory** (also called the "zonal hypothesis"): American cities expand radially outward from their center in five discernible circular patterns. Each circle represents a zone with distinct demographic and physical characteristics (see Figure 8.1). The first zone, where businesses are most concentrated, is the core. The second zone, which circles the core, is the "area of transition"—a place of high mobility, constantly being invaded by small businesses and light manufacturing. The third zone houses the working class who have escaped the area of transition but who work in industries located within that second zone. Zone IV, the "residential zone," consists of high-class apartment buildings and single family dwelling units. Zone V is the commuters' region.

In Chicago, the area of transition (zone II) was where delinquency, youth gangs, crime, poverty, spousal desertion, abandoned infants, and serious health problems seemed most concentrated. A contact with a juvenile court was used as the measure of delinquency. Even when the population density of the districts in relation to the number of juvenile court cases was taken into account, delinquency was higher in zone 2 than in other zones. This ratio—the rate of delinquency—was a new statistical concept that Burgess considered invaluable in promoting sociology as an empirical science. It is important to note that Burgess never *declared* that the zonal pattern was represented in Chicago's structure; he was *proposing* a pattern that seemed to have some testability.

FIGURE 8.1 Illustration of Burgess's concentric circles model

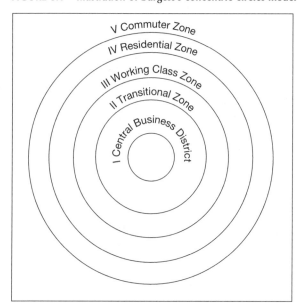

THE MAJOR FORCE IN EARLY STUDIES ON DELINQUENCY: SHAW AND McKAY

While Thrasher was observing youth gangs, researchers at the Chicago Institute for Juvenile Research were working on a systematic project covering 20 years of study on the ecological distribution of delinquency. Clifford R. Shaw and Henry D. McKay were the leaders of this group. Shaw, a former probation and parole officer who developed strong compassion for the powerless and poor, became a research associate at the Institute while still a graduate student at the University of Chicago. In 1926 he was appointed director of the new sociology research section, which was created after a group of private citizens raised money to fund research into the causes and cures of delinquency. As a result, Shaw became the link that connected the Chicago School to the Institute. The close working relationship that developed between these two institutions was to last for nearly three decades.

Under Burgess's tutelage, Shaw became keenly interested in the ecological distribution of delinquency. He and his colleague Henry D. McKay embarked upon a project that probably did more to transmit the essence of American social ecological research than any other project to date. As Shaw freely acknowledged, however, it was not the first geographical study of its type.

Geographical or ecological studies of crime and delinquency had been conducted in Europe at least as early as the first half of the nineteenth century. These studies reported on crime distributions city by city or province by province, but they did not focus on areas and regions within a city. In the United States, Sophonisba Breckenridge and Edith Abbott of the Chicago School of Civics and Philanthropy (later the School of Social Service Administration) published a 1912 report illustrating the geographic distribution of juvenile delinquency within the city of Chicago. The Breckenridge–Abbott article, "The Delinquent Child and the Home," was significant because it underscored the city's zonal patterns much as did the urban ecological studies of the Chicago School. Breckenridge and Abbott used as their index of delinquency all the cases that came to the attention of the Cook County Juvenile Court during the years 1899–1909. They constructed a map pinpointing the homes of the children, illustrating the fact that a disproportionately large number of the juveniles were from impoverished areas of the city where housing was inadequate. For example, 76 percent of the delinquent boys and 89 percent of the delinquent girls came from homes where the family's financial status was described by Breckenridge and Abbott as "poor" or "very poor."

The Breckenridge–Abbott maps depicted only the absolute numbers of cases in the various districts, however. Rates of delinquency—number of cases in relation to the population density—were not calculated. Consequently, it was not possible to conclude whether the observed concentrations of delinquent cases were due to anything other than high population density compared with other areas. Shaw and his associates intended to analyze delinquency rates throughout Chicago, as had Park and Burgess. However, their study would go beyond statistical analysis and would attempt to interpret the information they obtained and offer recommendations for society's response to what they saw as a mounting delinquency problem.

In a report written for the 1929 **Illinois Crime Survey**, Shaw, McKay, and their colleagues offered a comprehensive interpretation of the nature of the delinquency problem, its causes, and the shortcomings of existing treatment methods. Delinquency, they declared, was clearly a product of the social situation. Its roots could be found in community characteristics, the family situation, and peer companionship, including gang membership.

Using an elaborate system for plotting the home addresses of more than 100,000 juveniles processed by the Juvenile Court of Cook County between 1900 and 1927, the Shaw group found that the regions having the highest rates of delinquency corresponded roughly to Burgess's concentric circles theory. Specifically, areas of high delinquency were characterized by deteriorating buildings, widespread poverty, and residences interspersed with industry and commerce. These areas had not only the highest rates of delinquency but also the highest rates of adult crime. Shaw and his colleagues posited that criminal adults were deviant models for the young.

In addition, delinquency was especially high in areas with high concentrations of recent immigrants. As the economic status of these immigrants improved, they often moved to more attractive outlying regions. The "hotbeds" of delinquency—areas of high poverty— remained the same. Once a family moved to better surroundings, the children apparently did not continue their previous behavior, because rates of delinquency in the new areas were not high. This recurring pattern of high delinquency even in areas of high resident mobility suggested to the Shaw–McKay group that delinquency was not due primarily to cultural or ethnic background but to a "delinquency tradition" transmitted from older to younger youth within a specific geographical area, year after year.

The Continuance of the Life-History Method

Shaw and McKay compared features of two living areas: The better residential areas and rental areas where residential mobility was high. In the better residential neighborhoods, they found attitude similarities among families. These families adopted conventional values, such as the desirability of a general health program, education, and the promotion of constructive use of leisure time. There were also subtle pressures throughout the community to keep the children engaged in conventional activities, as well as some blatant condemnation directed at those who violated the community's standards of conduct. By contrast, in sections with high delinquency rates, attitudes and values varied widely. Families were so mobile and hard-pressed economically that they paid little attention to what others did or thought. Furthermore, in the better residential areas, the youth were generally insulated from direct contact with deviant forms of behavior engaged in by older models. In other words, the "delinquency tradition" was absent.

Shaw and McKay believed that many of the relationships between delinquency and social factors were too complex to be unraveled strictly by statistical data. Clearly, not all youth living in delinquency-prone areas became delinquent. For those who became delinquent, the developmental path was often very different from those who did not. Shaw in particular became an advocate of the "life history" method, to which he had been introduced by his mentor, Burgess. In addition to compiling maps and official data, Shaw and his colleagues asked some youth to tell about various experiences of their lives. The information was recorded, often in the youth's own words, written as an autobiography, as a diary, or presented in the format of an interview. According to Shaw (1931), the life-history or own-story method revealed important information on three aspects of delinquent behavior: (1) the point of view of the delinquents, (2) the social and cultural situation within which they live, and (3) the relevant experiences in their lives that had an extended impact on their point of view. Three classic books by Shaw illustrate the life-history method: *The Jack Roller: A Delinquent Boy's Own Story* (1930), *The Natural History of a Delinquent Career* (1931), and *Brothers in Crime* (1938).

The Jack-Roller is perhaps one of the best-known qualitative case studies in the field of juvenile delinquency. (A jack roller is one who robs intoxicated persons or individuals sleeping on city streets.) The book is biographical of "Stanley," an adolescent boy who grew up in a poor neighborhood near the Chicago stockyards. Stanley's story is continued in the book *The Jack-Roller at Seventy*, written by Jon Snodgrass (1982).

Some writers (e.g., Bennett, 1981; Geis, 1982) have alleged that Shaw's case-history books appear to be more directed at convincing his audience of the powerful influences of community exosystems than providing new scientific data. The life-history method was an effective medium through which to communicate Shaw's solution to the delinquency problem and improve the community exosystem (Bennett, 1981). Shaw also believed that delinquents were essentially alike; they were good kids striving to acquire what society advertised.

The life-history approach easily falls prey to criticisms about objectivity. The work of the Chicago School, for example, did not include middle- or upper-class delinquents. All of Shaw's case studies consisted of delinquents residing in areas characterized by social disorganization. Nor did he include life histories of youth who did not become delinquent but yet were exposed to many of the same life events as were those who did become delinquent. Despite questions about its ability to produce generalizeable data, the life history can provide valuable insights into how particular individuals perceive and mentally construct their worlds. Consider the following.

A 17-year-old boy was arrested and charged with the murder of a pregnant woman and her two children in a small New England town. The boy allegedly raped the mother and shot her through the head. Next, he drowned her 5-year-old son in a bathtub. He then waited for her 7-year-old daughter to come home from school and drowned her in a separate bathtub.

For some time, residents of the upper-middle-class neighborhood had been concerned about the boy's behavior. Approximately a year before the triple murder, he took a family of four hostage, surprising them when they arrived home by jumping out of a closet, wearing a black ninja mask and an Indian headdress, and waving a hatchet. He stuck knives into the woodwork and smeared mayonnaise and ketchup on the walls. Eventually, the terrified family managed to barricade themselves in a bedroom and were able to escape. The 17-year-old was awaiting trial on the earlier incident when he allegedly murdered the mother and the children.

This case is clearly atypical. Most delinquents, even serious or LCP delinquents, do not commit such bizarre or brutal crimes. A life-history approach, however, would be extremely valuable in reconstructing how this youth arrived at his version of the world. How much influence might be attributed to television, parenting, temperament, peers, or the community? As Solomon Kobrin (1982, p. 153) points out, the life-history method ". . . can serve as a test of the adequacy of the theory purporting to explain delinquency . . . and suggest neglected variables in theory building. These are typically the more elusive elements of deviant behavior that are often difficult to capture in quantifiable variables. . . ."

Conclusions from Shaw and McKay

The extensive and carefully accumulated Shaw and McKay data supported Park and Burgess's earlier conclusions that the distribution of juvenile delinquency corresponded to the physical layout and social organization of the American city. Delinquency, the researchers found, was concentrated near the center of the city, where physical deterioration and social disorganization were most in evidence. Dilapidated housing, proximity to railroad yards, crowded neighborhoods, and industry represented the physical structure. Adult crime, poverty, disease, suicide, mental disorders, and family instability represented the social disorganization element. As one moved away from the city's core, the rate of delinquency decreased until it almost vanished in the residential areas with better physical environments and less social disorganization.

The Shaw–McKay research also supported Thrasher's contention that delinquency is principally a group activity, because 82 percent of the juveniles brought before the juvenile court had committed their offenses in the company of others. Shaw and McKay (1931) noted, however, that delinquent acts are typically committed by a few partners who were members of the same gang, but not by the gang as a whole. Furthermore, like Thrasher, they were careful to say that gangs did not "cause" illegal actions but rather facilitated them. Traditions of delinquency are transmitted through successive generations in much the same way that language, social roles, and attitudes are transmitted. Shaw and McKay did not specify the process of becoming a delinquent. This was left to later theorists, including Edwin Sutherland (1939) with his theory of differential association.

Members of a gang helped and encouraged one another to engage in unconventional actions, but a major factor contributing to delinquency was lack of parental control. According to Shaw and McKay, when parental influence and control over children were weakened or hampered, delinquent behavior increased dramatically. For example, newly arrived immigrants often found themselves living partly in their own old-world traditions and partly in the new-world expectations. Many children, sensing the confusion, were drawn more to their peer world and less to the traditional lifestyle, which peers rejected. Under these conditions, parents lost much of their influence over their children. The youth also had little respect for the parentally supported conventional institutions such as the church or the school.

Shaw and McKay observed that many of the alienated youth developed their own splintered subcultures wherein certain forms of conduct were expected and particular symbols took on group-specific meanings. Thus, whereas Thomas believed that delinquency could be explained by a lack of socialization, Shaw and McKay saw it as the result of an alternate mode of socialization into a deviant subculture. Both the Thomas and Shaw–McKay perspectives, however, posited that the seeds of delinquency were fundamentally a lack of parental and social control. Shaw and McKay stressed that the deviant subcultures were not independent of the ethnic cultural context in which they developed, nor were they autonomous of mainstream American society. Rather, these youth subcultures *interacted* with several cultural and social contexts simultaneously, adopting some aspects of one, some of another. In essence, they saw the deviant subculture as one system within many systems.

Shaw and McKay's theoretical orientation shifted over the years as they continued to accumulate ecological data. Whereas their early writings reflect the strong influence of Thomas and his concepts of social disorganization and social control, their later writings lean toward a "strain" perspective. The most notable shift can be detected in their 1942 publication *Juvenile Delinquency and Urban Areas*. Here, rather than emphasize the impact of severed traditional family ties on juvenile conduct, they highlighted a discrepancy between delinquent areas and mainstream society in the achievement of goals. Furthermore, whereas Thomas had focused on the effects of social control (or lack of it) on individuals, Shaw and McKay now began to develop interest in the discrepancies between subgroups and mainstream society.

Shaw and McKay found that most delinquents they studied had internalized the central values of mainstream society but had difficulty reconciling them with their present predicament. Youth in deprived areas wanted what society advertised that everyone should have, including material goods, education, and prestige. Yet these youth did not have the legitimate avenues to obtain what society valued. Delinquency provided a means of securing some of these valued aspects of mainstream society.

> Groups in areas of lowest economic status find themselves at a disadvantage in the struggle to achieve the goals idealized in our civilization. Those persons who occupy a disadvantageous position are involved in a conflict between the goals assumed to be attainable in a free society and those actually unattainable for a large proportion of the population. It is understandable, then, that the economic position of persons living in the areas of least opportunity should be translated at times into unconventional conduct (Shaw & McKay, 1942, p. 233).

In summary, youth living in delinquency-prone areas are pulled toward the activities and material acquisitions that society advocates, but they have no legitimate way to obtain them. This creates a conflict or a **strain** in the youth, who may turn to illegitimate activities in order to ease it. This perspective anticipates the strain theory that will be discussed shortly. In fact, it is possible that, by 1942, Shaw and McKay had been exposed to Robert Merton's seminal 1938 article, which introduced what was to become known as strain theory in criminology. The Thomas perspective, on the other hand, viewed delinquency as the result of a "push" toward deviant groups because conventional groups were ineffective in promoting a reasonable quality of life.

One last point about the Shaw and McKay research should be noted. Female delinquents were generally not included in their investigations. This was not unusual. As stated previously in the text, many contemporary theorists and researchers have remarked that early criminologists gave scant attention to female offenders and that the classic theories were formulated almost exclusively by studying males (Klein, 1973; Leonard, 1982; Chesney-Lind, 1986). Martin Gold (1987) suggests that, because male offenders accounted for the vast majority of the official data on delinquency, Shaw and McKay may have been drawn to what appeared to be the more pressing social problem of male offending. Gold also cites evidence, however, that shows Shaw and McKay did *not* believe that their eco-logical theory applied equally to all delinquency. He speculates that they ". . . probably believed that the offenses of most female delinquents, with whom they had little personal experience, were of a different nature" (Gold, 1987, p. 71).

THE CHICAGO AREA PROJECT

Shaw had repeatedly found that areas with high delinquency rates lacked ade-quate neighborhood organizations or any community life. This, in addition to his experiences in probation and parole, convinced him that the most effective way of reducing rates of delinquency was to improve the community and give its mem-bers a sense of control over their fate. This led to the famous Chicago Area Project (CAP), which Shaw as director consistently and vigorously moved forward. The fact that Shaw never completed his Ph.D. work at the University of Chicago sug-gests that the project may have consumed his career. His initiative and the CAP itself account for sociology's success at challenging and counteracting the power-ful stronghold that psychiatry and psychology had on the treatment of delin-quency.

The Chicago Area Project (CAP) was an experimental program to test vari-ous methods of preventing delinquency. According to one of its participants, Shaw wished to apply information derived from ecological and sociopsychologi-cal research in delinquency (Kobrin, 1959). It is important to note that Shaw con-sidered the CAP a social experiment and never made extravagant claims about its capacity to prevent delinquency. The project was initiated in 1932, incorporated in 1934, and essentially terminated with Shaw's death 25 years later, although its actual life span was 30 years. It had 4 goals: (1) to provide less formal treatment of delinquents; (2) to emphasize that juvenile offenders needed understanding, not punishment; (3) to demonstrate the Chicago School's belief that environmental influences were far more critical than dispositional factors; and (4) to show that working with the delinquent within his own community is a more effective strategy than institutional confinement (Bennett, 1981).

The project has been described as a combination of recreation, communal self-renewal, and mediation. Shaw and his associates hypothesized that a significant amount of delinquency could be prevented if residents of disadvantaged areas could be persuaded to get involved, especially if the residents formed community groups designed for collective action and were willing to take communal responsibility for delinquency prevention.

The Chicago Area Project has been referred to extensively in criminology literature, but it is rarely described in detail. Noting this, two scholars, relying on archival data, have recently provided an excellent description of the day-to-day activities in the South Chicago neighborhood of Russell Square (Schlossman & Sedlak, 1983). The CAP took 15 months to become fully operational. It began with an initial identification of natural juvenile leaders and the formation of a basketball league. Shortly after this, street workers were dispatched to hang out with youth, help structure recreation, and offer problem-solving advice—a feature of the project referred to as "curbstone counseling." The street workers took copious notes and elicited life stories of local youth. Because Shaw was intent upon keeping youths away from juvenile courts, it was not unusual for the CAP street workers to mediate with police, schools, and police departments. "On the other hand, CAP workers tried to persuade local youth—in a low-keyed, tolerant, nonabusive manner—why it was both morally right and ultimately in their best interest to conform to the values and expectations of conventional society" (Schlossman & Sedlak, 1983, p. 48). Eventually, adults in the community were persuaded to get involved.

The CAP developed a number of subsidiary programs and projects, including a school guidance clinic staffed by a social worker, psychologists, psychiatrists, a camping program, and a parole program. The parole program in particular indicates that the project did not shy away from serious offenders and actually became one of the CAP's most-often-cited successes (Schlossman & Sedlak, 1983). The Schlossman and Sedlak article also details the political intrigues that were associated with the CAP, including the frustration and incremental victories experienced by both the community and the researchers.

For a variety of reasons, it is difficult to evaluate the overall "success" of the project. Shaw himself welcomed impartial measurements of the results, yet he doubted that these could be obtained (Bennett, 1981). Many criticisms of the program came from adults in the community, including school officials or mental-health workers who believed that their roles were being appropriated. Community organizer Sol Alinsky, an early CAP worker, eventually concluded that its mediation tactics were ineffective in comparison with more confrontational styles (Bennett, 1981). The CAP was most successful in communities with some effective conventional institutions already in place, including churches, schools, or kinship group, or even cohesive youth gangs. It was less effective in communities lacking these fundamental groups and activities. Because delinquency is most prevalent in disorganized communities, the CAP's success was limited in the communities where it was most needed. The CAP's apparent low impact on high-delinquency areas may account for the project's lack of replication in other cities (Finestone, 1976b). Schlossman and Sedlak, however, believe that the project itself had merit. "In a field where a quest for perfect knowledge has proved so frustrating and where there is no consensus on appropriate designs for research or evaluation, the numerous distinctive features that separated the Chicago Area Project from virtually all other experiments in delinquency prevention would appear to warrant serious study and reconsideration" (p. 461).

STRAIN AND ANOMIE: ROBERT K. MERTON

Robert K. Merton was one of the earliest American sociologists not affiliated with the Chicago School to make major contributions to the field of crime and delinquency. Merton received his Ph.D. from Harvard in 1936 and spent most of his professional career on the faculty of Columbia University. His contributions to sociology were multiple and diverse and hardly restricted to the sociology of deviance. In some circles, Merton is regarded as the father of modern sociology, because of his pioneering work on the relationship between empirical evidence and theory. For our purposes, we are most concerned with a paper published in 1938, "Social Structure and Anomie," which was to become the most-cited (and reprinted) article on the sociology of deviance.

Merton was born in 1910 and grew up in a south Philadelphia slum. His parents were immigrants from eastern Europe, not unlike those immigrants who were subjected to intense scrutiny by early sociologists of the Chicago School. His father barely made a living by alternating between carpentry and truck driving. Merton, the younger of two children, was an immigrant child; he was also a faithful gang member. Had the family lived in Chicago, Merton may well have qualified as a juvenile delinquent (probably adolescence-limited) in the Shaw and McKay descriptions being published around that same time. Nevertheless, he was different from his peers in one important aspect: He was an avid reader. As early as age eight, he was a regular visitor to the neighborhood public library.

Merton was in graduate school during the Great Depression. Because of his background, he was a sensitive observer of the plight of the disadvantaged during these years. He noted a wide discrepancy between the "American dream" and the realistic opportunities for the disadvantaged to reach that dream. Because he was well read and acquainted with the work of European social theorists, it was only natural that Merton looked there for some guidance in explaining what was happening to American society.

Merton's Strain Theory

Merton was drawn to the concept of anomie described by the French sociologist Emile Durkheim. Like the Austrian psychiatrist Sigmund Freud, Durkheim believed that humans are born with intense biological desires that must be held in check by society. He was convinced that people are incapable of controlling or limiting their biological needs without society's help and controls. Without social controls, an individual's desires expand until he or she aspires to everything and is satisfied with nothing. Thus, when social controls are weak or nonexistent, individual needs run rampant, resulting in chaos and normlessness. Durkheim labeled this state of affairs "anomie."

Although Merton liked some aspects of the concept of anomie, he rejected Durkheim's view of human nature. He did not accept the view that people are driven by innate impulses and desires. Merton believed that one's wants and goals in life were acquired as a result of living in a given society. Culture, not biology, determines an individual's motivation. Culture sets the individual's goals and designates the appropriate means for achieving them. Thus, whereas Durkheim's position viewed humans as driven by innately programmed physiological needs, Merton's suggested that humans follow the values and opportunities set forth by a given society. Whereas Durkheim believed that humans had a propensity to "sin," Merton identified society as the facilitator of "sin." Furthermore, Merton's theory is proposed as an explanation of utilitarian, profit-oriented crime and delinquency. It does not purport to explain violent crime, sexual crime, or other crimes such as drug abuse. The theory tries to account for deviant behavior at the larger cultural or societal level and not at the individual or family level. In this sense, it is more concerned with predicting and explaining delinquency rates and distributions, not why certain individuals engage in criminal conduct. For example, instead of attempting to explain why Johnnie burglarized and Tom did not, the theory's strength lies in its ability to explain why the rates of profit-oriented crime are so high in one society (e.g., the United States) and so low in another (e.g., England).

Merton posited that deviance (including crime and delinquency) occurred when there was a discrepancy between the values and goals cherished by a society and the legitimate means for reaching these cultural goals. If a society communicated to its members that the accumulation of wealth was paramount but offered few acceptable ways for most people to do so, strain would develop. Groups experiencing this strain would be inclined to violate norms and thus contribute to anomie.

Merton—probably ever mindful of his childhood experiences—was disenchanted with American culture, with its emphasis on economic success and its persuasive communication that all the symbols representing wealth should be valued. Merton believed that although American society myopically and fanatically pushed economic success, it failed to put much emphasis on the norms regulating the means to reach these goals. In short, he found a troubling discrepancy in American society between cultural goals and available means for reaching these goals. For some who accepted the importance of wealth, only illegitimate conduct could bring economic success.

One of the more interesting and most-discussed aspects of Merton's strain theory was his suggestion that individuals differed in their acceptance of society's view of what is important and the means for obtaining what is important. According to Merton, there were five possible strategies or modes of adaption: conformity, retreatism, ritualism, rebellion, and innovation.

Merton believed that most individuals accept and therefore conform to both the goals advocated by society and the means to achieve them. Merton suggested that if this conformity did not occur, the stability and continuity of society would be threatened. **Conformity**, then, is the rule rather than the exception. **Retreatism**, the rejection of both goals and means, is the least common strategy. Individuals who rely on this form of adaptation are considered aliens within a given society. Merton believed that the emotionally disturbed, vagrants, vagabonds, tramps, alcoholics, and drug addicts are all examples of retreatism. **Ritualism** occurs when a person accepts the means but rejects the goals because they are beyond reach. In Merton's view, many law-abiding citizens go through the motions: They work hard but believe that certain goal attainment is impossible. **Rebellion** occurs when a person rejects both the means and the goals of the social mainstream and replaces them with new ones. Rebels deviate from the social mainstream perspective and try to introduce a "new social order."

The fifth mode of adaptation, **innovation**, is the most relevant to the study of crime and delinquency, because innovative persons very often engage in criminal conduct. They have accepted the cultural emphasis on success, but not the prescribed means for achieving it. The innovative person rejects institutional or approved practices but retains the culturally induced goals. This is most likely to occur when the person has little access to conventional means for attaining such success. Innovative individuals, therefore, adopt unapproved means, such as theft or burglary.

Violence occurs as a result of anger and frustration over lack of opportunity to fulfill the American dream. Persons who engage in violence are angry about being blocked from attaining widely prized aspirations by the existing structure of society. In effect, angry, frustrated individuals can constitute any of the five modes of adaption outlined by Merton.

Strain theory is a comprehensive statement intended to explain most profit-oriented crime at the culture or societal level. Merton's theory is essentially a class-based theory of crime. He assumed that official crime statistics accurately portray the amount and class distribution of criminal offenses and, because the lower socioeconomic class was greatly overrepresented in these official statistics, it experienced the greatest pressure toward anomie. According to Stephen Cole (1975), had Merton looked upon anomie as a feature of the entire society, creating high rates of deviance across society, most of the criticism directed at his theory would have been avoided.

NEIGHBORHOOD AND COMMUNITY SYSTEMS

In recent years there has been a resurgence of interest in the role of the neighborhood or the community in preventing and controlling criminal activity (e.g., *Communities and Crime*, edited by Albert J. Reiss Jr. and Michael Tonry; *Social*

Ecology of Crime, edited by James M. Byrne and Robert J. Sampson). Traditionally, ecological studies examined geographic or demographic correlates of delinquency at one point in time and did not consider the dynamic processes underlying such distributions (Bursik & Webb, 1982). Thus, important differences between static and process factors were lost in the interpretation of empirical results. According to Bursik and Webb (1982), if such cross-sectional data are to be used as a basis of generalization, researchers must at least be mindful of the ever-changing processes within the community before drawing conclusions.

Just as many criminologists believe that longitudinal research is essential when individual-level variables are studied, many also believe that longitudinal procedures are necessary when examining macrosystem variables. Communities age, change, deteriorate, or are gentrified, and industries move in and they fold. Each of these processes has an effect on crime and delinquency.

To underscore this point, Bursik and Webb analyzed the changes in male delinquency rates in relation to changes in ecological processes. Four demographic variables were examined in 74 areas of Chicago that corresponded roughly to areas studied by Shaw and McKay. The researchers examined data from the census years 1940, 1950, 1960, and 1970. The variables were (1) population, 2) percentage of foreign-born whites, (3) percentage of nonwhites, and (4) levels of household density (the percentage of households with more than one person per room). Delinquency was measured by the number of referrals to the Chicago Juvenile Court per 1,000 males between the ages of 10 and 17.

In their analysis of changes from 1940 to 1950, Bursik and Webb discovered that ecological change was not related to changes in delinquency rates. This was consistent with the repeated finding of the Shaw–McKay investigations that delinquency was confined to specified areas and was not affected by the coming and going of their inhabitants. This finding had prompted Shaw and McKay to formulate their **cultural transmission hypothesis**, which states that delinquent values are passed on among the children in specified neighborhoods, even if populations within the area are constantly coming and going.

Bursik and Webb's analysis of the changes between 1950 and 1960, and again between 1960 and 1970, seriously questioned the cultural transmission hypothesis, however. During those decades, the stability of the neighborhoods (social networks) strongly correlated with the rates of delinquency. When neighborhoods were stable, as defined by low residential mobility, the delinquency rates dropped correspondingly. The Bursik–Webb results suggest that until the social networks and informal social support systems are crystallized, we can expect high rates of delinquency within a neighborhood. Bursik and Webb suggest that when social networks stabilize, delinquency will be dramatically reduced.

The results of the Bursik–Webb analysis should keep us mindful of two important points. First, Shaw and McKay worked within a specific historical context and based their interpretation on a model of ecological processes that has changed substantially over the past three or four decades. Based on the nature of their data, they were justified in making their conclusions. Second, cross-sectional studies cannot capture the dynamic changes of neighborhoods or communities.

Static analysis is very helpful for evaluating the characteristics of a particular community at a specific point in time. Conclusions based on this data must consider chronosystems and the likely impact of change on all components of the social system. Many criminologists in recent years have turned to time series analysis, a research method that specifically enables them to take into account specific changes over time. Monitoring trends and ecological changes across time allows investigators to better diagram the multicausal flow of events associated with any phenomenon, including delinquency.

Most neighborhoods are fairly stable social systems for a period of years (Skogan, 1986), changing very slowly. An exception to this slow change may occur when an unexpected series of events propels the neighborhood into demographic and economic flux. Numerous events can trigger this neighborhood instability, but Wesley Skogan (1986) identifies four factors that have major influence: (1) disinvestment, (2) demolition and construction, (3) demagoguery, and (4) deindustrialization.

The quality and appearance of a neighborhood depend partly on the building, repair, and maintenance of property, as decided by landlords and other owners. When homeowners do not invest time or money, physical deterioration begins to set in. Once this happens, other powerful and influential interests (such as mortgaging institutions and insurance companies) lose faith in an area, warning others that the neighborhood is declining. This process describes **disinvestment**.

Ever since the pioneering studies of Shaw and McKay (and certainly before), neighborhood physical deterioration has been linked to crime and delinquency. Physical deterioration communicates that residents feel helpless and ineffective, do not care, or are financially unable to improve the situation. Overgrown or cluttered vacant lots, littered streets, stripped and abandoned cars, and boarded-up buildings are all closely associated with high crime in urban settings. In these same neighborhoods, bands of teenagers, public drunkenness, street prostitution, open gambling, and drug use soon become prevalent. "Just as unrepaired broken windows in buildings may signal that nobody cares and lead to additional vandalism and damage, so untended disorderly behavior (drunks, gangs, prostitutes, pan handling, remarks to passers-by) may also communicate that nobody cares . . . and thus lead to increasingly aggressive criminal and dangerous predatory behavior" (Kelling, 1987, p. 93).

Although it is a common belief that crime causes deterioration, many criminologists believe that neighborhood deterioration causes crime. Richard Taub and his colleagues noted that the relationship is not unidirectional. "[T]he presence of deterioration and crime together does not necessarily mean that one caused the other. Nor does it mean that causal relations only go one way. Deterioration could either cause crime or create the conditions that allow crime to flourish. Arson by property owners is one dramatic example" (Taub, Taylor, & Dunham, 1984, p. 1).

The quality of a neighborhood is also strongly affected by land-use patterns. Skogan (1986) notes that freeways built during the 1950s tore through the hearts of low-income minority neighborhoods where land was cheaper and easier to pry loose from owners. These road networks were extremely destructive to neighborhoods and to individuals' sense of community. They not only consumed land but also created rigid boundaries between communities, dramatically decreased land values, and lowered the overall appeal and attractiveness of neighborhoods. Skogan terms this process **demolition** and **construction**. Another example is the tearing down of older homes in favor of high-rise apartment complexes for low-income tenants. Although the original intentions may have been laudatory, the plans were short-sighted. They had the unintended consequences of destabilizing neighborhoods and destroying whatever social networks had existed therein. There is clearly nothing well-meaning, however, to investors' appropriation of neighborhoods and the subsequent displacement of the residents without any provision for alternative housing. Impersonal high-rise buildings that crowd low-income residents together and isolate them from the streets below do little to cultivate a sense of community and concern for the neighborhood.

Albert J. Reiss Jr. (1986) also notes how federal legislation, the administration of federal programs, and judicial decisions can adversely affect the physical, moral, and social order of communities. "These changes often are incremental, and their cumulative effects can ultimately destroy the integrity of communities as viable collectivities to control the behavior of their inhabitants" (Reiss, 1986, p. 20). As an illustration, Reiss describes the redevelopment process in Boston's West End, a project that virtually eliminated the village as a viable social system. "[C]ommunities have a delicate balance of moral and social integration that rarely survives rapid change," he notes (Reiss, 1986, p. 20).

Anthony Bottoms and Paul Wiles (1986) scrutinize the important process of how residents get into a residential area in the first place, a point often neglected by ecologically oriented criminologists. Bottoms and Wiles, basing their conclusions on a study of British public housing communities, found that national housing plans and policies can have dramatic effects on an area's crime statistics. Policies may help to maintain, increase, or reduce the crime rates in particular communities. More specifically, those British researchers were interested in crime rates in specific areas affected by public local housing authority policies. They found that similar housing areas, even when matched for social class, ethnic origin, age, sex, household size, and education level, showed differential rates of crime. One factor that led to these differential rates was the method that local housing authorities used to assign housing. In Britain, public rental housing is controlled and assigned by local authorities within the community. The housing differs in desirability and often has waiting lists. Desirability is partly dictated by the crime rate. Areas with high crime rates are highly undesirable. In fact, waiting lists are excellent barometers of the desirability of the housing. The more people on the lists and the longer the wait, the more desirable the location. On the other hand, certain families and potential residents with a variety of social problems are desperate for housing and cannot wait—even though rents between desirable and undesirable locations may be the same. Bottoms and Wiles found that local housing authorities often assigned housing on the basis of ability to wait as well as the nature of the family's social problems. A common practice of the housing authority was to "dump" renters with social problems and a known propensity toward crime into specific areas, a procedure that contributed directly to differential crime rates between the public estates.

The Bottoms–Wiles study is important because it underscores the importance of understanding the process—how residents got there in the first place—in differential crime rates within geographical areas. A strictly social structure analysis, on the other hand, would have revealed a differential crime rate in relation to a geographical area but would not have provided answers as to why. Bottoms and Wiles conclude: ". . . if indeed it is obvious that to study the criminality of a particular area we need to know something about how the residents got there in the first place, we can only say that most criminologists have shown a remarkable lack of interest in the details of the process" (p. 151).

Similarly, Robert J. Bursik Jr. (1987) suggests that political dynamics can affect the delinquency rate in a community. He offers the example of the politically planned construction of a new public housing project in Chicago that immediately affected the residential stability of local neighborhoods. The project introduced a new source of instability into the local neighborhood that essentially decreased the community's ability to regulate itself. Specifically, the construction of public housing itself appeared to be enough to set off a chain of events that dramatically accelerated the instability of the neighborhood, resulting in an increase in the rate of delinquency.

Social networks and informal support systems are crucial to the prevention of crime and delinquency. Delinquency is encouraged by low levels of surveillance and supervision by concerned adults. In stable neighborhoods, residents supervise activities of youths, watch over one another's property, and challenge those who seem to be "up to no good" (Skogan, 1986). They offer a sense of security and peace of mind for the parent, feelings that translate into a more relaxed and positive stance toward the task of child rearing. This aspect appears to be especially important for the poor who are trapped in their surroundings. The more affluent can escape to another neighborhood or purchase necessary resources or support systems.

Skogan's concept of **demagoguery** concerns the process whereby unscrupulous real estate agents or other vested-interest parties frighten residents into leaving the area in order to gain substantial profits. This is similar to but more subtle than the outright appropriation of neighborhoods alluded to earlier. Usually, the scare tactics center on crime and racial threats. Real estate agents have been known to frighten white residents into selling their homes at reduced prices by planting rumors of increasing crime or a potential influx of ethnic groups, a practice known as "block busting" (Goodwin, 1979). Homes are resold at inflated prices to persons desperate for housing. Even Shaw and McKay in their early work made reference to these tactics, noting that social disorganization reflected concerted efforts at market manipulation by entrepreneurs trying to reap quick profits at the expense of residents (Bursik, 1986).

Playing on one's fear of crime is certainly an effective tactic. Second-hand information, even if it conflicts with official reports of crime, can increase fear that may accelerate neighborhood decline (Skogan, 1986). People make extensive use of information gathered second-hand through social networks, especially in tight-knit communities. When members of a community perceive and communicate that crime is rampant, this information may affect resident decisions more than officially reported crime and victimization rates (Greenberg, 1986). Fear encourages some residents, especially those more educated and in the higher income brackets, to move out. Those less fortunate, or those who do not wish to relocate, often withdraw physically and psychologically from community life. Fearful people stay at home more often and become discouraged about efforts to curb the crime problem. In other words, they avoid contact with unfamiliar neighbors and avoid monitoring the neighborhood.

Deindustrialization refers to the loss of jobs and the general economic decline of an area; these affect both the industry and the people living there. Crime-plagued urban neighborhoods have considerable concentrations of unemployment and poverty (McGahey, 1986). On the other hand, low-crime neighborhoods are characterized by stable, relatively affluent households, willing and able to maintain their homes and neighborhoods (McGahey, 1986). The economic status of the neighborhood is very much dependent upon a higher social system—the metropolitan and national economies. Jobs, income, and social status depend on both the state of the national and local economy and how much corporations and businesses are willing to invest in the community.

All four factors, Skogan reminds us, are typically dependent upon the decisions of persons in positions of political and financial power. "They reflect the interests of banks, manufacturing firms, government agencies, and others with large economic and political stakes in what they do" (Skogan, 1986, p. 207).

PHASES OF NEIGHBORHOOD DETERIORATION

Leo Schuerman and Solomon Kobrin (1986) likewise note that ecological research has continually shown a link between severely declining urban neighborhoods and rates of delinquency. They too conclude that deteriorated residential areas generally have the highest crime and delinquency rates. These researchers were more interested in discovering the **processes** neighborhoods follow in evolving into high-crime areas, however. Using a developmental model, they analyzed longitudinal data spanning a 20-year period (1950–70) in Los Angeles County's highest-crime areas. Their data consisted of census figures and official crime rates. In addition, Schuerman and Kobrin measured community structure through four basic social structural dimensions: (1) land use, (2) population composition, (3) socioeconomic status (SES), and (4) subculture. Land-use measures included such factors as the concentration and distribution of single- and multiple-family dwellings, industrial and commercial parcels, and traffic-generating establishments (such as offices, restaurants, and shopping centers). Population-composition measures included size and density of neighborhood populations, residential mobility, and household composition (number of parents, number of children, and so on). SES measures consisted of occupation, unemployment, education, and housing conditions. Subculture variables involved indicators of the ethnic make-up of the neighborhood.

The data suggested that in the initial stage of neighborhood change, land use and population composition are the early signs of impending change in neighborhood crime levels. Once in the initial stage, land use shows a shift from single to multiple dwellings, combined with rising numbers of commercial establishments. Eventually, in the more advanced stages of neighborhood decay, there is a gradual trend toward abandonment of the area; properties are sought by very few home buyers, renters, or investors. The population-composition variables then shift toward higher population density, increased mobility, and an increase in single-parent families and unattached individuals. These trends proceed at an increasing rate, eventually to a point where the social and cultural character of a neighborhood is qualitatively altered.

During the later stages of neighborhood deterioration, SES and subculture changes become more prominent. The Schuerman and Kobrin data indicate that high-crime areas evolve from initial ecological physical decay to social and cultural decay at the advanced stages of neighborhood deterioration. During the later stages, there is a sizeable decrease in professional and skilled occupational groups and in the educational level of the population. Conversely, unskilled laborers, unemployed persons, and overcrowded and deteriorated housing all increase. The data also showed decline in the white and Hispanic populations, but no change in the black population. At the advanced stage of deterioration, the neighborhood is characterized by instability, a breakdown in social controls, and an increase in normative ambiguity.

In Schuerman and Kobrin's study, changes in the crime rate paralleled the SES and subcultural changes described here. Neighborhood crimes increased steadily through the physical changes, changes in population composition, changes in SES characteristics, and changes in prevailing normative controls. Schuerman and Kobrin identified three distinct phases of neighborhood changes in crime rates. In the **emerging** stage, neighborhoods once relatively free of crime began to exhibit moderate crime rates. In the **transitional** stage, crime increased from a moderate to a high level. The **enduring** stage was characterized by persistent, ongoing high crime rates over long periods of time. Property was abandoned, the populations became increasingly unemployed and discouraged, and there was little social control over deviant behavior beyond token police patrols.

Schuerman and Kobrin also examined the **velocity** of these neighborhood changes. They discovered that speed of change was crucial in the process. The greater the velocity of structural change in the neighborhood, the more precipitous the rise in crime rates. Crime rates radically increased with rapid changes in SES and subcultural variables.

The researchers unfortunately assert that neighborhoods characterized by a high level of crime over a period of several decades may be considered "lost" for purposes of effective crime-reduction. In other words, some neighborhoods are so infested with crime that crime reduction strategies are futile. Schuerman and Kobrin suggest that police resources, police planning, and other forms of formal social control and social services be directed at communities in the emerging and transition stages of crime infiltration. At these stages, there is hope that the eventual slide into persistently high crime rates may be avoided.

NEIGHBORHOOD SOCIAL CONTROL AND FAMILY STRUCTURE

Families and communities are mutually connected, and to the extent that families are disrupted, we can expect communities to be similarly disrupted. It is important to note here that we are not speaking only of the traditional nuclear family of parents and children but rather of the nuclear group that constitutes a household. As we have seen, delinquency most often occurs in neighborhoods or communities in which informal social controls are reduced or absent. This is not to deny that youths living in stable neighborhoods commit crime. Explanations for the phenomenon of delinquency among youths of higher-SES levels are more likely to be found at the individual or microsystem level, however. Keep in mind that in this chapter we are discussing macrosystems and concentrating upon theories and data that transcend the boundaries of a youth's very personal situation.

As mentioned earlier in the chapter, surveillance and supervision by parents and concerned adults are the principal means for informal control and prevention. If parents are in marital conflict or unsupported in caregiving, their ability to monitor the activities of their own children, let alone those of others, is seriously hampered. More often than not, single parents are forced to work outside the home. Many parents work extended work days and must leave adolescents unsupervised, sometimes for long periods of time. Accordingly, communities that have extended clusters of single-parent homes, especially with low incomes, should have higher rates of delinquency. Robert J. Sampson has made some attempts to test this hypothesis.

Sampson (1986b) postulates that widespread marital and family disruption concentrated in certain neighborhoods is linked to the crime and delinquency rates of those areas, even when racial composition, poverty, or income are controlled. As noted previously, family disruption (divorce, family conflict, separation) had the effect of removing family members from active participation in their community and reducing informal social controls. Sampson hypothesized, in line with Marcus Felson (1986b), that communities with high concentrations of family disruption had low rates of participation in voluntary organizations and local affairs. A high level of family disruption, he notes, "interferes with the individual and collective efforts of families to link youth to the wider society through institutional means such as schools, religion, and sports" (1986b, p. 278). In other words, conflictful families develop fewer networks that would link their children to mainstream institutions and society in general.

Conflictful families may be less able to supervise their children and others in the neighborhood. In neighborhoods characterized by stable families, children are generally supervised and even reprimanded by adults other than own parents. Neighbors take note of strangers, question them, watch over one another's property, and often intervene in local disturbances. This adult surveillance, supervision, and intervention is apt to have substantial effects on the delinquency rate of a particular area.

Sampson tested his hypotheses by examining robbery and homicide rates in 171 American cities with populations over 100,000. Because the number of juvenile offenders involved in homicide was too small to suggest meaningful inferences, he focused on juvenile robbery. Family disruption was defined in two ways: (1) proportion of intact black and white families within a given area (with "intact" defined as married-couple families); and (2) the divorce rate within that targeted area. He examined a wide range of variables, including neighborhood instability, income heterogeneity, percent nonwhite, percent living alone, and percent over age 65. Sampson concluded that "Of all city characteristics . . . family structure clearly has the strongest effects on juvenile robbery offending for both sexes" (Sampson, 1986b, p. 298). Unfortunately, Sampson did not take direct measures of informal controls, such as parental and adult supervision of children, adolescents, and groups. Still, his project brings us one step closer toward understanding the complicated and bi-directional effects of family and neighborhood structure. Families can alter the delinquency characteristics of the neighborhood, and the neighborhood, in turn, can affect the security and well-being of the family.

A similar argument was advanced by Marcus Felson and Lawrence Cohen (1980), who emphasized the importance of guardianship and adult supervision in preventing delinquency within the community. They suggested that the quality and extent of this supervision has been eroded by the changing structure of modern American society. The primary lifestyle of most Americans today requires that family members be separated from one another and from their homes for extended periods of time. This reduces the amount of supervision over both households and juveniles. The home is unattended for long hours, increasing its chances of being burglarized or vandalized. Youngsters are left with idle time to pursue delinquent activities. Thus, neighborhood family structure is an important community-level factor in explaining offender rates and victimization risk. Of course, theories such as this one assume that when opportunity lurks, budding delinquents rise to the occasion, a supposition that would be challenged by other theories of delinquency.

In summary, this section sampled some of the contemporary work being done on process factors as potential explanations of delinquency. This section illustrates how macrosystem or social structure findings can be used as benchmarks for pursuing process variables.

BIAS CRIMES

One topic at the higher level that needs to be addressed is discrimination, which is reflected in bias-related crime. Bias or "hate" crimes are violent attacks, intimidation, arson, or property damage, that are directed at a person or group of persons because of race, religion, sexual orientation, or ethnicity. The motive for the crime is the presumed hatred of the victim because he or she belongs to the different group. Many states have added other categories, including gender, military status, physical disability, or age.

The Hate Crime Statistics Act of 1990 mandates data collection of crimes in which there is evidence the act was committed because of prejudice. Documenting hate or bias crimes is difficult because the intentions of the crime are not always that clearcut. Recent data suggest that about 18 percent of hate crimes are motivated by religious bias, 66 percent by racial hatred, and 12 percent because of sexual orientation (Schmalleger, 1997).

Victimization data, however, indicate that bias-related crime may be the most frequent kind of victimization experienced by lesbian, gay or bisexual youth (D'Augelli & Dark, 1994). Nearly 40 percent of gay youth reported they had been victims of severe physical violence because of their sexual orientation (Remafedi, Farrow, & Deisher, 1991). In addition, the psychological consequences of these victimizations may be far more severe for adolescents than adults. For example, as a result of being victimized, lesbian and gay youth are two to three times more likely to commit suicide than their heterosexual peers (Gibson, 1989). About 40 percent of street youth and runaways are lesbian, gay, or bisexual who have been rejected by their families.

The number of bias crimes against homosexual youth is increasing. Contemporary lesbian, gay and bisexual youth have been increasingly willing to express their sexual orientation in recent years. This increased openness often puts them in direct conflict with family, peers, and the traditional institutions such as schools (D'Augelli & Dark, 1994). In addition, those youths who are seriously hurt as a result of violent attacks are often victimized again when seeking help by a non-accepting American society. According to Anthony D'Augelli and Lawrence Dark (1994, p. 187), "It is reasonable to hypothesize that such youth, especially if they are young . . . and have little or no support in coping with attacks, will suffer more deleterious consequences . . ."

NETWORK ANALYSIS

Network analysis was developed primarily as a strategy for examining the nature of relationships within a group. The more extensive and varied one's personal networks, the greater the commitment toward the conventional thinking of the total social network. It is important to remember, however, that we often select and to some extent influence our personal networks.

Network analysis—both as an analytic strategy and as a theory—can serve as a bridge between different levels of explanations. This will be illustrated here, beginning with the work of Marvin D. Krohn, who has refined network analysis and, in the process, made more explicit its theoretical potential. We will also examine how Krohn applies his modification specifically to delinquency. Next, we will discuss the neighborhood and community as macrosystems and review current research focusing on the **processes** of these higher systems. Within this context, we include some discussions of chronosystems. The chapter concludes with a brief sketch of comparative criminology, a field that studies the broadest macrosystem. For illustration purposes, we will concentrate on Japan, because it exemplifies an industrialized, modern society with an exceedingly low crime rate (compared with that of the United States) and complex systems of social networks and community involvement.

Refinement and Application of Network Analysis

Marvin D. Krohn (1986) has proposed a promising theory of delinquency with considerable potential for explaining it across neighborhoods, cultures, and even nations. **Network analysis theory** has its roots in the work of Georg Simmel (1922) and, generally, cultural anthropology.

Krohn's version of network theory incorporates observations made by both Hirschi and Sutherland. Krohn and Hirschi agree that an adolescent's belief in and conformity to conventional norms is dependent upon his or her attachment to people and institutions. The Hirschi theory suggests that these links are additive: The more links the adolescent has, the stronger the bond to conventional society will be. If the links are weakened or broken, the adolescent is released from constraints, increasing the chances that he or she will slip into delinquency. Krohn notes that although Hirschi's theory has received modest empirical support (e.g., Hindelang, 1973; Krohn & Massey, 1980; Wiatrowski, Griswold, & Roberts, 1981; Krohn et al., 1983), it does not adequately explain the causes of delinquency. The **interactions** adolescents have with their peers, families, and the community at large are also crucial. Thus, Krohn accepts Sutherland's contention that behavior is learned through associations with significant others in the social environment.

Four concepts are at the root of network theory: **social network**, **personal network**, **multiplexity**, and **density**. "Social network" refers to sets of **groups** or organizations linked by the web of social relationships, such as friendships or memberships. It describes the structure and relationships among aggregates of people. As such, it has many of the features found in Bronfenbrenner's exosystems and macrosystems. "Personal network" refers specifically to the **participant** and the links that he or she has with other people. In many ways, this level is similar to the individual system, microsystems, and mesosystems. Personal networks are those social relationships experienced by a participant, whereas "social networks" refers to a **set** of social relationships between social groups and organizations. A simple strategy for determining a personal network is to ask a person to list all the units or individuals to which he or she is "linked" or associated. Identification of a social network, on the other hand, would require asking randomly selected samples of participants to list the units or individuals to which they are linked. Any number of ways may be employed to construct the social network—surveys, interviews, observations.

"Network multiplexity" refers to the number of contexts (microsystems) in which the same people interact jointly. The extent to which people go to school together, work together, go to religious services together, party together, or even live in the same neighborhood reflects network multiplexity. Multiplexity of social relationships fosters consistency in behavior and individual conformity. A person who interacts with the same people in different settings (microsystems) knows that the way he or she acts in one setting will affect how others expect him or her to behave in another. "Thus, multiplexity in social relationships is likely to constrain the individual's behavior" (Krohn, 1986, p. 83).

Inappropriate behavior in one microsystem may have adverse effects on participation in another, however. Becoming drunk, hostile, and obscene at the office party may have adverse consequences for the individual when promotion time comes. The individual's actions may negatively affect other microsystems, such as the local church or country club. For the gang member, telling on her friends under pressure is apt to promote dire consequences for her within the microsystem of the gang.

Krohn hypothesizes that the greater the number of contexts (such as family, church, school clubs, or other activities) in which there is network multiplexity, the lower the probability of delinquent behavior. In other words, youth who participate together in a number of conventional activities are less likely to engage in serious antisocial delinquency. He observes that Hirschi's theory is restrictive because it concentrates primarily upon the degree of adolescent attachment to parents. Krohn's network theory expands the explanation beyond the family context. In fact, he suggests that the concept of multiplexity can be expanded to describe relationships at even higher levels of social aggregation, such as among neighborhoods, cities, and society as a whole (all relationships that he calls "social units"). "In general, social units with higher levels of multiplexity will constrain behavior more than those with less multiplexity" (Krohn, 1986, p. 84). To put it another way, those neighborhoods whose residents demonstrate high levels of multiplexity will show lower rates of delinquency. Homogeneous neighborhoods where the members have similar values, such as we might find in ethnic neighborhoods, should show low rates of delinquency, compared with more heterogeneous neighborhoods. Multiplexity may also help explain the lower rates of delinquency in countries like Japan, Sweden, and Switzerland.

"Network density" refers to the extent to which individuals in a particular social network (or social system) are connected by direct relationships or ties, or the extent to which they know and interact with one another directly. Density answers, "How well do the inhabitants of a particular neighborhood know one another and talk to one another?" It does not refer simply to the *number* of contacts within a certain social group. Network density is usually measured as the **ratio** of actual social ties in a network to the maximum number of possible ties. A social network reaches maximum density when everyone knows one another, such as we might find in a small town. In this case, the behavior of each town member is potentially subject to the reactions of *all* town members. Under these conditions of maximum network density, the behavior of all the members will be under close scrutiny and maximum constraint. Therefore, we would expect the delinquency rate in isolated rural towns to be very low because of the very high network density.

Moreover, "There is a possibility that personal network density and social network density interact to produce different behavioral outcomes in different contexts" (Krohn, 1986, p. 85). That is, high-density networks at one ". . . level of aggregation may inhibit the formation of social networks at a larger aggregate" (p. 85). If a group of people know one another well and are close interpersonally, they may see themselves as self-sufficient, with little need to develop networks beyond their circle of friends and relatives. They may even view outside systems as infringements upon their own network. Although behavior within their group may be constrained, the group's behavior in the larger context of other systems may not be so constrained. Hence, a group of boys who develop a network may feel little need or social pressure to constrain their behavior to the expectations of a larger network, such as the school environment or the community.

It is clear from the available ecological research that the rate of crime and delinquency in urban areas is significantly greater than the rate in suburban or rural areas (Toby, 1979; Lylerly & Skipper, 1981; Krohn, Kanza-Kaduce, & Akers, 1984). Krohn suggests that this may be due to population density, an important structural component of a community or neighborhood. He hypothesizes that as population density increases, network density will decrease. Remember that network density is measured by the ratio of the number of people whom members of a social area know and interact with to the number of the potential people to know and interact with within that area. As population density increases, the number of potential contacts also increases. Because it is not likely that the individual will interact with everyone, network density is likely to be low. Krohn assumes—logically—that there is a limit to the number of people with whom a person can maintain social relationships. Because network density increases constraints on behavior, it follows that as population increases, the rate of delinquent behavior will increase.

Both self-report and official data indicate a significant relationship between population density for both crime and delinquency rates. It is also clear that this relationship will hold up only to a certain point. At that point, further increases in population will not affect the already high delinquency rate. As population density of an area goes up, delinquency rates will correspondingly go up in a similar fashion. It is expected that the delinquency rate will eventually reach a saturation point so that further increases in population density will have little effect on the rate (Roncek, 1975).

A large population also provides for the expression of widely diverse interests. This increases the number of contexts or systems around which social networks can be developed. As the number of potential contexts increases in a given area, the proportion of social relationships that are multiplex will decrease. Thus, Krohn hypothesizes that as the diversity of interests and potential contexts increases, it follows that delinquency will also increase.

A number of other predictions can be made from network theory. There is some evidence to suggest that people who live in houses are more likely to have social relationships with those locally than those who live in apartments (Fischer et al., 1977). This is especially true for multiple-family units, where it becomes difficult to know a high ratio of one's neighbors. "Therefore, I would expect there to be a lower social network density and multiplexity in communities having a high proportion of multiple-family housing and, hence, a higher rate of delinquent behavior" (Krohn, 1986, p. 87).

A high rate of residential mobility also changes the complexion of an area, as we have seen from the pioneering work of Shaw and McKay and others. When residents move often, it is difficult for members of the community to get to know one another or to establish social networks. Therefore, we can expect that areas of considerable residential turnover will have high rates of delinquency. Countries with low levels of residential mobility—for example, Switzerland—can be expected to show low levels of delinquency (Clinard, 1978).

Krohn further reminds us that limited financial resources make it difficult for individuals of lower SES to participate in volunteer and other community-oriented organizations (e.g., parent-teacher organizations, church groups, family activities) within their locale. Possible reasons for this include a need to work longer hours, a need to work nights, or feelings of being unaccepted by the community. Subsequently, lower-SES families will be less involved in microsystems within which to develop multiplex relations than middle- or upper-SES groups. Krohn also supposes that lower-SES juveniles are less likely to participate in extracurricular activities than their middle- and upper-SES peers. Thus, the social networks of lower-SES juveniles are apt to be less extensive (multiplex). The range of constraints on their behavior will be limited and the probability of delinquent involvement increased.

ROLE RELATIONSHIP THEORY

In 1976 Paul C. Friday and Jerald Hage launched a theory that has interesting parallels to network theory and, to some extent, to systems theory. Friday and Hage's **role relationship theory** may be applied across cultures and across levels of explanation. It posits that to understand delinquency, we must consider five patterns of role relationships that play a key role in the socialization and integration of youth into society. To avoid confusion and to coordinate Friday and Hage's theory with the theme of this chapter, we will refer to patterns of role relationships as "social networks."

The five social networks are: (1) kin relations, including the extended family; (2) community or neighborhood; (3) school; (4) work; and (5) peers not otherwise included in the four other networks. Friday and Hage postulated that delinquency depends upon the extent to which a person is enmeshed into these five social networks. The more enmeshed, the lower the probability of delinquent behavior. Friday and Hage see the five social networks as interconnected, in somewhat the same way Bronfenbrenner talks about mesosystems. The stronger the links between the social network systems, the lower the delinquency and general tendency to deviate from societal norms. Therefore, it is not so much a matter of whether a youth lives in a ghetto or has unemployed parents but rather how well that youth is worked into the social network of a society.

Two other concepts are crucial in the Friday–Hage model: the number of relationships and the intimacy of those relationships. A person may have a large number of relationships within a single network or a large number within different networks. Role relationship theory implies that many relationships within different networks—network diversity—are likely to ward off delinquency. The more diverse the youth's contacts with family, school, work, peers, and community, the fewer the chances for deviance. In this sense, role relationship theory emphasizes the interrelationships and interactions across all five networks rather than just one, as many traditional theories of delinquency have done. For example, Hirschi has focused upon the importance of the family, school, and peers. Role relationship theory expands the network into other areas, across different levels of network systems. Furthermore, it stresses the frequency of interactions (behaviors), rather than abstract attitudes and beliefs.

"Intimacy" in Friday and Hage's theory refers to the nature or quality of the relationships. In other words, what matters is not simply the number of relationships or passing acquaintances a youth has with the five networks but rather the closeness or significance of those relationships.

> The general hypothesis then becomes that if youth have intimate role relationships in all five areas or kinds, they are much less likely to engage in youth crime. Or, to put this more dynamically, as the intimacy declines both within certain areas and across all of them, the youth is less integrated into society and more likely to be involved in various kinds of crime (Friday & Hage, 1976, p. 350).

Like Krohn's network analysis theory, role relationship theory suggests that integration into the family, the school, work, friends, and the community constrains us toward conformity. The more socially isolated and unintegrated the youth, the greater the tendency toward deviation. Delinquency, then, arises among youth who are alienated because of being outside much of the social system.

Friday and Hage attributed increases in delinquency throughout many countries of the world to industrialization. Growing needs for skilled and educated workers restrict opportunities for many adolescents, particularly those youth who drop out of school, to become integrated into society. Friday and Hage contended that many youths of today are precluded from integration into society by virtue of their age, talents, and skills. Feeling alienated and cut off from social networks, they gravitate to youth gangs that become a barrier for future opportunities and interactions with other networks.

Industrialization also encourages residential mobility, with skilled, trained, or professional workers constantly on the move to better and different jobs. High residential mobility undercuts neighborhood stability, an important ingredient for informal control of deviant or delinquent activity. Residential mobility also diminishes the chances for community members to develop meaningful and extensive networks within the community.

Although the Friday–Hage model neither drew much interest nor generated research testing, we should not interpret this seeming lack of interest as evidence of poor theory. Research and scholarly interest also depend upon the inclinations of the criminology community at the time a theory is formulated. Stephen Cole (1975) wrote that ". . . the acceptance or rejection of a theory is not primarily dependent on empirical evidence. It is dependent on the way the theory fits in with the other interests of the community of scientists and the ability of the theory to fulfill what might be called its 'functional requirements'" (Cole, 1975, p. 212).

It may be time for theories or hypotheses which advance arguments that can be applied across levels of explanations to fit in with the interests of the research community. These theories may well receive increased attention by criminologists in the years ahead. This is not to advocate integration of the wide assortment of delinquency theories proposed over the past 50 years. On the contrary, it is important to keep in mind that each theory is a statement about how one or more persons view the world. Theories are constructions seen from different perspectives and construct systems, built on different assumptions. These ways of viewing the world would be difficult, if not impossible, to integrate without distorting or damaging the original statements. On the other hand, Krohn and Friday and Hage have made provocative and heuristic proposals from a different perspective from those of traditional theories of criminology. They are offered here as frameworks for the research that will be reviewed in the remainder of in this chapter.

SUMMARY AND CONCLUSIONS

This chapter introduces some of the research and theory on the exosystems and macrosystems as they affect delinquency. Historically, this level of analysis is found in the early foundations of sociology and ecology, beginning in the United States with the Chicago School. The ecological research of the Chicago School revolutionized the study of crime and delinquency. In effect, it can be considered the beginning of American criminology from a sociological perspective. Prior to the Chicago School, explanations of delinquency were dominated by a biologically based social science which asserted that crime and delinquency were due to individual deficiencies. "Poverty, crime, suicide, mental abnormality, and other behavioral defects of slum dwellers were seen as inborn legacies from their defective ancestors who had been reproducing at a higher rate than the normal population" (Faris, 1967, p. 62). One proposed remedy was to prevent deficient members of society from reproducing, an idea that included forced sterilization. This assumed biological deficit doctrine even received support from Supreme Court Justice Oliver Wendell Holmes, who proclaimed in an often-cited and much criticized decision allowing sterilization: "Three generations of imbeciles is enough."

The ecological research of the Chicago School shifted attention away from the individual–biological approach toward social factors as causal agents of crime and delinquency. It emphasized the effects of social disorganization and deteriorating physical environments, and it rejected notions of genetic and biological inferiority. Once policymakers and the public began to understand that crime and delinquency were not an inevitable biological aftermath of genetic coding or defective evolutionary development, more attention could be directed at the social, emotional, and physical environment as a powerful factor in the development of delinquency.

Two names that should be highlighted are Clifford R. Shaw and Henry D. McKay, two of the most influential researchers in criminology during the twentieth century. They are known not so much for any specific theory (primarily because they kept changing their explanations with each new set of data) but for their painstaking descriptions and geographical mapping of crime and delinquency in various urban areas. They were also pioneers in attempts to prevent delinquency by involving the community and its existing social networks. Their preventive strategy was epitomized in the Chicago Area Project, an approach that lasted more than three decades. Shaw also emphasized that delinquency is largely a group activity rather than an individual one. Furthermore, he was instrumental in bringing the life-history or case-study method to sociological research on delinquency, although the overall value of the method as a scientific tool remains much debated (see Geis, 1982; Short, 1982).

There are other significant names as well. William I. Thomas is best known for his elaboration of the concept of social disorganization. He also added invaluable insights into symbolic interactionism, characterized by his oft-cited dictum, "If men define situations as real, they are real in their consequences" (Thomas & Thomas, 1928, p. 572). This quotation suggests that the key to evaluating behavior is to understand how a person perceives and construes a situation. For Thomas, all human behavior was situationally oriented, and personal constructions of that situation dictated behavior.

The careful reader may wonder how Thomas, an integral member of the Chicago School, could have been toying with individual factors when we have just emphasized that the ecological perspective was the Chicago hallmark. The Chicago School, however, did not represent a unified system of thought. The term "Chicago School" was not even used until the 1950s. Lee Harvey (1987, p. 255) notes, "There are virtually no references to the 'Chicago School of Sociology' in the published literature during the first half of the century." Furthermore, interviews with the early Chicagoans reveal that they hardly considered themselves a "school of thought" during first 30 years after the founding of the sociology department (Kurtz, 1984; Harvey, 1987). Instead, they remember the University of Chicago as vibrant, full of energy, and a collection of people with wide interests. Thus, it is wiser to use "the Chicago School" loosely, to represent those divergent and influential thinkers associated with the University of Chicago's department of sociology who were keenly interested in crime and other social problems.

The ecological perspective of Burgess and Park and the highly influential work of Robert Merton on strain theory were discussed. The effects of neighborhood or community changes on the rates of crime and delinquency were also examined. We explored the important contributions of Krohn in his proposal for a network analysis theory of delinquency. The theory encourages social scientists to bridge and integrate all levels of the social systems.

A social systems orientation presumes finer gradients of social influence rather than simply an individual versus the environmental perspective.

Furthermore, a social systems perspective underscores the continual mutual influence of the systems at all levels. Delinquency as a social phenomenon cannot be meaningfully understood without careful consideration of family, peers, siblings, school, neighborhood, the chronosystem, cultures, and ethnic backgrounds within which all these systems are embedded. An understanding of highly aggressive or antisocial individuals requires an examination of their construct systems and an appreciation of other higher-level systems of influence.

KEY CONCEPTS

concentric circles theory
conformity
construction
cultural transmission hypothesis
deindustrialization
demagoguery
demolition
density
disinvestment
emerging stage
enduring stage
Illinois Crime Survey
innovation
multiplexity
network analysis theory

new experience
personal network
rates of delinquency
rebellion
recognition
response
retreatism
ritualism
role relationship theory
security
social disorganization
social network
transitional stage
velocity

9

Prevention, Intervention, and Treatment

The number of intervention, prevention, and treatment programs that have been tried on children at risk is overwhelming. Unfortunately, very few programs designed to reduce delinquent or predelinquent behavior have been effective or have shown lasting effects (Zigler, Taussig, & Black, 1992). This lack of success is especially true of programs that attempt to change serious delinquent offenders (Borduin et al., 1995), or those whom we have been referring to throughout the text as life-course-persistent (LCP) delinquents (Moffitt, 1993a). According to Dodge (1993a), no controlled study has demonstrated the long-term prevention of severe conduct disorders among high-risk children. Nonetheless, there are promising approaches on the horizon, as will be noted in this chapter.

CHARACTERISTICS OF SUCCESSFUL INTERVENTION

The reasons for the ineffectiveness of programs in preventing and changing antisocial behavior are multiple. However, by no means are all intervention or prevention programs ineffective. Some interventions have shown very promising results, and those that have been effective have some features in common.

Specifically, Zigler, Taussig, and Black (1992) concluded in their review that delinquency can be prevented by early childhood intervention programs that promote children's competence across multiple systems in which they are embedded. For example, crisis-oriented programs emphasizing counseling or social casework have been ineffective largely because they come too late. "By the time children reach these programs, often after referral by court personnel, they are already entrenched in a long history of antisocial interaction with parents, schools, and community that is not easily reversed" (Zigler, Taussig, & Black, 1992, p. 997). Nancy Guerra and her colleagues (Guerra et al., 1995) recommend that interventions begin no later in life than age eight and preferably before the first grade. There appears to be a mysterious jump in antisocial behavior between the first and second grade for many children, and, therefore, prevention programs enacted later than the first grade will need to be more intensive. Leonard Eron and his colleagues (Eron, Huesmann & Zelli, 1991) find that unusually aggressive behavior and violent tendencies crystallize by age eight or before. Guerra et al. (1995) have made the intriguing observation that aggressive and antisocial behavior begins to develop much earlier in children living in the most economically deprived urban neighborhoods, indicating that intervention and prevention programs must begin even earlier for some children. This observation appears to hold for both boys and girls (Tolan & Thomas, 1995). In addition, there is evidence to suggest that the earlier the signs of antisocial behavior appear, the more serious or violent the antisocial behavior or delinquency will be later (Tolan & Thomas, 1995). Terrie Moffitt (1993b; Moffitt et al., 1996) presents convincing evidence that the LCP delinquent manifests discernible indicators of antisocial behavior as early as age three. As discussed in previous chapters, early antisocial indicators often forecast a life of crime. As noted by Rolf Loeber (1990, p. 6), "[T]here is considerable *continuity* among disruptive and antisocial behavior over time, even though they may manifest themselves differently at different ages." Loeber also finds that as children and adolescents progress toward more serious delinquent behavior, they tend to move toward diversification, rather than from one specific deviant behavior to another. Thus, it is clear that without early intervention many children who are at risk for delinquency are more likely to engage in increasing levels of serious, chronic offending as they grow older.

There is little doubt that living conditions in the poorest inner-city neighborhoods are extremely harsh and that the daily onslaught of violence, substance abuse, child abuse, and hopelessness is highly disruptive to a child's normal development. For the child exposed to an adverse family life and inadequate living arrangements with little opportunity to develop even the rudiments of social and interpersonal skills for dealing effectively with others, the damage may be irreparable. Clearly, the longer a child is exposed to this adverse environment, the more difficult it will be to modify his or her life course away from crime and delinquency. Hence, intervention programs must not only begin as early as possible but also must be intensively directed at as many causes and negative influences as possible. Programs that have shown long-term success have used multipronged approaches concentrating on treating children through their broad social environment, and with particular sensitivity to the family's cultural background and heritage. Intervention programs that neglect gender, ethnicity, socioeconomic status, and other demographic markers that affect the development of antisocial behavior are destined to fail. Even poverty may affect individuals differently on the basis of their ethnicity and the meaning of poverty within a given cultural context (Guerra et al., 1995).

Effective intervention programs should also include prenatal and perinatal medical care and intensive health education for pregnant women and mothers with young children (Coordinating Council, 1996). These services reduce the delinquency risk factors of head and neurological injuries, exposure to toxins, maternal substance abuse, nutritional deficiencies, and perinatal difficulties.

Research has continually shown that the most successful interventions concentrate on the family system. It is clear that certain family relationships and parenting practices strongly relate to serious delinquency. More important, these family characteristics seem to be linked to delinquency regardless of ethnic or socioeconomic status (Gorman-Smith et al., 1996). The family characteristics most closely associated with serious delinquency are poor parental monitoring of the child's activities, poor and inconsistent discipline, and a lack of family closeness or cohesion. According to Thomas Dishion and David Andrews (1995), studies have consistently shown that negative, coercive exchanges between parents and children are predictive of child antisocial behavior (e.g., Patterson, 1986a), delinquent behavior (e.g., Bank & Patterson, 1992), and adolescent substance abuse (e.g., Dishion & Loeber, 1985). Research also indicates that emotional closeness and family cohesion—wherein the child receives emotional support, adequate communication, and love—are essential in the prevention of antisocial behavior and delinquency (Gorman-Smith et al., 1996).

Peer systems are critically important, and research has shown that negative peer associations are significant predictors of both substance abuse and delinquency (O'Donnell, Hawkins, & Abbott, 1995). Thus far, intervention programs have been unsuccessful in using peer groups as effective change agents in modifying these antisocial behaviors. Interventions that are peer-focused can actually have unintended negative effects if they require increased contact with antisocial peers (Vitaro & Tremblay, 1994). Similarly, Dishion and Andrews (1995) found that placing high-risk teens into groups together encouraged escalations in both tobacco use and problem behaviors in school. Dishion and Andrews discovered that bringing high-risk peers together may have actually served to increase contact with deviant peers and in the long run exacerbated their antisocial involvement. They recommended that intervention programs that use antisocial peers as change agents be discouraged unless such programs are very carefully designed. Likewise, research indicates that group homes for delinquents may increase delinquent behavior (Chamberlain, 1996). Antisocial peers model and encourage other antisocial peers.

In summary, effective prevention and treatment programs begin early, deal with multiple systems, focus on the family, and recognize the cultural, socioeconomic, and developmental influences affecting on the child.

SYSTEMS-BASED INTERVENTION PROGRAMS

Treating children through multiple systems rather than focusing on one isolated factor is an approach called **systems-based intervention**. Systems-based programs try to influence factors operating within the social environment that are believed to put the child at risk of delinquency. At the least, these programs try to reduce the situational opportunities that may lead to delinquency. **"At risk,"** as described in Chapter 2, denotes that an individual youth or a group of youths is in danger of future delinquency or crime. **Individual-based interventions**, on the other hand, try to change the beliefs, attitudes, skills, and behaviors of the *individual* child. Examples include improving academic performance, social and interpersonal skills, self-control and regulation, and social cognitive processes of particular youths.

Because of the many intervention and treatment programs that have been tried with children, some organizing structure is necessary to present the programs in a systematic way. In this chapter, we will follow the public health model of prevention, originally proposed by Gordon (1983) and elaborated upon further by Guerra, Tolan, and Hammond (1994) and Mulvey, Arthur, and Reppucci (1993). The model divides prevention strategies into three somewhat overlapping categories: (1) **primary prevention**, (2) **secondary prevention**, and (3) **tertiary** or **treatment prevention**.

Types of Prevention Programs

Primary prevention is designed to prevent delinquent behavior *before* any signs of the behavioral pattern emergences. Thus, primary prevention programs are installed early in the developmental sequence of a child, preferably before the ages of seven or eight. Typically, primary prevention programs are conducted within the school setting and focus on large groups of individuals.

Secondary prevention consists of working with children and adolescents who demonstrate some early signs of aggressive, antisocial, conduct disorder, or delinquent behavior but have not yet been formally classified as delinquent. In many instances, these prevention programs focus on young individuals who may have had contacts with the police but have not yet been adjudicated "delinquent" by the court (Mulvey, Arthur, & Reppucci, 1993). The basic assumption in secondary prevention is that early detection and early intervention will prevent the child from "graduating" into more serious, habitual offending. A well-known example of this prevention tactic is juvenile diversion, a strategy to be discussed more fully in Chapter 11. An advantage of secondary prevention programs is that they focus on those individuals who should benefit most from the services (Guerra, Tolan, & Hammond, 1994). That is, the effort can be concentrated on those at risk rather than on an entire group of children, many of whom may show no risk factors at all.

The third or "tertiary" prevention strategy is often described in the delinquency literature as "treatment." As noted by Guerra, Tolan, and Hammond (1994), the distinction between secondary and tertiary prevention is often fuzzy and unclear. This is because both approaches demand the identification of at-risk children for the intervention services and sometimes provide similar services. However, we will reserve the terms "tertiary prevention" (or "treatment") for those programs designed to reduce serious, extant delinquent behavior. More often than not, these fully involved delinquents have been referred for psychological care or have been committed to day treatment or residential correctional facilities. In most cases, tertiary prevention or treatment strategies for serious delinquents are carried out in residential (institutional) settings.

Types of Intervention Programs

Another useful way of classifying the three prevention strategies was proposed by Tolan and Guerra (1994), who outlined three types of intervention based not so much on *when* in the developmental sequence of delinquency intervention is enacted but more *to whom* the intervention is directed. The Tolan–Guerra classification system identifies: (1) **universal intervention**, wherein participants are included in the program regardless of possible differences in risk for delinquency; (2) **selected intervention**, wherein specific individuals believed to be at risk receive intervention; and (3) **indicated intervention**, wherein the intervention focuses on already fully involved delinquents.

Universal intervention is basically a primary prevention approach whereby the intent is to prevent the *onset* of delinquency among entire populations. Universal intervention programs attempt to increase the resources, skills, and competencies of the participants. They are usually less intensive than other forms of intervention because of the large number of participants. Many universal intervention strategies do have some focus in mind, such as the youth within a particular neighborhood or the disadvantaged youth within a certain sector of a city. Most such programs have focused on very young children, often before they attend formal schooling. The programs have generally concentrated on improving behavior-management skills, family relations, and the social and academic skills of the children. Excellent examples of universal intervention methods can be found in preschool programs such as Headstart.

Selected intervention programs rely heavily on a secondary prevention approach. As noted by Tolan and Guerra, the effectiveness of selected programs rests primarily with the quality of the screening of the participants. That is, a major objective of the program is to identify youths who demonstrate behaviors assumed to lead to more serious and diversified delinquency somewhere down the line.

Indicated interventions attempt to lessen the seriousness, chronicity, or continuation of already existing delinquency. Basically, indicated interventions are tertiary efforts because they are designed to prevent the long-term consequences of an ongoing problem. Indicated programs tend to be more intense and costly than other approaches.

PRIMARY INTERVENTION STRATEGIES

Mulvey, Arthur, and Reppucci (1993) divide primary prevention approaches into three major strategies, depending on where within the youth's systems the focus is placed: (1) family-based interventions, (2) school-based interventions, and (3) community-based interventions.

Family-based Programs

The most logical place to begin in preventing delinquency is the family. Family-based intervention is designed to help families cope with the stresses of child rearing by either training the caregivers on family management techniques or by developing a supportive network for the family. The strategy of the latter method is to provide a broad range of services to the family, such as day care, medical care, counseling, casework, and appropriate referrals to other agencies. A classic example of this approach is the Cambridge–Somerville Youth Study, described in Chapter 1. Although the Cambridge–Somerville project resulted in more negative effects than anticipated, recent family-support approaches have shown significantly more positive short-term outcomes. However, the long-term effects on delinquency remain unknown (Mulvey, Arthur, & Reppucci, 1993).

The **Yale Child Welfare Research Program** was an intervention program that provided "a coordinated set of social work, pediatric, child care, and psychological services for 30 months following birth to low income mothers and their firstborn children" (Mulvey, Arthur, & Reppucci, 1993, p. 137). Each family interacted with a small team of persons: a home visitor (social worker or psychologist), a pediatrician, primary day-care worker, and a developmental examiner (Seitz, Rosenbaum, & Apfel, 1985). The primary goal of the project was to reduce the negative impact of the many stressors experienced by economically disadvantaged mothers.

In a 10-year follow-up, boys in the program had better school attendance, demonstrated fewer conduct problems in the classroom, and generally exhibited less predelinquent behavior than a comparison group of boys. However, we must be very cautious in generalizing the results to other disadvantaged mothers. Participants (mothers and first-borns) were screened so thoroughly that any indications of physical problems at birth in the infant or any signs of serious psychological or cognitive problems in the mother were sufficient reasons to eliminate the family from further consideration in the project. Furthermore, there were only 18 children in both the intervention group and the control group, hardly a large enough sample to generalize to other economically disadvantaged mothers in other cities. In addition, the children were still pre-adolescent at the time of the 10-year follow-up and, therefore, were probably too young to be evaluated for delinquent behaviors. Still, the results of the Yale study suggest at least one very promising lead in the development of effective strategies for dealing with possible determinants of delinquency: Start early with strategies directed at multisystems.

School-Based Prevention Programs

Preschool Programs   School-based prevention programs focus on working with children or young adolescents within the school environment (including preschool), although family and community systems are sometimes included in the program. Excellent examples of preschool prevention programs are Project Headstart and the Perry Preschool Project.

Project Headstart began in 1965 as a 6- to 8-week summer program for 3- to 5-year-olds from economically disadvantaged families. However, professionals involved quickly realized that a longer educational program was necessary, and so Headstart was lengthened to 2 years. In 1992, Headstart enrolled approximately 600,000 preschoolers at a cost of $2.2 billion (Zigler, 1994).

The fundamental assumption underlying Headstart is that disadvantaged children are at risk for low academic achievement and that these factors ultimately can lead to persistent poverty and unfulfilled, unproductive lives. The program has 4 major components: education (including a creative preschool program), health (both physical and mental), parental involvement (in all planning and administrative aspects of each program), and a broad range of social services. However, it should be emphasized that the 2,000 or more Headstart programs often vary significantly in the type and quality of the services they render (Zigler & Stevenson, 1993). For example, some are center-based, whereas others are home-based.

Project Headstart does appear to produce significant and meaningful gains in intellectual performance and socioeconomic development at the end of the two years of intervention, and this improvement seems to last for at least two to three years thereafter. However, it is debatable how long after the initial intervention these gains continue without some re-intervention at a later time. Many effects seem to disappear by elementary school, although these findings may reflect variation in the quality of the Headstart program and differences in outcome measures used in the evaluations (Gamble & Zigler, 1989; Mulvey, Arthur, & Reppucci, 1993). Unfortunately, evaluations of Headstart's effectiveness at preventing delinquency remain sparse and inconclusive (Mulvey, Arthur, & Reppucci, 1993). The results from Headstart do suggest, however, that many children get a jump on their academic and social lives and that these effects significantly reduce their risk for later delinquency.

The most widely publicized evaluation of a preschool program was the **Perry Preschool Project**, started in 1962. This project was an organized educational program directed at the intellectual and social development of young children and was designed to prevent educational failure in high-risk children, mostly from low-income African American families (Berrueta-Clement et al., 1987). This early intervention program included either 1 or 2 years of preschool education, frequent parent meetings, and weekly home visits by teachers. The lasting effects of this intervention program were assessed annually from ages 4 to 11 and at 14, 15, and 19 years of age. Youth involved in the program received better grades, scored higher on standardized achievement tests, and had better high school graduation rates, higher employment rates, fewer acts of misconduct, and lower arrest rates (Berrueta-Clement et al., 1987). In summary, preschool programs designed to include the family system and lasting for at least a year or two do seem to play a substantial role in the prevention of delinquency. These programs may be especially effective in reducing the LCP trajectory toward a life of crime.

Formal School-based Prevention School-based prevention programs that begin in the early years of formal schooling, such as in the first grade, have a captive audience (under the law, all children must attend school) compared with preschool programs wherein participation in the preschooling curriculum is voluntary. Therefore, schools have been a popular setting for universal and primary programs of prevention (Tolan & Guerra, 1994). Examples of school-based programs include cognitive–behavorial interventions and social-process interventions.

Cognitive–behavioral interventions are based on "the idea that conduct disorders such as juvenile delinquency and substance abuse can result from an inability to develop and maintain positive social relationships due to deficits in social skills" (Mulvey, Arthur, & Reppucci, 1993, p. 139). According to Mulvey, Arthur, & Reppucci (1993), these interventions can be described as either interpersonal cognitive problem solving (ICPS) or behavioral social-skills-training (BSST) programs. ICPS programs concentrate on having the child interpret social cues and the intentions of others in more appropriate ways, as well as on having the child develop alternative solutions to conflict and interpersonal problems he or she may encounter in daily life. BSST programs concentrate on teaching specific behaviors on how to get along in peer groups, such as accepting criticism, giving compliments, and resisting peer pressure. Usually, BSST and ICPS programs are combined into a part of a school curriculum. Evaluations of the effectiveness of ICPS and BSST programs have shown some short-term improvements, but the evidence for long-term gains remains unclear (Mulvey, Arthur, & Reppucci, 1993).

Social-Process Interventions

One problem of many school-based programs is that, because they focus on children during the school day within the school setting, they often do not extend to other developmental contexts such as the family (Tolan & Guerra, 1994). Rarely do school-based programs specifically assess the long-term effects of the intervention on delinquency. Occasionally, though, the evaluations do examine some related antisocial behaviors such as aggression and truancy. Aggressive and truant children do not necessarily become delinquents, however. Consequently, it is difficult to evaluate properly the effectiveness of many school-based programs as prevention approaches to delinquency.

Tolan and Guerra (1994) note that delinquency prevention strategies that focus on multiple systems show greater promise than single-system-focused programs. They describe a program developed by Hawkins and his colleagues (Hawkins, Von Cleve, & Catalano, 1991) wherein first- and second-grade schoolchildren from low-income urban schools were taught social problem-solving skills. Teachers were also trained in classroom management and interactive teaching skills, and parents were trained in family management skills. Thus, the program encompassed both the school and the family systems. The program's underlying assumption was that aggressive and antisocial behaviors in the early elementary school grades are precursors of delinquency in adolescence. If these antisocial behaviors can be substantially reduced or terminated early, the chances for later involvement in delinquency are correspondingly reduced.

The program was evaluated at the end of the second grade. Lower rates of aggressiveness were found for boys in the classrooms that used the intervention strategies when compared with controls who did not receive any intervention strategies. In addition, boys who received the intervention were less likely to be extremely antisocial, compared with the control groups. Children in the intervention classrooms showed increased interest in school, and their families improved in management skills. Troubling, however, is the finding that the intervention strategies had virtually no effect on improving the classroom behavior of the African American children, a feature that *may* have been due to differences in parental participation. That is, the caretakers of the African American children often were unable to participate because of occupational or family commitments. Alternatively, parents may have been discouraged from participating by a perception that the program was not sensitive to their African American culture. Overall, the study does provide a limited demonstration that improved teacher instructional methods together with improved family management skills can reduce antisocial behavior in young children of a particular cultural background.

In another school-based project, Tremblay et al. (1995) developed an intervention program that concentrated on disruptive kindergarten boys from inner-city (Montreal), low-SES neighborhood schools. Disruptive behavior was assessed by school teachers using the Social Behavior Questionnaire (SBQ). Boys who scored above the seventieth percentile on the SBQ were considered to be at risk for later antisocial behavior and delinquency. The 2-year program included home-based parental training and school-based social skills training. Both training strategies were implemented by a multdisciplinary team consisting of child-care workers, a psychologist, and a social worker. The parental training sessions involved teaching parents to monitor their children's behavior and to give children positive reinforcement for socially appropriate behaviors, training parents to discipline appropriately, and teaching parents family crisis management techniques. The control group consisted of a group of disruptive boys who did not receive any of the interventions given the treatment groups. Delinquency was assessed by self-reports provided by the youths and court records. The court records did not reveal any significant differences between the groups. The results did show, however, that the treated boys reported fewer delinquent behaviors at yearly assessments from 10 to 15 years of age than the controls. Overall, the preventive intervention appeared to have a significant long-term impact on the social development of the disruptive kindergarten boys, although the effects appeared to decrease with time. The researchers recommended, therefore, that young adolescents be given "booster" sessions of similar treatments to reduce the risk for delinquency during the teen years. **Booster sessions** are periodic follow-up sessions added to help maintain the effects of the initial intervention.

COMMUNITY EFFORTS AT DELINQUENCY PREVENTION

Community-based prevention interventions include programs called Community Organization and Youth Recreation. One of the earliest programs in community-based prevention was the Chicago Area Project (CAP) discussed in Chapter 8. Although there was some evidence that delinquency rates in the CAP neighborhoods decreased by almost 50 percent during the 1930s, the Project was never empirically evaluated or researched (Mulvey, Arthur, & Reppucci, 1993). Consequently, the effectiveness of the CAP as a delinquency-prevention approach remains in question.

Many youth recreation programs (e.g., Police Athletic League, Boys' and Girls' Clubs, supervised intramural sports, and the Fresh Air Fund) have been introduced over the years to offer constructive activities for children and teens in an attempt to reduce their involvement in antisocial activity (Mulvey, Arthur, & Reppucci, 1993). According to Edward Mulvey and his co-workers, more than 20 million youths aged 6 to 15 currently participate in some form of organized recreational activity. Whether these activities actually reduce delinquency to any significant extent is unknown.

The problem with any community-based or organized recreation programs is that neighborhood organizing *by itself* does not significantly reduce delinquency (Mulvey, Arthur, & Reppucci, 1993). This is especially the case for life-course-persistent delinquents. Any effective community-based program will need to fully encompass the family system, the school system, and peer influences, with particular emphasis directed at the family.

The Virginia Youth Violence Project

One ongoing violence-prevention program which bears watching is the Virginia Youth Violence Project, which began as a grassroots effort in Virginia Beach in 1993 (Sheras, Cornell, & Bostain, 1996). Concerned about an apparent increase in incidents of gun and knife possession in the schools, parents, school officials, human-service workers, business leaders, and representatives of the law-enforcement community met to develop a prevention strategy. This initial meeting led to a broad, comprehensive program delivered to educators and human-service professionals throughout the state. A key component of the program was the dissemination of knowledge about violence to those who were working on a regular basis with violent or potentially violent youth.

The project, which was multidisciplinary in focus and action-oriented, involved continuing-education workshops intended to offer a message of hope to more than 1,000 participants. The participants were taught, for example, to recognize the hyperbole in many media accounts of the crime problem. They were also given information about the "risk factor" approach, which rejects simplistic explanation for violent behavior.

> A risk factor approach . . . conceptualizes violence in terms of a hierarchy of factors that may interact and cumulatively increase the risk of violent behavior. A risk factor model allow participants to recognize the role of multiple factors in the etiology of violence, which range from innate differences in temperament to family learning experiences, and to incorporate concepts of cognitive and affective development as well as societal influences (Sheras et al., 1996, p. 402).

In their descriptions of the Virginia Youth Violence Project, Sheras and colleagues note that educators across the country are continually barraged with information about unidimensional approaches to dealing with violence. For example, it is not unusual for teachers to receive mail offering training sessions, videotapes, or other materials on conflict resolution or peer mediation. Without an understanding of the causes of violence or the multitude of alternative strategies for dealing with it, however, these materials are incomplete.

The goal of the Virginia Youth Violence Project was to provide educators with "an overview of the nature and scope of youth violence, a conceptual basis for understanding aggression and analyzing the problem in a local context, and an introduction to intervention and prevention strategies" (Sheras et al., 1996, p. 402). The project made use of lectures as well as video-assisted presentations. For example, high school principals, law-enforcement officers, members of a juvenile gang, and youthful victims of crimes all shared their experiences on tape for program participants. Throughout the project, directors responded to media requests for interviews in order to disseminate information to a wider audience.

Although the project is ongoing, early results are promising. It was clear from pre- and post-testing measures that knowledge about the subject of youth violence increased significantly as a result of the workshops. Additionally, participants were required to plan and implement violence-awareness projects in their schools and communities. Some projects involved surveying students or community residents and holding forums on the results of the survey. Others encouraged students to produce plays, develop mediation programs, or form groups to discourage fighting and aggressive behavior in the schools.

The Virginia project is mentioned here as a good illustration of the multidisciplinary systems-based approach necessary to tackle the problem of youth violence. Significant community involvement and the use of community resources are critical components of the program.

SECONDARY PREVENTION INTERVENTIONS

Most of the secondary interventions, such as diversion, will be reviewed in Chapters 10 and 11. One secondary intervention method that merits mention in this chapter is family therapy and skills training. As noted by Mulvey, Arthur, and Reppucci (1993), family therapy and skills training have been a popular strategy for more than 25 years in the treatment of children with conduct disorders. Since the late 1980s, the method has become popular for dealing with delinquent and drug-abusing adolescents. Some research indicates that family skills training approaches may cut recidivism rates by nearly half compared with other forms of family and individual therapy (Gordon & Arbuthnot, 1987).

Some caution is necessary when drawing any conclusions concerning the effectiveness of the family skills training approach, however. Most of the studies evaluating this method have discovered that nearly 50 percent of the participants dropped out of the program before completion (Mulvey, Arthur, & Reppucci,

1993). Dropout rates were especially prevalent among families with older children and those characterized by few support systems, marital difficulties, and limited financial resources. More important, success rates were particularly unimpressive for families with older, chronic delinquents compared with families with younger, aggressive children. Again, later intervention with already involved serious delinquents has a very poor track record compared with very early intervention.

TREATMENT APPROACHES

Treatment usually involves some form of psychotherapy. "Psychotherapy" is defined by Kazdin (1994, p. 359) as "a wide range of interventions designed to decrease or eliminate problem behaviors and maladjustment and to improve adaptive and prosocial functioning." Treatment interventions most often rely upon interpersonal interaction or counseling, and they focus on how persons feel (affect), think (cognition), and act (behavior) (Kazdin, 1994).

Researchers have identified more than 230 different treatment methods currently being used for children (Kazdin, 1994). The effectiveness of most of these techniques has yet to be evaluated or empirically investigated. The small amount of research that has been conducted strongly indicates that treatment programs which concentrate on changing thought processes hold considerable promise. Treatment programs that include the family, school, peers, and community clearly show the greatest promise.

A very wide range of treatment methods has been tried with juvenile delinquents. In a common scenario, the juvenile court refers a persistent delinquent youth to an outpatient mental-health clinic for counseling and psychotherapy. The traditional approach relies on a one-on-one strategy of providing psychotherapy to an individual. Most commonly, the relationship with the therapist is the primary medium through which change is achieved (Kazdin, 1987). Presumably, the treatment provides a corrective experience by providing insight and exploring new ways of behaving (Kazdin, 1987). In some instances, the delinquent youth may receive individual counseling from a member of the juvenile court staff (Borduin, 1994). Delinquent youth who require a more restrictive setting are usually placed in a residential facility in which group therapy is more common than individual counseling. However, the effectiveness of delinquency treatment within the juvenile justice system is difficult to assess. Many factors influence the disposition of the juvenile, including the availability of treatment facilities or personnel.

Treatment programs for the LCP delinquent, whether provided in community or residential settings, have had little success historically (Borduin, 1994). Even treatment programs that have worked on mild or adolescence-limited offenders have been unsuccessful when applied to LCPs or serious delinquents. In most instances, as soon as youths leave the therapeutic milieu and return to their natural social environments, the antisocial behavior reemerges.

The poor track record with LCPs has prompted some professionals and policymakers to resist providing rehabilitative or treatment services to the serious offender (Borduin, 1994). However, an examination of the failures reveals that reha-bilitation and treatment services have often been too simplistic or narrowly focused. They have failed to include or even recognize the many influences (family, peers, school, media) that unwittingly promote and contribute to antisocial behavior. Not only must effective treatment approaches be multisystemic, but they must also be intensive and long-lasting if they are going to affect LCP teens who have already become deeply entrenched in their antisocial behavioral patterns. LCP behaviors are often severe, pervasive, and well learned. Although treatment for them is not hope-less, LCP delinquents will require innovation and extreme patience for the many frustrating setbacks that will certainly occur over the long haul.

One community-based treatment program that has shown considerable suc-cess in working with already involved delinquents is multisystemic therapy. It is called "multisystemic" because it deals with the many systems surrounding the offender.

Multisystemic Therapy

Scott Henggeler and his colleagues have designed a treatment approach for serious juvenile offenders that is responsive to many of the social systems influencing the child's delinquent behavior (Henggeler & Borduin, 1990; Henggeler, Melton, & Smith, 1992; Scherer et al., 1994). The focus of **multisystemic therapy** (MST) is the family microsystem, and a major ingredient of the treatment is that the family must be actively involved in the program. Together, counselors and family collaborate to develop pertinent treatment goals as well as appropriate plans to meet these goals (Henggeler, 1996). Impediments to the plan, such as uncooperative family mem-bers, teachers, and school administrators, are worked with directly and actively. MST is an action-based treatment program in that it tries to get the involved fami-ly members to take "action" (behaviorally do something) rather than just talk.

MST is an intensive, time-limited form of intervention wherein trained ther-apists have daily contact with the adolescent and his or her family for approxi-mately 60 hours over 4 months. The caseload of the therapist is small, averaging 4 to 6 families per counselor. Multisystemic therapists identify both strengths and problem areas within the individual, the family, and the other social systems, such as peers, school, social service agencies, and parents' workplace. Basically, MST focuses on the strengths of the family. The program tries to identify family strengths and provide the parent(s) with the resources needed for effective parent-ing and for developing a better-functioning and more cohesive family unit. For example, the therapists might work with the parents on improving communication and problem-solving skills, being less susceptible to manipulation by the child, enhancing their consistency in administering discipline and rewards, helping them find ways to reduce stress, and reducing parental drug and alcohol abuse.

Multisystemic therapists also work with the target youth to remediate deficits in interpersonal skills that hinder acceptance by prosocial peers. Youth and therapist may work on modifying thought processes and coping mechanisms that may interfere with the family, peer, school, and neighborhood microsystems.

Other MST strategies include decreasing the teenager's antisocial peer contacts and increasing affiliation with prosocial peers and activities. Another strategy is developing strategies to monitor and promote the youth's school performance. For example, the therapist might work toward opening and maintaining effective lines of communication among parents, teachers, and administrators.

In one outcome study, Henggeler, Melton, and Smith (1992) found that, in comparison with the typical intensive probation services, teenagers from families participating in their treatment had a significantly lower rearrest rate at a 2.4-year follow-up. This is a relatively long follow-up compared with those of most intervention studies and demonstrates that the program has considerable promise. In another study (Borduin et al., 1995), MST was found effective in reducing long-term rates of violent offending, drug-related offending, and other criminal offending, compared with individual, office-based therapy.

One point that needs to be emphasized here is that the *delivery* model followed for this MST program was the **family preservation model**. The word "delivery" is italicized because the family preservation model *is* a delivery system and not a form of therapy. Specifically, family preservation is a model of service delivery based on the philosophy that the most effective way to help children and adolescents is by helping the family.

RESIDENTIAL TREATMENT

Restrictive interventions for serious juvenile offenders, such as residential treatment and incarceration, have simply not been effective and are extremely expensive (Henggeler, 1996). According to Henggeler (1996, p. 139), "Restrictive out-of-home placements neither address the known determinants of serious antisocial behavior nor alter the natural ecology to which the youth will eventually return. Indeed, data show that incarceration may not even serve a community protection function."

The average cost of incarcerating a juvenile for just one year is close to $34,000, and some estimates go as high as $64,000 (Coordinating Council, 1996). In addition, the total cost of a young adult's (ages 18 to 23) persistent violent criminal career is estimated to be $1.1 million (Coordinating Council, 1996). Headstart, on the other hand, costs $4,300 per year per child. Multisystemic therapy costs approximately $4,000 per case.

We will discuss residential treatment and community-based strategies more fully in Chapter 13.

SUMMARY AND CONCLUSIONS

There is accumulating evidence that multicomponent, multicontext interventions are required to reduce antisocial behavior in children and adolescents. In addition, extensive knowledge of the myriad risk factors and developmental processes is essential if one is to design effective intervention programs. Some interventions are successful for dealing with some risk factors at specific developmental stages but unsuccessful with other risk factors at different developmental stages (Loeber, 1990). Specifically, what may work for a 6-year-old plagued by school adjustment problems may not work for a 16-year-old living in an inner-city neighborhood where violence is the norm.

The evidence is clear that intervention must begin early, preferably during the preschool years. Early intervention is especially critical for children growing up in inner-city neighborhoods where risk factors for delinquency are more prevalent. Research strongly indicates that intervention becomes more labor intensive and faces more intransigent behavior patterns from teenagers who exhibit antisocial behavior from an early age. This well-established observation is a primary reason for the frequent failure of intervention and treatment programs with serious, violent delinquency. The life-course-persistent offender who enters adolescence fully engaged in delinquent behavior is usually highly resistant to behavioral change. The adolescence-limited offender, on the other hand, is far more likely to be responsive to intervention and treatment strategies during the teen years. Adolescence-limited offenders are also more likely to show spontaneous recovery from their delinquency patterns as they embark on a more responsible, post-adolescent life style.

The evidence is also clear that the microsystem of the family must be the focus of the intervention and treatment. Some youth who experience poverty, neighborhood violence, delinquent peers, poor health care, and other risk factors do not become violent and antisocial. Their resilience can most often be attributed to close relationships with parents and other role models who provide support and encourage prosocial beliefs and values. Delinquency is often associated with families characterized by poor family management practices, excessively severe or inconsistent discipline, and parental (or caretaker) failure to monitor or supervise children's activities. Consequently, the teaching of effective parenting techniques, behavior-management skills, and adequate supervision and monitoring is a critical intervention strategy for some families. In some instances, parents may require additional guidance for dealing with children characterized by difficult temperaments and negative social orientations. The development of child competence and self-efficacy is also important. The family, however, cannot do it alone. The family needs help through various resources and support services that control and alter the many social systems that put the child at risk for delinquency and violence.

Effective intervention targets the *known* risk factors that occur along the child's developmental path. Before birth, intervention begins with ensuring prenatal health care and maternal nutrition and with elimination or control of toxic materials in the environment, intrafamilial abuse, and maternal alcohol or drug abuse (including that of tobacco). For children born into disadvantaged families living in inner cities, serious exosystem and macrosystem efforts must be directed at reducing the extreme economic deprivation that exists, especially among ethnic minorities. This effort includes dealing with low neighborhood attachment and community disorganization. It also includes addressing community norms for violence, the availability of guns, and the media portrayals of violence. On a broader level, it involves exposing the activities of powerful groups, including businesses, that victimize residents of inner cities.

The training in interpersonal and social skills for some children is essential, especially for highly aggressive children who are avoided by peers at an early age. Peer avoidance appears to accelerate quite early in the development of highly aggressive children, robbing them of the opportunity to develop effective interpersonal and social skills for dealing appropriately with others. Early academic problems also need to be identified, assessed, and effectively dealt with, particularly in children who demonstrate the behavioral patterns of ADHD or antisocial behavioral patterns. Youth must be discouraged from associating with antisocial peer groups, especially if the group is dominated by LCP youth.

Unfortunately, some very large gaps in our knowledge about intervention and prevention still remain. For instance, it is essential that more culturally sensitive and culture-specific interventions are developed. Researchers and practitioners alike need to develop an understanding, appreciation, and integration of the benefits of culturally diverse perspectives in dealing with highly aggressive and violent children and adolescents. "Prepackaged" interventions that do not recognize cultural diversity have a very high probability of failure.

It is also important for research to examine whether the developmental course of antisocial behavior varies by gender and ethnicity. The precise mechanisms and processes implicated in the development of antisocial behavior may vary by gender and ethnicity as well as by other demographic distinctions. Effective interventions must consider these mechanisms and processes in their conceptualization, implementation, and evaluation.

Surprisingly, very few studies have focused specifically on low-income urban minority children where living conditions are more harsh (Guerra et al., 1995). It is especially important that research focus on young children in this area who are particularly sensitive to environmental and social influences. The full implications of child abuse and emotional maltreatment on delinquency and career-long violence need to be more fully investigated.

KEY CONCEPTS

at-risk youth	Project Headstart
booster sessions	secondary prevention
cognitive–behavioral interventions	selected intervention
family preservation model	systems-based intervention
indicated intervention	tertiary or treatment prevention
individual-based interventions	universal intervention
multisystemic therapy (MST)	Virginia Youth Violence Project
Perry Preschool Project	Yale Child Welfare Research Program
primary prevention	

10

Juvenile Justice: Origins and Overview

"Juvenile justice" was officially ushered into the United States on the last day of the 1899 session of the Illinois legislature, when that body passed the seminal Juvenile Court Act. This comprehensive child welfare law created a juvenile court in Illinois and gave it jurisdiction over delinquent, dependent, or neglected children.

Although other states had adopted various procedures and regulations to deal with their "wayward" and neglected youth, the Illinois Juvenile Statute of 1899 represented the first comprehensive attempt at codification and at establishing a separate system. Other states rapidly passed similar laws. By 1925, all but two states (Maine and Wyoming) had established juvenile courts (Tappan, 1949). Wyoming was the last state to do so, enacting a juvenile court law in 1945.

The first juvenile court within the federal court system was created in 1906 in the District of Columbia, with jurisdiction over delinquent, dependent, incorrigible, and truant children. Other federal jurisdictions followed suit. In 1938 a federal juvenile court law was passed.

Before juvenile courts existed, children in need of care or at risk of committing delinquent acts were routinely handled by criminal courts. If judges believed they could not remain with their own families, they could be placed in private homes or in homes for wayward youth. Some were apprenticed to work at low or nonexistent wages. Juveniles 16 and older could also be sent to reformatories. In this chapter we will discuss these options and other developments leading up to and following the establishment of juvenile courts.

HOUSES OF REFUGE

In the second quarter of the nineteenth century, poor children living in urban areas were subject to being placed in houses of refuge, which were essentially the first residential institutions intended solely for juveniles. Reformers during this period, led by prominent Quakers, had established penitentiaries for adult criminals to work in silence and presumably repent their offenses against society. Young people, however, were believed to need a less punitive, more reparative environment. Furthermore, there was concern that children living in poverty were in danger of becoming adult criminals. The houses of refuge, therefore, were intended not only for juveniles who had committed crimes but also for those who were in danger of doing so as a result of lack of adult supervision.

The first house of refuge opened its doors in New York City to "six unhappy, wretched girls and three boys, clothed in rags, and with squalid countenances" on the first day of January 1825 (Peirce, 1869, p. 78). The following year (1826), the Boston House of Reformation opened, followed by the Philadelphia House of Refuge in 1828. Bernard (1992) notes that by the end of its first year, the New York House of Refuge had received a total of 73 children; one had been convicted of grand larceny, nine of petty larceny, and 63 of vagrancy, stealing, running away from poorhouses, or a combination of the three.

Strongly influenced by Quaker reformers, the houses of refuge emphasized firm discipline, punishment, and carefully constructed and scrupulously observed daily work schedules. Although they were promoted as *schools* to educate and save children who might go, or who were going, astray, they were far from educational enterprises. Children in the typical house of refuge spent only 4 hours a day in the classroom: 2 for moral indoctrination and 2 for "mental improvement." The rest of the day (8 hours) was spent at labor for industries to which the house had subcontracted the children's services. Many children left, often after about a year in the house of refuge, to be apprenticed to farmers until they reached the age of 21. Until the mid–nineteenth century, 90 percent of all releases from houses of refuge were accounted for through this system of apprenticeship (Bernard, 1992).

THE CONCEPT OF *PARENS PATRIAE*

The most common way for a child to be placed in a house of refuge was through the criminal courts. The courts derived their authority to do this under the doctrine of *parens patriae*, which was based on the belief that government had a right to intervene in the lives of children whose parents or guardians defaulted in their care-giving duties. This authority was made clear in a noteworthy Pennsylvania case, *Ex parte Crouse* (1838). Mary Ann Crouse was a 15-year-old girl who was committed by a court to the Philadelphia House of Refuge upon her mother's complaint and without her father's knowledge. Although Mary Ann had not been convicted of a criminal offense, her mother alleged that "by reason of vicious conduct," the daughter was out of control, which "made it manifestly requisite that in regard to the moral and future welfare of the said infant she should be placed under the guardianship of the managers of the House of Refuge" (Curtis, 1976, p. 901).

Mary Ann's father, who had been away at sea at the time of the commitment, tried to have her released. He filed a *habeas corpus* petition on her behalf, arguing that she was being held illegally because she had committed no crime. The Pennsylvania Supreme Court, however, unanimously rejected this view. The justices considered Mary Ann in danger of falling prey to the "corrupting influence of improper associates." The objective of the house of refuge, the court said, was to train children for citizenship and furnish them with a means to earn a living— much like any school. This was to be accomplished through work and moral and religious training. "To this end, may not the natural parents, when unequal to the task of education, or unworthy of it, be superseded by the *parens patriae*, or common guardian of the community?" (4 Wharton 9 (Pa, 1838) p. 11).

The Latin phrase *parens patriae* (literally, "parent of the country") has had a long and ambiguous history, dating as far back as ancient Roman law, where it was applied loosely to situations in which the state considered the head of the family incompetent and in danger of wasting his estate. The state was then vested with the power to declare him mentally incompetent and commit him and the estate to the care of curators or tutors designated by the praetor. *Parens patriae*, then, was a doctrine applicable more to persons with valuable property holdings and wealth than to the general population.

The concept was later adopted from Roman law in the eleventh century by the Anglo-Saxon king Athelred II and further developed and expanded during the early years of Edward I's reign (1272–1307) (Kittrie, 1971). The doctrine was first codified in 1324 during the reign of Edward II in the statute Prerogativa Regis, which gave the king the power to protect the lands and profits of "idiots" and "lunatics" until their mental restoration (Cogan, 1970). Although the main focus of the statute was on those who were mentally deficient, it soon began to include a wide range of "disabilities" and incapacitating behaviors, such as poverty and card playing. The doctrine has a history of being misinterpreted and misused and remains controversial to this day, especially as it is applied to juveniles.

At the time the colonies were being settled, English law still empowered the king to act as the general guardian of "infants, idiots, and lunatics" and those individuals "incompetent" to take care of themselves (Developments in the Law, 1974). After the American Revolution, the *parens patriae* power was imbued in the state legislatures, which, in turn, delegated the principal authority to the state courts.

Throughout its early history, *parens patriae* was used in the service of dependent persons, usually with propertied status. In the case of children, it was originally used only to replace parents who had died. The property of the parents was kept by the state until the child reached the age of 21. The doctrine authorized the state to substitute and enforce its decisions believed to be in the best interest of persons who presumably cannot or will not take care of themselves. Therefore, the *parens patriae* doctrine is used as the basis of state laws protecting the interests of minors, establishing guardianships, and providing for the involuntary commitment of the mentally ill.

Crouse was the first legal decision incorporating the power of *parens patriae* into American juvenile law (Schlossman, 1977). The case represents "the first explicit judicial resort to *parens patriae* as justification for seeking to instill virtue in children who would otherwise be doomed to a life of depravity" (Fox, 1970, p. 1206). It is important to note that the doctrine was used even though the parents were living. Thus, *parens patriae* allowed the court to supersede the authority of the parents.

Used in this context, the doctrine did not have immediate widespread acceptance, however. In 1868, in a situation with many parallels to that of Mary Ann Crouse, the Illinois Supreme Court ordered the release of a youth who had committed no criminal offense. Daniel O'Connell, like Mary Ann Crouse, had been sent to a house of refuge until the age of 21. The committing court had found that Daniel appeared to be in danger of growing up to be a pauper. His parents challenged his commitment and the Illinois Supreme Court rejected *parens patriae* as support for institutionalizing a juvenile who had committed no crime.

Shortly after the turn of the twentieth century, the Pennsylvania Supreme Court once again affirmed the doctrine of *parens patriae,* in allowing the commitment of a 14-year-old youth charged with larceny to the Philadelphia House of Refuge, where he would remain until the age of 21. Although Frank Fisher's father argued that the punishment was disproportionate to the offense, the Supreme Court noted—consistent with *parens patriae*—that the youth was being helped, not punished.

Although these decisions were issued in different states, they illustrate the ambivalence that courts have displayed in the appropriate use of this doctrine. As we will see shortly, the U.S. Supreme Court itself has, over the years, both severely criticized and strongly endorsed the concept of *parens patriae.*

REFORMATORY MOVEMENT

By the mid–nineteenth century, houses of refuge had started to earn reputations for being both cruel and ineffective, a fact that may have influenced the Illinois Supreme Court in the Daniel O'Connell case. Some superintendents blamed the deterioration on the presence of older children who were "seriously prejudicial" to the younger boys and girls. Managers of the Philadelphia House of Refuge, for example, concluded, "[E]xperience has shown that after the child has reached fifteen or sixteen years there is little hope of reformation" (Peirce, 1869, p. 165). Supporters of the New York House of Refuge expressed similar sentiments and argued that such institutions should not be used for older children who could not be "rescued." It was undesirable to mix young children whose prognosis was more optimistic with older, more seasoned youths.

In the opinions of many reformers, however, it was also undesirable to mix youthful offenders with adult criminals, particularly if the youth had just begun their criminal activity. This need for special placement for young, first-time offenders led to the reformatory movement in the United States.

During the nineteenth century, it was widely believed that adults who violated the criminal law should be incarcerated. Massive penitentiaries, the precursors of our modern prisons, were built. The two competing models for these penitentiaries was a **solitary system**, where both male and female inmates were confined to individual cells, and a **congregate model**, where male inmates worked in silence at hard labor through the day. Female inmates, in this latter model, were generally confined in makeshift, separate quarters, often in one large room (Rafter, 1990).

A third model of institutionalization, the **reformatory model**, gradually emerged and is most relevant to our discussion here. Youthful first-time offenders, because they were presumably more amenable to rehabilitation, were placed in facilities that were intended to provide them with education, vocational training, and individualized treatment. Inmates who cooperated with their jailers were promised early release or, as we know it today, parole. Although reformatories—alternately called "reform schools," "training schools," or "industrial schools"—housed adult offenders up to the age of 30, youth aged 16, 17, and 18 were considered adults. Additionally, special "training schools" for younger juveniles were also opened.

Throughout the late nineteenth and early twentieth centuries, these reformatories were increasingly used to hold what we now refer to as **status offenders** as well as youth who had committed crimes. Offenses such as truancy, incorrigibility, waywardness, immorality, or unmanageability were cited as justification for incarceration. As mentioned in the earlier chapters, girls were disproportionately represented for these status offenses. Schlossman and Wallach (1978) note that approximately 5 reformatories per decade were opened between the years 1850 and 1910. This trend accelerated in the succeeding decade. In the short span of 2 years (1919–20), 23 were opened.

The prototype reformatory opened in 1876 under the direction of Zebulon Brockway, who was its superintendent for approximately 30 years. A number of writers have characterized Brockway as a zealot intent upon indoctrinating inmates in the name of "moral purification" (e.g., Rothman, 1980; Pisciotta, 1983; Jenkins, 1984). Brockway apparently ruled by fear, and there is ample evidence of physical abuse of the inmates in his care (Johnson, 1996).

Reformatories, then, became the placement of choice for youthful offenders. Not all children age 16 and older convicted of crimes or status offenses were sent to reformatories, however. Superintendents had wide latitude in their choice of inmates and routinely rejected those who they believed had little rehabilitative potential. Consequently, these young offenders could be housed in adult penitentiaries. Alternately, and far more common, as the concept of probation began to be developed, criminal court judges who were reluctant to send young offenders to harsh penitentiaries placed them in community supervision.

PROBATION

Probation is the system of keeping convicted offenders under the supervision of the court but outside of an institution. A prison sentence is suspended, conditioned upon the individual's meeting court-imposed standards of behavior. Standard conditions require the probationer to be home by a certain time each evening, refrain from using alcohol, and report periodically to a probation officer. Special conditions might require the probationer to attend counseling sessions or literacy classes.

In the United States, probation began "unofficially" in Massachusetts in 1841 when John Augustus, a bootmaker living in Boston, volunteered to supervise in the community persons, both adults and juveniles, convicted of nonserious offenses (Cromwell et al., 1985). For this reason, Augustus is regarded by many as the "father of probation." In 1878, twenty years after his death, the citizens of Boston authorized their mayor to appoint a member of the police force to serve as a paid probation officer (Cromwell et al., 1985). Statewide probation was developed in Massachusetts in 1890, but the law specified that the officer could not be a member of any regular police force. By 1925 probation was authorized by statutes in all 48 states. During that same year, Congress passed the National Probation Act, which authorized the federal district courts to appoint salaried probation officers.

Officially, juvenile probation developed later than adult probation, becoming recognized in six states by 1899. Massachusetts and Vermont had enacted adult and juvenile probation statutes in 1898, and Rhode Island did the same a year later. Colorado, Minnesota, and Illinois enacted statutes that specifically recognized juvenile probation. According to the provisions of the Illinois Juvenile Court Act, probation officers (initially unpaid volunteers) were to provide judges with all the appropriate information to help them understand the personality and social environment of the youth who appeared in court. The probation agents were encouraged to become surrogate parents as well as instructors in parenting. They had the authority to go into homes, investigate circumstances, and offer parents suggestions on how to fulfill their responsibilities. We will discuss juvenile probation in more detail in the following sections as we review the features of the juvenile courts.

THE JUVENILE COURT

By the end of the nineteenth century, the system of treating children who had committed a crime or were believed to be in danger of such activity was in disarray. Conditions in houses of refuge had deteriorated; the most visible reformatory at Elmira, New York, was under investigation (Pisciotta, 1983); and reform schools as a whole had not lived up to their expectations. The exploitation of child labor, particularly by way of apprenticeship to farms, industries, and private homes, was being challenged. In urban areas, population density was accompanied by social disorganization and confusion. It was not surprising, then, that social reformers began to push for new laws that presumably would protect children.

The Illinois Statute

As noted at the beginning of this chapter, the state of Illinois took the lead in passing a comprehensive law establishing the first juvenile court. For our purposes, we discuss only the sections of the statute that pertained to delinquents, originally defined as children under the age of 16 who violated a state criminal law or any village or city ordinance. The law was soon revised (in 1905) to specify a delinquent as any boy under 17 or girl under 18 who violated any criminal law of the state. This differential age criterion for males and females, which remained in the law for more than 50 years, is reflective of the sexist approach that juvenile justice has taken with respect to girls. We will return to this topic shortly.

The Illinois juvenile statute had four essential features. Briefly, the statute: (1) refined the definition of delinquency; (2) removed the jurisdiction of juvenile cases from the adult criminal court; (3) authorized the placement of juveniles in separate facilities, away from adult offenders and for limited time periods; and (4) provided for a system of probation that allowed the state to supervise the child outside the confines of an institution.

The first feature separated the concept of "delinquency" from "neglect" and "dependency." In previous legislation, "delinquency" had been used as a catch-all term often overlapping with "dependency" or even indistinguishable from it. Now, the courts would focus on the behavior of the child as separate from that of her or his caretakers. A child who broke the law presumably would be treated differently from one who was not properly cared for by his or her guardians. This is not to say that the new statute specified precisely what courts should do about delinquent behavior; in fact, it remained so vague in this respect that, for all practical purposes, it placed no limits on the court's decision-making latitude.

The second feature of the Juvenile Court Act was its provision for a separate hearing of children's cases in a chancery court rather than a criminal court. A chancery court, derived from English law, is a court of equity, operating under a philosophy of "fairness" or "best interest." Equity "is the power to apply moral standards of justice in a given case by allowing the Chancellor the discretion to modify or soften the application of strict legal rules and thereby adapt or gear the relief in light of the circumstances of the particular case" (cited in Smith, 1993, p. 31). Considering this definition, the wide latitude given juvenile judges is not surprising.

The Illinois juvenile statute circumvented the usual formalities of the criminal process and provided new options for intervening in the lives of the child as well as for incarceration. It provided for nonadversarial proceedings that focused more on the child and his or her protection than on the nature of the offense. The proceedings were to be conducted informally, whereby an intimate, friendly relationship presumably would be established between the judge and the child. Even the physical layout of the court was to reflect a benevolent philosophy. Hearings were usually conducted in a small, private room, often in the judge's chambers, with a simple table arranged so that the judge would appear less intimidating and authoritative. Uniformed officers were excluded from the hearings, and no record was kept of the proceedings or of the disposition of the cases.

The statute also encouraged the court to try to understand and help the child rather than to blame or condemn. With the help of probation officers, courts investigated the social background, psychological makeup, and level of maturity of the child and prescribed strategies to draw the child away from his or her misguided ways. Children were to remain with their parents if at all possible; in some cases, parental surrogates who maintained contact with the courts were assigned as guardians. Thus, the juvenile courts under this statute were able to use their authority to reach into homes they considered undesirable and intervene before children developed a hopelessly errant lifestyle. The court hearing and all collateral investigations were meant to focus upon the needs of the child, not upon guilt or innocence. Ostensibly, the court's purpose was not to punish but to "save." In short, the apparent underlying intent of legislators was to encourage the juvenile court to function as the primary institution for the resocialization of the wayward child.

The third feature of the statute was its authorization of temporary detention and incarceration separate from adult offenders, reflecting a belief that young, malleable minds were corruptible. Until then, young people were subject to all the criminal processes applicable to adults and could be detained with adults awaiting trial. If convicted, they could be sent to adult institutions. As noted previously, judges also had the options of probation, houses of refuge, and, for older juveniles, reformatories.

Illinois legislators believed that when immature and highly impressionable children were exposed to hardened adults, they would easily learn to be deviant and antisocial. Furthermore, the adults might prey upon and victimize the children. When institutionalization was deemed necessary, therefore, it was crucial that the facilities be separate from those of adults. As critics have noted, however, the legislature did not provide funds for the building of separate detention facilities (Fox, 1970). Institutionalization, if it occurred, was meant to be only temporary, until the natural home situation improved or an alternate home could be found. The proponents of the act were opposed to long-term placement in houses of refuge or reform schools.

The fourth feature of the Illinois statute was its provision for a system of probation so that the child and his or her parents would receive the proper supervision and training necessary to prevent future delinquent behavior. Under the new law, probation officers were to work closely with the juvenile court and were given considerable power in making decisions. In reality, the probation component was a weak link in the system, because the officers were too few in number and often not trained to deliver the needed services to the children and their families.

As we noted at the beginning of this chapter, the Illinois law was a model for law in other states. The juvenile court movement also extended to many parts of the world. Juvenile courts were officially established in Canada in 1909, the first in Winnipeg in accordance with the National Juvenile Delinquents' Law passed in 1908 (Lou, 1927). Shortly thereafter, juvenile court legislation was passed in Great Britain in 1908; Geneva (Switzerland) in 1910; France, Austria, and Belgium in 1912; Hungary in 1913; Croatia in 1918; and Argentina and Austria in 1919.

The Child Saver Movement

The Juvenile Court Act was the culmination of many years of discussions and experiments on the part of public and private organizations, legislators and judicial officials. The initial impetus for the statute, however, came from prominent women's groups in the Chicago area, especially the Chicago Women's Club and the National Congress of Mothers (forerunner to the PTA). The sustaining impetus came from Ben Lindsey, a Denver judge who lobbied state legislatures and spoke and wrote extensively and cogently throughout the early part of the twentieth century about the merits of the juvenile court (see Box 10.1).

The motivations and the precise influence of the women's groups on the Juvenile Court Act are obscure and debatable. Despite encouragement from and consultation with the Chicago Bar Association, there is little evidence that these groups clearly understood the legal system or were able to specify how the juvenile court, as they saw it, should be structured (Sutton, 1985). This was not their goal. Their main purpose was to guarantee that wayward children would receive an approximation of the care, custody, and discipline given by loving parents. The reformers were critical of existing criminal law for failing to distinguish between young offenders and adult criminals and for considering the two moral and psychological equals (Ryerson, 1978). They hoped that the court could become a benevolent surrogate for ineffective parents and "corrupt subcultures." The purpose of the juvenile court should be child saving, not criminalizing.

We should realize that this was during the child-oriented Progressive Era, a time when reformers were instrumental in establishing child-labor legislation, compulsory-education laws, kindergartens, playgrounds, and municipal bureaus of child health and hygiene (Rothman, 1980). Within this social context, the arguments advanced by the Chicago women's groups were not all that controversial and therefore met with little opposition. Nevertheless, the bill passed the Illinois legislature only after considerable cutting of costly items.

Many writers have questioned the motives behind these reforms, however (e.g., Platt, 1969b; Rothman, 1980; Sutton, 1985; Bernard, 1992). Anthony Platt (1969), for example, asserted that the child-saving movement that led to the juvenile court was not simply a humanistic enterprise on behalf of the lower classes; on the contrary, its proponents were middle- and upper-class people who were seeking new forms of social control to protect their privileged positions in American society against crime. The child-saving movement did attract women from a variety of political and class backgrounds, but it was dominated by daughters of the old landed gentry and wives of the upper-class *nouveau riche*. True, many may have been genuinely concerned about alleviating human misery and

Box 10.1

JUDGE BEN LINDSEY

One of the most outspoken and colorful juvenile court judges was Judge Ben Lindsey. Schlossman (1977, p. 56), who has praise for Lindsey, writes:

Lindsey stood in relation to the court movement much as John Dewey did to progressive education and Jane Addams did to social settlements. All were popularly acknowledged as leaders of their respective institutions, yet all differed considerably from the rank and file of reformers who identified with them. Just as Dewey's grasp of the educational needs of an industrial democracy and Addams's insight into the psychological and cultural mainstreams of immigrant behavior far surpassed their followers' understanding of the issues in both sensitivity and sophistication, so Lindsey's understanding of the possibilities and limitations of the court was more profound than that of most partisans.

Tireless and energetic, Lindsey spoke to various charitable groups and organizations across the country, lobbied legislatures in several states, and wrote voluminously about the advantages of the juvenile court. He believed that individuals were not by nature bad or corrupt but that the environment was the main determinant of human behavior. Sutton (1985) calls him the "most active evangelist" of the juvenile court movement during the early twentieth century.

Lindsey's exploits also extended into the courtroom. He independently organized a personalized juvenile court in 1899 under the so-called "school law" in Denver, which gave the court limited jurisdiction over delinquent children of school age. Lindsey managed to expand it (at least in his own courtroom) to include any child he believed was moving along the "wrong path." Lindsey single-handedly created a juvenile court in Denver in 1901, without statutory authorization. At this time, he may or may not have been aware of the similar court established in Chicago two years previously.

David Rothman (1980), however, notes that Lindsey's court took on an arbitrary quality and was questionably effective. He refers to Lindsey's activity pejoratively as a "one-man traveling road show" (p. 215). He notes that Lindsey's flamboyant personality dominated—indeed, monopolized—the juvenile court's proceedings. His courtroom was his stage from which he performed various dramatics and gave powerful speeches and pleading sermons to groups of offending youths.

Although his court took on an arbitrary quality and self-promotion and egotism may well have been dominant characteristics of this early judge, he clearly had an important role in promoting the acceptance of separate courts for children. Although strong documentation is lacking, a number of historical accounts conclude, chiefly on the basis of anecdotal evidence, that Lindsey was quite effective in positively changing the life course of many of the children who appeared before him.

---

improving the lives of the poor, but, Platt insisted, the child savers and other progressive reformers were predominantly concerned that crime, rising from the "lowest orders," was threatening to engulf respectable society like a virulent disease.

John Sutton (1985), another critic of juvenile court philosophy, contends that the establishment of the juvenile court allowed the legal system to *appear* responsive to the demands for individualized, therapeutic justice without any real alteration in routine decision-making practices. Furthermore, it allowed juvenile justice agencies to maintain their ideology and discretionary authority. In other words, the creation of the juvenile court may have changed procedures, but it was not truly a substantive reform.

Sanford Fox (1970) argues that the primary motivating force for the Juvenile Court Act was a genuine desire to change institutional conditions for predelinquent children. Given this assumption, the reformers' trek to the Illinois capital in the spring of 1899 was a colossal failure, because institutional conditions hardly changed as a result of the legislation. Moreover, nothing was done about children in poorhouses, or local jails, both of which often housed youths as well as adults. The only change was the provision that children under the age of 12 were not to be detained in a jail or police station. Furthermore, the statute did not provide funds for leasing, building, or otherwise finding suitable places even for temporary detention. According to Fox, the Juvenile Court Act passed by the rural and conservative Illinois legislature represented a victory for private enterprise and sectarianism.

Bernard (1992) argues persuasively that the juvenile court represented a shift in the idea of delinquency. Whereas delinquency in the nineteenth century had been associated with pauperism, delinquency in the new century became associated with dependency and neglect. It was assumed that children who lacked the supervision of kind and firm parents would exhibit a variety of problem behaviors, one of which was to engage in criminal and status offenses. The poor remained the targets of the intervention, however. Bernard also suggests that, as juvenile justice developed, efforts to change the social conditions that were the main causes of delinquency proved futile, so the juvenile court reverted to the approach of changing the child. "Eventually, social workers stopped trying to change the rich and powerful and started trying to change the poor and powerless. The seeds of both casework and social reform had been present at the beginning of the juvenile court, but only the seeds of casework sprouted and grew. The seeds of social reform withered and died" (p. 102).

It is important not to lose sight of the fact, however, that the turn-of-the-century reform represented a marked change from viewing children as nonentities or even chattel in the legal system to acknowledging that they had a measure of legal rights. As one scholar noted, "While the legal reforms may now seem in the light of revisionist histories, to have been catalyzed by questionable motives, they did give children certain legally enforceable rights not previously held" (Rodham, 1973, p. 495). These did not include, however, rights to an adversary hearing or lawyer. Rodham made the important point that "Whenever reforms have been enacted—the rights they provide are those which the state decides are in the best interests of the public and the child" (p. 496).

This "best interest" philosophy, derived from the legal doctrine of *parens patriae*, became the foundation of the juvenile justice system. Those who fought to establish the first juvenile courts would have disagreed vehemently with the long-term institutionalization of Mary Ann Crouse, yet they would have accepted the court's rationale that it acted in the best interest of the child. In their zeal to remove offending youth from what they saw as the rigidities, technicalities, and harshness of criminal law, however, they ignored or deprived children of rights that were due adults. Sanford Fox (1970) suggested that this was because early reformers melded, in their own minds, the terms "dependency," "neglect," and "delinquency." That is, even though the statute attempted to separate the concepts, the root causes of all were, in the minds of the legislators, poverty, dire home conditions, or faulty parenting—all conditions over which the child had no personal control. Thus, "delinquent" children were not criminal; they were misguided and unsocialized. Because they could not be held responsible for their predicament, criminal procedure, determinations of responsibility, sentencing, and punishment were simply not appropriate.

The reformers tried to make the court a benevolent parent intent on care and welfare rather than a forum for procedures, due process, fairness, and resolution. But this presumably benevolent role invited arbitrary behavior by those who assumed it. Furthermore, the children who came before the juvenile courts and were increasingly sent to institutions were almost invariably the offspring of the poor. As Bernard (1992) has remarked, through parens patriae the juvenile court "established a new legal basis for the old practice of sending poor urban children to rural institutions for their own good" (p. 101).

Gender and the Juvenile Court

It is well documented that from its inception the juvenile justice system has treated girls differently from boys. You may recall that on its first day, the New York House of Refuge opened its doors to twice as many girls as boys. This ratio continued throughout the years (Bernard, 1992). Several researchers have documented that girls were more likely than boys to be sent to reformatories for status offenses (e.g., Schlossman & Wallach, 1978; Shelden, 1981; Rafter, 1990). In the first quarter of the twentieth century, virtually all girls who appeared before the courts were charged with immorality or waywardness, and they were frequently incarcerated (Federle & Chesney-Lind, 1992). In Chicago, for example, over the 10-year-period 1900–09 more than half the girls but only one-fifth of the boys were sent to reformatories (Rosenbaum & Chesney-Lind, 1994). There were also clear differences in the "reformatory regime" and apprenticeships offered to girls as opposed to boys. Girls, for example, would be taught to accept the traditional domestic role and to be subservient to the men who headed the household and were not infrequently apprenticed as domestic workers in private homes (Rafter, 1990).

In a classic article on girls and juvenile justice, Meda Chesney-Lind (1982, p. 81) refers to the family (or juvenile) court's "exclusive preoccupation with female sexuality." The disparate incarceration of girls noted in the preceding paragraph reflected the strong *parens patriae* rationale of the juvenile courts, because it was argued that this was done for the girls' own protection and in their best interests. The court acted as the guardian of morality; urged on by reformers, juvenile judges believed that girls who came under their aegis could benefit from institutionalization, where they would presumably be taught proper morality. "Between 1888 and 1950 the percentage of girls incarcerated in juvenile correctional facilities grew from 19 percent to 34 percent" (Federle and Chesney-Lind, 1992, p. 166). Additionally, many state statutes allowed girls to be retained under the control of the juvenile justice system for longer than boys. These laws continued well into the twentieth century, when they were found to violate the constitutional guarantee of equal protection of the law. As we will see, however, disparities in treatment of boys and girls continue to plague the juvenile justice system.

COMMUNITY DELINQUENCY PREVENTION PROGRAMS

In 1930, the approach to juvenile offending took a dramatic turn when University of Chicago sociologists collaborated with researchers at the Institute for Juvenile Research (formerly William Healy's diagnostic clinic) on the Chicago Area Project (CAP), a monumental effort to involve communities in the solution of their delinquency problems. The project paved the way for reassessment of the existing programs based on individual psychological or psychiatric treatment. It also represented the first systematic challenge by sociologists to the domination of psychologists and psychiatrists in both private and public juvenile programs (Schlossman & Sedlak, 1983).

The CAP, which we discussed in Chapter 8, has been amply described, praised, and criticized. Essentially, it immersed researchers and volunteers, including erudite sociologists from the Chicago School, into communities with higher-than-average rates of delinquency. The researchers obtained oral histories and accounts of juvenile activities, offered "curbstone counseling," and mediated with police and juvenile justice agencies on behalf of community youth. An important component of the CAP was to encourage members of the community to make their own decisions and initiate their own self-help programs, such as recreation activities, discussion groups, or after-school tutoring programs. Therefore, CAP workers served as advisors to neighborhood committees or community organizers rather than as directors of the various projects undertaken.

There was a distrust of juvenile courts on the part of many CAP workers, because the courts were increasingly sending juveniles to institutions "for their own good." Furthermore, there were too few full-time trained probation officers to work closely with the youth and their families. Therefore, community committees began to try to work with the courts, particularly with liaison probation officers, to help reintegrate youthful offenders into the community.

The Chicago Area Project and programs like it in other major cities ushered in an era of delinquency prevention focusing on organized community efforts. In Boston, a project operated by professional social workers involved gang members, the community, and families. Known as the Midcity Project, it involved volunteers and community reaching out to gang members as well as social workers doing intensive psychiatric casework with families deemed in need of support. An evaluation of the Midcity Project, however, indicates there were few significant decreases in a wide range of inappropriate behaviors. Improvements were found in school-related behaviors, and there was some decrease in minor offending and in illegal activity by girls (Miller, 1962).

In New York, a project known as Mobilization for Youth (MFY) provided a wide range of activities and programs to convince youths of the value of education, work, and community service. Unlike the Boston project, MFY did not emphasize intensive casework, although efforts were made to provide families with needed services. Roberts (1989b) notes that MFY became the prototype project for the wide variety of federally funded "war on poverty" programs developed during the Kennedy and Johnson administrations in the 1960s.

THE SHIFT TO DUE PROCESS

The philosophy and procedures of the juvenile courts remained largely unchanged until the second half of the twentieth century. The court and its ancillary institutions became firmly established. Judges, probation officers, social workers, and police officers whose primary role was to work with juveniles increased in number and acquired considerable prestige and power. At the same time, there was apparent collusion between those working in the juvenile justice system and those who were asked to rehabilitate young offenders. Most programs directed at preventing or treating juvenile delinquency were created and managed by psychiatrists, psychologists, or social workers, who promoted extensive testing, individual counseling, and therapy for youthful offenders. The courts, trusting that these approaches were beneficial, responded favorably. Illinois remained the pioneer in this area, having the first clinic to provide psychiatric diagnoses to juvenile courts, the Juvenile Psychopathic Institute.

Throughout this time, volunteers and volunteer agencies continued to be associated with juvenile courts. The reader may recall that probation itself began as a volunteer service and gained stature as an official service under juvenile court statutes. In the first half of the twentieth century, however, probation services, requirements for officers, and degree of training varied widely. Additionally, many juvenile courts continued to rely on volunteers associated with child-saving agencies rather than on professionally trained officers (Roberts, 1989a).

By the early 1960s, serious juvenile crime was an issue of major public concern. This was fueled by the work of influential sociologists who were concerned about conditions in the inner cities and who directed much of their research attention to youth gangs. At the same time, the issue of children's constitutional rights began to receive attention. This was a logical extension of changes wrought by the various civil rights movements of the late 1950s and 1960s, by controversies over the effectiveness of social welfare programs, and later—at least where female delinquents were concerned—by the resurgence of the women's movement.

The academic community, which had long contributed to the intellectual climate assessing the juvenile justice system, was experiencing its own transformation. Alongside the traditional research on the control, prevention, and cure of juvenile delinquency, research focusing on the shortcomings of the system made its appearance. The juvenile court was not only criticized as ineffective in preventing delinquency; it was also accused of fostering juvenile crime through its labeling or stigmatizing of young norm-violators as "delinquents." In short, the juvenile justice system was itself becoming viewed as harmful to the juvenile.

Some warned that the extensive criticism of the court should not result in its demise, however. The legal scholar Francis A. Allen (1964, p. 56), for example, advocated a reassessment of the court's function in society. "[T]he tendency to describe the court only by reference to its therapeutic or rehabilitative potential creates the peril of unrealistic and unrealizable expectations." Allen noted that the court had a role in protecting the community from the violent or predatory acts of some children for whom rehabilitation was not realistic. In such cases, the primary function was the temporary incapacitation of children. He added, however, that this should be done only if the children were given the same procedural safeguards as were adults accused of criminal acts. Allen's philosophy was reflected in some measure in subsequent decisions of the U.S. Supreme Court, to which we now turn.

Landmark U.S. Supreme Court Decisions

Arguments questioning the proceedings of juvenile courts and the wisdom of the doctrine of *parens patriae* gained legal support with the Supreme Court decisions of *Kent v. U.S.* (1966), *In re Gault* (1967), *In re Winship* (1970), and *Breed v. Jones* (1975). Other decisions, such as *McKeiver v. Pennsylvania* (1971) and *Schall v. Martin* (1984), however, represented the resilience of *parens patriae* and made it clear that juvenile offenders remained in a separate category. We will focus on decisions of the U.S. Supreme Court, but readers should keep in mind that lower appellate courts frequently rule on juvenile matters. Cases involving juveniles at every stage of the juvenile process are often decided in these lower appellate courts.

Kent v. U.S. (1966) was the first case in which the Supreme Court extended limited due process guarantees to juveniles. Just as important, however, it signaled the Court's disenchantment with the operation of the juvenile courts: "Juvenile Court history has again demonstrated that unbridled discretion, however benevolently motivated, is frequently a poor substitute for principle and procedure. . . . [T]he absence of substantive standards has not necessarily meant that children receive caring, compassionate, individualized treatment. The absence of procedural rules based upon Constitutional principle has not always produced fair, efficient, and effective procedures" (387 U.S. 1 (1966), p. 17).

Morris A. Kent Jr. was a 16-year-old charged with housebreaking, robbery, and rape while on probation under the jurisdiction of the District of Columbia Juvenile Court. When arrested, Kent admitted to the offenses and was placed in a receiving home (detention center) for children. The juvenile court transferred Kent's case to adult criminal court over the objections of Kent's lawyer, who argued that the boy had rehabilitative potential. The lawyer also requested that the court review his client's social service records, a request the court denied. In criminal court, Kent was found not guilty by reason of insanity on the rape charge but guilty of housebreaking and robbery. He was sentenced to 30 to 90 years and transferred to St. Elizabeth's Hospital for the mentally ill.

In reviewing Kent's appeal, the U.S. Supreme Court first recognized that there was no constitutional requirement for a separate juvenile court system. When such a system does exist, however, a juvenile court may not waive jurisdiction over a juvenile without a hearing and accompanying safeguards. "There is no place in our legal system for reaching a verdict of such serious consequences without a hearing, without effective assistance of counsel, and without a statement of the reasons" (383 U.S. at 554). Additionally, the Court provided guidelines to lower court judges for making the waiver decision, listing eight factors to be taken into consideration. We will review these in more detail in Chapter 12.

The Court's opinion, written by Justice Abe Fortas, strongly criticized the operation of the juvenile court. The case foreshadowed a decision the following year that extended broad procedural safeguards to juveniles charged with criminal conduct and would have a profound impact on the juvenile court process.

This second decision, *In re Gault*, involved a 15-year-old Arizona boy, Gerald Gault, who was accused of making an "obscene" phone call to a neighbor. The Supreme Court later referred to the telephone remarks as "of the irritatingly offensive, adolescent, sex variety." Gerald Gault was taken into police custody at about 10 A.M. without his parents' knowledge and placed in a juvenile detention center. When his mother arrived home that evening, she dispatched her older son to search for Gerald and soon learned of his whereabouts. The mother and older brother went to the detention center and were informed that a hearing was scheduled for the following afternoon.

Gault, his mother, his older brother, and two probation officers appeared before the juvenile court judge in chambers. The father was working out of town and could not attend. The complaining neighbor was not in attendance. Gerald had no attorney. The judge questioned the boy, but no transcript or recording was made of the hearing. Later, there was conflicting information about what was said. A week later, at a second hearing, Gerald was declared a "delinquent" and committed to the State Industrial School until he reached the age of 21. At that time, it was a misdemeanor to make lewd or obscene phone calls in the State of Arizona. Had Gerald been an adult and been convicted, his maximum penalty would have been $50 or two months' imprisonment.

When the U.S. Supreme Court ruled on the Gault case, it held that juveniles appearing before a juvenile court have the following constitutional rights: (1) to adequate written notice of the charges against them, in order to afford them a reasonable opportunity to prepare a defense; (2) to the assistance of counsel and, if indigent, to the appointment of counsel; (3) to invoke the privilege against self-incrimination; and (4) to confront and cross-examine witnesses. Gerald Gault had received none of those protections at his hearing.

In 1970, the Court in *In re Winship* held that before a juvenile may be adjudicated a delinquent there must be proof beyond a reasonable doubt of every fact necessary to constitute the offense with which he or she is charged. Until the *Winship* ruling, juvenile courts routinely found delinquency on the basis of less stringent standards. The Court was not persuaded by the argument that juvenile proceedings were noncriminal and were intended to benefit the child.

Finally, in *Breed v. Jones*, the Supreme Court clarified the protection against double jeopardy found in the Fifth Amendment. Gary Jones, a 17-year-old charged with armed robbery, was first adjudicated a delinquent in a juvenile court. The judge then proceeded to transfer his case to criminal court, where he was tried as an adult, convicted, and sentenced to prison. The Supreme Court ruled that this violated the Constitution. Once a juvenile court, at the adjudicatory hearing, begins to hear evidence against the juvenile, the proceedings become tantamount to a criminal trial, and the same case cannot then be retried in a criminal court.

Critics of the four decisions discussed here feared that they would alter juvenile court proceedings dramatically. By providing juveniles with many of the constitutional safeguards provided adult offenders, these and related decisions severely undercut the juvenile court's emphasis on informal "humanitarian" proceedings (Mennel, 1983). As we will discuss in Chapter 13, however, there were many unanticipated outcomes. *In re Gault*, in particular, produced far fewer changes than had been projected. Researchers have learned that despite the fact that juveniles have a constitutional right to a lawyer in delinquency proceedings, they are commonly unrepresented. "In the decades since Gault, the promise of counsel remains unrealized" (Feld, 1992, p. 79). Feld mentions a variety of explanations for this phenomenon, including parents' reluctance to retain attorneys, a judge's subtle encouragement to waive the right to a lawyer, and judicial hostility to the advocacy role in the juvenile court.

Although Supreme Court decisions in the 1960s and 1970s brought due process to juveniles, the Court stopped short of extending all constitutional protections to juveniles. In *McKeiver v. Pennsylvania* (1971), for example, the Supreme Court rejected the contentions of juveniles in two states that they were entitled to a jury trial similar to that given to adults. The Pennsylvania juveniles had argued that the juvenile proceedings in that state were virtually identical to those of adults. They were detained before their hearings in buildings similar to adult prisons, plea bargaining was allowed, and the proceedings were open to the press and public (which is unusual in juvenile proceedings). The Pennsylvania juveniles believed that the right to a jury trial was also theirs. In North Carolina, juveniles argued that the adjudication of facts was indistinguishable from a criminal trial and that a jury would provide a protective factor. The Supreme Court, however, believed that juries would substantially change the nature of juvenile hearings and refused to impose that requirement on states. The Court added that states were free to offer juries if they wished, however.

The Court also reinforced the doctrine of *parens patriae* in *Schall v. Martin* (1984) by allowing the preventive detention of juveniles before their scheduled hearings for up to 18 days when charged with serious crime or a maximum of 6 days otherwise. If there was any doubt that *parens patriae* still lives, it was resolved with the Schall decision, which will be discussed again in Chapter 13. The juveniles' interest in freedom was "qualified," the Court said, "by the recognition that juveniles, unlike adults, are always in some form of custody." If their parents faltered in controlling them, government could appropriate that role.

The Juvenile Justice and Delinquency Prevention Act

In addition to the attention they have received from the U.S. Supreme Court, juveniles also have been the focus of congressional initiatives. In 1974, following more than a decade of hearings on juvenile crime and the state of juvenile courts and institutions, Congress passed the Juvenile Justice and Delinquency Prevention Act (JJDPA). As the statute's name suggests, its philosophy was preventive. This significant federal law altered the course of juvenile justice more than any other legislative action since the passage in 1899 of the Chicago Juvenile Court Act.

The federal government was only minimally involved in the prevention or control of delinquency prior to the late 1940s. The Children's Bureau, established in 1912, represented the extent of its leadership. With respect to delinquency, this agency limited itself to keeping voluntarily submitted data on the activity of juvenile courts. Shortly after World War II, however, the public began to perceive delinquency as an increasingly serious problem. In response to this concern, the Interdepartmental Committee on Children and Youth was established in 1948. Its primary function was to develop better relationships among existing federal agencies totally or peripherally concerned with youth. It had no power or funds to advise or assist state or local governments in their attempts to prevent or control delinquency.

In early 1961, as an outgrowth of the White House Conference on Children and Youth, the President's Commission on Juvenile Delinquency and Youth Crime was established. The commission was able to recommend and secure enactment of the Juvenile Delinquency and Youth Offenses Control Act of 1961 and its amendments of 1964 and 1965. This statute authorized the secretary of Health, Education and Welfare (HEW) to provide grants to state, local, and private agencies to conduct various projects in search of improved methods for the prevention and control of juvenile delinquency. The Control Act of 1961 was replaced by the broader (and better financed) Juvenile Prevention and Control Act of 1968. In 1971, the Control Act of 1968 was superseded by the Juvenile Delinquency Prevention Act (JDPA), which was designed to provide grants to support community-based juvenile delinquency prevention programs. The ultimate result of this bureaucratic leap-frogging was the historic Juvenile Justice and Delinquency Prevention Act (JJDPA) of 1974, the focus of our attention.

The 1974 statute contains a broad mandate for reform and qualifies as the most comprehensive federal juvenile justice legislation ever enacted (Krisberg et al., 1986). The legislation has had broad-based support from juvenile justice and child welfare professionals, public interest groups, and Congress itself (Krisberg et al., 1986). The original bill passed in the House of Representatives by a vote of 329 to 20 and received only one dissenting vote in the Senate. The statute boosted efforts at juvenile justice reform already in progress at the state level and stimulated nationwide reforms. It was intended to deinstitutionalize status offenders (e.g., "incorrigibles," truants, runaways); provide alternatives to incarceration for nonserious youthful offenders; provide additional funds to localities to improve delinquency prevention programs; establish a federal assistance program to deal with the problems of runaway youth; and ensure that juveniles would not be detained in the same facilities as adults.

The JJDPA is often thought of as promoting the four D's: decriminalization, deinstitutionalization, diversion, and due process, which can be summarized as follows:

- Decriminalization: Status offenses should not be considered "delinquency."
- Deinstitutionalization: Juveniles should be sent to institutions only as a last resort, status offenders should not be institutionalized (DSO); juveniles in adult jails and correctional facilities should be separated from adults by sight and sound.
- Diversion: Alternatives to juvenile court should be considered and used.
- Due Process: The Constitutional rights of juveniles should be recognized.

Note that the concept of **deinstitutionalization**, as addressed in the JJDPA, referred to several groups of juveniles. First, and perhaps most prominently featured, were status offenders, who until that time were commonly placed in training schools with youths who had committed criminal offenses. Second, many members of Congress felt that nonserious delinquents—those found to have committed nonviolent offenses, for example—should not be institutionalized. The JJDPA, therefore, strongly encouraged the development of alternatives to incarceration for dealing with delinquent youth (Krisberg & Schwartz, 1983). Finally, the JJDPA reflected concern about the problem of juveniles held in adult jails. It initially called on states to keep juveniles "out of sight and sound" of adult offenders and eventually mandated that they be kept out of adult facilities altogether. Although we use the abbreviation DSO to refer specifically to status offenders, it is important to keep in mind the other aspects of deinsitutionalization as well.

Proponents of the JJDPA assumed that juveniles, because of their age and inexperience, are less culpable than adult offenders and more amenable to treatment and rehabilitation, both of which are difficult if not impossible to achieve in punitive or coercive institutional settings (Smith et al., 1980). This assumption was based on the time-honored observations of the nature of institutions and the powerful effects of peers. Despite good intentions of early juvenile courts, it was widely documented that juveniles were institutionalized more than was necessary. Institutions were believed to encourage brutality and inhumane treatment. Furthermore, the social systems that developed among the juveniles promoted recalcitrance and resistance to treatment (Smith et al., 1980). It was believed that deinstitutionalization would bypass these group systems.

The JJDPA also created the Office of Juvenile Justice and Delinquency Prevention (OJJDP), which had four major functions: (1) information collection and dissemination, (2) research and evaluation, (3) development and review of standards, and (4) training through National Training Institutes. Also established were an independent Runaway Youth Program to be administered by the Department of Health, Education and Welfare (which has since been divided into the Department of Education and the Department of Health and Human Services) and a National Institute of Corrections within the U.S. Justice Department.

Because the deinstitutionalization of status offenders was a major emphasis of the statute, we will give it special attention here. It should be noted, however, that this topic will be revisited in Chapter 11, where current information covered very briefly in this historical chapter will be readdressed.

Deinstitutionalization of Status Offenders (DSO)   At the time Congress debated the bill that later became the JJDPA, the public was hearing consistently through the media that more than one million children per year run away from home, that they leave at younger ages than before (more than 40 percent between the ages of 11 and 14), and that many resorted to illegal activities to support themselves or their drug habits. Moreover, the runaway problem seemed to be primarily a white, middle-class phenomenon involving girls, many of whom allegedly turned to prostitution. There were few reliable data available to support or refute these media proclamations.

The Runaway Youth Act authorized the secretary of the then HEW to provide assistance to local groups to operate temporary shelter care programs in areas where runaways tended to congregate. Runaways would be provided with a place to stay and immediate assistance, such as medical care and counseling. Although they were to be encouraged to contact their families, they were not to be forced to do so. The statute also authorized funds to conduct research on the scope and nature of the runaway problem and the characteristics of children who left their homes. Congress wished to determine the age, sex, and socioeconomic background of runaway children as well as the places from which and to which they ran and the relationship between running away and other behavior.

At the time the law was passed, it was estimated that 40 percent of all institutionalized children under the control of the juvenile justice system were status offenders or dependent and neglected youth, primarily in the runaway category. They were juveniles who had done nothing that could be considered a violation of the criminal code.

At first glance, the DSO movement appeared to benefit girls. Before the passage of the JJDPA, it was common for states to file delinquency petitions against status offenders. As we noted earlier in the chapter, these petitions were disproportionately filed against girls, and girls were far more likely than boys to be institutionalized for status offending. If juvenile courts determined them to be delinquent, they could then be incarcerated in a juvenile training school together with juveniles who had committed criminal offenses. The new law, with its emphasis on decriminalization as well as DSO, discouraged this practice.

You may recall the earlier figure that by 1950, girls accounted for 34 percent of incarcerated youth. By 1989, however, the percentage of girls incarcerated had dropped to 11.9 percent (Federle and Chesney-Lind, 1992). This is by no means the last word on this topic, as we will see shortly in a discussion of JJDPA amendments.

States adopted different strategies to deinstitutionalize status offenders. Among the two dominant strategies were **decarceration** and **divestiture**. States that adopted a divestiture strategy—by far the less common approach—essentially relinquished their authority over youth who had committed no criminal offense. Status offenders would no longer appear in their juvenile statutes. Juvenile courts would not consider petitions or detain, adjudicate, or dispose of youths on the basis of behavior that previously was identified as a status offense.

More commonly, states used a decarceration strategy. They treated status offenders in much the same way as they did before the JJDPA was passed, with the exception that the status offenders were no longer called delinquents. Status offenders were brought before the juvenile court on a petition that they were children in need of supervision (CHINS) (or, alternately, PINS, MINS, JINS—person, minor, juvenile). A hearing followed, and, if the facts outlined in the petition were upheld, the youth was typically placed under the authority of a public social agency, such as a Division of Child Welfare or Social and Rehabilitative Services. That agency would then determine whether the child was to be kept under supervision in his or her own home or needed out-of-home placement in a foster home, group home, or other nonsecure facility.

Note that deinstitutionalization did not mean that juvenile status offenders could not be removed from their own homes. They could be placed, as noted in the previous paragraph, in foster homes, group homes, or nonsecure residential treatment programs. In fact, the original JJDPA presumed that states often would place status offenders in some form of shelter care. They simply could not be placed in secure institutions operated by juvenile correctional officials, commonly called "training schools." They were to be diverted from juvenile justice processing to alternative services and treatment facilities. Because these facilities could be residential, some status offenders were in effect still confined, though not technically institutionalized.

The philosophy behind DSO was commendable, but the practice brought numerous unanticipated consequences. It was widely acknowledged that there was wide resistance to DSO on the part of juvenile court judges, many of whom did not wish to relinquish control over status offenders. Social service agencies had the task of finding nonsecure placements and community services and devising new methods of enforcing compliance with court-ordered treatment and out-of-home placements.

JJDPA Amendments

Congress has made significant revisions to the original JJDPA. In 1976, Congress asserted that states were in "substantial compliance" with the DSO mandate if they had accomplished a 75 percent reduction over a period of two years. (The original law had mandated DSO within a one-year period.) In 1977, Congress created a category of "non-offenders," to distinguish them from status offenders. Non-offenders—who were dependent and neglected children—were to come under the DSO mandate as well. The 1977 amendment to the JJDPA also encouraged states to seek a wider variety of alternative placements, including nonplacement. In other words, it was not presumed that states should keep status offenders and non-offenders in shelter care if they could be better served in their own homes. Congress also extended the compliance period, giving states up to five years to meet the DSO mandate.

In 1980, partially as a result of lobbying by the National Association of Juvenile Court Judges, the JJDPA was revised to allow judges to institutionalize or to hold in contempt a juvenile who violated a valid court order (VCO). This represented a major revision of the JJDPA. Critics of this change note that these violations allowed judges to turn status offenders into "delinquents," who could then be institutionalized (Schwartz, 1992). Although there is debate over whether this remains a common practice today (Holden & Kapler, 1995), a number of researchers have documented the disproportionate effect of this amendment on girls, particularly runaway girls, compared with boys (e.g., Schwartz, 1989; Chesney-Lind, 1995).

The 1980 amendment also mandated the removal of juveniles from adult jails and lockups. The JJDPA of 1974 had called for the separation of juveniles by sight and sound from adults in jails and lockups. The separation requirement led to some juveniles' being kept in worse conditions than adults: drunk tanks, segregation units, abandoned sections of jails, or makeshift cells in storage areas (Schwartz, 1989). Considering the potential for psychological trauma and even suicide attempts, advocates for children convinced Congress that this practice was unacceptable.

The amendment of 1980, therefore, explicitly prohibited states receiving federal funds from detaining or confining juveniles in the same facility with adults who were charged in or convicted of a crime. State legislatures appeared to be slow in developing statutes that clearly spelled out the need for separation, and Congress sought to put "more teeth" into the Act. Interestingly, however, there was resistance to this mandate, just as there was resistance to the DSO mandate.

As Schwartz (1989) has noted, jurisdictions argued that there were no alternatives to jail and that the costs of building detention facilities for juveniles were prohibitive. Schwartz adds, though, that alternatives are relatively inexpensive and do not require secure facilities for the vast majority of juveniles. Resistance to the mandate to remove juveniles from jails also arose because "judges and probation and parole staffs were locking many kids up in jails 'to get their attention' or 'to give them a taste' of what a harsh, prisonlike experience would be like" (p. 76).

Issues dealing with status offenders and with the problem of children in adult jails will be readdressed in Chapter 12. Although recent data indicate that 49 states are in full compliance with the DSO provision (Holden & Kapler, 1995), there is still considerable disagreement about how the juvenile justice system should deal with status offenders. Furthermore, for some juveniles, public institutionalization has been supplanted by private institutionalization in mental-health facilities, substance-abuse treatment centers, or a wide variety of facilities for youths who have committed no crime but are perceived to be at risk. This phenomenon, called transinstitutionalization, appears to have affected girls more than boys (Schwartz,

1989; Federle & Chesney-Lind, 1992). Additionally, there is some suspicion that the gains in deinstitutionalization made in the wake of the JJDPA are beginning to be eroded. Specifically, it appears that girls are increasingly being detained and committed for different and less serious offenses than boys (Federle & Chesney-Lind, 1992, p. 171). Federle and Chesney-Lind also point out the racial disparities relating to DSO. Although girls and white boys benefited from the JJDPA's mandates, minority youth rarely did. Additionally, although most states are in compliance with jail removal (Holden & Kapler, 1995), it is increasingly apparent that juveniles are being unlawfully detained in facilities with adults.

In 1992, Congress dealt with the issue of minority overrepresentation in the juvenile justice system. States were told that the proportion of minors confined in their detention and correctional facilities should not exceed the aggregate proportion of minorities in the general population. To receive grants, states were required to develop and implement plans for reducing the overrepresentation.

Rarely has a session of Congress not seen some debate over the JJDPA. In 1996, for example, Congress considered proposals that would have placed more emphasis on juvenile crime control than rehabilitation. In fact, one of the proposals called for the elimination of the OJJDP, to be replaced by an Office of Juvenile Crime Control. Although these efforts did not succeed, it is expected that perceptions of a growing juvenile crime problem will elicit additional attempts at controlling juvenile behavior. Under its current administrator, however, the Office of Juvenile Justice and Delinquency Prevention is funding preventive programs within the community that are likely to reach a wide group of juveniles and their families.

EXPLAINING SHIFTS IN JUVENILE POLICIES

In an attempt to understand some of the shifts in thinking about juveniles alluded to in the preceding section, it is helpful to turn to the ideas of a number of prominent criminologists, many of whom remind us that "get tough" approaches to juveniles are not new, nor are perceptions of dramatic increases in the juvenile crime rates. Lloyd Ohlin (1983b), for example, identifies the get-tough approach as the third wave of changes in federal policy toward juveniles since the 1960s.

In the early 1960s, largely because of the history of the Chicago Area Project and others like it, federal policymakers drew upon community *organization* strategies to foster community responsibility for juvenile misbehavior. A variety of social programs toward that end were funded. The programs in general were not successful, however, partly because of naïveté and partly because of the massive social changes that were occurring in society during that period. Ohlin noted that "the growing gap between expectation and achievable results fostered disillusionment, alienation, social unrest, and ultimately, abandonment of the programs themselves" (Ohlin, 1983b, p. 464).

The second shift in social policy, a multifaceted approach to official prevention, deinstitutionalization, and community treatment, was spearheaded by a series of presidential commissions studying the broad problems of crime and violence. In 1967 the first of these commissions, the President's Commission on Law Enforcement and Administration of Justice, set the tone. Its primary task was to recommend ways to identify and control delinquents and status offenders. Its recommended strategies, which were reflected in the JJDPA, discussed earlier, emphasized both formal and informal programs intended to prevent delinquency, extend rights to juveniles, and move them out of institutions whenever possible. Implicit in these recommendations was a pervasive distrust of institutions and a prevalent assumption that delinquents are not as much guilty of crimes as they are victims of social and economic deprivation. The fundamental premise was that families, group homes, and peer groups would provide suitable alternatives to the discredited courts and institutions. Ohlin noted that, although the commission's recommendations were well received, implementation of the strategies was "spotty," and their effectiveness was difficult to assess.

A "law-and-order" commitment began in the mid-1970s, with the public demanding quicker punishments and mandatory sentencing procedures, first for adults and eventually for juveniles. Ohlin noted that this focus reflected in part a strong conservative reaction to "liberal" policies of rehabilitation and community treatment programs advocated in the 1960s. Ohlin wrote (1983b, p. 467), "We are now in one of those periods of conservative reaction where the prevailing views about crime express beliefs about retribution, deterrence, and incapacitation that are deeply rooted in our religious and cultural heritage. . . .Our policies are now being developed by those who believe that the traditional system of punishment can be fine-tuned to control offenders by increasing the predictability and certainty of punishment."

The criminologist Frank Hellum (1979) identified a twofold orientation and philosophy toward juvenile justice that emerged during the mid- to late 1970s. On the one hand, a "velvet glove" was to be extended to noncriminal status offenders in the form of restrictions on confinement. On the other, there was an emerging "iron fisted," punitive approach to nonstatus offenders. There were calls for remanding juveniles to adult criminal courts or for demanding accountability akin to that demanded of adults, including the imposition of fines or imprisonment.

This "iron fisted" philosophy was specifically directed at the violent and repetitive offender, whom the JJDPA of 1974 (and its amendment of 1977) seemed to ignore. The overall primary mission of the JJDPA was to strengthen the ties of "common delinquents" to their families, school, and work (Galvin & Blake, 1984). It sought to develop a strong and comprehensive national policy on prevention. The common nonserious or status offender constituted about 95 percent of total delinquent population, and the serious offender made up the residual 5 percent. These approximate figures continue to be representative, with serious delinquency hovering between the 5 and 10 percent figures. It is important to note, however, that the figures refer to individuals, not to crimes, a distinction that will soon be discussed. When the JJDPA was being debated, it seemed more important to respond to the greatest percentage of the juvenile problem, represented by nonserious and status offenders. Nevertheless, those who supported the JJDPA hoped that the policies it advocated would address serious delinquency as well. Beginning in 1981, the Reagan administration instituted an agenda that changed the direction of national policy from one of prevention to one of control. The target now became the serious or repetitive offender, the youth who committed persistent violent acts. The White House announced that it wished to prevent the victimization of children, reduce school violence, support the nuclear family and traditional values, compensate the victims of juvenile crime, and restore the concept of accountability or "just deserts" to the juvenile justice system. There was indication that even status offenders might not escape the iron fist, however. A 1984 report by the National Advisory Committee for Juvenile Justice and Delinquency Prevention recommended that grants to states to accomplish the deinstitutionalization of status offenders not be renewed.

Those who agreed with the shift in attention pointed out not only that 80 percent of serious juvenile crime is committed by less than 10 percent of juvenile offenders but also that a third of all serious crime is committed by juveniles. Furthermore, some juvenile offenders were allegedly committing as many as 150 to 200 felonies per year, much like their adult counterparts. Juvenile justice policies, according to these observers, must be directed at identifying and incapacitating these serious, violent, chronic offenders.

The Reagan administration further believed that for too long the juvenile justice system had been overly concerned with the juvenile offender at the expense of society and the victim. Traditionally, juvenile courts since 1899 had emphasized what was in the best interest of the offending child rather than what was in the best interest of society and the child's victim. It was time to change all that. Recommendations and procedures for restitution were advanced. Restitution, the requirement that an offender make amends to the victim, meant for the most part that offenders should pay back their victims monetarily what they had stolen, damaged, or destroyed.

According to this approach, the philosophy reflected in the JJDPA of 1974 was all wrong. The administrator of the Office of Juvenile Justice and Delinquency Prevention commented, "To a great extent, the system has been based on the Rousseauvian notion that people are born good, but corrupted by institutions" (Regnery, 1986, p. 49). Delinquents now would be considered as having rational choice; they were no longer at the mercy of forces beyond their control. They must accept the consequences of their behavior, and courts must hold them accountable. Furthermore, whereas the intent behind the original JJDPA was to have the federal government provide leadership, states and local communities were now encouraged to solve their delinquency problems in their own way.

The Reagan administration also argued that the underlying cause of delinquency was the erosion of traditional values and the disruption of the family structure, as reflected by the number of broken homes, the high incidence of child abuse and neglect, the fact that some 1.5 million children a year apparently ran away from home, and the recorded 7 million births out of wedlock annually. This observation seems to contradict the iron-fisted approach, however. If children are delinquent because they have been abused or neglected, their individual choices have been restricted by social conditions beyond their control. To be consistent, one would call for an assessment of the conditions that lead to delinquency and meaningful intervention before delinquency occurs; in other words, we still need a strategy of formal prevention rather than one of control, which is what the original JJDPA was intended to be.

THE SHIFT TOWARD PUNISHMENT

In recent years we have seen many requests for a get-tough stance toward juvenile offenders. The surge in juvenile violent-crime rates, the publicity given to illustrations of particularly heinous juvenile offending, and the apparent failure of many rehabilitation programs to deliver law-abiding youths have all led to calls for reform. In the 1990s, for example, almost every state has changed its juvenile justice laws to make it easier for youth to be tried in criminal courts and at younger ages. A considerable amount of juvenile justice legislation, both state and federal, has facilitated the transfer of serious juvenile offenders to adult criminal courts. This reflects a greater concern about chronic, violent offenders, who actually constitute a very small proportion of the juvenile offender population. We will discuss this issue in more detail in Chapter 12.

Thomas Bernard (1992) has offered perceptive comments about such shifts in policy. In *The Cycle of Juvenile Justice*, Bernard argues that perceived rises in the juvenile crime rate are invariably followed by increased public pressure for harsh punishments. Next, new reformers appear on the scene and argue successfully against the punitive approach. The well-intentioned reformers, however, suggest methods of "helping" juveniles that ignore due process. Meanwhile, despite these changes in philosophy, juvenile crime rates remain high, because juveniles have always been a high-crime-rate group. And so, the cycle of juvenile justice will be perpetuated until we give up the belief "that an as-yet undiscovered juvenile justice policy will transform juveniles into a low-crime-rate group" (p. 165). Rather than changing the system, Bernard urges us to change our "ideas" of delinquency by dividing delinquents into two groups. The vast majority are "naïve risk-takers" who do not understand the consequences of their actions. Most delinquents, he notes, "are adolescents acting the way adolescents always have: wild and crazy" (p. 167). Others, the few, are "rational calculators" who are fully aware of the consequences of their actions. This second group of offenders, he argues, should be transferred to criminal courts.

CURRENT TRENDS

As we approach the twenty-first century, then, we are faced with several competing models for dealing with juvenile delinquency. The law-and-order approach has continued through the 1990s, as evidenced by new state laws, federal initiatives, and an apparent reluctance on the part of the courts to interfere with legislative initiatives that are tougher on juveniles. The retributive response is particularly apparent against adolescents involved in serious violence (Grisso, 1996).

Nevertheless, there are renewed calls for rehabilitation of juvenile offenders, both within the community and when necessary in secure juvenile facilities. Most importantly, communities are focusing on crime-prevention programs targeting a youthful population in the community. In 1994, U.S. Attorney General Janet Reno invited criminologists to participate in a variety of "task forces," including one on delinquency in the inner cities. The task force's recommendations (American Society of Criminology, 1995) focused on prevention, particularly early child–parent intervention and education. Among other things, the criminologists recommended that parent training programs be made widely available and that the federal government fund pilot residential and community schools offering comprehensive services to children and their families. The task force recognized that law-enforcement alternatives are still needed, however, "to detect and punish those who make life intolerable for others" (p. 16). "Since even the best preventive programs need considerable time to bear fruit, we have no choice but to immediately upgrade our law enforcement alternatives" (p. 16). Preventive programs must not take second place to retributive policies, however. Many communities across the United States are recognizing that efforts at crime prevention, tailored to their needs, deserve their support.

SUMMARY AND CONCLUSIONS

In this chapter, we traced the legislative and judicial origins of contemporary juvenile justice and the early formulation of the term "juvenile delinquency." In the nineteenth century, children experienced the first attempts by social reformers to institutionalize them "for their own protection," specifically in houses of refuge and reformatories. Until these institutions were created, juveniles who had committed crime were dealt with in criminal courts, where they were subject to being sent to—but not likely to be sent to—penitentiaries.

The houses of refuge signaled a change in that they supervised not only juveniles who had committed criminal acts but also those "in danger of falling into depravity." Invariably, these were the children of the poor and tended to be girls more than boys. Similarly, reformatories housed youthful offenders who were believed to be rehabilitatable. Young women were more likely than young men to be sent to reformatories for minor offenses.

The watershed year for juvenile justice was 1899, when the Illinois legislature passed a law that represented the first comprehensive attempt to define juvenile delinquency and provide for the care of the offender. The statute emphasized the need to separate adult from child offenders for purposes of definition, processing, and treatment. It was followed by similar statutes establishing juvenile courts in nearly every state. Closely connected with the juvenile court were concepts of probation, social work, and child guidance clinics.

Social and political factors significant to the evolution of the Illinois statute were summarized. The motives of those who prompted and sustained reforms in the treatment of juveniles have been questioned (e.g., Platt, 1969b; Rothman, 1980). Were the child savers associated with the juvenile court movement truly well-meaning individuals responding to appalling conditions in institutions that housed juveniles, or were they righteous members of the privileged classes intent upon protecting themselves against crime? Does the history of juvenile justice reflect an excessive focus on the "offensive" behavior of the poor and a double standard with respect to the treatment of girls? Even if well meaning, did their reforms harm more than help juveniles? Whatever the answers to these questions, reformers received legal support in the doctrine of *parens patriae*, the care-giving principle that continues to pervade legal opinions in cases involving juveniles.

We saw that interests in community strategies for the prevention of delinquency shifted the focus from individual treatment of delinquents to attempts at producing social change. To this day, community efforts hold great promise for juveniles, as we will see in later chapters.

In the 1960s, scholars, courts, and legislatures began to reflect a growing disenchantment with the system of juvenile justice. The U.S. Supreme Court began to extend due process guarantees to juveniles. Although juveniles now have many of the same constitutional rights as adults, it is not unusual for them to waive the rights at various stages in the juvenile process. Additionally, in later decisions the Court refused to extend to juveniles the full panoply of protections given to adults, reflecting a reluctance, in the name of the "best interest of the child," to bury the *parens patriae* doctrine. The due process approach of the Supreme Court had a parallel in federal law, specifically with the passage of the JJDPA.

Observers have remarked upon discernible shifts not only in judicial but also in legislative and social policy with reference to juveniles. Beginning in the mid-1970s, a trend toward tougher policies became evident. States passed laws enabling criminal courts to have jurisdiction of an increasing number of juveniles, and at younger ages.

As we enter the twenty-first century, we can expect to continue to see many approaches competing for prominence. Although there are continuing calls for the abolition of juvenile courts or for treating more and more juveniles as adults in criminal courts, many practitioners, scholars, and members of the public are still optimistic about the preventive and rehabilitative potential of the juvenile justice system. In 1991, the Center for the Study of Youth Policy at the University of Michigan conducted the first National Public Opinion Survey on Juvenile Crime (Schwartz, 1992). The survey indicates that the public favors giving juveniles the same due process rights as adults and adjudicating those who commit serious crimes in adult courts. By an overwhelming majority, however, the public wants juvenile courts to retain their emphasis on treatment and rehabilitation. As Schwartz (1992, p. 222) notes, "[T]he public does not appear to be nearly as punitive and demanding of retribution toward juvenile offenders as many politicians and, in some instances, juvenile justice officials have made them out to be. When politicians and others claim to be speaking for the community, they may well be representing a much smaller group than is typically thought to be the case."

KEY CONCEPTS

Illinois Juvenile Court Act of 1899
houses of refuge
parens patriae
reformatory model
solitary and congregate systems
Zebulon Brockway
probation
John Augustus
Ben Lindsey
Progressive Era
CAP
Midcity Project

Mobilization for Youth
JJDPA
decriminalization
deinstitutionalization
diversion
due process
DSO
decarceration strategy
divestiture strategy
CHINS
National Public Opinion Survey on
    Juvenile Crime

Early Processing

11

The typical juvenile—particularly the juvenile male—is far more likely to come into informal, direct contact with the juvenile justice system than the typical adult is with the criminal justice system. Studies consistently document that between 20 and 50 percent of adolescent males have some police contact, for example (e.g., Wolfgang, Figlio, & Sellin, 1972; Farrington, Ohlin, & Wilson, 1986). Self-report studies indicate that even higher proportions of juveniles report at least one illegal act before turning 18 (e.g., Huizinga, Loeber, & Thornberry, 1994).

As Grisso (1996, p. 235) has commented, "refraining from crime during adolescence is statistically aberrant." Late childhood and adolescence, particularly the latter, are times of exploration and boundary pushing. Bernard (1992) notes that adolescence is a time for acting wild and crazy, and most juveniles who come into contact with the law are "naïve risk-takers" who truly do not understand the consequences of their actions. A group of teenagers in one community, for example, recently undertook "the great license-plate caper," an evening of switching plates on a variety of cars parked in motel parking lots. Tampering with license plates in this manner presents numerous problems for the car owner and involves direct and indirect costs. Consider, for example, the family on vacation, the traveling salesperson, the person in town to interview for a job, the person who may be attending a funeral, the time spent by victims obtaining new license plates. It is unlikely that youths planning this caper thought about the possible impact of their behavior, either on themselves or their victims. How should the juvenile justice system respond to these youths?

Similarly, underage drinking, stealing signs, vandalism, illegal drug use, shoplifting, and fights are often part of growing up for a significant number of youths. It is widely believed that the juvenile justice system should be initially lenient toward youth involved in these activities. If juveniles were referred to family or juvenile courts for every violation of the law, those courts would be immobilized and juveniles themselves would be needlessly stigmatized. Even police arrests are often not referred. In 1992, 30 percent of all juveniles arrested were handled within the police department and then released (Snyder & Sickmund, 1995). The balance were referred to juvenile court or, far less frequently, to criminal courts for prosecution as adults. Bernard (1992) notes that adults working at each stage of the juvenile justice system offer a series of "escalating threats," "convincer punishments," and—if necessary—"coerced treatments" to the naïve risk takers who come to their attention. Police, for example, have always exercised a variety of informal diversion methods that may be seen as "threats" to deal with mischievous behavior by youths. The officer encountering a group of youths smoking marijuana cigarettes may confiscate the drugs, give a stern warning to the group, and report their behavior to parents or guardians. Some officers, by choice or by department policy, would not report such one-time behavior to parents. Alternately, a department may operate its own diversion program, which may include "convincer punishments." One police chief, for example, regularly "invites" juveniles engaged in mischief to wash and polish police cruisers and fire trucks on Saturday mornings. Failure to appear may result in "an escalating threat" to refer the youth to court. Even though the chief may be aware that the court is unlikely to go forward with a case, the implied threat sends a message to the youth that his or her behavior is taken seriously in the community.

This chapter will address the important decisions made when juveniles first come to the attention of the justice system. We begin with the moment of police contact and proceed through the intake process and the issues associated with the decision whether to detain a juvenile prior to an adjudication hearing.

THE DECISION TO ARREST

Although it is often remarked that "it's hard for juveniles to get arrested," the fact remains that juveniles appear in police arrest records disproportionately to adults. Police clearance data in 1991 revealed that juveniles under 18 were responsible for approximately 10 percent of all violent crimes, 19 percent of burglaries, 23 percent of larcenies, 23 percent of motor vehicle thefts, and 40 percent of all arsons.

The decisions made by the police officer when he or she first meets the juvenile often set the stage for what will transpire later. This includes decisions that will be made by other representatives of the juvenile justice system as well as the juvenile's own attitudes about law, law enforcement, and the courts.

In juvenile law, states usually distinguish between "taking a juvenile into custody" and "arresting" the juvenile. All arrests involve taking juveniles into custody, but not all takings into custody are arrests. The typical statute allows law-enforcement officers to take runaways into custody, for example, or to take juveniles into custody if they are endangered by their environments. "Arresting" a juvenile, by contrast, requires probable cause to believe that a crime has been committed and that the juvenile was the one who committed it.

Research in the area of taking juveniles into custody has focused on the decision as to whether to arrest. Such research indicates that, in nonserious cases, police routinely abdicate their discretion to the complainant. If the complainant prefers that the youth not be arrested, police are likely to honor his or her wishes. Another factor that affects the arrest decision is the demeanor of the juvenile. Juveniles who are hostile or uncooperative are more likely to be taken into custody than those who appear frightened or are respectful of police; on the other hand, juveniles who are obsequious or too cooperative are likely to be looked upon with suspicion. Interestingly, the training an officer has obtained with regard to procedures involving youth affects the arrest decision. Officers with little training in juvenile procedures are less likely to arrest juveniles, presumably because they are not sure of the appropriate measures to take once the youths are in their custody.

CONSTITUTIONAL RIGHTS OF JUVENILES

Juveniles, like adults, are entitled to constitutional protections, including those relating most closely to police actions. Like adults, juveniles have a First Amendment right to congregate in groups. Under the Fourth Amendment, police officers may not conduct unreasonable searches and seizures of a juvenile's person or possessions, and under the Fifth Amendment juveniles have a right against self-incrimination. As this right has been interpreted, police must warn juveniles in their custody of the right to remain silent before interrogation begins. The U.S. Supreme Court itself, while recognizing these broad rights, has issued rulings restrictive of them, however. In *New Jersey v. T.L.O.* (1985), for example, the Court allowed the search of a high school student's purse by a school official who had reasonable suspicion that the student was breaking a school rule against smoking in the lavatory. Marijuana was found, and the school principal called in police. Courts also have allowed school officials to use canines to search student lockers, classrooms, and student clothing. In 1995, the Supreme Court allowed random drug testing as a condition for playing on school sports teams (*Vernonia School District v. Acton*).

Police officers are far more likely to break up a group of juveniles meeting on the street or in a mall than a group of adults. They are also more likely to ask—or order—juveniles to empty their pockets or handbags without any reasonable suspicion that they are involved in illegal activity. It is common, as well, for police officers to interrogate juvenile suspects who have been urged—often by their parents—to waive their privilege against self-incrimination and their right to an attorney.

There is considerable debate in the juvenile justice literature with respect to these occurrences. On the one hand, many argue that the law-enforcement community is protective of juveniles and is acting in their best interest. Police will say that they break up small gatherings of juveniles only as a last resort and often at the request of townspeople or merchants. The groups are thought to breed trouble, and "We want to stop trouble before it starts." Random searching is done as a deterrent, even though evidence obtained in such a search would likely not be admissible in court. In the interrogation process, when lawyers are involved, they "tell the kids to shut up" and interfere with the rehabilitation process.

In *Fare v. Michael C.* (1979), the U.S. Supreme Court recognized a juvenile's right to a lawyer before custodial interrogation but stopped short of setting a constitutional requirement that the juvenile be allowed to see a substitute adult, even a parent. Michael C., a 16-year-old charged with murder, waived his right to a lawyer but asked to see his probation officer before talking to police. In a 6-3 decision, the Court ruled that the rights outlined in *Miranda v. Arizona* applied to juveniles as well as to adults but did not include the right to see a lawyer substitute, whether it be a parent, probation officer, or trusted friend.

Research suggests that most juveniles are not represented by lawyers during police interrogation (Feld, 1988; Schwartz, 1989). This does not mean that they have not been informed of their rights; rather, it is more likely that they have waived them. Despite the fact that the Supreme Court in *Fare v. Michael C.* did not require anyone but a lawyer, many departments by policy do not question juveniles suspected of a crime unless their parents or guardians are present. In some jurisdictions, a special juvenile rights form is used (see Box 11.1). Nevertheless, juveniles routinely waive their right to a lawyer during custodial interrogation. Numerous advocates for juveniles have questioned the common practice of allowing juveniles to do this, with or without the presence of parents or guardians. Barry Feld, for example, argues vehemently that juveniles should not be allowed to waive their right to a lawyer at this phase of the proceeding, because they are unable to understand the consequences of this action.

Parents also are not always the best protectors of children's rights (e.g., Schwartz, 1989). Parents themselves may be unaware of the consequences of waiving a constitutional right, or they may pressure their children to confess out of fear or even out of anger at the child. Alternately, parents may assume the benevolence of police and the juvenile courts. Grisso and Ring (1979) studied the attitudes of 753 middle-class parents with respect to children's legal rights in arrest situations. Although three-quarters of the parents believed that juveniles should have the same legal rights as adults in concept, just over half said they would advise a juvenile to obtain a lawyer before custodial interrogation. Fifty to 60 percent of the parents also believed that juveniles should not be allowed to withhold information from police or courts when they are suspected of a crime.

Box 11.1

EXAMPLE OF A JUVENILE RIGHTS FORM

Child in Custody _____
Place _____
Date _____ Time Child taken into custody _____
Time this form was read _____

(The following is to be read and explained by the officer, and the child shall read it before signing.)

Before I am allowed to ask you any questions, you must understand that you have certain rights, or protections, that have been given to you by law. These rights make sure that you will be treated fairly. You will not be punished for deciding to use the rights. I will read your rights and explain them to you. You may ask questions as we go along so that you can fully understand what your rights are. Do you understand me so far?   YES ___ NO ___

1. You have the right to remain silent. This means that you do not have to say or write anything. You do not have to talk to any one or answer any questions we ask you. You will not be punished for deciding not to talk to us. Do you understand this right? YES ___ NO ___

2. Anything you say can and will be used against you in a court. This means that if you do say or write anything, what you say or write will be used in a court to prove that you may have broken the law. Do you understand this? YES ___ NO ___

3. You have the right to talk to a lawyer before any questioning. You have the right to have the lawyer with you while you are being questioned. The lawyer will help you decide what you should do or say. The things you say to the lawyer cannot be used in court to prove that you may have broken the law. If you decide you want a lawyer, we will not question you until you have been allowed to talk to the lawyer. Do you understand this right? YES ___ NO ___

4. If you want to talk to a lawyer and you cannot afford one, we will get you a lawyer at no cost to you before any questioning begins. This means that if you want a lawyer and you cannot pay for one, you still may have one. Do you understand this right? YES ___ NO ___

5. You can refuse to answer any or all questions at any time. You also can ask to have a lawyer with you at any time. This means that if you decide, at any time during questioning, that you do not want to talk, you may tell us to stop and you cannot be asked any more questions. Also, if you decide you would like to talk to a lawyer at any time during questioning, you will not be asked any more questions until a lawyer is with you. Do you understand this right? YES ___ NO ___

6. (In Felony Cases Only) There is a possibility that you may not be brought to juvenile court but instead will be treated as an adult in criminal court. There you could go to a county jail or the State Prison. If you are treated as an adult you will have to go through the adult criminal system, just as if you were 18 years old. If that happens, you will not receive the protections of the juvenile justice system. Do you understand this? YES ___ NO ___

7. Do you have any questions so far? YES ___ NO ___

(This portion is now to be read by the child.)

I can read and understand English. YES ___ NO ___

I have been read and I have read my rights as listed above. I fully understand what my rights are. I do not want to answer any questions at this time and I would like to have a lawyer.

Signature of Child _____
Date _____ Time _____

WAIVER OF RIGHTS

(This portion is to be read by the child.)

I can read and understand English. YES ___ NO ___

I have been read and I have read my rights as listed above. I fully understand what my rights are. I have been asked if I have any questions and I do not have any. I am willing to give up my right to silence and answer questions. I give up my right to have a lawyer present. I do not wish to speak to a lawyer before I answer any questions. No promises or threats or offers of deals have been made to me to make me give up my rights. I understand that I may change my mind, it will not affect what I have already done or said.

Signature of Child _____
Date _____ Time _____
Signature of Witness _____
Date _____ Time _____

DECISION MAKING IN ADOLESCENCE

The issue of whether juveniles should be allowed to waive their right to an attorney relates to decision-making capacity. Many studies have found that the cognitive capacities of mid-adolescents (who are the most likely to appear in arrest records) are not significantly inferior to those of adults (Grisso, 1996). This suggests that an adolescent's decision to waive the right to remain silent and the right to an attorney, or both, is an informed one and should be allowed. Grisso (1996), however, raises two critical points about this assumption. First, "few studies have examined decision-making abilities among adolescents with poor intellectual abilities, low socioeconomic status, and cultural characteristics typical of delinquent populations" (p. 233). Second, laboratory experimental conditions do not simulate decisions made under stress and "on the street." According to Grisso, "Especially relevant when considering delinquent populations are special sources of negative emotion and stress that are said to influence adolescents differently than adults because of their social and developmental status. Numerous studies describe the sense of 'futurelessness' and fatalism that is experienced by adolescents whose dependent status does not allow them to escape neighborhoods in which violent death is a daily occurrence . . . " (p. 234).

Although Grisso was relating the foregoing to adolescents' making decisions relating to the perpetration of violent behavior, the concepts are also relevant to adolescents in an arrest situation. A juvenile's decision to waive his or her right to remain silent or the right to an attorney is without doubt one made under negative emotion and stress.

Earlier studies by Grisso can be brought to bear more directly to this topic as well. In order for a waiver to be valid, it must be made knowingly, intelligently, and voluntarily. Grisso (1980) compared juveniles and adults on their respective ability to comprehend *Miranda* warnings and appreciate their significance. He learned that capacity was poor for juveniles below 14 as a group. For juveniles between the ages of 15 and 17, factors such as intelligence and lack of experience with the law significantly impeded the ability to understand. We cannot assume that judges, who have the task of determining that a waiver was intelligent, knowing, and voluntary, are aware of the developmental research in this area.

POLICE JUVENILE PROGRAMS

In recent years, many police departments have consciously engaged in a process of rethinking their approaches to juveniles, specifically in line with a "community policing" approach. Community policing has alternately been thought of as a philosophy and a program. Although critics have seen it as a form of glorified public relations, supporters see it as a way of facing some of the most intractable issues facing law enforcement today. Recognizing that police are often out of touch with the communities they serve, many departments have initiated programs in which they work with the community and attempt to break down the

barriers that have resulted in mutual distrust. These community policing models hold promise for juvenile justice in the years ahead, particularly if they are
able to produce attitudinal changes in both law-enforcement officers and in the
juveniles themselves.

Recent literature on policing suggests that strategies which keep the law-
enforcement officer physically closer to the community and in a better position to
communicate with citizens encourage citizen participation in crime-control
efforts. Lawrence Sherman (1986) has reviewed and assessed a variety of these
strategies. They include such varied approaches as opening police storefront centers, holding meetings to assess citizen needs, distributing newsletters, and organizing neighborhood cleanup efforts. Research evaluating these efforts generally
focuses on what impact these community policing strategies have on fear of crime
or reporting victimization to police. Sherman reports mixed results. There appears
to be greater success when the strategies do not depend upon extensive citizen
participation, however. According to Sherman, there is indication that such citizen
involvement increases fear of crime and leaves citizens with an exaggerated perception of the crime problem in the community. He also notes, however, that programs involving citizens may not work because police themselves may not be
supportive. In some communities, for example, citizens may believe that they can
handle crime better than the police, or that the police budget has grown out of
hand. "It is therefore no surprise that many police unions are suspicious of citizen-
involvement programs" (Sherman, 1986, p. 374).

We should be careful not to blame the community when citizen–police partnerships in crime prevention are minimally effective, however. Police–community relations also may be damaged as a result of the public's lack of trust in the
police. Citizens who see their police officers abusing their power, failing to provide adequate protection, engaging in illegal activities, or otherwise overlooking
their sworn duty to serve and protect cannot be expected to work with police in
an ongoing effort to prevent crime.

One of the trends in policing today is to involve officers in more formalized
delinquency prevention programs. The prime example is DARE (Drug and
Alcohol Resistance Education), a program that was initiated in Los Angeles in
1983 and has been widely adopted throughout the country. The typical DARE
program sends trained officers to local schools to teach fifth and sixth graders
about drugs, self-esteem, peer resistance, stress management, assertiveness, and
healthful alternatives to drug use. The DARE curriculum lasts about 17 weeks.
Although an early, preliminary evaluation found that participation in DARE
lowered drug use (DeJong, 1987), later and more methodologically sound studies have not been so positive. Some evaluations (e.g., Clayton, Cattarello, &
Walden, 1991; Ringwalt, Ennett, & Holt, 1991) did find changes in attitudes
toward drug use, but they did not find differences in actual use. In one recent
evaluation, a one-year follow up of students who had participated in DARE in
36 schools in Illinois (Rosenbaum et al., 1994), researchers found no significant
differences in drug use or in attitudes or beliefs about drugs between participants and nonparticipants.

Despite these discouraging findings, very few are calling for the scrapping of the DARE program. Supporters point to the likely positive effect of having police in the schools as role models for juveniles. Others suggest that DARE facilitates the work of law enforcement. For example, there are numerous anecdotal accounts of juveniles' reporting their own victimization to DARE officers or of officers' being able to work better with youth in the community as a result of knowing them through their work with DARE. On the other hand, unanticipated outcomes treading on civil liberties have also been associated with DARE in some communities. Children have been known to report their parents to police for using drugs in the home. In one case, a 17-year-old Maine girl who reported her parents to police when she was 12 and participating in a DARE program is at this moment suing the town and its police chief. Police had arrested and charged her parents despite their assurances to her that they would not do so. Her father pleaded guilty to cultivating marijuana and was placed on probation for a year. Although the program itself should not be blamed for these developments, it is clear the police should exercise judgment in using information they obtain in the process of teaching the DARE curriculum.

INFORMAL PROCESSING

Recall that one-third of juvenile arrests are handled informally within the police department, a process sometimes referred to as "station-house adjustment." Numerous police departments today, particularly in urban areas, sponsor special programs for juveniles at this early stage of their contact with the juvenile justice system. The programs are both preventive and diversionary in nature. That is, they are meant not only to target juvenile crime but also to work with juveniles who might be at risk of additional offending.

Some departments have begun to assign officers to run sports and recreation programs or work with youth on a one-to-one basis or in small groups in such areas as anger management or conflict resolution. In Columbia, South Carolina, the police department operates substations in city housing projects. Officers plan or co-sponsor youth activities, such as camping trips or community talent shows. Police Athletic Leagues (PALs) in more than 500 communities across the United States sponsor community service projects, educational field trips, and recreational activities. In Jacksonville, Florida, officers sponsor an after-school program in low-income, gang-plagued neighborhoods. The officers serve as mentors for youths and provide informal guidance on a wide range of health and safety topics (DeJong, 1995).

Preventive and diversionary programs also may involve the juvenile's family. In Honolulu, Hawaii, police established a Saturday-morning program whereby juveniles arrested for minor offenses were given the option of being referred to juvenile court or reporting weekly to a community center for classes on decision making, anger management, and conflict resolution. Interestingly, the parents of the juveniles were also expected to attend. While juveniles were put through role-playing exercises in decision making, parents were given information about community resources and tips on dealing with children and adolescents. Failure to attend the program resulted in juveniles' referral to the juvenile court.

Family-based models are popular internationally as well. In Australia, for example, a "Family Group Conference" model is being widely implemented (Moore, 1993). A derivative of that model, the Wagga model (named after the New South Wales city in which it has been implemented), is operated by police with strong support of a local committee representing citizens. When a juvenile is arrested, a panel of police sergeants decides—within 14 days—whether the case is appropriate for a Family Group Conference. If it is, a police sergeant convenes a meeting of relatives of both the juvenile and his or her victims for a thorough airing of the issue. The sergeant has the authority to order restitution, settle the case without further intervention, or refer the juvenile and his or her family for professional counseling or other services. Proponents of the model note that victims almost invariably forgive the offenders.

The Wagga model is praised for its emphasis on community involvement. Furthermore, the model avoids the stigmatizing effect of the formal justice system while still holding juveniles accountable for their actions. Those who object to the net-widening effect of many diversionary programs are also appeased. As Moore (1993, p. 8) has observed, "[T]he Family Group Conference helps to ensure that this narrowing of the net of state control does not produce a dangerous social vacuum. As the net of state control is narrowed, the net of community or civic control is widened."

Although police-sponsored programs such as those mentioned in this section are proliferating, most have not been submitted to rigorous evaluation, particularly with respect to the issue of recidivism. Moreover, the programs vary so widely that an evaluation of one could not be easily generalized to others. Those programs that are less coercive in nature have received the most favorable reviews, however.

INTAKE PROCEDURES

In recent years police nationwide have referred approximately two-thirds of juvenile arrestees to juvenile courts. Additionally, almost all juvenile court delinquency cases reach the court via police referrals. In 1992, for example, law-enforcement referrals accounted for 85 percent of all delinquency cases referred to juvenile courts (Snyder & Sickmund, 1995).

Intake is, for most juveniles, the first step in the juvenile court process. The intake worker is one of the most powerful yet most unstudied individuals in the juvenile justice system. Although there is ample description of the intake worker's role and recommendations for how it should be carried out, we have very little information about the actual intake process. Additionally, courts have given broad discretionary power to intake workers, who are the front-line officials in the juvenile courts.

Intake workers are often associated with juvenile probation offices and may be either probation officers or social workers. Occasionally, the intake function is performed by the prosecutor's office. The state of Washington has led the way in taking this approach, which is more consistent with a justice or due process model than a *parens patriae* model. In Washington, prosecutors make the decision as to whether or not to file a petition of delinquency in all felony cases.

Intake workers in most jurisdictions have the authority to send juveniles back home, refer them informally to community services, detain them, refer them to juvenile court clinics for assessment, refer them to formal diversion programs, or send them forward for court processing, which involves filing a petition alleging delinquency or status offending. Even in this traditional intake model, however, the decision to file a petition must be approved by the prosecutor, who will look not only at the legal sufficiency of the evidence but also at social factors in determining whether to proceed. Intake workers also may make recommendations for treatment plans.

Jurisdictions do not always keep statistics on the percentage of cases referred to juvenile courts that are subsequently petitioned (Feld, 1991). Available data from 1992 indicate that approximately 51 percent of the 1,471,200 delinquency cases processed by the juvenile courts were petitioned (Butts, 1994). Cases that are handled informally at the intake process are said to be "adjusted."

Research on the intake decision-making process, particularly qualitative research, is not widely available, and those studies that have been published have yielded mixed results. Although there is evidence that the seriousness of the offense and the prior record of the juvenile are critical components, there is suspicion that race and social-class variables come into play in the decisions made by intake workers (e.g., Sampson & Laub, 1993).

Rosenbaum and Chesney-Lind (1994), for example, found evidence of both sexism and racial stereotyping in the comments of juvenile intake workers in California and Hawaii in the 1960s and more recently in Hawaii in the 1980s. The researchers found that comments about the girls' appearance—particularly related to their physical maturity or attractiveness—were liberally sprinkled throughout case records prepared by male intake workers, who did 71 percent of the intakes and mentioned appearance in 63 percent of the cases. The physical descriptions were significantly linked to charges of "immorality" but not to more serious offenses. Additionally, it was not unusual to find comments negating the attractiveness of girls of color, such as the following: "S. is a tall pretty Mexican girl whose appearance belies her Mexican heritage" (p. 255).

The researchers also examined more recent data from California Youth Authority files in 1990 and Hawaii Youth Correctional Facility files in 1989. In California only 8 of 214 records mentioned appearance. In Hawaii, however, appearance comments were found regularly in the files of girls, whereas none were found in files of boys.

One may ask, What is the harm of mentioning a juvenile's appearance in a case file? Is it not logical to describe height, weight, body build, eye color, and manner of dress, for example? Consider, however, descriptions that are not neutral observations but subjective appraisals of attractiveness primarily associated with sexuality—as was discovered in the records studied in the preceding paragraphs. Boys are rarely described as being "on the brink of physical maturity" or as dressing "seductively," but these comments are not uncommon in the files of girls. Finally, it is important to recognize the racist tone of descriptions that imply imperfection if juveniles do not conform to white standards of beauty.

Although the foregoing research is limited to a relatively small number of records from two states, Rosenbaum and Chesney-Lind express concern that states which are especially resistant to the deinstitutionalization of status offenders may continue to use suspected sexual behavior as a reason to detain them early in the juvenile justice process or even institutionalize them after they have been adjudicated. In California, which no longer incarcerates girls for noncriminal offenses, the attractiveness and physical maturity statements have all but disappeared from intake files; in Hawaii, where incarceration still persists, the statements remain (p. 259).

Intake workers' subjective appraisals of attractiveness and appearance are rarely studied by contemporary researchers. Neither are the stereotypes of sex, race, and class that may influence individual decisions made by juvenile justice professionals. There is, in fact, a great need for more qualitative research on this issue (Conley, 1994). In light of the powerful position of the intake worker, this issue clearly should be addressed.

In the following sections we will take a closer look at two common decisions made by intake workers, the decision to divert and the decision to detain. In the process of discussing the decision to divert we will review issues and research relating to diversion as both a process and a program in juvenile justice.

FORMAL DIVERSION PROGRAMS

In the 1960s, the labeling perspective in criminology was strong. As described in Chapter 5, sociologists in particular argued strongly that youth who were identified, tagged, and processed through the formal court system were likely to see themselves as deviant and to live up to this label. You may recall that this perspective had its origins in the work of Frank Tannenbaum, whose concept of "dramatization of evil" set the stage for the labeling perspective. According to Tannenbaum (1938, p. 19), "The first dramatization of evil which separates the child from the group for special treatment plays a greater role in making the criminal than any other experience."

Tannenbaum's work was continued in the writings of Howard Becker, Edwin Lemert, Edwin Schur, and other labeling theorists (as introduced in Chapter 5). This theoretical perspective appealed to policymakers during the 1960s. "Most juvenile justice professionals felt that the court would do a better job by focusing on the smaller number of serious juvenile offenders and by developing alternative approaches for youth charged with less serious offenses" (Ezell, 1992). Consequently, the federal government provided funding for communities that were willing to initiate formal diversion programs.

"Juvenile diversion" can be defined in various ways. At the least, diversion involves steering youth away from the formal system. As it most commonly occurs, it also provides alternative programs and services. It is useful, therefore, to make a distinction between the diversion *process* and a diversion *program* (Rutherford & McDermott, 1976). The process—which can occur in a very short span of time—is essentially the decision to steer the youth away from formal processing. Depending on the jurisdiction, this referral decision may be made by police, the intake worker, the prosecutor, or the juvenile court judge. The further along into the system the decision is made, however, the less it represents the "true" diversion process.

Diversion as a *program* offers services to the youth in the hope that intervention will prevent recidivism. It is very rare today to see a diversion process occurring without an accompanying program, but the programs vary widely in the extent and type of services they offer. This variation makes it very difficult to assess their effectiveness.

It should be noted also that diversion ideally should be an option only for juveniles who would otherwise be sent to juvenile court. Some critics charge that it is increasingly used for juveniles who would otherwise have been diverted informally by police, as in the station-house adjustments discussed earlier (Ezell, 1992). This "net-widening" aspect of diversion will be discussed again in this chapter.

Diversion programs are operated under different auspices, including private groups, probation offices, social services, or even the juvenile courts themselves. One typical model involves a board of community volunteers (often including other youths) who interview the youth and decide on what will be required to make amends. Youths under diversion may be required to write letters of apology to their victims, rake leaves in the town park, work to give restitution, provide volunteer tutoring services, enroll in a mediation program (see Box 11.2), tour correctional facilities, or attend week-long boot camps. Some programs also include job training or referral to community agencies for family counseling, group therapy, or substance-abuse treatment. In agreeing to participate in a diversion program the youth admits his or her culpability for the offense charged, signs a contract, and—upon completion of the terms of the contract—is left with no record.

In some jurisdictions, the maximum length of diversion intervention is specified in the statutes. According to a study of diversion programs nationwide (Gensheimer et al., 1986), the median length of intervention was 15 weeks. This study, which was an attempt to distill information garnered from 103 studies on diversion, will be discussed again shortly.

Teen Courts

Over the past decade, many states have begun to experiment with **teen courts**, usually as part of a diversion program. The typical teen court is composed of high school students who serve as a jury in the cases of juveniles charged with first-time, nonviolent offenses. As a rule, teen courts do not serve as triers of fact, deciding on the issue of guilt. Rather they are a "sentencing" tribunal, fashioning an appropriate punishment for a juvenile who has admitted to committing a crimi-

Box 11.2

MEDIATION

Over the past 25 years, we have heard a good deal about the so-called "litigation explosion," referring to the increasingly large number of civil and criminal suits being filed in courts. Juvenile court dockets have steadily increased as well. Numerous commentators have suggested alternative dispute resolution (ADR) as a way of dealing with court overcrowding.

ADR—or mediation, as it is often called—is a voluntary process through which disputants meet with a neutral third party and attempt to arrive at a mutually agreeable solution to an underlying dispute. Thus, for example, rather than go to court over a boundary dispute, two neighbors are urged to work out a peaceful settlement with a trained mediator. Among many advantages, ADR is hailed as being less expensive, less time-consuming, and far more likely to resolve underlying conflicts in a dispute. Participants in ADR programs have reported being more satisfied with the outcome than individuals who have gone through a more formal court process. Thus, victim–offender mediation fits in well with the concept of reparative justice.

In the juvenile justice system, the court mediation programs were almost always associated with diversion. Today it is not uncommon for courts to require mediation as a condition of juvenile probation. In an extensive assessment of juvenile victim–offender mediation programs in four states, which involved observation of mediation sessions as well as 1,153 interviews with victims and offenders, Umbreit and Coates (1993) found that juveniles who participated were significantly more likely to complete restitution than those in comparison groups. Furthermore, victims were significantly more likely to perceive that the justice system was fair. We should keep in mind that mediation appears to work better if the incident is fresh in the minds of the juvenile and the victim, however (Chown & Parham, 1995).

Supporters of mediation programs in juvenile justice maintain that they are an important way of encouraging juveniles who have committed relatively minor offenses to recognize the consequences of their actions. Victims communicate to the offender the extent of their suffering and are encouraged to have meaningful input into the resolution of a case, including restitution or reparation for the wrong done to them. Chown & Parham (1995), who would like to see mediation programs be part of every juvenile court and probation system, propose that these programs be offered to all first-time offenders accused of minor offenses. On the basis of their encouraging assessment of mediation programs, Umbreit and Coates (1993) recommend that they be extended to a wider variety of property crimes as well as to some violent crimes. We must keep in mind, though, that the option to mediate cannot be offered without the consent of the victim. Furthermore, the offender must not be coerced to participate. Overall, Umbreit and Coates did not find coercion to be a significant factor in their study, although there was indication that juveniles in one site had a relatively low rate (71 percent) of voluntary participation.

Mediation programs such as those described here are still the exception rather than the rule, especially in the juvenile context. Critics of the programs fear that both victims and juveniles will be pressured to participate or that, when the participants know one another, the mediators may not have the necessary training to help resolve a serious underlying conflict between them. However, although mediation programs are too few and too new to be given enthusiastic endorsement, the Umbreit and Coates research is encouraging.

nal act. In some jurisdictions, however, an adversarial model is used, whereby a "prosecutor" represents the community and a "defense lawyer" forces the "state" to prove its case beyond a reasonable doubt. A "judge" is the neutral arbiter, and a "jury" decides the defendant's fate.

The recently established teen court in Windsor County, Vermont, gave high school students there an important civics lesson. They proposed a statute, saw it go to a legislative committee, attended hearings on the bill, and saw it passed into law by the state legislature for a three-year tryout. The high school students have now begun to hear the first cases brought to their attention.

Studies of teen courts suggest that rates of recidivism are impressively low compared with rates in traditional juvenile courts (Schiff & Wexler, 1996). The cases themselves, of course, are likely to involve minor offenses, and the teens who agree to go before these courts are probably well motivated to clear their records and move on with their lives. Nonetheless, the approach is so different from that of the traditional juvenile court model controlled by adults that the nature of the teen court itself may have a positive impact.

The teen court model has been hailed as one that is consistent with the concept of "therapeutic jurisprudence" in law. "Therapeutic jurisprudence is a discipline that looks at the therapeutic impact of the law on the various participants involved" (Schiff & Wexler, 1996). According to this perspective, law and legal processes have the potential of being beneficial or helpful without sacrificing due process. The teen court model, while focusing on legal aspects, is also believed to be therapeutic to both young people who serve on the courts and those who appear before them charged with crimes. Most teen courts allow defendants to have input in proposing their own sentences. Schiff and Wexler (1996) suggest that these teens are more likely to perceive the justice system as fair if they participate in making decisions, than if they do not. This perception will encourage them to obey the law in the future.

RESEARCH ON DIVERSION

Formal diversion programs have become so entrenched in the juvenile justice system that it is unlikely they will disappear in the foreseeable future. There is something very appealing about giving first-time juvenile offenders a second chance, together with the guarantee that they will not have a juvenile record if they cooperate with the intervention strategies. Nevertheless, critics object to diversion on many grounds, not the least of which is the wide variation in program requirements. The existing research on the effectiveness of diversion programs provides fuel for these objections.

Labeling

As noted earlier in the chapter, diversion programs first developed as a result of sympathy with the labeling perspective in criminology. It was assumed that juveniles are less likely to re-offend if we avoid the stigma associated with the court process and the tagging of the individual as a delinquent. Studies have indicated, though, that diversion itself "labels" the person in a negative way, at least as perceived by the youth. Elliott, Dunford, and Knowles (1978), for example, found that youth who were diverted perceived high levels of labeling. Additionally, this labeling was perceived whether the diversion program operated through an independent diversion agency or through a court-associated system.

Arnold Binder and Gilbert Geis (1984), strong supporters of diversion, assert that there is no cogent evidence that the label affixed to a youth by the diversion process will have the lasting impact on peers and family that repeat offending and more formalized juvenile justice processing would have. This assumes again, of course, that youth *not* diverted will continue their illegal behavior. Binder and Geis's literature review suggests, however, that there is no evidence that the child's self-concept will suffer irreparable damage from diversion.

Net Widening

Numerous scholars have pointed out that diversion programs expand the reach of the juvenile justice system, bringing more youth under governmental social control (e.g., Klein, 1979; Blomberg, 1983; Saul & Davidson, 1983; Polk, 1984). In other words, rather than steering away youth who would otherwise go to court, diversion pulls in youth whose cases would otherwise be dropped or who would be informally adjusted in other ways, such as through warnings, referrals or police-sponsored programs. Blomberg (1983) has argued that this net widening is likely to have harmful effects because the state focuses its attention on a family without evidence that this attention is really needed.

Research by Ezell (1989) has documented the net-widening effect of diversion. Ezell found that arrested youth were no less likely to be under court supervision when diversion programs are in existence. In other words, the juvenile court was just as likely to have control over arrested youth as it was without a diversion program in the community. More significant, youth who did not successfully complete their diversion program were more likely to be placed on probation and more likely to be sent to a residential program than youth who had not participated in diversion programs.

Binder and Geis (1984), however, believe that widening the net is not necessarily a bad thing. The term "conjures up visions of a mesh net that is thrown over thrashing victims, incapacitating them, as they flail about, desperately seeking to avoid captivity" (Binder & Geis, 1984, p. 315). They argue, instead, that diversion offers a wide variety of services to youth who might not otherwise obtain them. Without diversion, some youths could eventually go deep into the system, ending in long-term confinement. They add that, "Among those redirected [juveniles], at least some would benefit from such services as employment counseling, family counseling, a requirement of restitution, a relationship with a Big Brother or a Big Sister, substance abuse education, or even psychotherapy" (1984, p. 326).

Recidivism

Although there have been studies assessing individual diversion programs, the variances in program approaches allow diversion as a general strategy to elude empirical assessment. Gensheimer et al. (1986), however, have published a helpful meta-analysis of 103 outcome studies on diversion that questions the efficacy of diversion programs. Overall, "diversion interventions produce no strong positive or strong negative effects with youth diverted from the juvenile justice system" (Genshemier et al., 1986, p. 52). Nevertheless, they recommend refining the programs rather than doing away with them. They found, for example, that both age and contact hours were correlated with program effectiveness: The younger the youth, the more successful the intervention; the greater the number of contact hours, the more positive the effect.

Ezell (1992) believes that the debate over whether diversion reduces recidivism asks the wrong question. "A more appropriate question is What alternative works best for which types of youths?" (p. 55). This is the question that we must continually ask when we try to make some sense of the numerous options available to us within the juvenile justice arena.

In the juvenile justice literature, debates over diversion seem to have attenuated. Additionally, research on diversion as a general process has given way to research on specific approaches associated with programs (e.g., mediation, family preservation efforts, peer counseling). This is a good thing, because it helps us to answer the question Ezell (1992) posed in the preceding paragraph: "What alternative works best for which types of youths?"

A complicating factor in this research relates to the timing of the program. A mediation program, for example, may be offered as an alternative to the formal court process (true diversion) or in conjunction with juvenile probation after the youth has been adjudicated delinquent. We cannot assess the effectiveness of mediation as a diversion program unless outcomes on diversion clients are separated from outcomes on post-adjudicated delinquents.

Important questions remain about diversion as a process. There is still concern that formal diversion programs are more likely to be offered to nonminority youths. Ezell (1992) also notes that questions such as who works with the diverted youth, what are their credentials and training, and what theoretical rationale guides the intervention they receive still need to be addressed.

THE DECISION TO DETAIN

The term "juvenile detention" is very widely used to refer to any form of residential placement for juveniles, both before and after an adjudication of delinquency. Technically (and as it will be used here), however, detention is a *temporary* disposition pending further court proceedings, and the decision to detain a juvenile is made early in the process. A juvenile detention center, therefore, is the equivalent of an adult detention center or jail (although adult jails also hold persons who have been convicted of misdemeanors or are awaiting sentencing after a felony conviction).

The initial decision to detain a juvenile may be made by an intake worker, who traditionally is a juvenile probation officer. Law-enforcement officials may also detain a youth in police or sheriff's lockups, which are temporary holding facilities maintained on department premises. Surprisingly, recent figures suggest that on a typical day 750 juveniles, or 1 in 10 juvenile arrestees, were placed in lockups (Snyder & Sickmund, 1995). All states require that a youth's detention be reviewed by a juvenile court judge or magistrate within a few days, and generally within 24 hours. In the juvenile system, detention is intended to be both protective and preventive in nature, meaning that it is intended to protect juveniles from harm and prevent them from being involved in further delinquent activity. As we will note shortly, conditions in many detention centers nationwide raise questions about the protective nature of detention.

Detention itself may be both secure and nonsecure. A juvenile may be "detained" in a nonsecure group home or private home and yet be able to attend school in the community on a daily basis. Home detention, sometimes accompanied by electronic monitoring, may also be available. Youth in secure detention are kept within a locked facility under the presumably close supervision of juvenile workers. For our purposes, we will focus on this secure detention, which has received the most research attention.

Most juveniles are not detained. From 1988 through 1992, for example, approximately 20 percent of all delinquency cases involved secure detention. In terms of raw numbers, however, the number of youth detained has consistently increased, from 237,200 in 1988 to 296,100 in 1992. A one-day count of juveniles in detention centers on February 15, 1991, found nearly 19,000 in public detention centers. Nearly half of these youth were held in 4 states: California, Florida, Michigan, and Ohio. The great majority (95 percent) of detained youth were charged with delinquency offenses, but 3 percent were status offenders and 2 percent were non-offenders. The great majority of status offenders held in detention were charged with violating court orders (42 percent of all status offenders) or running away (32 percent). Property offense cases have the lowest likelihood of detention and, interestingly, drug cases have the greatest likelihood of detention. The average number of days juveniles are held in secure detention has increased steadily, reaching 2 weeks in 1990.

The decision to keep a juvenile in detention may have numerous consequences. Studies have found that detention per se has a negative effect on the disposition of the case (e.g. McCarthy, 1987; Feld, 1989). In other words, controlling for other factors, juveniles who were kept in detention received more restrictive dispositions than those who were not.

Thomas Grisso and his colleagues (Grisso, Tomkins, & Casey, 1988), reviewed standard criteria for detention across the United States and found that the great majority of states allow detention (1) for juveniles' protection, (2) if they are likely to flee, or (3) if they are a danger to the community. They found that one of more of these 3 standards was in the juvenile codes of 43 states. Other standards for continuing detention were less frequent in the statutes. These included the unavailability of adequate supervision in the community or a juvenile's own request for protection. With just a few exceptions, most states did not give examples of the type of information to be considered in making the decision to detain.

The decision to detain based on the youth's alleged danger to the community involves making a **risk assessment**, or engaging in a procedure for estimating the probability that the juvenile will commit another offense. Such predictions of offending may be clinical or actuarial. Clinical predictions are based on a decision maker's subjective interpretation of the situation and may or may not include an interview with the individual. Actuarial predictions—often referred to as "objective risk assessments"—are based on demonstrated statistical relationships between a characteristic and an outcome. For example, a history of violence is a good predictor of future violence.

Because there is a long line of research supporting the accuracy of actuarial predictions over clinical predictions, the former are widely recommended, and most jurisdictions today have **risk-assessment scales** for use by decision makers. These scales represent probabilities and are no guarantee that a particular individual will fit into the group prediction. Therefore, intake workers, as well as other decision makers in the juvenile process, may be tempted to make clinical prediction, based on their judgment. Additionally, some workers resist "check-list decision-making," which allows a form to be filled in simply from the paperwork in the file, without any need to meet the individual. Unfortunately, however, subjective judgments may lead to discriminatory outcomes.

Over the past decade, researchers have also brought considerable attention to gender, racial, and geographical differences in detention. For example, although boys are more likely than girls to be detained for property offenses, girls are significantly more likely than boys to be detained for status offenses (such as running away from home, truancy, or curfew violations) and for contempt of court (Federle & Chesney-Lind, 1992). (Recall that holding a juvenile in contempt for disobeying a court order was one way "around" the DSO mandate of the JJDPA, discussed in Chapter 10.)

Research on ethnic and racial differences in detention also uncovers disturbing trends. Increasingly, minority youth constitute greater percentages of the population in public detention facilities. In the late 1980s, they made up about 55 percent of the population (Federle & Chesney-Lind, 1992). By the mid-1990s, white youth were less likely to be detained than African American youth or youth of other ethnic/racial groups. One-fourth of all delinquency cases involving African American juveniles resulted in detention, compared with 22 percent of those involving other ethnic/racial groups and 18 percent of those involving white youth. African American youth were nearly twice as likely as other youth to be detained for drug offenses (47 percent, compared with 19 percent for other ethnic/racial groups and 26 percent for whites).

Edmund McGarrell (1993) analyzed trends in juvenile detention in 17 states by comparing cases of white and nonwhite juveniles processed in 1985 and 1989. He found a 41.5 percent increase in the number of nonwhite detentions at the same time that there was a 12.6 percent decrease in the detention of white youths. Detentions for drug-related offenses were especially noticeable. The increases in nonwhite detentions also exceeded what would be expected by an increase in referrals to juvenile court, which McGarrell also found. McGarrell also notes that the trends he uncovered were not universal, with a significant minority of the counties he studied not experiencing the increase in nonwhite detention. He recommends that these atypical counties be compared with those that have experienced increases to learn why these differences might exist.

Robert Sampson and his colleagues have done extensive work on macrolevel variables associated with juvenile justice processing (e.g., Sampson, 1986a; Sampson & Laub, 1993; Sampson & Wilson, 1993). Of particular note is the interaction between racial inequality and underclass poverty. In a study of 538,000 case records representing 6,000 youths aged 10 to 17 in 21 states, Sampson and Laub (1993) found that African American youth living in urban poverty were more likely to get secure detention and out-of-home placement for crimes against persons, property crimes, and drug offenses than were white youth for comparable offenses.

The increase in secure detention of minority youth cannot be simply explained by a greater likelihood of their being involved in juvenile crime. In the 1980s, as Federle and Chesney-Lind (1992) point out, "[a]rrest rates for serious crimes among white and minority youth [were] quite stable, with minorities accounting for about 30 percent of total index arrests." Sampson and Laub (1993) note that, although rates of drug violations prior to the 1980s were about equal for African American and white juveniles, African American arrest rates for drug offenses increased markedly during the 1980s. The perception that minorities are, thus, more dangerous contributes to a greater likelihood of secure detention.

Sampson and Laub stress that their research is preliminary, particularly because possible differences in the organizational structure of the juvenile courts in their sample were not taken into consideration. Nevertheless, the results are disturbing enough to support their call for careful consideration of the macrolevel variables that affect living conditions in the inner cities, which have become repositories for the economically disadvantaged. Community stereotypes of minorities (e.g., the young African American male dealing drugs in the inner city) lead to a desire for more social control by the juvenile justice system. Differences in juvenile justice processing of African Americans and whites, then, may well be explained by differences in community perceptions of being threatened by minority populations.

Schall v. Martin

The only U.S. Supreme Court case on juvenile detention can be interpreted as a "loss for juveniles" but a victory for the doctrine of *parens patriae*. In *Schall v. Martin* (1984) the Court upheld a New York statute allowing the preventive detention of juveniles if there was a serious possibility that they would be involved in *any* crime, felony or misdemeanor, before their next court appearance. Although this suggests a societal-protection rationale, it has been justified as being in the juvenile's best interest or for her or his protection. As a result of that case, we know, for example, that—unless the law in the state says otherwise—a youth charged with shoplifting can be held in secure detention if the court is concerned that he or she will commit any other crime before the next court appearance. This is clearly a very different approach from the one taken with adults, who are granted bail or released on their own recognizance for minor offenses.

Schall v. Martin began as a class-action suit brought by juveniles being held at Spofford, a secure detention facility in New York City. They alleged that they were denied equal protection of the law because the statute allowed their detention, even for minor offenses, whereas adults charged with the same offenses would have the benefit of bail. The average length of stay at the time was 17 days.

Conditions at Spofford during the late 1970s and early 1980s have been described as "disorganized, demoralized, deteriorating, and chaotic" (Soler, 1992, p. 139). The three Justices who dissented in the Supreme Court case noted that numerous studies of Spofford attested to its "unsavory characteristics." They also noted that, because juveniles are impressionable, the experience of detention for them might be more injurious than pretrial detention for adults. "[A]ll too quickly juveniles subjected to preventive detention come to see society at large as hostile and oppressive and to regard themselves as irremediably 'delinquent.'" In a footnote, the dissenters noted that one of the youths had been arrested for enticing others to play three-card monte, behavior that did not come under the provisions of the penal law. He had been detained at Spofford for five days, after which the petition against him was dismissed.

The Justices in the majority, however, indicated that there were adequate procedural protections for youths prior to being placed at Spofford and that the remedy for bad conditions was not to release juveniles into the community but to fix the conditions. Preventive detention was justified, the justices said, to protect society from the crimes juveniles who are at large might commit and to protect the juveniles themselves from the "downward spiral of criminal activity into which peer pressure may lead [them]."

Interestingly, conditions at Spofford dramatically improved in the late 1980s under the leadership of Ellen Schall, who became commissioner of the New York Department of Juvenile Justice in 1983, and Rose Washington, who became director of Spofford itself. Today, juveniles entering Spofford are assigned caseworkers immediately. They receive comprehensive needs assessments and individualized plans for services both while in the facility and in aftercare, if the children and families want these services (Soler, 1992). Nevertheless, it is important to keep in mind that juveniles and adults are treated very differently with respect to preventive detention. Adults are eligible for pretrial release unless they are found dangerous by clear and convincing evidence; in most jurisdictions, dangerousness is presumed if the crime allegedly committed was a capital offense. Preventive detention for juveniles, on the other hand, has been allowed, both to protect the community from *any* crime, not necessarily violent ones, and to protect juveniles from themselves or from the influence of peers.

Conditions in detention centers across the United States have been the subject of numerous lawsuits. The one-day count in 1991 indicated that 53 percent of detention center residents were in facilities operating above their design capacity. Additionally, 30 percent of the juveniles were held in undersized rooms, as defined by the accreditation standards of the American Correctional Association (Snyder & Sickmund, 1995).

In one noteworthy lawsuit, youths detained at the Broward County Regional Juvenile Detention Center in Fort Lauderdale, Florida, filed a class-action suit challenging the conditions of their care. They cited inadequate physical and psychological safety, unsanitary and dangerous physical conditions, and abusive punishment, including the inappropriate use of isolation. They also argued that they were denied medical and psychological care and appropriate education and programming.

Dale and Sanniti (1993) reviewed the genesis and results of this class-action suit. They note that within 3 years after a consent decree was signed, conditions in the detention center had improved significantly, chiefly because the population had decreased from 147 youths (in a facility with capacity for 109 beds) to 67. Children charged with serious or repeat offenses were still held in secure detention, but alternative nonsecure placements had been found for those charged with lesser felonies or misdemeanors. The overuse of detention and the reluctance on the part of many states to look for less secure alternatives is a problem that litigation may be required to solve.

DETENTION PROGRAMS

The programs offered to juveniles in detention facilities have received considerable attention in the literature. Although youths are not technically there for "rehabilitation" (because they have not been adjudicated delinquent), it is hoped that their days will be spent doing more than avoiding altercations with others and watching television. The most documented problem with detention nationwide is the lack of ongoing educational and recreational programs. Health services, however, are also of growing concern.

The OJJDP has used six criteria to determine whether adequate health services are available to juveniles in confinement. They are as follows:

1. Initial health screening within one hour of admission.
2. Complete health appraisal for juveniles held more than seven days.
3. Information on access to health services provided during orientation.
4. Appropriate number of "sick calls" per week, allowing juveniles to bring medical problems to the attention of health-care staff.
5. Written arrangements for emergency health care.
6. Staff training in first aid and CPR.

Although most juveniles seem to be held in facilities that provide basic health services, just under half (48 percent) of all detainees were in facilities that met all six criteria (Snyder & Sickmund, 1995).

Several writers have pointed to the need for health education with regard to HIV transmission, AIDS, and sexually transmitted diseases. The typical juvenile held in a detention facility is sexually active, but he or she is not likely to have information about prevention. In 1988, the American Correctional Association conducted a survey of juvenile correctional facilities that included 29 detention centers. One-third provided no information about AIDS or HIV.

In a pilot project carried out in the Alabama juvenile correctional system, Mark Lanier and Belinda McCarthy (1989) discovered that although knowledge about HIV and AIDS was widespread, almost 80 percent of the youths questioned did not feel that they were at high risk of becoming infected. Moreover, despite the fact that the youths reported that they took precautions, only one-half of those who were sexually active reported the regular use of condoms. Youths 14 and under were the least knowledgeable and least likely to think they should take preventive measures. After an education program was initiated, participants had more accurate knowledge about HIV-infection and AIDS than youths who did not receive the instruction and were more likely to report that they would take precautions with respect to sexual activity and intravenous drug use.

There are many reasons why detention programming is not always considered a priority in juvenile corrections. Detention, by definition, is temporary. The short length of stay (two weeks on average) discourages officials from implementing educational or counseling programs. Furthermore, the date of a youth's release from detention is unpredictable; the next court appearance could mean freedom or a less restrictive setting. Many detention centers are overcrowded and understaffed. The juveniles themselves, particularly those who are experiencing their first stay in a detention center, are confused, frightened, and often withdrawn, uncooperative, or displaying a false bravado. Despite these obstacles, some detention facilities do offer juveniles health, educational, and recreational services. Considering the positive results AIDS education programs have had, it is wise, cost-effective, and compassionate to offer them to youths in detention facilities.

JUVENILES IN ADULT JAILS

A discussion of juvenile detention is incomplete without consideration of the special issue of juveniles who are detained in adult facilities. You may recall that the JJDPA of 1974 sought to separate juveniles from adults by sight and sound. In 1980, when it became apparent that "sight and sound" separation often relegated juveniles to highly substandard quarters, Congress mandated total removal. The 1980 amendment required that by 1988 there would no longer be any juveniles held in adult jails. Arguing that costs were prohibitive, however, states successfully obtained extensions to the deadline mandating removal of all juveniles from adult jails.

In the 1980s and '90s, the problem of juveniles' being housed in adult jails remains an issue. Even though some progress has been made, 100 percent removal has never been achieved. Between 1986 and 1993, for example, the one-day count of juveniles held in adult jails more than doubled, from 1,708 to 4,300 (Maguire &

Pastore, 1995). These figures included only juveniles who were so defined by a state's statutes, however. In 1994, when the definition was changed to include all persons under age 18 held in jails, the one-day count jumped to 6,725. Still omitted from these data—collected from an annual survey of inmates in local jails—are 5 states with a combined jail/prison system. The figures also do not include short-term lockups or state-administered (as opposed to locally administered) jails. It should also be noted that a one-day count does not indicate the number of juveniles who are affected by this practice in a given year.

The issue of juveniles in adult prisons is a bit different, and the statistics are more difficult to obtain. First, only juveniles tried as adults would be eligible to go to adult prisons. These juveniles, if convicted, are often sent to juvenile facilities until they reach the statutory age of adulthood, when they are then transferred to adult prisons. Critics of this practice argue that any rehabilitative gains made in the juvenile institution are lost upon transfer to the adult facility.

Some states, however, do imprison juveniles tried as adults in adult prisons. Under federal law, they must be separated from adult offenders by sight and sound until they reach the statutory age of adulthood in that state. This often involves keeping juveniles in protective custody, where they are less likely to benefit from programs designed for rehabilitative purposes. We will return to a discussion of this issue in the following chapter.

To the many critics of the practice of holding juveniles in adult jails, the fact that they are held for short periods of time only does not detract from its unacceptability. We have had graphic and horrible descriptions of the physical and emotional victimization that can occur to both girls and boys in an adult jails (Schwartz, 1989; Chesney-Lind, 1988). Youths in adult jails are eight times more likely to commit suicide than youths in juvenile detention centers. Schwartz (1989, p. 79) noted that, although a substantial number of juveniles are jailed because of lack of alternatives, "most are jailed for convenience, 'to get their attention,' or 'to teach them a lesson.'" Additionally, they have often been accused of minor crimes.

Today, many states prohibit the confinement of juveniles in adult facilities, including police lockups. Even so, a six-hour grace period allowing the temporary holding of juveniles is usually available to allow arrangements to be made. Furthermore, there continues to be resistance to the jail removal mandates. Beger (1996) suggests that minors in rural areas often are detained in jails and adult lockups even though state and federal regulations prohibit the practice. Like other child advocates, Beger notes that lack of secure and nonsecure facilities, which is often cited as the reason, is no excuse for holding a juvenile in an adult jail. Alternatives such as home detention, crisis foster care, and emergency shelter care can meet the needs of many youths who might otherwise be kept in a secure detention facility. For those youths who *need* secure detention, transportation to secure juvenile facilities should be provided.

On the political front, the jail removal issue is high on the agenda. In 1996 two bills were introduced in Congress easing the requirement on states to house juveniles separately. In keeping with the current trend against "coddling" juveniles, supporters of the bills argued that states should be allowed to hold juveniles, particularly violent offenders, in adult facilities (both jails and prisons) if they are deemed in need of these restrictive placements. One of the bills, introduced by Florida Republican Representative Bill McCollum, would also dismantle the OJJDP and replace it with a new Office of Juvenile Crime Control. A spokesperson for President Bill Clinton said that the administration would like to keep the principle of separation but recognizes the high costs of building separate facilities for juveniles. The administration appears ready to allow juveniles to be kept in separate wings, sharing such facilities as gyms and cafeterias, as long as they are used by adults and juveniles at different times and the sight and sound separation is met (Butterfield, 1996).

SUMMARY AND CONCLUSIONS

The early stages of the juvenile justice process involve numerous decisions that have serious consequences for young offenders. As we have seen, adults at every phase of this early process have considerable leeway in applying their judgment to the situation at hand. Police officers in their decision to arrest determine whether a youth will be brought into the system. Approximately one-third of these arrests, however, are not referred to the juvenile court but instead are handled informally within the department.

Over the past decade, police-initiated preventive programs directed at youths have burgeoned. Juvenile units now exist in virtually every large police department, and even departments of only 25 and 30 officers may have a juvenile officer. These special police officers focus on the needs of youth in their community, visit schools, and plan a variety of preventive programs targeting youths who have become involved in crime or are believed to be at risk for offending.

Although law-enforcement agencies are increasingly recognizing the need to sponsor such programs, we must recognize that criminal investigation is still a critical function of police. Juveniles are not immune to being interrogated or searched by police. The U.S. Supreme Court has ruled that juveniles require no "special" *Miranda* rights and do not have a constitutional right to see anyone other than a lawyer prior to in-custody interrogation. Many departments today will not allow juveniles to be interrogated before parents or guardians are notified. Even so, it is common for juveniles to waive their right against self-incrimination. Children's-rights advocates have criticized this practice, suggesting that neither the parents nor the juveniles themselves may understand the consequences of these waivers.

Juvenile court intake workers wield consider power in the system, particularly given that their decisions are seldom scrutinized. In many jurisdictions, intake is a function of the probation office. Intake workers have a wide variety of options, including warnings, referrals to community agencies, diversion, informal probation, or filing a petition of delinquency or status offending. Approximately half of all cases that come to the attention of intake workers result in petitions. In most jurisdictions, the intake worker also makes the initial detention decision.

The diversion process and diversion programs are well entrenched in virtually every state, despite criticisms that they widen the net of social control unnecessarily, are not significantly less stigmatizing than the juvenile court process, and do not significantly reduce recidivism. Supporters of diversion argue that some youths are helped and that it has the advantage of not leaving the juvenile with a juvenile court record.

The secure detention of juveniles early in the juvenile justice process is an area that has attracted extensive commentary, research, and legal challenges. Although only about 20 percent of all youth who come to the attention of the juvenile justice system are detained, the numbers themselves are rising and the length of stay in detention centers is increasing. Researchers have documented disturbing trends in the use of detention for female status offenders and for nonwhite youths, particularly those charged with drug-related offenses. The war on drugs, as several researchers have noted, has disproportionately targeted minority youths. Although it is important to take jurisdictional differences into account, many detention centers nationwide are overcrowded and understaffed and are housing youths under conditions that are harmful to their health and safety.

The problem of juveniles held in adult jails has attenuated but has not been solved. Although OJJDP reports indicate that states have made significant progress in this area, most states continue to allow the practice in "exceptional" circumstances and for a limited period of time. Children's-rights advocates argue, however, that even a six-hour placement in an adult facility is unacceptable, even though the juvenile may be awaiting an initial court appearance and may be separated from adults by sight and sound. Legislation directed at loosening the jail removal mandate has surfaced over the past few years, in keeping with a punitive stance toward juvenile offenders.

The early stages of the juvenile justice process involve critical decisions on the part of many different adults. The informality of these stages, particularly with respect to the law-enforcement officer and intake workers, encourages broad discretion not subjected to public scrutiny. Even if we grant that discretion is usually exercised to the benefit of the juvenile and society, some research suggests that racial and ethnic minorities and the economically disadvantaged may not benefit from favorable discretionary decisions. It is important, therefore, that researchers continue to focus attention on these early stages of the juvenile justice process.

KEY CONCEPTS

arrest	formal diversion
take into custody	labeling
waiver of rights	dramatization of evil
community policing	net widening
DARE	teen courts
station-house adjustment	therapeutic jurisprudence
family preservation models	detention
intake	risk-needs assessment

12

Delinquency Hearings and Criminal Trials

The early stages of the juvenile process described in the preceding chapter screen out more than half of all juvenile offenders who come into contact with police. Rather than referring all juveniles to intake, for example, police officers employ a range of measures that include warnings, referrals to community agencies, or "station-house adjustments." Approximately half of the cases reaching the intake stage result in the filing of a delinquency petition (Snyder & Sickmund, 1995).

Although many commentators are highly critical of the juvenile justice system, Thomas Bernard (1992) argues cogently that the system is not a failure. You may recall Bernard's dichotomy of "naïve risk-takers" and "rational calculators," discussed in Chapter 10. According to Bernard (1992, p. 170), "the function of the juvenile justice system should be to communicate that actions have consequences. Such communication should involve the minimum consequences possible." He suggests that this communication occur through an escalating series of "threats," "eye-openers or convincer punishments," and "coerced treatments." The adult participants in the process—police officers, intake workers, juvenile judges, and probation officers, for example—use this approach, particularly with naïve risk takers, who constitute the great majority of juvenile offenders.

To illustrate Bernard's model, an intake worker may send a youth home with a warning (threat) to him and to parents that another contact will not be so palatable. A second appearance before the intake worker may result in referral to a diversion program, where the youth will be expected to fulfill some contractual obligation, such as the performance of community service work or apology to his victim (eye opener). The third appearance at intake may lead the intake officer to file a petition of delinquency (coerced treatment).

Prior to the intake worker's communication, the youth will have been given similar communications by law-enforcement officers. Except in high-profile, serious cases, therefore, a youth's appearance before a juvenile court on a petition of delinquency is most likely to happen after screening-out efforts early in the process have apparently failed to communicate the importance of obeying the law. As the juvenile judge enters the case, he or she also applies the escalating series.

Bernard is not suggesting that every adult in the system applies every type of communication to every juvenile. Rather, these mechanisms of communication are available and are routinely used by adults at their discretion. Furthermore, "[f]ew juveniles go through all stages. A juvenile whose first offense is very serious might be waived to criminal court despite having no prior records. A juvenile who commits many trivial offenses might be handled entirely by police officers and never be referred to juvenile court" (p. 172).

FIGURE 12.1   The juvenile justice "funnel"

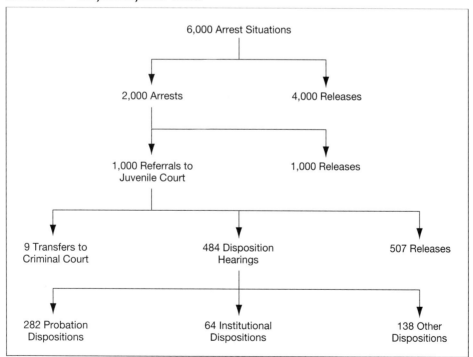

SOURCE: From *The Cycle of Juvenile Justice* by Thomas Bernard. Copyright © 1991 by Thomas Bernard. Used by permission of Oxford University Press, Inc.

Bernard sees this as a highly successful method of handling the large majority of juveniles with whom the system deals. He offers a "juvenile justice funnel" (see Figure 12.1) to demonstrate. Of 6,000 arrest situations, the only "failures" of the system are represented by 9 transfers to criminal court and 64 institutional dispositions, which is a better than 96 percent success rate. Even counting the 282 probation dispositions as failures, the system has an 82 percent success rate.

Bernard believes that perceptions of a weak or failing juvenile justice system can be explained by the tendency to focus on the failures, rather than on the successes who have been processed through the system at earlier stages. Convinced by research that crime peaks at age 16 or 17 and then declines rapidly, Bernard also argues that youthful offenders will not go on to become adult criminals. "Given this widespread agreement [about the relationship between crime and age], we can confidently expect that most juveniles who were involved in the juvenile justice system do not become further involved in the adult system" (Bernard, 1992, p. 175).

With Bernard's ideas as a backdrop, we will focus in this chapter on the two main avenues that lead a youth to adjudication. The first, and by far the more common, is the filing of a petition alleging that a youth has committed a delinquent act or is in need of supervision as a status offender. The second avenue involves a waiver of the juvenile court's jurisdiction and leads youths to criminal, rather than juvenile, court.

PETITIONS OF DELINQUENCY AND STATUS OFFENDING

In most states, delinquency and status offender petitions are initiated by intake workers (who are usually probation officers) and reviewed by the prosecutor. The delinquency petition is the equivalent of a prosecutor's information or charges in an adult case. It outlines the behaviors allegedly committed by the youth and the relevant sections of the statute that were violated. A small minority of states, led by Washington, have adopted a "justice model" whereby prosecutors, rather than intake workers, file petitions in felony cases.

Youths may be adjudicated delinquent either after admitting to the charges or after a judge finds sufficient evidence to prove beyond a reasonable doubt that the youth has indeed committed them. Note that juveniles do not have a constitutional right to a trial by jury in juvenile court, although approximately ten states do allow jury trials in delinquency proceedings.

In 1992, juvenile courts formally processed 743,700 delinquency cases, representing a 31 percent increase since 1988. Fifty-seven percent of these cases resulted in an adjudication of delinquency. (All figures relating to the processing of juveniles are taken from Snyder and Sickmund, 1995.)

The delinquency petitions indicated gender and race differences. Girls were charged in only 15 percent of delinquency cases. As will be noted shortly, girls were far more likely to appear in the status offender processing. African Americans were formally processed at more than three times the rate for white and other-race juveniles. Specifically, juvenile courts processed 66 delinquency petitions for every 1,000 African American juveniles age 10 or above, whereas the white rate was 21 and the rate for youth of other races was 20.

Status offense caseloads for juvenile courts in 1992 were much smaller, constituting approximately 10 percent of all juvenile court cases. The number of status offender cases, 97,000, represented an 18 percent increase over a 5-year period, however. More specifically, running away increased by 31 percent, truancy by 21 percent, and status liquor by 15 percent. Cases alleging "ungovernability" declined by 22 percent.

The historical trend of girls' being disproportionately overrepresented in the status offender category and underrepresented in the delinquency category has continued. Although girls were charged in only 15 percent of the delinquency cases, they were processed by the juvenile courts in 42 percent of the status offense cases. Running away represented the most disproportionate category, with girls accounting for 62 percent of all the cases.

As in the delinquency processing, racial differences in status offender processing are also evident. Although the overall differences were not major, there were substantial racial differences in specific offenses. The runaway, truancy, and ungovernability cases involving African American juveniles doubled those involving white juveniles, for example. Liquor violations for white juveniles were three times as high as for African American juveniles. Liquor violations involve the purchase or possession of alcohol by minors.

Just over half of all status offender cases (56 percent) resulted in an adjudication, or judicial determination that the juvenile was indeed a status offender. The majority of these juveniles (65 percent) were placed on probation, but 17 percent were removed from their homes. About 15 percent of the cases resulted in sanctions such as fines, restitution, or community service. This last group of status offenders consisted primarily of juveniles involved in liquor violations.

THE JUVENILE COURT HEARING

As we discussed in Chapter 10, the U.S. Supreme Court in 1967 made it clear that juveniles had important constitutional rights in delinquency hearings (*In re Gault,* 1967). These rights included the right to written notification of the charges against them, to be represented by an attorney, to be protected from self-incrimination, to call witnesses on their behalf, and to confront witnesses against them. It is important to note that the Supreme Court did *not* give these protections to status offenders. Even today, "[m]any procedural safeguards that delinquent youths receive are denied to those charged with noncriminal misconduct" (Feld, 1992, p. 63).

Even in light of the JJDPA mandate that status offenders be deinstitutionalized, juvenile courts are still able to remove them from their homes, as happened to 17 percent of the status offenders processed in 1992 (Snyder & Sickmund, 1995). Nonsecure placements can be very restrictive, however. Placements in group homes, wilderness camps, foster homes, and ranches, for example, certainly limit a juvenile's freedom, despite good intentions on the part of adults who have recommended or made these placements. For these reasons, if juvenile courts are to retain jurisdiction over status offenders, these juveniles should be afforded constitutional protections similar to those afforded juveniles charged with delinquency.

Delinquency proceedings themselves have raised questions, however. Barry Feld (1992) argues that the *Gault* decision has led to a "criminalizing" of the juvenile court, which he defines as a primarily punitive orientation toward juveniles. He notes that the delinquency proceeding has been contracted, omitting the "soft" or status offense cases and the "hard" or serious cases that are transferred to the adult criminal courts. The former, because they do not come under the requirements of *Gault*, continue to be processed informally. The transferred cases provide the juveniles with identical due process protections as given to adults. The juveniles who remain on the court's delinquency caseloads are presumably given procedural justice. Feld notes, though, that "[a]lthough theoretically the formal procedural safeguards of juvenile courts closely resemble those of criminal courts, in reality the quality of justice routinely afforded juveniles is far lower than the minimum insisted upon for adults" (1992, p. 60).

In part this happens because the delinquency hearing retains an aura of informality in most jurisdictions. Juveniles do not have the constitutional right to trial by jury (*McKeiver v. Pennsylvania*, 1971). The U.S. Supreme Court in *McKeiver* expressed the belief that jurors would formalize the juvenile court process too much, rendering it virtually identical to that of the criminal court. Furthermore, delinquency hearings are closed to the public, presumably to protect youth from the glare of publicity. Closed courtrooms, however, have the disadvantage of not allowing the press or the public to be informed and to observe possible miscarriages of justice.

Juveniles do, of course, have the constitutional right to be represented by an attorney in delinquency proceedings. Research has consistently demonstrated, however, that fewer than half of all youths are represented by lawyers in juvenile courts (Coleman & Guthrie, 1984; Feld, 1984, 1992). Orlando and Crippen (1992) note that counsel is not routinely provided, even to juveniles who are at high risk of secure institutionalization. Like many critics of the juvenile court process, Orlando and Crippen believe that the lack of legal protections and the disparities observed within and across jurisdictions make this a "dangerous system" for juveniles. They note that even the euphemistic language used prevents observers from obtaining accurate perceptions of what occurs. "Confinement is commonly called 'treatment' or 'shelter care.' . . . Training school confinement blocks are called 'cottages.' . . . Solitary confinement is called 'quiet time.' This modern double-speak explains many of the problems of the juvenile court, and it defeats reformers who are satisfied with words of promise from those who support its authority" (p. 96).

Interestingly, some research has indicated that juveniles who are not represented by lawyers may receive less punitive dispositions than those who are (e.g., Feld, 1989). In a study of legal representation in six states, Feld found evidence suggesting that juvenile judges may be sympathetic to juveniles who appear before them without the assistance of counsel. Nevertheless, juveniles at risk of institutionalization did not benefit from this apparent leniency.

JUVENILE COURT JUDGES

Throughout the history of the juvenile court, juvenile court judges have been idealized as wise, caring individuals who had the best interest of the juveniles in mind when they rendered their decisions. Recall the discussion of Judge Ben Lindsey in Chapter 10, whose energy, personality, and courtroom demeanor won him many admirers and few detractors. Despite growing evidence that many juvenile court judges were not happy with their assignment, untrained, or despotic (Rothman, 1980), their courtroom remained their domain, and their decisions were rarely questioned. Until the 1960s, in fact, it was unusual to have either a prosecutor or a defense lawyer in juvenile court; the judge essentially assumed these roles (Emerson, 1969).

The Supreme Court's decisions in *Kent v. U.S.* (1966) and *In re Gault* (1967) encouraged more scrutiny of juvenile judges. With the recognition of the constitutional rights of juveniles in delinquency proceedings, prosecutors and defense lawyers have assumed expanded roles in juvenile court, although there is no constitutional requirement that a juvenile be represented by a lawyer if he or she waives that right. Similarly, as we discussed in Chapter 11, juveniles can and do commonly waive their right to have a lawyer present during custodial interrogation.

In the juvenile court system, the judge's basic role traditionally has been to assure that decisions are made "in the child's best interest." As we described in Chapter 10, this "best interest" standard, which goes hand in hand with the court's *parens patriae* role, invited widespread discretion and decisions that often abrogated the legal rights of juveniles. Juvenile courts today are still expected to make decisions "in the child's best interest," but they are increasingly being required to protect the constitutional rights of the child and his or her family and to consider the welfare of the community as well (Grisso & Melton, 1987).

Many juvenile court judges nationwide are represented by the National Council of Juvenile and Family Court Judges, an organization that offers training to juvenile court judges and disseminates information to its members about issues in juvenile justice. The Council is also a powerful lobbying group in Congress and in some state legislatures. It successfully convinced Congress to pass the 1980 amendment to the JJDPA that allowed them to hold status offenders in contempt of court if they violated a valid court order. The Council also has come out strongly in favor of mediation programs in the juvenile justice context.

Individual juvenile court judges do not often speak out on issues related to their profession. One notable exception is Judge Theodore Rubin (1985a, 1985b, 1989), who has argued vehemently that the juvenile justice system must try to meet the needs of all youths, even those whom Bernard (1992) would call "rational calculators." He has questioned the wisdom of keeping status offenders under the jurisdiction of juvenile courts, however. Rubin has described in rich detail the experience of being a juvenile court judge and has been one of the most consistent judicial voices for the compassionate and due process–oriented treatment of juvenile offenders. We will revisit Judge Rubin's views later in the chapter when we discuss the waiver process.

More recently, Judge Judith Sheindlin has received extensive media attention as a result of her book *Don't Pee on My Leg and Tell Me It's Raining* (1996). The title aptly captures Judge Sheindlin's no-nonsense approach to juveniles. As one who has served on the bench for nearly a quarter of a century, she recites a familiar refrain that the system is "too easy" on juveniles and should hold them accountable for the bad choices they make. Sheindlin also indicts parents for their failure to meet their responsibilities toward their children.

An occasional hint of sympathy appears in her work. She recounts, for example, the tale of a girl whom she placed on probation. The probation officer helped the girl find an apartment. The judge contributed furniture that had been stored in her own basement. It is her get-tough stance, however, that predominates. She is particularly critical of entitlements (although she certainly would resist the term):

> I have seen so many programs that are society's giveaways: housing, welfare, special education, free medical care, free transportation, adoption subsidies, social security disability for alcoholics and drug addictions. The list is endless, and the results have not produced a more responsible or productive population. There may be a few isolated success stories paraded by the media, but the whole picture does not justify the billions spent by taxpayers. (p. 234)

Judge Scheindlen advocates charging individuals for public defenders and charging parents with the cost of their children's incarceration. She is also very critical of "kinship foster care," a system that pays adults for caring for the dependent children of their relatives.

We include Judge Scheindlen's views in some detail here because they represent a perspective that is very different from that presented thus far in this text. Although Judge Sheindlin doubtless has the support of many members of the public who believe that the justice system in general is too soft on offenders, no research evidence suggests that a "tough" style has a lasting, positive influence on juveniles and their families. Recall, also, the results of the first national public opinion survey on juvenile crime described at the end of Chapter 10, which suggest that "the public's views about the juvenile crime problem and what should be done about it are relatively enlightened, compassionate, and probably more cost-effective than existing policies or policies being enacted in most states" (Schwartz, 1992, p. 225).

Although juvenile court judges do make the critical adjudication decisions in delinquency proceedings, it would be a mistake to overlook the influence of other individuals on the judges' decisions. These include prosecuting and defense attorneys, court-appointed guardians, intake and probation officers, social workers, and mental-health professionals. As Thomas Grisso and Gary Melton (1987, p. 150) have noted, "many decisions about children in the juvenile justice system are not merely judicial decisions, but 'juvenile court' decisions involving many non-judicial personnel." Grisso and Melton were making the point that in order for research on child development to be disseminated widely, these groups must be informed about the research along with juvenile court judges.

JUSTICE BY GEOGRAPHY

A growing body of research in recent years documents differences in the processing of juveniles across jurisdictions (e.g., Schwartz, 1992). As a result of this research, it is clear that saying juvenile courts today are therapeutically "*parens patriae* oriented," legalistically "due process oriented," or "punitive" is too simplistic. The latest national report on juvenile offenders and victims, for example, indicates that juvenile courts in rural areas process cases very differently from the way courts in urban areas do (Snyder & Sickmund, 1995).

Stapleton, Aday, and Ito (1982) conducted a mail and telephone survey of 150 metropolitan juvenile courts across the United States (obtaining data on 130) in an effort to study variations in structure and procedure. They suspected that contradictions in past research, particularly involving race and social-class variables, might be explained by measurable differences among the courts. They were able to identify a typology of 12 different "clusters" of metropolitan courts. The predominant cluster, cluster 1, comprised 32 courts. These courts: (1) had jurisdiction over status offenders; (2) had broad control over probation, detention, and restitution services along with other juvenile court functions; (3) were informal; (4) rarely involved prosecutors; and (5) gave strong discretion to intake officers, although the court still maintained control over the intake process. According to the researchers, "Cluster 1 courts may be said to approximate the traditional juvenile court described in the literature. The court is all-inclusive; it *is* the juvenile justice system" (p. 557). Only 14 courts (in cluster 8) were characterized as highly formal. In 38 courts (clusters 7, 8, and 9), the prosecutor's role was far more salient, and probation was administered by probation services rather than by the court.

Although we have not reviewed all of the clusters, the reader should discern that variations among the courts may well affect decision making, outcomes, or even "success," however it is measured. As Stapleton et al. note, research on juvenile courts that does not consider differences in structure and process is extremely limited in value. The 12 typologies they have identified should be helpful to future researchers studying outcomes and determinants of decision making in juvenile courts.

Barry Feld (1991) used a similar approach to study differences in juvenile court processing among urban, suburban, and rural courts in Minnesota. Feld studied the cases of 17,195 juveniles who reached the juvenile court under petitions of delinquency or status offending. The study did not include those who had been referred to juvenile court intake but had been diverted or otherwise disposed of without filing.

Feld's research indicates that a juvenile's place of residence may well determine the harshness of the juvenile justice system's response. Although juveniles were more likely to be represented by lawyers in urban courts, they also received the toughest sentences. This occurred even when controlling for prior record and the offense itself. In an earlier study (1989), Feld found similar differences between juveniles with and without lawyers during their delinquency proceedings.

The Minnesota study revealed interesting interactions between geography and gender as well. Rural courts were lenient on sentencing compared with urban and suburban courts, but girls received more severe dispositions than boys. There were no significant gender differences in sentencing patterns in the other two types of courts. Rural courts also focused attention heavily on status offenders, hence the probable explanation, given that girls have historically been charged more than boys with status offenses. Suburban courts focused more on juveniles charged with felonies. Urban courts, which dealt with a great diversity of offenses, had a higher proportion of status offenses and minor crimes, interestingly, than rural or suburban courts. They made greater use of detention and also were more likely to intervene early in the life of the juvenile than were suburban and rural courts.

The importance of factoring in geography when discussing the operation of the juvenile courts cannot be overemphasized. It is clear from Feld's research that urban courts are more formalized and punitive than rural courts, which seem to maintain informality and a more individualized justice. This individualized type of justice, however, may also connote a double standard between girls and boys, with girls treated with more severity. The informality of rural courts also may represent a disadvantage to the juvenile nonresident who appears before them. Scholars who have studied rural courts (e.g., Fetter, 1977; Fahnestock, 1990) discuss the fact that judges, defense attorneys, prosecutors, defendants, and victims often know one another quite well. This may be to the advantage of local juveniles, particularly if the community feels a collective responsibility for the actions of its children, but those who are unknown in the area may be looked upon with distrust (Beger, 1996).

In Feld's study, suburban courts were almost as formal as urban courts, but they tended to be more like the rural court in their individualized approach to juvenile justice. They also were most likely to focus on serious offenders, screening out of the court process status offenders and misdemeanants.

CLINICAL ASSESSMENT

From the early days of the juvenile courts, clinicians have been closely associated with the juvenile justice process. Recall the work of William Healey, whose clinic furnished juvenile courts in Boston with lengthy reports on juveniles' backgrounds, mental abilities, emotional adjustment, and prospects for rehabilitation. This attempt to bring psychological understanding to juvenile behavior has continued, and in most juvenile courts it has retained a pivotal role. Grisso (1984) studied juvenile courts in 127 large jurisdictions and learned that almost one-third employed full-time mental-health professionals to perform psychological evaluations. "Millions of dollars are spent by juvenile courts for traditional psychological and social assessment of delinquent youths each year in the hope of providing the court with information to determine the most appropriate and individualized dispositional alternative" (Niarhos & Routh, 1992).

Courts traditionally have received little guidance on how to use clinical assessments (Grisso, 1986), and some have suggested that these assessments are of limited use. A high correlation between a clinician's recommendations and final court dispositions does not necessarily mean that the court is taking the advice of the clinician; it may simply mean that the clinician is a good predictor of court dispositions.

A good illustration of this is a study by Niarhos and Routh (1992) that examined the cases of 234 male juveniles evaluated by a juvenile court mental-health clinic in Florida. The researchers were studying the relationship between clinical assessment and (1) the court's disposition and (2) subsequent recidivism. The clinic staff gathered extensive data on the juveniles, including demographic variables, offense-related information, school records, associations with peers, parent information, evidence of behavioral disorders, and psychological functioning in such areas as self-control and capacity to form interpersonal relationships.

Niarhos and Routh learned that the offender's past criminal behavior was the most significant factor predicting court disposition. Also significant were the seriousness of the crime and whether or not the juvenile had been in detention prior to the delinquency hearing. The recommendation of the clinician also correlated highly with the final outcome. The researchers also found that recidivism was predicted most significantly by the same legal variable, the number of prior arrests, and not by psychological variables. The impact of the assessment report, Niarhos and Routh concluded, was "minimal."

Thomas Grisso has done extensive research on the topic of a wide range of clinical assessments for courts (e.g., Grisso, 1986). A theme of Grisso's work is to encourage clinicians to avoid a surplus of irrelevant information and to hone in on specific material that will be the most helpful. In one such study (Grisso, Tomkins, & Casey, 1988), for example, the researchers tried to identify factors that were relevant to the detention decision, the decision to transfer or waive a youth to criminal court, and the disposition decision. One of the most critical uses of clinical assessment is in making the waiver decision, which is discussed in the next section.

WAIVERS TO CRIMINAL COURT

In most states, juvenile courts have jurisdiction over all juveniles in the state under age 18. In 8 states (Georgia, Illinois, Louisiana, Massachusetts, Michigan, Missouri, South Carolina, and Texas) the age cut-off is 17, and in four states (New York, Connecticut, North Carolina, and Vermont) the cutoff is 16 (Snyder & Sickmund, 1995). In the past decade, however, states have allowed the transfer of increasingly more juveniles to criminal courts. The first national survey of public opinion on juvenile offending (Schwartz, 1992) indicated that the public is supportive of having serious offenders handled by criminal courts.

Virtually every state allows juveniles to be tried as adults, at least for some crimes. A growing number of states are *mandating* that those 14 and older who are charged with violent offenses be tried in criminal courts. These moves are intended to see that juveniles considered threats to public safety are subjected to the more punitive adult system, wherein defendants are held accountable for their actions. The waiver of jurisdiction is an extremely consequential action, one that " . . . strips individuals of the allegedly protective status of 'juvenile' and subjects them to the punitive force of the adult criminal justice system" (Bortner, 1986, p. 53).

The issue of relegating juvenile cases to criminal courts is hotly debated in the juvenile justice literature. After a description of the waiver process and a review of some recent statistics in this area, we will review the arguments on both sides of this issue.

WAIVER PROCESS

There are three avenues for transferring juvenile offenders to the adult criminal justice process. The first, the **judicial waiver** of jurisdiction, involves case-by-case decisions by the juvenile court judge, weighing a variety of factors including the nature of the crime and the juvenile's potential for treatment. **Legislative waivers** are laws allowing (and sometimes mandating) that juveniles of specified ages accused of certain serious offenses be tried as adults in criminal court. In many states, however, criminal court judges are allowed to transfer these cases back to juvenile courts. Legislative waivers are sometimes called statutory exclusions or waivers by statute. A third option is the **prosecutorial waiver**, by which the prosecutor is given the discretion to decide in which court a petition or case shall be filed.

Reverse waivers, by which a case begins in criminal court and the judge transfers it to juvenile court, are less frequent. Also less frequent are cases in which juveniles (through their lawyers) are allowed to certify themselves to criminal courts, a process called a **demand waiver**. A 15-year-old accused of robbery, for example, may prefer to take his chances with a jury, which might acquit him, or with a criminal court judge, who might place him on probation, rather than with a juvenile court where he may be sent to a juvenile facility until the age of 18 or, in some cases, 21.

In federal courts, the minimum age at which juveniles can be prosecuted has been lowered from 16 to 15. They may be prosecuted for any felony involving violence or for certain drug offenses. Furthermore, transfer is mandatory, if the government requests it, for youths who repeat serious crimes. As noted earlier, however, the federal government prefers not to deal with juvenile offenders and not infrequently waives its own jurisdiction to the states.

Judicial waiver appears to be the most common method by which juvenile cases are heard in criminal courts. Increasingly, more youths are being moved into the adult system by legislative or prosecutorial waiver, however (Snyder, Sickmund, & Poe-Yamagata, 1996). In a study prepared for Congress by the General Accounting Office (GAO), researchers were unable to obtain data on the numbers of juveniles appearing in criminal court via avenues other than judicial waivers (GAO, 1995). We know, therefore, that the legislative waivers are popular with state legislators, but we do not know how many criminal court cases are the result of this option.

You may recall from Chapter 10 that a case involving judicial waivers reached the U.S. Supreme Court in 1966. In *Kent v. U.S.*, a federal judge had made the decision to transfer Morris Kent's case to criminal court over the objections of the defense attorney and without granting the juvenile a hearing to allow him to challenge the transfer.

The Court made it clear that the waiver decision should not be taken lightly. The lower court's denial of a hearing violated Kent's Fifth Amendment right to due process of law; failure to rule on his attorney's motions to challenge the waiver in a hearing and to allow access to his social service records violated his Sixth Amendment right to the adequate assistance of counsel.

In an appendix to its decision, the Court gave judges guidelines for making the waiver decision. The Justices noted that the following eight factors should be considered before a youth is transferred to criminal court. Champion and Mays (1991, p. 62) have summarized them as follows:

1. The seriousness of the alleged offense to the community and whether the protection of the community requires waiver;

2. Whether the alleged offense was committed in an aggressive, violent, premeditated, or willful manner;

3. Whether the alleged offense was against persons or against property, greater weight being given to offenses against persons, especially if personal injury resulted;

4. The prosecutive merit of the complaint—that is, whether there is evidence upon which a grand jury may be expected to return an indictment;

5. The desirability of trial and disposition of the entire offense in one court when the juvenile's associates in the alleged offense are adults;

6. The sophistication and maturity of the juvenile by consideration of [his or her] home, environmental situation, emotional attitude, and pattern of living.

7. The record and previous history of the juvenile, including previous contacts with . . . law-enforcement agencies, juvenile courts and other jurisdictions, prior periods of probation . . . or prior commitments to juvenile institutions;

8. The prospects for adequate protection of the public and the likelihood of reasonable rehabilitation of the juvenile (if found to have committed the alleged offense) by the use of procedures, services, and facilities currently available to the juvenile court.

Champion and Mays note that the foregoing factors may be divided into two broad considerations: danger to the public and amenability to treatment. Both assume that, to some extent, predictability is possible. That is, they assume that the juvenile judges and/or the adults who have influence on their decisions (e.g., clinicians or probation officers) will be able to ascertain the likelihood of future offending.

Partly as a result of *Kent v. U.S.*, judicial waivers of jurisdiction are often accompanied by hearings, called "bindover," "transfer," certification," or "waiver" hearings. In cases involving serious crimes, and where it is presumed that a youth has much to lose by being tried in criminal court, these hearings can be very extensive. They may involve testimony and cross-examination of witnesses for both the defense and prosecution.

STATISTICS ON WAIVERS

The National Center for Juvenile Justice has published a report that includes valuable statistics on juvenile waivers (Snyder, Sickmund, & Poe-Yamagata, 1996). Between 1989 and 1993, the number of cases judicially waived to criminal court increased 41 percent. According to the researchers, this increase in judicial transfers cannot be explained simply by an increase in juvenile court caseloads. During the same period, offenses by juveniles against persons increased by 58 percent while transfers of juveniles charged with these crimes increased by 115 percent. Likewise, public order cases (e.g., public intoxication or disturbing the peace) increased 37 percent, whereas while public order transfers increased 75 percent. Interestingly, drug cases increased 15 percent, but drug cases judicially transferred declined 11 percent.

Snyder et al. suggest that the increases in transfers could be attributed to a number of factors, none of which as of yet are supported or refuted by empirical evidence. The factors include perceived increases in the level of violence, perceived declines in the amenability of youths for treatment, increase in the willingness of juvenile courts to transfer, a decline in available treatment options within the juvenile justice system, and an expansion of the pool of juveniles eligible for transfer. The last possibility relates to legislation across the country that allows transfer of more and more juvenile offenders.

In a study sponsored by the Government Accounting Office (GAO, 1995), researchers took a close look at data from six states and found some gender and race differences in the judicial waiver decision. Controlling for other factors, those most likely to be transferred were older male juveniles with prior referrals to juvenile court. In four of the six states, African Americans were more likely to be transferred than whites.

In apparent contradiction of Feld's research (1991), a breakdown of metropolitan and nonmetropolitan cases revealed few consistent differences. When faced with these contradictions, we are reminded of the work of Stapleton, Aday, and Ito (1982), which suggests that a closer look at the structure and process of different courts is warranted. If the courts were classified according to the clusters those researchers identified, it might be possible to discover some metropolitan courts that differed significantly from nonmetropolitan ones in the waiver decision, as well as in other outcomes.

WHO GETS TRANSFERRED?

Snyder, Sickmund, and Poe-Yamagata (1996) report data on the most serious offense of judicially waived cases in 1993. Offenses against persons accounted for 42 percent of the waivers, followed by property offenses (38 percent), drug offenses (10 percent), and public order offenses (9 percent). It should not be assumed, then, that only violent juveniles get sent to criminal court, or even that violent juveniles make up a majority of those transferred. Legislative waivers cover a broad range of juvenile offenses. With reference to judicial waivers, courts are encouraged to consider the age of the youth, the availability of treatment in the juvenile system, and protection of the community, among other things. Additionally, the youth's own attitude toward treatment may be factored into the decision. The type of crime committed by the juvenile may be less important than the other factors, depending upon the weight given to each by the presiding judge and influence by others in the juvenile court.

After an extensive review of the research on transfers, Champion and Mays (1991) have concluded that juvenile transferees fall into four distinct groups: the "bad," the "mad," the uncooperative, and those who have nothing else to lose. The "bad" are the most dangerous or persistent offenders, for whom the transfer process was originally intended. The "mad" are youths who are both delinquent and mentally disordered. Because states lack treatment resources for these delinquents, they may prefer to transfer them to adult justice systems where treatment may be more readily available. Those in the uncooperative group could be helped in the juvenile justice system, but they refuse to be. As Champion and Mays remark, the transfer action "often occurs from a sense of frustration, or in order to 'teach those kids a lesson'" (p. 75).

The juveniles who have nothing to lose are those who are persistent but minor property offenders. Members of this group are likely to be treated with leniency in adult courts, because they "look good" compared with the adult offenders. Although there is research evidence to support this leniency (e.g., Sagatun, McCollum, & Edwards, 1985), the most recent data indicate that we cannot assume it will occur. We will return to this issue shortly, when we discuss outcomes of the transfer process.

Champion and Mays ask us to consider whether the juveniles who get transferred might not actually be the ones who need the most help from the juvenile justice system. In similar fashion, juvenile court Judge Theodore Rubin (1989) has challenged the juvenile justice system to retain jurisdiction over all youth. Rubin maintains that a commitment to finding creative alternatives for juvenile offenders would reverse the trend toward increasing the numbers of juveniles being dealt with in the adult system. Specifically, he suggests eight alternatives: intensive probation supervision, expanded work programs, special school programs, full-day school and work programs, school combined with adventure programs, short-term secure residential placements, specialized foster homes combined with an alternative school, and long-term residential programs.

OUTCOMES OF THE WAIVER PROCESS

Some research has indicated that transfer to criminal court leads to more lenient sentencing for juveniles. M. A. Bortner (1986), for example, found that only about 30 percent of a sample of 214 "serious" delinquents transferred to adult courts were convicted and imprisoned. Slightly more than half (55 percent) of these transferees had been charged with felonies against persons; the remainder were charged with property felonies or drug offenses. This leniency assumption has been challenged by other studies, however.

There is some evidence of harsher treatment in criminal court, however. Rudman et al. (1986) studied 117 violent youths transferred to adult criminal courts in Boston, Newark, Phoenix, and Memphis. They found that more than 90 percent of the transferred violent youth were convicted, that criminal court sanctions were more severe than we would expect from juvenile court, and that 90 percent of those convicted were incarcerated—72.6 percent in prisons, 17.7 percent in jails. *Prisons* are for convicted felons. *Jails* are for people detained temporarily before trial and people convicted of misdemeanors.

The national report (Snyder & Sickmund, 1995) notes that transfer may increase the length of confinement for some of the most serious offenders, but the majority of transferred juveniles receive sentences comparable to sanctions already available in the juvenile justice system. Likewise, in a recent essay on society's retributive response to juvenile violence, Thomas Grisso (1996) notes that "for serious offenses, conviction rates and severity of sentencing in criminal courts are about the same for adolescents as for adults" (p. 231).

The GAO report cited above (GAO, 1995), looked at criminal court data from six states and found that conviction rates ranged widely (32 to 100 percent for serious violent offenses, 26 to 97 percent for serious property offenses, 27 to 100 percent for drug cases). Likewise, incarceration rates differed (e.g., 14 to 98 percent for serious violent crimes).

ARGUMENTS AGAINST WAIVERS

Researchers and commentators who oppose transferring juvenile cases to criminal courts generally concede that transfers may be appropriate in some cases. However, they argue that for the great majority of juveniles, even those charged with violent offenses, transfer is inappropriate. Particularly objectionable are the automatic or legislative transfers, where the decision is made based on the age of the offender and type of offense rather than on the individual's likelihood of rehabilitation.

Grisso (1996) points out that these automatic transfer provisions immediately subject the youth to the glare of publicity that accompanies criminal court proceedings. This is suffered, he notes, "not only by antisocial youths, but also by those who are not guilty of the alleged offense and those who are vulnerable by way of mental disorders or developmental disabilities" (p. 231).

In a discussion of the robust body of research on decision making among adolescents, Grisso notes that adolescent decision making is qualitatively different from adult decision making under conditions of heightened emotion. "Especially relevant when considering delinquent populations are special sources of negative emotion and stress that are said to influence adolescents differently than adults because of their social developmental status" (p. 234). He notes that adolescents as a group seem to be at a greater risk of making maladaptive choices, although he cautions that this decision making research is still evolving.

More clear-cut, however, is research documenting the widespread diversity among juveniles, including juveniles involved in violent offenses. Recall the work of Terrie Moffitt and her colleagues (Moffitt, 1993a; 1993b; 1994), who have identified life-course-persistent (LCP) delinquents (whose offending began early and has persisted over many years) and adolescence-limited (AL) delinquents (who begin in adolescence and whose offending desists). Grisso contends that automatic transfers based on a youth's age or alleged offense are unwarranted, given the differential rehabilitative prognosis of these groups. We will return to this issue shortly when we focus on juveniles who kill.

Finally, Grisso expresses concern about the possible mental disorder experienced by adolescents charged with serious crimes. Such disorders are particularly difficult to identify in adolescents, because of the confounding aspects of the normal turmoils associated with adolescent development. He notes that a mental disorder is more likely to be uncovered during the individualized and rehabilitation-oriented juvenile court process than the criminal process.

There is also concern about the effect of imprisonment on juveniles. In most states, a juvenile tried in criminal court and sentenced to incarceration would not be sent to an adult prison until he or she reached the age of adulthood in that state. He or she will be kept in a secure juvenile facility, where rehabilitation is an important goal. Any gains made in the juvenile facility, however, may be lost upon transfer to the adult prison. Young offenders in adult facilities are notoriously problematic for prison administrators. One study of juveniles in adult prisons, for example, found them to be twice as likely as adult offenders to need protective custody and to be disciplinary problems. They were significantly less likely to be involved in job-training programs and to earn "good time" toward release (McShane & Williams, 1989).

A DIFFERENT VIEW

Sanborn (1994) takes issue with much of the literature objecting to juveniles' being waived to criminal courts. This literature, he argues, fails to recognize that some juveniles are "beyond rehabilitation." He believes that treatment resources are wasted on this group of juveniles and that the juvenile justice system lacks the intensive resources needed for their care. In addition, these hard-core juveniles may contaminate others, thereby frustrating the other juveniles' chances of rehabilitation.

Sanborn conducted a study in which he held open-ended interviews with 100 juvenile workers in three juvenile courts. He found widespread support for the waiver option, with 88 percent of his sample saying that the juvenile court needed the certification option. However, more than three-fourths (77.3 percent) indicated that some juveniles were beyond rehabilitation. The professionals interviewed were not harsh in their outlook toward juveniles, however, and they wanted the waiver decision to be made carefully, preferably by a judge rather than by the prosecutor.

Sanborn, like Feld (1991), found jurisdictional differences in the likelihood of transfers. They were virtually nonexistent in the rural court; there were significantly more drug cases transferred in the suburban court; and the urban court was rife with political struggle, with the prosecutor wishing to maintain control over the waiver decision.

Sanborn's study is limited in that it covered only three courts, but it raises interesting questions about the support for the waiver decision among juvenile justice workers. Although Sanborn's respondents indicated that they supported waivers for the most heinous of crimes or under limited circumstances, they also reported the actual waiver decision as being arbitrary, too inconsistent, and too likely to be used as a plea bargaining tool. In that sense, therefore, the study confirms the problems identified in the literature to date about the process of waiving juveniles to adult courts.

Juvenile court Judge Theodore Rubin (1989) takes issue with the increasing tendency to waive juveniles to criminal courts. He suggests that waived juveniles are often precisely those who need the most help from a specialized rehabilitative system. Rubin suggests a wide variety of alternatives that should be considered rather than giving over the jurisdiction of juveniles to criminal courts. Among these alternatives are intensive community supervision, day reporting programs, specialized treatment programs for serious juvenile offenders, alternative school placements, and wilderness experiences.

It may be true that a small percentage of juveniles are "beyond rehabilitation," at least insofar as the juvenile justice system can offer it. It seems foolhardy to waste resources, particularly if this impedes the rehabilitation of those youths who can benefit from the wide variety of programming options offered to juveniles. However, we still face the prospect of misidentification, particularly in giving up on those juveniles who are deemed "hopeless." The fact remains that an increasing number of juveniles today seem to be inappropriately transferred to criminal courts.

SPECIAL ISSUE: JUVENILES WHO KILL

It is clear that there is considerable diversity among juveniles who are convicted of murder (Ewing, 1990). Nevertheless, juveniles who commit murder are often treated as a unified group in state statutes. For example, the trend today is to mandate criminal court jurisdiction for juveniles charged with murder, and states that do not have this automatic waiver provision at least allow the transfer, in some cases as young as age ten.

Traditionally, researchers have studied juveniles who kill as a part of the larger group of violent juvenile offenders, on the premise that what began as a robbery or an aggravated assault can end in a homicide. A significant body of research has begun to focus exclusively on youths who kill in an attempt to identify distinctive categories, however.

Three distinct types of juvenile murderers have emerged from the literature (e.g., Cornell, 1990; Toupin, 1993; Grisso, 1996). The first type comprises juveniles who kill during other crimes, such as a robbery or a rape. The second type comprises those who kill during an interpersonal conflict, such as an altercation between a parent and a child or a "turf war" among members of rival gangs. The third type involves mentally disordered juveniles, specifically those who are under the influence of psychosis. Most juvenile murderers appear to fall about evenly divided between the first two categories, with only a small percentage in the psychotic category (Cornell, 1990). Grisso (1996) observes, however, that even so, a long line of research supports the conclusion that "many youths who commit murders suffer from nonpsychotic disorders, including depression, neurological disorders, and neurotic forms of character disorders" (p. 236). Researchers also have discovered that a substantial proportion of youths convicted of murder had no prior juvenile or criminal court record. In Cornell's study (1990), this was true of one-third of the sample.

As noted earlier in the chapter, automatic waiver statutes do not take into account the wide diversity among juveniles charged with murders. Can we assume that judges in criminal courts will take this diversity into account in making a sentencing decision? In 19 jurisdictions, judges are expected to abide by sentencing guidelines, which discourage individualized sentencing. Guidelines focus primarily on the seriousness of the offense and the prior record of the offender. Automatic waiver provisions also do not take into account promising programs being developed that deal with the rehabilitation of even serious, violent juvenile offenders (e.g., Hengeller, Melton, & Smith, 1992).

THE DEATH PENALTY FOR JUVENILES

Cries for a tougher stance on juvenile crime are often accompanied by assertions that juveniles should be treated exactly like adults, including imposing the death penalty for murder. In the 1980s, the U.S. Supreme Court issued four decisions directly relating to the age at which juveniles could be sentenced to death. Taken as a whole, the decisions place limitations on the identical treatment of juveniles and adults with respect to capital punishment.

Supreme Court Decisions

The U.S. Supreme Court has ruled on the issue of capital punishment for juveniles in four landmark cases: *Eddings v. Oklahoma* (1982), *Thompson v. Oklahoma* (1988), *Stanford v. Kentucky* (1989), and *Wilkins v. Missouri* (1989). Because *Stanford* and

Wilkins were companion cases, with the decisions issued concurrently, we will treat them as one here. Each of the four cases presented questions about the age at which juveniles could receive the death penalty, but in one of the cases, *Eddings*, the Court did not treat age as a critical issue.

Monty Lee Eddings and a few friends ran away from home in a car owned by Eddings's older brother. In the car were rifles stolen from Eddings's father. When an Oklahoma State Highway Patrol officer stopped the car, the 16-year-old Eddings stuck a shotgun out the window and killed him. Eddings's case was waived to criminal court by prosecutorial motion and he was tried, convicted, and sentenced to death. The sentencing judge considered his age a mitigating factor, but not his unhappy childhood and emotional disturbance.

Eddings's lawyers and a number of interested parties who submitted *amicus curiae* briefs to the Court urged the justices to rule that sentencing to death someone who was 16 years old at the time of the offense constituted "cruel and unusual punishment." In fact, the briefs argued that the line should be drawn at 18. The U.S. Supreme Court did not directly address the age issue, however. Instead, it noted that the judge should have treated the offender's dysfunctional background as a mitigating factor. (In death penalty cases, before the sentence of death is actually imposed, the judge or jury must weigh mitigating factors; in most states, they must also find at least one aggravating factor.) The Court's silence on the age issue allowed states to execute if an offender was 16 at the time of the offense, if they wished to do so.

Thompson v. Oklahoma was decided by the Court in 1988. Here, a 15-year-old had been convicted of killing his former brother-in-law, who had been suspected of abusing his (the 15-year-old's) sister. The youth, William Wayne Thompson, had disclosed to his mother his intention to kill the victim. The case was transferred to criminal court under legislative waiver. The sentencing judge considered, among other things, the mitigating factor of his age (15) and the aggravating factor of the heinousness of the crime. (Thompson had shot the victim twice in the head, placed him in a river, and had slit his throat, abdomen, and chest "so the fish could eat his body.") Thompson was sentenced to death.

The U.S. Supreme Court used this case to draw the line below which a youth could not be sentenced to death, concluding that "the Eighth and Fourteenth Amendments prohibit the execution of person who was under 16 years of age at the time of the offense." There was still the question, however, of whether the execution of a *16-year-old* was permissible, because the Court had not addressed that in *Eddings*.

The *Stanford* and *Wilkins* cases, decided in 1989, involved a 17-year-old and a 16-year-old, respectively. Kevin Stanford and an accomplice robbed a gas station and repeatedly raped, sodomized, and finally shot to death the woman who was on duty. Heath Wilkins robbed a convenience store, also with an accomplice, and repeatedly stabbed the clerk while she begged unsuccessfully for her life. Both were sentenced to death by judges.

The U.S. Supreme Court, with two dissenting votes, upheld the death sentences, a decision that effectively set the line at age 16. In other words, once a person has reached his or her sixteenth birthday at the time of the crime, a state is free to impose the death penalty as long as other constitutional requirements are met. If a person commits a capital offense prior to that time, however, imposition of the death penalty amounts to "cruel and unusual punishment" in violation of the Eighth Amendment of the Constitution.

Both survey and experimental research indicate that the public is ambivalent in its support of the death penalty for juveniles. Whereas current public support for the death penalty as a general concept is strong, that support decreases when the issue of juveniles is raised (Bohm, 1991).

Finkel et al. (1994) conducted two experiments with subjects who were **death qualified**. (A death-qualified person is someone who is not so opposed to the death penalty that he or she would be unable to find a defendant guilty or sentence the person to death.) Subjects were given research booklets that included detailed descriptions of cases whose facts closely resembled the facts in the four Supreme Court cases just discussed. The researchers varied the ages of the perpetrator, from 13 to 25. The first experiment was done with 85 undergraduates, 47 females and 38 males. In the second experiment both undergraduates and 174 nonstudent adults were used.

The results of both experiments indicated significant age effects relating to the offenders. Between 65 and 75 percent of the "jurors" refused to impose the death penalty on the 13 to 15 or the 16 to 18 age groups, whereas they did impose it on the 25-year-old perpetrator. In the second experiment, the jurors were given the option of life without parole, but that option made no difference.

Finkel et al. concluded from the experiment that the public is not ready for the "man-sized" punishment of the death penalty for persons who commit their crimes—even egregious crimes—-as juveniles. Although the jurors were more likely to find a juvenile responsible when the facts of the case were particularly vicious and the defendant directly committed the murder (as opposed to being an accomplice), the great majority of these jurors, who were philosophically in favor of the death penalty, stopped short of imposing the death sentence.

The death penalty issue involves a very small proportion of all juveniles transferred to criminal courts. With the Supreme Court's placement of age restrictions, it becomes increasingly difficult to argue that a 16-year-old should be given favorable treatment over an 18-year-old simply on the basis of age. As noted previously, public support for the death penalty does seem to waver when juveniles are involved (Bohm, 1991). Nevertheless, opponents of the death penalty for juveniles today are also likely to be those who oppose the death penalty as a general policy.

SUMMARY AND CONCLUSIONS

More than 25 years ago the U.S. Supreme Court began to issue decisions that observers predicted would have a revolutionary effect on the juvenile justice process. Both *Kent v. U.S.* (1966) and *In re Gault* (1967) marked the beginning of due process protections in the juvenile court, specifically in transfer and delinquency proceedings. Juvenile-rights advocates, however, suggest that the spirit of each of these decisions has not been honored by the juvenile courts.

Despite the procedural protections offered in *Gault*, for example, fewer than one-half of all juveniles are represented by lawyers in delinquency proceedings. Although some research suggests that they gain more lenient dispositions when not represented, the most serious offenders do not benefit from this leniency. Additionally, juveniles who appear before judges on status offender petitions are not afforded the same due process protections as those who appear in delinquency petitions. Considering the fact that recent research indicates nearly 20 percent of status offenders are removed from their homes, the lack of due process is questionable.

Early in the chapter we discussed the work of Bernard (1992,) who argues that the juvenile justice system is working if we consider the many cases that are successfully screened out early in the process. Although Bernard's point is well taken, the fact remains that the system's "failures," or those youths who are transferred to criminal courts or are institutionalized, deserve our attention. Specifically, we must ask whether the process, even if well intended, served these juveniles in a fair manner. Historians have consistently documented the harms done by persons with good intentions. The absence of lawyers in juvenile court has led some critics to suggest that the system itself should be abolished in favor of one that is virtually identical to the adult system.

The waiver process, whereby juveniles are transferred to criminal courts, was discussed extensively in this chapter. Judicial waiver decisions are accompanied by the procedural safeguards that require judges to conduct hearings and encourage them to weigh a variety of factors. Legislative and prosecutorial waivers are under no such requirements, however. Although prosecutorial waivers do allow individualized decisions, the prosecutor is allowed the discretion to decide where the juvenile's case will be heard. Legislative waivers involve an automatic decision that does not take into account the many developmental differences among adolescents and their decision-making processes. Even in states in which reverse waivers are possible, criminal court judges are reluctant to transfer juveniles to the juvenile court, perhaps in deference to state legislators.

Juvenile waivers are increasing in number and in types of offenses. Critics of this phenomenon argue that the system is giving up too easily on the juvenile offenders who are most in need of its help. They note that the wide range of alternatives available for the rehabilitation of juveniles is not adequately explored.

The chapter ended with a discussion of the special issue of juveniles who kill. It is common for these juveniles to be automatically waived to criminal courts, particularly from the age of 14 and up. If convicted, these are the youths who are most likely to be sent to adult prisons—if not immediately, then when they reach the age of adulthood in their respective states. Research indicates that young offenders in adult prisons, regardless of the nature of their crime, are particularly likely to be disruptive or to need protective custody, and they are particularly unlikely to be involved in work and training programs or gain "good time" toward early release.

The Supreme Court has placed an age limit on the imposition of capital punishment for those who committed murder. In *Stanford v. Kentucky*, the Court ruled that it was cruel and unusual punishment to execute someone who was 15 years old at the time of his crime. This decision appears to be in keeping with public opinion on this issue, as both public-opinion surveys and experimental research indicate the public is not strongly in support of capital punishment for young offenders.

KEY CONCEPTS

threats/eye-openers/convincer
   punishments
delinquency petition
due process at delinquency hearing
justice by geography
clinical assessments
legislative waivers
judicial waivers

prosecutorial waivers
reverse waivers
demand waivers
protective custody
death-qualified juries
public opinion on juvenile death penalty
Kent waiver guidelines

13

Juvenile Rehabilitation: Community and Institutional Strategies

The juvenile justice system rests on two assumptions. The first is that juveniles are accountable for their offenses, but not as accountable as adults considering their age and developmental differences. Second, juveniles are more likely to be rehabilitated than adults, presumably because their behavior is not as entrenched. In recent years these assumptions have been questioned, however. Hirschi and Gottfredson (1993, p. 262), for example, argue cogently that distinctions based on age are arbitrary and "probably cause more trouble than they are worth." In a provocative essay, Hirschi and Gottfredson assert that one model of justice should be used for all offenders: specifically, the model that favors less incarceration and less procedural formality but demands accountability of all offenders, regardless of their age. Some adults, they say, are just as deserving of the leniency associated with the juvenile system as are some juveniles; on the other hand, some juveniles are just as deserving of harsh punishment as are some adults.

Hirschi and Gottfredson, along with many other critics of the juvenile justice system, are skeptical of its ability to rehabilitate juveniles through elaborate treatment efforts. More importantly, they are skeptical of the *need* to rehabilitate the great majority of delinquents who desist from criminal activity in late adolescence or shortly thereafter. In effect, the juvenile justice system does indeed operate this way. That is, at the early stages of the juvenile justice process, rehabilitation is not necessarily a consideration. If we accept Bernard's (1992) comment that adolescence is a time for acting wild and crazy, we can state with confidence that most juveniles will stop offending. The system of threats, eye-openers, and coerced treatment applied early in the process will successfully sift juveniles out of the system.

Adjudicated juveniles, however, or those whom courts have found to have committed crimes, present a different picture. For these juveniles, the rehabilitative component of the juvenile justice system is supposed to be applied. Although we have discussed in previous chapters a wide variety of preventive programs, we have not discussed—with a few exceptions—the treatment of adjudicated juveniles. Following an overview of the data on dispositions given to juveniles by juvenile courts, therefore, this chapter will provide examples of rehabilitation-oriented approaches used in both institutional and community settings.

JUVENILE PROBATION

Probation is the most frequently dispensed disposition for juvenile offenders and has been since as far back as the middle of the nineteenth century. Even before the first juvenile courts were established, probation officers—who were often volunteers—were asked to provide support to youth who came before the criminal courts and their families. From the establishment of the first juvenile courts in the early nineteenth century, probation officers were closely involved. You may recall from Chapter 10, however, that these early probation workers were often untrained and overburdened with cases.

Juvenile probation today continues to be very closely aligned with juvenile courts and serves as a vehicle for providing a wide variety of services to juveniles. A recent report from the Office of Juvenile Justice and Delinquency Prevention (Torbet, 1996) indicates that of the 1.5 million delinquency cases handled by juvenile courts in 1993, virtually every juvenile had contact with a probation officer at some point.

We should note that juvenile probation is used both early in the system (informal probation) and after adjudication (formal probation). In Chapter 11 we discussed the intake process and the fact that probation departments are usually involved in screening cases and making such decisions as whether juveniles should be detained or referred to diversion programs, or whether delinquency or status offender petitions should be filed. Additionally, probation departments sometimes are allowed to put juveniles on "informal" probation and require that they meet certain conditions if they are to avoid formal processing. In the present chapter we will discuss the role of probation departments at later stages of the juvenile process, most specifically as related to delinquency proceedings and their aftermath. We will also discuss a variety of variants of probation that are available to the juvenile justice system.

In 1993, 56 percent of all juveniles adjudicated delinquents in juvenile courts received probation as the most severe disposition. (All statistics relating to the 1993 data are gathered from Torbet [1996].) Most of these youths were adjudicated for property offenses, 21 percent for offenses against persons, 18 percent for public order offenses, and 7 percent for drug offenses. Although all categories increased since 1989, the largest increase (45 percent) was in offenses against persons, which included homicides, rapes, robberies, assaults, and kidnappings. It may be surprising to learn that juveniles can be placed on probation for violent offenses, but as we discuss the variety of probation options available—including intensive supervision programs—this disposition may become more acceptable.

Torbet (1996) calls juvenile probation the "workhorse" of the juvenile justice system. Depending upon the jurisdictions, probation departments may have sole or shared responsibility for the intake process in addition to their investigative and supervisory responsibilities. In some jurisdictions, probation offices administer detention facilities and programs. In others, they are responsible for providing aftercare services to youths who have been released from institutions.

The typical juvenile probation officer is a college-educated white male, 30 to 49 years old, with 5 to 10 years of experience in the field. Average caseloads consist of 41 juveniles, but the size of caseloads reported ranges from 2 to more than 200 cases (Torbet, 1996). Not surprisingly, mean urban caseloads are the highest, at 47 cases. Nevertheless, even rural probation officers report mean caseloads of 30 juveniles.

Torbet (1996) notes that one of the biggest issues facing the field of juvenile probation is on-the-job safety. Almost one-third of probation officers responding to a survey sponsored by the National Center for Juvenile Justice (NCJJ) reported that they had been assaulted on the job at some point in their careers. Almost half said they were usually or always concerned about their personal safety.

THE RESTORATIVE JUSTICE APPROACH

Both adult and juvenile probation have long been plagued by a role-conflict problem. On the one hand, probation officers are enforcers of the law and have the important task of supervising the behavior of the probationers in their charge. Juvenile probation officers have broad discretion to place requirements on their clients, including curfews and restrictions on persons with whom they associate. On the other hand, the probation officer is also expected to provide support to the juvenile and help him or her become reintegrated into the community. In this sense, the probation officer may be regarded as a friend or a trusted adult. You may recall the case of *Fare v. Michael C.*, discussed in Chapter 11, in which Michael preferred to see his probation officer rather than an attorney before custodial interrogation.

In recent years, growing recognition of safety concerns has led to a new look at the function of probation officers. The discussion has centered on a need for the community to give assistance to both the probation officer and the juvenile. This has led to calls for a "balanced approach" to probation and "restorative justice" (Umbreit, 1989). A balanced approach means that probation must recognize the importance of community protection as well as treatment for the juvenile and accountability for law-abiding behavior. Restorative justice is a concept that encourages victims and the community to be involved in re-integrating the offender (Torbet, 1996).

INTENSIVE SUPERVISION PROGRAMS

One of the fastest-growing community-based programs in adult corrections is that of intensive supervision (Clear & Hardyman, 1990; Petersilia & Turner, 1995). A variant of "regular" probation, intensive supervision and services are given offenders who are presumed to need not institutionalization but more frequent contacts with probation or parole officers than other probationers or parolees. The typical intensive supervision program (ISP) involves multiple weekly contacts with a supervising officer, random drug testing, unannounced visits and drug tests, strict enforcement of the conditions of probation or parole, and requirements to participate in rehabilitation-oriented programs and hold a job (Petersilia & Turner, 1995).

Juvenile intensive supervision programs (JISP) have many of the some features, although the emphasis on rehabilitation is usually more pronounced. Troy Armstrong (1988) has published the results of a national survey on JIS programs. Approximately one-third of the jurisdictions responding to the survey reported a JIS program.

JISP is intended to be an alternative to residential treatment for juveniles. This is an important point to keep in mind. Critics of ISPs in general, for both adults and juveniles, have cautioned that the process may be overused, as a needless alternative to regular probation. In other words, if a person could do just as well or better on regular probation, he or she is not an appropriate candidate for an ISP.

Juvenile intensive supervision has gained supporters from a variety of camps. Those who are concerned about the high costs of keeping juveniles in residential facilities—with figures often around $50,000 per year—are pleased to hear that JIS is less than one-third the cost of commitment (Barton & Butts, 1990). The research on intensive supervision, although just gaining momentum, suggests that it is at least as effective as residential treatment at reducing recidivism (Krisberg et al., 1994). Furthermore, as we have noted consistently throughout this text, considering the numerous problems associated with the institutionalization of juveniles throughout the history of juvenile justice, secure residential options should be exercised only as a last resort and for carefully selected delinquents.

ISPs vary widely according to the jurisdictions in which they are used. For our purposes, we will describe them according to recommendations published by the OJJDP (Krisberg et al., 1994), wherein ISP is defined as "postadjudication, non-residential programs for serious juvenile offenders as an alternative to long-term institutional placement" (p. 2). Two groups of delinquents should be considered for ISP. The first comprises chronic offenders who have committed a multitude of nonviolent offenses and have not responded well to traditional probation or to other attempts by the juvenile justice system to intervene. The second group comprises serious but nonviolent property and drug-trafficking offenders. (Recall that hardliners might want each of these groups to be transferred to criminal courts.) Krisberg et al. (1994) caution that selecting a population which would otherwise be institution-bound is the "single most important element in the implementation of the [program]" (p. 3). They also caution against selecting low-risk offenders who would not otherwise be placed in an institution.

A model ISP combines rehabilitation and close supervision. It is individualized in the sense that the needs of the juvenile have been carefully assessed, and services are provided to address the needs. A case plan is developed, listing the goals to be achieved for the juvenile and the resources available to reach these goals.

The ISP, which ranges from about 11 to 18 months, may begin with a short (15 days to one month) stay in a juvenile facility. Decreasing amounts of restrictiveness follow, involving community treatment and regular probation supervision and ending in a one- to two-month period of discharge from the program.

The model ISP suggested by the OJJDP has a theoretical base in Elliott, Huizinga, and Ageton's (1985) concept of integrated social control (ISC). As we noted in an earlier chapter, the 1980s and '90s saw a trend among criminologists to integrate key points of two or more theories in an attempt to better explain crime and delinquency. Delbert Elliott and his colleagues used aspects of social control theory, strain theory, and social learning theory to account for delinquency. According to this approach, delinquency is caused by a combination of factors that include a weakening of the bond to society (social control), a perceived lack of opportunity to reach society's goals (strain), and the influence of delinquent peers (social learning).

Each of the foregoing theories separately would suggest strategies to take for preventing delinquency. Combined, they suggest a cohesive case plan. Thus, a case plan may call for disengaging from a crowd and for obtaining information about a vocational school. The success of this approach is highly dependent upon the willingness of the youth and his or her family to engage in the process. Additionally, it is clear that this type of ISP approach will seek staff who are committed to rehabilitation.

Armstrong's (1988) descriptive report on intensive supervision programs nationwide suggests that many jurisdictions have established carefully thought-out programs that comport with the model suggested by Krisberg et al. (1994). Armstrong found that, although enforcement was the main goal of the greatest percentage of the programs, both enforcement and rehabilitative concerns were important to all. More than 90 percent of the programs referred juveniles to other community services, such as job-training programs, substance-abuse treatment, or family counseling. The typical juvenile under intensive supervision was a male between the ages of 15 and 17 who had a history of repeat offending. Although the programs reported being selective in their choice of youths, a minority reported that they automatically accepted some juveniles, such as arsonists, gang members, prostitution cases, or repeat drug offenders.

Although Armstrong found that evaluations of these intensive supervision programs were virtually nonexistent, juvenile ISPs are now beginning to come under the research microscope. Wiebush (1993) compared juvenile felony offenders who were sentenced to three alternative forms of intervention: intensive supervision in lieu of incarceration, incarceration followed by parole supervision, and traditional probation supervision. The youths on intensive supervision were repeat offenders with an average of almost three felonies each. They had frequent face-to-face contacts with their probation officers and were referred to a wide variety of rehabilitation-oriented community services. Furthermore, ISP officers were not reluctant to use their power to "punish" the youths for technical violations. (Technical violations are rule-breaking violations of probation as opposed to the commission of new crimes.) In other words, the youths in the program were carefully supervised and were held accountable for their behavior.

Results over an 18-month-period indicated that recidivism rates were no worse than those of youths who had been institutionalized. Nevertheless, the rates were high, with 63 percent of the youth committing a new offense, 47 percent a new felony. ISPs, as Wiebush notes, should not be regarded as panaceas in the juvenile justice system, but they clearly seem to hold promise as alternatives to incarceration.

Minor and Elrod (1990, 1994) have evaluated a program yielding less favorable results, however. Numerous programs in juvenile corrections show positive results while the program is in progress but are unable to show long-term effects. Such was the apparent fate of Project Explore, a probation alternative operating under the aegis of the Kalamazoo County, Michigan, juvenile court. As we review this program, however, it will become evident that it is not a pure JIS program, and this may affect the results.

Project Explore was an experimental program combining life opportunities and relationship enhancements for juveniles aged 12 to 17 who were both delinquents and status offenders. Youths who were both on "regular" probation and intensive supervision were eligible for the program. It included four job-preparation workshops, a three-day outdoor adventures experience, and seven family workshops that focused on improving family communication. Program designers sought to improve the self-concept of juveniles in the program, encourage them to take greater responsibility for their behavior, and improve their perceptions of the juvenile justice system.

Minor and Elrod (1990, 1994) have published 2 evaluations of the program based on 45 youths (23 in the experimental condition, 22 as controls). Each predominantly male (82 percent) group was also divided between youths who were on intensive supervision and those who were on "normal" or moderate supervision. All youths were followed up over 18 months after completing the program. In the first study (1990), the researchers found no significant differences between the experimental and control group on either self-reported or official delinquency. This suggests that the extra attention received by the experimental group made no difference and that a net-widening effect is in operation. The juveniles could just as well have been on regular probation.

In the second study, on the premise that offense reduction should not be the sole criterion by which to measure the effectiveness of a program, the researchers looked at cognitive benefits that might have been derived from the program. Again, the differences failed to reach levels of significance.

Nonetheless, interesting observations could be made about possible reasons for the program's apparent "failure." The job-preparation component was only moderately successful; although attendance was good, participation was not, which suggested to the researchers that acquiring job skills was not a salient issue to most of the juveniles, whose average age was 15. The most successful of the three components appeared to be the outdoor components, where youths' participation was good and their self-esteem was improved, but only for the short term. On the third day, however, which was to include parents, only one-half of the parents appeared. Although it would be tempting to assume that some parents could not afford to take time from work, the researchers suggest that parents were not interested in what the youths were doing. Even parents who did attend were often half-hearted about participation. Finally, the family workshops were poorly attended by parents.

Minor and Elrod tried hard to salvage the program by suggesting a variety of reasons why good results were not achieved. They noted that, although the court ordered the participation, it did not enforce the order, enabling the youths and their families to attend only sporadically or to drop out altogether. Additionally, they suggest that the program design should have involved parents and youths, including early feedback from them—if involved in the planning, they would be more likely to be committed. The intensity and duration of the intervention were also questioned. The outdoor component in particular, which seemed to have produced good results, should have been extended.

The project included such a range of youths, both in terms of age and offending, that it may have been trying to do too much. Targeting a population of youths under intensive supervision, or a population of status offenders, or a population of violent offenders, may have been a better approach.

FAMILY PRESERVATION PROGRAMS

The fact that Project Explore tried to include parents in the intervention leads to a discussion of a variety of programs in the juvenile justice area that have family preservation as a major goal. Family preservation is a model of delivering services to families in the hope that they will be able to remain intact. You will recall that we discussed one program under this model, multisystemic therapy (Henggeler & Borduin, 1990), in Chapter 9. MST will not be covered again here, although it is important to keep it in mind as a community treatment approach with juveniles that is being promoted as a highly successful way of working with serious juvenile offenders.

At the other end of the continuum, status offenders are also the target of family preservation programs. The predominant example of this is the Homebuilders Model, which began in Washington state in 1974 and extended to approximately 28 states within a decade (Haapala & Kinney, 1988). Homebuilders is an intensive family treatment program delivered by social service workers over a period lasting one month. Families referred to Homebuilders have one or more children in the home who are status offenders at risk of out-of-home placement.

Homebuilders is unique in that it combines counseling services with tangible help. Families are given such help as assertiveness training, values clarification, behavior modification, and client-centered therapy. Additionally, they are helped to obtain needed services, such as math tutoring for a child or a battery for the family car.

The Homebuilders model is intended for families who have encountered numerous problems, sometimes over years, and for whom traditional counseling or social-work interventions have been ineffective. One or more of the children are plagued by problems such as truancy, substance abuse, teen pregnancy, or attempted suicides.

Homebuilders staff work, sometimes in teams of two, with only one or two families per month. Meetings occur in the home, sometimes more than once a day. The Homebuilder worker is all but living in the home with the family. Professional therapists are also on call 24 hours a day. A major goal of the program is to help families learn to communicate with one another, solve problems, and make efficient use of community services.

The one-month duration of the program may lead one to be skeptical about its success. How can anything reasonably be accomplished in only 30 days? Haapala and Kinney (1988) report favorable results with 678 Homebuilder clients. Over a four-year period, 87 percent of the families were able to avoid out-of-home placement of their children. If family preservation is the aim, the Homebuilders model appears to be a good way of achieving it.

Family preservation models are not always enthusiastically endorsed, however. Critics assert that we should be willing to acknowledge that some juveniles must be helped to separate from a dysfunctional family and become independent if they are to succeed.

Jill Rosenbaum (1993), for example, describes the apparent futility of a community program that included intensive supervision of girls and seemed highly focused on preserving the family unit. In 1961 the California Youth Authority (CYA) experimented with a project designed to keep delinquents in their own homes in the community, under intensive supervision. Rosenbaum examined adult records of 159 women who had been part of that program as juveniles. She found that 96 percent had been arrested as adults. More significant, however, was that 82 percent had been convicted of at least one moderately serious crime, excluding such crimes as prostitution, drug possession, and theft of less than $100.

Rosenbaum posits that family dysfunction was a critical factor in the adult criminality of the women. Multiple marriages, parental criminal activity, conflict, and family violence were common in the sample. Daughters followed the generational cycle set by their mothers: They bore children at an early age and chose men "who had a striking resemblance to those chosen by their mothers. Many were significantly older than the girls and had criminal records" (p. 407). Rosenbaum's findings suggest that without attention to the family variables that seem to have a strong effect on both delinquency and subsequent adult criminality, a community-based program involving intensive supervision is unlikely to have long-lasting positive effects. Rosenbaum notes that today's policies are less likely to advocate the return of youths to ineffectual parents. Although attempts are made to work out problems within families, "we no longer do so at the youth's expense" (p. 411). She suggests that the need for transitional shelters and emancipation programs is becoming well recognized. "Given our more realistic appraisal of family viability today, perhaps the current counterparts [of the delinquent girls of the 1960s] will stand a better chance" (p. 411).

BOOT CAMPS

In the 1980s, many states developed a system of "shock incarceration"—commonly called boot camps—for adult offenders. Initially based on a military model, shock incarceration was intended to provide an intensively structured, short-term alternative to prison, primarily for nonviolent offenders. By the end of the decade, the "model" boot-camp programs included military-style discipline, a rehabilitative component (such as substance-abuse treatment), and community follow-up, or "aftershock." Although there continue to be serious questions raised about the success of the boot-camp model, shock incarceration seems destined to remain an intermediate sanction for some adult offenders (MacKenzie & Hebert, 1995).

Boot camps were not immediately adopted in the juvenile system, primarily because there were questions about their appropriateness. Faced with increased overcrowding in juvenile facilities, however, juvenile justice policymakers began to consider the possibility of the boot-camp alternative for less serious juvenile offenders who were believed to need more structure than the typical community probation experience and less structure than an institution. In the early 1990s, the Office of Juvenile Justice and Delinquency Prevention (OJJDP) funded demonstration projects at three sites to develop a model boot-camp program for male juveniles aged 13 to 18. The sites were Cleveland, Ohio; Denver, Colorado; and Mobile, Alabama.

The ambitious goals of the boot-camp programs, as reported in a recent report (Bourque et al., 1996), were as follows:

- Serve as a cost-effective alternative to institutionalization;
- Promote discipline through physical conditioning and teamwork;
- Instill moral values and a work ethic;
- Promote literacy and increase academic achievement;

- Reduce drug and alcohol abuse;
- Encourage participants to become productive, law-abiding citizens;
- Ensure that offenders are held accountable for their actions.

The boot-camp experience included a 90-day residential program that was heavily focused on military drills, discipline, and physical conditioning. The regime included uniforms, military jargon, and an exhausting daily routine from 5:30 or 6:00 A.M. until 9:00 or 10:00 P.M. To a lesser extent, rehabilitative activities such as remedial education, life-skills education and counseling, and substance-abuse education were included.

The boys in the programs had committed a wide range of offenses, including property, drug, and other felonies but excluding violent offenses. The programs "targeted male delinquents likely to become further involved in the juvenile justice system and excluded youths with violent criminal histories" (Bourque et al., 1996, p. 3). Interestingly, the sites differed in their choice of staff and correctional philosophy. Although all three sought staff with military experience, only one site, Cleveland, also wanted staff to have counseling backgrounds. Denver "avoided instructors with counseling or therapy backgrounds for fear that they would have difficulty with the more militaristic aspects of the programs" (Bourque et al., 1996, p. 4). In Cleveland, therapeutic counseling was a central part of the programming.

In all three sites, the programs demonstrated short-term success during the residential phase. In all three sites, at least 80 percent of the boys graduated from boot camp (with a high of 94 percent in Cleveland). The boys improved in educational performance, physical fitness, and behavior, and staff noted their improvement in respect for authority, self-discipline, teamwork, and physical appearance. The youths themselves rated their experience positively, noting that they believed they had significantly changed the direction of their lives.

The aftercare components of the program were discouraging, however, and raise important questions about the effectiveness of boot camps for juvenile offenders. A variety of aftercare services were made available, depending upon the site. These included specially created aftercare centers, mainstreaming into local Boys' Clubs, academic instruction, drug counseling, and support services. Over a one-year follow-up, all three sites reported high rates of noncompliance, absenteeism, and new arrests. "No site graduated more than 50 percent of its aftercare participants, and terminations were most commonly caused by new arrests in two sites" (Bourque et al., 1996, p. 7). Denver had a notably low rate of completion, 26.2 percent, compared with 44.6 percent in Cleveland and 49.5 percent in Mobile.

In assessing what went wrong, Bourque and his colleagues suggest, among other things, that a more appropriate balance between militaristic and rehabilitative elements is needed. Although discipline can be an important motivating tool, they note, the educational, psychological, and emotional needs of the youths must be better addressed. They also suggest fine-tuning the selection of youths, in particular noting that youths with prior incarceration were less likely to survive the aftercare component. Additionally, two programs seemed to include too many serious offenders, whereas a third was overrestrictive, selecting youths who could have done just as well or better in another probation alternative. This last problem is another illustration of the "netwidening" that has haunted the juvenile justice system since its inception.

It should not be surprising to anyone that a short-term residential program that is so discipline-oriented is unlikely to produce positive long-term results. (It should be noted that the Denver program, which had the least educational and life-skills orientation, also had the lowest success rate with respect to aftercare.) In fact, in its guidelines for implementing the demonstration projects, the OJJDP should have required a better balance, particularly in light of research from adult boot-camp programs that indicates better long-term results when rehabilitative components are implemented (MacKenzie, 1996). Even so, it is questionable whether meaningful change can be produced given the short length of stay and the quick return to the juveniles' previous environments. It would seem far more logical to develop alternatives within the community setting for the great majority of juvenile offenders who do not need institutionalization.

INSTITUTIONAL PROGRAMS

Obtaining statistics on the precise number of juveniles incarcerated is a challenge. The best source for this information is the OJJDP's *Children in Custody* census, which gathers data from both private and public facilities on a biannual basis. Unfortunately, the response rate from private juvenile facilities has never reached 100 percent. Although it is well recognized that private facilities are able to offer outstanding programs for the juveniles in their care, there are strong concerns about trends toward privatization in some of its aspect. Writers such as Schwartz (1989) and Federle and Chesney-Lind (1995), for example, express grave concerns about the use of private psychiatric facilities for juveniles. We will return to this issue later in the chapter.

According to Butts et al. (1995), of every 1,000 delinquency cases referred to juvenile courts in 1992, 85 resulted in out-of-home placement. All but two of these involve cases that were handled formally by the juvenile courts (i.e., through the delinquency-hearing process). Proportionally, out-of-home placement occurred in 28 percent of all adjudicated delinquency cases. Figure 13.1 displays these differences in dispositions.

Another way of categorizing juvenile facilities relates to their degree of physical security and community access. The *Children in Custody* census distinguishes between whether they have "open" or "institutional" environments. Institutional facilities are those with the heaviest security. As a general rule, juveniles are allowed out of these facilities only under close supervision of staff. A juvenile in an institutional setting, for example, may be accompanied to a court hearing, to a medical appointment, or to a family funeral. Juveniles who show progress in rehabilitation programs also may be taken into the community for recreational or educational events. Open facilities are intended for youth who are believed not to need the secure confinement of the traditional training-school model. Open facilities include group

FIGURE 13.1   Delinquency dispositions in 1992

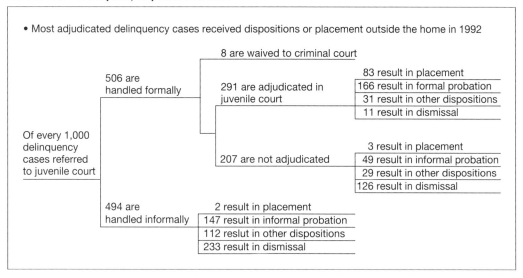

• Most adjudicated delinquency cases received dispositions or placement outside the home in 1992

Of every 1,000 delinquency cases referred to juvenile court

506 are handled formally

8 are waived to criminal court

291 are adjudicated in juvenile court
- 83 result in placement
- 166 result in formal probation
- 31 result in other dispositions
- 11 result in dismissal

207 are not adjudicated
- 3 result in placement
- 49 result in informal probation
- 29 result in other dispositions
- 126 result in dismissal

494 are handled informally
- 2 result in placement
- 147 result in informal probation
- 112 reslut in other dispositions
- 233 result in dismissal

SOURCE: Butts, J., et al. 1995. *Juvenile Court Statistics 1992.*

homes, halfway houses, forestry or wilderness camps, ranches, or farms. Open facilities also may hold both adjudicated delinquents and status offenders. Additionally, they sometimes include voluntary placements, a term used to refer to youths whose parents or guardians have placed them there.

In 1990, 97,732 juveniles were admitted to public long-term facilities throughout the United States. Nearly twice as many were admitted to institutional as to open facilities. The average length of stay in these facilities was 182 days, or about 6 months (OJJDP, *Children in Custody*, 1993). Recall that the average length of stay in secure detention facilities is approximately two weeks. Interestingly, however, when juveniles were detained in detention units of a long-term treatment center, the average length of stay was three weeks.

A one-day count of juveniles held in facilities in 1991 (OJJDP, *Children in Custody*, 1993) indicated that 36,000 juveniles were held in public long-term facilities, three-fourths of which were of the institutional model. By contrast, of the 34,000 juveniles held in private facilities, 80 percent were in open environments.

One of the most disturbing and consistent findings with respect to children held in custody is the disproportionate number of minority youth who are held in both public and private facilities. In 1991, 69 percent of all children held in public facilities were members of ethnic minority groups, while minorities constituted 51 percent of all children held in private facilities. You may recall from Chapter 10 that the 1992 amendment to the JJDPA requires states to address this disproportionate representation of minorities in institutional settings.

Snyder and Sickmund (1995) have reported other interesting findings regarding private facilities. The proportion of status offenders was 12 percent (compared with 1 percent in public facilities). It may be surprising to learn, also, that 37 percent of the youth in private facilities were non-offenders, voluntarily admitted on referral by parents or school officials.

It is important to note that, although the number of status offenders in public facilities has declined in keeping with the JJDPA's DSO mandate discussed in Chapter 10, the number in private facilities has increased markedly. Because the private facilities usually are group homes or similar nonsecure, open settings, it may appear that there is little cause for alarm. Increasing privatization in juvenile corrections, however, could mean that increasingly more status offenders will be turned over to those who operate private institutions. This is a trend that should be watched very carefully.

TRANSINSTITUTIONALIZATION

A number of writers have begun to identify what they consider a "hidden" private juvenile correctional system, one that is associated with hospitalization for mental-health treatment (e.g., Schwartz, Jackson-Beeck, & Anderson, 1984; Weithorn, 1988; Schwartz, 1989; Federle & Chesney-Lind, 1992). Such hospitalizations, which have a disproportionate effect on girls (approximately 60 percent versus 40 percent boys), are considered voluntary placements because parents have willingly brought the juvenile to the facility. Ira Schwartz (1989) calls private psychiatric facilities the "new jails" for middle-class children. The cost of care is typically borne by insurance programs, and, according to Schwartz, the juvenile is typically "cured" when the insurance runs out. The term **transinstitutionalization** refers to the shift from incarcerating juveniles in detention centers to hospitalizing them in private facilities.

Weithorn (1988) has estimated that fewer than one-third of all juveniles admitted to these restrictive private facilities have severe or acute mental disorders. Additionally, the juvenile rarely consents freely to the admission. A 1979 U.S. Supreme Court decision, *Parham v. J.R.*, however, gave parents the authority to admit their children to mental-health facilities over the child's objections and without the requirement of an external judicial review process. Criteria for admission to private mental-health facilities often include the same behaviors that were used by juvenile courts to control status offenders prior to the DSO mandates. In some facilities, for example, vague criteria such as "incorrigibility," "troublesome behavior," or "sexual promiscuity" qualify the youths for institutionalization (Federle & Chesney-Lind, 1992).

INSTITUTIONAL TREATMENT

The out-of-home placement of youth, particularly in secure institutional facilities, is widely believed by advocates for juveniles to be the least desirable option, one to be used only if other community-based attempts have failed. The early history of treatment of juvenile in institutional settings is rife with evidence of neglect, brutalization, inefficiency, high financial as well as societal costs (e.g., Rafter, 1990; Rothman, 1980).

In the mid-1960s, many states began to rethink their approaches to the institutionalization of juveniles. In Massachusetts, for example, Youth Commissioner Jerome Miller fought a lengthy battle to close down all large juvenile training schools and replace them with community-based treatment programs or small rehabilitation centers for juveniles. As we have seen, despite the fact that the trend is clearly toward dealing with youthful offenders in the community if possible, institutional settings remain very much a part of the juvenile justice system and are unlikely to go away. They are likely to remain the placement of choice for chronic offenders for whom other alternatives are not believed feasible. Furthermore, unless the juvenile justice system becomes virtually indistinguishable from the adult justice system, the preeminent goal will remain the rehabilitation of these offenders.

As a rule, chronic juvenile offenders, particularly chronic violent offenders, do not seem to respond to rehabilitation, which we define here as planned intervention designed to change an offender's behavior or situation and presumably prevent him or her from offending in the future. Although a variety of rehabilitative strategies have been attempted, their effectiveness has not been promising. Such strategies are extremely difficult to evaluate, however.

The most recent approach to evaluating treatment effectiveness is to employ meta-analysis, which is a statistical method allowing us to compare many studies on common variables (e.g., Garrett, 1985; Andrews et al., 1990; Lipsey, 1991). Meta-analyses have suggested results that are slightly more promising than those of earlier research. Garrett (1985), for example, analyzed 111 studies on the effectiveness of residential treatment for juveniles and concluded that there was positive change. The change was primarily associated with institutional behavior and psychological adjustment within the institution, however. The Lipsey (1991) and Andrews et al. (1990) meta-analyses looked at a wide range of interventions in the community as well as institutional settings. The most positive results were in community settings.

Even if a violent, repetitive offender is willing and able to change and rehabilitation appears to have been achieved within an institutional setting, the youth generally returns to the social systems whence he or she came. Youths discharged from institutions usually go back to the same home, the same neighborhood, the same community, the same peer network, and the same systems that teach, encourage, and support the same deviant behaviors. This is one of the reasons why research such as that of Henggeler et al. (1996), discussed in Chapter 9, gives reason for optimism. In the following few pages we will review research on selected programs within institutional settings that are believed to have promise.

Paint Creek Youth Center

One of the most closely watched private residential treatment programs for serious juvenile offenders is called Paint Creek Youth Center, nestled in an isolated, rural community in Ohio. It is an open facility that serves up to 34 male youths aged 13 to 18 who have been convicted of first- or second-degree felonies ranging from burglaries to manslaughter. The great majority of youths are 16 and 17, however, and robbery and assault are the most common violent crimes. Paint Creek is also part of a controlled experiment, with researchers from the Rand Corporation closely following the progress of the juveniles sent to Paint Creek compared with juveniles in more typical training schools.

The program includes a wide array of intensive individual and group treatments, including educational, work-training, and aftercare services. Juveniles—all boys—are encouraged to take responsibility for their crimes and to empathize with their victims through role-playing exercises. The average length of stay is one year. As the youths progress through the program, they enter different levels or phases that carry greater responsibilities as well as privileges. Juveniles at the highest level, for example, have the opportunity to participate in a "Freedom Factory," where they not only learn valuable work skills but also earn a weekly salary, a portion of which is used to pay restitution to victims.

Critics are hard-pressed to find shortcomings in the program. It is a small, carefully structured approach based on sound principles of social learning. Its director, Dr. Vikki Agee, is a clinical psychologist with many years of experience. Nonetheless, the first published evaluation of the Paint Creek program was discouraging (Greenwood & Turner, 1993).

The experimental design included random assignment of youths to Paint Creek or one of two public training schools also in Ohio. One was an antiquated facility that provided a minimum of therapy but did offer remedial education and vocational training. The other was a more modern, less secure facility offering similar services. Neither facility approached the intensity of services available to Paint Creek boys.

Seventy-five boys in each of the three placements were studied. As Greenwood and Turner (1993) note, the Paint Creek program had many of the features hypothesized to be marks of effective programming. For example, the 75 boys at Paint Creek were more likely to have jobs while in custody, have family visits and obtain counseling, get drug and alcohol counseling, have home furloughs, and see the program in a positive light. Additionally, while in aftercare the Paint Creek boys saw workers often. Seventy-four percent saw their workers at least twice a week, compared with 19 percent of the controls. More than half the Paint Creek boys saw aftercare workers more than six times a week.

The Paint Creek staff were more favorable to their program director and to the program and were happier with their jobs than workers at the other two facilities. Paint Creek staff also demonstrated a more favorable attitude toward the boys in their care.

In a one-year follow-up period, recidivism was not significantly different between the experimental and control groups. Both official and self-report data were obtained. Official records indicated that the Paint Creek boys were less likely to have another arrest, but the difference was not significant. On self-reported measures, 75 percent of the experimental group reported at least one serious infraction, whereas 62 percent of the controls did. Again, this difference was not significant. The control group reported slightly more drug offending, but again the difference was not significant.

The Paint Creek model promotes intensive, residential and aftercare services for small groups of youths found to have committed serious crimes. The cost is slightly higher (approximately $29,653 per youth, compared with $26,137 in the control facilities). On the basis of this one study, it may be tempting to conclude that youth are just as well served in an institution without the advantage of the special programs offered to Paint Creek youth. It cannot be said that Paint Creek doesn't work; it is simply not documented that it works better than the traditional public training schools with which it was compared.

Supporters of the Paint Creek model stress, however, that long-term evaluations are yet to come and may indicate more favorable results. Additionally, allowing the private facility to determine specifically which types of offenders could best benefit by its services could make a difference in its success rate.

Glen Mills School

A very different type of program operates at the Glen Mills School, which was once the Philadelphia House of Refuge. This is a large institution, located on a 779-acre campus, with capacity for approximately 600 boys. According to Grissom and Dubnov (1989), who have described the program in detail in their book *Without Locks and Bars*, Glen Mills is a success story in juvenile corrections primarily because it communicates a sense of responsibility and positive regard to the boys in its care.

Glen Mills was on the verge of closing in 1975 when a new director, Cosimo "Sam" Ferrainola, came on board determined to demonstrate that large schools for delinquents can indeed work. The school uses a "guided group interaction" approach, a system of rehabilitation that uses peer pressure to encourage juveniles to behave. Glen Mills staff and students (they are not called residents, inmates, or delinquents) are expected to abide by a system of "norms," rather than "rules."

Like many private residential facilities, Glen Mills is able to choose the students it accepts. Because the program is based heavily on peer culture and learning, directors say they are unable to work with juveniles for whom this type of learning is contraindicated. They will not accept, for example, juvenile arsonists or those who are mentally ill. The program promotes itself as being most effective with streetwise, urban gang members. "There is strong preference for older, 'socialized' delinquents for whom peer pressures have played a significant role in misbehavior" (Grissom & Dubnov, 1989, p. 113).

Glen Mills focuses on the student, encouraging the development of life skills such as obtaining a GED, solving problems without resorting to violence, and learning to manage financial affairs. Field trips offering exposure to cultural and recreational activities are frequent. There is, however, no emphasis on reintegration into the community. The Glen Mills program does not involve work with the family, on the premise that most of the boys will be independent upon leaving the school. Resources are focused on promoting attitudinal and habit changes that presumably will follow the boys into adulthood. Peer pressure is used to induce the boys to respect the dignity and property of others, adopt good work habits and habits of personal care, and avoid illegal activity.

Grissom and Dubnov note that Glen Mills is noteworthy for its ongoing evaluations, designed to identify weaknesses as well as strengths. The evaluations are based predominantly on institution records as well as surveys of all students approximately two years after discharge. The interviews are either by phone or in person, and the student himself is interviewed whenever possible. A chapter on program effectiveness cites positive outcomes on a variety of measures, including reduction of negative behaviors in the program, continuance of education after discharge, and recidivism compared with traditionally run training schools. Glen Mills has not been evaluated by an independent source, however.

We should keep in mind, however, that Glen Mills has the power to select as well as to expel students who do not fit into the program, unlike public facilities, which do not generally have these powers. These sifting-in and shifting-out processes clearly affect a program's likelihood of success. Nevertheless, it is important to keep in mind that there is room in the juvenile justice system for programs which recognize that they cannot be all things to all juveniles and are able to target those with whom they can work best.

SUMMARY AND CONCLUSIONS

Since the inception of the first juvenile courts, the juvenile justice system has been plagued by largely unsuccessful efforts at rehabilitating juveniles. Research on the wide variety of programs offered to juveniles once adjudicated delinquent has had discouraging results, particularly when the juveniles are in residential treatment. Nevertheless, it is important to keep in mind the large percentage of juveniles who have been sifted out early in the juvenile process, either by police, prosecutors, intake workers, diversion, or a system of informal probation. These early decisions operate as a way of steering juveniles through the crime-prone adolescent years with a minimum of scarring or stigmatizing.

To those juveniles who are adjudicated delinquent, however, the system owes some responsibility to attempt rehabilitation. Otherwise, the rationale for maintaining a separate justice system becomes less clear. If we do not try to produce change in a juvenile's behavior or life situation, then why not simply process the juvenile through the adult system? The adult system, after all, does include some rehabilitative component as well. Despite the fact that the rehabilitation of juvenile offenders in the juvenile justice system has not met expectations, proponents of the separate system assert that there are enough successes to warrant optimism.

About half of all adjudicated delinquents are placed on probation, allowing community supervision accompanied by a wide range of services. Probation officers have broad discretion in relation to the requirements they are able to place upon the probationers under their supervision. Nevertheless, their workload in recent years has increased along with fears for their personal safety. An important variant of probation, intensive supervision, offers greater protection to the community and provides the officer with a smaller caseload and more ability to offer services to nonviolent juvenile offenders who have not responded well to regular probation but are not considered in need of institutional placement. Thus far, research on intensive supervision programs indicates that recidivism rates, although high, are no greater than those for juveniles who are released from institutions. There is continuing need to fine tune the programs and to identify which juveniles are best suited to which type of intensive supervision program.

There is considerable debate about whether juveniles are better off with their families, particularly if families display numerous dysfunctional characteristics. Family preservation models posit that all efforts should be made to keep families together, including the provision of a wide range of services and intensive, frequent contacts with social service agencies. Henggeler's MST approach, discussed in Chapter 9, used with serious delinquents, is a good illustration of this perspective. Another is Homebuilders, a program for families with at least one status offender at risk of out-of-home placement. Programs such as these offer multifaceted treatment to family members within the community in which they reside.

We discussed the boot-camp phenomenon, which reached the juvenile justice system in the late 1980s. Boot camps have had considerable popular appeal: They appear to provide for juveniles a disciplined, structured experience on a short-term basis at relatively low cost. Results of evaluations of boot-camp model programs, however, have been disappointing. The camps emphasize the militaristic approach at the expense of the educational, psychological, and emotional needs of the juveniles. Additionally, there is concern that boot camps may be overly restrictive, selecting youths who could have done just as well or better in another probation alternative.

Institutionalization of juveniles is generally considered the least desirable disposition in the juvenile justice system, even though juvenile institutions today are less likely to be characterized by the physical brutality of the past. In recent years writers have begun to draw attention to the transinstitutionalization process, which occurs when juveniles are placed, usually by their parents, in private psychiatric hospitals. This is particularly a problem for juvenile girls. Studies of the effectiveness of residential treatment of juvenile delinquents have not been supportive of this approach. Although some meta-analyses suggest that effective programs are available and should be continually improved, the most beneficial programs are yet to be identified.

KEY CONCEPTS

probation	residential treatment
restorative justice	shock incarceration/boot camps
intensive supervision programs	*Children in Custody*
mediation	transinstitutionalization
Project Explore	meta-analysis
Homebuilders	Paint Creek evaluation
Jerome Miller	Glen Mills School

References

ABADINSKY, H. (1993). *Drug abuse* (2nd ed.). Chicago: Nelson-Hall.

ADAMS, D. (1992). Biology does not make men more aggressive than women. In K. Bjorkquist & P. Niemela (Eds.), *Of mice and women: Aspects of female aggression*. San Diego, CA: Academic Press.

ADLAF, E. (1993). *Alcohol and other drug use*. Ottawa: Health Canada.

ADLAF, E., SMART, R., & WALCH, G. (1993). *The Ontario student drug use surveys: 1977-1993*. Toronto: Addiction Research Foundation.

ADLER, F. (1975). *Sisters in crime*. New York: McGraw-Hill.

ADLER, R., NUNN, R., NORTHAM, E., LEBNAN, V., & ROSS, R. (1994). Secondary prevention of childhood firesetting. *Journal of the American Academy of Child and Adolescent Psychiatry, 33*, 1194-1202.

AGETON, S. S. (1983). The dynamics of female delinquency, 1976-1980. *Criminology, 21*, 555-584.

AGNEW, R. (1996). Foundation for a general strain theory of crime and delinquency. In P. Cordella & L. Siegel (Eds.), *Readings in contemporary criminological theory*. Boston: Northeastern University Press.

AKERS, R. L. (1977). *Deviant behavior: A social learning approach* (2nd ed.). Belmont, CA: Wadsworth.

AKERS, R. L. (1985). *Deviant behavior: A social learning approach* (3rd ed.). Belmont, CA: Wadsworth.

ALLEN, F. A. (1964). *The borderland of criminal justice*. Chicago: University of Chicago Press.

ALLPORT, G. (1961). *Pattern and growth in personality*. New York: Holt, Rinehart & Winston.

ALTSHULER, D., & BROUNSTEIN, P. J. (1991). Patterns of drug use, drug trafficking and other delinquency among inner city adolescent males in Washington, DC. *Criminology, 29*, 589-622.

AMERICAN PSYCHIATRIC ASSOCIATION (APA). (1994). *Diagnostic and statistical manual (DSM-IV)*. Washington: Author.

AMERICAN SOCIETY OF CRIMINOLOGY (1995). Task Force Reports, Delinquency: A new vision for inner-city schools, *The Criminologist, 20*, 1-6.

ANDERSON, E. J. (1990). *Streetwise: Race, class, and change in an urban community*. Chicago: University of Chicago Press.

ANDREWS, D. A., ZINGER, I., HOGE, R. D., BONTA, J., GENDREAU, P., & CULLEN, F. T. (1990). Does correctional treatment work?: A clinically relevant and psychologically informed meta-analysis. *Criminology, 28*, 369-404.

APPLEGATE, J. L., BURLESON, B. R., BURKE, J. A., DELIA, J. G., & KLINE, S. L. (1985). Reflection-enhancing parental communication. In I. E. Sigel (Ed.), *Parental belief systems*. Hillsdale, NJ: Erlbaum.

ARMSTRONG, T. (1988). National survey of juvenile intensive probation supervision, parts I and II. *Criminal Justice Abstracts, 2*, 342-348; 497-523.

AUSTIN, R. L. (1978). Race, father-absence, and female delinquency. *Criminology, 15*, 487-504.

BALL, J. C., SHAFFER, J. W., & NURCO, D. N. (1983). The day-to-day criminality of heroin addicts in Baltimore—A study in the continuity of offense rates. *Drug and Alcohol Dependence, 12*, 119-142.

BANDURA, A. (1977). *Social learning theory*. (2nd edition). Englewood Cliffs, NJ: Prentice-Hall.

BANDURA, A., & WALTERS, R. H. (1959). *Adolescent aggression*. New York: Ronald.

BANDURA, A., & WALTERS, R. H. (1963). *Social learning and personality development*. New York: Holt, Rinehart.

BARDONE, A. M., MOFFITT, T. E., & CASPI, A. (in press). Adult mental health and social outcomes of adolescent girls with depression and conduct disorder. *Development and Psychopathology*.

BARTOLLAS, C. (1988). Survival problems of adolescent prisoners. In H. Toch & R. Johnson (Eds.), *The pains of imprisonment*. Prospect Heights, IL: Waveland.

BATES, J. E. (1980). The concept of difficult temperament. *Merrill-Palmer Quarterly, 26*, 299-319.

BECKER, H. S. (1963). *Outsiders: Studies in the sociology of deviance*. New York: Free Press.

BECKER, T., Samet, J., Wiggins, C., & Key, C. (1990). Violent death in the west: Suicide and homicide in

New Mexico, 1958-1987. *Suicide and Life-Threatening Behavior, 20*, 324-334.

BEGER, R. R. (1996). Rural juvenile courts. In T. D. McDonald, R. A. Wood, & M. A. Pflug, M.A. (Eds.), *Rural criminal justice: Conditions, constraints and challenges*. Salem, WI: Sheffield.

BELL, R. R. (1981). *Worlds of friendship*. Beverly Hills, CA: Sage.

BELSKY, J., LERNER, R. M., & SPANIER, G. B. (1984). *The child in the family*. New York: Random House.

BENNETT, J. (1981). *Oral history and delinquency: The rhetoric of criminology*. Chicago: University of Chicago Press.

BENSING, R. C., & SCHROEDER, O. (1960). *Homicide in an urban community*. Springfield, IL: Charles C. Thomas.

BERGSMANN, I. R. (1989). The forgotten few: Juvenile female offenders. *Federal Probation, 53*, 73-78.

BERKOWITZ, L. (1993). *Aggression: Its causes, consequences, and control*. Philadelphia: Temple University Press.

BERKOWITZ, L. (1994). Guns and youth. In L. D. Eron, J. H. Gentry, & P. Schlegel (Eds.), *Reason to hope: A psychosocial perspective on violence and youth*. Washington: American Psychological Association.

BERKOWITZ, L., & HEIMER, K. (1989). On the construction of the anger experience: Aversive events and negative priming in the formation of feelings. In L. Berkowitz (ed.), *Advances in experimental social psychology* (Vol. 22). New York: Academic Press.

BERNARD, T. J. (1992). *The cycle of juvenile justice*. New York: Oxford University Press.

BERNDT, T. (1979). Developmental changes in conformity to peers and parents. *Developmental Psychology, 15*, 608-616.

BERNSTEIN, B. (1974). *Class, codes, and control: Theoretical studies towards a sociology of language*, Vol. 1. (rev ed.) New York: Schocken.

BERRUETA-CLEMENT, J. R., SCHWEINHART, L. J., BARNETT, W. S., & WEIKART, D. P. (1987). The effects of early educational intervention in adolescence and early adulthood. In J. D. Burchard & S. N. Burchard (Eds.), *Prevention of delinquent behavior*. Newbury Park, CA: Sage.

BERTALANFFY, L. VON. (1968). *General system theory*. New York: George Braziller.

BIJOU, S. W., & BAER, D. M. (1961). *Child development*. New York: Appleton-Century-Crofts.

BINDER, A., & GEIS, G. (1984). Ad populum argumentation in criminology: Juvenile diversion as rhetoric. *Crime and Delinquency, 30*, 309-333.

BIXENSTINE, V. E., DESORTE, M. S., & BIXENSTINE, B. A. (1976). Conformity to peer-sponsored misconduct at four grade levels. *Developmental psychology, 12*, 226-236.

BLECHMAN, E. A. (1982). Are children with one parent at psychological risk? A methodological review. *Journal of Marriage and the Family, 44*, 179-195.

BLOCK, C. R. (1988). Lethal violence in the Chicago community, 1965-1981. In research conference proceedings, *Violence and homicide in Hispanic communities*. Los Angeles: University of California Press.

BLOCK, H. A., & NIEDERHOFFER, A. (1958). *The gang: A study in adolescent behavior*. New York: Philosophical Library.

BLOCK, R., & BLOCK, C. R. (1993, November). Street gang crime in Chicago. *National Institute of Justice research in brief*. Washington: U.S. Department of Justice.

BLOMBERG, T. G. (1983). Diversion's disparate results and unresolved questions: An integrative evaluation perspective. *Journal of Research in Crime and Delinquency, 20*, 24-38.

BLOOMQUIST, E. R. (1970). The use and abuse of stimulants. In W. G. Clark & J. DelGiudice (Eds.), *Principles of psychopharmacology*. New York: Academic Press.

BLUMSTEIN, A. (1995). Violence by young people. Why the deadly nexus? *National Institute of Justice Journal, 229*, 2-9.

BOHM, R. (1991). *The death penalty in America: Current research*. Cincinnati, OH: Anderson.

BONEY-MCCOY, S., & FINKELHOR, D. (1995). Psychosocial sequelae of violent victimization in a national youth sample. *Journal of Consulting and Clinical Psychology, 63*, 726-736.

BORDUIN, C. M. (1994). Innovative models of treatment and service delivery in the juvenile justice system. *Journal of Clinical Child Psychology, 23*, 19-25.

BORDUIN, C. M., MANN, B. J., CONE, L. T., HENGGELER, S. W., FUCCI, B. R., BLASKE, D. M., & WILLIAMS, R. (1995). Multisystemic treatment of serious juvenile offenders: Long-term prevention of criminality and violence. *Journal of Consulting and Clinical Psychology, 63*, 569-578.

BORTNER, M. A. (1986). Traditional rhetoric, organizational realities: Remand of juveniles to adult court. *Crime and Delinquency, 32*, 53-73.

BOTTOMS, A. E., & WILES, P. (1986). Housing tenure and residential community crime careers in Britain. In A. G. Reiss Jr., & M. Tonry (Eds.), *Communities and crime*. Chicago: University of Chicago Press.

BOURQUE, B. B., CRONIN, R. C., FELKER, D. B., PEARSON, F. R., HAN, M., & HILL, S. M. (1996). *Boot camps for juvenile offenders: An implementation evaluation of three demonstration programs*. Research in Brief. Washington: National Institute of Justice.

BOWDEN, K. M., WILSON, D. W., & TURNER, L. K. (1958). A survey of blood alcohol testing in Victoria (1951-56). *Medical Journal of Australia, 45*, 13-15.

BOYKIN, A. W. (1986). The triple quandary and the schooling of Afro-American children. In U. Neisser (Ed.), *The school achievement of minority children.* Hillsdale, NJ: Erlbaum.

BOYKIN, A. W. (1994). Harvesting talent and culture: African-American children and educational reform. In R. Rossi (Ed.), *Schools and students at risk.* New York: Teachers College Press.

BRECKINRIDGE, S., & ABBOTT, E. (1912). *The delinquent child and the home.* New York: Russell Sage Foundation.

BRIERE, J. (1992). *Child abuse trauma.* Newbury Park, CA: Sage.

BRITISH COLUMBIA MINISTRY OF HEALTH AND MINISTRY RESPONSIBLE FOR SENIORS (1992). *1990 British Columbia student drug use survey: Summary report.* Vancouver: Ministry of Health and Ministry Response for Seniors, Province of British Columbia.

BROMBERG, W. (1939). Marihuana: A psychiatric study. *Journal of the American Medical Association, 113,* 4-12.

BRONFENBRENNER, U. (1979). *The ecology of human development: Experiment by nature and design.* Cambridge, MA: Harvard University Press.

BRONFENBRENNER, U. (1986a). Ecology of the family as a context for human development: Research perspectives. *Developmental Psychology, 22,* 723-742.

BRONFENBRENNER, U. (1986b). Recent advances in research on the ecology of human development. In R. K. Silbereisen, K. Eyferth & G. Rudinger (Eds.), *Development as action in context.* Berlin: Springer-Verlag.

BRONFENBRENNER, U., & CROUTER, A. C. (1982). Work and family through time and space. In S. B. Kamaman & C. D. Hayes (Eds.), *Families that work: Children in a changing world.* Washington: National Academy Press.

BRUNET, B. L., REIFFENSTEIN, R. J., WILLIAMS, T., & WONG, L. (1985-1986). Toxicity of phencyclidine and ethanol in combination. *Alcohol and Drug Research, 6,* 341-349.

BUREAU OF THE CENSUS. (1995). *Current population reports, population projection of the U.S., by age, sex, race and Hispanic origin: 1995 to 2050.* Washington: Author.

BURGESS, E. W., & AKERS, R. L. (1966). A differential association-reinforcement behavior. *Social Problems, 14,* 128-147.

BURGESS, E. W., & BOGUE, D. J. (1967). The delinquency research of Clifford R. Shaw and Henry D. McKay and associates. In E. W. Burgess & D. J. Bogue (Eds.), *Urban sociology.* Chicago: University of Chicago Press.

BURSIK, R. J., Jr. (1987). *Political decision-making and ecological models of delinquency: Conflict and consensus.* The Albany Conference: Theoretical Integration in the Study of Deviance and Crime, May 7-8.

BURSIK, R. J., Jr., & WEBB, J. (1982). Community change and patterns of delinquency. *American Journal of Sociology, 88,* 24-43.

BURTON, R. V. (1963). Generality of honesty reconsidered. *Psychological Review, 70,* 481-499.

BURTON, R. V. (1976). In T. Lickona (Ed.), *Moral development and behavior.* New York: Holt, Rinehart & Winston.

BUSS, A. H., & PLOMIN, R. (1975). *A temperament theory of personality development.* New York: Wiley.

BUSS, A. H., & PLOMIN, R. (1984). *Temperament: Early developing personality traits.* Hillsdale, NJ: Erlbaum.

BUTTERFIELD, F. (1996, June 24). Republicans challenge notion of separate jails for juveniles. *New York Times,* p. A1.

BUTTERFIELD, F. (1996, August 9). After ten years, juvenile crime begins to drop. *New York Times,* pp. 1, A25.

BUTTS, J. A. (1994). *Offenders in Juvenile Court 1992.* Juvenile Justice Bulletin. Washington: U.S. Department of Justice.

BUTTS, J. A. (1996). *Offenders in juvenile court, 1993.* Washington: U.S. Government Printing Office.

BUTTS, J., SNYDER, H., FINNEGAN, T., AUGHENBAUGH, A., TIERNEY, N., SULLIVAN, D., POOLE, R., SICKMUND, M., & POE, E. (1995). *Juvenile court statistics, 1992.* Washington: Office of Juvenile Justice and Delinquency Prevention.

BYRNE, J. M., & SAMPSON, R. J. (Eds.). (1986). *The social ecology of crime.* New York: Springer-Verlag.

CAIRNS, R. B. (1983). The emergence of developmental psychology. In P. H. Mussen (Ed.), *Handbook of Child Psychology, Vol. 1.* (4th ed.). New York: Wiley.

CAIRNS, R. B., & CAIRNS, B. D. (1991). Social cognition and social networks: A developmental perspective. In D. J. Pepler & K. H. Rubin (Eds.), *The development and treatment of childhood aggression.* Hillsdale, NJ: Erlbaum.

CAMP, C. (1980). *School dropouts.* Sacramento, CA: Assembly Office of Research.

CAMPAGNA, A. F., & HARTER, S. (1975). Moral judgment in sociopathic and normal children. *Journal of Personality and Social Psychology, 31,* 199-205.

CAMPBELL, A. (1984). *The girls in the gang.* Oxford: Basil Blackwell.

CAMPBELL, A. (1993). *Men, women, and aggression.* New York: Basic Books.

CAMPOS, J. J., BARRETT, K. C., LAMB, M. E., GOLDSMITH, H. H., & STENBERG, C. (1983). Socioemotional development. In P. H. Mussen (Ed.), *Handbook of child psychology* (Vol. 4). (4th ed.). New York: Wiley.

CANTNER, R. (1981). *Family correlates of male and female delinquency.* Boulder, CO: Behavioral Institute.

CAREY, J. T. (1975). *Sociology and public affairs: The Chicago school.* Beverly Hills, CA: Sage.

CARNEGIE COUNCIL ON POLICY STUDIES IN HIGHER EDUCATION (1979). *Giving youth a better chance:*

Options for education, work and service. San Francisco: Jossey-Bass.

CARRAHER, T. N., CARRAHER, D., & SCHLIEMANN, A. D. (1985). Mathematics in the streets and schools. *British Journal of Developmental Psychology, 3,* 21-29.

CASPI, A., ELDER, G. H., JR., & BEM, D. J. (1987). Moving against the world: Life course patterns of explosive children. *Developmental Psychology, 23,* 308-313.

CENTERS FOR DISEASE CONTROL (1991). Weapon-carrying among high school students—United States, 1990. *Morbidity and Mortality Weekly Report, 40,* 681-684.

CHAMBERLAIN, P. (1996). Treatment foster care for adolescents with conduct disorders and delinquency. In P. S. Jensen & D. Hibbs (Eds.), *Psychological treatment research with children and adolescents.* Rockville, MD: National Institute of Mental Health.

CHAMPION, D. J., & MAYS, G. L. (1991). *Transferring juveniles to criminal courts.* New York: Praeger.

CHEN, S. A. (Ed.) (1992). *In pursuit of justice: National Anti-Asian Violence Task Force report and guidelines for citizen actions.* Washington: Organization of Chinese Americans.

CHEN, S. A., & TRUE, R. H. (1994). Asian/Pacific Island Americans. In L. D. Eron, J. H. Gentry, & P. Schlegel (Eds.), *Reason to hope: A psychosocial perspective on violence and youth.* Washington: American Psychological Association.

CHESNEY-LIND, M. (1982). Guilty by reason of sex: Young women and the juvenile justice system. In B. R. Price & N. J. Sokoloff (Eds.), *The criminal justice system and women.* New York: Clark Boardman Ltd.

CHESNEY-LIND, M. (1986). Women and crime: The female offender. *Signs, 12,* 78-96.

CHESNEY-LIND, M. (1988). Girls and status offenses: Is juvenile justice still sexist? *Criminal Justice Abstracts, 20,* 144-160.

CHESNEY-LIND, M. (1995). Girls, delinquency, and juvenile justice: Toward a feminist theory of young women's crime. In B. R. Price & N. J. Sokoloff (Eds.), *The criminal justice system and women* (2nd ed.). New York: Clark Boardman Ltd.

CHOWN, P. L., & PARHAM, J. (1995). Can we talk? Mediation in juvenile justice. *The FBI Law Enforcement Bulletin, 6,* 21.

CLAYTON, R. R., CATTARELLO, A., & WALDEN K. P. (1991). Sensation seeking as a potential mediating variable for school-based prevention interventions: A two-year follow-up of DARE. *Journal of Health Communications, 3,* 229-239.

CLEAR, T. R., & HARDYMAN, P. L. (1990). The new intensive supervision movement. *Crime and Delinquency, 36,* 42-60.

CLEVELAND, F. P. (1955). Problems in homicide investigation IV: The relationship of alcohol to homicide. *Cincinnati Journal of Medicine, 36,* 28-30.

CLINARD, M. (1978). *Cities with little crime: The case of Switzerland.* New York: Cambridge University Press.

CLOWARD, R. A., & OHLIN, L. E. (1960). *Delinquency and opportunity: A theory of delinquent gangs.* Glencoe, IL: Free Press.

COGAN, N. H. (1970). Juvenile law before and after the entrance of "parens patriae." *South Carolina Law Review, 22,* 147-181.

COHEN, A. K. (1955). *Delinquent boys: The culture of the gang.* Glencoe, IL: Free Press.

COHEN, A. K. (1965). The sociology of the deviant act: Anomie theory and beyond. *American Sociological Review, 30,* 5-14.

COHEN, A. K. (1980). The sociology of the deviant act: Anomie and beyond. In S. H. Traub & C. B. Little (Eds.), *Theories of deviance* (3rd ed.). Itasca, IL: Peacock.

COHEN, B. (1981). Reporting crime: The limits of statistical and field data. In A. S. Blumberg (Ed.), *Current perspective on criminal behavior* (2nd ed.). New York: Knopf.

COHEN, P., COHEN, J., & BROOK, J. (1993). An epidemiological study of disorders in late childhood and adolescence—II. Persistence of disorders. *Journal of Child Psychology and Psychiatry, 34,* 869-877.

COHN, V. (1986). Crack use. *NIDA Notes, 1,* 6.

COIE, J. D., BELDING, M., & UNDERWOOD, M. (1988). Aggression and peer rejection in childhood. In B. Lahey & A. Kazdin (Eds.), *Advances in clinical child psychology,* Vol. 2. New York: Plenum.

COIE, J. D., DODGE, K., & KUPERSMITH, J. (1990). Peer group behavior and social status. In S. R. Asher & J. D. Coie (Eds.), *Peer rejection in childhood.* Cambridge, England: Cambridge University Press.

COLBY, A., KOHLBERG, L. GIBBS, J., & LIEBERMANN, M. (1983). A longitudinal study of moral judgment. *Monographs of the Society for Research in Child Development, 48* (Nos. 1-2, Serial No. 200).

COLCORD, J. C. (1932). Discussion of "Are broken homes a causative factor in juvenile delinquency?" *Social Forces, 10,* 525-527.

COLE, K. E., FISHER, G., & COLE, S. S. (1968). Women who kill. *Archives of General Psychiatry, 19,* 1-8.

COLE, S. (1975). The growth of scientific knowledge: Theories of deviance as a case study. In L. A. Coser (Ed.), *The idea of social structure: Papers in honor of Robert K. Merton.* New York: Harcourt Brace Jovanovich.

COLEMAN, J. C. (1976). *Abnormal psychology and modern life* (5th ed.). Glenview, IL: Scott, Foresman.

COLEMAN, S., & GUTHRIE, K. (1984). *Directions: How today's juvenile justice trends have affected policy.* St. Paul, MN: Criminal Justice Statistical Analysis Center, Minnesota State Planning Agency.

CONGER, J. J., & MILLER, W. C. (1966). *Personality, social class and delinquency.* New York: Wiley.

CONLEY, D. J. (1994). Adding color to a black and white picture: Using qualitative data to explain racial disproportionality in the juvenile justice system. *Journal of Research in Crime and Delinquency, 312,* 135-148.

COORDINATING COUNCIL ON JUVENILE JUSTICE AND DELINQUENCY PREVENTION (1996). *Combating violence and delinquency: The national juvenile justice action plan.* Washington: U.S. Government Printing Office.

CORNELL, D. (1990). Prior adjustment of violent juvenile offenders. *Law and Human Behavior, 14,* 569-577.

CORTES, J. B., & GATTI, F. M. (1972). *Delinquency and crime: A biopsychological approach.* New York: Seminar Press.

COX, A. D., COX, D., ANDERSON, R. D., & MOSCHIS, G. P. (1993). Social influences on adolescent shoplifting—theory, evidence, and implications for the retail industry. *Journal of Retailing, 69,* 234-246.

CRESSEY, D. R. (1960). The theory of differential association: An introduction. *Social Problems, 8,* 2-5.

CRITCHLOW, B. (1986). The powers of John Barleycorn: Beliefs about the effects of alcohol on social behavior. *American Psychologist, 41,* 751-764.

CROMWELL, P. F., JR., KILLINGER, G. C., KERPER, H. B., & WALKER, C. (1985). *Probation and parole in the criminal justice system* (2nd ed.). St. Paul, MN: West.

CURTIS, G. B. (1976). The checkered career of parens patriae: The state as parent or tyrant? *DePaul Law Review, 25,* 895-915.

DALE, M. J., & SANNITI, C. (1993). Litigation as an instrument for change in juvenile detention: A case study. *Crime and Delinquency, 39,* 167-184.

DALGARD, O. S., & KRINGLEN, E. (1976). A Norwegian twin study of criminality. *British Journal of Criminology, 16,* 213-232.

DALY, K., & CHESNEY-LIND, M. (1988). Feminism and criminology. *Justice Quarterly, 5,* 497-535.

DATESMAN, S. K., & SCARPITTI, F. R. (1975). Female delinquency and broken homes: A reassessment. *Criminology, 13,* 33-54.

D'AUGELLI, A. R., & DARK, L. (1994). Lesbian, gay, and bisexual youths. In L. D. Eron, J. H. Gentry, & P. Schlegel (Eds.), *Reason to hope: A psychosocial perspective on violence and youth.* Washington: American Psychological Association.

DEJONG, W. (1987). A short-term evaluation of project DARE (Drug Abuse Resistance Education): Preliminary indications of effectiveness. *Journal of Drug Education, 17,* 279-294.

DEJONG, W. (1995). *Preventing interpersonal violence among youth.* U.S. Department of Justice: National Institute of Justice.

DELORTO, T. E., & CULLEN, F. T. (1985). The impact of moral development on delinquent involvement. *International Journal of Comparative and Applied Criminal Justice, 9,* 128-139.

DERVILLE, P., L'EPEE, P., LAZARIN, H. J., & DERVILLE, E. (1961). Statistical indications of a possible relationship between alcoholism and criminality: An inquiry into the Bordeaux region. *Revue Alcoholisme, 7,* 20-21.

DEVELOPMENTS IN THE LAW (1974). Civil commitment of the mentally ill. *Harvard Law Review, 87,* 1190-1406.

DiIULIO, J. J., Jr. (1995, November 27). The coming of the super-predators. *The Weekly Standard,* pp. 23-28.

DISHION, T. J. & ANDREWS, D. W. (1995). Preventing escalation in problem behaviors with high-risk young adolescents: Immediate and 1-year outcomes. *Journal of Consulting and Clinical Psychology, 63,* 538-548.

DISHION, T. J., & LOEBER, R. (1985). Male adolescent marijuana and alcohol use: The role of parents and peers revisited. *American Journal of Drug and Alcohol Abuse, 11,* 11-25.

DODGE, K. A. (1993a). The future of research on the treatment of conduct disorder. *Development and Psychopathology, 5,* 311-319.

DODGE, K. A. (1993b). Social-cognitive mechanisms in the development of conduct disorder and depression. *Annual Review of Psychology, 44,* 559-584.

DONNERSTEIN, E., SLABY, R. G., & ERON. L. D. (1994). The mass media and youth aggression. In E. Eron, J. H. Gentry, & P. Schlegel (Eds.), *Reason to hope: A psychosocial perspective on violence and youth.* Washington: American Psychological Association.

DORNBUSCH, S. M. (1983). *Social class, race and sex differences in family influence upon adolescent decision making.* Paper presented at the meeting of the Pacific Sociological Association, San Jose, CA.

DORNBUSCH, S. M., CARLSMITH, J. M., BUSCHWALL, S. J., RITTER, P. L., LEIDERMAN, H., HASTORF, C., & GROSS, R. T. (1985). Single parents, extended households, and the control of adolescents. *Child Development, 56,* 326-341.

DOUGLAS, J. W. B., ROSS, J. M., & SIMPSON, H. R. (1968). *All our future.* London: Peter Davies.

DOWNES, D., & ROCK, P. (1982). *Understanding deviance.* Oxford: Clarendon Press.

DUCK, S. W., & CRAIG, G. (1978). Personality similarity and the development of friendship: A longitudinal study. *British Journal of Social and Clinical Psychology, 17,* 237-242.

EISENBERG, N., & LENNON, R. (1983). Sex differences in empathy and related capacities. *Psychological Bulletin, 94,* 100-131.

ELLINWOOD, E. H. (1971). Assault and homicide associated with amphetamine abuse. *American Journal of Psychiatry, 127,* 90-95.

ELLIOTT, D. S., & AGETON, S. S. (1980). Reconciling race and class differences in self-reported and official estimates of delinquency. *American Sociological Review, 45,* 95-110.

ELLIOTT, D. S., AGETON, S. S., & CANTER, R. J. (1979). An integrated theoretical perspective on delinquent behavior. *Journal of Research in Crime and Delinquency, 16*, 3-27.

ELLIOTT, D. S., DUNFORD, F. W., & KNOWLES, B. (1978). *Diversion: A study of alternative processing.* Boulder, CO: Behavioral Institute.

ELLIOTT, D. S., & HUIZINGA, D. (1983). Social class and delinquent behavior in a national youth panel. *Criminology, 21*, 149-177.

ELLIOTT, D. S., & HUIZINGA, D. (1984). *The relationship between delinquent behavior and ADM [Alcohol, Drug, and Mental Health] problems.* Boulder, CO: Behavioral Research Institute.

ELLIOTT, D., HUIZINGA, D., & AGETON, S. (1985). *Explaining delinquency and drug use.* Beverly Hills, CA: Sage.

ELLIOTT, D. S., & VOSS, H. L. (1974). *Delinquency and dropout.* Lexington, MA: Lexington Books.

ELLIOTT, D. S., VOSS, H. L., & WENDLING, A. (1966). Capable dropouts and the social milieu of the high school. *Journal of Educational Research, 60*, 180-186.

EMERY, R. E. (1982). Interparental conflict and the children of discord and divorce. *Psychological Bulletin, 92*, 310-330.

EPPS, P., & PARNELL, R. W. (1952). Physique and temperament of women delinquents compared with women undergraduates. *British Journal of Medical Psychology, 25*, 249-255.

EREL, O., & BURMAN, B. (1995). Interrelatedness of marital relations and parent-child relations: A meta-analytic review. *Psychological Bulletin, 118*, 108-132.

ERNST, C., & ANGST, J. (1983). *Birth order: Its influence on personality.* Berlin: Springer-Verlag.

ERON, L. D., HUESMANN, L. R., & ZELLI, A. (1991). The role of parental variables in the learning of aggression. In D. J. Pepler & K. H. Rubin (Eds.), *The development and treatment of childhood aggression.* Hillsdale, NJ: Erlbaum.

ERON, L. D., & SLABY, R. G. (1994). Introduction. In L. D. Eron, J. H. Gentry, & P. Schlegel (Eds.), *Reason to hope: A psychosocial perspective on violence and youth.* Washington: American Psychological Association.

EWING, C. (1990). *When children kill: The dynamics of juvenile homicide.* Lexington, MA: Lexington Books.

EYSENCK, H. J. (1977). *Crime and personality* (2nd ed.). London: Routledge & Kegan Paul.

EYSENCK, H. J. (1983). Personality, conditioning, and antisocial behavior. In W. S. Laufer & J. M. Day (Eds.), *Personality, theory, moral development, and criminal behavior.* Lexington, MA: Lexington Books.

EYSENCK, H. J. (1984). Crime and personality. In D. J. Miller, D. E. Blackman, & A. J. Chapman (Eds.), *Psychology and the law.* Chichester, England: Wiley.

EYSENCK, H. J. (1996). Personality and crime: Where do we stand? *Psychology, Crime, & Law, 2*, 143-152.

EYSENCK, H. J., & GUDJONSSON, G. H. (1989). *The causes and cures of criminality.* New York: Plenum.

EZELL, M. (1989). Juvenile arbitration: Net-widening and other unintended consequences. *Journal of Research in Crime and Delinquency, 26*, 358-377.

EZELL, M. (1992). Juvenile diversion: The ongoing search for alternatives. In I. M. Schwartz (Ed.), *Juvenile justice and public policy.* New York: Lexington Books.

FAGAN, J., & WEXLER, S. (1987). Family origins of violent delinquents. *Criminology, 25*, 643-669.

FAHNESTOCK, K. L. (1990). *Time to justice: Caseflow in rural general jurisdiction courts.* Montpelier, VT: Rural Justice Center.

FARIS, R. E. L. (1967). *Chicago sociology: 1920-1932.* San Francisco: Chandler.

FARRINGTON, D. P. (1979). Environmental stress, delinquent behavior, and conviction. In I. G. Sarason & C. D. Spielberger (Eds.), *Stress and anxiety*, Vol. 6. Washington: Hemisphere.

FARRINGTON, D. P. (1989). Early predictors of adolescent aggression and adult violence. *Violence and Victims, 4*, 79-100.

FARRINGTON, D. P. (1991). Childhood aggression and adult violence: Early precursors and later life outcomes. In D. J. Pepler & K. H. Rubin (Eds.), *The development and treatment of childhood aggression.* Hillsdale, NJ: Erlbaum.

FARRINGTON, D. P., GUNDRY, G., & WEST, D. J. (1975). The familial transmission of criminality. *Medicine, Science and the Law, 15*, 177-186.

FARRINGTON, D. P., OHLIN, L. E., & WILSON, J. Q. (1986). *Understanding and controlling crime.* New York: Springer-Verlag.

FAUPEL, C. E. (1991). *Shooting dope: Career patterns of hard-core heroin users.* Gainesville, FL: University of Florida Press.

FEDERAL BUREAU OF INVESTIGATION (1995). *Uniform crime reports-1994.* Washington: U.S. Department of Justice.

FEDERAL BUREAU OF INVESTIGATION (1996). *Uniform crime reports-1995.* Washington: U.S. Department of Justice.

FEDERLE, K. H., & CHESNEY-LIND, M. (1992). Special issues in juvenile justice: Gender, race, and ethnicity. In I. M. Schwartz (Ed.), *Juvenile justice and public policy.* New York: Lexington Books.

FEINDLER, E. L., & BECKER, J. V. (1994). In L. D. Eron, J. H. Gentry, & P. Schlegel (Eds.), *Reason to hope: A psychosocial perspective on violence and youth.* Washington, DC: American Psychological Association.

FELD, B. C. (1984). Criminalizing juvenile justice: Rules of procedure for juvenile court. *Minnesota Law Review, 69*, 141-276.

FELD, B. C. (1988). *In re Gault* revisited: A cross-state comparison of the right to counsel in juvenile court. *Crime and Delinquency, 34*, 393-424.

FELD, B. C. (1989). Right to counsel in juvenile court: An empirical study of when lawyers appear and the difference they make. *Journal of Criminal Law and Criminology, 79*, 1185-1201.

FELD, B. C. (1991). Justice by geography: Urban, suburban, and rural variations in juvenile justice administration. *The Journal of Criminal Law and Criminology, 82*, 156-210.

FELD, B. C. (1992). Criminalizing the juvenile court: A research agenda for the 1990s. In I. M. Schwartz (Ed.), *Juvenile justice and public policy*. New York: Lexington Books.

FELSON, M. (1986). Linking criminal choices, routine activities, informal social control, and criminal outcomes. In R. Clarke & D. Cornish (Eds.), *The reasoning criminal*. New York: Springer-Verlag.

FELSON, M., & COHEN, L. E. (1980). Human ecology and crime: A routine activity approach. *Human Ecology, 8*, 389-406.

FETTER, T. (1977). Rural courts. In S. D. Cronk (Ed.), *A beginning assessment of the justice system in rural areas*. Washington: Joint Conference Report, National Rural Center/American Bar Association.

FILSTEAD, W. J. (1970). *Qualitative methodology: First hand involvement in the social world*. Chicago: Markham.

FINESTONE, H. (1976a). The delinquent and society: The Shaw and McKay tradition. In J. F. Short Jr. (Ed.), *Delinquency, crime and society*. Chicago: University of Chicago Press.

FINESTONE, H. (1976b). *Victims of change: Juvenile delinquents in American society*. Westport, CT: Greenwood Press.

FINKEL, N. J., HUGHES, B. A., SMITH, S. F., & HURABIELL, M. L. (1994). Killing kids: The juvenile death penalty and community sentiment. *Behavioral Sciences & the Law, 12*, 5-20.

FINKELHOR, D., & DZIUBA-LEATHERMAN, J. (1994). Victimization of children. *American Psychologist, 49*, 173-183.

FISCHER, C. S. (1982). *To dwell among friends: Personal networks in town and city*. Chicago: University of Chicago Press.

FISCHER, C. S., JACKSON, R. M., STUEVE, C. A., GERSAU, K., JONES, L. M., & BALDASSARE, M. (1977). *Networks and places*. New York: Free Press.

FISHER, R. S. (1951). Symposium on the compulsory use of chemical tests for alcoholic intoxication. *Maryland Medical Journal, 3*, 291-292.

FOREHAND, R., WIERSON, M., FRAME, C. L., KEMPTOM, T., & ARMISTEAD, L. (1991). Juvenile firesetting: A unique syndrome or an advanced level of antisocial behavior? *Behavioral Research and Therapy, 29*, 125-128.

FOX, S. J. (1970). Juvenile justice reform: An historical perspective. *Stanford Law Review, 22*, 1187-1239.

FRIDAY, P. C., & HAGE, J. (1976). Youth crime in postindustrial societies: An integrated perspective. *Criminology, 14*, 347-368.

FRIEND, T. (1996, August 21). Today's youth just don't see the dangers. *USA Today*, pp. 1-2.

GALVIN, J., & BLAKE, G. F. (1984). Youth policy and juvenile justice reforms. *Crime and Delinquency, 30*, 339-346.

GAMBLE, T. J., & ZIGLER, E. (1989). The headstart synthesis project: A critique. *Journal of Applied Developmental Psychology, 10*, 267-274.

GARBARINO, J. (1976). A preliminary study of some ecological correlates of child abuse: The impact of socioeconomic stress on mothers. *Child Development, 47*, 178-185.

GARBARINO, J. (1982). Sociocultural risk: Dangers to competence. In C. B. Kopp & J. B. Krakow (Eds.), *The child: Development in a social context*. Reading, MA: Addison-Wesley.

GARBARINO, J., & ASP, C. E. (1981). *Successful schools and competent students*. Lexington, MA: Lexington Books.

GARCIA, A. (1991). The changing demographic face of Hispanics in the United States. In M. Sotomayer (Ed.), *Empowering Hispanic families: A critical issue for the '90s*. Milwaukee, WI: Family Service America.

GARDNER, H. (1983). *Frames of mind: The theory of multiple intelligences*. New York: Basic Books.

GARDNER, H. (1986). The waning of intelligence tests. In R. J. Sternberg & D. K. Detterman (Eds.), *What is intelligence?* Norwood, NJ: Ablex.

GARDNER, H. (1993). *Multiple intelligences*. New York: Basic Books.

GARRETT, C. J. (1985). Effects of residential treatment on adjudicated delinquents: A meta-analysis. *Journal of Research in Crime and Delinquency, 22*, 287-308.

GEIS, G. (1965). *Juvenile gangs*. Washington: U.S. Government Printing Office.

GEIS, G. (1982). The Jack-roller: The appeal, the person, and the impact. In J. Snodgrass (Ed.), *The Jack-roller at seventy*. Lexington, MA: Lexington Books.

GELLES, R. J. (1982). Domestic criminal violence. In M. E. Wolfgang & N. A. Weiner (Eds.), *Criminal violence*. Beverly Hills, CA: Sage.

GENERAL ACCOUNTING OFFICE (1995). *Juveniles processed in criminal court and case dispositions: Letter report*. Washington: U.S. Government Printing Office.

GENSHEIMER, L. K., MAYER, J. P., GOTTSCHALK, R., & DAVIDSON, W. S. (1986). Diverting youth from the juvenile justice system: A meta-analysis of intervention efficacy. In S. J. Apter & A. P. Goldstein (Eds.), *Youth violence: Programs and prospects*. New York: Pergamon Press.

GERBNER, G. (1994). The politics of media violence: Some reflections. In C. Hamelink & O. Linne (Eds.),

Mass communication research: On problems and policies. Norwood, NJ: Ablex.

GERBNER, G., & GROSS, L. (1976). Living with television: The violence profile. *Journal of Communications, 26,* 173-199.

GERBNER, G., MORGAN, M., & SIGNORIELLI, N. (1993). *Television violence profile No. 16: The turning point for research to action.* Annenberg School of Communication, University of Pennsylvania.

GERWITZ, J. L. (1961). A learning analysis of the effects of normal stimulation, privation, and deprivation on the acquisition of social motivation and attachment. In B. M. Foss (Ed.), *Determinants of infant behavior.* New York: Wiley.

GIBBENS, T. C. N. (1963). *Psychiatric studies of Borstal lads.* London: Oxford University Press.

GIBSON, H. B. (1969). Early delinquency in relation to broken homes. *Journal of Child Psychology and Psychiatry, 10,* 195-204.

GIBSON, P. (1989). Gay male and lesbian youth suicide. In *Report of the Secretary's Task Force on Youth Suicide* (DHHS Publication No. ADM 89-1623, Vol. 3. Washington: U.S. Government Printing Office.

GILLIES, H. (1965). Murder in West Scotland. *British Journal of Psychiatry, 111,* 1087-1094.

GILLIGAN, C. (1982). *In a different voice.* Cambridge, MA: Harvard University Press.

GLASER, D. (1978). *Crime in our changing society.* New York: Holt, Rinehart & Winston.

GLUECK, S., & GLUECK, E. T. (1930). *Five hundred criminal careers.* New York: Knopf.

GLUECK, S., & GLUECK, E. T. (1934). *One thousand juvenile delinquents.* Cambridge, MA: Harvard University Press.

GLUECK, S., & GLUECK, E. T. (1937). *Later criminal careers.* New York: Commonwealth Fund.

GLUECK, S., & GLUECK, E. T. (1943). *Criminal careers in retrospect.* New York: Commonwealth Fund.

GLUECK, S., & GLUECK, E. T. (1950). *Unraveling juvenile delinquency.* Cambridge, MA: Harvard University Press.

GLUECK, S., & GLUECK, E. T. (1956). *Physique and delinquency.* New York: Harper and Brothers.

GLUECK, S., & GLUECK, E. T. (1957). Working mothers and delinquency. *Mental Hygiene, 41,* 327-352.

GLUECK, S., & GLUECK, E. T. (1968). *Delinquents and nondelinquents in perspective.* Cambridge, MA: Harvard University Press.

GOLD, M. S. (1984). *800-cocaine.* New York: Bantam.

GOLD, M. (1987). Social ecology. In H. C. Quay (Ed.), *Handbook of juvenile delinquency.* New York: Wiley.

GOLDSMITH, H. H., BUSS, A. H., PLOMIN, R., ROTHBART, M. K., THOMAS, A., CHESS, S., HINDE, R. A., & McCALL, R. B. (1987). Roundtable: What is temperament? Four Approaches. *Child Development, 58,* 505-529.

GOLDSMITH, H. H., & CAMPOS, J. J. (1982). Toward a theory of infant temperament. In R. N. Emde & R. J. Harmon (Eds.), *The development of attachment and affiliative systems.* New York: Plenum.

GOLDSTEIN, A. P. (1991). *Delinquent gangs: A psychological perspective.* Champaign, IL: Research Press.

GOLDSTEIN, A. P., & SORIANO, F. I. (1994). Juvenile gangs. In L. D. Eron, J. H. Gentry, & P. Schlegel (Eds.), *Reason to hope: A psychosocial perspective on violence and youth.* Washington: American Psychological Association.

GOODMAN, N. (1978). *Ways of worldmaking.* Indianapolis: Hackett.

GOODWIN, C. (1979). *The Oak Park strategy: Community control of racial change.* Chicago: University of Chicago Press.

GORDON, D. A., & ARBUTHNOT, J. (1987). Individual, group, and family interventions. In H. C. Quay (Ed.), *Handbook of juvenile delinquency.* New York: Wiley.

GORDON, M. (1971). *Juvenile delinquency in the American novel, 1905-1965.* Bowling Green, OH: Bowling Green University Popular Press.

GORDON, R. (1983). An operational definition of prevention. *Public Health Reports, 98,* 107-109.

GORMAN-SMITH, D., TOLAN, P. H., HUESMANN, L. R., & ZELLI, A. (1996). The relation of family functioning to violence among inner-city minority youths. *Journal of Family Psychology, 10,* 115-129.

GOTTFREDSON, M., & HIRSCHI, T. (1986). The true value of Lambda would appear to be zero: An essay on career criminals, criminal careers, selective incapacitation, short studies and related topics. *Criminology, 24,* 213-234.

GOTTFREDSON, M., & HIRSCHI, T. (1987). The methodological adequacy of longitudinal research on crime. *Criminology, 25,* 581-614.

GOTTFREDSON, M., & HIRSCHI, T. (1990). *A general theory of crime.* Stanford, CA: Stanford University Press.

GOVE, W., & CRUTCHFIELD, R. D. (1982). The family and delinquency. *The Sociological Quarterly, 23,* 301-319.

GREENBERG, B. S. (1986). Minorities in the mass media. In J. Bryant & D. Zillmann (Eds.), *Perspectives on media effects.* Hillsdale, NJ: Erlbaum.

GREENBERG, D. F. (1985). Age, crime and social explanation. *American Journal of Sociology, 91,* 1-21.

GREENBERG, D. F. (1991). Modeling criminal careers. *Criminology, 25,* 17-46.

GREENBERG, D. F. (1992). Comparing criminal career models. *Criminology, 30,* 141-147.

GREENWOOD, P. W., & TURNER, S. (1993). Evaluation of the Paint Creek Youth Center: A residential program for serious delinquents. *Criminology, 31,* 263-280.

GRINNELL, R. M., & CHAMBERS, C. A. (1979). Broken homes and middle class delinquency. *Criminology, 17,* 395-400.

GRISSO, T. (1980). Juveniles' capacities to waive Miranda rights: An empirical analysis. *California Law Review, 68*, 1134-1166.

GRISSO, T. (1984). Psychological concepts in juvenile law. (Final report of Research Grant No. MH-35090.) Rockville, MD: Center for Studies of Antisocial and Violent Behavior, National Institute of Mental Health.

GRISSO, T. (1986). *Evaluating competencies: Forensic assessments and instruments.* New York: Plenum.

GRISSO, T. (1996). Society's retributive response to juvenile violence: A developmental perspective. *Law and Human Behavior, 20*, 229-247.

GRISSO, T., & MELTON, G. (1987). Getting child development research to legal practitioners: Which way to the trenches? In G. Melton (Ed.), *Reforming the law: Impact of child development research.* New York: Guilford Press.

GRISSO, T., TOMKINS, A., & CASEY, P. (1988). Psychosocial concepts in juvenile law. *Law and Human Behavior, 12*, 403-437.

GRISSOM, G. R., & DUBNOV, W. L. (1989). *Without locks and bars: Reforming our reform schools.* New York: Praeger.

GUERRA, N. G., HUESMANN, L. R., TOLAN, P. H., VAN ACKER, R., & ERON, L. D. (1995). Stressful events and individual beliefs as correlates of economic disadvantage and aggression among urban children. *Journal of Consulting and Clinical Psychology, 63*, 518-528.

GUERRA, N. G., TOLAN, P. H., & HAMMOND, W. R. (1994). Prevention and treatment of adolescent violence. In L. D. Eron, J. H. Gentry, & P. Schlegel (Eds.), *Reason to hope: A psychosocial perspective on violence and youth.* Washington: American Psychological Association.

HAAN, N. (1977). *Coping and defending: Processes of self-environment organization.* New York: Academic Press.

HAAN, N. (1978). Two moralities in action contexts: Relationships to thought, ego regulation, and development. *Journal of Personality and Social Psychology, 36*, 286-305.

HAAPALA, D. A., & KINNEY, J. M. (1988). Avoiding out-of-home placement of high-risk status offenders through the use of intensive home-based family preservation services. *Criminal Justice and Behavior, 15*, 334-348.

HAGAN, J. (1987). Micro and macro-structure of delinquency causation and power-control theory of gender and delinquency. *Albany conference on theoretical integration in the study of deviance and crime.* State University of New York at Albany, May 7-8.

HAMMOND, W. R., & YUNG, B. R. (1994). African Americans. In L. D. Eron, J. H. Gentry, & P. Schlegel (Eds.), *Reason to hope: A psychosocial perspectives on violence and youth.* Washington: American Psychological Association.

HAMPARIAN, D. M., ESTER, L. K., MUNTEEN, S. M., PRIESTINO, R. R., SWISHER, R. G., WALLACE, P. L., & WHITE, J. L. (1982). *Youth in adult courts: Between two worlds.* Washington: U.S. Government Printing Office

HAMPARIAN, D. M. SCHUSTER, R., DINITZ, S., & CONRAD, J. D. (1978). *The violent few.* Lexington, MA: Lexington Books.

HANSELL, S., & WIATROWSKI, M. D. (1981). Competing conceptions of delinquent peer relations. In G. G. Jensen (Ed.), *Sociology of delinquency: Current issues.* Beverly Hills, CA: Sage.

HARE, R. D. (1983). Diagnosis of antisocial personality disorders in a prison population. *American Journal of Psychiatry, 140*, 887-890.

HARE, R. D., FORTH, A. E., & STACHAN, K. E. (1992). Psychopathy and crime across the life span. In R. D. Peters, R. J. McMahon, & V. L. Quinsey (Eds.), *Aggression and violence throughout the life span.* Newbury Park, CA: Sage.

HARE, R. D., MCPHERSON, L. M., & FORTH, A. E. (1988). Male psychopaths and their criminal careers. *Journal of Consulting and Clinical Psychology, 56*, 710-714.

HARTUP, W. W. (1983). Peer relations. In P. H. Mussen (Ed.), *Handbook of child psychology, Vol. 4* (4th ed.). New York: Wiley.

HARVEY, L. (1987). The nature of "schools" in the sociology of knowledge: The case of the "Chicago School." *The Sociological Review, 35*, 245-278.

HATHAWAY, S. R., & MONACHESI, E. D. (1957). The personalities of pre-delinquent boys. *Journal of Criminal Law, Criminology, and Police Science, 48*, 149-163.

HATHAWAY, S. R., & MONACHESI, E. D. (1963). *Adolescent personality and behavior.* Minneapolis: University of Minnesota Press.

HAWKINS, D. F. (1993). Inequity, culture and interpersonal violence. *Health Affairs, 12*, 80-95.

HAWKINS, J. D., VON CLEVE, E., & CATALANO, R. F. (1991). Reducing early childhood aggression: Results of a primary prevention program. *Journal of the American Academy of Child and Adolescent Psychiatry, 30*, 208-217.

HEALY, W. (1915). *The individual delinquent.* Boston: Little, Brown.

HEALY, W., & BRONNER, A. F. (1926). *Delinquents and criminals: Their making and unmaking.* New York: Macmillan.

HEILBRUN, K., HAWK, G., & TATE, D. C. (1996). Juvenile competence to stand trial: Research issues in practice. *Law and Human Behavior, 20*, 573-578.

HELLUM, F. (1979). Juvenile justice: The second revolution. *Crime and Delinquency, 25*, 299-317.

HENGGELER, S. W. (1996). Treatment of violent juvenile offenders—We have the knowledge: Comment on

Gorman-Smith et al. *Journal of Family Psychology*, 10, 137-141.

HENGGELER, S. W. & BORDUIN, C. M. (1990). *Family therapy and beyond: A multisystemic approach to treating the behavior problems of children and adolescents*. Pacific Grove, CA: Brooks/Cole.

HENGGELER, S. W., MELTON, G. B., & SMITH, L. A. (1992). Family preservation using multisystemic therapy—An effective alternative to incarcerating serious juvenile offenders. *Journal of Consulting and Clinical Psychology*, 60, 953-961.

HENKER, B., & WHALEN, C. K. (1989). Hyperactivity and attention deficits. *American Psychologist*, 44, 216-224.

HENNESSY, M., RICHARDS, P. J., & BERK, R. A. (1978). Broken homes and middle class delinquency: A reassessment. *Criminology*, 15, 505-528.

HENRY, B., CASPI, A., MOFFITT, T., & SILVA, P. A. (in press). Temperamental and familial predictors of violent and non-violent criminal convictions: From age 3 to age 18. *Developmental Psychology*.

HETHERINGTON, E. M., COX, M., & COX, R. (1979). Family interaction and the social, emotional, and cognitive development of children following divorce. In V. Vaughn & T. Brazelton (Eds.), *The family: Setting priorities*. New York: Science & Medicine.

HILL, H. M., SORIANO, F. I., CHEN, S. A., & LAFROMBOISE, T. D. (1994). Sociocultural factors in the etiology and prevention of violence among ethnic minority youth. In L. D. Eron, J. H. Gentry, & P. Schlegel (Eds.), *Reason to hope: A psychosocial perspective on violence and youth*. Washington: American Psychological Association.

HINDELANG, M. J. (1973). Causes of Delinquency: A partial replication and extension. *Social Problems*, 20, 471-487.

HINDELANG, M. J. (1979). Sex differences in criminal activity. *Social Problems*, 27, 143-156. 471-487.

HINDELANG, M. J., HIRSCHI, T., & WEIS, J. G. (1981). *Measuring delinquency*. Beverly Hills, CA: Sage.

HIRSCHI, T. (1969). *Causes of delinquency*. Berkeley: University of California Press.

HIRSCHI, T. (1983). Crime and family policy. *Journal of Contemporary Studies*, Winter, 3-16.

HIRSCHI, T. (1987). Exploring alternatives to integrated theory. *Albany conference on theoretical integration in the study of deviance and crime*. State University of New York at Albany, May 7-8.

HIRSCHI, T., & GOTTFREDSON, M. (1983). Age and the explanation of crime. *American Journal of Sociology*, 89, 552-584.

HIRSCHI, T., & HINDELANG, M. J. (1977). Intelligence and delinquency. *American Sociological Review*, 42, 571-587.

HIRSCHI, T., & HINDELANG, M. J. (1978). Reply to Ronald L. Simons. *American Sociological Review*, 43, 610-613.

HIRSCHI, T., & SELVIN, H. C. (1967). *Delinquency research: An appraisal of analytical methods*. New York: Free Press.

HOFFMAN, M. L. (1977). Sex differences in empathy and related behaviors. *Psychological Bulletin*, 84, 712-722.

HOFMANN, F. G. (1975). *A handbook on drug and alcohol abuse: The biomedical aspects*. New York: Oxford University Press.

HOGAN, R., & JONES, W. H. (1983). A role-theoretical model of criminal conduct. In W. S. Laufer & J. M. Day (Eds.), *Personality theory, moral development and criminal behavior*. Lexington, MA: Lexington Books.

HOLCOMB, W. R., & ANDERSON, W. P. (1983). Alcohol and multiple drug abuse in accused murderers. *Psychological Reports*, 52, 159-164.

HOLDEN, G. A., & KAPLER, R. A. (1995). Deinstitutionalizing status offenders: A record of progress. *Juvenile Justice*, 2, 3-10.

HOTALING, G. T., & STRAUS, M. A. (1989). Infrafamily violence, and crime and violence outside the family. In L. Ohlin & M. Tonry (Eds.), *Family violence, Vol. 11*. Chicago: University of Chicago Press.

HUDGINS, W., & PRENTICE, N. M. (1973). Moral judgments in delinquent and nondelinquent adolescents and their mothers. *Journal of Abnormal Psychology*, 82, 145-152.

HUESMANN, L. R. (1988). An information processing model for the development of aggression. *Aggressive Behavior*, 14, 13-24.

HUESMANN, L. R., & ERON, L. D. (Eds.). (1986). *Television and the aggressive child: A cross-national comparison*. Hillsdale, NJ: Erlbaum.

HUIZINGA, D. H., LOEBER, R., & THORNBERRY, T. (1994). *Urban delinquency and substance abuse: Initial findings*. Washington, D.C.: Office of Juvenile Justice and Delinquency Prevention.

HUSTON, A. C., DONNERSTEIN, E., FAIRCHILD, H., FESHBACH, N. D., KATZ, P. A., & MURRAY, J. P. (1992). *Big world, small screen: The role of television in American society*. Lincoln: University of Nebraska Press.

INABA, D. S., & COHEN, W. E. (1993). *Uppers, downers, all arounders: Physical and mental effects of psychoactive drugs* (2nd ed.). Ashland, OR: CNS Productions.

INCIARDI, J. A. (1981). Crime and alternative patterns of substance abuse. In S. E. Gardner (Ed.), *Drug and alcohol abuse*. Rockville, MD: National Institute on Drug Abuse.

INCIARDI, J. A. (1986). *The war on drugs: Heroin, cocaine, crime and public policy*. Palo Alto, CA: Mayfield.

INCIARDI, J. A. (Ed.) (1991). *The drug legalization debate*. Newbury Park, CA: Sage.

INCIARDI, J. A., PATTIEGER, A. E., FORNEY, M. A., CHITWOOD, D. D., & MCBRIDE, D. C. (1991). Prostitution, IV drug use, and sex-for-crack exchanges among serious delinquents: Risk for HIV infection. *Criminology, 29,* 221-235.

INSTITUTE FOR LAW AND JUSTICE (1994). *Gang prosecution in the United States.* U.S. Department of Justice. Washington: U.S. Government Printing Office.

JACKSON, H. F., GLASS, C., & HOPE, S. (1987). A functional analysis of recidivistic arson. *British Journal of Clinical Psychology, 26,* 175-185.

JAFFE, J. H., BABOR, T. F., & FISHBEIN, D. H. (1988). Alcoholics, aggression and behavior. *Journal of Studies on Alcohol, 49,* 211-218.

JARVIS, G., & PARKER, H. (1989). Young heroin users and crime. *British Journal of Criminology, 29,* 175-185.

JEGLUM-BARTUSCH, D. R., LYNAM, D. R., MOFFITT, T. W., & SILVA, P. A. (1997). Is age important? Testing a general versus a developmental theory of antisocial behavior. *Criminology, 35,* 13-48.

JENKINS, P. (1984). Temperance and the origins of the new penology. *Journal of Criminal Justice, 12,* 551-565.

JENNINGS, W. S., KILKENNY, R., & KOHLBERG, L. (1983). Moral development theory and practice for youthful and adult offenders. In W. S. Laufer & J. M. Day (Eds.), *Personality theory, moral development, and criminal behavior.* Lexington, MA: Lexington Books.

JESNESS, C. F. (1987). Early identification of delinquent-prone children: An overview. In J. D. Burchard & S. N. Burchard (Eds.), *Prevention of delinquent behavior.* Newbury Park, CA: Sage.

JESSOR, R. (1986). Adolescent problem drinking: Psychosocial aspect and developmental outcomes. In R. K. Silbereisen, K. Eyferth, & G. Rudinger (Eds.), *Development as action in context.* Berlin: Springer-Verlag.

JOHNSON, R. E. (1986). Family structure and delinquency: General patterns and gender differences. *Criminology, 24,* 64-80.

JOHNSON, R. (1996). *Hard time: Understanding and reforming the prison* (2nd ed.). Monterey, CA: Brooks/Cole.

JOHNSON, R. E., MARCOS, A. C., & BAHR, S. J. (1987). The role of peers in the complex etiology of adolescent drug use. *Criminology, 25,* 323-340.

JOHNSTONE, J. W. C. (1978). Juvenile delinquency and the family: A contextual interpretation. *Youth and Society, 9,* 299-313.

JOHNSTONE, J. W. C. (1980). Delinquency and the changing American family. In D. Schichor & D. H. Kelly (Eds.), *Critical issues in juvenile delinquency.* Lexington, MA: Lexington Books.

JONAS, S. (1991). The U.S. drug problems and the U.S. drug cultures: A public health solution. In J. A. Inciardi (Ed.), *The drug legalization debate.* Newbury Park, CA: Sage.

JOSEPH, J. (1995). *Black youths, delinquency, and juvenile justice.* Westport, CT: Praeger.

JULIEN, R. M. (1975). *A primer of drug action.* San Francisco: Freeman.

JULIEN, R. M. (1995). *A primer of drug action.* (7th ed.). New York: Freeman.

JURKOVIC, G. J., & PRENTICE, N. M. (1977). Relation of moral and cognitive development to dimensions of juvenile delinquency. *Journal of Abnormal Psychology, 86,* 414-420.

KAFREY, D. (1980). Playing with matches: Children and fire. In D. Canter (Ed.), *Fires and human behaviour.* Chichester, England: Wiley.

KALISH, C. B. (1983). *Prisoners and alcohol.* Washington: U.S. Government Printing Office.

KANDEL, D. B. (1978). *Longitudinal research on drug use.* Washington: Hemisphere.

KANDEL, D. B. (1984). Marijuana users in young adulthood. *Archives of General Psychiatry, 41,* 200-209.

KANDEL, D. B. (1986). Process of peer influences in adolescence. In R. K. Silbereisen, K. Eyferth, & G. Rudinger (Eds.), *Development as action in context.* Berlin: Springer-Verlag.

KANDEL, D. B., & LESSER, G. S. (1972). *Youth in two worlds.* San Franciso: Jossey-Bass.

KAZDIN, A. E. (1987). Treatment of antisocial behavior in children: Current status and future directions. *American Psychologist, 102,* 187-203.

KAZDIN, A. E. (1993). Adolescent mental health, prevention and treatment programs. *American Psychologist, 48,* 127-141.

KAZDIN, A. E. (1994). Psychotherapy for children and adolescents. In A. E. Bergin & S. L. Garfield (Eds.), *Handbook of psychotherapy and behavior change* (4th ed.). New York: Wiley.

KELLAM, S. G., ADAMS, R. G., BROWN, H. C., & ENSMINGER, M. E. (1982). The long term evolution of the family structure of teenage and older mothers. *Journal of Marriage and the Family, 44,* 539-554.

KELLAM, S. G., BRANCH, T. D., BROWN, C. H., & RUSSELL, G. (1981). Why teenagers come for treatment: A ten year prospective epidemiological study in Woodlawn. *Journal of the American Academy of Child Psychiatry, 20,* 477-495.

KELLING, G. L. (1987). A taste for order: The community and police. *Crime and Delinquency, 33,* 90-102.

KELLY, D. H. (1980). The educational experience and evolving delinquent careers: A neglected institutional link. In D. Schichor & D. H. Kelly (Eds.), *Critical issues in juvenile delinquency.* Lexington, MA: Lexington Books.

KELLY, G. A. (1955). *The psychology of personal constructs.* New York: Norton.

KELLY, G. A. (1963). *A theory of personality: The psychology of personal constructs.* New York: Norton.

KING, C. H. (1975). The ego and the integration of violence in homicidal youth. *American Journal of Orthopsychiatry,* (45), 134-144.

KITTRIE, N. N. (1971). *The right to be different: Deviance and enforced therapy.* Baltimore: Johns Hopkins University Press.

KLEBER, H. D. (1988). Epidemic cocaine abuse: America's present, Britain's future. *British Journal of Addiction, 83,* 1359-1371.

KLEIN, D. (1973). The etiology of female crime. *Issues in Criminology, 8,* 3-30.

KLEIN, M. (1971). *Street gangs and street workers.* Englewood Cliffs, NJ: Prentice-Hall.

KLEIN, M. W. (1979). Deinstitutionalization and diversion of juvenile offenders: A litany of impediments. In N. Morris & M. Tonry (Eds.), *Crime and justice: An annual review of research.* Chicago: University of Chicago Press, 145-201.

KLEIN, M., MAXSON, C. L., & CUNNINGHAM, L. C. (1988). *Gang involvement in cocaine 'rock' trafficking.* Project Summary/Final Report, Center for Research and Crime Control, Social Science Research Institute, University of Southern California, Los Angeles.

KLEMKE, L. W. (1992). *The sociology of shoplifting: Boosters and snitches today.* Westport, CT: Praeger.

KOBRIN, S. (1959). The Chicago Area Project—A 25 year assessment. *The Annals of the American Academy of Political and Social Science, 322,* 19-29.

KOBRIN, S. (1982). The uses of the life-history document for the development of delinquency theory. In J. Snodgrass (Ed.), *The Jack-roller at seventy.* Lexington, MA: Lexington Books.

KOHLBERG, L. (1969). Stage and sequence: The cognitive developmental approach to socialization. In D. A. Goslin (Ed.), *Handbook of socialization theory and research.* Chicago: Rand-McNally.

KOHLBERG, L. (1976). Moral stages and moralization: The cognitive developmental approach. In T. Lickona (Ed.), *Moral development and behavior,* New York: Holt, Rinehart, & Winston.

KOHLBERG, L. (1977). The child as a moral philosopher. In CRM, *Readings in developmental psychology today,* New York: Random House.

KOHLBERG, L., & FREUNDLICH, D. (1973). Moral judgment in youthful offenders. In L. Kohlberg & E. Turiel (Eds.), *Moralization, the cognitive development approach.* New York: Holt, Rinehart and Winston.

KOHN, M. L. (1977). *Class and conformity: A study in values* (2nd ed.). Chicago: University of Chicago Press.

KOLKO, D. J. (1985). Juvenile firesetting: A review and methodological critique. *Clinical Psychology Review, 5,* 345-376.

KOLKO, D. J., & KAZDIN, A. E. (1986). A conceptualization of firesetting in children and adolescents. *Journal of Abnormal Child Psychology, 17,* 157-176.

KORNHAUSER, R. R. (1978). *Social sources of delinquency: An appraisal of analytic models.* Chicago: University of Chicago Press.

KOZOL, J. (1992). *Savage inequalities: Children in America's schools.* New York: Harper Perennial.

KOZOL, J. (1995). *Amazing grace: The lives of children and the conscience of a nation.* New York: Continuum.

KRATCOSKI, P. C., & KRATCOSKI, L. D. (1996). *Juvenile delinquency* (4th ed.). Upper Saddle River, NJ: Prentice-Hall.

KRISBERG, B. (1995). The legacy of juvenile corrections. *Corrections Today, 57,* 122-126.

KRISBERG, B., NEUENFELDT, D., WIEBUSH, R., & RODRIGUEZ, O. (1994). *Juvenile intensive supervision: Planning guide.* Washington: National Council on Crime and Delinquency.

KRISBERG, B., & SCHWARTZ, I. (1983). Rethinking juvenile justice. *Crime and Delinquency, 29,* 333-364.

KRISBERG, B., SCHWARTZ, I., FISHMAN, G., ELSIKOVITZ, Z., GUTTMAN, E., & KAREN, J. (1987). The incarceration of minority youth. *Crime and Delinquency, 33,* 173-205.

KRISBERG, B., SCHWARTZ, I. M., LITSKY, P., & AUSTIN, J. (1986). The watershed of juvenile justice reform. *Crime and Delinquency, 32,* 5-38.

KROHN, M. D. (1986). The web of conformity: A network approach to the explanation of delinquent behavior. *Social Problems, 33,* 81-93.

KROHN, M. D., KANZA-KADUCE, L., & AKERS, R. L. (1984) Community context and theories of deviant behavior: An examination of social learning and social bonding theories. *Sociological Quarterly, 25,* 353-371.

KROHN, M. D., & MASSEY, J. L. (1980). Social control and delinquent behavior: An examination of the elements of the social bond. *Sociological Quarterly, 21,* 529-544.

KROHN, M D., MASSEY, J. L., SKINNER, W. F., & LAVER, R. (1983). Social bonding theory and adolescent cigarette smoking: A longitudinal analysis. *Journal of Health and Social Behavior, 24,* 337-349.

KUBY, R. W., & CSIKSZENTMIHALYI, M. (1990). *Television and the quality of life: How viewing shapes everyday experience.* Hillsdale, NJ: Erlbaum.

KURTZ, L. R. (1984). *Evaluating Chicago sociology: A guide to the literature with an annotated bibliography.* Chicago: University of Chicago Press.

LAMB, M. E. (1977). The effects of divorce on children's personality development. *Journal of Divorce, 2,* 163-174.

LANG, A. R., GOECKNER, D. J., ADESSO, V. G., & MARLATt, G. A. (1975). Effects of alcohol on aggression in male social drinkers. *Journal of Abnormal Psychology, 84,* 508-518.

LANGE, J. (1928). *Crime as destiny.* London: George Allen and Unwin.

LANGNER, T. S., GERSTEN, J. C., & EISENBERG, J. G. (1977). The epidemiology of mental disorders in children: Implications for community psychiatry. In G. Serban (Ed.), *New trends of psychiatry in the community.* Cambridge, MA: Ballinger.

LANIER, M., & McCARTHY, B. (1989). AIDS awareness and the impact of AIDS education in juvenile corrections. *Criminal Justice and Behavior, 16*(4), 395-411.

LAUB, J. H. (1983). Trends in serious juvenile crime. *Criminal Justice and Behavior, 10*, 485-506.

LAW ENFORCEMENT ASSISTANCE ADMINISTRATION (1976). *Survey of inmates of state correctional facilities, 1974: Advance report.* Washington: U.S. Government Printing Office.

LEES, J. P., & NEWSON, L. J. (1954). Family or sibship position of some aspects of juvenile delinquency. *British Journal of Delinquency, 5*, 46-55.

LEFKOWITZ, M. M., ERON, L. D., WALDER, L. O., & HUESMANN, L. R. (1977). *Growing up to be violent.* New York: Pergamon.

LEMERT, E. M. (1951). *Social pathology.* New York: McGraw-Hill.

LEMERT, E. M. (1983). Interview with E. M. Lemert, March 16, 1979. In J. H. Laub (Ed.), *Criminology in the making: An oral history.* Boston: Northeastern University Press.

LENROOT, K. R. (1932). Discussion of "Are broken homes a causative factor in juvenile delinquency?" *Social Forces, 10*, 527-529.

LEONARD, E. B. (1982). *Women, crime, and society.* New York: Longman.

LESTER, D. (1991). Crime as opportunity: A test of the hypothesis with European homicide rates. *British Journal of Criminology, 31*, 186-188.

LIPSEY, M. W. (1991). Juvenile delinquency treatment: A meta-analytic inquiry into the variability of effects. In T. D Cook, H. Cooper, D. S. Cordaray, H. Hartmann, L. V. Hedges, R. J. Light, T. A. Louis, & F. Mosteller (Eds.), *Meta-analysis for explanation: A casebook.* New York: Russell Sage Foundation.

LIPSEY, M. W. (1995). What do we learn from 400 research studies on the effectiveness of treatment with juvenile delinquents? In J. McGuire (Ed.), *What works: Reducing reoffending.* New York: Wiley.

LO, L. (1994). Exploring teenage shoplifting behavior: A choice and constraint approach. *Environment and Behavior, 26*, 613-639.

LOEBER, R. (1990). Development and risk factors of juvenile antisocial behavior and delinquency. *Clinical Psychology Review, 10*, 1-41.

LOEBER, R., & STOUTHAMER-LOEBER, M. (1986). Family factors as correlates and predictors of juvenile conduct problems and delinquency. In N. Morris & M. Tonry (Eds.), *Crime and justice: An annual review of research,* Vol. 7. Chicago: University of Chicago Press.

LOMBROSO, C., with FERRERO, W. (1895). *The female offender.* London: Fisher Unwin.

LOU, H. H. (1927). *Juvenile courts in the United States.* New York: Arno.

LYLERLY, R. R., & SKIPPER, J. K., JR. (1981). Differential rates of rural-urban delinquency: A social control approach. *Criminology, 19*, 385-399.

MACCOBY, E. E. (1986). Social groupings in childhood. In D. Olweus, J. Block, & M. Radke-Yarrow (Eds.), *Development of antisocial and prosocial behavior.* Orlando, FL: Academic Press.

MACCOBY, E. E., & JACKLIN, C. N. (1980). Sex difference in aggression: A rejoinder and reprise. *Child Development, 51*, 964-980.

MACKENZIE, D. L. (1996). Boot camp prisons: Examining their growth and effectiveness. In K. C. Haas & G. P. Alpert (Eds.), *The dilemmas of corrections* (3rd ed.). Prospect Heights, IL: Waveland Press.

MACKENZIE, D. L., & HEBERT, E. (Eds.) (1995). *Correctional boot camps: A tough intermediate sanction.* Washington: National Institute of Justice.

MAGNUSSON, D. (1981). *Toward a psychology of situations: An interactional perspective.* Hillsdale, NJ: Erlbaum.

MAGNUSSON, D., & ALLEN, V. L. (1983). Implications and applications of an interactional perspective for human development. In D. Magnusson & V. L. Allen (Eds.), *Human development: An interactional perspective.* New York: Academic Press.

MAGUIRE, K., & PASTORE, A. (Eds.) (1995). *Sourcebook of criminal justice statistics.* Washington: U.S. Department of Justice, Bureau of Justice Statistics.

MAHAR, L., & CURTIS, R. (1995). In search of the female urban "gangster": Change, culture, and crack cocaine. In B. R. Price & N. J. Sokoloff (Eds.), *The criminal justice system and women,* 2nd ed. New York: McGraw-Hill.

MANICAS, P. T., & SECORD, P. F. (1983). Implications for psychology of the new philosophy of science. *American Psychologist, 38*, 399-413.

MANN, C. R. (1984). *Female crime and delinquency.* University: University of Alabama Press.

MANN, C. R. (1993). Maternal filicide of preschoolers. In A. V. Wilson (Ed.), *Homicide: The victim/offender connection.* Cincinnati, OH: Anderson.

MANNHEIM, H. (1965). *Comparative criminology.* Boston: Houghton Mifflin.

MARLATT, G. A., & ROHSENOW, D. J. (1980). Cognitive processes in alcohol use: Expectancy and the balanced placebo design. In N. K. Mello (Ed.), *Advances in substance abuse: Behavioral and biological research.* Greenwich, CT: JAI Press.

MATSUEDA, R. (1982). Testing control theory and differential association: A causal modeling approach. *American Sociological Review, 47*, 489-504.

MAWBY, R. (1980). Sex and crime. *British Journal of Sociology, 31*, 525-543.

MAYFIELD, D. (1976). Alcoholism, alcohol, intoxication and assaultive behavior. *Diseases of the Nervous System, 37*, 288-291.

McCandless, B. R., Persons, W. S., & Roberts, A. (1972). Perceived opportunity, delinquency, race and body build among delinquent youth. *Journal of Consulting and Clinical Psychology, 38*, 281-287.

McCarthy, B. (1987). Preventive detention and pretrial custody in the juvenile court. *Journal of Criminal Justice, 15*, 185-200.

McCord, J. (1978). A thirty-year follow up of treatment effects. *American Psychologist, 33*, 284-289.

McCord, J. (1979). Some child rearing antecedents of criminal behavior in adult men. *Journal of Personality and Social Psychology, 37*, 1477-1486.

McCord, J. (1986). Instigation and insulation: How families affect antisocial behavior. In D. Olweus, J. Block, & M. Radke-Yarrow (Eds.), *Development of antisocial and prosocial behavior*. Orlando, FL: Academic Press.

McCord, W., McCord, J., & Zola, I. K. (1959). *Origins of crime: A new evaluation of the Cambridge-Somerville study*. New York: Columbia University Press.

McGahey, R. M. (1986). Economic conditions, neighborhood organization, and urban crime. In A. J. Reiss Jr. & M. Tonry (Eds.), *Communities and crime*. Chicago: University of Chicago Press.

McGarrell, E. (1993). Trends in racial disproportionality in juvenile court processing: 1985-1989. *Crime and Delinquency, 39*, 29-48.

McGuire, S. (1996, October 28). The Dunblane effect. *Newsweek*, p. 46.

McKenzie, D., & Williams, B. (1995). Licit and illicit drugs. Canadian Profile: Alcohol, Tobacco and Other Drugs. http://www.ccsa.ca/cpdruge.htm.

McShane, D. A., & Plas, J. M. (1984a). Response to a critique of the McShane & Plas review of American Indian performance on the Wechsler Intelligence Scales. *School Psychology Review, 13*, 83-88.

McShane, D. A., & Plas, J. M. (1984b). The cognitive functioning of American Indian Children: Moving from the WISC to the WISC-R. *School Psychology Review, 13*, 61-73.

McShane, M. D., & Williams, F. P. (1989). The prison adjustment of juvenile offenders. *Crime and Delinquency, 35*, 254-269.

Mechoulam, R. (1970). Marihuana chemistry. *Science, 168*, 1159-1166.

MEGG Associates (1996). *NIBRS now! A NIBRS overview report*. Richmond, VA: Author.

Menard, S., & Morse, B. J. (1984). A structuralist critique of the IQ-delinquency hypothesis: Theory and evidence. *American Journal of Sociology, 89*, 1347-1378.

Mennel, R. M. (1983). Attitudes and policies toward juvenile delinquency in the United States: A historiographical review. In M. Tonry & N. Morris (Eds.), *Crime and justice: Annual review of research, Vol. 4*. Chicago: University of Chicago Press.

Merton, R. K. (1938). Social structure and anomie. *American Sociological Review, 3*, 672-682.

Messner, S., & Rosenfeld, R. (1994). *Crime and the American dream*. Belmont, CA: Wadsworth.

Miczek, K. A., DeBold, J. F., Haney, M., Tidey, J., Vivian, J., & Weerts, E. M. (1994). Alcohol, drugs of abuse, aggression, and violence. In A. J. Reiss & J. A. Roth (Eds.), *Understanding and preventing violence, Vol. 3. Social Influences*. Washington: National Academy Press.

Miller, T. R., Cohen, M. A., & Wiersema, B. (1996). *Victim costs and consequences: A new look*. Washington: National Institute of Justice.

Miller, W. B. (1958). Lower class culture as a generating milieu of gang delinquency. *Journal of Social Issues, 14*, 5-19.

Miller, W. B (1962). The impact of a "total-community" delinquency control project. *Social Problems, 10*, 168-191.

Miller, W. (1975). *Violence by youth gangs and youth groups as a crime problem in major American cities*. Washington: U.S. Government Printing Office.

Miller, W. B. (1980). Gangs, groups, and serious youth crime. In D. Schichor & D. H. Kelly (Eds.), *Critical issues in juvenile delinquency*. Lexington, MA: Lexington Books.

Miller, W. (1982). *Crime by youth gangs and groups in the United States*. Washington: U.S. Government Printing Office.

Miller, W. R., & Hester, R. K. (1989). Treating alcohol problems: Toward an informed eclecticism. In R. K. Hester & W. R. Miller (Eds.), *Handbook of alcoholism treatment approaches: Effective alternatives*. New York: Pergamon Press.

Minor, K. I., & Elrod, H. P. (1990). The effects of a multi-faceted intervention on the offense activities of juvenile probationers. *Journal of Offender Counseling, Services, and Rehabilitation, 15*, 87-108.

Minor, K. I., & Elrod, P. (1994). The effects of a probation intervention on juvenile offenders' self-concepts, loci of control, and perceptions of juvenile justice. *Youth & Society, 25*, 490-511.

Moffitt, T. E. (1990). Juvenile delinquency and attention deficit disorder: Boys' developmental trajectories from age 13 to age 15. *Child Development, 61*, 893-910.

Moffitt, T. E. (1993a). Adolescence-limited and life-course-persistent antisocial behavior: A developmental taxonomy. *Psychological Review, 100*, 674-701.

Moffitt, T. E. (1993b). The neuropsychology of conduct disorder. *Development and Psychopathology, 5*, 135-151.

Moffitt, T. E., Caspi, A., Dickson, N., Silva, P., & Stanton, W. (1996). Childhood-onset versus adolescent-onset antisocial conduct problems in males: Natural history from ages 3 to 18. *Development and Psychopathology, 8*, 399-424.

MOFFITT, T. E., & SILVA, P. A. (1988). Self-reported delinquency, neuropsychological deficit, and history of attention deficit disorder. *Journal of Abnormal Child Psychology, 16*, 553-569.

MONAHAN, T. P. (1957). Family status and the delinquent child: A reappraisal and some new findings. *Social Forces, 35*, 250-258.

MONTEMAYOR, R. (1978). Men and their bodies: The relationships between body types and behavior. *Journal of Social Issues, 34*, 48-64.

MOORE, D. B. (1993). Shame, forgiveness, and juvenile justice. *Criminal Justice Ethics, 12*, 3-25.

MORASH, M. A. (1981). Cognitive development theory. *Criminology, 19*, 360-371.

MORASH, M. A. (1983). An explanation of juvenile delinquency: The integration of moral reasoning theory and sociological knowledge. In W. S. Laufer & J. M. Day (Eds.), *Personality theory, moral development, and criminal behavior*. Lexington, MA: Lexington Books.

MORRIS, T. P. (1957). *The criminal area: A study in social ecology*. London: Routledge & Kegan Paul.

MOTT, J. (1986). Opoid use and burglary. *British Journal of Addiction, 81*, 671-677.

MULVEY, E. P., ARTHUR, M. W., & REPPUCCI, N. D. (1993). The prevention and treatment of juvenile delinquency: A review of the research. *Clinical Psychology Review, 13*, 133-167.

MURPHY, G. H., & CLARE, C. H. (1996). Analysis of motivation in people with mild learning disabilities (mental handicap) who set fires. *Psychology, Crime & Law, 2*, 153-164.

MURRAY, C. (1976). *The link between learning disabilities and juvenile delinquency: Current theory and knowledge. Executive Summary*. Washington: U. S. Government Printing Office.

NADELMAN, E. A. (1991). The case for legalization. In J. A. Inciardi (Ed.), *The drug legalization debate*. Newbury Park, CA: Sage.

NAGEL, I. H., & HAGAN, J. (1983). Gender and crime: Offense patterns and criminal court sanctions. In M. Tonry & N. Morris (Eds.), *Crime and justice: An annual review of research, Vol. 4*. Chicago: University of Chicago Press.

NAGIN, D. S., FARRINGTON, D. P., & MOFFITT, T. (1995). Life-course trajectories of different types of offenders. *Criminology, 33*, 111-139.

NAGIN, D. S., & LAND, K. C. (1993). Age, criminal careers, and population heterogeneity: Specification and estimation of a nonparametric, mixed Poisson model. *Criminology, 31*, 163-189.

NATIONAL CENTER FOR THE ANALYSIS OF VIOLENT CRIME (1992). *Annual report*. Quantico, VA: FBI Academy.

NATIONAL COMMISSION ON MARIHUANA AND DRUG ABUSE (1972). *Marihuana: A signal of misunderstanding*. Appendix, Vol. 1. Washington: U.S. Government Printing Office.

NATIONAL COMMISSION ON MARIHUANA AND DRUG ABUSE. (1973). *Drug use in America: Problem in perspective* (2nd Report). Washington, DC: U.S. Government Printing Office.

NATIONAL INSTITUTE OF JUSTICE (November, 1995). *Drug use forecasting: 1994 annual report on adult and juvenile arrestees*. Washington: U.S. Government Printing Office.

NATIONAL INSTITUTE OF MENTAL HEALTH (1982). *Television and behavior: Ten years of scientific progress and implications for the eighties*. Summary Report (Vol. 1). Washington: U.S. Government Printing Office.

NATIONAL INSTITUTE ON ALCOHOL ABUSE AND ALCOHOLISM (1990). *Alcohol and health: Neuroscience*. Rockville, MD: U.S. Government Printing Office.

NATIONAL INSTITUTE ON DRUG ABUSE (1978). Drug abuse and crime. In L. D. Savitz & N. Johnson (Eds.), *Crime in society*. New York: Wiley.

NEILSEN, A., & GERBER, D. (1979). Psychological aspects of truancy in early adolescence. *Adolescence, 41*, 313-326.

NEISSER, U., et al., (1996). Intelligence: Knowns and unknowns. *American Psychologist, 51*, 77-101.

NELSON, R. J., SMITH, D. J., & DODD, J. (1990). The moral reasoning of juvenile delinquency. *Journal of Abnormal Child Psychology, 18*, 231-239.

NETTLER, G. (1984). *Explaining crime*. (3rd ed.). New York: McGraw-Hill.

NIARHOS, F. J., & ROUTH, D. K. (1992). The role of clinical assessment in the juvenile court: Predictors of juvenile dispositions and recidivism. *Journal of Clinical Child Psychology, 21*, 151-159.

NICHOL, A. R., GUNN, J. C., GRISTWOOD, J., FOGGETT, R. H., & WATSON, J. P. (1973). The relationship of alcoholism to violent behaviors resulting in long-term imprisonment. *British Journal of Psychiatry, 23*, 47-51.

NORLAND, S., SHOVER, N., THORNTON, W., & JAMES, J. (1979). Intrafamily conflict and delinquency. *Pacific Sociological Review, 22*, 233-237.

NYE, F. I. (1958). *Family relationships and delinquent behavior*. New York: Wiley.

O'DONNELL, J., HAWKINS, J. D., & ABBOTT, R. D. (1995). Predicting serious delinquency and substance abuse among aggressive boys. *Journal of Consulting and Clinical Psychology, 63*, 529-537.

OFFICE OF JUVENILE JUSTICE AND DELINQUENCY PREVENTION (1993). *Children in custody census 1990/1991*. Washington: U.S. Government Printing Office.

OFFORD, D. R., BOYLE, M. C., & RACINE, Y. A. (1991). The epidemiology of antisocial behavior in childhood and adolescence. In D. J. Pepler & K. H. Rubin (Eds.), *The development and treatment of childhood aggression*. Hillsdale, NJ: Erlbaum.

OGBU, J. U. (1974). *The next generation: An ethnography of education in an urban neighborhood*. New York: Academic Press.

OHLIN, L. E. (1983a). Interview with Lloyd E. Ohlin, June 22, 1979. In J. H. Laub (Ed.), *Criminology in the making: An oral history*. Boston: Northeastern University Press.

OHLIN, L. E. (1983b). The future of juvenile delinquency policy and research. *Crime and Delinquency, 29*, 463-472.

OHLIN, L., & TONRY, M. (1989). Family violence in perspective. In L. Ohlin & M. Tonry (Eds.), *Family violence, Vol. 11*. Chicago: University of Chicago Press.

OLWEUS, D. (1978). *Aggression in the schools*. New York: Wiley.

OLWEUS, D. (1980). Familial and temperamental determinants of aggressive behavior in adolescent boys: A causal analysis. *Developmental Psychology, 16*, 644-660.

PAGELOW, M. D. (1989). The incidence and prevalence of criminal abuse of other family members. In L. Ohlin & M. Tonry (Eds.), *Family violence, Vol. 11*. Chicago: University of Chicago Press.

PARK, R. E., & MILLER, H. A. (1921). *Old world traits transplanted*. New York: Harper and Brothers.

PARKER, H., & NEWCOMBE, R. (1987). Heroin use and acquisitive crime in an English community. *British Journal of Sociology, 38*, 331-350.

PARKER, J. G., & ASHER, S. R. (1987). Peer relations and later personal adjustment: Are low-accepted children at risk? *Psychological Bulletin, 102*, 357-389.

PATTERSON, G. R. (1982). *Coercive family process*. Eugene, OR: Castalia Press.

PATTERSON, G. R. (1986a). Performance models for antisocial boys. *American Psychologist, 41*, 432-444.

PATTERSON, G. R. (1986b). The contribution of siblings to training for fighting: A microsocial analysis. In D. Olweus, J. Block, & M. Radke-Yarrow (Eds.), *Development of antisocial and prosocial behavior*. Orlando, FL: Academic Press.

PATTERSON, G. R., DISHION, T. J., & BANK, L. (1984). Family interaction: A process model of deviance training. *Aggressive Behavior, 10*, 253-267.

PEARSON, F., & WEINER, N. A. (1985). Toward an integration of criminological theories. *Journal of Criminal Law and Criminology, 76*, 116-150.

PEELE, S. (1984). The cultural context of psychological approaches to alcoholism. *American Psychologist, 39*, 1337-1351.

PEIRCE, B. K. (1969/1869). *A half century with juvenile delinquents*. Montclair, NJ: Patterson Smith.

PEPLER, D. J., BYRD, W., & KING, G. (1991). A social-cognitively based social skills training program for agressive children. In D. J. Pepler & K. H. Rubin (Eds.), *The development and treatment of childhood aggression*. Hillsdale, NJ: Erlbaum.

PEPLER, D. J., & SLABY, R. G. (1994). Theoretical and developmental perspectives on youth and violence. In L. D. Eron, J. H. Gentry, & P. Schlegel (Eds.), *Reason to hope: A psychosocial perspective on violence and youth*. Washington, DC: American Psychological Association.

PETERSILIA, J., & TURNER, S. (1995). Evaluating intensive supervision probation/parole: Results of a nationwide experiment. In K. C. Haas, & G. P. Alpert (Eds.), *Dilemmas of corrections* (3rd ed.). Prospect Heights, IL: Waveland Press.

PETERSON, D. R., & BECKER, W. S. (1965). Family interaction and delinquency. In H. C. Quay (Ed.), *Juvenile delinquency: Research and theory*. Princeton, NJ: Van Nostrand.

PETRAITIS, J., FLAY, B. R., & MILLER, T. Q. (1995). Reviewing theories of adolescent substance use: Organizing pieces in the puzzle. *Psychological Bulletin, 117*, 67-86.

PFOHL, S. J. (1985). *Images of deviance and social control: A sociological history*. New York: McGraw-Hill.

PHARES, E. J. (1972). Applications to psychopathology. In J. B. Rotter, J. E. Chance, & E. J. Phares (Eds.), *Applications of a social learning theory of personality*. New York: Holt, Rinehart and Winston.

PIAGET, J. (1948). *The moral judgment of the child*. New York: Free Press.

PISCIOTTA, A. W. (1983). Scientific reform: The `new penology' at Elmira, 1876-1900. *Crime and Delinquency, 29*, 613-630.

POE-YAMAGATA, E., & BUTTS, J. A. (1996). *Female offenders in the juvenile justice system*. Washington: Office of Juvenile Justice and Delinquency Prevention.

POLLAK, O. (1950). *The criminality of women*. New York: A. S. Barnes.

POWERS, E., & WITMER, H. (1951). *An experiment in the prevention of delinquency*. New York: Columbia University Press.

RADA, R. T. (1975). Alcoholism and forcible rape. *American Journal of Psychiatry, 121*, 776-783.

RAFTER, N. (1990). *Partial justice: Women, prisons and social control*. New Brunswick, NJ: Transaction Books.

RAINE, A. (1993). *The psychopathology of crime: Criminal behavior as a clinical disorder*. San Diego, CA: Academic Press.

RANKIN, J. H. (1983). The family context of delinquency. *Social Problems, 30*, 466-479.

RATNER, M. S. (1993). Sex, drugs, and public policy: Studying and understanding the sex-for-crack phenomenon. In M. S. Ratner (Ed.), *Crack pipe as pimp: An ethnographic investigation of sex-for-crack exchanges*. New York: Lexington Books.

RAY, O. (1972). *Drugs, society and human behavior*. St. Louis, MO: C. V. Mosby.

RAY, O. (1983). *Drugs, society and human behavior* (3rd ed.). St. Louis, MO: C. V. Mosby.

RECKLESS, W. C. (1961). *The crime problem* (2nd ed.). New York: Appleton-Century-Crofts.

RECKLESS, W. C. (1973). *The crime problem* (5th ed.). New York: Appleton-Century-Crofts.

RECKLESS, W. C., & DINITZ, S. (1967). Pioneering with self-concept as a vulnerability factor in delinquency. *Journal of Criminal Law, Criminology and Police Science, 63*, 515-523.

REGNERY, A. S. (1986). A federal perspective on juvenile justice reform. *Crime and Delinquency, 32*, 39-51.

REICHENBACH, H. (1947). *Elements of symbolic logic*. New York: Macmillan.

REID, J. B. (1993). Prevention of conduct disorder before and after school entry: Relating interventions to developmental findings. *Development and Psychopathology, 5*, 243-262.

REISS, A. J., Jr. (1951a). Unraveling juvenile delinquency: An appraisal of the research methods. *American Journal of Sociology, 52*, 115-120.

REISS, A. J., Jr. (1951b). Delinquency as the failure of personal and social controls. *American Sociological Review, 16*, 197-207.

REISS, A. J., Jr. (1986). Why are communities important in understanding crime? In A. J. Reiss Jr. & M. Tonry (Eds.), *Communities and crime*. Chicago: University of Chicago Press.

REISS, A. J., & RHODES, A. L. (1961). The distribution of juvenile delinquency in the social class structure. *American Sociological Review, 26*, 720-732.

REISS, A. J., & ROTH, J. A. (Eds.) (1993). *Understanding and preventing violence*. Washington: National Academy Press.

REISS, A. J., & TONRY, M. (Eds.) (1986). *Communities and crime*. Chicago: University of Chicago Press.

REMAFEDI, G., FARROW, J. A., & DEISHER, R. W. (1991). Risk factors for attempted suicide in gay and bisexual youth. *Pediatrics, 87*, 222-225.

REST, J. R. (1979). *Revised manual for the defining issues test: An objective test of moral judgment development*. Minneapolis, MN: Moral Research Projects.

RINGWALT, C. L., ENNETT, S. T., & HOLT, K. D. (1991). An outcome evaluation of project DARE. *Health Education Research: Theory and Practice, 6*, 327-337.

RITVO, E., SHANOK, S. S., & LEWIS, D. O. (1983). Firesetting and nonfiresetting delinquents: A comparison of neuropsychiatric, psychoeducational, experiential, and behavioral characteristics. *Child Psychiatry and Human Development, 13*, 259-267.

ROBERTS, A. R. (1989a). The emergence of the juvenile court and probation services. In A. R. Roberts (Ed.), *Juvenile justice: Policies, programs, and services*. Chicago: Dorsey Press.

ROBERTS, A. R. (1989b). Community strategies with juvenile offenders. In R. A. Roberts (Ed.), *Juvenile justice: Policies, programs, and services*. Chicago: Dorsey Press.

RODHAM, H. (1973). Children under the law. *Harvard Education Review, 43*, 493-497.

RODMAN, H., & GRAMS, P. (1967). Juvenile delinquency and the family: A review and discussion. *Task force report: Juvenile delinquency and youth crime*. Washington: U. S. Government Printing Office.

RODRIQUEZ, K. (1996, Sept 22). Crime hurting college football's image. Knight-Ridder Service. Reported in *The Rutland Herald and Sunday Times Argus*, pp. B1, B4.

ROFF, J. D., & WIRT, D. (1984). Childhood aggression and social adjustment as antecedents of delinquency. *Journal of Abnormal Child Psychology, 12*, 111-126.

ROFF, M. (1975). Juvenile delinquency in girls: A study of a recent sample. In R. D. Wirt, G. Winokur, & M. Roff (Eds.), *Life history research in psychopathology: Vol. 4*. Minneapolis: University of Minnesota Press.

ROFF, M., & SELLS, S. B. (1968). Juvenile delinquency in relation to peer acceptance-rejection and socioeconomic status. *Psychology in the Schools, 5*, 3-18.

RONCEK, D. W. (1975). Density and crime. *American Behavioral Scientist, 18*, 843-860.

ROSECAN, J. S., SPITZ, H. I., & GROSS, B. (1987). Contemporary issues in the treatment of cocaine abuse. In H. I. Spitz & J. S. Rosecan (Eds.), *Cocaine abuse: New directions in treatment and research*. New York: Brunner/Mazel.

ROSEN, L. (1985). Family and delinquency: Structure or function. *Criminology, 23*, 553-573.

ROSENBAUM, D. P., FLEWELLING, R. L., BAILEY, S. L., RINGWALT, C. L., & WILKINSON, D. I. (1994). Cops in the classroom: A longitudinal evaluation of Drug Abuse Resistance Education (DARE). *Journal of Research in Crime and Delinquency, 31*, 3-31.

ROSENBAUM, J. L. (1975). The stratification of socialization processes. *American Sociological Review, 40*, 42-54.

ROSENBAUM, J. L. (1993). The female delinquent: Another look at the role of the family. In R. Muraskin & T. Alleman (Eds.), *It's a crime: Women and justice*. Englewood Cliffs, NJ: Regents/Prentice-Hall.

ROSENBAUM, J. L., & CHESNEY-LIND, M. (1994). Appearance and delinquency: A research note. *Crime and Delinquency, 40*, 250-261.

ROTHBART, M. K. (1986). Longitudinal observation of infant temperament. *Developmental Psychology, 22*, 356-365.

ROTHBART, M. K., & DERRYBERRY, D. (1982). Emotion, attention and temperament. In M. E. Lamb & A. L. Brown (Eds.), *Advances in developmental psychology*, Vol. 1. Hillsdale, NJ: Erlbaum.

ROTHMAN, D. J. (1980). *Conscience and convenience*. Boston: Little, Brown.

ROUSE, J. J., & JOHNSON, B. D. (1991). Hidden paradigms in morality debates about drugs: Historical and policy shifts in British and American drug policies. In J. A. Inciardi (Ed.), *The drug legalization debate*. Newbury Park, CA: Sage.

ROWE, D. C., & OSGOOD, D. W. (1984). Heredity and sociological theories of delinquency: A reconsideration. *American Sociological Review, 49*, 526-540.

RUBIN, H. T. (1985a). *Behind the black robes: Juvenile court judges and the court*. Beverly Hills, CA: Sage.

RUBIN, H. T. (1985b). *Juvenile justice: Policy, practice, and law* (2nd ed.). New York: Random House.

RUBIN, H. T. (1989). The juvenile court landscape. In A. R. Roberts (Ed.), *Juvenile justice: Policies, programs, and services*. Chicago: Dorsey Press.

RUBIN, S. (1951). Unraveling juvenile delinquency: Illusions in a research project using matched pairs. *American Journal of Sociology, 52*, 107-114.

RUDMAN, C., HARDSTONE, E., FAGAN, J., & MOORE, M. (1986). Violent youth in adult court: Process and punishment. *Crime and Delinquency, 32*, 75-96.

RUTHERFORD, A., & MCDERMOTT, R. (1976). *National evaluation program Phase I Summary Report*. U.S. Department of Justice, Law Enforcement and Criminal Justice. Washington: U.S. Government Printing Office.

RUTTER, M., & GILLER, H. (1984). *Juvenile Delinquency: Trends and perspectives*. New York: Guilford Press.

RYERSON, E. (1978). *The best-laid plans*. New York: Hill and Wang.

SAGATUN, I., MCCOLLUM, L. L., & EDWARDS, L. P. (1985). The effect of transfers from juvenile court to criminal court: A loglinear analysis. *Journal of Crime and Justice, 8*, 65-92.

SAMPSON, R. J., & LAUB, J. H. (1993). Structural variations in juvenile court processing: Inequality, the underclass, and social control. *Law and Society Review, 27*, 285-311.

SAMPSON, R. J., & LAURITSEN, J. L. (1994). Violent victimization and offending: Individual, situational and community-level risk factors. In A. T. Reiss, Jr., & J. Roth (Eds.), *Understanding and preventing violence: Social influences*, Vol. 3. Washington: National Academy Press.

SAMPSON, R. J., & WILSON, W. J. (1993). Toward a theory of race, crime, and urban inequality. In J. Hagan and R. Peterson (Eds.), *Crime and inequality*. Stanford, CA: Stanford University Press.

SANBORN, J. B. (1994). Certification to criminal court: The important policy questions of how, when, and why. *Crime and Delinquency, 40*, 262-281.

SAPIR, E. (1921). *Language*. New York: Harcourt Brace & World.

SATTERFIELD, J., SWANSON, J., SCHELL, A., & LEE, F. (1994). Prediction of antisocial behavior in attention-deficit hyperactivity disorder boys from aggression/defiance scores. *Journal of the American Academy of Child and Adolescent Psychiatry, 33*, 185-191.

SAUL, J. A., & DAVIDSON, W. S. (1983). Implementation of juvenile diversion programs: Cast your net on the other side of the boat. In J. R. Kluegel (Ed.), *Evaluating juvenile justice*. Beverly Hills, CA: Sage.

SAUNDERS, E. B., & AWAD, G. A. (1991). Adolescent female firesetters. *Canadian Journal of Psychiatry, 36*, 401-404.

SCARR, S., & MCCARTNEY, K. (1983). How people make their own environments: A theory of genotype-environment effects. *Child Development, 54*, 424-435.

SCHACTER. D. L. (1986). Amnesia and crime: How much do we really know? *American Psychologist, 41*, 286-295.

SCHAFER, W. E., & POLK, K. (1967). Delinquency and the schools. *Task force report: Juvenile delinquency and youth crime*. Washington: U.S. Government Printing Office.

SCHERER, D. G., BRONDINO, M. J., HENGGELER, S. W., MELTON, G. B., & HANLEY, J. H. (1994). Multisystemic family preservation therapy: Preliminary findings from a study of rural and minority serious adolescent offenders. *Journal of Emotional and Behavioral Disorders, 2*, 198-206.

SCHLOSSMAN, S. L. (1977). *Love and the American delinquent*. Chicago: University of Chicago Press.

SCHLOSSMAN, S. & SEDLAK, M. (1983). The Chicago Area Project revisited. *Crime and Delinquency, 29*, 398-462.

SCHLOSSMAN, S., & WALLACH, S. (1978). The crime of precocious sexuality: Female delinquency in the Progressive Era. *Harvard Educational Review, 48*, 65-94.

SCHMALLEGER, F. (1997). *Criminal justice today* (4th ed.). Upper Saddle River, NJ: Prentice Hall.

SCHUERMAN, L., & KOBRIN, S. (1986). Community careers in crime. In A. J. Reiss, Jr. & M. Tonry (Ed.), *Communities and crime*. Chicago: University of Chicago Press.

SCHWARTZ, I. M. (1989). *(In)Justice for juveniles: Rethinking the best interests of the child*. Lexington, MA: Lexington Books.

SCHWARTZ, I. M. (1992). Juvenile crime-fighting policies: What the public really wants. In I. M. Schwartz (Ed.), *Juvenile justice and public policy. Toward a national agenda*. New York: Lexington Books.

SCHWARTZ, I. M., Jackson-Beeck, M., & Anderson, R. (1984). The "hidden" system of juvenile control. *Crime and Delinquency, 30*, 371-385.

SCHWARTZ, H., & JACOBS, J. (1979). *Qualitative sociology: A method to the madness*. New York: The Free Press.

SCOTT, K. E. (1992). Childhood sexual abuse: Impact on a community's mental health status. *Child Abuse and Neglect, 16*, 285-295.

SEBALD, H. (1986). Adolescents' shifting orientations toward parents and peers: A curvilinear trend over recent decades. *Journal of Marriage and the Family, 48*, 5-13.

SEITZ, V., ROSENBAUM, L. K., & APFEL, N. H. (1985). Effects of family support intervention: A ten-year follow-up. *Child Development, 56*, 376-391.

SHAW, C. R. (1930). *The Jack-roller: A delinquent boy's own story*. Chicago: University of Chicago Press.

SHAW, C. R. (1931). *The natural history of a delinquent career*. Philadelphia: Lippincott.

SHAW, C. R. (1938). *Brothers in crime*. Chicago: University of Chicago Press.

SHAW, C. R., & MCKAY, H. D. (1931). Social factors in juvenile delinquency. In *Report on the causes of crime*, Vol. 2. Washington: National Commission on Law Observance and Enforcement.

SHAW, C. R., & MCKAY, H. D. (1932). Are broken homes a causative factor in juvenile delinquency? *Social Forces, 10*, 514-533.

SHAW, C. R., & MCKAY, H. D. (1942). *Juvenile delinquency and urban areas*. Chicago: University of Chicago Press.

SHEINDLIN, J. (1996). *Don't pee on my leg and tell me it's raining*. New York: HarperCollins.

SHELDEN, R. (1981). Sex discrimination in the juvenile justice system: Memphis, Tennessee, 1900-1971. In M. Q. Warren (Ed.), *Comparing male and female offenders*. Beverly Hills, CA: Sage.

SHELDON, W. H., HARTL, E. M., & MCDERMOTT, E. (1949). *Varieties of delinquent youth: An introduction to constitutional psychiatry*. New York: Harper.

SHERMAN, L. W. (1986). Policing communities: What works In A. J. Reiss & M. Tonry, M. (Eds.), *Communities and crime*. Chicago: University of Chicago Press.

SHIDELER, E. H. (1918). Family disintegration and the delinquent boy in the United States. *Journal of Criminal Law, Criminology, and Police Science, 261*, 21-37.

SHIFF, A. R., & WEXLER, B. (1996). Teen court: A therapeutic jurisprudence perspective. *Criminal Law Bulletin*, 342-357.

SHORT, J. F., Jr. (1979). On the etiology of delinquent behavior. *Journal of Research on Crime and Delinquency, 16*, 28-33.

SHORT, J. F., JR., (1982). Life history, autobiography, and the life cycle. In J. Snodgrass (Ed.), *The Jack-roller at seventy*. Lexington, MA: Lexington Books.

SHORT, J. F., JR., & Strodtbeck, F. L. (1965). *Group process and gang delinquency*. Chicago: University of Chicago Press.

SHUNTICH, R. J., & TAYLOR, S. P. (1972). The effects of alcohol on human physical aggressions. *Journal of Experimental Research on Personality, 6*, 34-38.

SILVA, P. A. (1990). The Dunedin Multidisciplinary Health and Development Study: A fifteen year longitudinal study. *Pediatric and Perinatal Epidemiology, 4*, 96-127.

SILVERMAN, D. (1985). *Qualitative methodology and sociology: Describing the social world*. Hants, England: Gower.

SIMON, R. (1975). *Women and crime*. Lexington, MA: Lexington Books.

SIMONS, R. L. (1978). The meaning of the IQ-delinquency relationship. *American Sociological Review, 43*, 268-270.

SIMPSON, S. (1996). Feminist theory, crime and justice. In P. Cordella & L. Siegel (Eds.), *Readings in comtemporary criminological theory*. Boston: Northeastern University Press.

SINGER, S. (1993). The automatic waiver of juveniles and substantive justice. *Crime and Delinquency, 39*, 253-261.

SKOGAN, L. W. (1986). Fear of crime and neighborhood change. In A. J. Reiss Jr., & M. Tonry (Eds.), *Communities and crime*. Chicago: University of Chicago Press.

SKOVRON, S. E., SCOTT, J. E., & CULLEN, F. T. (1989). The death penalty for juveniles: An assessment of public support. *Crime and Delinquency, 35*, 546-561.

SLOAN, J., KELLERMANN, A., REAY, D., FERRIS, J., KOESPELL, T., RIVARA, F., RICE, C., GRAY, L., & LoGERFO, J. (1988). Handgun regulation, crime, assaults, and homicides. *New England Journal of Medicine, 319*, 1256-1262.

SMART, R. G. (1986). Cocaine use and problems in North America. *British Journal of Criminology, 28*, 109-128.

SMART, R. G., & ADLAF, E. M. (1992). Recent studies of cocaine use and abuse in Canada. *Canadian Journal of Criminology, 34*, 1-13.

SMITH, C. E. (1993). *Courts, politics, and the judicial process*. Chicago: Nelson-Hall.

SMITH, C. P., & ALEXANDER, P. S. (1980). *A national assessment of serious juvenile crime and the juvenile justice system: The need for a rational response, Vol. 1. Summary*. Washington: U.S. Government Printing Office.

SMITH, C. P., ALEXANDER, P. S., KEMP, G. L., & LEMERT, E. N. (1980). *The national assessment of serious juvenile crime and the juvenile justice system: The need for a rational response, Vol. 3*. Washington: U.S. Government Printing Office.

SMITH, C., & KROHN, M. D. (1995). Delinquency and family life among male adolescents: The role of ethnicity. *Journal of Youth and Adolescence, 24*, 69-94.

SMITH, D., & VISHER, C. (1980). Sex and involvement in deviance/crime: A quantitative review of the empirical literature. *American Sociological Review, 45*, 691-701.

SNAREY, J. R., & VAILLANT, G. E. (1985). How lower and working class youth become middle-class adults: The association between ego defense mechanisms and upward social mobility. *Child Development, 56*, 899-910.

SNODGRASS, J. (1982). *The Jack-roller at seventy*. Lexington, MA: Lexington Books.

SNYDER, H. N., & SICKMUND, M. (1995). *Juvenile offenders and victims: A focus on violence*. Pittsburgh, PA: National Center for Juvenile Justice.

SNYDER, H. N., SICKMUND, M., AND POE-YAMAGATA, E. (1996). *Juvenile offenders and victims: 1996 update on violence*. Washington: Office of Juvenile Justice and Delinquency Prevention.

SNYDER, J., & PATTERSON, G. (1987). Family interaction and delinquent behavior. In H. C. Quay (Ed.), *Handbook of juvenile delinquency*. New York: Wiley.

SOBELL, M. B., & SOBELL, L. C. (1973). Individualized behavior for alcoholics. *Behavior Therapy, 4*, 49-72.

SOLER, M. (1992). Interagency services in juvenile justice systems. In I. M. Schwartz (Ed.), *Juvenile justice and public policy*. New York: Lexington Books.

SORIANO, F. I. (1994). U.S. Latinos. In L. D. Eron, J. H. Gentry, & P. Schlegel (Eds.), *Reason to hope: A psychosocial perspective on violence and youth*. Washington: American Psychological Association.

SPERGEL, I. A. (1995). *The youth gang problem*. New York: Oxford University Press.

SPERGEL, I. A., Ross, R. E., Curry, G. D., & Chance, R. (1989). *Youth gangs: Problem and response*. Washington: Office of Juvenile Justice and Delinquency Prevention.

SPIVACK, G., & CIANCI, N. (1987). High-risk early behavior patterns and later delinquency. In J. D. Burchard & S. N. Burchard (Eds.), *Prevention of delinquent behavior*. Newbury Park, CA: Sage.

STAFFORD, M. (1984). Gang delinquency. In R. F. Meier (Ed.), *Major forms of crime*. Beverly Hills, CA: Sage.

STAPLETON, V., ADAY, D. P., & ITO, J. A. (1982). An empirical typology of American metropolitan juvenile courts. *American Journal of Sociology, 88*(3), 549-564.

STEFFENSMEIER, D. (1978). Crime and the contemporary woman: An analysis of changing levels of female property crime, 1969-1975. *Social Forces, 57*, 566-584.

STEFFENSMEIER, D. (1980). Sex differences in patterns of adult crimes 1965-1977: A review and assessment. *Social Forces, 58*, 1080-1108.

STEFFENSMEIER, D. (1995). Trends in female crime: It's still a man's world. In B. R. Price and N. J. Sokoloff (Eds.), *The criminal justice system and women* (2nd ed). New York: McGraw-Hill.

STEFFENSMEIER, D. J., & STEFFENSMEIER, R. H. (1980). Trends in female delinquency. *Criminology, 18*, 62-85.

STEINBERG, L. (1986). Latchkey children and susceptibility to peer pressure: An ecological analysis. *Developmental Psychology, 22*, 443-439.

STEINBERG, L. (1987). Single parents, stepparents, and the susceptibility of adolescents to antisocial peer pressure. *Child Development, 58*, 269-275.

STERNBERG, L., BLINDE, P. L., & CHAN, K. S. (1984). Dropping out among language minority youth. *Review of Educational Research, 54*, 113-132.

STERNBERG, R. J. (1985). *Beyond IQ: A triarchic theory of human intelligence*. New York: Cambridge University Press.

STERNBERG, R. J. (1995). *In search of the human mind*. Fort Worth, TX: Harcourt Brace.

STEVENSON, H. W., & STIGLER, J. W. (1992). *The learning gap*. New York: Summit Books.

STOKES, J. & LEVIN, I. (1986). Gender differences in predicting loneliness from social network characteristics. *Journal of Personality and Social Psychology, 51*, 1069-1074.

STRAUS, M. (1991). Discipline and deviance: Physical punishment of children and violence and other crime in adulthood. *Social Problems, 38*, 133-154.

SUBSTANCE ABUSE AND MENTAL HEALTH SERVICES ADMINISTRATION (September, 1995). *Preliminary estimates from the 1994 national household survey on drug abuse*. Advance Report number 10. Washington, DC. U.S. Government Printing Office.

SURGEON GENERAL'S SCIENTIFIC ADVISORY COMMITTEE ON TELEVISION AND SOCIAL BEHAVIOR (1972). *Television and growing up: The impact of television violence*. Washington: U.S. Government Printing Office.

SUTHERLAND, E. H. (1939). *Criminology* (3rd ed.). Philadelphia: Lippincott.

SUTHERLAND, E. H. (1973). *On analyzing crime*. Chicago: University of Chicago Press.

SUTHERLAND, E. H., & CRESSEY, D. R. (1974). *Criminology* (9th ed.). Philadelphia: Lippincott.

SUTTON, J. R. (1985). The juvenile court and social welfare: Dynamics of progressive reform. *Law and Society Review, 19*, 107-146.

SYKES, G. M., & MATZA, D. (1957). Techniques of neutralization: A theory of delinquency. *American Sociological Review, 22*, 664-670.

TAKAKI, R. (1989). *Strangers from a different shore: History of Asian Americans*. Boston: Little, Brown.

TANNENBAUM, F. (1938). *Crime and the community*. Boston: Ginn.

TAPPAN, P. W. (1949). *Juvenile delinquency*. New York: McGraw-Hill.

TAUB, R. P., TAYLOR, D. G., & DUNHAM, J. D. (1984). *Paths of neighborhood change: Race and crime in urban America*. Chicago: University of Chicago Press.

TAYLOR, S. P., & GAMMON, C. B. (1975). Effects of type and dose of alcohol on human physical aggression. *Journal of Personality and Social Psychology, 32*, 169-175.

TAYLOR, S. P., GAMMON, C. B., & CAPASSO, D. R. (1976). Aggression as a function of the interaction of alcohol and threat. *Journal of Personality and Social Psychology, 34*, 938-941.

TAYLOR, S. P., & LEONARD, K. E. (1983). Alcohol and human physical aggression. In R. G. Geen & E. I. Donnerstein (Eds.), *Aggression: Theoretical and empirical reviews*, Vol. 2. New York: Academic Press.

TAYLOR, S. P., SCHMUTTE, G. T., LEONARD, K. E., & CRANSTON, J. W. (1979). The effects of alcohol and extreme provocation on the use of highly noxious shock. *Motivation and Emotion, 3*, 73-81.

TAYLOR, S. P., & SEARS, J. D. (1988). The effects of alcohol and persuasive social pressure. *Aggressive Behavior, 14*, 237-244.

THOMAS, A., & CHESS, S. (1977). *Temperament and development*. New York: Brunner/Mazel.

THOMAS, W. I. (1923). *The unadjusted girl*. Boston: Little, Brown.

THOMAS, W. I. (1931). *The unadjusted girl* (rev. ed.). Boston: Little, Brown.

THOMAS, W. I., & THOMAS, D. S. (1928). *The child in America*. New York: Knopf.

THOMAS, W. I., & ZNANIECKI, F. (1927). *The Polish peasant in Europe and America*. New York: Knopf.

THORNBERRY, T. P. (1987). Toward an interactional theory of delinquency. *Criminology, 25*, 863-891.

THURMAN, Q. C., GIACOMAZZI, A., & BOGEN, P. (1993). Research note: Cops, kids, and community policing. An assessment of a community policing demonstration project. *Crime and Delinquency, 39*, 554-564.

TINKLENBERG, J. R. (1973). Alcohol and violence. In P. G. Bourne (Ed.), *Alcoholism: Progress in research and treatment*. New York: Academic Press.

TINKLENBERG, J. R., & STILLMAN, R. C. (1970). Drug use and violence. In D. Daniels, M. Gilula, & F. Ochberg (Eds.), *Violence and the struggle for existence*. Boston: Little, Brown.

TOBY, J. (1957). The differential impact of family disorganization. *American Sociological Review, 22*, 505-512.

TOBY, J. (1979). Delinquency in cross-cultural perspective. In L. T. Empey (Ed.), *Juvenile justice: The progressive legacy and current reform*. Charlottesville: University of Virginia Press.

TOLAN, P. H. & GUERRA, N. G. (1994). Prevention of delinquency: Current status and issues. *Applied & Preventive Psychology, 3*, 251-273.

TOLAN, P. H., GUERRA, N. G., & KENDALL, P. C. (1995). A developmental-ecological perspective on antisocial behavior in children and adolescents: Toward a unified risk and intervention framework. *Journal of Consulting and Clinical Psychology, 63*, 579-584.

TOLAN, P. H., & LORION, R. P. (1988). Multivariate approaches to the identification of delinquency-proneness in males. *American Journal of Community Psychology, 16*, 547-561.

TOLAN, P. H., & THOMAS, P. (1995). The implications of age of onset for delinquency II: Longitudinal data. *Journal of Abnormal Child Psychology, 23*, 157-169.

TORBET, P. M. (1996). *Juvenile probation: The workhorse of the juvenile justice system*. Washington: Office of Juvenile Justice and Delinquency Prevention.

TOULMAN, S. (1961). *Foresight and understanding: An inquiry into aims of science*. New York: Harper.

TOUPIN, J. (1993). Adolescent murderers: Validation of a typology and study of their recidivism. In A. Wilson (Ed.), *Homicide: The victim/offender connection*. Cincinnati, OH: Anderson.

TRASLER, G. (1987). Biogenetic factors. In H. C. Quay (Ed.), *Handbook of juvenile delinquency*. New York: Wiley.

TREMBLAY, R. E., PAGANI-KURTZ, L., MASSE, L. C., VITARO, F., & PIHL, R. O. (1995). A bimodal preventive intervention for disruptive kindergarten boys: Its impact through mid-adolescence. *Journal of Consulting and Clinical Psychology, 63*, 560-568.

UMBREIT, M. S. (1989). Victims seeking fairness, not revenge: Toward restorative justice. *Federal Probation, 53*, 52-57.

UMBREIT, M. S., & COATES, R. B. (1993). Cross-site analysis of victim-offender mediation in four states. *Crime and Delinquency, 39*, 565-585.

U.S. DEPARTMENT OF JUSTICE (1983). *Report to the nation on crime and justice: The data*. Washington: U.S. Government Printing Office.

VINCENT, K. R. (1991). Black/white IQ differences: Does age make the difference? *Journal of Clinical Psychology, 47*, 266-270.

VITARO, F., & TREMBLAY, R. P. (1994). Impact of a prevention program on aggressive children's friendships and social adjustment. *Journal of Abnormal Child Psychology, 22*, 457-476.

VOLD, G. B. (1979). *Theoretical criminology* (2nd ed.). New York: Oxford University Press.

WADSWORTH, M. E. J. (1975). Delinquency in a national sample of children. *British Journal of Criminology, 15*, 167-174.

WADSWORTH, M. (1979). *Roots of delinquency: Infancy, adolescence and crime*. Oxford: Martin Robinson.

WATSON, J. B. (1913). Psychology as the behaviorist views it. *Psychological Review, 20*, 158-177.

WEILER, B. L., & WIDOM, C. S. (1996). Psychopathy and violent behaviour in abused and neglected young adults. *Criminal Behaviour and Mental Health, 6*, 253-272.

WEIS, J. G. (1989). Family violence research methodology and design. In L. Ohlin & M. Tonry (Eds.), *Family violence, Vol. 11*. Chicago: University of Chicago Press.

WEIS, J. G., & SEDERSTROM, J. (1981). *The prevention of serious delinquency: What to do?* Washington: Center for Law and Justice.

WEISHEIT, R. A. (1992). *Domestic marijuana: A neglected industry*. New York: Greenwood Press.

WEISS, R. D., & MIRIN, S. M. (1987). *Cocaine.* Washington: American Psychiatric Press.

WEITHORN, L. A. (1988). Mental hospitalization of troublesome youth: An analysis of skyrocketing admission rates. *Stanford Law Review, 40,* 773-838.

WELLFORD, C. F. (1987). Towards an integrated theory of criminal behavior. *Albany conference on theoretical integration in the study of deviance and crime.* The State University of New York at Albany, May 7-8.

WELLS, L. E., & RANKIN, J. H. (1985). Broken homes and juvenile delinquency: An empirical review. *Criminal Justice Abstracts, 17,* 249-272.

WELLS, L. E., & RANKIN, J. H. (1986). The broken homes model of delinquency: Analytic issues. *Journal of Research in Crime and Delinquency, 23,* 68-93.

WELTE, J. W., & ABEL, E. L. (1989). Homicide: Drinking by the victim. *Journal of Studies on Alcohol, 50,* 197-201.

WERNER, E. E. (1987). Vulnerability and resiliency in children at risk for delinquency: A longitudinal study from birth to young adulthood. In J. D. Burchard & S. N. Burchard (Eds.), *Prevention of delinquency.* Newbury Park, CA: Sage.

WERNER, E. E., BIERMAN, J. M., & FRENCH, F. E. (1971). *The children of Kauai: A longitudinal study from the prenatal period to age ten.* Honolulu: University of Hawaii Press.

WERNER, E. E., & SMITH, R. S. (1977). *Kauai's children come of age.* Honolulu: University of Hawaii Press.

WERNER, E. E., & SMITH, R. S. (1982). *Vulnerable, but invincible: A longitudinal study of resilient children and youth.* New York: McGraw-Hill.

WERNER, H. (1957). The concept of development from a comparative and organismic point of view. In D. B. Harris (Ed.), *The concept of development.* Minneapolis: University of Minnesota Press.

WEST, D. J. (1982). *Delinquency: Its roots, careers and prospects.* Cambridge, MA: Harvard University Press.

WEST, D. J., & FARRINGTON, D. P. (1973). *Who becomes delinquent?* London: Heinemann.

WEST, D. J., & FARRINGTON, D. P. (1977). *The delinquent way of life.* London: Heinemann.

WHITE, P. T., & AZEL, J. (1989, January). Coca—an ancient herb turns deadly. *National Geographic,* pp. 3-47.

WHORF, B. L. (1956). Science and linguistics. In J. B. Carroll (Ed.), *Language, thought, and reality: Selected writings of Benjamin Lee Whorf.* Cambridge, MA: MIT Press.

WIATROWSKI, M. D., GRISWOLD, D., & ROBERTS, M. K. (1981). Social control theory and delinquency. *American Sociological Review, 46,* 525-541.

WIDOM, C. S. (1992, October). The cycle of violence. *National Institute of Justice: Research in brief,* pp. 1-4.

WIEBUSH, R. G. (1993). Juvenile intensive supervision: The impact on felony offenders diverted from institutional placement. *Crime and Delinquency, 39,* 68-89.

WILGOSH, L., & PAITICH, D. (1982). Ratings of parent behaviors for delinquents from two-parent and single-parent homes. *International Journal of Social Psychiatry, 28,* 141-143.

WILKINSON, K. (1974). The broken family and juvenile delinquency: Scientific explanation or ideology? *Social Problems, 21,* 736-739.

WILSON, J. Q. (1975). *Thinking about crime.* New York: Vintage Books.

WILSON, J. Q., & HERRNSTEIN, R. J. (1985). *Crime and human nature.* New York: Simon and Schuster.

WISH, E. D. (1986). PCP and crime: Just another illicit drug? In D. H. Clouet (Ed.), *Phencyclidine: An update.* Rockville, MD: National Institute on Drug Abuse.

WOLFGANG, M. E. (1958). *Patterns in criminal homicide.* Philadelphia: University of Pennsylvania Press.

WOLFGANG, M. E. (1983). Delinquency in two birth cohorts. *American Behavioral Scientist, 27,* 75-86.

WOLFGANG, M. E., FIGLIO, R. M., & SELLIN, T. (1972). *Delinquency in a birth cohort.* Chicago: University of Chicago Press.

YATES, A., BEUTLER, L. E., & CRAGO, M. (1983). Characteristics of young, violent offenders. *Journal of Psychiatry and Law, 11,* 137-149.

YORBURG, B. (1973). *The changing family.* New York: Columbia University Press.

YUNG, B. R., & HAMMOND, W. R. (1994). Native Americans. In L. D. Eron, J. H. Gentry, & P. Schlegel (Eds.), *Reason to hope: A psychosocial perspective on violence and youth.* Washington, DC: American Psychological Association.

ZEICHNER, A., & PIHL, R. O. (1979). Effects of alcohol and behavior contingencies on human aggression. *Journal of Abnormal Psychology, 88,* 152-160.

ZEICHNER, A., & PIHL, R. O. (1980). Effects of alcohol and instigator intent on human aggression. *Journal of Studies on Alcohol, 41,* 265-276.

ZIGLER, E. (1994). Reshaping early childhood interventions to be a more effective weapon against poverty. *American Journal of Community Psychology, 22,* 37-47.

ZIGLER, E. F., & STEVENSON, M. F. (1993). *Children in a changing world: Development and social issues* (2nd edition). Pacific Grove, CA: Brooks/Cole.

ZIGLER, E., TAUSSIG, C. & BLACK, K. (1992). Early childhood intervention: A promising preventative for juvenile delinquency. *American Psychologist, 47,* 997-1006.

ZILLMAN, D. (1979). *Hostility and aggression.* Hillsdale, NJ: Erlbaum.

ZILLMAN, D. (1983). Arousal and aggression. In R. G. Geen & E. I. Donnerstein (Eds.), *Aggression:*

Theoretical and empirical reviews, Vol. 1. New York: Academic Press.

ZOCCOLILLO, M. (1993). Gender and the development of conduct disorder. *Development and Psychopathology, 5*, 65-78.

CASES CITED

Breed v. Jones, 421 U.S. 519 (1975).

Eddings v. Oklahoma, 102 S.Ct. 869 (1982).

Ex parte Crouse, 4 Whart. 9 (1839).

Fare v. Michael C., 442 U.S. 707 (1979).

Commonwealth v. Fisher, 213 Pa. 48 (1905).

In re Gault, 387 U.S. 1 (1967).

Kent v. U.S., 383 U.S. 541 (1966).

McKeiver v. Pennsylvania, 403 U.S. 528 (1971).

Miranda v. Arizona, 384 U.S. 436 (1966).

New Jersey v. T.L.O., 469 U.S. 325 (1985).

Parham v. J.R., 442 U.S. 584 (1979).

Schall v. Martin, 104 S.Ct. 2403 (1984).

Stanford v. Kentucky, 109 S.Ct. 2969 (1989).

Thompson v. Oklahoma, 108 S.Ct. 2687 (1988).

Vernonia School District v. Acton, 115 S.Ct. 2386 (1995).

Wilkins v. Missouri, 109 S.Ct. 2969 (1989).

In re Winship, 397 U.S. 358 (1970).

Author Index

Blomberg, T. G., 301
Bloomquist, E. R., 65
Blumer, H., 204
Blumstein, A., 29, 44
Bogue, D. J., 213
Bohm, R., 331
Boney-McCoy, S., 169, 170
Borduin, C. M., 242, 253, 254, 255, 340
Bortner, M. A., 322, 326
Bottoms, A. E., 227, 228
Bourque, B. B., 342, 343
Bowden, K. M., 74
Boykin, A. W., 141, 142
Boyle, M. C., 99
Breckinridge, S., 160, 215
Briere, J., 169
British Columbia Ministry of Health and
    Ministry Responsible for Seniors, 55
Bromberg, W., 62
Bronfenbrenner, U., 82, 83, 84, 86, 87, 88, 149,
    202, 203, 207, 237
Bronner, A. F., 160
Brook, J., 100
Brounstein, P. J., 56, 57, 58
Brown, H. C., 60
Brunet, B. L., 64
Bureau of the Census, 29
Burgess, E. W., 86, 123, 212, 213, 214, 215, 216,
    217, 220, 240
Burman, B., 84, 85
Bursik, R. J., 225, 228
Burton, R. V., 126
Buss, A. H., 93, 94
Butterfield, F., 27, 310
Butts, J. A., 7, 13, 14, 296, 337, 340, 344
Byrd, W., 132
Byrne, J. M., 225

Cairns, B. D., 145
Cairns, R. B., 114
Camp, C., 44, 199
Campagna, A. F., 128
Campbell, A., 6, 51, 178, 179, 190, 191
Campos, J. J., 92, 95, 96
Canter, R. J., 83
Cantner, R., 197
Capasso, D. R., 77, 78
Carey, J. T., 211
Carnegie Council on Policy Studies in Higher
    Education, 199
Carraher, D., 142
Carraher, T. N., 142
Casey, P., 303, 321
Caspi, A., 102, 103, 104
Catalano, R. F., 249

Cattarello, A., 293
Centers for Disease Control, 31
Chamberlain, P., 244
Chambers, C. A., 161
Champion, D. J., 323, 325
Chen, S. A., 42
Chesney-Lind, M., 37, 86, 191, 211, 220, 269, 277,
    279, 280, 296, 297, 304, 305, 309, 344, 346
Chess, S., 92, 95
Chown, P. L., 299
Cianci, N., 102
Clare, C. H., 36
Clayton, R. R., 293
Clear, T. R., 337
Cleveland, F. P., 74
Clinard, M., 237
Cloward, R. A., 179, 186, 187, 188, 189, 190
Coates, R. B., 299
Cogan, N. H., 260
Cohen, A. K., 179, 180, 181, 182, 183, 184, 186,
    188, 191
Cohen, B., 9
Cohen, J., 99
Cohen, L. E., 232
Cohen, P., 99
Cohen, W. E., 53, 66, 67
Cohn, V., 68
Coie, J. D., 89
Colby, A., 128
Colcord, J. C., 160
Conger, J. J., 194
Conley, D. J., 297
Coordinating Council on Juvenile Justice and
    Delinquency, 2, 169, 170, 244, 255
Cornell, D., 251, 329
Cortes, J. B., 110
Cox, A. D., 34
Cox, D., 34
Cox, M., 162, 163
Cox, R., 162, 163
Craig, G., 195
Cressey, D. R., 121, 122
Critchlow, B., 73, 75, 77
Cromwell, P. F., 263
Crouter, A. C., 203
Crutchfield, R. D., 148, 163, 164
Csikszentmihalyi, M., 119
Cullen, F. T., 129
Cunningham, L. C., 177
Curtis, G. B., 260
Curtis, R., 6

D'Augelli, A. R., 233
Dale, M. J., 307
Dalgard, O. S., 107

Subject Index